Maintenance Matters
The Guide to Periodical Payments upon Divorce
and Dissolution of Civil Partnerships

SIMON JOHNSON
BARRISTER
STOUR CHAMBERS
MILL STUDIO
17A STOUR STREET
CANTERBURY CT1 2NR
01227 764899
DX 5342 CANTERBURY 1

Maintenance Matters
The Guide to Periodical Payments upon Divorce and Dissolution of Civil Partnerships

Andrew Commins

Barrister, St John's Chambers, Bristol

Family Law

Published by Family Law
A publishing imprint of Jordan Publishing Limited
21 St Thomas Street
Bristol BS1 6JS

British Library Cataloguing-in-Publication Data

A catalogue record for this book is available from the British Library.

ISBN 978 1 84661 299 2

Typeset by Letterpart Ltd, Caterham on the Hill, Surrey CR3 5XL

Printed in Great Britain by CPI Antony Rowe Limited, Chippenham and Eastbourne

FOREWORD

I have always maintained that no proper understanding of our present family law and in particular of what is now called 'financial remedies' can be gained without a clear vision of the historical perspective. Thus it is my humble view that no-one should be allowed to embark on a career as a family lawyer until he or she has read Laurence Stone's great trilogy (*Road to Divorce: England, 1530–1987* (1990), *Uncertain Unions: Marriage in England, 1660–1753* (1992), and *Broken Lives: Separation and Divorce in England, 1660–1857* (1993)); Joseph Jackson's seminal work *The Formation and Annulment of Marriage* (2nd edn 1969); and Stephen Cretney's extraordinary exegesis *Family Law in the Twentieth Century: A History* (2005). So it was with very great pleasure that I discovered that Andrew Commins's new book *Maintenance Matters: The Guide to Periodical Payments upon Divorce and Dissolution of Civil Partnerships* contained in Chapter 2 nearly 20 pages of historical background to our present law of maintenance.

Indeed the historical excursus touches on aspects of social history of which I had mere fleeting knowledge. I had assumed that wife-sales were a figment of Thomas Hardy's imagination; but was astounded to learn that the practice was fact not fiction, was widespread, and endured from the 11th to the mid-19th centuries. It is of course well-known that the principles which inform an award of maintenance have their roots firmly in the jurisprudence of the ecclesiastical courts but Andrew Commins demonstrates this with clarity, pleasingly laced with amusing anecdotal evidence. He tells us that 'repeated appeals, failed appearances, recalcitrance, and even judicial inadequacy abound in the alimony suits of the late medieval English courts', which only goes to show that plus ça change, plus c'est la même chose. The section on private separation deeds illustrates this aphorism further at a time when we excitedly await the Law Commission's report which will address the legal treatment of marital agreements. I had not realised that a private parliamentary divorce almost invariably included an annuity for the ex-wife (of course, dum sola et casta) or that there was a parliamentary official known as the 'Ladies' Friend' whose task was to ensure its provision and adequacy.

The history from the dawn of judicial divorce in 1857 is traced with great learning, clever tropes and not a little wit. The more recent history following the tectonic decision of the House of Lords in *White* in 2000 is analysed perceptively and objectively. The author describes his chapter 2 as a 'potted history' which to my mind takes self-effacement to extremes. I have not enjoyed reading a legal history as much as this one in a long while.

The present law is examined, dissected and analysed in pitiless detail and conspicuous clarity in the pages which follow. This extends to the minefields of child support, bankruptcy and enforcement, and in each instance a safe route through has been charted. My only concern is that perhaps this text is premature. The author acknowledges that in September 2012 the Law Commission launched a consultation dealing with marital property, needs and agreements and states that 'the results of the consultation, and any proposals for reform, are awaited'. As I write this in early February 2014 press reports about the forthcoming report, no doubt based on secret unattributable briefings, have recently appeared in the press. If those reports are right then a mighty revolution will be inflicted on our present law of maintenance, requiring no doubt a re-alignment of this book by a substantial expansion of the historical section.

I have been concerned by the number of references to a certain Mostyn QC or Mostyn J, but a specific word count reveals that that frequency is far exceeded by references to Thorpe LJ. The book pays proper tribute to the titanic contribution of Mathew Thorpe to the development of this branch of our law. I would go so far as to say that no single judge, not even Ormrod LJ, has made such a telling and important contribution to our jurisprudence. Whatever the Law Commission decides his influence will echo down the generations.

This is an excellent book which every family lawyer ought to own, and not merely for professional reasons.

Finally, I would take mild exception with the suggestion in **7.4** that my own view in *B v S (Financial Remedy: Marital Property Regime)* that save in exceptional cases, a periodical payments claim should be determined or settled by reference to the principle of need alone and should not be obscured by the introduction of the concept of sharing future income and earning capacity is '*perhaps controversial*'. On the contrary, I would suggest that it was not controversial at all but a proper interpretation of the (perhaps less than pellucidly clear) pronouncements from the summit. At all events, it will be interesting to see whether the Law Commission agrees. By the same token it will be interesting to learn if the Law Commission suggests that a formulaic approach should be adopted. Society's experiment with formulae in the realm of child support has not been an unqualified success (to put it mildly). The author in a number of instances advances formulaic yardsticks for dealing with certain phenomena (eg Chapter 10 on bonus payments), and of course *Duxbury* (see Chapter 15) is a present example of a formulaic method. Whether this work will be classed as a harbinger remains to be seen.

Nicholas Mostyn
5 February 2014

PREFACE

Marriage and civil partnerships are fraught with uncertainties about their future. Separation always remains an unforeseen possibility. When a relationship fails, the financial inequalities of the exiting parties are often obvious and enduring: an order for periodical payments is one significant and often strategic method to effect a re-balancing and re-organisation of such unfairness. The aim of The Guide is to expose the strengths, weaknesses, application and limitations of orders for periodical payments in all their different guises. The intention is to provide the reader with a programmatic and informative resource to offer guidance and support when dealing with both the fundamental and more demanding aspects of such orders.

With special thanks to my father for his invaluable linguistic guidance and to Sheila for her secretarial wizardry. I would also like to express gratitude to David Lockett, Martha Maher, Christopher Sharp QC and Jody Atkinson for taking the time to proof-read and offer comment on some of the chapters in The Guide.[1] Thanks are also owed to my clerking team for their patience and support and to all those members of Jordan Publishing, in particular Greg Woodgate, Kate Hather and Gillian Pickering, for their assistance, partnership and encouragement throughout this project. Finally, I would like to dedicate this book to Sue, who has constantly supported and inspired me.

I have attempted to set out the law as at 1 January 2014 and my interpretation of the law – whether taken from statute or reported cases – is a matter of personal opinion only: after all, the law of financial remedies is a discretionary affair offering significant leeway for diverging interpretation!

Andrew Commins

---

[1]   David Lockett (Chapter 19), Martha Maher (Chapter 13), Christopher Sharp QC (Chapter 10), Judy Atkinson (Chapter 20).

CONTENTS

Foreword   v
Preface   vii
Table of Cases   xxi
Table of Statutes   xxix
Table of Statutory Instruments   xxxiii

Chapter 1
How to Use The Guide   1
Purpose and scope   1
The phenomenon of periodical payments orders   2
Layout and design   2
  Layout   2
  Design   3
Terminology in The Guide   3
Readership   4
Searching for fairness ...   4

Chapter 2
The Historical Perspective: Maintenance, Alimony and Periodical
Payments from Medieval England to Modern-day Proposals for
Reform   5
Introduction   5
'Maintenance' in medieval England   6
Two lives: one flesh   6
Achieving separation and financial support   7
  The wife-sale   7
  Ecclesiastical courts and the divorce *a mensa et thoro*   9
  Private separation deeds   12
  An action for criminal conversation (a crim. con. action)   13
  Divorce by Parliamentary Act   14
The position by 1857: privilege, collusion and connivance   15
Victorian feminists, pressure for reform and the Divorce Act 1857   16
Financial provision and the Matrimonial Causes Acts of 1857 and
    beyond   17
Introducing the concept of breaking cleanly away   19
Case-law and the measure of maintenance   20
  Pre-1970   21

Post-1970   21
   The one-third rule   21
   Reasonable requirements   22
   Need, generously interpreted   23
Conclusion   24

Chapter 3
A Synopsis: The Orders and Issues   25
Categories of 'maintenance' and periodical payments orders   25
   'Failure to maintain' orders   25
   Orders for maintenance pending suit   25
   Costs allowances/orders for payment in respect of legal services   26
   Substantive periodical payments orders   26
   Nominal periodical payments orders   26
   Interim periodical payments orders (nominal or substantive)   26
   Secured periodical payments orders   27
   Married couples and civil partners: orders in relation to children   27
   Unmarried couples: orders in relation to children   27
   Pension orders   27
   Periodical payments orders after an overseas divorce   28
   Maintenance agreements   28
Associated issues   28
   Expenditure, income need and 'maintenance' budgets   28
   Variation, discharge and suspension   28
   Capitalisation and supplemental orders (upon variation)   29
   Capitalisation and *Duxbury* calculations (original final orders)   29
   The clean break (immediate and deferred)   29
   Extendable and non-extendable term orders for periodical payments   29
   Periodical payments and bankruptcy   30
   Periodical payments, remarriage and cohabitation   30
   Enforcement (in England and Wales)   30

Chapter 4
Failure to Provide Reasonable Maintenance   31
Introduction   31
Statutory basis   31
Applicability   31
Interim orders   32
Final orders   32
The failure to maintain   32
Reasonable maintenance   33
Duration   33
Prior liabilities and expenses   34
Children   34
Procedure   35
Costs   35
Points of practice and theory   36

Chapter 5
Maintenance Pending Suit   37
Introduction   37
Legal basis   37
Applicability   37
Applicant's procedure   38
Respondent's procedure   38
General good practice: the hearing   38
Interim maintenance pending suit   39
Key concepts and principles   39
    Maintenance – what it is and what it is not   40
    Reasonableness and discretion   41
    Standard of living   42
    Third-party support for the applicant (the intended payee) 42
    Assumptions and inferences   43
    Third party support for the respondent (the intended payer) 44
    Balancing interests   46
    Arrears   46
    The impact of an agreement   46
Variation   47
Costs   48
Translating an order for maintenance pending suit into an order for
    periodical payments   48
Points of practice and theory   49

Chapter 6
Maintenance Pending Suit, Costs Allowances and Orders for Payment
in Respect of Legal Services   51
Introduction   51
The old law: costs allowances   52
    Rationale   52
    Legal basis (statutory)   52
    Applicability   52
    Legal basis (case-law)   53
        Minimum standards   53
        Discretionary standards   55
    The burden of proof   56
    Amount   56
    Duration   56
The new law   57
    Dismissing 'costs allowances' and the changes introduced by LASPO 57
    Applicable proceedings   57
    Legal services and timing   58
    Payment, security and enforcement   59
    Minimum standards and the burden of proof   61
    Exercising the discretion   62
    Variation and duration   63
    Costs   64

Points of practice and theory   65

Chapter 7
Needs, Budgets and Expenditure: Exaggeration and Broad-brushes
versus Evidence and Realism   67
Introduction   67
The budget, the client and MCA 1973, s 25(2)   68
  The purpose of a budget   68
  Documents   69
  How to approach drafting or challenging a budget: case-law
      guidance   69
    Realistic assessment   70
  The broad brush versus the fine toothcomb   70
  The perils of exaggeration   71
  Budgets and the duty of full and frank disclosure   72
  Particular expenditure for particular people in particular
      circumstances   73
  Common traps and pitfalls   74
Bringing the strands together: a macro- rather than micro-economic
    approach   74
Points of practice and theory   77

Chapter 8
The Basics of Periodical Payments Orders: Absolutes, Game Rules and
Forms   79
Introduction   79
The absolutes   79
  The elements of a periodical payments order   79
  Start date, interim payments and backdating   80
  Variability and capitalisation   80
  An application for a periodical payments order is barred by the
      payee's remarriage   81
  A default term of joint lives applies: termination on death or
      remarriage   81
  Decree absolute is required to make the order effective   81
  A s 28(1A) bar is required to prevent an extension of any term for
      payment   82
  Leave is required to enforce longer-term arrears   82
  Non-taxable position   82
  Net income calculations   83
The game rules   83
  Payment: fixed amount and percentages   83
  Attachment of earnings, standing order payments and bank accounts 84
  Indexation   84
  Flexibility and the definition of maintenance   85
  The remittance of arrears of periodical payments   86
The forms   86

Chapter 9
The Quantification of Orders for Periodical Payments   89
Introduction   89
Back to basics   90
   The two-stage approach   90
   In pursuit of the elusive concept of fairness   90
      Periodical payments and the three requirements of fairness   91
Capital division and income provision   93
   Marriage as a partnership: financial provision after separation   94
Financial need and compensation for relationship-generated
      disadvantage   94
   What exactly is 'financial need'?   94
   Reasonable requirements   95
   Need 'generously interpreted'   95
   Real need   96
   Caution: need, the marital standard of living and the duration of the
      marriage   97
   A broad conclusion: one man's real need may be another man's
      luxury   98
Understanding and quantifying compensation   99
   The very high income case and compensation/exceptional sharing   101
Conclusions as to quantification/points of practice and theory   102

Chapter 10
The Bonus and Periodical Payments   105
Introduction   105
The bonus analysis: information and disclosure   105
The bonus analysis: income or capital?   108
Broad principles: future financial resources   109
Big[ger] money, clean break cases and bonus payments received after
      separation   109
Something other than equal sharing   110
The transition or 'run-off' award   111
Cases in which a periodical payments order is made and the treatment
      of (future) receivable bonus payments   114
   The 'all-in' income method (Scenarios 1 and 3) 115
   The exclusion method (Scenario 4)   116
   The capped method (Scenario 3)   116
   The transition method (Scenarios 1 and 3)   119
   The deferred clean break method   119
   The other agreed methods   120
Conclusion   120

Chapter 11
**Terminating Financial Dependency: The Immediate and Deferred Clean
Break and [Non]-extendable Term Orders**   123
Introduction   123

The goal of autonomy and self-sufficiency versus the realities of life
    post- divorce   124
The objective of the clean break   125
The legal basis for the clean break   126
To break cleanly or not?   127
   Indicators in favour of a clean break   128
   Indicators against a clean break   130
To term or not to term?   133
   Adjusting without undue hardship to the termination of financial
     dependence   133
   Adjusting: evidence not expectation   134
   Term orders: whose uncertainty and whose burden?   137
   The short marriage and the clean break/term order   139
To bar or not to bar? The deferred clean break   142
   The broad approach   142
   Dates, life-events and the length of the term for periodical payments   143
   The presence of children   144
Points of practice and theory   145
   Clean break   145
   Term orders for periodical payments   145

Chapter 12
Orders for Nominal Periodical Payments: Justification and
Transmutability   147
Introduction   147
Justification for a nominal order   148
   Legal basis   148
   The clean break versus the nominal order   148
   Uncertainties and risks: the nominal order as a 'safety valve', 'last
     backstop' and 'long stop'   149
     The safety valve   150
     The last backstop   150
     The long stop   151
   Practicalities: addressing financial imbalance   151
   The dependence of children and nominal periodical payments orders   152
   Short marriages, dependent children and nominal periodical
     payments orders   153
   Balancing risk and opportunity   154
   Avoiding further litigation   155
   Cohabitation and nominal periodical payments   155
The transmutability of a nominal order   156
   Special rules do not apply   156
   Transmuted orders and the limits of the safety net   156
   Transmutability and the reasoning behind the original nominal order   158
Points of practice and theory   159

Chapter 13
Bankruptcy and Periodical Payments 161
Introduction 161
Core principles 161
  The bankruptcy petition and discharge 161
  Application to annul a bankruptcy order 162
  The general effects of bankruptcy 164
  Void payments 164
  After-acquired property, income increases and the bankrupt's duty to
    give notice 165
  Income payments orders 166
Legal basis for an income payments order 166
  Income payments orders (IA 1986, s 310) 166
The limits of an income payments order and its interaction with an
    order for periodical payments 167
  Limits: reasonable domestic needs 167
  Limits: defining the 'family' 168
  Interaction 168
  Will the bankruptcy court allow for an order for periodical
    payments when quantifying an income payments order? 169
Periodical payments and bankruptcy: effect and impact 170
  The [potential] bankrupt in receipt of periodical payments 171
  Periodical payments and the proof of debts 171
    Provable debts 172
    Bankruptcy debts 172
    Discretionary release 172
  Bankruptcy and an order for secured periodical payments 174
  Miscellaneous trustee powers: obtaining information from an
    ex-spouse 174

Chapter 14
**The Impact of Remarriage and Cohabitation on Orders for Periodical
Payments** 175
Introduction 175
Cohabitation: the statistics 176
The effect of remarriage on an order for periodical payments 177
  Remarriage of the *payee* of a periodical payments order 177
  Remarriage of the *payer* of a periodical payments order 177
  A brief historical review: the payer's remarriage 178
  The modern approach: the payer's remarriage 179
Cohabitation 181
  Stage 1: defining and proving cohabitation: the difficulty with labels 181
    Proving cohabitation 183
    Cohabitation: opportunities for disclosure, interrogation and
      adverse inferences 184
  Stage 2: the financial consequences of cohabitation on the
    payer/payee 186

Stage 3: the extent to which cohabitation and its financial
    consequences may affect an order for periodical payments   186
Orders that terminate a periodical payments order on the payee's
    cohabitation   188
Points of practice and theory   189

Chapter 15
Periodical Payments and *Duxbury* Calculations: The Fable of the
'Tool' and the 'Paradox'   **191**
What is a *Duxbury* calculation?   191
When is a *Duxbury* calculation useful?   192
The fundamental assumptions within a *Duxbury* calculation   192
    Fiscal assumptions   192
Physical assumptions   193
Why is a *Duxbury* calculation a 'tool and not a rule'?   194
Negotiating the '*Duxbury* Paradox'   195
Departing from the *Duxbury* calculation: final orders versus orders for
    capitalisation on an application to vary a periodical payments
    order   196
Circumstances in which it may be appropriate to depart from a
    Duxbury calculation   197
    Providing additional financial security and enabling discretionary
        expenditure   197
    Meeting concerns as to the assumed rate of return   197
    Foreign investment and tax   198

Chapter 16
Orders to Provide Security for Periodical Payments   **199**
Introduction   199
Legal basis, interpretation and procedure   199
The provision of security   200
Flexibility versus finality   200
Documents, deeds and decrees   201
    Factors for the court's consideration   202
Points of practice and theory   205

Chapter 17
Variation, Discharge, Suspension and Revival: Quantum and Term   **207**
Introduction   207
Quantum variation   208
    Legal basis   208
    Procedure   208
    Case analysis on a variation application   209
    Principles on which the court acts (statutory)   209
        Principles on which the court acts (case-law)   212
    Cohabitation   219
    Comparing the percentage of income payable or receivable under
        the original order with that payable under the variation order   219

Backdating upon an application to vary a periodical payments order 220
  Arrears 221
  Costs 221
Variation of the term of a periodical payments order 222
  When to apply to extend the term 222
  The reasons for the original term order 222
  Applying to extend the term for periodical payments and the
    requirement of 'exceptional justification'? 224
Points of practice and theory 227

Chapter 18
Capitalisation upon an Application to Vary a Periodical Payments
Order 229
Introduction 229
Legal basis 230
Applicability and procedure 231
Orders available on an application for 'capitalisation' 231
The benefits and disadvantages of capitalisation upon a variation
  application 232
Capitalisation and the prohibition against capital readjustment 234
The staged-assessment approach (lump sum payment) 235
  Stage 5: Quantification of the lump sum 236
  The use of a *Duxbury* calculation 236
    The *Duxbury* calculation and the capitalisation of a term order
      for periodical payments 238
    Special factors justifying a departure from the *Duxbury*
      calculation 238
    The '*Duxbury* paradox', old age and ill-health 238
    Arrears and miscellaneous compensation 239
    The payee's cohabitation/shorter marriages 240
  Stage 6: pension sharing orders and capitalisation 241
    Pension peculiarities 242
  Stage 7: Is it right and fair to capitalise?: resources and uncertainty 243
Points of practice and theory 244

Chapter 19
Pension Orders & Periodical Payments: Attachment, Sharing &
Interaction 245
Introduction 245
Terminology 246
Pension benefits 246
The nature of a pension attachment order: primary and secondary
  powers 246
  Primary power 247
  Secondary powers 248
  Pension attachment orders versus pension sharing orders 249
Valuations and expert evidence in pension matters 250
Pension attachment orders and variation 252

Contributions and pension benefits accrued before, during and after
    the marriage: general approach   252
Contributions and pension benefits accrued before, during and after
    the marriage: pension attachment   254
Pensions and bankruptcy   254
  Bankruptcy and pensions in payment   254
  Bankruptcy and pensions not in payment but capable of payment   255
Pension attachment orders and alternatives   256
Comparing the pension sharing order and the pension attachment
    order   256
  Advantages of Pension Attachment   258
Clean break   258
Pension attachment orders and statutory prohibitions   259
Procedure   259
Pension sharing and orders for periodical payments   260
Points of practice and theory   262

Chapter 20
Periodical Payments for the Benefit of a Child: School Fees, Disability
Expenses, Top-up Assessments and Written Agreements   263
Introduction and context   263
A basic overview of the statutory child support system   264
The court's residual jurisdiction   268
  Legal basis: school fees   269
  Legal basis: disability expenses   271
  Legal basis: 'top-up' order   272
  Legal basis: written agreements   273
  Legal basis for quantification and payment: child maintenance in
    cases of a petition for divorce   273
Defining a 'child of the family'   274
Factors for the court's consideration   275
The number and duration of orders   276
Quantification of an order for child periodical payments   277
Procedure   277
Segal orders   277

Chapter 21
Maintenance Agreements and MCA 1973, ss 34–35   279
Introduction   279
Legal basis: elements and effect of a maintenance agreement   280
The alteration of maintenance agreements: varying, revoking and
    inserting financial arrangements   281
  Process, procedure and costs   281
  Conditions for altering a maintenance agreement   281

Chapter 22
Enforcement of Maintenance Orders and Arrears within England &
Wales   283
Introduction   283
Securing location and financial information in relation to a judgment
    debtor   284
Enforcing the payment of arrears under a periodical payments order   286
    Granting leave to enforce arrears or remitting them   286
Enforcing an order for periodical payments   288
    'Pre-emptive' enforcement   288
        Enforcement pursuant to the Maintenance Enforcement Act 1991
            (MEA 1991)   288
        Post-default enforcement   291
        The Family Procedure Rules 2010   291
The methods of enforcement   292
    An attachment of earnings order   292
    Enforcement against the earnings of members of the Armed Forces   293
    Charging order   294
Judgment summons   294
    Judgment summons and 'the means to pay'   297
Points of practice and theory   299

Appendix 1
Statutes   301
Attachment of Earnings Act 1971   301
Child Support Act 1991   317
Debtors Act 1869   322
Insolvency Act 1986   323
Maintenance Enforcement Act 1991   335
Matrimonial Causes Act 1973   337

Appendix 2
Statutory Instruments   375
Armed Forces (Forfeitures and Deductions) Regulations 2009,
    SI 2009/1109   375
Child Support (Meaning of Child and New Calculation Rules)
    (Consequential and Miscellaneous Amendment)
    Regulations 2012, SI 2012/2785   380
Civil Procedure Rules 1998, SI 1998/3132   389
Family Procedure Rules 2010, SI 2010/2955   423
Insolvency Rules 1986, SI 1986/1925   444

Appendix 3
Forms   445
Form N349 Application for Third-party Debt Order   446
Form N337 Request for Attachment of Earnings Order   448
Form N379 Application for Charging Order on Land or Property   449
Form EX140 Record of Examination   451

Form D62 Request for Issue of Judgment Summons   463
Form P2 Pension Attachment Annex under [section 25B or 25C of the
    Matrimonial Causes Act 1973] [paragraph 25 or 26 of
    Schedule 5 to the Civil Partnership Act 2004]   464
Form PPF2 Pension Protection Fund (PPF) Attachment Annex to a
    Pension Compensation Attachment Order [section 25F of the
    Matrimonial Causes Act 1973] [paragraph 34A of Schedule 5 to
    the Civil Partnership Act 2004]   467

Index   471

TABLE OF CASES

References are to paragraph numbers.

A (A Minor) (Child of the Family), Re [1998] 1 FLR 347, [1998] 1 FCR
    458, [1998] Fam Law 14, CA   20.28
A v A (Maintenance Pending Suit: Provision for Legal Fees) [2001] 1 WLR
    605, [2001] 1 FLR 377, [2001] 1 FCR 226, [2001] Fam Law 96,
    (2000) 97(44) LSG 45, (2000) 144 SJLB 273, FD   6.6, 6.20
A v A [2004] EWHC 2818 (Fam), [2006] 2 FLR 115, [2006] Fam Law 435   12.19
A v L (Departure From Equality: Needs) [2011] EWHC 3150 (Fam), [2012]
    1 FLR 985, [2012] Fam Law 395   11.11
AB v CB (Divorce and Maintenance: Discretion to Stay) [2012] EWHC 3841
    (Fam), [2013] 2 FLR 29, [2013] Fam Law 384   4.13
Acworth v Acworth [1943] P 21, [1942] 2 All ER 704   2.35
AH v PH [2013] EWHC 3873 (Fam)   15.3, 15.6
Albert v Albert (A Bankrupt) [1996] BPIR 232   13.1, 13.19
AR v AR (Treatment of Inherited Wealth) [2011] EWHC 2717 (Fam), [2012]
    2 FLR 1, [2012] WTLR 373, [2012] Fam Law 15, (2011) 109(44)
    LSG 19   7.15, 10.27, 15.9, 15.11
Arif v Anwar [2013] EWHC 624 (Fam), [2013] BPIR 389   13.5
Arif v Zar [2012] EWCA Civ 986, [2012] BPIR 948   13.5
Artman v Artman [1996] BPIR 511   13.4
Ashley v Blackman [1988] Fam 85, [1988] 3 WLR 222, [1988] 2 FLR 278,
    [1988] FCR 699, [1988] Fam Law 430, (1988) 152 JPN 770, (1989)
    133 SJ 206, FD   9.1
Atkinson v Atkinson [1988] Fam 93, [1988] 2 WLR 204, [1987] 3 All ER
    849, [1988] 2 FLR 353, [1988] FCR 356, [1988] Fam Law 392,
    (1988) 152 JPN 126, (1988) 132 SJ 158   14.21

B v B (Ancillary Relief) [2008] EWCA Civ 284, [2008] 1 WLR 2362, [2008]
    2 FLR 1627, [2008] 1 FCR 613, [2008] Fam Law 611, (2008)
    152(13) SJLB 29   1.1
B v B (Ancillary Relief: Post-Separation Income) [2010] EWHC 193 (Fam),
    [2010] 2 FLR 1214, [2010] Fam Law 905   10.8, 10.11
B v B (Assessment of Assets: Pre-Marital Property) [2012] EWHC 314
    (Fam), [2012] 2 FLR 22, [2012] Fam Law 516   9.17, 19.12
B v B (Consent Order: Variation) [1995] 1 FLR 9, FD   8.13
B v B (Financial Orders: Proportionality) [2013] EWHC 1232 (Fam), [2013]
    Fam Law 1374   10.10, 10.15
B v B (Injunction: Restraint on Leaving Jurisdiction) [1998] 1 WLR 329,
    [1997] 3 All ER 258, [1997] 2 FLR 148, [1997] 3 FCR 262, [1997]
    Fam Law 538, (1997) 94(14) LSG 25, (1997) 141 SJLB 93   22.15
B v B (No. 1) (Financial Provision Proceedings) [1995] 2 FCR 813   11.12
B v C (Maintenance: Enforcement of Arrears) [1995] 1 FLR 467, [1995] 2
    FCR 678, [1995] Fam Law 243   22.7
B v S (Financial Remedy: Marital Property Regime) [2012] EWHC 265
    (Fam), [2012] 2 FLR 502, [2012] 2 FCR 335, [2012] Fam Law 648   7.4, 9.8
Barker v Barker [1952] P 184, [1952] 1 All ER 1128, [1952] 1 TLR 1479,
    (1952) 96 SJ 358   16.7

Bhura v Bhura [2012] EWHC 3633 (Fam), [2013] 2 FLR 44, [2013] 3 FCR
    142   22.23, 22.25
BN v MA [2013] EWHC 4250 (Fam)   5.29, 6.24
Borthwick, Re, Borthwick v Beauvais [1949] Ch 395, [1949] 1 All ER 472,
    [1949] LJR 752, (1949) 93 SJ 147   2.36

C v C (Financial Relief: Short Marriage) [1997] 2 FLR 26, [1997] 3 FCR
    360, [1997] Fam Law 472, CA   11.17, 11.18, 11.20, 11.28, 16.12
C v C (Maintenance Pending Suit: Legal Costs) [2006] 2 FLR 1207, [2006]
    Fam Law 739   6.8, 6.11
C v F (Disabled Child: Maintenance Orders) [1998] 2 FLR 1, [1999] 1 FCR
    39, [1998] Fam Law 389   20.19
C v S (Maintenance Order: Enforcement) [1997] 1 FLR 298, [1997] 3 FCR
    423, [1997] Fam Law 236, (1997) 161 JPN 629   22.8
CF v KM (Financial Provision for a Child: Costs of Legal Proceedings)
    [2010] EWHC 1754 (Fam), [2011] 1 FLR 208, [2010] Fam Law 1060   20.22
Charman v Charman [2006] EWHC 1879 (Fam), [2007] 1 FLR 593, [2007]
    1 FCR 33, [2006] WTLR 1349, (2006-07) 9 ITELR 173, [2006] Fam
    Law 1018, (2006) 103(35) LSG 33, (2006) 150 SJLB 1111   5.1, 9.1, 9.16
Charman v Charman (No 4) [2007] 1 FLR 1246   9.3
CO v CO (Ancillary Relief: Pre-marriage Cohabitation) [2004] EWHC 287
    (Fam), [2004] 1 FLR 1095, [2004] Fam Law 406   15.6
Constantinides v Constantinides [2013] EWHC 3688 (Fam)   22.1, 22.27
Corbett v Corbett [2003] EWCA Civ 559, [2003] 2 FLR 385, [2003] Fam
    Law 474   22.29
Cornick v Cornick (No 2) [1995] 2 FLR 490, CA   17.31
Cornick v Cornick (No 3) [2001] 2 FLR 1240, [2001] Fam Law 871, (2002)
    99(9) LSG 27   12.25, 17.16, 17.17, 17.22
CR v CR [2007] EWHC 3334 (Fam), [2008] 1 FLR 323, [2008] 1 FCR 642,
    [2008] Fam Law 198   9.21, 11.11, 15.8
Currey v Currey (No 2) [2006] EWCA Civ 1338, [2007] 2 Costs LR 227,
    [2007] 1 FLR 946, [2007] Fam Law 12, (2006) 156 NLJ 1651,
    (2006) 150 SJLB 1393   6.4, 6.7–6.9, 6.11, 6.12

D v D (Financial Provision: Periodic Payments) [2004] EWHC 445 (Fam),
    [2004] 1 FLR 988, [2004] Fam Law 407   11.13, 11.31, 17.37, 19.24, 19.35
D v D [2010] EWHC 138 (Fam)   7.11
D v D (Production Appointment) [1995] 2 FLR 497, [1995] 3 FCR 183,
    [1995] Fam Law 670   14.19
DB v CMEC [2010] UKUT 356 (AAC)   20.15
Delaney v Delaney [1990] 2 FLR 457, [1991] FCR 161, [1991] Fam Law
    22, (1990) 154 JPN 693, CA   14.7
Dencourt v Mervyn Canterbury U. 41, fols, 70r-70v (1394)   2.11
Dharamshi v Dharamshi [2001] 1 FCR 492, [2001] Fam Law 98   15.3, 15.7
Dixon v Marchant [2008] EWCA Civ 11, [2008] 1 FLR 655, [2008] 1 FCR
    209, [2008] Fam Law 304, (2008) 152(5) SJLB 28   15.6
Dorney-Kingdom v Dorney-Kingdom [2000] 2 FLR 855, [2000] 3 FCR 20,
    [2000] Fam Law 794, (2000) 97(30) LSG 39, CA   20.36
DR v GR & Others (Financial Remedies: Variation of Overseas Trust)
    [2013] EWHC 1196 (Fam), [2013] 2 FLR 1534, [2013] WTLR 1123,
    16 ITELR 281   15.10
Duxbury v Duxbury (Note) [1992] Fam 62, [1991] 3 WLR 639, [1987] 1
    FLR 7, [1990] 2 All ER 77, [1987] Fam Law 13, CA   15.6

Ella v Ella [2008] EWHC 3258 (Ch), [2009] BPIR 441   13.4

F v F (Ancillary Relief: Substantial Assets) [1995] 2 FLR 45, [1996] 2 FCR
    397, [1995] Fam Law 546, FD   5.11, 5.20, 15.13
F v F (Clean Break: Balance of Fairness) [2003] 1 FLR 847, [2003] Fam Law
    311   11.12

F v F (Duxbury Calculation: Real Rate of Return) [1996] 1 FLR 833   15.2, 15.3

F v F (Financial Remedies: Premarital Wealth) [2012] EWHC 438 (Fam),
    [2012] 2 FLR 1212, [2012] WTLR 1079, [2012] Fam Law 1198   21.2

Fallon v Fallon [2008] EWCA Civ 1653, [2010] 1 FLR 910, [2010] Fam
    Law 13, (2008) 105(46) LSG 16, (2008) 152(46) SJLB 29   12.17

Fisher v Fisher [1989] 1 FLR 423, CA   11.13

Flavell v Flavell [1997] 1 FLR 353, [1997] 1 FCR 332, [1997] Fam Law
    237, CA   11.12, 11.15, 17.5

Fleming v Fleming [2003] EWCA Civ 1841, [2004] 1 FLR 667, [2004] Fam
    Law 174   11.24, 14.21, 17.38–17.40

Fournier v Fournier [1998] 2 FLR 990, [1999] 2 FCR 20, [1998] Fam Law
    662   11.11

Frary v Frary [1993] 2 FLR 696, [1994] 1 FCR 595, [1993] Fam Law 628   14.19

Furniss v Furniss (1982) 3 FLR 46, (1982) 12 Fam Law 30   14.8

G v B [2013] EWHC 3414 (Fam)   9.9

G v G (Financial Remedies: Short Marriage: Trust Assets) [2012] EWHC
    167 (Fam), [2012] 2 FLR 48, [2012] Fam Law 652   11.12, 11.26, 17.1, 17.40

G v G (Maintenance Pending Suit: Legal Costs) [2002] EWHC 306 (Fam),
    [2003] 2 FLR 71, [2002] 3 FCR 339, [2003] Fam Law 393   5.11, 5.14, 5.23, 6.26

G v G (Periodical Payments: Jurisdiction to Vary) [1998] Fam 1, [1997] 2
    WLR 614, [1997] 1 All ER 272, [1997] 1 FLR 368, [1997] 1 FCR
    441, [1996] Fam Law 722, (1997) 161 JPN 86   17.35, 20.27

Grey (No 3), Re [2010] EWHC 1055 (Fam), [2010] 2 FLR 1848, [2010]
    Fam Law 1261   14.15, 14.16

Grey v Grey [2009] EWCA Civ 1424, [2010] 1 FLR 1764, [2010] 1 FCR
    394, [2010] Fam Law 440   12.21, 17.30

Grey v Grey [2010] 1 FLR 1764, [2010] 1 FCR 394, [2010] Fam Law 440   14.15, 14.19, 14.21,
    14.22, 14.27

Grocholeswka-Mullins v Mullins [2013] EWCA Civ 1121   8.23, 18.7

GS v L (Financial Remedies: Pre-Acquired Assets, Needs) [2011] EWHC
    1759 (Fam), [2013] 1 FLR 300, [2012] Fam Law 800   19.17

GW v RW (Financial Provision: Departure from Equality) [2003] EWHC
    611 (Fam), [2003] 2 FLR 108, [2003] Fam Law 386, [2003] All ER
    (D) 40 (May), FD   20.33

H v C [2009] EWHC 1527 (Fam), [2009] 2 FLR 1540, [2009] Fam Law
    802   20.22

H v H (Financial Provision) [2009] EWHC 494 (Fam), [2009] 2 FLR 795,
    [2009] Fam Law 787   5.30, 10.21

H v H (Financial Provision: Application to Terminate Wife's Right to
    Periodical Payments) [1993] 2 FLR 35, [1993] 2 FCR 357   12.20

H v H (Financial Provision: Capital Allowance) [1993] 2 FLR 335, [1993] 2
    FCR 308, [1993] Fam Law 520   12.11, 19.16

H v H [2007] EWHC 459 (Fam), [2007] 2 FLR 548, [2008] 2 FCR 714,
    [2007] Fam Law 578, (2007) 151 SJLB 503   10.10, 10.13, 10.14

H v H [2009] EWHC 3739 (Fam), [2010] 2 FLR 173, [2010] Fam Law 575   10.7

H-J (Children), Re [2012] EWCA Civ 1080   14.15

Hamilton v Hamilton [2013] EWCA Civ 13, [2013] Fam 292, [2013] 2
    WLR 1440, [2014] 1 FLR 55, [2013] 2 FCR 343, [2013] Fam Law
    539, (2013) 157(4) SJLB 43   10.31, 16.9, 17.3

Harb v King Fahd Bin Abdul Aziz [2005] EWCA Civ 1324, [2006] 1 WLR
    578, [2006] 1 FLR 825, [2006] WTLR 609, [2006] Fam Law 96,
    (2005) 102(45) LSG 28   4.12

Harris v Harris [2001] 1 FCR 68, CA   18.1, 18.4, 18.11, 18.14

Hayes v Hayes [2012] EWHC 1240 (Ch), [2012] BPIR 739   13.29, 13.30

Hedges v Hedges [1991] 1 FLR 196, [1990] FCR 952, [1991] Fam Law 267   11.11

Hellyer v Hellyer (Lump Sum Payments) [1996] 2 FLR 579, [1997] 1 FCR
    340, [1997] BPIR 85, [1997] Fam Law 14   13.6

Hill v Haines [2007] EWCA Civ 1284, [2008] Ch 412, [2008] 2 WLR 1250,
    [2008] 2 All ER 901, [2008] 1 FLR 1192, [2007] 3 FCR 785, [2007]
    BPIR 1280, [2008] WTLR 447, [2008] Fam Law 199, [2007] 50 EG
    109 (CS), (2007) 151 SJLB 1597, [2007] NPC 132   13.7
Hodgson v Trapp 1989] AC 807, [1988] 3 WLR 1281, [1988] 3 All ER 870,
    (1988) 138 NLJ Rep 327, (1988) 132 SJ 1672   15.1
Huxley v Child Support Officer [2000] 1 FLR 898, [2000] 1 FCR 448,
    [2000] Fam Law 465   20.1
Hvorostovsky v Hvorostovsky [2009] EWCA Civ 791, [2009] 2 FLR 1574,
    [2009] 3 FCR 650, [2009] Fam Law 1019, (2009) 106(31) LSG 18,
    (2009) 153(30) SJLB 28   17.21, 17.29

J (SR) v J (DW) [1999] 2 FLR 176, [1999] 3 FCR 153, [1999] Fam Law 448   12.15, 12.25
J v V (Disclosure: Offshore Corporations) [2003] EWHC 3110 (Fam),
    [2004] 1 FLR 1042, [2004] Fam Law 398   15.6
Jones v Jones [2011] EWCA Civ 41, [2012] Fam 1, [2011] 3 WLR 582,
    [2011] 1 FLR 1723, [2011] 1 FCR 242, [2011] Fam Law 455, (2011)
    161 NLJ 210   9.9, 11.12
Jones v Jones (Periodical Payments) [2001] Fam 96, [2000] 3 WLR 1505,
    [2000] 2 FLR 307, [2000] 2 FCR 201, [2000] Fam Law 607, (2000)
    97(17) LSG 34, (2000) 144 SJLB 203   17.36

K v K (Periodical Payment: Cohabitation) [2005] EWHC 2886 (Fam), [2006]
    2 FLR 468, [2006] Fam Law 518   14.1, 14.23, 14.26, 18.23
Kimber v Kimber [2000] 1 FLR 383, [2000] Fam. Law 317   14.15
King v Bunyon [2007] EWHC 3281 (Admin), [2008] 1 FLR 1564, [2008]
    Fam Law 308   22.8

L v L (Financial Remedies: Deferred Clean Break) [2011] EWHC 2207
    (Fam), [2012] 1 FLR 1283, [2012] Fam Law 518   11.19, 17.40
L v L (School Fees: Maintenance: Enforcement) [1997] 2 FLR 252, [1997] 3
    FCR 520, [1997] Fam Law 658   22.22
Lauder v Lauder [2007] EWHC 1227 (Fam), [2007] 2 FLR 802, [2008] 3
    FCR 468   9.22, 17.20, 17.28, 18.9, 18.19, 18.20
Lawrence v Gallagher [2012] EWCA Civ 394, [2012] 2 FLR 643, [2012] 1
    FCR 557, [2012] Fam Law 646   9.16
Livesey (formerly Jenkins) v Jenkins [1985] AC 424, [1985] 2 WLR 47,
    [1985] 1 All ER 106, [1985] FLR 813, [1985] Fam Law 310, (1985)
    82 LSG 517, (1985) 134 NLJ 55   5.23, 7.11, 14.18
Lumsden v Lumsden (unreported) 11 November 1998   22.7, 22.8

M v M (Financial Provision) [2010] EWHC 2817 (Fam), [2011] 1 FLR
    1773, [2011] Fam Law 469   4.5, 5.21
M v M (Financial Relief: Substantial Earning Capacity) [2004] EWHC 688
    (Fam), [2004] 2 FLR 236, [2004] Fam Law 496   2.39, 7.7
M v M (Maintenance Pending Suit) [2002] EWHC 317 (Fam), [2002] 2 FLR
    123, [2002] Fam Law 510, FD   5.11, 5.19, 5.24
M v M (Maintenance Pending Suit: Enforcement: on Dismissal of Suit)
    [2008] EWHC 2153 (Fam), [2009] 1 FLR 790, [2009] Fam Law 8   22.20
M v M (Third Party Subpoena: Financial Conduct) [2006] EWHC 2250
    (Fam), [2006] 2 FLR 1253, [2006] 2 FCR 555   14.19
M-D v D [2008] EWHC 1929 (Fam), [2009] 1 FLR 810, [2009] 1 FCR 731,
    [2009] Fam Law 181   11.25
Mawson v Mawson [1994] 2 FLR 985   11.33
McCartney v Mills McCartney [2008] EWHC 401 (Fam), [2008] 1 FLR
    1508, [2008] 1 FCR 707, [2008] Fam Law 507, (2008) 105(13) LSG
    28   7.10, 7.12, 9.18
McFarlane v McFarlane [2009] EWHC 891 (Fam), [2009] 2 FLR 1322,
    [2009] Fam Law 1020, (2009) 153(25) SJLB 28   9.24, 12.25, 17.16, 17.40

McRoberts v McRoberts [2012] EWHC 2966 (Ch), [2013] 1 WLR 1601,
    [2013] BPIR 77   13.29, 13.30

Mekarska v Ruiz & Boyden [2011] EWHC 913 (Fam), [2011] 2 FLR 1351,
    [2011] 2 FCR 608, [2011] BPIR 1139, [2011] Fam Law 802   13.5

MET v HAT [2013] EWHC 4247 (Fam)   5.15, 6.26

Miller v Miller; McFarlane v McFarlane [2006] UKHL 24, [2006] 2 AC 618,
    [2006] 2 WLR 1283, [2006] 3 All ER 1, [2006] 1 FLR 1186, [2006]
    2 FCR 213, [2006] Fam Law 629, (2006) 103(23) LSG 28, (2006)
    156 NLJ 916, (2006) 150 SJLB 704   2.34, 2.42, 3.18, 5.12, 7.3, 7.4, 8.24, 9.6, 9.8, 9.11,
          9.12, 9.14, 9.16, 9.21, 9.22, 11.4, 11.6, 11.12, 11.24, 15.7, 17.11,
          17.16, 17.18

Minton v Minton [1979] AC 593, [1979] 2 WLR 31, (1978) FLR Rep 461,
    [1979] 1 All ER 79, HL   11.1, 12.5, 18.11

Mohan v Mohan [2013] EWCA Civ 586, [2013] CP Rep 36, [2014] 1 FCR
    40, [2013] Fam Law 959   22.23

Moore v Moore (Maintenance Pending Suit: Enforcement on Dismissal of
    Suit) [2009] EWCA Civ 1427, [2010] 1 FLR 1413, [2010] Fam Law
    443, [2010] Fam Law 335, (2009) 106(42) LSG 23   5.13, 5.27

Morton v Morton [1954] 1 WLR 737, [1954] 2 All ER 248, (1954) 98 SJ
    318   4.9

Moses-Taiga v Taiga [2005] EWCA Civ 1013, [2006] 1 FLR 1074, [2008] 1
    FCR 696, [2006] Fam Law 266   5.3, 5.28, 6.9

MT v OT (Financial Provision: Costs) [2007] EWHC 838 (Fam), [2008] 2
    FLR 1311, [2008] Fam Law 209   16.12

Mubarak v Mubarak [2001] 1 FLR 698, [2001] 1 FCR 193, [2001] Fam
    Law 178   22.24

Murphy v Murphy [2009] EWCA Civ 1258, [2011] 1 FLR 537, [2010] 3
    FCR 222, [2010] Fam Law 1163, (2009) 153(36) SJLB 29   11.11, 12.6

N v F (Financial Orders: Pre-acquired Wealth) [2011] EWHC 586 (Fam),
    [2011] 2 FLR 533, [2012] 1 FCR 139, [2011] Fam Law 686   9.17, 9.20, 20.33

N v N (Consent Order: Variation) [1993] 2 FLR 868, [1994] 2 FCR 275,
    [1993] Fam Law 676, CA   11.33, 17.10

N v N (Financial Orders: Appellate Role) [2011] EWCA Civ 940, [2012] 1
    FLR 622, [2011] Fam Law 1069   17.37

N v N [2006] EWHC 3269 (Fam), [2007] 1 FCR 749, [2007] Fam Law 294   12.23

NA v MA [2006] EWHC 2900 (Fam), [2007] 1 FLR 1760, [2007] Fam Law
    295   21.7

NG v SG (Appeal: Non-disclosure) [2011] EWHC 3270 (Fam), [2012] 1
    FLR 1211, [2012] Fam Law 394   5.23, 18.6

North v North [2007] EWCA Civ 760, [2008] 1 FLR 158, [2007] 2 FCR
    601, [2008] Fam Law 508, (2007) 151 SJLB 1022   12.23, 12.24, 17.23

O'Farrell v O'Farrell [2012] EWHC 123 (QB), [2013] 1 FLR 77, [2012]
    Fam Law 514   22.5

OS v DS (Oral Disclosure: Preliminary Hearing) [2004] EWHC 2376 (Fam),
    [2005] 1 FLR 675, [2005] 1 FCR 494, [2005] Fam Law 11, FD   13.5

P (A Child) (Financial Provision), Re [2003] EWCA Civ 837, [2003] 2 FLR
    865, [2003] 2 FCR 481, [2003] Fam Law 717, (2003) 100(33) LSG
    27   20.22

P v P (Post-Separation Accruals and Earning Capacity) [2007] EWHC 2877
    (Fam), [2008] 2 FLR 1135, [2008] Fam Law 614   9.9, 10.10, 10.12

Parlour v Parlour; McFarlane v McFarlane [2004] EWCA Civ 872, [2005]
    Fam 171, [2004] 3 WLR 1480, [2004] 3 All ER 921, [2004] 2 FLR
    893, [2004] 2 FCR 657, [2004] Fam Law 714   9.9

Parr v Parr [2013] EWHC 4105 (Fam)   6.26, 10.29

Parra v Parra (Divorce: Financial Provision: Clean Break) [2002] EWCA Civ
    1886, [2003] 1 FLR 942, [2003] 1 FCR 97, [2003] Fam Law 314   20.15

Paulin v Paulin [2009] EWCA Civ 221, [2010] 1 WLR 1057, [2009] 3 All
　　ER 88, [2009] 2 FLR 354, [2009] 2 FCR 477, [2009] BPIR 572,
　　[2009] Fam Law 567, (2009) 159 NLJ 475　　　　　　　　　　　　13.2, 13.4
Pearce v Pearce [2003] EWCA Civ 1054, [2004] 1 WLR 68, [2003] 2 FLR
　　1144, [2003] 3 FCR 178, [2003] Fam Law 723, (2003) 100(36) LSG
　　39　　　　　　　　　　　15.9, 18.6, 18.9, 18.10, 18.12, 18.15, 18.22, 18.25
Porter v Porter [1969] 1 WLR 1155, [1969] 3 All ER 640, (1969) 113 SJ
　　163, CA　　　　　　　　　　　　　　　　　　　　　　　　　　　5.18
Price v Price [1951] P 413, [1951] 2 All ER 580 (Note), (1951) 115 JP 468
　　(Note), (1951) 95 SJ 560　　　　　　　　　　　　　　　　　　　2.35
Purba v Purba [2000] 1 FLR 444, [2000] 1 FCR 652, [2000] Fam Law 86,
　　CA　　　　　　　　　　　　　　　　　　　　　　　　　　　7.8, 22.8

Q v Q (Ancillary Relief: Periodical Payments) [2005] EWHC 402 (Fam),
　　[2005] 2 FLR 640, [2005] Fam Law 539　　　　　　　　　　　　8.19, 10.31

R (on the application of Green) v Secretary of State for the Department for
　　Work and Pensions [2010] EWHC 1278 (Admin), [2011] Fam Law
　　462, (2010) 154(29) SJLB 32　　　　　　　　　　　　　　　　20.15
R (on the application of Kehoe) v Secretary of State for Work and Pensions
　　[2005] UKHL 48, [2006] 1 AC 42, [2005] 3 WLR 252, [2005] 4 All
　　ER 905, [2005] 2 FLR 1249, [2005] 2 FCR 683, [2005] HRLR 30,
　　[2006] UKHRR 360, [2005] Fam Law 850, (2005) 155 NLJ 1123,
　　(2005) 149 SJLB 921　　　　　　　　　　　　　　　　　　20.1, 20.2
R (on the application of Smith) v Secretary of State for Defence and
　　Secretary of State for Work and Pensions [2004] EWHC 1797
　　(Admin), [2005] 1 FLR 97, [2004] Pens LR 323, [2005] ACD 15,
　　[2004] Fam Law 868, (2004) 101(34) LSG 30　　　　　　　　19.1, 19.25
R v R (Financial Remedies) [2012] EWHC 2390 (Fam), [2013] 1 FLR 106,
　　[2013] Fam Law 28　　　　　　　　　　　　　　　　　　　　11.12
R v R (Financial Remedies: Needs and Practicalities) [2011] EWHC 3093
　　(Fam), [2013] 1 FLR 120, [2012] Fam Law 653　　　　　　　　11.12
R v R [2009] EWHC 1267　　　　　　　　　　　　　　　　　　　7.8
Radmacher v Granatino [2010] UKSC 42, [2011] 1 AC 534, [2010] 3 WLR
　　1367, [2011] 1 All ER 373, [2010] 2 FLR 1900, [2010] 3 FCR 583,
　　[2010] Fam Law 1263, (2010) 107(42) LSG 18, (2010) 160 NLJ
　　1491, (2010) 154(40) SJLB 37　　　　　5.29, 9.17, 11.4, 21.1, 21.4, 21.8
Raithatha v Williamson [2012] EWHC 909 (Ch), [2012] 1 WLR 3559,
　　[2012] 3 All ER 1028, [2012] BPIR 621　　　　　　　　　　　19.22
Rayatt (a Bankrupt), Re [1998] BPIR 495, [1998] 2 FLR 264, [1998] Fam
　　Law 458, ChD　　　　　　　　　　　　　　　　　　　　　13.16
Roberts v Roberts [1970] P 1, [1968] 3 WLR 1181, [1968] 3 All ER 479,
　　(1969) 133 JP 8, (1968) 112 SJ 964　　　　　　　　　　　　　14.8
Robson v Robson [2010] EWCA Civ 1171, [2011] 1 FLR 751, [2011] 3
　　FCR 625, [2011] Fam Law 224, (2010) 107(43) LSG 20, (2010) 160
　　NLJ 1530　　　　　　　　　　　2.42, 7.8, 9.16, 9.19, 11.11, 16.12
RP v RP [2006] EWHC 3409 (Fam), [2007] 1 FLR 2105, [2008] 2 FCR
　　613, [2007] Fam Law 581　　　　　　　　　　　　　　　　9.21, 11.11
Russell v Russell (1985) [1986] 1 FLR 465, [1986] Fam Law 156, (1985)
　　135 NLJ 829　　　　　　　　　　　　　　　　　　　　　　22.7

S v B (Ancillary Relief: Costs) [2004] EWHC 2089 (Fam), [2005] 1 FLR 474　　12.16
S v M (Maintenance Pending Suit) [2012] EWHC 4109 (Fam), [2013] 1 FLR
　　1173, [2013] Fam Law 271　　　　　　　　　　　　　　　　　5.25
S v S [2008] EWHC 519 (Fam), [2008] 2 FLR 113, [2008] 3 FCR 533,
　　[2008] Fam Law 616　　　　　　　　　　　　　　　　　　7.12, 11.23
S v S, Note [1987] 2 FLR 342, [1987] 1 WLR 382, [1987] 2 All ER 312,
　　[1987] Fam Law 312, CA　　　　　　　　　　　　　　　　17.31, 17.32
Scallon v Scallon [1990] 1 FLR 194, [1990] FCR 911, [1990] Fam Law 92　　12.9
Scott v Davis [2003] BPIR 1009　　　　　　　　　　　　　　　　13.16

Scott v Scott [1951] P 245, [1951] 1 All ER 216   4.10
Shaw v Shaw [2002] EWCA Civ 1298, [2002] 2 FLR 1204, [2002] 3 FCR
    298, [2002] Fam Law 886   22.7
Slater v Slater (1982) 3 FLR 364   14.9
Stockford v Stockford (1982) 3 FLR 52, (1982) 12 Fam Law 30 2.38, 14.9
Supperstone v Lloyd's Names Working Party [1999] BPIR 832   13.12
Suter v Suter [1987] Fam 111, [1987] 3 WLR 9, [1987] 2 All ER 336,
    (1987) 151 JP 593, [1987] 2 FLR 232, [1987] Fam Law 239, (1987)
    151 JPN 174, (1987) 84 LSG 1142, (1987) 131 SJ 471   11.21
SW v RC [2008] EWHC 73 (Fam), [2008] 1 FLR 1703, [2008] 2 FCR 663,
    [2008] Fam Law 400   20.33

T v T (Financial Provision: Private Education) [2006] EWHC 2119 (Fam),
    [2006] 1 FLR 903, [2006] Fam Law 182   20.16
T v T (Financial Relief: Pensions) [1998] 1 FLR 1072, [1998] 2 FCR 364,
    [1998] OPLR 1, [1998] Pens LR 221, [1998] Fam Law 398   19.25
Tavouleras v Tavouleras [1998] 2 FLR 418, [1999] 1 FCR 133, [1998] Fam
    Law 521   16.12
Teeling v Teeling [1984] FLR 808, CA   20.28
Thompson v Thompson [1986] Fam 38, [1985] 3 WLR 17, [1985] FLR 863,
    [1985] 2 All ER 243, CA   17.6
TL v ML (Ancillary Relief: Claim against Assets of Extended Family) [2005]
    EWHC 2860 (Fam), [2006] 1 FLR 1263, [2006] 1 FCR 465, [2006]
    Fam Law 183   5.11, 5.23, 6.8, 6.11, 6.25
Tracey v Tracey [2006] EWCA Civ 734, [2007] 1 FLR 196, [2006] 2 FCR
    481, [2006] Fam Law 838, (2006) 150 SJLB 666   16.9, 20.16, 20.17
Turner v Royal Bank of Scotland [2000] BPIR 683, [2001] EWCA Civ 64,
    [2001] 1 All ER (Comm) 1057, CA   7.8

V v V (Ancillary Relief: Prenuptial Agreement) [2011] EWHC 3230(Fam),
    [2012] 1 FLR 1315, [2012] 2 FCR 98, [2012] Fam Law 274, (2012)
    109(4) LSG 17   9.17, 11.4
V v V (Financial Relief) [2005] 2 FLR 697, [2005] Fam Law 684 11.12
Vaughan v Vaughan [2010] EWCA Civ 349, [2011] Fam 46, [2010] 3 WLR
    1209, [2010] 2 FLR 242, [2010] 2 FCR 509, [2010] Fam Law 793   14.10–14.12, 18.10,
                                                                   18.15
VB v JP [2008] EWHC 112 (Fam), [2008] 1 FLR 742, [2008] 2 FCR 682   8.23, 9.23, 17.19,
                                                                   17.21

W v C (Financial Remedies: Appeal: Non-Disclosure) [2012] EWHC 3788
    (Fam), [2013] 2 FLR 115, [2013] Fam Law 953   14.18
W v W (Financial Provision: Form E) [2003] EWHC 2254 (Fam), [2004] 1
    FLR 494, [2003] 3 FCR 385   15.12
W v W (Periodical Payments: Variation) [2009] EWHC 3076 (Fam), [2010]
    2 FLR 985, [2010] Fam Law 691   7.14, 7.15, 17.21, 17.22, 18.10, 18.23, 18.28
Waterman v Waterman [1989] 1 FLR 380, [1989] FCR 267, [1989] Fam
    Law 227   11.33
WF v HF (Financial Remedies: Premarital Wealth) [2012] EWHC 438 (Fam),
    [2012] 2 FLR 1212, [2012] WTLR 1079, [2012] Fam Law 1198 7.1
Whaley v Whaley [2011] EWCA Civ 617, [2012] 1 FLR 735, [2011] 2 FCR
    323, [2011] WTLR 1267, 14 ITELR 1, [2011] Fam Law 804, [2011]
    NPC 53   9.26, 18.8, 20.29
White v White [2001] 1 AC 596, [2000] 3 WLR 1571, [2000] 2 FLR 981,
    [2001] 1 All ER 1, [2000] 3 FCR 555, [2001] Fam Law 12, (2000)
    97(43) LSG 38, (2000) 150 NLJ 1716, (2000) 144 SJLB 266, [2000]
    NPC 111, HL   2.30, 2.39, 2.40, 9.15, 9.16, 15.7, 18.14, 19.15
Whiting v Whiting [1988] 2 FLR 189, [1988] 1 WLR 565, [1988] 2 All ER
    275, CA   12.10
Wilford v Berkeley (1758) 1 Burr 609   2.20
Wilson v National Coal Board (1980) 130 NLJ 146, HL   12.23

X (A Bankrupt), Re [1996] BPIR 494   13.21
X v Y (Maintenance Arrears: Cohabitation) [2012] EWHC 1 (Fam)   14.15

Y v Y (Financial Orders: Inherited Wealth) [2012] EWHC 2063 (Fam),
    [2013] 2 FLR 924, [2013] Fam Law 535   15.6
Yates v Yates [2012] EWCA Civ 532, [2013] 2 FLR 1070, [2012] Fam Law
    951   17.25, 18.16
Young v Young [2012] EWHC 138 (Fam), [2012] Fam 198, [2012] 3 WLR
    266, [2012] 2 FLR 470, [2012] 2 FCR 83, [2012] Fam Law 655   22.15

Z v Z (No 2) (Financial Remedy: Marriage Contract) [2011] EWHC 2878
    (Fam), [2012] 1 FLR 1100, [2012] Fam Law 136   12.12
Zuk v Zuk [2012] EWCA 1871, [2013] 2 FLR 1466   22.22, 22.26

TABLE OF STATUTES

References are to paragraph numbers.

Administration of Justice Act 1970	22.9
Armed Forces Act 1996	
s 356(4)(a)	22.19
Attachment of Earnings Act 1971	22.9,
	22.15, 22.19
s 6	22.15
s 6(2)	22.15
s 6(5)	22.16
s 7	22.17
s 9(4)	22.17
s 13(2)	22.18
s 16	22.15
s 24	22.15
s 24(2)(b)	22.19
Charging Orders Act 1979	22.20
s 2	22.21
s 3	22.21
Child Support Act 1991	1.2, 3.9, 4.15,
	13.27, 13.28, 20.3, 20.19, 20.36
s 8	20.13, 20.14, 20.34, 20.36
s 8(3)	20.36
s 8(3A)	20.13
s 8(6)	20.22
s 8(6)(a)	20.22
s 8(6)(b)	20.22
s 8(8)	20.19
s 8(9)	20.19
s 8(10)	20.13
s 8(11)	20.14
s 9	20.34
s 44(2A)	4.15
Children Act 1989	3.10, 6.16, 20.5, 20.19
s 17(11)	20.19
Sch 1	3.10, 13.21, 14.2, 16.12, 20.14,
	20.22
Civil Partnership Act 2004	1.8, 6.14, 6.16,
	17.3
Pt 11	6.16
Sch 5	6.16, 20.14
Pt 1	
para 2(1)(a)	8.26
para 2(1)(b)	8.26, 16.2
para 2(1)(d)	20.25
para 2(1)(e)	16.2
para 4	8.11
Pt 3	
para 12	8.14
Pt 4	
para 18	18.7

Civil Partnership Act 2004—*continued*	
Sch 5—*continued*	
Pt 5	
para 23	11.7
Pt 6	19.8
para 25	19.1
para 26	19.1
Pt 8	
para 38	5.1
para 38A	6.1
para 38B	6.1
Pt 9	
paras 39–45	4.1
para 39(1)(b)	4.15
para 39(3)	4.5
para 40	4.5
para 41(1)	4.6
Pt 10	
para 47(2)	8.8
para 47(5)	8.12
Pt 11	8.7, 17.5
para 52	17.33
para 52(1)	8.25
para 53	18.5
para 53(2)(a)–(d)	18.7
para 54	18.7
para 59(4)	17.14
Sch 6	20.14
Sch 7	20.14
Companies Act 1989	20.19
s 17	20.19
Debtors Act 1869	22.24, 22.25, 22.27
s 5	22.22, 22.25
Divorce Act 1857	2.24
Domestic Proceedings and Magistrates'	
Courts Act 1978	
s 1	4.2
Equality Act 2010	20.19
s 6	20.19
s 198	4.10
Family Law Act 1986	5.15
Family Law Act 1996	14.14
s 62(1)(a)	14.14
s 66	11.24

Income Tax (Trading and Other
    Income) Act 2005
    s 454   8.15
Inheritance (Provision for Family and
    Dependants) Act 1975   4.12, 16.9
Insolvency Act 1986   13.15, 13.17, 13.19,
                           13.21, 13.25, 13.29
    s 272(1)   13.4
    s 278(1)(a)   13.3
    s 279(1)   13.3
    s 281(1)   13.3
    s 281(5)   13.28, 13.30
    s 281(5)(b)   13.29
    s 282   13.2
    s 282(1)   13.2, 13.4
    s 284(1)   13.7
    s 284(4)(a)   13.7
    s 285(1)   13.23
    s 306   13.7
    s 307   13.8
    s 307(2)(c)   13.8
    s 307(4)(a)   13.10
    s 307(5)   13.11
    s 310   13.11, 13.13
    s 310(1)   13.12
    s 310(1A)   13.12
    s 310(2)   13.15
    s 310(5)   13.12
    s 310(6A)   13.19, 13.24
    s 310(7)   13.12
    s 310A   13.12
    s 333(2)   13.9
    s 366(1)   13.32
    s 385   13.17, 13.20
    s 436   13.6, 13.8

Legal Aid, Sentencing and Punishment
    of Offenders Act 2012   3.4, 6.1, 6.2,
        6.14, 6.16, 6.22–6.24, 6.26, 6.27,
                                            6.30
    ss 49–54   6.13

Magistrates' Courts Act 1980
    s 93(6)   22.27
Maintenance Agreements Act 1957   21.1
Maintenance Enforcement Act 1991   8.20,
                                   22.8, 22.9
    s 1(1)   8.20
    s 1(4)(b)   8.20, 22.9
    s 1(5)(a)   8.20
    s 1(5)(b)   8.20
    s 1(6)   8.20
Married Women (Maintenance in
    Cases of Desertion) Act 1886   2.27
Matrimonial and Family Proceedings
    Act 1984   2.32, 3.12, 5.15
    Pt III   5.21, 6.16
    s 46(2)   5.15
Matrimonial Causes Act 1857
    s 21   2.25
    s 22   2.25
    s 32   2.25
    s 35   2.25

Matrimonial Causes Act 1857—*continued*
    s 59   2.19
Matrimonial Causes Act 1866   2.26
    s 1   2.26
Matrimonial Causes Act 1878   2.27
    s 4(1)   2.27
    s 5(c)   2.27
Matrimonial Causes Act 1884   2.28
    s 2   2.28
Matrimonial Causes Act 1907   2.29
Matrimonial Causes Act 1950   2.29
    s 23   2.29
    s 28(3)   2.29
Matrimonial Causes Act 1973   2.30, 2.40,
        4.6, 6.16, 6.26, 8.3, 8.25, 9.14,
            9.15, 9.18, 10.12, 10.31, 11.6,
        11.11, 11.13, 11.14, 12.18, 12.23,
            13.6, 14.5, 14.6, 14.14, 15.3,
        16.8, 17.6, 17.22, 18.6, 18.11,
    19.23, 19.37, 20.19, 20.25, 20.28,
        20.31, 20.36, 21.1–21.3, 21.6,
                                            22.7
    Pt II   6.15, 20.14, 22.14
    s 4   16.1
    s 5D(4)   19.9
    s 8(7)   20.15
    s 22   3.3, 5.2, 5.11, 5.12, 6.5, 6.20
    s 22(2)   6.14
    s 22ZA   6.20, 6.22
    s 22ZA(3)   6.24
    s 22ZA(4)(a)   6.24, 6.25
    s 22ZA(4)(b)   6.24
    s 22ZA(6)   6.20
    s 22ZA(6)(b)   6.21
    s 22ZA(8)   6.28
    s 22ZA(9)   6.29
    s 22ZA(10)   6.17
    s 22ZA(11)   6.18
    s 22ZB(1)(c)–(h)   6.26
    s 22ZB(3)   6.26
    s 23   6.22, 8.24, 20.25, 20.28
    s 23(1)   20.26, 21.4
    s 23(1)(a)   5.12, 8.9, 8.13, 8.24, 8.26,
                11.7, 12.4, 14.26, 20.36
    s 23(1)(b)   3.8, 8.26, 11.7, 16.2
    s 23(1)(c)   11.7
    s 23(1)(d)   20.15, 20.25, 20.27
    s 23(1)(e)   3.8, 16.2
    s 23(2)   20.26
    s 23(4)   20.28, 20.30
    s 23(5)   8.11, 13.31
    s 23(6)   18.7
    s 24   6.22, 11.7
    s 24A   11.7, 16.8
    s 24A(1)   6.22
    s 24B   11.7
    s 24B(3)   18.7, 18.27, 19.36
    s 24B(4)   18.27
    s 24B(5)   19.29
    s 24F   19.24
    s 25   2.42, 5.18, 9.16, 9.21, 11.17, 14.19,
                                    15.7, 17.21
    s 25(1)   2.30, 6.22, 8.24, 9.2, 9.5, 12.14,
                                    16.12, 17.9

Matrimonial Causes Act 1973—*continued*

s 25(2)	2.30, 2.42, 4.6, 5.18, 6.26, 8.24, 9.2, 9.5, 9.16, 10.9, 10.12, 12.4, 16.12, 17.9–17.11, 17.22, 18.18
s 25(2)(a)	9.9, 9.23, 10.2, 11.7, 11.8, 11.18, 22.27
s 25(2)(b)	7.3, 9.14, 9.16, 9.23, 14.6
s 25(2)(c)	7.3, 9.16, 9.18, 9.19
s 25(2)(d)	9.16, 9.23
s 25(2)(e)	9.16
s 25(2)(f)	7.3, 9.23, 19.15
s 25(3)(e)	20.29
s 25(4)	20.28
s 25A	2.32, 11.6, 11.7, 11.23, 17.14
s 25A(1)	12.4
s 25A(2)	12.4, 17.40
s 25B	19.8
ss 25B–25D	3.11
s 25B(1)(a)	19.5
s 25B(1)(b)	19.5
s 25B(5)	19.7
s 25B(7)	19.9
s 25B(7B)	19.28
s 25C(2)(a)	19.9
s 25C(2)(b)	19.9
s 25C(4)	19.28
s 25F	19.24
s 26(1)	5.3
s 27	3.3, 4.1, 4.2, 4.5, 4.13
s 27(1)(b)	4.7, 4.15
s 27(2)	4.4
s 27(3)	4.6
s 27(5)	4.5, 4.6
s 27(6)	4.6
s 27(7)(a)	4.14
s 27(7)(b)	4.14
s 28	21.9
s 28(1)	11.33, 14.5, 17.4
s 28(1)(a)	11.17
s 28(1)(b)	16.5
s 28(1A)	3.6, 3.19, 8.12, 8.13, 11.1, 11.3, 11.8, 11.17, 11.27, 11.32, 11.33, 17.3, 17.35, 17.37, 19.24
s 28(2)	8.9, 17.4
s 28(3)	8.8, 14.5
s 28(b)	14.26
s 29(1)	20.31
s 29(1A)	19.35
s 29(2)(b)	20.31
s 29(3)	20.30, 20.31
s 30(a)	16.10
s 31	6.16, 11.8, 12.24, 17.3, 17.5, 17.6, 17.23, 17.32, 17.38, 19.14
s 31(1)	17.5
s 31(2)	3.15, 22.29
s 31(2)(a)	5.30
s 31(2)(a)–(c)	17.3
s 31(2)(b)	19.14

Matrimonial Causes Act 1973—*continued*

s 31(2)(c)	16.9
s 31(2)(d)	16.9
s 31(2)(dd)(ii)	19.14
s 31(2)(dd)(iii)	19.14
s 31(2)(g)	19.25
s 31(2A)	5.30, 8.25, 17.33
s 31(2B)	19.14
s 31(4A)	19.25
s 31(6)	16.9
s 31(7)	6.11, 10.31, 12.22, 13.25, 14.6, 17.9, 17.14, 18.5
s 31(7)(a)	5.30, 11.17, 18.9, 18.10
s 31(7A)	11.24, 15.9, 18.6
s 31(7B)	8.7, 11.24, 18.6
s 31(7B)(a)	15.3, 18.7
s 31(7B)(b)	18.7
s 31(7B)(ba)	18.7, 18.25
s 31(7B)(bb)	18.7
s 31(7B)(c)	17.4, 18.7
s 31(7C)	18.7
s 31(7E)	18.7
s 31(8)	16.9
s 31(9)	16.9
s 31(10)	17.4
s 31(14)	17.30
s 32(1)	8.14, 8.25, 13.28, 22.6
s 32(2)	8.25, 22.6
s 34	21.1, 21.2, 21.4
ss 34–36	3.13
s 34(2)	21.2
s 34(2)(b)	21.2
s 34(6)	21.4
s 35	21.1, 21.4, 21.6
s 35(1)	21.7
s 35(2)(b)(i)	21.5
s 35(2)(b)(ii)	21.5
s 35(3)	21.6
s 36	21.6
s 52(1)	20.28, 21.3

Matrimonial Proceedings and Property
    Act 1970   2.30, 2.37

Mental Health Act 1983	20.19
s 1(2)	20.19
Pension Schemes Act 1993	13.13
Poor Relief Act 1601	
s 7	20.2

Summary Jurisdiction (Married
    Women) Act 1895

s 5(c)	2.27

Welfare Reform and Pensions Act 1999

s 11	13.13
s 12	13.13

TABLE OF STATUTORY INSTRUMENTS

References are to paragraph numbers.

Armed Forces (Forfeitures and
   Deductions) Regulations 2009,
   SI 2009/1109   22.19
   reg 7   22.19

Child Support (Variations) Regulations
   2000, SI 2001/156
   reg 13   20.15
Civil Procedure Rules 1998,
   SI 1998/3132
   r 52.3(1)(a)(i)   22.22
   Pt 70   22.10
   Pt 71   22.5
   r 71.2(1)   22.5
   r 71.2(6)   22.12
   r 71.2(7)   22.12
   r 71.6   22.12
   r 71.6(3)(b)   22.12
   PD 71   22.12
     para 2.2   22.12
   r 71(3)   22.5
   r 71(8)   22.5
   r 72.1(1)   22.5
   r 72.1(2)   22.5
   r 72.6   22.5
   Pt 73   22.20
   r 73.4   22.21
   r 73.10   22.21

Divorce etc (Pensions) Regulations
   2000, SI 2000/1123   19.12

Family Procedure Rules 2010,
   SI 2010/2955   4.16, 4.17, 17.34,
      19.32, 22.1, 22.5, 22.10, 22.11,
                   22.30
   r 1.1(2)(c)   6.4
   r 2.3   5.31, 6.13, 16.4, 19.1, 19.11,
                 20.34, 21.6
   r 2.3(1)   4.16, 6.15, 6.16, 17.5
   PD 6C   22.5
   Pt 9   17.5, 20.34, 21.6
   r 9.1   17.5
   r 9.3   6.16, 17.34
   r 9.3(1)   6.16, 17.5
   r 9.7(1)(a)   5.4
   r 9.7(1)(d)   5.31
   r 9.7(3)   5.5
   r 9.7(4)   5.7

Family Procedure Rules 2010,
   SI 2010/2955—*continued*
   r 9.8   5.32
   r 9.9   5.32
   r 9.10   20.35
   r 9.14(5)(a)   14.19
   r 9.14(5)(c)   14.19
   r 9.15(7)(a)   5.9
   r 9.17(2)   5.9
   r 9.33   19.31
   r 9.33(1)(a)–(c)   19.30
   Pt 18   5.32
   r 18.7(2)   5.6
   PD 27A
     para 2.4(a)   5.9
   Pt 28   6.1
   r 28.1   4.17
   r 28.3(4)   17.34
   r 28.3(4)(b)   4.17, 6.29, 16.4
   r 28.3(4)(b)(i)   5.31, 21.6
   r 28.3(5)   6.29, 17.34
   r 28.3(7)   6.26, 17.34
   r 29.8   20.34
   Pt 32   22.10
   Pt 33   22.10, 22.25
   r 33.1(2)   22.26
   r 33.2   22.10
   r 33.3(2)   22.11
   r 33.10–33.18   22.25
   r 33.11(3)   22.25
   r 33.14(2)   22.24
   r 33.16(1)   22.29
   r 33.16(1))   22.26
   r 33.16(1)(b)   22.29
   r 33.16(2)   22.28
   r 33.16(4)(b)   22.28
   r 33.23   22.5
   r 33.24   22.5
   r 33.25   22.20
   PD 33A   10.17, 10.32
     paras 2.1–2.4   22.13, 22.14
   Pt 34   22.10

Insolvency Rules 1986, SI 1986/1925
   r 13   13.27

Pensions on Divorce etc (Provision of
   Information) Regulations 2000,
   SI 2000/1048   19.12

CHAPTER 1

HOW TO USE THE GUIDE

'One of the frustrations of family law, as well as one of its fascinations, is that no two cases are ever the same. Since the essence of any judicial discretion lies in its application to particular facts, and since each case requires its own resolution, the concept of fairness becomes essentially a matter of judgment'[1]

PURPOSE AND SCOPE

1.1 'The Guide To ...' ('The Guide') is designed to provide an accessible, readable and practice-orientated manual to steer the reader through the many complexities inherent in applying for, advising on and litigating orders for maintenance and periodical payments in family finance cases ('periodical payments orders'[2]). Any assessment of these orders provides a fascinating insight into the peculiarities and inequalities of human relationships and the structures designed by Parliament and developed by judges to manage the financial disorder and uncertainty when those relationships fail. The analysis of periodical payments orders also raises fundamental questions about the legal, socio-economic and moral responsibility (and fairness) of an individual to continue to provide for the financial needs of an ex-partner, and to compensate, or share with, that person any future income and financial resources. Furthermore, periodical payments orders occupy that invidious position between, on the one hand, the endemic inequality of wealth so often revealed upon a family's separation and, on the other, the 'clean-break' rhetoric of equality and self-sufficiency. The Guide has been conceived both to help expose these various tensions and to assist the reader in resolving them by offering analysis, commentary, targeted guidance, and practical assistance.

1.2 The Guide's chapters tackle the principal types of periodical payments orders available to parties to a divorce or dissolution of a civil partnership, and on occasion, children themselves. The Guide also confronts key issues such as the quantification, duration, termination, variation and capitalisation of periodical payments orders.[3] The Guide provides analysis of, and commentary on, case-law and, wherever possible, draws together consistent threads of

---

[1] *B v B (Ancillary Relief)* [2008] EWCA Civ 284, [2008] 2 FLR 1627, at [54], per Ward LJ.
[2] Or orders for periodical payments.
[3] Given the number of excellent texts covering financial provision upon the death of a partner or spouse and the application of the Child Support Act 1991, The Guide does not cover these topics in any detail.

judicial opinion and guidance. The ultimate purpose is to offer a single point of reference for any reader interested in, advising on, pursuing or responding to a claim for a periodical payments order in any form or at any stage before or after the instigation of legal proceedings.

1.3   The Guide addresses periodical payments orders relevant to parties to a marriage or a civil partnership, unless otherwise specified. However, for ease of reference only, the text assumes to deal with a husband and wife. Periodical payments orders for the benefit of children are dealt with in a separate chapter. Furthermore, unless otherwise indicated, The Guide is directed to the study of unsecured periodical payments. Chapter 16 deals in more detail with the law and practice relevant to orders for secured periodical payments.

THE PHENOMENON OF PERIODICAL PAYMENTS ORDERS

1.4   The Guide seeks, as far as possible,[4] to isolate periodical payments orders from the range of other orders available to the court when determining a family finance case. Unlike orders for the payment of a lump sum, for property adjustment or for pension sharing, periodical payments orders are uniquely adaptable, flexible and reactive. Orders are available in one form or another from a period during the subsistence of the marital relationship itself through, for example, to the division of income upon retirement many years after the parties to a marriage have divorced. Periodical payments orders can also be tailored to fit with – and respond to – the specific facts of a case from the earliest hint of litigation to a point in time decades after a final order has been made, when a party may seek further orders for variation or capitalisation. Additionally, the phenomenon of periodical payments orders demands a detailed assessment of the applicability of a 'clean break', an understanding of the role of orders for nominal periodical payments and an appreciation of the methods for enforcing such orders. Therefore, the considerable variety of periodical payments orders available (and the distinctive principles governing their imposition, application and extent) benefit from a separate and focused appraisal.

LAYOUT AND DESIGN

Layout

1.5   The Guide begins with an examination of the history and development of alimony and maintenance payments in order to provide some context to the modern-day orders with which parties and the courts grapple on a daily basis. Thereafter, the Guide's chapters are principally divided to deal either with the

---

[4]   It is fully recognised that a final periodical payments order will be determined only by considering all the other orders available to the court in the ultimate pursuit of fairness (in cases of divorce and dissolution of civil partnerships).

different categories of periodical payments orders available or specific issues relevant to the applications for those orders. The Guide's chapters follow a largely chronological sequence from orders available during a marriage on the basis of a failure to provide reasonable maintenance to orders relating to future pension provision. This arrangement is interspersed with chapters dealing with the design and use of maintenance budgets and agreements, the clean break principle, the treatment of bonus payments, the interaction with bankruptcy proceedings and orders available for the benefit of the children of the family.

Design

1.6   In order to maintain consistency, each chapter follows a similar format, wherever practicable. Chapters generally begin with an introduction to the application or issue in hand, which is followed by an examination of the legal basis (statutory or otherwise), the applicable procedure, the principles on which the court acts and any relevant costs consequences. Case references or practice points that provide particularly important or clear guidance are highlighted in boxes. Most chapters also include a quick-reference guide to the key points of **practice** and **theory** relevant to each application or issue. This quick-reference guide is designed to offer practical and appropriate recommendations to the practitioner in addition to highlighting the key principles of law that apply.

1.7   Each chapter is written as a self-contained examination of an application for a specific type of periodical payments order or a related issue. However, as in all areas of family law, it is almost impossible to assess an application or an issue in *complete* isolation. Therefore, the chapters highlight when cross-reference should be made to other sections within The Guide.[5]

TERMINOLOGY IN THE GUIDE

1.8   The phrase 'maintenance' is an umbrella term to encompass all orders for periodic or maintenance payments and includes, for example, orders for periodical payments (secured or otherwise), maintenance pending suit and income payments from pension arrangements. For the purpose of The Guide, therefore, a periodical payments order is interpreted as **any order or agreement for the periodic payment of money (which is not a lump sum payment by instalments) from one party to another or to a relevant child.** Furthermore, to ensure some consistency throughout the chapters, The Guide describes the person making a periodic payment as the **payer** and the recipient as the **payee**, where a neutral description is possible. In deference to readability only, The Guide otherwise refers throughout the text to the 'husband' and 'wife' when considering any issue inapplicable to cohabitants. However, the principles of

---

[5]   For example, an application to capitalise a periodical payments order requires the court first to determine an application for variation, which itself involves a consideration of expenditure budgets and the applicability of a clean break.

law and points of practice apply equally to civil partners, unless otherwise indicated, and each chapter refers to the main corresponding sections of the Civil Partnership Act 2004.[6]

READERSHIP

1.9 The Guide is intended to be of practical and theoretical benefit to a wide range of readers; from law students through to solicitors, barristers, mediators and finance professionals, whether generalist or specialising in family law. The Guide seeks not only to deconstruct the periodical payments order in order to expose its basic features but also tackles the wide range of more complex issues relevant to such orders. For the lawyer, The Guide aims to provide a clear assessment of the relevant legal theory so as to function as a practical tool, whether at court or in the office, to assist in giving the correct advice to clients in all manner of cases involving periodical payments orders.

SEARCHING FOR FAIRNESS ...

1.10 It is axiomatic of family law that its study and practice do not permit of an 'all-answers' approach to any issue within its compass. The Guide does not pretend to offer a comprehensive set of solutions to the myriad challenges posed by periodical payments orders. However, it is hoped that The Guide does more to 'fascinate' than 'frustrate' by helping the reader to advise, and argue on behalf of, clients in family finance cases in the unremitting search for that elusive concept of fairness.

---

[6]   At the time of writing, the Marriage (Same Sex Couples) Bill has received Royal Assent.

CHAPTER 2

THE HISTORICAL PERSPECTIVE: MAINTENANCE, ALIMONY AND PERIODICAL PAYMENTS FROM MEDIEVAL ENGLAND TO MODERN-DAY PROPOSALS FOR REFORM

'That is why a man leaves his father and mother and is united to his wife, and they become one flesh'[1]

INTRODUCTION

2.1   This chapter offers an overview of the historical development of the concepts of alimony, maintenance and financial support after the breakdown of a marriage. The history provides a unique and fascinating insight into the past inequality of marriage, the vulnerability of wives and children, the tension between the sanctity of the marital union and the fallibility of human relationships and, ultimately, the struggle for gender equality. This chapter can do nothing more than briefly chart the progress from the apparent brutality of late-medieval wife-sales to the complexity of modern-day concepts of sharing and non-discrimination in an attempt to provide some perspective to the contemporary analysis of [periodic] financial provision on divorce.

2.2   The concept of divorce – understood as a legal act permitting re-marriage and terminating the contractual, financial and legal ties of marriage – is modern; even when it was introduced to the civil court system in 1857, divorce continued to prejudice women. Prior to 1857, achieving a legal divorce[2] was an exclusive privilege reserved to wealthy husbands in positions of power or influence. Therefore, alternative processes developed over the centuries to achieve and legitimise some degree of separation between spouses and, to significantly varying degrees, to provide financial support to wives and their children. Spouses negotiated private deeds of separation, approached ecclesiastical courts[3] for limited decrees enabling their separation or, in very few cases, petitioned for a full divorce by an Act of Parliament. Pressure for change, particularly from Victorian feminist campaigners, led to the reforms of 1857,

---

[1]   Genesis 2:24.
[2]   Allowing the husband to re-marry.
[3]   Ecclesiastical courts were bound to the principle of the indissolubility of marriage.

which introduced a civil legal system for divorce. Parliament adopted the first Matrimonial Causes Act in 1857, which included some codification of laws providing for the payment of alimony by the husband. Latterly, this chapter charts the fundamental statutory advancements from 1857 relevant to the principles, and the assessment, of maintenance, alimony and, later, periodical payments. The chapter concludes by considering the judicial constructs that have developed and, ultimately, have been rejected, in abortive attempts to explain and apply Parliament's intention in affording maintenance after divorce.

'MAINTENANCE' IN MEDIEVAL ENGLAND

2.3 'Maintenance' is a medieval word, which had – and can still have – both positive and negative connotations. It is not a word originally associated with the institution of marriage or the obligations of a husband to his wife; instead, it was used to describe the action of interfering (often illegally) in a lawsuit in favour of one of the parties. Beyond this negative definition, 'maintenance' also involved being provided with – or providing to another – the wherewithal to live. In medieval England, maintenance was crucial to the general business and cohesion of the community, as everyone sought some level of maintenance from another and, in turn, provided some level of support to someone else.[4] This mutuality of obligation differs from the modern pursuit for autonomy, which, unfortunately, associates the word 'maintenance' with idleness, unnecessary dependence and a lack of self-reliance.

TWO LIVES: ONE FLESH

2.4 Marriage in medieval England made husband and wife 'one flesh', as decreed in scripture. The romance and exclusivity associated with this unity was undermined by an institution which could act to entrench and perpetuate inequality. Kennedy draws an analogy between the medieval husband and wife and the relationship of lord and servant; a relationship of closeness and, on occasion, love but one ultimately based on a foundation of service, subservience, inequality and discrimination.[5] The biblical order to convert spouses into 'one flesh' dictated that, at law, medieval wives existed in a legal fiction that stripped them of their legal personality and subsumed their existence into that of their husbands. Premodern wives survived in the legal state of *coverture* in which they were 'covered' by their husbands and unable to express personhood, individuality or agency, save through their spouse. A wife's commission of a civil offence, for example, would demand the trial of both the husband and wife: a contractual debt incurred by the wife was one for which the husband was responsible. This state of *coverture* was a legal fiction because, day-to-day, women did indeed trade goods, contract to sell, promise to pay for

---

[4]   Kennedy, K, *Maintenance, Meed and Marriage in Medieval English Literature* (Palgrave, 2009), p 4.

[5]   Ibid, p 5.

and receive services, and, on occasion, commit offences. Nevertheless, the supremacy of the husband over the wife was enshrined in the law as well as custom. For example, the 1352 Statute of Treason provided that a wife who killed her husband was guilty of the crime of petty treason for committing the murder of her lawful superior:

> 'Women who slew their husbands were guilty not only of violating the social hierarchy but also of undermining the gender hierarchy. In this climate, their crime was as egregious and socially disruptive as an attack on the life of the king.'[6]

The doctrine of unity was the common law's interpretation of the principle of husband and wife existing as 'one flesh' and its application of the theory of *coverture*. The doctrine of unity – the embodiment of patriarchy[7] – relied upon the fact that marriage combined the legal personalities of the spouses such that, as *Blackstone* stated:

> '... the very being or legal existence of the woman is suspended during the marriage, or at least is incorporated and consolidated into that of the husband; under whose wing, protection and cover, she performs everything ...'[8]

ACHIEVING SEPARATION AND FINANCIAL SUPPORT

2.5   England did not entertain any civil procedure for divorce until 1857. For the vast majority of the population, poverty and the indissolubility of marriage forbade the finality of 'divorce', as it is now understood. Therefore, customs and legal practices developed to provide for the possibility of separation and, on occasion – and with varying degrees of success – for the financial support of the wife.

The wife-sale[9]

2.6   Thomas Hardy's *The Mayor of Casterbridge* opens with Michael Henchard's scheme to sell his wife, Susan:

> '"For my part I don't see why men who have got wives and don't want 'em shouldn't get rid of 'em as these gypsy fellows do their old horses," said the man in the tent. "Why shouldn't they put 'em up and sell 'em by auction to men who are in need of such articles? Hey? Why, begad, I'd sell mine this minute if anybody would buy her!"'

The practice of wife-selling was fact rather than fiction. It was an exercise independent of the formal social institutions of the day and was most prevalent between 1750 and 1850, although Menefee suggests that sales occurred as early

---

[6]   Butler, S M, *The Language of Abuse: Marital Violence in Later Medieval England* (Brill, 2007), p 88.
[7]   *Bromley's Family Law*, (Oxford University Press, 10th edn, 2006) p 108.
[8]   Blackstone, W, Sir, Commentaries on the Laws of England, Book 1, Chapter 15.
[9]   Desertion was also a means of achieving a de facto separation.

as 1073.[10] Thomas Hardy portrays Henchard's decision to sell his wife as impulsive, illegitimate and immoral. However, from the late seventeenth to early nineteenth century, the process of selling a wife was not so uncommon at all, nor was it necessarily viewed as morally repugnant by the communities involved. For poor, working-class rural communities, a wife-sale typically legitimized the consensual end of a marriage in a world in which a legally valid divorce was almost impossible to obtain.[11]

2.7　　The 'sale' was normally preceded by local publicity and conducted at market to generate maximum local interest for the event and to guarantee the highest number of witnesses to the renunciation of the husband's obligations to his wife, financial or otherwise. Although the concept of the wife-sale suggests that the transaction was a unilateral one, motivated and controlled by the husband alone, EP Thompson describes the success of the process as being conditional upon the consent of the wife. EP Thompson states that the legitimacy of the sale often relied upon the approval of the wife, who was able to exercise her veto in respect of an [unsuitable or unwanted] potential purchaser.[12]

2.8　　This custom of self-divorce amongst the rural working classes severed marital ties and obligations and permitted remarriage, at least in the eyes of the parties involved. The sale would relieve the 'seller' husband of his duties to maintain and support his wife, which would transfer to the 'purchaser' husband. Menefee comments, therefore, that wife-sales were tied to market mechanisms: the sale allowed the husband to avoid his responsibility for maintaining his wife and children and transferred this 'commercial' obligation to another man.[13] Wife-sales gained notoriety through the rise of the popular press,[14] which willingly reported both the salacious details of the transactions and the apparent abhorrence of the intellectual classes:

> 'On Friday a butcher exposed his wife to Sale in Smithfield Market, near the Ram Inn, with a halter about her neck, and one about her waist, which tied her to a railing, when a hog-driver was the happy purchaser, who gave the husband three guineas and a crown for his departed rib. Pity it is, there is no stop put to such depraved conduct in the lower order of people.' (*The Times*, 1797)[15]

2.9　　Despite the ubiquity of wife-sales, the transactions had no legal basis, nor were they representative of a custom approved by the courts. Husbands (and purchasers) risked prosecution for conducting wife-sales and, in any subsequent case in which the wife sought financial maintenance from the 'seller' husband,

---

[10]　Menefee, Samuel Pyeatt, *Wives for Sale: An Ethnographic Study of British Popular Divorce* (Basil Blackwell, 1981) p 2.

[11]　Suk, Julie C, '*The Moral and Legal Consequences of Wife Selling in the Mayor of Casterbridge*', March 2011, electronic copy available at http://ssrn.com/abstract=1777555.

[12]　Thompson, EP, *Customs in Common: Studies in Traditional Popular Culture* (The New Press, 1994) p 433.

[13]　Menefee, p 66.

[14]　Kenny, C, '*Wife Selling in England*', (1929) 45 LQR 494.

[15]　Page 3, Col B, 18 July 1797.

any plea by him that the sale had freed him from all responsibility for, and liability to, her, was rejected.[16] Nevertheless, this formal illegality does not appear to have affected the widespread belief in the effectiveness of a wife-sale to achieve an enforceable divorce and relief from financial liability. Wife-sales continued to be popular across the country and were, on occasion, accompanied by written contracts specifying the terms on which the purchaser took the wife, whether those were 'with all right, property, claim, services and demands whatsoever' or, in rather more simple terms, 'free from me for ever, to do as she has a mind'.[17] The formalities of the transaction, which often involved local publicity, public witnesses, a halter around the wife's neck, a written contract, an auction and on occasion an auctioneer, belied the informality of the sale's consequences. However, for the working classes, wife-selling developed into an institution-of-resort for achieving separation from an unhappy or incompatible union and for achieving a measure of financial freedom for the seller-husband and a replacement source of economic security for the wife.

Ecclesiastical courts and the divorce *a mensa et thoro*

2.10 In the *comparatively* more gentle surroundings of the ecclesiastical courts[18] of the Middle Ages and beyond, judges were competent to order a declaration of nullity, annulment[19] or divorce *a mensa et thoro* (from bed and board). The latter effected the equivalent of a judicial separation of the parties on the limited grounds of adultery,[20] cruelty or heresy. The divorce *a mensa et thoro* did not permit either party to re-marry but simply released them from the obligations of the conjugal debt.[21] Helmholz states that a practice developed whereby ecclesiastical courts would make an award of alimony to the wife upon a sentence of divorce *a mensa et thoro* – originally, only if agreed by the parties – which provided some slender relief to a wife left destitute after a separation.[22] Blackstone's Commentaries record the financial relief available as 'alimony', which was a payment in the discretion of the ecclesiastical judge and dependent upon a now-familiar assessment of 'all the circumstances of the case':

> 'In case of a divorce *a mensa et thoro*, the law allows alimony to the wife: such is that allowance which is made to a woman for her support out of the husband's estate: being settled at the discretion of the ecclesiastical judge, on consideration of

---

[16] Menefee, p 66.

[17] Menefee, p 97.

[18] The ecclesiastical courts had undisputed jurisdiction in matrimonial causes from at least the twelfth century.

[19] Divorce *a vinculo*; a ruling that the marriage had never been valid on the grounds of coercion, minority, consanguity etc.

[20] Adultery and life-threatening cruelty if proposed on the basis of the husband's actions.

[21] To cohabit and to have sexual relations.

[22] Helmholz, RH, *The Oxford History of the Laws of England*, Vol I (Oxford University Press, 2004), pp 558–559.

SALE OF
A WIFE.

A full and particular Account of the Sale of a Woman, named Mary Mackintosh, which took place on Wednesday Evening, the 16th of July, 1828, in the Grass Market of Edinburgh, accused by her Husband of being a notorious Drunkard; with the Particulars of the bloody Battle which took place afterwards.

ON Wednesday evening last, in the Grass-market, Mary Mackintosh was brought down about six o'clock by her husband, for the purpose of being sold. Her crime was drunkenness and adultery. She was held by a straw rope tied round her middle, and the words, " To be sold by public auction" in front of her bosom. Several thousand spectators were assembled to witness this novel occurrence. John F——a, pensioner, and knight of the hammer, commenced business, but the acclamations of the people were so great, that no one could get a hearing for ten minutes, to bid for the unfortunate woman.

When the crowd got a little quiet the people began to examine the countenance of the woman; a Highland Drover stepped through the crowd, and pulled out his purse, and said, " She be a good like lassie, I will gie ten and twenty shillings for her." This caused great cheering among the crowd—then a stout Tinker made a bolt into the crowd, and said she should never go to the Highlands—he then bid sixpence more for her. At this time, one of the KILLARNEY PIG JOBBERS, with his mouth open as wide as a turnpike gate, and half drunk, cried loudly, Excellencies, I will give two shillings more, for she is a pretty woman. A Brogue maker, from Newry, coming out of a public house, as drunk as 50 cats in a wallet, came up to the Killarney man, and hits him in the bread bag, and he lay there for the space of ten minutes, which made the woman for sale, laugh heartily, and the cheers of the crowd at this time was long and incessant.— The Brogue-maker being a supposed friend to the woman, went up to the auctioneer, and told him there were three bidders; he was so enraged, he knocked the auctioneer down, and made his claret flow desperately. Great cheering among the people, at the expense of the knight of the hammer.— The women of the neighbourhood gathered to the number of 700, and armed themselves with stones, some threw them, and others put them in their stockings and handkerchiefs, and made a general charge through the mob, knocking every one down that came in their way, until they got up to the auctioneer, when they scratched and tore his face in a dreadful manner, in consequence of the insult the fair sex had received. One resolute woman came up with a stone and knocked down Thomas M'Guisgan, husband to the woman who was exposed for sale. This woman, a true female hero, and a SWEEP'S WIFE, displayed great courage in favour of her sex, and said I will learn you to auction your wife again, you contaminated villain; Tom returned the blow, and hit her between the eyes, and made them like two October cabbages. The sweep seeing his wife struck, made a sally with his bag and scrapper; the women all took the sweep's part, and cried with a loud voice, mill him the old boar, a general battle ensued, and only for the interference of the police, there would have been lives lost. After the disturbance was quelled, the husband insisted she should be sold. She was brought up again, and the auctioneer declared that if he could not be protected, he would have no more call to her. Some young fellows shouted he should, and the sale began again. An old pensioner, a Jack tar, stepped forward, saying, damn my tarry top-lights and chain plates she is a tight little frigate, and well rigged too, and I will give half a crown more than the last bidder. Well done, cried the mob to the sailor, you are a spirited fellow, and you must get her; when a farmer, who was a widower, bade two pound five shillings for her, he being a friend to the sex, and the auctioneer knocked her down. The farmer took her up behind him on his horse, and away they went amidst the cheers of the populace.

W. BOAG, PRINTER, NEWCASTLE.

all the circumstances of the case. This is sometimes called her *estovers*, for which, if he refuses payment, there is besides the process of excommunication, a writ at common law ... in order to recover it.'[23]

2.11   In his influential study of marriage litigation in medieval England, Helmholz states that few records of awards of alimony have survived, particularly those that were imposed on husbands rather than agreed by the parties.[24] One such record of an agreement, however, from the early case of *Dencourt v Mervyn*, sheds some light on the periodic nature of the husband's financial responsibility upon a divorce *a mensa et thoro*:

> 'And it was agreed then and there between them that the aforesaid Richard should pay or cause to be paid to the aforesaid Joan Dencourt his wife every year to the end of her life the sum of five marks sterling'.[25]

2.12   The ecclesiastical court's custom of awarding alimony to a separated spouse extended when the Privy Council licensed branches of the Court of High Commission to make orders (not necessarily by agreement) for 'reasonable alimony and maintenance' in cases of divorce *a mensa et thoro*. Stone states that 'the amount [of alimony] varied according to the degree of turpitude of the husband, his net income, the size of the portion and estate brought to him on his marriage with the wife, and the cost of child maintenance'.[26] The practice of ordering financial support was adopted by the lower ecclesiastical courts, although not without controversy, as it was seen by some as an encouragement to wives to disobey and challenge their husbands.

2.13   One London Guildhall record demonstrates how the recognisable factors of the length of the marriage and the conduct of the parties were brought into consideration in determining the level of alimony:

> 'In these articles it is good to laie howe longe the wife hath beene married to the husband, what portion shee brought, what parentage shee is of, how longe she hath been wrongd etc.'[27]

2.14   The object of awarding alimony upon a sentence of divorce *a mensa et thoro* was to provide ongoing maintenance to the wife (and, therefore, indirectly to the children) as a matter of social economy: there was, of course, no welfare state or other support available. The quantum of the alimony was within the discretion of the ecclesiastical judges who were evidently entitled to take account of the spouses' financial contributions to the marriage as well as

---

[23]   *Blackstone Commentaries*, Vol 1, p 355.
[24]   Helmholz, RH, *Marriage Litigation in Medieval England*, (Cambridge Studies in English Legal History, Cambridge University Press, 2007), p 106.
[25]   Canterbury U. 41, fols, 70r-70v (1394).
[26]   Stone, L, *Broken Lives: Separation and Divorce in England 1660–1857* (Oxford University Press, 1993) p 210. He suggests that by the end of the nineteenth century, permanent alimony was between a third and half of joint income.
[27]   From Helmholz, *Roman Canon Law in Reformation England*, Cambridge University Press, 1990, p 78 (internal reference London Guildhall MS. 11448, f. 147).

the needs of the children. Vernier has studied the historical records of such awards and provides the following analysis:

> '... the husband's obligation to support the children was not ignored in fixing the amount which he could appropriately be called upon to pay for the wife's support. Actually, however, the order for permanent alimony involved more than a mere judicial measurement of the husband's legal duty as husband to support the wife. If he acquired wealth from the wife by virtue of the marriage, he could not be compelled to disgorge, but that fact was of influence in fixing the amount of the award. Finally, in the minds of some of the judges at least, the notion of punishment depending upon the degree of the husband's moral delinquency played some part in the process.'[28]

2.15   Despite the availability of alimony, methods to enforce its payment were almost non-existent, particularly for the wife who had little means to pursue a disobedient husband through the complicated and fragmented court system. As Musson makes clear, the Church lacked adequate powers to force the payment of alimony by the husband:

> 'Penance, fines and public humiliation were only useful if a husband chose to co-operate with the court; however, if a separated husband were accommodating by nature and spiritually conscientious, he probably would not have defaulted on his payments in the first place. Even the threat of excommunication, the church's most powerful weapon, failed to rouse the fears of social exclusion and eternal damnation for most medieval Englishmen by the late Middle Ages. Thus, repeated appeals, failed appearances, recalcitrance, and even judicial inadequacy abound in the alimony suits of the late medieval English courts.'[29]

Private separation deeds

2.16   Separation suits in the ecclesiastical courts that included a claim for alimony became more popular in the late eighteenth century. However, if the husband sued the wife for a divorce *a mensa et thoro* (see above) on the basis of her adultery, the court would refuse her alimony payments on account of her infidelity. Additionally, if the parties to a separation wished to avoid the cost and local publicity of the ecclesiastical court, they were forced themselves to settle and codify the terms of their severance. The early 1700s and 1800s, therefore, witnessed a rise in the popularity of private separations, particularly for the rich and elite, in which the husband and (usually) a trustee on behalf of the wife agreed terms in a deed to govern the spouses' separation and its limited financial consequences.[30]

---

[28]   Vernier, CG and JB Hulbut, 'The Historical Background of Alimony Law and its Present Statutory Structure', (1939) 6(2) Law and Contemporary Problems (Spring) 197–212, 199.

[29]   Musson, A, *Boundaries of the Law: Geography, Gender and Jurisdiction in Medieval and Early Modern Europe* (Ashgate Publishing, 2005), p 76.

[30]   Vleeschouwess van Melkebeek, M, 'Separation and Marital Property in Late Medieval England and the Franco-Belgian Region' in M Korpiola, *Regional Variations in Matrimonial Law and Customs in Europe 1150–1600* (Brill, 2011), p 79.

2.17 Separation deeds normally contained two fundamental clauses: first, the promise by the husband to provide his wife with an annual maintenance allowance and, secondly, a reciprocal indemnity given by the wife to the husband in relation to her debts. In addition, the deed's clauses would invariably free the wife from the position of *coverture* and thereby allow her to act as a sole agent, provide protection to her from the husband's future molestation or any action in the ecclesiastical courts[31] and allow her to live where and with whom she pleased.[32] The deed would entitle both parties to cohabit freely or to remarry, despite such freedom having no formal legal basis. In common with modern separation agreements, Stone states that these deeds proved popular with husbands seeking privacy in relation to the circumstances of the separation. For wives, a separation deed gave a measure of economic freedom and security by providing an annual maintenance payment as well as the right to act independently as a single woman or *femme sole*, both privately and professionally.

2.18 In Stone's *Broken Lives* he details the protracted separation of the Duke and Duchess of Grafton, which is a history that relies on a remarkable set of private correspondence between the spouses.[33] The Grafton's turbulent marriage was eventually terminated by an Act of Parliament (see **2.21**), but the parties' initial separation was governed by an agreement. Despite the Duchess's early pleas for reconciliation, the Duke was determined to separate. Instead of lawyers, family friends were engaged to negotiate and settle the terms of the Grafton's separation, which provided an allegedly generous sum of £3,000 per annum for the Duchess and additional funds for the children of the marriage.[34] However, the Duke's financial generosity was not matched by his demands regarding the children. As part of the agreement, he insisted that his eldest son was sent to the Duchess's mother, which reflected the common law's position that a husband at the time had absolute and inalienable power to 'dispose' of his children as he wished.[35]

An action for criminal conversation (a crim. con. action)

2.19 The late seventeenth century witnessed the development of a common law action enabling a husband to sue his wife's lover for damages in cases of alleged adultery – a crim. con. action. The action, which was a writ of trespass, was founded on the theory of the wife being the absolute property of the husband. The basis of injury to the plaintiff was the loss of consortium resulting from the act of adultery.[36] The actions were relatively rare and, if pursued, were often prohibitively expensive for the majority of the population. An action for

---

[31] In particular, a prosecution for the restitution of conjugal rights.
[32] Stone L, *Road to Divorce* (Oxford University Press, 1990), p 153.
[33] Stone, *Broken Lives*.
[34] Stone, *Broken Lives*, p 144.
[35] Stone, *Broken Lives*, p 20.
[36] The transcript of evidence in the action for criminal conversation brought in 1782 by Sir Richard Worsley against Captain George Maurice Bisset is available to view at http://freespace.virgin.net/robmar.tin/worsley/lady.htm.

crim. con. commonly had three motives: revenge for the injury and insult inflicted on the husband; financial compensation to fund future litigation against the wife; and necessity, as a crim. con. action became a condition precedent for securing a Parliamentary Divorce in the nineteenth century (see **2.21**). The crim. con. action did not constitute a divorce nor did it affect the financial position of the wife, and such prosecutions lost favour and popular support prior to their abolition in 1857:[37]

> 'The reason for this passionate sense of shame about crim. con. stemmed from the fact that it confused the external world of commerce and the market-place with the private world of Victorian domesticity and love, two spheres which the public mind was coming increasingly to view as entirely separate ... The Victorians had finally come to believe that wives were also entitled to a share of the world's virtue and honour, and that neither should be traded for money.'[38]

2.20 Prior to their abolition, successful crim. con. actions would invariably result in large awards of damages made by the jury, which were utterly disproportionate to the means of the defendant. For example, Oldham makes reference to the case of *Wilford v Berkeley*, in which the jury's verdict of £500 was upheld on a motion for a new trial despite the defendant's total income from his employment as a clerk being just £50 a year. The damages payable made both a public example as well as effecting a private recompense.[39]

Divorce by Parliamentary Act

2.21 The growing demand for a 'full' divorce to enable the husband's re-marriage, principally emanating from members of the aristocracy, led to the development of a formal parliamentary process to secure the necessary decree. Divorce by an Act of Parliament was a seldom-used procedure that was limited to a suit on the ground of adultery. The process for seeking an Act was extremely costly, cumbersome and protracted. The Act, if eventually passed by Parliament, was the result of an open investigation and trial that often exposed the most intimate and scandalous details of the marriage. The process became standardised by the early nineteenth century but proved unpopular, with a maximum of 55 petitions for an Act in the years 1841–50 rising from only 10 petitions in the period 1761–1770.[40]

2.22 If Parliament acceded to the husband's petition,[41] it would award an annuity to the wife. Rayden records that the House of Commons included a functionary known as the 'Ladies' Friend' whose duty it was to see that a husband petitioning for divorce made some suitable but moderate financial

---

[37] Matrimonial Causes Act 1857, s 59. However, a modified procedure was retained in the Divorce Act 1857 which allowed the judge in his discretion to distribute any damages awarded between the husband, wife and children.

[38] Stone, *Road to Divorce*, p 291.

[39] (1758) 1 Burr 609. Oldham, J, *English Common Law in the Age of Mansfield* (University of North Carolina Press, 2004), p 341.

[40] Stone, *Road to Divorce*, p 325.

[41] For it was a process predominantly for husbands.

provision for his divorced wife.[42] However, although the husband was freed by an Act of Parliament to re-marry and pursue his life as he wished, the annuity for the wife was conditional upon her remaining chaste and unmarried. Vernier further comments that, even if the annuity or its amount was not agreed, it became common practice for Parliament to *insist* upon pecuniary provision for the support of the 'guilty' (adulterous) wife as a condition to granting the husband a divorce. In contrast to the divorce *a mensa et thoro,* divorce by Parliamentary Act achieved a complete termination of the marriage and, therefore, any subsisting duty of the husband to maintain the wife. Thus, if an Act was passed, Parliament's insistence upon pecuniary provision for the wife 'was a novel and significant development in the law of divorce, flying in the face of the then accepted legal and moral dogmas'.[43]

> 'The Parliamentary practice of requiring the injured husband to make a provision for his delinquent wife had not much to commend it, either morally or legally. Morally it seems monstrous to compel a man to support through life the woman who has dishonored him; legally, she has no claim whatever, because after she has committed adultery, the husband may turn her out of doors ... What, therefore, can appear more strange than to call upon the husband to secure her maintenance? Yet this was constantly done in Parliament, sometimes in the upper but often in the lower assembly.'[44]

THE POSITION BY 1857: PRIVILEGE, COLLUSION AND CONNIVANCE

2.23 By the mid-nineteenth century, divorce was the privilege of the elite and the rich. The cumbersome and peculiar procedures and conditions for its achievement were routinely undermined and exploited by those with sufficient means to do so to achieve the desired end – separation and an ability to re-marry. For the working classes, the procedure for achieving a separation was equally expensive, confusing and localised. The custom of wife-selling was without legal basis and increasingly losing its popularity and public mandate. The provision of financial support to a separated wife was irregular and devoid of any proper or widely accessible enforcement procedures. The unenviable position in which a spouse seeking a manageable and inexpensive separation found [him/her]self was most acutely described by Maule J when addressing a prisoner in a bigamy case. The unfortunate man had been convicted of bigamy for re-marrying after his [first] wife had committed adultery and deserted him:

> '... you have been convicted of the offence of bigamy, that is to say, of marrying a woman while you have a wife still alive, though it is true that she has deserted you, and is still living in adultery with another man. You have, therefore, committed a crime against the laws of your country, and you have also acted under a very

---

[42]   *Rayden and Jackson on Divorce and Family Matters* (Butterworths Law, looseleaf), p x.

[43]   Vernier, G and Hurlbut, J, 'The Historical Background of Alimony Law and its Present Statutory Structure' in *Law and Contemporary Problems* (1939) p 197, at 200.

[44]   MacQueen, *A Practical Treatise on Divorce and Matrimonial Jurisdiction under the Act of 1857 and New Orders* (London: Maxwell, Sweet and Stevens, 1858), p 55.

serious misapprehension of the course which you ought to have pursued. You should have gone to the ecclesiastical court and there obtained against your wife a decree a mensa et thoro. You should have then brought an action in the courts of common law and recovered, as no doubt you would have recovered, damages against your wife's paramour. Armed with these decrees you should have approached the legislature, and obtained an Act of Parliament, which would have rendered you free, and legally competent to marry the person whom you have taken on yourself to marry with no such sanction. It is quite true that these proceedings would have cost you many hundreds of pounds, whereas you probably have not as many pence. But the laws knows no distinction between rich and poor ...'[45]

The system for divorce desperately needed urgent reform to usher in a new period of consistency and accessibility.

VICTORIAN FEMINISTS, PRESSURE FOR REFORM AND THE DIVORCE ACT 1857

2.24

'Why is England the only country obliged to confess she cannot contrive to administer justice to women? ... Simply because our legists and legislators [will never] succeed in acting on the legal fiction that married women are "non-existent", and man and wife are still "one", in cases of alienation, separation, and enmity, when they are about as much as "one" as those ingenious twisted groups of animal death we sometimes see in sculpture; one creature wild to resist and the other fierce to destroy.'[46]

Victorian feminists pursued a crusade for the law's recognition that marriage was not always a union of happiness and that its romantic sentimentality often gave cover to abuse and misery: they sought to free women from the necessity of marriage and to open the institution to those who chose to marry for love rather than money, security, status or privilege.[47] The campaigners' initial success crystallised in the Divorce Act 1857. Stone argues that the debates in Parliament prior to this Act demonstrated that the 'predominant morality ... was not one of liberalism but of nervously defensive conservatism'.[48] Nevertheless, the first Divorce Act revolutionised the system of matrimonial litigation by wresting the jurisdiction for divorce from the ecclesiastical courts

---

[45] Holdsworth, W, *A History of English Law*, Vol I, (London: Methuen, 1922), p 623.

[46] From Caroline Norton, *A letter to the Queen on Lord Chancellor Cranworth's Marriage and Divorce Bill* (1855), p 28. Caroline Norton was an outspoken feminist and supporter of women's rights upon separation or divorce. She was in a violent and unhappy marriage with George Norton, who sued his wife for divorce on the grounds of adultery with the then Prime Minister, Lord Melbourne.

[47] Shanley, ML, *Feminism, Marriage and the Law in Victorian England*, (Princeton University Press, 1933).

[48] Stone, *Road to Divorce*, p 383.

and by creating a centralised civil court for all divorce and matrimonial causes. Shanley recognises the fundamental transformation inherent in the Divorce Act's provisions:

> 'Despite the misogynistic and patriarchal tenor of many of [the parliamentary debates regarding the Marriage and Divorce Bill of 1857], the discussions of the grounds for a wife's divorce contained the seeds of the idea that marriage could not properly be understood solely as an institution for sexual or reproductive bonding, but must also be regarded as a locus for companionship and mutual support. In rejecting the ecclesiastical doctrine of the indissolubility of marriage … Parliament had opened the door a crack to further the debate about the purpose and nature of marriage itself'.[49]

FINANCIAL PROVISION AND THE MATRIMONIAL CAUSES ACTS OF 1857 AND BEYOND[50]

2.25 The Divorce Act was accompanied by the first Matrimonial Causes Act 1857 (MCA 1857[51]), which laid the foundations for all the subsequent Acts of Parliament that shared its name. The MCA 1857 provided the first codification – and limited statutory extension – of principles governing financial provision on divorce. The MCA 1857 offered a very limited degree of protection for the earnings and property acquired by a wife after desertion by her husband.[52] More importantly, s 32 of the MCA 1857 also permitted the court, at its discretion, to order the husband to *secure* the payment of alimony to the wife, as follows:

> 'The Court may, if it shall think fit … order that the husband shall to the satisfaction of the Court secure to the wife such gross sum of money, or such annual sum of money for any term not exceeding her own life, as, having regard to her fortune (if any), to the ability of the husband, and to the conduct of the parties it shall deem reasonable … and upon any petition for dissolution of marriage, the Court shall have the same power to make interim orders for payment of money, by way of alimony or otherwise, to the wife, as it would have in a suit instituted for judicial separation …'

The application of s 32 of the MCA 1857 relied heavily on the historical practice in the ecclesiastical courts, in conformity with which the civil courts were bound by law to act.[53] The court was also empowered to make such provision as it deemed just and proper with respect to the custody, maintenance and education of the children of the marriage.[54] The action for criminal conversation (crim. con. action) was abolished, but the jurisdiction to award

---

[49] Shanley, p 44.
[50] It is not possible to chart all the statutory developments but the principal ones will be considered.
[51] Hereafter, all Matrimonial Causes Acts will be abbreviated as 'MCA' and only the relevant date will change.
[52] MCA 1857, s 21.
[53] MCA 1857, s 22.
[54] MCA 1857, s 35.

damages to the husband in cases of a wife's adultery was retained, albeit that the court could order that the whole or any part of an award of damages could be settled for the benefit of the children of the marriage or paid as 'maintenance' to the wife.

2.26 It was not until the MCA 1866 that the court was granted the power to order the husband to *pay* – rather than merely to secure – a monthly or weekly sum of alimony to the wife. Section 1 of the MCA 1866 enabled the court to order such payments during the parties' joint lives 'of such monthly or weekly sums for [the wife's] maintenance and support as the court may think reasonable'. Additionally, the court was empowered to discharge or modify the payments by the husband or to suspend or revive the order.

2.27 Despite these early statutory developments, many women continued to suffer from a marital relationship characterised by obedience and subordination and, on occasion, significant violence. The MCA 1878 further extended the court's powers so that if a husband was convicted of an aggravated assault upon his wife, the court could order that she was no longer bound to cohabit with him and could make an additional order for the husband to pay 'such weekly sum as the court or magistrate may consider to be in accordance with [the husband's] means and with any means which the wife may have for her support'.[55] The Married Women (Maintenance in Cases of Desertion) Act 1886 enlarged the power of the court by entitling deserted women, who would otherwise be condemned to the workhouse, to compel husbands to maintain them and their family.[56] Later, the Summary Jurisdiction (Married Women) Act 1895 empowered women to separate from their husbands on the basis of persistent cruelty and to apply for a separation decree, custody of the children of the family and maintenance up to the sum of £2 per week.[57] By allowing a wife to leave a husband *before* seeking assistance from the court, the Act of 1895 recognised the need for greater autonomy for a wife who had been subjected to cruelty in her marriage.

2.28 It was not until the MCA 1884 that the concept of **'periodical payments'** was introduced into the matrimonial lexicon. Section 2 of the MCA 1884 entitled the court to order the husband, upon a decree for the restitution of conjugal rights, 'to make to the petitioner such periodical payments as may be just …'.

2.29 The Matrimonial Causes Acts of the twentieth century incrementally advanced the court's powers to order alimony, maintenance and periodical payments and introduced statutory tests and principles which remain familiar to lawyers even in 2014. The MCA 1907 extended the powers of the court to grant maintenance and alimony on decrees for dissolution and nullity of marriage. The MCA 1950 gave jurisdiction to the court to order the husband to

---

[55] MCA 1878, s 4(1).
[56] If the husband had wilfully neglected or refused to provide such maintenance despite having the means to do so.
[57] Summary Jurisdiction (Married Women) Act 1895, s 5(c).

pay periodical payments to the wife (during the subsistence of the marriage) if he was found guilty of wilful neglect to provide reasonable maintenance to his wife or infant children.[58] Section 28(3) of the MCA 1950 also permitted the court to vary or discharge any order for the payment of alimony and maintenance by having regard to all the circumstances of the case, including any increase or decrease in the means of either of the parties to the marriage.

2.30   In the wake of the subsequent divorce reforms of 1969, The Matrimonial Proceedings and Property Act 1970 (MPPA 1970) provided a fresh start to an otherwise outdated and inadequate statutory regime governing financial provision on divorce, which was piecemeal, limited in its scope and continued to reflect the values of male-dominated Victorian society.[59] The MPPA 1970 introduced the concept of maintenance pending suit, replaced the terms 'alimony' and 'maintenance' with that of 'periodical payments'[60] for all final financial orders and introduced the essential list of discretionary factors that now dominate the principled search for fairness in every case.[61]

2.31   As can be seen from this brief summary, the Matrimonial Causes Acts – which led to the 1973 version still applicable today[62] – gradually required a comparatively more liberal approach to the treatment of separated and divorced wives and, later, spouses, who were otherwise exposed and impoverished when the marital partnership came to an end. The terminology of financial support also changed from 'alimony' and 'maintenance' (words originally linked to decrees for judicial separation and divorce or nullity respectively) to 'periodical payments' – an expression first introduced for decrees for the restitution of conjugal rights.[63]

INTRODUCING THE CONCEPT OF BREAKING CLEANLY AWAY

2.32   The Matrimonial and Family Proceedings Act 1984 (MFPA 1984) introduced one of the most fundamental and radical statutory provisions, viz the duty of the court to consider the appropriateness of a clean break between divorcing spouses.[64] The duty to consider whether termination of each party's financial dependence on the other could be achieved shifted the emphasis in financial provision from long-term financial support to the pursuit and achievement of self-sufficiency. The MFPA 1984 explicitly repudiated one of the fundamental principles of mid-twentieth-century marriage – women's 'meal ticket for life'. Auchmuty argues that, in doing so, 'many women concluded that the protection that marriage was supposed to offer them was illusory;

---

[58]   MCA 1950, s 23.
[59]   *White v White* [2000] 3 WLR 1571, per Lord Nicholls, at [20].
[60]   Which could be secured or unsecured.
[61]   Now found in MCA 1973, s 25(1) and (2).
[62]   As amended.
[63]   *Rayden's Practice and Law in the Divorce Division* (Butterworth & Co, 5th edn, 1949), p 471.
[64]   MCA 1973, s 25A.

marriage was, if anything, a risk, if you gave up so much to enter it and might get so little back when it ended'.[65] Later commentators remain equally critical of the clean break 'principle'[66] for its schizophrenic nature, which 'endorses financial independence and self-sufficiency whilst simultaneously stripping ex-wives of any financial stability with one off, inadequate capital awards'.[67] Nevertheless, the court's duties to consider, first, whether financial obligations can be terminated as soon after the divorce as is just and reasonable and, secondly, whether periodical payments orders should only last for a period sufficient to enable the payee to adjust without undue hardship to their termination, are now fully embedded in the statutory landscape.

CASE-LAW AND THE MEASURE OF MAINTENANCE[68]

2.33 The changing statutory environment from 1857 to the present day provides the foundation for the more modern concept, quantification and duration of periodical payments orders as a category of financial remedy available to the court. However, consideration of the legislative developments alone does not explain how judges grappled with – and interpreted – the concepts of maintenance, alimony and, later, periodical payments.

2.34 What exactly maintenance *means* and at what level a periodical payments order should be set are impossible questions to answer definitively. The level of financial support for the payee and the duration of its payment depend, and will continue to do so until Parliament intervenes, on the particular facts of each case as part of the ultimate search for fairness. Fairness – the holy grail of the modern law – is:

> '... an elusive concept. It is an instinctive response to a given set of facts. Ultimately, it is grounded in social and moral values. These values, or attitudes, can be stated. But they cannot be justified, or refuted, by any objective process of logical reasoning. Moreover they change from one generation to the next.'[69]

Nevertheless, the family courts have struggled to refine and define what maintenance actually *is* and how the level of a periodical payments order should be determined. The following brief analysis of case-law is divided into pre- and post-1970 authorities.

---

[65] Auchmuty, R, 'Law and the Power of Feminism: How Marriage Lost its Power to Oppress Women', (2012) 20(2) Feminist Legal Studies 79.

[66] As it is commonly referred to.

[67] Ouazzani, S, 'Ancillary Relief and the Public Private Divide' [2009] Fam Law 842.

[68] A phrase taken from the excellent article by Alexander Chandler 'What is the Measure of Maintenance? How Does the Court Quantify Spousal Periodical Payments?', [2009] Family Law Week.

[69] *Miller v Miller; McFarlane v McFarlane* [2006] 1 FLR 1186, at [4], per Lord Nicholls of Birkenhead.

Pre-1970

2.35 Maintenance, of course, necessitates dependence; it demands that one financially weaker party relies – and must continue to do so – on the financial assistance provided by the other. The historical power-imbalance occasioned by the traditional dependence of the wife on the husband is reflected in the language and approach of the older case law. In *Price v Price*,[70] a case in which the wife alleged that the husband had failed to maintain her during the marriage, the court interpreted 'maintenance' as the provision of the necessities of life. In *Acworth v Acworth*[71] 'maintenance' was described as:

'a very wide word, [which] should be read as covering everything which a wife may in reason want to do with the income which she enjoys. It includes much more than food, lodging, clothes, travelling, and so on. It includes, for instance, charity and making arrangements for the future, thus incurring various liabilities in her discretion, and it is wrong to limit it to any particular form of expenditure.'

2.36 In *Re Borthwick, Borthwick v Beauvais*[72] Harman J explained that:

'maintenance does not only mean the food a wife puts in her mouth. It also means her clothes, the house in which she lives, and the money which she is to have in her pocket, all of which vary according to the means of her husband. Maintenance [therefore] cannot mean only mere subsistence.'

Post-1970

2.37 In the period after the MPPA 1970, an order for periodical payments was increasingly viewed as one of a number of orders available to the court to regulate the division of family finances after a divorce. The courts have struggled to develop and then apply guidance, phrases and judicial concepts to provide some consistency to orders for financial provision, which have impacted on the quantification of orders for periodical payments: three of these concepts or constructs are most noteworthy; the 'one-third rule', the concept of 'reasonable requirements' and, most recently, the model of financial needs, which are often subject to a 'generous' interpretation.

The one-third rule

2.38 The one-third 'rule' developed in response to the philosophy of ongoing maintenance for the wife after divorce. One-third of the assets were judged as the right proportion to award to the wife, which frequently extended to the calculation of her ongoing level of maintenance payable by the husband. The calculation traditionally embraced one-third of the parties' joint incomes less the expenses of earning them.[73] The 'rule' was patently arbitrary and inappropriate to the vast number of separations, whether after a long or short

---

[70] [1951] P 413.
[71] [1943] P 21, CA, at 22, per Scott LJ.
[72] [1949] 1 All ER 472, at 475-476, per Harman J.
[73] Divide by three and deduct the payee's existing income.

marriage, and failed to properly represent the infinite variety of personal and financial circumstances in which divorcing spouses found themselves.[74]

Reasonable requirements

2.39   Prior to the House of Lords in the seminal case of *White v White*[75] expressly rejecting any gender discrimination in ancillary relief cases, the assessment of a wife's 'reasonable requirements' also limited her claim for financial provision. The concept of reasonable requirements was arguably a more generous estimation of a wife's future financial 'need' but, in *determining* the financial award to the wife, it allowed discrimination to infiltrate the court's assessment. The concept directly discriminated against women who, particularly at the end of a long marriage, often suffered the greatest financial disadvantage as a result of home-making, caring for children and sacrificing career prospects.[76] Ellman accurately summarises the extent of the inequality, as follows:

> 'Ending the marriage becomes even less expensive for men, while a wife's probable loss increases as the parties age. Thus, the traditional wife not only makes substantial investments early in expectation of a deferred return, but she depletes her capital assets while making those investments. She gives him "the best years of her life" – the years in which her sexual appeal are the highest, her fertility greatest, and her domestic services are most in demand – and she can never get those years back. At the same time, the man realizes gains from the marriage during its early years, in the form of increased earning capacity as well as the production of children, and his earning capacity has general value both in the marriage market [ie, for remarriage] and the commercial world. He can take much of the gain realized from his first marriage into a second, and he can more easily find a replacement mate.'[77]

2.40   In *White v White*, Lord Nicholls rejected the limitations artificially imposed by the concept of 'reasonable requirements' and encouraged a return to the statutory language of the MCA 1973 in order to properly recognise the flexible and relative nature of financial need:

> '... whatever the division of labour chosen by the husband and wife, or forced upon them by circumstances, fairness requires that this should not prejudice or advantage either party.'[78]

2.41   Duckworth and Hodson also vigorously attacked the reasonable requirements concept as having become 'a sort of mantra or shibboleth of a small magic circle, roughly translatable as "what we as specialist lawyers decide is the right amount according to the unknown and unwritten rules of our secret

---

[74]   See, for example, *Stockford v Stockford* (1982) 3 FLR 52.
[75]   [2001] 1 AC 596.
[76]   Baron J referred to 'reasonable requirements' as a 'discredited concept' in *M v M* [2004] 2 FLR 236, at [59].
[77]   Ellman, I, 'The Theory of Alimony' (1989) 77(1) California Law Review 1, at 44.
[78]   [2001] 1 AC 596, at 605.

society". And, of course, this was a licence to print money'.[79] Ultimately, the concept of 'reasonable requirements' artificially limited a wife's claims on divorce and compounded the financial predicament in which a 'traditional' wife found herself after devoting her time and effort to the family in expectation of future financial security. The husband's claims to wealth on divorce were based on entitlement, whereas the wife's claims relied upon a discretionary and capped redistribution of capital and income. The result was the *antithesis* of fairness.

Need, generously interpreted

2.42 In *Miller v Miller; McFarlane v McFarlane*[80] the House of Lords identified three particular strands of fairness, which should guide the discretionary exercise: need, compensation[81] and sharing. The court must strive to ensure that each party and their children have enough to supply their needs, set at a level as close as possible to the standard of living enjoyed during the marriage.[82] Baroness Hale identified financial need as a concept open to a 'generous interpretation'[83] but not so that those needs act as a ceiling on the level of any final award (whether of a capital or income nature). The notion of needs 'generously interpreted' started to assume a principled status, despite this concept not featuring within the statutory language. The risk is obvious, that whatever the interpretation given by higher courts to the words of the statute, such an interpretation can operate – if it is applied as a rule of law – to unduly fetter and limit the broad discretion of the judge. Therefore, subsequent judgments of the Court of Appeal have stressed the need for lawyers to return to the wording of the statutory checklist in seeking to advise their clients as to what a fair financial award may be in each particular case, whether of a capital or income nature. In *Robson v Robson*,[84] Ward LJ advised thus:

> '[43] Concentrate on s 25 of the Matrimonial Causes Act 1973 as amended because this imposes a duty on the court to have regard to all the circumstances of the case, first consideration being given to the welfare while a minor of any child of the family who has not attained the age of 18; and then requires that regard must be had to the specific matters listed in s 25(2). Confusion will be avoided if resort is had to the precise language of the statute, not any judicial gloss placed upon the words, for example by the introduction of "reasonable requirements" nor, dare I say it, upon need always having to be "generously interpreted".'

2.43 The application of any strict rule to determine the level of maintenance payments, whether that is for one-third or some other fractional division, is arbitrary, inflexible and unfair. The ceiling of 'reasonable requirements' is a relic. Instead, the court must strive to achieve fairness between the parties. The

---

[79] Duckworth, P and D Hodson, 'White v White – Bringing Section 25 Back to the People' [2001] Fam Law 24, 29.
[80] [2006] 1 FLR 1186.
[81] For relationship-generated disadvantage.
[82] [2006] 1 FLR 1186, at [138], per Baroness Hale.
[83] Ibid, at [144].
[84] [2011] 1 FLR 751.

concept of need 'generously interpreted' provides nothing more than a gloss on the statute, which directs the court to consider the financial needs, obligations and responsibilities of the parties now and in the foreseeable future. There is no upper or lower limit on those needs; they must be assessed as only one part of a full evaluation of the child-welfare considerations, financial resources and incomes, contributions to the welfare of the family, ages and the health status of the parties involved. Ultimately, the duty of the court is to have regard to all the circumstances of the case, which means that each case *requires* its own individual solution.[85]

Conclusion

2.44 This potted history of the development of alimony and maintenance is testament to the progression of the law from ad hoc, customary and informal rules and procedures to more structured, reasoned and enforceable orders. This evolution has largely followed the course of social and political advancements, particularly those that have emancipated women and rejected gender-discrimination. The current state of the law regarding periodical payments orders is as much a product of statute as it is a reflection of judicial efforts to achieve fairness in the financial division on divorce. However, even today, in 2014, the discretionary exercise imposed on the court is 40 years old. Judges continue to struggle to strike the right balance between appropriate provision for the financially disadvantaged party and encouraging a post-divorce economy based on independence and autonomy.

---

[85] In September 2012 the Law Commission launched a consultation dealing with marital property, needs and agreements. The consultation was extended to consider the extent and duration of the liability of an ex-spouse to meet a party's financial needs on divorce. The consultation considers, as one option, the introduction of formulas to determine appropriate levels of spousal support. The results of the consultation, and any proposals for reform, are awaited and are likely to be made public in the near future. These proposals may, if followed into law, have a profound impact on this historical survey and the future development of the law.

CHAPTER 3

A SYNOPSIS: THE ORDERS AND ISSUES

3.1   Orders for periodical payments and maintenance[1] are available in a number of different forms and guises at different stages of a relationship, separation and legal proceedings, and raise a variety of distinct and inter-related issues. This chapter summarises the main types of orders available and the corresponding issues that feature in The Guide.

CATEGORIES OF 'MAINTENANCE' AND PERIODICAL PAYMENTS ORDERS

'Failure to maintain' orders[2]

3.2   During a marriage and prior to any petition being issued by a party, the court is empowered to make an order for periodical payments against a payer who fails to provide reasonable maintenance for the payee. Orders in this category can also be made in favour of a child of the family. If the payee can demonstrate an immediate need for financial assistance, the court may make an interim order.

Orders for maintenance pending suit[3]

3.3   An order for maintenance pending suit (or pending outcome of dissolution[4]) is for the payment of maintenance by one party of the marriage to the other after a petition has been issued but before decree absolute, decree of judicial separation or its equivalent. The payment is designed to cater for a relatively short-term period, and is therefore limited to the more pressing and immediate financial outgoings of the payee. However, since maintenance pending suit applications are often the 'first taste' of litigation after separation – and in light of the significant financial dependence generated by many marriages – they are always important, sometimes complex, and their significance is often underestimated.

---

[1]   Used here as a term to include orders for maintenance pending suit and because 'maintenance' is a common umbrella-term used to categorise any non-capital order.
[2]   Matrimonial Causes Act 1973 (MCA 1973), s 27.
[3]   MCA 1973, s 22.
[4]   In cases of civil partnership.

Costs allowances/orders for payment in respect of legal services

3.4   Prior to April 2013 and the implementation of the Legal Aid, Sentencing and Punishment of Offenders Act 2012 (LASPO 2012), orders for maintenance pending suit could include an element of 'maintenance' enabling the payee to fund legal advice and representation (the 'costs allowance'). LASPO 2012, however, introduces a new statutory regime for 'orders for payment in respect of legal services' and removes the power of the court to order costs allowances as a component of an order for maintenance pending suit. The Guide presents an analysis of both regimes.

Substantive periodical payments orders

3.5   An order for periodical payments can be made at any time after a decree nisi has been pronounced. A 'substantive' order is one which provides for payment of an amount that is not merely nominal in nature (see **3.6** below), for example, £500 per month. Periodical payments orders can be made for any period up to the death of either party or the remarriage of the payee. A periodical payments order can provide for a party's future financial need, offer a means for compensating a party for economic disadvantage arising out of a relationship and, more controversially, may present an opportunity to share in the future financial prosperity of the payer.

Nominal periodical payments orders

3.6   An order for nominal periodical payments is a fully-fledged order for periodical payments save for one element only: that the payment is expressed as a nominal sum (eg £1 per annum). A nominal order is one which is often described as 'leaving the door ajar' at a later date for the payee, if the circumstances justify it, to seek an extension of the term for payments[5] or an order transmuting[6] the nominal order into a *substantive* periodical payments order. A transmuted order is also susceptible to the court's powers of capitalisation (see **3.16**). The nominal amount of the payment places such orders – in strict monetary terms – in a precarious position on the cusp of a 'clean break',[7] for a court has no power to order periodical payments that provide for the payment of nothing.[8] However, a nominal order fully engages the court's powers of variation, extension and capitalisation.

Interim periodical payments orders (nominal or substantive)

3.7   An order for periodical payments can be made on an interim or final basis. Interim orders are made when the payee requires financial support but

---

[5]   If the original order did not include a bar preventing such an application pursuant to MCA 1973, s 28(1A).

[6]   This is the terminology adopted in The Guide.

[7]   If all other claims for lump sum, property adjustment and pension orders are dismissed, settled or determined.

[8]   Ie a periodical payments order requires the **payment** of some amount to the payee.

the ultimate determination as to the term for, and amount of, payment will depend, for example, on further financial disclosure.

Secured periodical payments[9] orders

3.8   An order for secured periodical payments is an order against the payer to secure a fund out of which the future periodical payments for the payee are to be made. Such orders are not commonplace and are invoked, generally, where there is risk that the payer will default or the payer's future susceptibility to the jurisdiction of the court is in question.

Married couples and civil partners: orders in relation to children

3.9   In the limited circumstances in which the Child Support Act 1991 permits the court to retain jurisdiction, the court has residual powers to order periodical payments orders for the benefit of children of a marriage. Principally, this limited jurisdiction applies in cases in which funds are required to meet expenses connected with a child's education or disability and in situations where the payer's income exceeds the limits accounted for within the child support legislation ('top-up' cases).

Unmarried couples: orders in relation to children

3.10   The Children Act 1989[10] empowers the court to make orders for periodical payments directly to, and for the benefit of, children of unmarried parents. These orders are not dealt with in any detail in The Guide as there is a dedicated practitioner text available.[11]

Pension orders

3.11   The most common method for distributing pension provision upon divorce or dissolution is the pension sharing order. However, the court also has power to make pension attachment orders,[12] which are orders for periodical payments (and/or a lump sum), albeit that the payment is made directly to the payee by the pension scheme provider.[13] These orders for periodical payments can be made at a time when the payer is in receipt of pension income or they can be deferred in expectation of such income.

---

[9]   MCA 1973, s 23(1)(b) and (e).
[10]   Schedule 1 to the Act.
[11]   Bazley, J, QC et al, *Applications under Schedule 1 to the Children Act 1989* (Jordan Publishing, 2010).
[12]   In relation to petitions filed after 1 July 1996.
[13]   MCA 1973, ss 25B–25D.

Periodical payments orders after an overseas divorce

3.12 The Matrimonial and Family Proceedings Act 1984 empowers the court, in certain circumstances, to make orders for financial provision for parties after a divorce in a foreign jurisdiction. The orders available include orders for periodical payments.

Maintenance agreements

3.13 MCA 1973 also makes provision for parties to enter into binding maintenance agreements containing financial arrangements governing, inter alia, the making or securing of payments to one another.[14] These agreements are enforceable even though they may not ultimately result in a final consent order approved by the court. Maintenance agreements are subject to the court's powers to vary or revoke any of the financial arrangements made, or to provide for new financial arrangements within the agreement.

ASSOCIATED ISSUES

Expenditure, income need and 'maintenance' budgets

3.14 In all financial remedy cases, it is an essential task of legal advisors properly to plead, evidence and challenge budgets that seek to establish a party's actual or anticipated expenditure. The Guide considers what a budget is, what it should contain (and exclude), how it should be presented, to what extent the court is wedded to the budget in the determination of a claim for periodical payments and how the court deals with exaggerated and underestimated budgets. Fundamentally, the future budgets of both the payer and payee will be subject – by the court or in the process of financial disclosure – to both a micro- and a macroeconomic analysis.

Variation, discharge and suspension

3.15 The beauty and bane of an order for periodical payments[15] is that during its existence it is always variable[16] and vulnerable to discharge or suspension. These orders benefit from an innate capacity to respond to the changing financial circumstances and fortunes of both parties but also suffer from the consequential uncertainty demanded by such a level of responsiveness. The variability of periodical payments orders may be expressed as an increase or decrease to the quantum of the original order, by extension of the period for payment, by dismissal, suspension or revival of the order or by capitalisation of the order's future value to the payee.

---

[14]   MCA 1973, ss 34–36.
[15]   Here, the term includes orders for maintenance pending suit, interim maintenance, periodical payments and secured periodical payments (see MCA 1973, s 31(2)).
[16]   Up- and downwards in terms of its amount.

Capitalisation and supplemental orders (upon variation)

3.16 Capitalisation is principally the process of substituting an order of a capital nature[17] for an order for periodical payments, whether those payments are secured or not. Capitalisation is a method of achieving a clean break, which is available to either party upon an application for variation of an order for periodical payments. Capitalisation, if it is ordered, is the result of a staged assessment, which begins with the court's evaluation of an underlying variation application and ends with the capitalised order. Capitalisation represents income-freedom to the payer by terminating the obligation to pay maintenance. For the payee, capitalisation offers capital-security but the ultimate risk is one of under-payment. Any capital sum which seems appropriate at the time of the application may be shown, as a result of future events, to have worked in favour of, or against, one or other of the parties.

Capitalisation and *Duxbury* calculations (original final orders)

3.17 In certain cases in which the capital resources are sufficient, the payee's entitlement to periodical payments may be paid by way of a lump sum rather than by means of a periodic order. The court will often refer to the payment to the payee of a '*Duxbury* fund', which is a capital lump sum calculated on the basis that, if amortised and suitably invested by the payee, it will provide him/her with a broadly predictable income for life. However, the calculation is fraught with assumptions and issues that can undermine its use and effectiveness. The calculation may also be used to determine the appropriate level of security for a periodical payments order and to estimate the income that a payee can generate from residual capital under his/her control.

The clean break (immediate and deferred)

3.18 The court is under a duty to consider whether the financial obligations of each party to a divorce should be terminated as soon as is just and reasonable. Orders for periodical payments are the antithesis of the clean break: whereas the ultimate objective of financial orders is 'to give each party an equal start on the road to independent living',[18] the periodical payments order perpetuates financial dependence. The Guide will consider the case law that provides some guidance as to when a clean break is appropriate and whether it can be imposed immediately [after decree absolute] or at a later date [in deferral].

Extendable and non-extendable term orders for periodical payments

3.19 The default duration of a periodical payments order is until the death of either party or the payee's remarriage. However, the court can make a periodical payments order for any other such term as it considers appropriate.

---

[17] This can also be achieved by making a property adjustment or pension sharing order.

[18] *Miller v Miller; McFarlane v McFarlane* [2006] 1 FLR 1186, at [144], per Baroness Hale.

If the court imposes a 'term order', consideration must also be given to whether it is proper to prohibit the payee from applying to extend the term for payment.[19]

Periodical payments and bankruptcy

3.20 Levels of personal indebtedness in the United Kingdom have reached record levels. Bankruptcy is a process that can severely undermine the powers of the family court seeking to fairly distribute matrimonial assets, as bankruptcy places the assets and property of the bankrupt in the hands of the Trustee in Bankruptcy. Orders for periodical payments may survive a bankruptcy order but the quantum of such orders can be limited by orders available to the Bankruptcy Court. The Guide analyses the impact of the bankruptcy of, and on, the payer and payee and the interactions between the powers of the Bankruptcy Court and the Family Court.

Periodical payments, remarriage and cohabitation

3.21 Orders for periodical payments terminate automatically on the remarriage of the payee. However, the financial effect of the payer's remarriage and the cohabitation of either party on a periodical payments order remains to be determined within the court's discretion.

Enforcement (in England and Wales)

3.22 The methods for enforcing a periodical payments order are found in various ancient and modern statutes which, together, provide a thoroughly confusing and highly technical web of rules and processes. The situation is so dire that the Law Commission is undertaking a consultation which, the author hopes, will result in radical proposals for reform.[20] Pending any legislative changes, the Guide will highlight the most common means for enforcing an order for periodical payments and provide an overview of the essential processes.

---

[19] Pursuant to MCA 1973, s 28(1A) and often referred to as a 'bar' on the payee's ability to extend a term for payment.
[20] See http://lawcommission.justice.gov.uk/areas/family-financial-orders.htm for more details.

CHAPTER 4

FAILURE TO PROVIDE REASONABLE MAINTENANCE[1]

INTRODUCTION

4.1   Just as a decree of divorce, nullity or judicial separation may trigger an order for periodical payments, so can one party's 'failure to maintain' the other during the marriage, notwithstanding the absence of any such decree. Section 27 of the Matrimonial Causes Act 1973 (MCA 1973) is a rarely used – but nevertheless important – statutory provision, which enables the court to make a range of financial orders in favour of a party to the marriage or any child of the family where one party has failed to provide reasonable maintenance or to make a proper contribution towards reasonable maintenance.

STATUTORY BASIS

4.2   Section 27 of the MCA 1973 provides that:

'(1) Either party to a marriage may apply to a court for an order under this section on the ground that the other party to the marriage –

(a)   has failed to provide reasonable maintenance for the applicant, or

(b)   has failed to provide, or to make any proper contribution towards, reasonable maintenance for any child of the family.'

There is also power in the Domestic Proceedings and Magistrates' Courts Act 1978, s 1 for the magistrates' court to make similar orders for financial support. However, the magistrates' court's powers are more restricted as it is not empowered to make orders for secured periodical payments and the level of available lump sum provision is limited.

APPLICABILITY

4.3   Orders for failure to maintain are available without any petition for divorce. Therefore, an application for an order can be made whilst the marriage

---

[1]   In cases of civil partnership, the relevant provisions are to be found in the Civil Partnership Act 2004 (CPA 2004), Sch 5, Part 9, paras 39–45.

subsists or, in theory, after a petition for divorce, nullity or judicial separation. However, given the more extensive powers available to the court when considering an application for financial relief[2] upon a petition for divorce, orders for failure to maintain have a limited application.

4.4   The entitlement to apply for an order depends on the domicile of either party in England and Wales, the habitual residence of the applicant in the jurisdiction for one year or the respondent's residence on the date of the application.[3]

INTERIM ORDERS

4.5   The court may order interim provision whilst an application under MCA 1973, s 27 is proceeding. Interim orders are limited to periodical payments only.[4] The applicant must be in a position of 'immediate need'[5] of financial assistance in circumstances where is it not yet possible for the court to determine what order, if any, should be made on the application.[6] Any interim order ends with the court's final order on the application.

FINAL ORDERS

4.6   The orders available under MCA 1973, s 27 are for a lump sum and periodical payments, secured or otherwise, but not property adjustment orders.[7] The court must take into account all the familiar factors set out in MCA 1973, s 25(2) in deciding both whether one party has failed to provide reasonable maintenance for the other and, if so, the level of any award.[8]

4.7   The welfare of a child of the family is the first consideration for the court only when an application is made pursuant to MCA 1973, s 27(1)(b) (ie for the maintenance of a child of the family).

THE FAILURE TO MAINTAIN

4.8   The requirement that one party has failed to provide reasonable maintenance for the other is more neutral than the historical stipulation of a 'wilful neglect to maintain'. There is no case-law guidance as to what constitutes a *failure* to provide reasonable maintenance. This can only be determined by an assessment of the applicant's financial needs versus the

---

[2]   For example, lump sum and pension sharing orders.
[3]   MCA 1973, s 27(2).
[4]   No lump sum or other provision is available at the interim stage.
[5]   An 'immediate' need is one which is current rather than urgent, if analogy is taken with *M v M* [2011] EWHC 3574 (Fam) and [2010] EWHC 2817 (Fam).
[6]   MCA 1973, s 27(5); CPA 2004, Sch 5, Part 9, paras 39(3) and 40.
[7]   MCA 1973, s 27(6); CPA 2004, Sch 5, Part 9, para 41(1).
[8]   MCA 1973, s 27(3).

available resources of both parties in the context of the marital standard of living as well as the other discretionary factors. Jackson suggests that the statutory wording of 'has failed' (to provide reasonable maintenance) is equivalent to 'has not'.[9]

4.9   The previous statutory test of the husband's 'wilful neglect' to maintain (the wife) relied on a more conduct-led assessment of one party's behaviour, which does not form part of the more 'modern' test of failure. Whereas wilful neglect to provide reasonable maintenance 'imports some element of matrimonial misconduct',[10] failure to maintain suggests, rather, an ability and a responsibility to pay and a failure to pay, and nothing more.

REASONABLE MAINTENANCE

4.10   There are no modern authorities which assist to define what constitutes 'reasonable maintenance'. Older authorities must be treated with caution given social and legal developments. For example, in *Scott v Scott*[11] it was held that 'the word "reasonable" no doubt has to be interpreted against the background of the standard of life which [the husband] previously had maintained'.[12] The decision in *Scott* was made with reference to the husband's common law liability to maintain his wife and children; a liability which will be abolished by s 198 of the Equality Act 2010.[13]

4.11   Any modern interpretation of the term 'reasonable maintenance' will likely follow the guidance set out in Chapter 9 dealing with the quantification of periodical payments orders.

DURATION

4.12   Orders made as a result of a 'failure to maintain' are limited to the joint lives of the parties.[14] Upon the death of one party, the Inheritance (Provision for Family and Dependants) Act 1975 may be invoked as the statute of recourse if the surviving party considers that reasonable financial provision has not been made for them.

4.13   Orders for failure to maintain are only available to parties to a marriage and, therefore, end upon the pronouncement of decree absolute. In *AB v CB*[15] the court was faced with complicated proceedings in which applications for divorce and financial relief had been made in England and India. The wife's applications for maintenance pending suit and for an order for failure to

---

[9]   *Jackson's Matrimonial Finance* (9th edn), para 11.28.
[10]   *Morton v Morton* [1954] 2 All ER 248, at 252, per Singleton J.
[11]   [1951] P 245.
[12]   At 248, per Hodson J.
[13]   Not yet in force at the time of publication.
[14]   *Harb v King Fahd Bin Abdul Aziz* [2005] EWCA Civ 1324, [2006] 1 FLR 825.
[15]   [2012] EWHC 3841 (Fam).

maintain had been stayed in England (the latter resulting in an order for an interim payment of £844 per month). Bodey J considered that the wife's MCA 1973, s 27 application could theoretically stand alongside her application for maintenance pending suit. However, the former application was vulnerable to a strike-out application as a mere duplication of the essence of the latter application. Bodey J ultimately retained the stay on the wife's s 27 application but refused to dismiss it, as requested by the husband. Therefore, the wife could resurrect her application if the husband failed to make interim provision for her in the knowledge that her application pursuant to s 27 would be dismissed when a decree absolute was pronounced in India.

PRIOR LIABILITIES AND EXPENSES

4.14 The court has the additional power to order the payment of a lump sum for the purpose of discharging any liabilities or expenses reasonably incurred in maintaining the applicant (or child of the family) *before* the making of the application.[16] This important supplementary power to provide payment retrospectively permits the applicant to be recompensed for payments made by her when the respondent ought to have been providing reasonable maintenance.

CHILDREN

4.15 Orders can, in theory, be made against a party who has 'failed to provide, or to make proper contribution towards, reasonable maintenance for any child of the family'.[17] However, the Child Support Act 1991 (CSA 1991) significantly limits the court's jurisdiction to make orders relating to child maintenance. Briefly, the responsible government agency[18] does not have sole jurisdiction to determine maintenance for children if:

(1)   the child is over 16 and not in full-time education;

(2)   the child is 19 or over;

(3)   the child or one of the parents is habitually resident outside England and Wales;[19]

(4)   a written agreement is reached between the adult parties (which applies for 12 months before an application for an assessment can be made);

(5)   the matter requires a 'topping up' order in excess of the maximum assessment;

(6)   an order is required for additional educational expenses; or

(7)   an order is required for the support of disabled or blind children.

---

[16]   MCA 1973, s 27(7)(a), (b); such lump sum payment can also be made by instalments, if so ordered.

[17]   MCA 1973, s 27(1)(b); CPA 2004, Sch 5, Part 9, para 39(1)(b).

[18]   Child Support Agency or equivalent body (laws and regulations are in transition at the time of writing).

[19]   And not within one of the exceptions listed in CSA 1991, s 44(2A).

PROCEDURE

4.16 An application for an order is made pursuant to Part 9 of the Family Procedure Rules 2010 (FPR 2010).[20] An order made on the basis of a failure to provide reasonable maintenance is a 'financial remedy'[21] within the meaning provided for in the FPR 2010.

COSTS

4.17 Despite the fact that an order made on the basis of a failure to provide reasonable maintenance is a 'financial remedy', the application for such an order does not qualify as 'financial remedy proceedings' for the purpose of determining the issue of costs.[22] Therefore, the general rule that the court will not make an order requiring one party to pay the costs of the other does not apply. The court may at any time make such costs order as it thinks just,[23] and the relevant parts of the Civil Procedure Rules apply.

---

[20] SI 2010/2955.
[21] FPR 2010, r 2.3(1).
[22] FPR 2010, r 28.3(4)(b).
[23] FPR 2010, r 28.1.

POINTS OF PRACTICE AND THEORY

4.18

(1) There is no requirement for proceedings (for divorce, dissolution or any other suit) to be instituted.

(2) The right to bring an application for failure to maintain is limited to the joint lives of the parties.

(3) The relevance of these orders in favour of children is limited by the statutory body tasked with assessing and enforcing child maintenance calculations.

(4) Interim payments are available, which cease when the court makes a final order.

(5) The general rule of no order as to costs does not apply.

CHAPTER 5

MAINTENANCE PENDING SUIT[1]

INTRODUCTION

5.1   Maintenance pending suit (or pending the outcome of a dissolution[2]) is the payment of maintenance[3] by one party to the marriage or civil partnership to the other before decree absolute, a decree of judicial separation or its equivalent.[4] The maintenance is designed to cover a relatively short period and, therefore, is limited to the more pressing and immediate financial realities of life post-separation. However, since maintenance pending suit applications are often the 'first taste' of litigation after separation – and in light of the financial dependence generated by many marriages – they are always important, sometimes complex, and their significance is often underestimated.[5]

LEGAL BASIS

5.2   Maintenance pending suit has its statutory basis in MCA 1973, s 22:

> 'On a petition for divorce, nullity of marriage or judicial separation, the court may make an order for maintenance pending suit, that is to say, an order requiring either party to the marriage to make to the other such periodical payments for his or her maintenance and for such term, being a term beginning not earlier than the date of the presentation of the petition and ending with the date of the determination of the suit, as the court thinks reasonable.'

APPLICABILITY

5.3   An application for maintenance pending suit requires the filing of a petition.[6] Decree absolute prevents any application for maintenance pending suit. The application is available even if the respondent denies, for example, the

---

[1]   In cases of civil partnership, the relevant provision is CPA 2004 (CPA 2004), Sch 5, Part 8, para 38.

[2]   In the case of a civil partnership, CPA 2005, Sch 5, Part 8, para 38.

[3]   In big money cases, the court can give the option to the payer to pay on a monthly basis or by way of a single capital sum, see for example, *Charman v Charman* [2006] EWHC 1879 (Fam), [2007] 1 FCR 33, at [52].

[4]   After which, the payment is for 'interim periodical payments', which may continue through to a final order being made, at which point the payments lose their 'interim' nature.

[5]   Cleaver, M, 'An Uncertain Future for Maintenance Pending Suit?' [2013] Fam Law 290.

[6]   MCA 1973, s 26(1).

existence of the marriage or disputes the court's jurisdiction, for whatever reason.[7] The court has the power to backdate the order to the date of the presentation of the petition.

APPLICANT'S PROCEDURE

5.4   Maintenance pending suit is an application for an interim order pursuant to FPR 2010, r 9.7(1)(a). If the applicant makes an application at the time of filing his financial statement (Form E), s/he need do no more than include the proposed maintenance budget within the statement.

5.5   If the applicant applies for maintenance pending suit before filing his financial statement, written evidence must explain why the order is necessary and give up-to-date information about his/her financial circumstances.[8] This information should include all income from all sources, any capital assets capable of producing an income or being liquidated and a clear and reasoned schedule outlining the monthly financial needs.

5.6   As an interim application, FPR 2010, Part 18 applies. The notice of application must, therefore, include a draft of the order sought for maintenance pending suit.[9] Backdating should be requested in all cases in which the respondent's financial support has been lacking after presentation of the petition.

RESPONDENT'S PROCEDURE

5.7   If no financial statement has been filed, a statement of means must be filed and served on the applicant at least 7 days before the court hearing.[10] The statement of means should include information as to income and expenditure and any likely changes to those figures.

GENERAL GOOD PRACTICE: THE HEARING

5.8   The focus of the court's attention at a maintenance pending suit hearing will be the budget of the payee and the maintenance-paying ability of the payer. The key question will be whether the deficit in the payee's budget can fairly be met from the surplus in the payer's, pending the court making a final order (which requires a much more extensive level of disclosure and investigation).

5.9   If the application for maintenance pending suit is listed for consideration at the first directions appointment (FDA), the court may make an order for

---

[7]   *Moses-Taiga v Taiga* [2005] EWCA Civ 1013, [2008] 1 FCR 696.
[8]   FPR 2010, r 9.7(3).
[9]   FPR 2010, r 18.7(2).
[10]   FPR 2010, r 9.7(4).

maintenance pending suit at that hearing.[11] Hearings are often listed with optimistic time limits of one hour or less, irrespective of the complexity of the case. Practitioners should, if necessary, consider the need for seeking a longer time estimate to permit the court to examine the issues, read the relevant papers,[12] listen to submissions, take limited oral evidence (exceptionally)[13] and give judgment. If the FDA is also likely to be complex or lengthy, consideration should be given to requesting that the maintenance pending suit hearing is listed separately. If a financial dispute resolution appointment (FDR) fails to generate a final agreed order on the substantive application for a financial remedy, the judge hearing the FDR appointment is unable to thereafter determine an application for maintenance pending suit. The FDR judge 'must have no further involvement with the application, other than to conduct a further FDR appointment or to make a consent order or a further directions order'.[14]

INTERIM MAINTENANCE PENDING SUIT

5.10 An interim maintenance pending suit order can, in principle, be made if there is particular urgency, although such an application will be rare.

KEY CONCEPTS AND PRINCIPLES

5.11

> Maintenance pending suit hearings are often master classes in concise advocacy, whether written or oral. The court's examination of the financial positions of both parties is focused and limited. Submissions that mirror this approach are likely to have more success. In *TL v ML*[15] Nicholas Mostyn QC (sitting as a deputy High Court Judge) considered the leading cases relevant to an application for maintenance pending suit and elicited the following core principles:
>
> > '(i) The sole criterion to be applied in determining the application is "reasonableness" (s 22 of the Matrimonial Causes Act 1973), which, to my mind, is synonymous with "fairness".
> >
> > (ii) A very important factor in determining fairness is the marital standard of living (*F v F*). This is not to say the exercise is merely to replicate that standard (*M v M*).   →

---

[11]   FPR 2010, r 9.15(7)(a).
[12]   Pursuant to FPR 2010, PD 27A, para 2.4(a), a court bundle is not required for a hearing listed for one or hour less.
[13]   Jackson suggests that if the application is heard after decree nisi, it is then more likely that oral evidence will be heard by the court. It will depend on the complexity of the case. *Jackson's Matrimonial Finance* (9th edn), para 2.28.
[14]   FPR 2010, r 9.17(2) and see further '*Financial Dispute Resolution Appointment – Best Practice Guidance*' December 2012, [2013] 1 FLR 1109.
[15]   [2005] EWHC 2860 (Fam), [2006] 1 FLR 1263.

(iii) In every maintenance pending suit application there should be a specific maintenance pending suit budget which excludes capital or long-term expenditure more aptly to be considered on a final hearing (F v F). That budget should be examined critically in every case to exclude forensic exaggeration (F v F).

(iv) Where the affidavit or Form E disclosure by the payer is obviously deficient, the court should not hesitate to make robust assumptions about his ability to pay. The court is not confined to the mere say-so of the payer as to the extent of his income or resources (G v G, M v M). In such a situation the court should err in favour of the payee.

(v) Where the paying party has historically been supported through the bounty of an outsider, and where the payer is asserting that the bounty has been curtailed, but where the position of the outsider is ambiguous or unclear, then the court is justified in assuming that the third party will continue to supply the bounty, at least until final trial (M v M).'[16]

These key concepts and principles (and others of relevance) are worthy of further explanation.

Maintenance – what it is and what it is not

5.12 The claim is one for maintenance[17] for a relatively short period of time. Financial information is likely to be limited. Budgets that include, for example, capital expenditure or provision for savings will not assist and may lead the court to consider that the budget is unreasonably inflated.

5.13 An order for maintenance pending suit is 'designed to deal with short-term cash flow problems, which arise during divorce proceedings. Its calculation is somewhat rough and ready, as financial information is frequently in short supply at the early stage of the proceedings. It is nonetheless valid until discharged'.[18]

5.14 What amounts to 'maintenance' will depend on both the facts of the case and prevailing social and economic conditions. In *G v G (Maintenance Pending Suit: Costs)*, Charles J commented that 'what is or is not within the range of the meaning of the word 'maintenance' is something that has to be judged from time to time having regard to both general circumstances and the circumstances and context of the particular case'.[19]

---

[16]   Ibid, at [124].
[17]   MCA 1973, s 22 is to be contrasted with MCA 1973, s 23(1)(a). The former section specifies that periodical payments may be ordered for one party's 'maintenance' whereas the latter provides no such limitation. See also *McFarlane v McFarlane* [2006] UKHL 24, [2006] 1 FLR 1186 at [31] in which Lord Nicholls said: 'There is nothing in the statutory ancillary relief provisions to suggest Parliament intended periodical payments orders [pursuant to MCA 1973, s 23(1)(a)] to be limited to payments needed for maintenance'.
[18]   *Moore v Moore* [2009] EWCA Civ 1427, [2010] 1 FLR 1413, per Coleridge J.
[19]   [2002] EWHC 306 (Fam), [2003] 2 FLR 71, at [93], per Charles J.

5.15 The subject matter of the proceedings may also affect the outcome of any application for maintenance pending suit, particularly if the validity of the underlying divorce proceedings is in issue. For example, in *MET v HAT*[20] the wife applied for 'interim interim' maintenance for a very short period pending a further listed hearing. She was the fourth of four wives of the husband, who had valid polygamous marriages in his country of origin. The husband claimed a valid (non-proceedings[21]) talaq divorce. The wife's two petitions for divorce in England had been dismissed and struck out. It appeared to Mostyn J that the husband's talaq divorce may have been a valid non-proceedings divorce that was entitled to recognition in the UK. However, such recognition would not enable the wife to seek financial provision for herself pursuant to Part 3 of the Matrimonial and Family Proceedings Act 1984. The wife had issued a third petition for divorce in England but Mostyn J doubted the likelihood of that petition resulting in a decree. Mostyn J refused the wife's application for maintenance pending suit for herself and concluded that 'the court is entitled ... to have regard to the strength or otherwise of the claim that the court has jurisdiction, and the more uncertain the court is on a provisional basis that the court has jurisdiction, the more cautious it should be [in awarding maintenance pending suit].'[22] Maintenance pending suit would only be ordered – in such uncertain [jurisdictional] circumstances – to relieve an applicant's 'real predicament of [financial] need'.[23]

Reasonableness and discretion

5.16 Reasonableness is the only standard by which to assess the quantum of an order for maintenance pending suit. Reasonableness is synonymous with fairness, which is the driving force behind all resolutions of applications for financial relief.

5.17 Reasonableness is a criterion that permits the court huge flexibility in considering what constitutes the 'right' amount of maintenance in any individual case.

5.18 The court is not directed to consider the factors in MCA 1973, s 25(2) nor is the welfare of a child of the family the first consideration.[24] Nevertheless, the court will invariably have recourse to the familiar discretionary factors within MCA 1973, s 25 when determining an application for maintenance pending suit in order to guide its approach and decision. Ultimately, however, as identified in *Porter v Porter*[25] 'the discretion given to the court is complete and unfettered by anything in any statute or other instrument'.

---

[20] [2013] EWHC 4247 (Fam).
[21] In the sense of FLA 1986, s 46(2).
[22] Per Mostyn J, at [21].
[23] In the circumstances, and for similar reasons, the wife's application for a legal services payment order was also refused (see Chapter 6).
[24] See **5.30**, however, for how this changes on an application for variation.
[25] [1969] 3 All ER 640, at 643, CA.

Standard of living

5.19 The assessment of what is reasonable will take account of the marital standard of living. This is an important consideration by which to assess the reasonableness of any immediate financial support. If there are children involved, the court will strive to minimise any obvious changes to lifestyle in the immediate aftermath of separation, if this is reasonable and viable. If the standard of living during the marriage is of importance to the level of the order claimed,[26] it is sensible to include evidence in support of this standard (eg a schedule of expenditure during the marriage) in order to compare and contrast this with the proposed maintenance pending suit budget of the payee. However, the standard of living prior to separation is by no means the determining object of the exercise. In *M v M (Maintenance Pending Suit)*[27] the court considered and rejected the argument that an award should be set at a level 'designed to maintain the status quo or to establish a yardstick that more nearly reflects the marital standard of living and thus the status quo'.[28]

5.20 In *F v F (Ancillary Relief: Substantial Assets)*[29] the court faced a case involving a huge asset base. The husband claimed the 'millionaire's defence' alleging his worth at between £150m to £200m. He argued that the standard of living of the parties should not raise any award over the sum of £220,000 a year, a sum on which he claimed that anyone could live comfortably. The court rejected his argument and held that 'it is necessary to establish a yardstick that more nearly reflects the standard of living which has been the norm for the wife ever since marriage and for the husband for considerably longer'.[30] The standard of living was an important factor taken into consideration in assessing the subjective reasonableness of the award, albeit that it was not the determining one.

Third-party support for the applicant (the intended payee)

5.21 In the immediate aftermath of separation, friends and family often assist by loaning or giving money to enable the applicant to meet her needs, particularly if the respondent fails completely to provide financial support. However, it is wrong to assume that such support extinguishes the applicant's entitlement to maintenance pending suit. In *M v M (Financial Provision)*[31] the wife's friend had provided her with £12,000 per month to pay her rent, in addition to money for living and legal expenses. The husband resisted the wife's application for interim maintenance (this being a case pursuant to Part III of the Matrimonial and Family Proceedings Act 1984) by concentrating on the generosity of her friends as removing any 'immediate need' she had for interim

---

[26] Limited, in reality, to the larger money cases.
[27] [2002] EWHC 317 (Fam), [2002] 2 FLR 123.
[28] Ibid, at [123].
[29] [1995] 2 FLR 45.
[30] Ibid, at 50C.
[31] [2010] EWHC 2817 (Fam), [2011] 1 FLR 1773; an application pursuant to Part III MFPA 1984.

maintenance. King J rejected this principle and stated that 'such temporary assistance should not subsequently be used as a basis for resisting the making of an order for interim maintenance, which would otherwise be appropriate. The fact that the sums involved in this case are very considerable matters not; this is a family that lived at a very high level, as do their friends and acquaintances'.[32]

5.22 If third party support is provided by way of a loan, it is arguably good practice for those involved to enter into a loan agreement in order to demonstrate the need for, and terms of, repayment.

Assumptions and inferences

5.23 Just as in cases for final orders for financial relief, parties to a maintenance pending suit application may attempt to restrict their disclosure or conceal assets and income in an effort to curtail the court's ability to assess the level of, and make an order for, maintenance pending suit. The duty of the parties to give full and frank disclosure,[33] not merely to each other but, first and foremost, to the court, is the core requirement of the law of financial remedies.[34] In a maintenance pending suit application, the court *will* be realistic and pragmatic about the extent of the information that can be presented at such an early stage of the proceedings. Nevertheless, despite the more limited nature of the enquiry, without full, frank and clear disclosure, the 'court is thrown back on inference and guess-work within an exercise which inevitably costs a fortune and which may well result in an unjust result to one or other party'.[35]

In *G v G (Maintenance Pending Suit: Legal Costs)*[36] the husband was found to have failed to comply with his duty to provide full and frank disclosure and to have given an unclear, incomplete and poorly evidenced account of his business and financial affairs. The court was clear that, in such circumstances, it is not bound to 'accept and proceed on the basis of his … assertions as to means and an inability to pay'.[37] Instead, the court can 'take a broad and robust view of disputes as to means, which it is not then in a position to decide'.[38] This robust approach will be taken despite the court invariably not hearing oral evidence from either party.

Therefore, in a dispute as to the means of the payer, the court (and legal advisers) should consider:

(a)   the extent of the compliance by the paying party with his or her duty to make full and frank disclosure; and   ➝

---

[32]   Ibid, at [55].
[33]   *Livsey (formerly Jenkins) v Jenkins* [1985] AC 424, [1985] FLR 813, HL.
[34]   *NG v SG (Appeal: Non-disclosure)* [2011] EWHC 3270 (Fam) at [1] per Mostyn J.
[35]   Ibid.
[36]   [2003] 2 FLR 71.
[37]   Ibid, at [76], per Charles J.
[38]   Ibid, at [77].

(b)   the force of the points (about the payer's means) made by the
applicant in light of the disclosure made by the paying party and the
other evidence as to, for example, the lifestyle and spending of that
party.[39]

In *TL v ML*,[40] Nicholas Mostyn QC[41] considered that, in cases where the
court is faced with obviously deficient disclosure, it should 'err in favour
of the payee'.[42] The payer, if dissatisfied, is always able to make good the
deficiencies in his disclosure or to seek a variation of the level of payments
ordered. The unfortunate reality is that forensic examination by the court
of the extent of a party's disclosure will be limited by time and resources
at the impending maintenance pending suit hearing. Therefore, although
Mostyn J's collation of the guidance applicable to cases where adverse
inferences are drawn in *NG v SG (Appeal: Non-disclosure)*[43] is helpful,
the non-discloser at this interim stage must be prepared for the court to
take a broad, rough and robust approach to inexcusable or inexplicable
gaps in information. Such an approach may be to the payer's significant
detriment.

Third party support for the respondent (the intended payer)

5.24   As is often the case, the respondent may claim that the income available
during the marriage has or will suddenly reduce upon separation; and that this
reduction affects the immediate financial support available to the applicant. For
example, in *M v M (Maintenance Pending Suit)*[44] the parties enjoyed an
extremely high marital standard of living. At the hearing, and in a case
advanced with a sense of theatre to which Charles J was unused, the wife's
claim for maintenance pending suit was set at £510,000 per annum. The
husband claimed that the expenditure during the marriage had largely been
funded by his father, who was now no longer prepared to do so. Charles J was
underwhelmed by the husband's attempt to explain his inability to pay
maintenance at a level more commensurate with the standard of living during
the marriage. Charles J considered that the husband had failed to provide a
clear and full explanation of his father's position and the change in
circumstances he relied upon regarding a personal business venture.[45] The court
recognised the father's unfettered discretion as to whether he would fund the
husband's lifestyle but, nevertheless, proceeded to award a global sum of
£330,000 per annum by way of maintenance pending suit.

'If the father strongly disagrees with the reasoning or order of the court, he may
have some hard decisions to make, but at this stage I see no reason to assume that

---

[39]   Ibid, at [73].
[40]   [2005] EWHC 2860 (Fam), [2006] 1 FLR 1263.
[41]   As he then was and sitting as a deputy judge of the High Court.
[42]   *TL v ML*, at [124](iv).
[43]   [2011] EWHC 3270 (Fam), [2012] 1 FLR 1211.
[44]   [2002] EWHC 317 (Fam), [2002] 2 FLR 123.
[45]   Ibid, at [57].

this situation will arise or that the father's position is that he will not enable the husband to comply with orders of the court'.[46]

5.25 The case of *S v M (Maintenance Pending Suit)*,[47] however, cautions against formulating an order for maintenance pending suit on the basis of third-party support. In *S v M* the husband was 39 years of age and the wife 37. The marriage had lasted just one year and the parties did not have any children. The husband had been convicted of VAT fraud and his father had paid to the HMRC the resulting order for £1.5m. Upon separation, the wife moved to live in a property owned by a company, which in turn was owned by the husband's father. The father issued a notice to quit on the wife; she applied for an order for maintenance pending suit alleging that the husband's family had significant financial resourses and could and should be expected to support the wife as they had the husband. The husband disputed that the evidence demonstrated any historic pattern of financial support provided to him by his family. After a hearing listed only for 30 minutes, the deputy district judge made an order for maintenance pending suit in the wife's favour at the rate of £750 per month (in addition to a legal costs provision of £2,400 per month and payments towards her housing costs). At the hearing of the husband's appeal, the husband's father had filed a statement indicating that he was not prepared to provide financial resources to his son except on a strict and immediate needs basis. Coleridge J allowed the appeal and lamented the 'huge gulf in evidence' about the level of financial support to the husband (from his family) and from the husband (to his wife). In any case in which a third-party's financial support is in issue, the court's investigation must be suitably detailed and forensic:

'It seems to me of the essence in these type of family money cases to establish as clearly as one can what the true historical position is. In particular, the extent of the provision provided by the family to the payer and, just as importantly, the extent to which there has been an established payment stream or other regular financial provision to the claimant in the application. Those are not straightforward matters, as those of us who deal with these cases know only too well. They are certainly not matters which can be dealt with in a 30-minute hearing. They require much more than usual attention by the court to try to discern the underlying reality of the past arrangements.'[48]

The deputy district judge, with insufficient analysis, had been 'blinded by an aura of wealth which is referable certainly to the father but about which there can be no certainty as to the future, other than the husband will not be left on the breadline.'[49]

---

[46] Ibid, at [105].
[47] [2012] EWHC 4109 (Fam), [2013] 1 FLR 1173.
[48] At [35], per Coleridge J.
[49] At [48].

Balancing interests

5.26 Despite the focus of an application for maintenance pending suit on the applicant's immediate financial needs, it is equally important to consider the financial position of the respondent (intended payer). The court is required to balance the competing interests of the applicant for reasonable financial support with the need for the respondent to achieve a level of payment that does not unreasonably leave him unable to meet his own expenditure.

Arrears

5.27 Arrears arising out of an order for maintenance pending suit are enforceable, even if the originating suit is discontinued or fails. In *Moore v Moore*[50] the husband had accrued arrears of some £200,000 in a case in which he had been ordered to pay maintenance pending suit at the rate of £10,000 per month. The initial dispute had focused on whether Nigeria or England was the appropriate jurisdiction to deal with the divorce. Eventually, the Nigerian court granted the husband a divorce, the wife discontinued her proceedings in England and she sought to enforce the arrears of maintenance pending suit. The jurisdictional issue had taken two years to reach trial. The Court of Appeal held that, even if proceedings are discontinued, any arrears of maintenance pending suit nonetheless remain enforceable. Guidance was given that the (main suit) proceedings ought to be prioritised and dealt with as quickly as possible, so that the duration of any maintenance pending suit order can be kept to a minimum. If maintenance pending suit payments were not enforceable, there would, of course, be no incentive for the payer to make payment in any case in which a petition for divorce was being challenged, for whatever reason. In *Moore v Moore*, the only caveat placed on the general rule that arrears are enforceable was 'absence some special circumstance (sic)' (which was not clarified further).

5.28 The essential counterbalance to the general enforceability of arrears of maintenance pending suit is that, where a preliminary issue as to jurisdiction or forum conveniens[51] exists, strict case management must be pursued to ensure a swift resolution of the issue. Prioritising the preliminary issue will ensure that the duration of any order for maintenance pending suit 'is kept to a minimum to ensure that the payer is not put at risk of having to advance irrecoverable and unmerited moneys'.[52]

The impact of an agreement

5.29 The existence of a (pre- or post-)nuptial agreement may impact on the quantum of an award of maintenance pending suit. The Supreme Court in *Radmacher v Granatino*[53] identified the basic test applicable to nuptial agreements as follows: 'The court should give effect to a nuptial agreement that

---

[50] [2009] EWCA Civ 1427, [2010] 1 FLR 1413.
[51] Or, it is suggested, the validity of the marriage.
[52] *Moses-Taiga v Taiga* [2005] EWCA Civ 1013, [2006] 1 FLR 1074, at [29], per Thorpe LJ.
[53] [2011] 1 AC 534.

is freely entered into by each party with a full appreciation of its implications unless in the circumstances prevailing it would not be fair to hold the parties to their agreement.' In *BN v MA*[54] the marriage lasted just 15 months. After the engagement, the parties had negotiated a prenuptial agreement through solicitors, with the benefit of legal advice and mutual financial disclosure. The agreement provided for the wife to receive £96,000 pa by way of interim maintenance in addition to payments for the children of the marriage. In her application for maintenance pending suit the wife failed in evidence or through Counsel's submissions to expose any real basis for an argument that the agreement should not be upheld. Mostyn J made an order for interim maintenance at the level indicated in the agreement. Therefore, the court should seek to apply the terms of a valid nuptial agreement as 'closely and as practically as it can'[55] in determining interim maintenance if:

(a) the agreement specifies a level of interim maintenance that a payee is to receive upon separation; and

(b) the available evidence does not demonstrate a likely prospect of the payee satisfying the court that the agreement should *not* be upheld;[56] and

(c) the level of payment does not leave the payee in a predicament of financial need.

VARIATION[57]

5.30 Pursuant to MCA 1973, s 31(2)(a) the court retains the power to vary, discharge, suspend or revive an order for maintenance pending suit. The power to vary the order raises two important points of practice:

(1) Despite what is stated above in **5.27** regarding the enforceability of arrears, if a variation application is made, the court has the power to remit the payment of any arrears due.[58]

(2) A variation application invokes the court's duty to have regard to all the circumstances of the case, first consideration being given to the welfare of any minor child of the family, and to any change in any matters which the court considered pursuant to the original application.[59] In the original application for an order for maintenance pending suit, the only test is one of reasonableness and there is no statutory mandate to focus on the welfare of any minor child of the family.

---

[54] [2013] EWHC 4250 (Fam).

[55] [2013] EWHC 4250 (Fam), at [33].

[56] For example, by reference to undue influence, lack of sufficient legal advice or lack of material financial disclosure.

[57] For a full consideration of the principles applicable to an application for variation, see Chapter 17.

[58] MCA 1973, s 31(2A).

[59] MCA 1973, s 31(7)(a).

It must also be noted that an award of maintenance pending suit is retrospectively variable if it transpires at the (later) substantive hearing that the amount ordered was excessive or inadequate (whether the order for maintenance pending suit was imposed or agreed). For example, in *H v H (Financial Provision)*,[60] Singer J increased the wife's lump sum payment at a final hearing to account for a deficit identified, with the benefit of hindsight, between the inadequate award of maintenance pending suit and the proper level of such financial support.

COSTS

5.31 An order for maintenance pending suit is a financial order[61] and, therefore, a financial remedy. However, FPR 2010, r 28.3(4)(b)(i) makes it clear that the costs rules in financial remedy proceedings do not apply to orders for maintenance pending suit (or indeed any other form of interim order save for an interim variation order[62]). The general rule of no order as to costs does not apply.

TRANSLATING AN ORDER FOR MAINTENANCE PENDING SUIT INTO AN ORDER FOR PERIODICAL PAYMENTS

5.32 Obtaining a decree absolute is a bar to any application for, or payment of, maintenance pending suit. An order for maintenance pending suit should be drafted so as to indicate that, upon decree absolute, payments shall continue as interim periodical payments. In the event that an order is not drafted in this way, FPR 2010, r 9.8 provides for an application for periodical payments to continue at the same rate as an order for maintenance pending suit.[63] The FPR Part 18 procedure applies to any such application with the following conditions, that:

(1)   a decree nisi has been made; and

(2)   at or after the date of the decree nisi an order for maintenance pending suit is in force; and

(3)   the party in whose favour the decree nisi was made has made an application for periodical payments.

60   [2009] EWHC 494 (Fam), [2009] 2 FLR 795.
61   FPR 2010, r 2.3.
62   FPR 2010, r 9.7(1)(d).
63   For civil partners, the same rules apply in FPR 2010, r 9.9.

POINTS OF PRACTICE AND THEORY

5.33

(1)   Ensure that the time estimate is commensurate with the issues involved.

(2)   Focus on the applicant's immediate needs.

(3)   Reasonableness is the driving force behind an order for maintenance pending suit set within the context of the marital standard of living.

(4)   If either party has been in receipt of third-party financial support, consider filing evidence from the provider of such support as to its continuation or termination.

(5)   The court will be robust, realistic and pragmatic in drawing inferences against a party whose disclosure is unreasonably or inexcusably lacking.

(6)   The court must balance the financial interests of both parties, despite the focus being on the applicant's financial needs.

(7)   Arrears of maintenance pending suit are enforceable, even if the originating suit is discontinued or fails.

(8)   An order for maintenance pending suit remains variable, which may affect the remission of arrears.

CHAPTER 6

MAINTENANCE PENDING SUIT, COSTS ALLOWANCES AND ORDERS FOR PAYMENT IN RESPECT OF LEGAL SERVICES[1]

INTRODUCTION

6.1   The law governing applications by one party to a divorce or dissolution, or for a financial remedy for the other to pay a contribution towards the ongoing costs[2] of legal advice and representation is in a state of flux. In 2013[3] the Legal Aid, Sentencing and Punishment of Offenders Act 2012 (LASPO 2012) launched a new statutory regime introducing 'orders for payment in respect of legal services' (hereafter referred to as legal services orders). These orders replace the system of 'costs allowances', which developed through case-law as a constituent element of orders for maintenance pending suit. An order for the payment of a costs allowance was subject to the applicant satisfying certain minimum and discretionary standards developed through case-law, which are, to a certain extent, replicated in the new statutory regime. LASPO 2012 now explicitly prevents the extension of a maintenance pending suit order to cover continuing legal costs; instead, legal services orders are the modern and designated method for a party to secure funding for legal costs.

6.2   Given the nexus between the 'old' and 'new' law contained in LASPO 2012, and the possibility that older reported decisions may continue to be important in interpreting LASPO 2012's provisions, this chapter deals with both systems in order to provide context to LASPO 2012's statutory regime and to offer a comprehensive resource for practitioners advising and acting on a client's funding options.

---

[1]   In cases of civil partnership, the relevant provisions are found in the Civil Partnership Act 2004 (CPA 2004), Sch 5, Part 8, paras 38A and 38B.

[2]   In contrast to the law governing the payment of costs by one party to another due to 'litigation conduct' (Family Procedure Rules 2010, SI 2010/2955 (FPR 2010), Part 28).

[3]   Introduced 1 April 2013.

THE OLD LAW: COSTS ALLOWANCES

Rationale

6.3   The days of public funding for family finance cases are over. The reality of specialist solicitors, counsel and forensic accountants – who charge the corresponding fees of professional experts – dominate financial remedy litigation. Privately funded cases are often lengthy, and protracted litigation meant that costs allowances were not strictly limited to the 'big [or bigger] money' cases.

6.4   Costs allowances – as alternatives to self-funding (by whatever means) – catered for an 'unserved constituency'[4] of those litigants who were unable, through other means, to achieve rough equality of arms in their legal advice and representation. Costs allowances, therefore, could be seen in the context of the court's overriding objective to deal with cases justly and, as a priority in that pursuit, to ensure that parties to a case were on an equal footing.[5]

Legal basis (statutory)

6.5   Albeit that there was no express statutory basis for a costs allowance, the jurisdiction was found by extrapolation in the Matrimonial Causes Act 1973 (MCA 1973), s 22:

> On a petition for divorce, nullity of marriage or judicial separation, the court may make an order for maintenance pending suit, that is to say, an order requiring either party to the marriage to make to the other such periodical payments for his or her maintenance and for such term, being a term beginning not earlier than the date of the presentation of the petition and ending with the date of the determination of the suit, as the court thinks reasonable.

The costs allowance was expressed and interpreted as an element of 'maintenance' for the payee's benefit, payable at a level the court deemed reasonable and for a term concluding with the determination of the suit (decree absolute or final dissolution order).

Applicability

6.6   Albeit that costs allowances were normally part of a substantive claim for a financial remedy,[6] they were not limited to such claims and were also available in any case where one party challenged the court's jurisdiction. For example, in *A v A (Maintenance Pending Suit: Provision for Legal Fees)*[7] a costs allowance was made for the benefit of a wife for prosecuting a suit for divorce in which the husband contested the validity of the marriage.

---

[4]   *Currey v Currey (No 2)* [2006] EWCA Civ 1338, [2007] 1 FLR 946, at [21], per Wilson LJ.
[5]   FPR 2010, r 1.1(2)(c).
[6]   Ie for lump sums, periodical payments, pension orders and property adjustment orders.
[7]   [2001] 1 FLR 377.

Legal basis (case-law)

6.7   The leading case regarding the making and payment of a costs allowance is *Currey v Currey*.[8] In *Currey*, the rich wife ('W') was pitched against the relatively impoverished husband ('H') in ongoing financial remedy proceedings. W sought capitalisation of a periodical payments order made 3 years earlier against her in H's favour. In the process of resolving W's application, the district judge made an order increasing the original periodical payments order of £48,000 pa by £10,000 per month to fund H's ongoing legal costs. W argued that H had his own means to fund his litigation, which he was failing to apply properly towards the costs of his case. She also maintained that H's litigation conduct, which included ill-directed applications, poor financial disclosure and outstanding costs orders due to her, made any costs allowance wholly unsuitable in the circumstances. Wilson LJ clarified the law as it stood and the tests to be applied in any application for a costs allowance. Those tests can be divided into (what the author describes as) *minimum standards* and *discretionary standards*.

Minimum standards

6.8   The costs allowance was an alternative to a party self-funding the litigation; therefore certain minimum standards had to be met, which, if satisfied, opened the gateway to an application for a costs allowance. The overarching minimum standard[9] was that *the applicant must have demonstrated an inability to reasonably procure legal advice and representation by any other means*. In *Currey*, Wilson J explained this standard, as follows:

> 'Thus, to the extent that she has assets, the applicant has to demonstrate that they cannot reasonably be deployed, whether directly or as the means of raising a loan, in funding legal services. Furthermore, not to forget the third of Thorpe L.J.'s three features, she has also to demonstrate that she cannot reasonably procure legal services by the offer of a charge upon ultimate capital recovery. I would add, fourthly, that the court needs also to be satisfied that there is no such public funding available to the applicant as would furnish her with legal advice and representation at a level of expertise apt to the proceedings, ie, that the applicant does indeed in that regard fall within the unserved constituency ...'[10]

It is evident that 'reasonableness' was a criterion that applied to all independent sources of funding potentially available to the applicant. The overarching standard was met by the applicant demonstrating[11] to the court an inability to:

> (a)   *Reasonably deploy assets directly to fund legal services*: the applicant had to establish that she had insufficient assets under her control to →

---

[8]   [2007] 1 FLR 946.

[9]   What Wilson J called a 'necessary condition of making a [costs] allowance' in *Currey v Currey (No 2)* [2006] EWCA Civ 1338, [2007] 1 FLR 946, at [21].

[10]   *Currey v Currey*, at [20], per Wilson LJ.

[11]   Of course, on the balance of probabilities.

fund her legal costs, including assets that were capable of liquidity, even if not liquid at the time of the application. However, there was often an immediacy to applications for costs allowances, which did not justify a lengthy and complex course of action to liquefy assets. For example, in *Currey*, W had been ordered to pay £640,000 to trustees as a housing fund for H to be held as to one-half for him absolutely and as to the other half for him for life and thereafter to the children absolutely. At the time of H's costs allowance application, this fund had not been used to purchase the home, as originally planned. W complained that H had been recalcitrant in deploying those funds for their intended purpose. Chadwick LJ recognised that, as the FDR hearing was only 4 months away at the time of the application for a costs allowance, recourse to the housing fund did not provide an immediate solution to the funding problem faced by H.

(b) *Reasonably deploy assets indirectly to fund legal services*: the applicant had to show that she was not able, for example, reasonably to raise a loan against assets in which she had an interest (or, indeed, to loan the money from other sources, whether private, familial or commercial).[12]

The 'reasonableness' inherent in this and all minimum standards acted to limit simple arguments that *any* interest in *any* asset provided the basis for extracting cash by way of borrowing. For example, in *C v C (Maintenance Pending Suit: Legal Costs)*[13] the court rejected the husband's ('H') argument that the wife ('W') should raise a mortgage on her £500,000 interest (half share) in the family home. The court concluded that such a course of action would be unfair. All other assets were held in H's sole name. H's broader case in the proceedings was that no other capital could be raised to pay W a lump sum, despite his shareholding in a fast-developing company valued at £13 million. In those circumstances, the court regarded W's re-mortgage of the family home as wholly unfair in circumstances where no other capital provision was guaranteed (on H's own case) and where there was risk to her and the children's occupation of the family home.

In *TL v ML (Ancillary Relief: Claim against Assets of Extended Family)*[14] Nicholas Mostyn QC sitting as a deputy judge of the High Court indicated that the production by the applicant of correspondence between a party's solicitors and at least two banks would ordinarily be sufficient to satisfy the evidential test[15] relevant to this minimum standard.   ➡

---

[12] As William Healing asks in his excellent article, '*Interim Costs Orders: Where Are We Now?* A v A' [2012] Fam Law 56, 'why should one party extend the family's indebtedness if liquid assets clearly exist to pay the lawyers . . .?'.

[13] [2006] 2 FLR 1207.

[14] [2005] EWHC 2860 (Fam), [2006] 1 FLR 1263.

[15] Ibid, at [129].

> (c) *Reasonably enter into a 'Sears Tooth' agreement*: the Sears Tooth agreement is a deed of assignment of the client's rights to financial provision to enable the firm of solicitors instructed by her to settle outstanding fees at the conclusion of the financial remedy litigation. Few firms will countenance such agreements, particularly in times of recession and unstable housing and capital markets. In *TL v ML* it was suggested that a statement from a party's solicitors' firm confirming that they are not prepared to enter into such an agreement will ordinarily suffice.[16]
>
> (d) *Secure public funding*: public funding for financial remedy applications is almost extinct and, in any event, very few firms of solicitors now undertake such work.

Discretionary standards

6.9   Satisfaction of the minimum standards did not guarantee success in an application for a costs allowance. In *Moses-Taiga v Taiga*[17] Thorpe LJ reminded litigants that 'the dominant safeguard against injustice is the discretion of the trial judge ...'.[18] Therefore, discretionary standards led the court, on occasion, to decline to make an order for a costs allowance, despite the minimum standards having been met. These discretionary standards varied according to the facts of each particular case, but in *Currey v Currey*, Wilson LJ referred to the following considerations by way of example:

> 'The subject-matter of the proceedings will surely always be relevant; and, insofar as it can safely be assessed at so early a juncture, the reasonableness of the applicant's stance in the proceedings will also be relevant. So also will a variety of other features, including of the type which exist in the present case, in particular the arresting fact that the husband already owes £46,000 to the wife in respect of costs.'[19]

In *Currey v Currey (No 2)*, despite H owing significant costs orders to the wife, making inadequate disclosure and being subject of a civil restraint order, the Court of Appeal nevertheless dismissed W's appeal against the order for £10,000 per month by way of a costs allowance. A key reason for the dismissal of the appeal – despite H's previous poor litigation conduct – was that W's substantive application had been for the capitalisation of a periodical payments order; this was an application of profound importance to H and, against which, his cross-application was prima facie reasonable in the circumstances.[20]

---

[16] Ibid.
[17] [2005] EWCA Civ 1013, [2006] 1 FLR 1074.
[18] Ibid, at [25].
[19] *Currey v Currey*, at [21].
[20] *Currey v Currey (No 2)*, at [26], per Wilson LJ.

The burden of proof

6.10 The burden of proof rested on the applicant for the costs allowance to satisfy the minimum standards and, if necessary, any discretionary factors in support of an order for a costs allowance.

Amount

6.11 The amount of any costs allowance depended on the solicitor's charging rates, the likely disbursements and the complexity of the case. The applicant was advised to approach the court with a relatively detailed budget[21] explaining how the costs allowance was likely to be spent. The budget would be scrutinised as 'whenever a court decides to make a costs allowance, it ought to proceed with a judicious mixture of realism and caution as to both its amount and its duration'.[22] Practitioners were cautioned to think carefully and realistically about the ongoing legal costs budget. Of course, not all eventualities could be foreseen, but an unrealistically optimistic low initial claim could require further variation applications;[23] at the hearing of such an application, the court would consider whether the change in circumstances (exceeding the level of the initial allowance) could have been anticipated, both in relation to the principle of any variation as well as to the amount ordered. Once the court had determined the appropriate amount of the costs allowance, the court could give the payer the option to pay in monthly instalments or in one lump sum on account.[24]

Duration

6.12 Costs allowances were not open-ended vouchers to procure legal advice and representation. The court would invariably limit the duration of payment to significant junctures in the proceedings. The principal break-point was the FDR hearing. In *Currey v Currey (No 2)* the Court of Appeal explained its reasoning as follows:

> 'The FDR appointment is a watershed and all reasonable inducements to both parties there to negotiate positively in the light of informal judicial indications should be in place. The knowledge of a spouse in receipt of a costs allowance that, absent settlement at or in the immediate aftermath of the FDR, she will have to apply for a further allowance, which may or may not be granted, seems to me to amount only to a reasonable inducement, as opposed to improper pressure, to reach settlement.'[25]

---

[21] *TL v ML (Ancillary Relief: Claim against Assets of Extended Family)* [2005] EWHC 2860 (Fam), [2006] 1 FLR 1263.
[22] *Currey v Currey (No 2)*, at [28], per Wilson LJ.
[23] MCA 1973, s 31(7).
[24] See for example, *C v C (Maintenance Pending Suit: Legal Costs)* [2006] 2 FLR 1207, at [15].
[25] *Currey v Currey (No 2)*, at [28], per Wilson LJ.

THE NEW LAW

6.13 LASPO 2012 introduces an explicit statutory regime governing the payment of money by one party to enable another to fund legal advice and representation in matrimonial, civil partnership and financial relief[26] proceedings. The relevant ss 49 to 54 sandwiched in Part 2 of LASPO 2012 came into force in April 2013.[27]

Dismissing 'costs allowances' and the changes introduced by LASPO

6.14

First, LASPO 2012 changes the terminology and the applicable legal basis. Costs allowances become 'orders for payment in respect of legal services' (hereafter referred to as 'legal services orders'). Legal services orders are given an express statutory basis.

Second, LASPO 2012 removes legal services orders from the jurisdiction to award 'maintenance' pending suit. MCA 1973, s 22(2), as amended, makes it explicit that an order for maintenance pending suit 'may not require a party to a marriage (or a civil partner) to pay to the other any amount in respect of legal services for the purposes of the proceedings'.

Instead, and third, LASPO 2012 creates a new statutory basis for legal services orders. The MCA 1973 and the CPA 2004 have a number of new paragraphs inserted in order to define and guide the application of the court's discretion in deciding these new orders.

Applicable proceedings

6.15 Legal services orders are available both in proceedings for divorce, nullity of marriage or judicial separation (or dissolution, nullity or a separation order) and, separately, in proceedings for 'financial relief':

'**22ZA Orders for payment in respect of legal services**

(1) In proceedings for divorce, nullity or judicial separation, the court may make an order or orders requiring one party to the marriage to pay to the other ("the applicant") an amount for the purpose of enabling the applicant to obtain legal services for the purposes of the proceedings.

---

[26] Which is not, as a particular term, defined in FPR 2010, r 2.3, whereas the terms 'financial order' and 'financial remedy' are so defined.

[27] I have written an article on the impact of these provisions: Commins, A, 'The Costs Allowance Revolution in Proceedings for Financial Relief', [2012] Fam Law 1491. David Burrows has also written an article, in which he challenges the provisions as being discriminatory and contrary to the principle of affording the parties an equality of arms '*Costs Allowances and Legal Services Orders: MCA 1973, s 22ZA and s 22ZB*' [2013] Fam Law 318.

(2) The court may also make such an order or orders in proceedings under this part for financial relief in connection with proceedings for divorce, nullity of marriage or judicial separation.'

The FPR 2010 introduced and defined the now-familiar concepts of the 'financial order' and the 'financial remedy'.[28] 'Financial relief', however, is not defined as a concept within the FPR 2010, which raises an initial question as to which substantive applications may permit the applicant to also make an application for a legal services order.[29] The only reference to 'financial relief' is within Part II of the MCA 1973, which is entitled '*Financial Relief* for Parties to Marriage and Children of Family' (emphasis added).

6.16 A 'financial order', as defined in FPR 2010, r 2.3(1), incorporates the familiar financial claims available on divorce, as follows:

(a) an avoidance of disposition order;[30]

(b) an order for maintenance pending suit;

(c) an order for maintenance pending outcome of proceedings;

(d) an order for periodical payments or lump sum provision (but not for lump sum provision on the basis of the payer's failure to maintain the payee, whether under the MCA 1973 or the CPA 2004);

(e) a property adjustment order;

(f) a variation order;[31]

(g) a pension sharing order;

(h) a pension compensation sharing order.

The 'financial remedy' is a much broader concept, which includes all financial orders but, crucially, extends to orders with legal bases in statutes other than the MCA 1973 and the CPA 2004.[32] LASPO 2012, however, limits the legal services order to proceedings for married- or civil-partners. Therefore, it must be anticipated – without judicial interpretation to the contrary – that such orders will be available only for applications for a 'financial order' and/or a 'financial remedy' in cases which the parties are married or civil partners only.

Legal services and timing

6.17 MCA 1973, s 22ZA(10) defines those legal services that can be paid for by an order:

(a) providing advice as to how the law applies in the particular circumstances;

---

28   FPR 2010, r 2.3(1).
29   See also the article by David Burrows, 'Costs Allowances and Legal Services Orders: MCA 1973, s 22ZA and s 22ZB' [2013] Fam Law 318.
30   As defined in FPR 2010, r 9.3(1).
31   Defined in FPR 2010, r 9.3 as proceedings pursuant to MCA 1973, s 31 and pursuant to CPA 2004, Sch 5, Part 11.
32   For example, Children Act 1989, Sch 1 and MFPA 1984, Part III.

(b)   providing advice and assistance in relation to the proceedings;

(c)   providing other advice and assistance in relation to the settlement or other resolution of the dispute that is the subject of the proceedings; and

(d)   providing advice and assistance in relation to the enforcement of decisions in the proceedings or as part of the settlement or resolution of the dispute,

and they include, in particular, advice and assistance in the form of representation and any form of dispute resolution, including mediation.

6.18   Legal services orders may include payment for legal services specified in the court order (MCA 1973, s 22ZA(11)) or for legal services for a specified period or part of the proceedings (MCA 1973, s 22ZA(11)). The anticipation must be that each legal services order will expressly state the legal services, period or part of the proceedings for which the payment is designed to cater. Any application for, or draft of, an order sought by the applicant should do likewise.

6.19   Therefore, legal services orders – unlike costs allowances within an order for maintenance pending suit – do not appear to be time-limited by the determination of the suit (decree absolute or dissolution). They can apply to enforcement proceedings in addition to any form of dispute resolution, including mediation and, presumably, arbitration and other collaborative attempts to settle proceedings.[33] The identification of different legal services and periods within the proceedings may give greater latitude to the intended payer to argue that an order should not be made at all or be more limited (in amount and time) than may have been made under the current law. Equally, the payee may suffer from more restricted and time- or activity-limited funding in comparison with the older 'costs allowances'. The manner in which LASPO seeks to structure legal services orders will require a more strategic approach to litigation by the payee: orders will not be made on a 'blanket' basis to include *any* activities of legal representatives during a period of time within the proceedings, however determined by the payee in consultation with his/her legal representatives.

Payment, security and enforcement

6.20   Costs allowances under MCA 1973, s 22 were justified as a legitimate component of periodic 'maintenance' (pending suit) for the payee. In *A v A (Maintenance Pending Suit: Provision for Legal Fees)*,[34] the husband argued that periodical payments for legal costs were not payments for the 'maintenance' of the payee. This argument was roundly rejected by Holman J, who identified that the wife's legal costs represented her most urgent and pressing need and expense at the time (after housing and food):

---

[33]   There may be a need for proceedings to be adjourned for the purpose of engaging in such Alternative Dispute Resolution (ADR) processes.

[34]   [2001] 1 FLR 377.

'She could manage without holidays, though I have made some provision for them. She could no doubt manage for a while without buying new clothes. She could manage without her manicures, pedicures and yoga and keep fit classes, for all of which I have, on the facts of this case, made provision. She could even manage without the provision for forms of private medical care (to which the family has been accustomed) for, if necessary, she could fall back on the NHS. But she simply cannot make any progress with the dominating issue in her life if she cannot pay her lawyers, and for this the State will not provide.'[35]

MCA 1973, s 22ZA refers, in contrast, to the payment of an 'amount' for the purpose of enabling the applicant to obtain legal services. MCA 1973, s 22ZA(6) provides that this amount may be paid, in whole or in part, by instalments of specified amounts. These provisions arguably provide greater scope for legal services orders to reflect the fact that litigation often has periods of activity-drought and other periods where activity increases and costs multiply. Conversely, for the payee, it may require, first, an application more targeted to a specific event in the proceedings and, second, repeated applications to the court if the event already paid for does not lead to the resolution of proceedings.

6.21 Furthermore, MCA 1973, s 22ZA(6)(b) makes provision for the court to require that payments by instalments – if that is how the order is to be paid – can be secured to the satisfaction of the court.

6.22 Finally, LASPO 2012 amends MCA 1973, s 24A(1) to entitle the court – when making a legal services order – to make a further order requiring sale of property in which either or both of the parties to a marriage has or have a beneficial interest:

'**[24A Orders for sale of property]**

(1) Where the court makes an order under section 22ZA or makes under section 23 or 24 of this Act a secured periodical payments order, an order for the payment of a lump sum or a property adjustment order, then, on making that order or at any time thereafter, the court may make a further order for the sale of such property as may be specified in the order, being property in which or in the proceeds of sale of which either or both of the parties to the marriage has or have a beneficial interest, either in possession or reversion.

(2) Any order made under subsection (1) above may contain such consequential or supplementary provisions as the court thinks fit and, without prejudice to the generality of the foregoing provision, may include –

(a)   provision requiring the making of a payment out of the proceeds of sale of the property to which the order relates, and

(b)   provision requiring any such property to be offered for sale to a person, or class of persons, specified in the order.

---

[35]   *A v A*, at 382, per Holman J.

(3) Where an order is made under subsection (1) above on or after the grant of a decree of divorce or nullity of marriage, the order shall not take effect unless the decree has been made absolute.

(4) Where an order is made under subsection (1) above, the court may direct that the order, or such provision thereof as the court may specify, shall not take effect until the occurrence of an event specified by the court or the expiration of a period so specified.

(5) Where an order under subsection (1) above contains a provision requiring the proceeds of sale of the property to which the order relates to be used to secure periodical payments to a party to the marriage, the order shall cease to have effect on the death or re-marriage of, or formation of a civil partnership by, that person.

(6) Where a party to a marriage has a beneficial interest in any property, or in the proceeds of sale thereof, and some other person who is not a party to the marriage also has a beneficial interest in that property or in the proceeds of sale thereof, then, before deciding whether to make an order under this section in relation to that property, it shall be the duty of the court to give that other person an opportunity to make representations with respect to the order; and any representations made by that other person shall be included among the circumstances to which the court is required to have regard under section 25(1) below. (as amended).'

This extension to the court's power to order a sale of property may prove to be an important tool. In the context of LASPO 2012 and legal services orders, it is a quasi-enforcement provision, which (a) prevents the payer from relying on the court's inability to make orders for the payment of interim lump sums and (b) provides a useful interim mechanism for the payee to extract money from matrimonial resources.[36]

Minimum standards and the burden of proof

6.23 LASPO 2012 broadly retains the distinction between the *minimum* and *discretionary* standards central to the old costs allowance regime, albeit with modifications and extensions. LASPO 2012 proceeds on the [negative] basis that an order should **not** be made unless certain standards are met. The burden of proof to satisfy the court of the required standards continues to rest with the applicant.

6.24 The court must 'not make an order ... unless it is satisfied that, without the amount, the applicant would not reasonably be able to obtain appropriate legal services for the purposes of the proceedings or any part of the proceedings' (MCA 1973, s 22ZA(3)). In particular, the court must be satisfied that the applicant is not reasonably able to secure a loan to pay for the legal services and that the applicant is unlikely to be able to obtain legal services by granting a charge over any assets recovered in the proceedings (MCA 1973,

---

[36] See also the insightful article by Rhys Taylor, 'Funding Family Proceedings: The New Law' [2013] Family Law Week (28 March).

s 22ZA(4)(a) and (b)). The retention of the criterion of 'reasonableness' may give strength to a claim that pre-LASPO 2012 case-law continues to be of some use in arguing whether a party can reasonably deploy assets directly or indirectly to self-fund the litigation. In *BN v MA*[37] Mostyn J refused a wife's application for a legal services order on the basis that, firstly, she had received offers from litigation loan suppliers[38] and, secondly, her 'borderline irresponsible' claim for a costs allowance of £400,000 provided no detailed breakdown of how those costs had been calculated.

6.25 The law of costs allowances indicated that the production of correspondence between a party's solicitors and at least two banks would ordinarily be sufficient to satisfy the court that a loan is not available. Furthermore, a simple statement from a party's solicitors stating that they were not prepared to enter into a Sears Tooth charge would ordinarily be satisfactory (*TL v ML*, at [129]). Given the proliferation of companies providing litigation loans, it will be prudent to address the specific requirements of MCA 1973, s 22ZA(4)(a) in any narrative statement in support of an application for a legal services order; to provide as much documentary evidence as is proportionate to demonstrate that a litigation loan is unaffordable, inappropriate or unacceptable in the circumstances. This may be, for example, a letter from a loan company refusing to provide funds or information as to unaffordable and disproportionate rates of interest that may be charged.

Exercising the discretion

6.26

In deciding whether and, if so, how to exercise its power to make a legal services order, the court must have regard to a list of factors similar to those in MCA 1973, s 25(2) , which include the familiar subjects of income, earning capacity, property, financial resources, needs, obligations and responsibilities of both the payer and payee. In addition, MCA 1973, s 22ZB(1)(c)–(h) codifies a number of additional factors (some common to the old case-law), which the court must weigh in the balance, as follows:

(c)   the subject matter of the proceedings, including the matters in issue in them,[39]

(d)   whether the paying party is legally represented in the proceedings,

(e)   any steps taken by the applicant to avoid all or part of the proceedings, whether by proposing or considering mediation or otherwise,

(f)   the applicant's conduct in relation to the proceedings,   ➡

---

[37]   [2013] EWHC 4250 (Fam).
[38]   Albeit at a fairly steep rate of interest!
[39]   See also *MET v HAT* [2013] EWHC 4247 (Fam), and discussed further at **5.15**.

(g) any amount owed by the applicant to the paying party in respect of costs in the proceedings or other proceedings to which both the applicant and the paying party are or were party, and

(h) the effect of the order or variation on the paying party.

The applicant's conduct[40] from the very start of proceedings (or indeed, beforehand, and in relation to *other unrelated* proceedings) will be of significance to the court's discretionary exercise. In a case in which a legal services order may be necessary, particular attention must be paid to pre-issue conduct, the making and consideration of offers and the proportionate and streamlined progress of the case. In *Parr v Parr*[41] Eleanor King J made reference to Mostyn J's refusal of the wife's prior application for a legal services order. Mostyn J refused the application on the basis that the wife had been unreasonable in her approach to mediation: first, she had insisted on using a 'top-drawer' and 'top-price' mediator and, second, she had insisted on legal representation at the mediation, which was unnecessary, unusual and unreasonable.

LASPO 2012 also introduces a single statutory counter-balance to the rigorous examination of the position and conduct of the party applying for the legal services order. MCA 1973, s 22ZB(3) requires the court to have regard, in particular, to whether making or varying an order is likely to cause undue hardship to the payer or prevent the payer from obtaining legal services him/herself. This provision reflects the previous case-law, particularly *G v G (Maintenance Pending Suit: Costs)*[42] in which Charles J stated that:

> 'Fairness is a "two-way street" and therefore the power to include an element in respect of the costs of the ancillary relief proceedings has to be exercised having regard to the positions of both the husband and the wife and thus to the possibility that such an order could or would be unfair to the paying party as well as to the advantages and disadvantages to the other party that would flow from the making or refusal of the order.'

Variation and duration

6.27 LASPO 2012 is silent as to legal services orders being time-limited as an incentive to achieve settlement. However, LASPO 2012 does make it explicit that legal services orders may be made on more than one occasion (as an order or orders) or for a specified period or a specified part of the proceedings. It is submitted that it is likely that the practice of time-limiting orders to provide a reasonable inducement to settle will continue.

---

[40] Perhaps, by analogy, to be examined in a manner consistent with the identifying factors of 'litigation conduct' relevant to the costs rules in FPR 2010, r 28.3(7).

[41] [2013] EWHC 4105 (Fam), a case in which Eleanor King J made reference to a previous ruling of Mostyn J.

[42] [2002] EWHC 306 (Fam), [2003] 2 FLR 71, at [65].

6.28   The court is given the power 'at any time' to vary an order if 'it considers that there has been a material change of circumstances since the order was made' (MCA 1973, s 22ZA(8)). The factors for the court's consideration on an application to vary are the same as those applicable to an original application.

Costs

6.29   In the reckoning for costs, s 22ZA(9) of the MCA 1973, provides that 'for the purposes of the assessment of costs in the proceedings, the applicant's costs are to be treated as reduced by any amount paid to the applicant pursuant to an order under this section for the purposes of those proceedings'. What remains unclear at the time of writing is whether a legal services order will be classified as a 'financial remedy' in the meaning given to that term in FPR 2010, r 28.3(4)(b), thereby engaging the general rule in financial remedy proceedings that the court will not make an order upon dealing with the application requiring one party to pay the costs of the other party (FPR 2010, r 28.3(5)).

POINTS OF PRACTICE AND THEORY

6.30

(1) LASPO 2012 applies from April 2013. Costs allowances as an element of maintenance pending suit are extinct.

(2) Orders for legal services are available for ADR processes as well as court proceedings.

(3) Minimum standards apply, which direct the court not to make an order unless it is satisfied that, without the amount requested, the applicant will not reasonably be able to obtain the appropriate legal services.

(4) Discretionary standards also apply, which focus some attention on the applicant's pre- and post-issue conduct.

(5) The applicant will likely need to demonstrate with evidence that s/he cannot obtain a litigation loan, third-party funding from other sources or an agreement with her legal representatives as to deferred payment. The statement in support of an application for a legal services order should address the statutory checklist provided in LASPO 2012.

CHAPTER 7

NEEDS, BUDGETS AND EXPENDITURE: EXAGGERATION AND BROAD-BRUSHES VERSUS EVIDENCE AND REALISM

'The wife's budget for the purpose of establishing her maintenance needs was opened as "aspirational". It is entirely unrealistic and without historical basis or reasonable future projection. The husband's opening gambit as to his own maintenance needs are excessive and form no useful comparison ...'[1]

INTRODUCTION

7.1 In many cases, periodical payments orders are predominantly made to provide for the ongoing financial needs of the payee (whether those needs are capable of a generous interpretation or not). However, if the income of the payer is sufficient and the circumstances warrant it, periodical payments orders can extend to incorporate payments for compensation for relationship-generated disadvantage and perhaps, more controversially, some sharing of the fruits of the marital partnership in the form of one party's high earning capacity.[2]

7.2 This chapter does not engage in the more esoteric debate as to the role of a periodical payments order. Instead, it has its focus practically on how the financial needs of the payee (and the payer) are established, evidenced and challenged, whether during negotiation, mediation or at a court hearing. For most cases, the agreement to, or determination of, the level of the ongoing financial need of the payee is pivotal to resolving a claim for periodical payments. In the first instance, the payee's financial needs must be ascertained by reference to a budget or expenditure list. This chapter considers what a budget is, what it should contain (and exclude), how it should be presented, to what extent the court is wedded to the budget and how the court deals with exaggerated and underestimated budgets. Ultimately, this chapter concludes that the proper procedure in most cases is to approach the drafting and analysis of a budget on a macro- rather than micro-economic basis.[3]

---

[1] *WF v HF* [2012] EWHC 438 (Fam). Macur J dealt with a case in which the parties' combined legal costs had reached £2.4m. The wife had relinquished her career on marriage and had been a home-maker. See heading 'maintenance needs', at [74].

[2] For further analysis, see Chapter 9 on Quantification.

[3] That is, by challenging those particular budget entries that are unjustifiable, inaccurate and

THE BUDGET, THE CLIENT AND MCA 1973, S 25(2)

The purpose of a budget

7.3

> The budget is the most appropriate document by which to ascertain and evidence a client's current and future financial needs. However, the budget also has a much wider significance, which can extend throughout the litigation process, as follows:
>
> (1) The budget is a demonstration of the financial needs, obligations and responsibilities which a party has or is likely to have in the foreseeable future.[4]
>
> (2) The budget, particularly when it is prepared on the basis of historical expenditure, is instructive as to the standard of living enjoyed by the family before the breakdown of the marriage.[5]
>
> (3) In appropriate cases, the budget may be important in revealing how a party is to fund (in income terms) the 'gentle transition'[6] from the marital standard of living to a standard expected of a self-sufficient individual.
>
> (4) One party's budget – especially when it is compared with the other party's – can be used to demonstrate any particular continuing economic disadvantage (or advantage) arising out of the marriage or the way in which the parties organised their married life.[7]
>
> (5) The budget may serve to establish the financial cost of a party's future contributions to the welfare of the family[8] by listing the expenditure relevant to maintaining a child of the family.

7.4   For some separating couples, the first time they draw up a budget or list of expenditure will be in response to their respective solicitor's prompts. For others, they will have lived to a strict regime of planned spending during the marriage. For both parties to a divorce, whether a budget novice or expert, the schedule of expenditure for their future life as single persons is often a valuable tool to bring home the reality of the financial constraints they may face. In cases involving greater income-wealth, the budget can also present innumerable opportunities to exaggerate both spending and lifestyle. In all cases, however, the budget is usually the first step in demonstrating the basis of any claim for, or defence to, an application for periodical payments: it is, after all, the

---

without an evidential basis, whilst appreciating that a strict and narrow analysis of expenditure is inappropriate in most cases, as the budget must respond more broadly to the individual circumstances of each case.

[4]   Matrimonial Causes Act 1973 (MCA 1973), s 25(2)(b).
[5]   MCA 1973, s 25(2)(c).
[6]   Taken from the speech of Baroness Hale in *Miller v Miller; McFarlane v McFarlane*, at [158].
[7]   Taken from the speech of Lord Nicholls in *Miller v Miller; McFarlane v McFarlane*, at [32].
[8]   MCA 1973, s 25(2)(f).

evidential foundation for a party's future income need. In *B v S (Financial Remedy: Marital Property Regime)*[9] Mostyn J proposed, perhaps controversially, that, save in exceptional cases, a periodical payments claim[10] should be determined or settled by reference to the principle of 'need' alone and should not be obscured by the introduction of the concept of 'sharing' future income and earning capacity:

> 'Save in the exceptional kind of case exemplified by *Miller v Miller; McFarlane v McFarlane* a periodical payments claim (whether determined originally or on variation) should in my opinion be adjudged (or settled), generally speaking, by reference to the principle of need alone. Of course needs are elastic in concept and there is much room for the exercise of discretion in their assessment. But to allow consideration of the concept of sharing to intrude in the assessment of a periodical payments award seems to me to be based on a doubtful principle, and is replete with problems of quantification by any sure standard. The sharing principle in relation to matrimonial property is simple enough: it is usually 50/50, because in the division of the marital acquest equity (or fairness) is (usually) equality. But if the concept of sharing is going to uplift above the assessment of need a periodical payments award which will be paid from post-separation earnings, how does a judge set about doing it? Is it a third? Or 40%? Or 20%? There are not even any signposts along the road to a fair award.'[11]

Documents

7.5 Naturally, the Financial Statement (Form E) is normally the first express account of financial needs. However, the Form E limits the schedule of income needs to 'regular expenses'.[12] Often, it is desirable to have two separate schedules, one identifying the regular spending during the marriage and a separate document setting out the future proposed income needs upon separation. The former is a useful record of the standard of living during the marriage and the latter can inform the case for future financial support (for the payee, or, for the payer, it can identify the surplus income that may be available).

How to approach drafting or challenging a budget: case-law guidance

7.6 Assisting and guiding a client who is drafting a budget is not a task that permits strict adherence to a pro-forma because one person's need may be another's indulgence. There is no doubt that every family practitioner has experienced the inflated *and* understated budget, both of which are equally concerning; such as the husband who lived perfectly well on a monthly spend of £2,000 during the marriage but who, upon separation, magically 'needs' double that figure each month just to survive, or the parsimonious wife who minimises her expenditure due to a lack of financial awareness or a desire not to appear

---

[9]   [2012] EWHC 265 (Fam).
[10]   Whether an original or variation claim.
[11]   [2012] EWHC 265 (Fam), at [79].
[12]   See Part 5 of the Form E1.

'greedy'. There is no directive as to which items of expenditure should be included in, or excluded from, a budget, and all will depend on the peculiarities of each case, save for the very usual housing, motoring, food and clothing costs. However, as will be seen, the reported cases do give the practitioner some general guidance as to good practice in drafting schedules of expenditure.

Realistic assessment

7.7   The first obvious and generally applicable rule is to approach the budget with a sense of realism, however affluent or otherwise the marital lifestyle may have been. In *M v M (Financial Relief: Substantial Earning Capacity)*[13] the wife argued for an income need figure of £150,000 per annum and the husband claimed that her budget, in reality, amounted to £111,000 per annum. In finding that the wife needed no more than £125,000 per annum by way of income, Baron J recognised that the court was entitled to take a view about the wife's expressed budgetary needs and whether they were sensibly formulated and calculated:

> 'Those who practise in this field know that a budget is a work of art, and sometimes a work of artifice, but the court must be entitled to take a realistic view'.[14]

In approaching budgets with a sense of realism, a party's stated income needs are more likely to find approval if they are *justifiable, accurate and evidenced*. A *justifiable* expense is one that has an historical basis or a reasonable purpose; an *accurate* expense is one that is calculated rather than based on unsubstantiated guesswork; and an *evidenced* expense is one that can be verified through the disclosure process, if appropriate.

The broad brush versus the fine toothcomb

7.8   In order to assess whether a budget is realistic, the court must – to a greater or lesser extent – investigate the expenditure claimed by a party and the basis for it. However, there is usually a reluctance to encourage spending significant time and money on meticulous and exacting analyses of income-need budgets.[15] This tension between the pursuit of realism and reasonableness whilst not advocating detailed and costly investigations appears regularly in the body of reported cases. For example, in *Purba v Purba*[16] the husband's appeal criticised the judge at first instance for accepting the income-needs budget proffered by the wife at trial. Thorpe J stated that:

---

[13]   [2004] 2 FLR 236, at 258, per Baron J.
[14]   Ibid, at [69].
[15]   Such an approach would be a retrograde step to the era of 'reasonable requirements', in which litigation too often became an exercise in constructing or demolishing exaggerated budgets of income and housing needs (see Duckworth and Hodson, 'White v White – Bringing Section 25 Back to the People' [2001] Fam Law 24.)
[16]   [2000] 1 FLR 444.

'In this field of litigation, budgets prepared by the parties often have a high degree of unreality – usually the applicant wife's budget is much inflated. Most unusually, in this case the wife's budget seems to have been rather understated in many respects. It is true that one of the major items on the budget was substantial monthly expenditure for rent or mortgage. It is true that that could be said to be a superfluous item once the substantial lump sum was ordered. But the essential task of the judge is not to go through these budgets item by item but stand back and ask, what is the appropriate proportion of the husband's available income that should go to the support of the wife?'[17]

However, this broader and less stringent approach to budget assessment was not followed by Charles J in *R v R*,[18] who considered it inappropriate for the court to assess the reality of a budget using a broad brush in circumstances in which the evidence from each party focused on extremes of parsimony on one side and extravagance on the other. Charles J was critical of the wife's budget in which it was unclear whether items therein related to past, future, actual or anticipated expenditure:

'I repeat that I accept and urge that over analysis of, and disproportionate expense is avoided in respect of the preparation of, budgets. But equally in my judgment the bases of their preparation should be clear so that their relevance, accuracy and reliability can be assessed by reference to them. This it seems to me is an aspect of, and/or in accordance with the underlying purpose of, the duty to give full, frank and clear disclosure if the budget is related to past expenditure.'[19]

The extent of the analysis of a party's budget is, ironically, often greater in cases in which every pound counts than those cases in which money is less of an object or none at all. The extent of any assessment of a budget will depend on the circumstances of the case. However, if the guiding principle of ensuring each and every expenditure item is *justifiable, accurate and evidenced* is followed, the overall budget can avoid judicial criticism and better resist challenges by the other party.

The perils of exaggeration

7.9 The unsurprising reality is that budgets are often set too high in parties' financial statements on the understanding that the overall figure may be reduced through the process of negotiation or as a result of cross-examination. However, care must be taken at this early stage of drafting, as wildly inaccurate submissions bearing little relation to the marital finances and without an evidential basis can adversely affect the client's overall credibility.

7.10 One of the most outrageous examples of overstatement in a party's budget is found in the case of *McCartney v Mills McCartney*.[20] The wife's

---

[17] Ibid, at 449B.
[18] Although this case was successfully appealed in *Robson v Robson*, the Court of Appeal approved Charles J's criticism of the information provided to him regarding budgets.
[19] *R v R* [2009] EWHC 1267 (Fam), at [266].
[20] [2008] 1 FCR 707.

budget at trial after a marriage lasting just under 4 years was set at £3.25m per annum. The mere fact that her budget was unusually set out in the report of a chartered accountant did not lend the budget any special sense of authenticity. The wife's claimed expenditure was roundly criticised for being extraordinarily exaggerated and, in certain obvious respects, risible. This fact undermined the wife's credibility when it came to assessing the veracity of other elements of her case and arguably damaged the overall presentation of her case. Despite the huge sums involved, the salutary lesson given by Bennett J is one that is applicable to all cases:

> 'In the absence of a sensible proposal by the wife as to her income needs I must do the best I can on the material I have. If the wife feels aggrieved about what I propose she only has herself to blame. If, as she has done, a litigant flagrantly over-eggs the pudding and thus deprives the court of any sensible assistance, then he or she is likely to find that the court takes a robust view and drastically prunes the proposed budget'.[21]

Budget statements are not exercises in creative writing.

Budgets and the duty of full and frank disclosure

7.11   The Form E is a sworn document. The accuracy of information as to a party's capital and investments is just as important as the accuracy of a party's schedule of expenditure. It can all too often be forgotten that each party's solemn duty to give full and frank disclosure of all material and relevant facts to the court and the other party[22] extends to schedules of expenditure. In *D v D*,[23] Charles J criticised the wife for failing during either her written or oral evidence to provide a clear account of how she compiled her budget and further stated:

> '126. I repeat what I have said in other cases that in my view parties to ancillary relief proceedings should provide clear information as to how they have compiled their budgets. This should be a simple task because all they have to do is to set out the thinking behind, and thus the justification for, the figures advanced. Further, it should not involve the expenditure of disproportionate time and money on the preparation of budgets and supporting material because, when a figure is in effect a "guesstimate", this can be stated and it can then be considered whether more accuracy is appropriate. Rather, the provision of such supported information should (a) encourage realistic and sensible estimates with an appropriate explanation, (b) discourage speculative, excessive and aspirational budgets and (c) enable the court to reach an informed view on the appropriate level of future income need (generously assessed) without any detailed analysis or auditing of underlying figures.'

---

[21]   Ibid, at [230], per Bennett J.
[22]   *Jenkins v Livesey* [1985] 1 AC 424.
[23]   [2010] EWHC 138 (Fam).

Particular expenditure for particular people in particular circumstances

7.12 Whereas budgets will always include the ordinary everyday global costs of living, they are not limited to such routine matters. The court will not necessarily criticise or strike from a budget items of expenditure that are unusual or may appear to be extravagant in comparison with other families, if the circumstances of the case warrant their inclusion. For example, in *Mills v McCartney*,[24] – and despite the outrageous nature of many of the wife's items of claimed expenditure – Bennett J exceptionally included a figure of £50,000 per annum in the wife's budget to enable her to continue her charitable activities and to make charitable donations. The rationale behind this decision was based on her historical commitment to charitable giving, her genuine desire to continue that practice and the husband's similar approach to charity:

> '[238] Whatever else may be said about the wife, her devotion to her charities is very impressive. Over many years, and in particular during the marriage, the wife was very generous in her charitable giving and did much work on behalf of her selected charities. She very much wants to continue along this path. The husband, too, was, and continues to be, generous to charities. I do not think therefore that he can legitimately complain if the wife's budget includes such a sum.'

In *S v S*[25] the parties had been married for some 11 years until their separation. The sole issue for the judge at first instance had been the level and duration of periodical payments for the wife. Both parties had an interest in horses, had kept horses during the marriage and the wife was a talented rider. On appeal, Sir Mark Potter refused to accept the husband's contention that the district judge had wrongly maintained the wife's marital lifestyle despite the fact of separation, particularly in relation to the costs of keeping horses. Sir Mark Potter concluded that affording the wife the opportunity to retain and enjoy horses was consistent with the importance that such activities had assumed during the marriage, so long as it was within the husband's ability to finance this.

It is clear that unusual and costly items of expenditure may be legitimate within a budget, particularly if:

(1) they have a historical basis, and

(2) their past and future importance can be justified and explained, and

(3) they are affordable within the means of the paying party.

---

[24] [2008] 1 FLR 1508.
[25] [2008] 2 FLR 113.

Common traps and pitfalls

7.13 Budgets come under attack in most cases. It is impossible to list all the potential challenges to various items of expenditure – over and above those challenges based on justification, accuracy and evidence – but a few of the more common traps and pitfalls are:

- *Double-counting*: items of expenditure that are doubled-up either by inclusion twice under different headings or within separate personal and child-related budgets.

- *Capital or one-off expenditure*: items of capital expenditure should properly be listed as capital needs, whether the party seeks to save for such items or spread the cost over time.

- *Legal fees*: ongoing legal fees are identified both in the costs schedules (Form H) and by reference to depleting bank accounts and have no place in budgets.[26]

- *Guesstimates*: if the cost of a proposed item of expenditure is guesstimated, this is not illegitimate, but the party should explain how that estimate has been arrived at.

- *Changing values*: beware the budget that fluctuates wildly, whether from voluntary disclosure to Form E or from hearing to hearing! If disclosable, budgets that increase over time, particularly as the litigation process develops, can be a good indicator of exaggeration.

- *Unreasonably-adopted expenditure*: increasing personal indebtedness and monthly repayments or making unwise financial choices that incur significant costs immediately upon the parties' separation or during the currency of litigation may be challenged by the potential payer.

BRINGING THE STRANDS TOGETHER: A MACRO-RATHER THAN MICRO-ECONOMIC APPROACH

7.14 Budgets are an essential element of all family finance cases and are critical to any claim for a periodical payments order. The degree to which a budget may be scrutinised or criticised, reduced or increased will depend on the circumstances of the case. There is an identifiable and understandable reluctance on the part of the higher courts to sanction costly investigations of, and challenges to, expenditure schedules. Ultimately, once those items that are unjustified, inaccurate or lacking evidence have been removed from the budget, the court is more likely to consider the appropriate *total* monthly or annual sum claimed by the payee by reference to the standard of living during the marriage, the resources of the payer, the earning capacity of the payee, the duration of the marriage, the duration of anticipated support and the ages of the parties. Too strict and narrow an adherence to financial need gives too

---

[26] Unless specifically required upon an application for a costs allowance or an order for payment in respect of legal services; for more, see Chapter 6.

much weight to one discretionary factor, often to the detriment of others. After all, the budget is *a* tool and not *the* answer to determining the level of a periodical payments order as the principles of need, compensation and sharing are 'intended to be guides on the route to fairness and not obstacles to the achievement of fairness'.[27]

7.15 In *W v W*[28] the wife sought an increase to her periodical payments from £18,000 per annum to £42,000 per annum and to capitalise the payment at a figure of £840,000 after the husband sold his company for £11.4m. The husband's counsel had mounted a sustained attack against the wife's budget – both in principle and in relation to specific items – which had increased during the course of proceedings from £62,000 to £97,000 per annum. The wife's counsel argued that her budget was just a starting point, that it should not determine the level of her periodical payments order and that the court could order periodical payments at a level higher than the budget figure. Moylan J considered that, despite some individual items of expenditure being excessive, the husband had focused too unreasonably on the wife's schedule of expenditure. Instead, Moylan J sought to establish an *overall fair figure* for the wife's future income needs:

> '[76] I do not propose to address each of the items challenged by Miss Boyd. I accept that some of the items in the wife's budget, when viewed individually, could well be said to be excessive, although not to the extent submitted by Miss Boyd – for example, the sums claimed for replacing furniture and white goods, the contingency fund, and some of the other smaller items identified by Miss Boyd. In my view, however, the husband's case focuses too narrowly on the wife's income claim in purely budgetary terms. The question I ask myself is whether the global sum put forward by the wife is a fair sum for her current and future income needs. Having looked carefully at all the points identified by Miss Boyd, in my view, the global sum of £60,000 is fair and just.'

> The case of *AR v AR* (Treatment of Inherited Wealth)[29] also provides a good example of the court approaching the payee's budget on a macro- rather than strictly micro-economic basis. The wife's initial Form E budget of £77,000 per annum had increased to £136,000 per annum in further written evidence as the case progressed. The parties' relationship was a long one of some 25 years. However, the vast majority of the capital assets had been gifted to, or inherited by, the husband. In assessing the wife's income needs at a figure of £115,000 per annum consistent with capitalising the payment to meet those needs, Moylan J concluded that:
>
> > '[70] Next, turning to the issue of the wife's future income needs, it is trite to state that the nature and composition of these needs are likely to fluctuate significantly in the future. In assessing the wife's income needs, in particular ➡

---

[27] W *v* W [2010] 2 FLR 985, at [97].
[28] [2010] 2 FLR 985, a case in which the wife applied for an upward variation of a periodical payments order but the principles are applicable to all cases.
[29] [2011] EWHC 2717, [2012] 2 FLR 1, at [70] and [71].

for the purposes of determining what income fund she should be awarded, the analysis, as has been said on many occasions, is a broad one as the court is considering what income it would be fair for the wife to have available to her, in this case, for the next 30 or so years.

[71] To repeat what I have said in previous cases, in my judgment the court's task when addressing this factor is not to arrive at a mathematically exact calculation of what constitutes an applicant's future income needs. It is to determine the notional annual income which, in the circumstances of the case, it would be fair for the wife to receive. Further, in a case such as the present, in my judgment the wife is entitled to have sufficient resources to enable her to spend money on additional, discretionary, items which will vary from year to year and which are not reflected in her annual budget. The husband has provided examples of this, such as the (very substantial) loan to one of his children, the inheritance tax policy he has recently taken out, and treating others, including the parties' son, to a very expensive holiday. There is also the example from the marriage of £60,000–£80,000 being spent on a new kitchen in about 2006. I am not suggesting that the wife should be placed in an equivalent position, but it is reasonable for the wife to have the ability to incur expenditure which is not allowed for as part of her regular annual income needs as set out in the budget.

[72] As referred to earlier in this judgment, the level of expenditure incurred by the family during the latter years of the marriage, the husband's own Form E budget and the level of the husband's expenditure since the separation, are significantly greater than the budget proposed by the husband for the wife. As also referred to earlier in this judgment, the wife's proposed budget is too high in some respects.

[73] Taking all the evidence into account, in my judgment, a reasonable annual income need for the wife is £115,000. This would meet her regular annual income needs, but does not encompass what I have described as discretionary expenditure, individual items not being included as part of her regular expenditure.

POINTS OF PRACTICE AND THEORY

7.16

(1) The budget indicates financial needs, demonstrates the marital standard of living, reveals how a payee may fund the 'gentle transition' to independent living after divorce, illuminates any economic disadvantage experienced by the payee after separation and reveals the financial consequences of a party's future contributions to the welfare of the family.

(2) In appropriate cases, a separate budget may be necessary to demonstrate the marital standard of living.

(3) The budget must be drafted so it is realistic: each entry must be justifiable, accurate and evidenced.

(4) Exaggerated budgets may impact on the overall assessment of a party's credibility.

(5) Unusual and costly items of expenditure may be legitimate within a budget, particularly if:
    (a) they have a historical basis, and
    (b) their past and future importance can be justified and explained, and
    (c) they are affordable within the means of the paying party.

(6) The court's task is not to arrive at a mathematically exact calculation of what constitutes a payee's future income needs. It is to determine the notional annual income which, in the circumstances of the case, it would be fair for the payee to receive. Further, in certain cases, the payee may be entitled to have sufficient resources to enable him/her to spend money on additional, discretionary, items which will vary from year to year and which are not reflected in the annual budget.

CHAPTER 8

THE BASICS OF PERIODICAL PAYMENTS ORDERS: ABSOLUTES, GAME RULES AND FORMS

'Simplicity is the ultimate sophistication'[1]

INTRODUCTION

8.1   This short chapter presents some of the essential principles and fundamental points of practice relevant to the composition and formation of a periodical payments order. Even for the seasoned family lawyer, a reminder of the basics is often invaluable: stripping away the 'flesh' of the court's discretionary exercise reveals the 'skeleton' structure of the order, which, in turn, exposes its inherent strengths, weaknesses and complexities. This chapter is divided into three sections that cover different aspects of periodical payments orders: the absolutes, the game rules and the forms. *Absolutes* are the imperatives that apply to all periodical payments orders. *Game rules* are the various conventions and features of periodical payments orders that may or may not apply to an individual case, depending on the particular circumstances. The section on *Forms* identifies the different types of periodical payments orders that the court can make. This chapter is only an introduction to basic principles, which have importance – individually and in concert – throughout the other more detailed chapters in The Guide.

THE ABSOLUTES

8.2   Family law is so often driven by discretion, nuance and the uniqueness of facts and so seldom permits any absolutes, that it is instructive and positive to consider these first. Periodical payment orders[2] offer a limited number of imperatives, which relate both to their functioning and drafting.

The elements of a periodical payments order

8.3   The MCA 1973 clarifies the elements that are necessary in a properly drafted and executed periodical payments order. These elements can be distilled

---

[1]   Leonardo Da Vinci (1452–1519).
[2]   Upon a decree of divorce etc.

and listed with relative ease to ensure that any periodical payments order meets the demands of the statute as well as the individual circumstances of each case. Any periodical payments order must include the following:

(a)   a payment from one party of the marriage to another;[3]

(b)   identification of the amount of the payment (which can be nominal, substantive, fixed or percentage-based);[4]

(c)   expression of the frequency for payment;[5]

(d)   an indication of whether the payment is made in advance or in arrears;

(e)   the date on which payment begins;

(f)   the date or occasion(s) and event(s) on which payment ends;

(g)   if appropriate, a clause preventing an application to extend the term during which the payer is liable.

Start date, interim payments and backdating

8.4   A periodical payments order can be made on or at any time after granting a decree nisi. Prior to decree nisi, the court may order maintenance pending suit.[6] A periodical payments order can be backdated to the earliest date on which an application for the order was made, which may be the petition for divorce. A backdated order will place the payer in a position of immediate arrears, so the court must be careful to balance the needs of the payee against the payer's ability to pay the arrears in addition to the future payments.

8.5   The periodical payments order may be interim or final, depending on the stage of the proceedings at which it is made.

Variability and capitalisation

8.6   Secured and unsecured periodical payments orders are *always* susceptible to variation, discharge, suspension and revival. The variability of orders is critical to their proper functioning, flexibility and future-proofing. Whereas lump sum and property adjustment orders deal with more immediate financial provision based on existing (or immediately foreseeable) assets, periodical payments orders are made to endure, and will rely and depend on future income and financial needs and obligations. The court cannot order – and the parties cannot make an enforceable agreement – to delete this inherent susceptibility.

8.7   If, on an application to vary a periodical payments order, the court discharges a periodical payments order or varies such an order so that

---

3   No third party can be a payer or payee.
4   A nominal order is usually expressed as 5 pence per annum. Nominal orders are considered in detail in Chapter 12.
5   Eg, weekly, monthly or annually.
6   Which is dealt with in Chapter 5.

payments are to be made for only a limited term, the court can also make a lump sum, property adjustment or pension sharing order, even if the original order, whether by consent or otherwise, dismissed such claims.[7] The power to make these supplemental orders is termed 'capitalisation' within The Guide.[8]

An application for a periodical payments order is barred by the payee's remarriage

8.8　Remarriage or the formation of a civil partnership is an automatic bar to applying for – or pursuing an application for – a periodical payments order, even if the remarriage takes place after the application for a periodical payments order has been made. Remarriage of the applicant (intended payee) terminates any duties arising out of the first marriage:

> 'If after the grant of a decree dissolving or annulling a marriage either party to that marriage remarries whether at any time ... or forms a civil partnership, that party shall not be entitled to apply ... for a financial provision order in his or her favour, or for a property adjustment order, against the other party to that marriage.'[9]

A default term of joint lives applies: termination on death or remarriage

8.9　The court is entitled to make a periodical payments order 'for such term' as may be specified.[10] The maximum term for an unsecured periodical payments order is the death of either the payer or the payee or, where the periodical payments order is made on or after the grant of a decree of divorce or nullity, the remarriage of, or formation of a civil partnership by, the payee.[11] In the absence of any further instruction or indication as to timing within the court's order, the default term for an unsecured periodical payments order, therefore, is the joint lives of the parties.

8.10　A secured periodical payments order survives the death of the payer and automatically terminates only on the death (or remarriage) of the payee.[12]

Decree absolute is required to make the order effective

8.11　A periodical payments order can be made on granting a decree of divorce or 'at any time thereafter'. However, the order does not take effect unless the decree of divorce has been made absolute.[13]

---

[7]　Matrimonial Causes Act 1973 (MCA 1973), s 31(7B); Civil Partnership Act 2004 (CPA 2004), Sch 5, Part 11.

[8]　Albeit that a property adjustment order or a pension sharing order may not strictly be the transfer or payment of capital from the payer to payee, this umbrella term is used for convenience.

[9]　MCA 1973, s 28(3); CPA 2004, Sch 5, Part 10, para 47(2).

[10]　MCA 1973, s 23(1)(a).

[11]　See also MCA 1973, s 28(2).

[12]　See Chapter 16 on Secured Periodical Payments.

[13]　MCA 1973, s 23(5); CPA 2004, Sch 5, Part 1, para 4.

A s 28(1A)[14] bar is required to prevent an extension of any term for payment

8.12 If the court makes an order for periodical payments for a limited term, for example, for one year, 6 years or to a person's retirement, it has the power to order that the payee is not entitled to apply to extend that term for payment. This power acts as a 'bar' on any future variation application to extend the financial obligations of the payer beyond the term specified in the original order. If the court does not make such an order barring an extension, even a dismissal of claims for periodical payments at a future date will fail to invoke this important restriction.

8.13 In *B v B*,[15] a consent order had been made, which provided for reducing periodical payments for the wife over a 7-year period, at which point the wife's claims under s 23(1)(a) and (b) were to be dismissed. Correspondence between the solicitors at the time that the original consent order was agreed made it clear that the intention was that the wife would not be able to apply to extend the term for payments. However, the order did not include an express bar pursuant to s 28(1A) preventing her applying to extend the 7-year term. Thorpe J considered that the wife had received bad legal advice at the time of the original consent order. Although it was exceptional for the court to make an order despite contractual assurances in correspondence that pointed to both parties having intended to create a bar preventing an extension of the term for payment, Thorpe J exercised his discretion and varied the original order to run for the duration of the parties' joint lives.

Leave is required to enforce longer-term arrears

8.14 If the payer fails to pay periodical payments under a court order, the payee must act relatively swiftly to enforce those payments in order to increase the prospects of recovering any accrued arrears. The payer must seek and be granted leave by the court to enforce any arrears that become due more than 12 months before the enforcement proceedings begin.[16]

Non-taxable position

8.15 Save for rare cases in which one of the parties to the marriage was born before 6 April 1935,[17] periodical payments are not treated as the taxable income of the payee. Of course, the payer's income – from which the periodical payments are paid – will be subject to tax deductions (at source or otherwise), depending upon the form in which that income is derived.

---

[14]   In the case of civil partnership, CPA 2004, Sch 5, Part 10, para 47(5) applies.
[15]   [1995] 1 FLR 9.
[16]   MCA 1973, s 32(1); CPA 2004, Sch 5, Part 12. See Chapter 22 on Enforcement.
[17]   And the payment is a qualifying maintenance payment within the meaning of the Income Tax (Trading and Other Income) Act 2005, s 454.

Net income calculations

8.16 It is an obvious but important element of assessing the level of a periodical payments order, to calculate the incomes of both parties, particularly the payer, after the deduction of all taxes, costs and charges that may be levied against such income. The same applies for any costs of the payer necessary to generate the income.

THE GAME RULES

8.17 Game rules are a variety of important features of, and conventions that may apply to, periodical payments orders. These game rules are not appropriate in every case but they demonstrate the flexible nature of periodical payments orders.

Payment: fixed amount and percentages

8.18 It is trite to say that a periodical payments order requires a 'payment' of money, which can be nominal or substantive in nature. The payment can also be specified within the order as a fixed amount or as a percentage of the payer's income. The latter approach allows a periodical payments order, for example, to react to a fluctuating or uncertain income or future bonus payments.[18] The percentage approach can also prove useful in cases in which the payer's income is very high but time-limited. In any case in which a percentage approach is used, it is crucial to identify clearly within the order the type(s) of income of the payer against which the percentage calculation will be applied.[19]

8.19 In *Q v Q (Ancillary Relief: Periodical Payments)*,[20] Bennett J tackled the division of finances arising out of a divorce between a footballer husband and his wife, who cared for the four children of the marriage. The wife proposed that the husband pay to her 50% of his net income for an extendable term of 4 years. The husband contended for an order limiting his payments to 37.5% of net income, reducing upon certain events to 32.5% over the four year term. The husband's income fluctuated; it was likely to be high for four or five years but plummet thereafter and it included a basic wage, bonus and incentive payments as well as signing and publicity fees. Bennett J made an order for the husband to pay periodical payments at the rate of 40% of his net income for an extendable period of 4 years. This order was intended to be a 'bridge' to a

---

[18]   Unless otherwise dealt with by way of lump sum orders/payments. See further, Chapter 10 on Bonus Payments.

[19]   For example, if a bonus payment or investment income is anticipated but is to be excluded from the percentage calculation, this should be clear within the order. Often, the most effective way to ensure that the extent of the divisible income is unambiguous is to include a recital that (1) defines the types of income that fall within the periodical payments order calculation and (2) expressly excludes any other payments made to the payer. Care must also be taken if such an order is achieving a 'sharing' of the payer's income without a cap or limit on the amount. See further, Chapters 9 and 10 on Quantification and Bonus Payments.

[20]   [2005] 2 FLR 640.

potential clean break, as it provided the wife with maintenance that was at a level significantly higher than her income needs for the short anticipated period of the husband's high income.

Attachment of earnings, standing order payments and bank accounts

8.20 Pursuant to the Maintenance Enforcement Act 1991 (MEA 1991), the High Court or a county court has various powers to ensure the payment, or to determine the means of payment, of a periodical payments order.[21] At the time a periodical payments order is made or at any later time, the court can:

(a) make an attachment of earnings order, so that the payment is deducted at source from the payer's employed income;[22] or

(b) order that the payment is made by way of standing order[23] or any other method requiring the payer's authority for payment;[24] or

(c) order the payer to open an account to enable payment to be made, if the payer has been given an opportunity to open an account but, without reasonable excuse, has failed to do so.[25]

The use of these powers will depend on the circumstances of the case. If the history indicates that a payer may default, and with a view to preventing costly enforcement proceedings, it may be prudent to seek a 'means of payment order' pursuant to the MEA 1991 from the court at the time when the order is made.

Indexation

8.21 Periodical payments orders can endure for many years. In so doing, the payee may suffer a 'real value' reduction to the payments if the order does not include provision to adjust the level of payments in line with inflation. Inflation is the rate of change of prices for goods and services. Indexation, therefore, seeks to maintain the buying power of the periodical payments received by the payee. The two principal measures of inflation are the Retail Prices Index (RPI) and the Consumer Prices Index (CPI). These measures use different calculation methods, the most important difference being that the RPI includes housing costs, whereas the CPI does not. The data that underpins the RPI and CPI is available (in quarterly updated format) on the Office for National Statistics website.[26]

---

[21] Of its own motion or on the application of an interested party (MEA 1991, s 1(1)). The payer must be ordinarily resident in England and Wales for the maintenance payment to be a qualifying one, such that the provisions of the MEA 1991 are available.

[22] MEA 1991, s 1(4)(b).

[23] MEA 1991, s 1(5)(a).

[24] MEA 1991, s 1(5)(b).

[25] MEA 1991, s 1(6).

[26] http://www.ons.gov.uk/ons/.

8.22   The CPI is increasingly becoming the popular choice for the payer as RPI historically results in a higher inflationary figure.

8.23   A failure to include an indexation clause in any order for periodical payments that is not very short term in nature can have a significant detrimental impact on the relative value of future payments. In *VB v JP*[27] Sir Mark Potter was asked to replace a complicated claw-back indexation clause with a more standard precedent for index-linking. Sir Mark Potter refused to do so given that the parties had relatively recently agreed the terms of the more complicated formula, but highlighted the importance of indexation clauses, commenting as follows:

> 'It is, of course, the ordinary purpose of a (conventional) RPI clause to provide protection for the receiving spouse, usually the wife, against the erosive effects of inflation and hence to inhibit the likelihood of future litigation; as such, use of RPI clauses is to be encouraged, in my view.'[28]

Flexibility and the definition of maintenance

8.24   Periodical payments orders are inherently flexible as to their timing and amount and, importantly, their purpose. Courts often refer to the expression of 'maintenance' when considering the future financial support of the payee from the future income of the payer. However, periodical payments orders are not limited to payment only for an exclusive list of items, needs, objects or obligations, which may fall within a traditional understanding of 'maintenance'. In *Miller v Miller; McFarlane v McFarlane*,[29] Lord Nicholls, when considering whether periodical payments orders could be used to afford compensation to the payee for economic disadvantage arising out of the marriage, stated the following:

> '[31] I see no difficulty on this point. There is nothing in the statutory ancillary relief provisions to suggest Parliament intended periodical payments orders to be limited to payments needed for maintenance. Section 23(1)(a) empowers the court, in quite general language, to order one party to the marriage to make to the other 'such periodical payments, for such term, as may be specified in the order'. In deciding whether, and how, to exercise this power the statute requires the court to have regard to all the circumstances of the case: s 25(1) of the 1973 Act. The court is required to have particular regard to the familiar wide-ranging checklist set out in s 25(2). These provisions, far from suggesting an intention to restrict periodical payments to the one particular purpose of maintenance, suggest that the financial provision orders in s 23 were intended to be flexible in their application.'

---

[27]   [2008] 1 FLR 742.
[28]   Ibid, at [88]; although in *Grocholeswka-Mullins v Mullins* [2013] EWCA Civ 1121, Patten LJ, in a permission to appeal ruling, did not accept that the judge's failure to apply an RPI index increase to an order for periodical payments amounted to an error of law (this was a variation and capitalisation case).
[29]   [2006] 1 FLR 1186.

Therefore, periodical payments orders can provide for compensation as well as financial need and they can be used, for example, to assist the payee to amass capital with a view to a future clean break if the payer's income is high but short-lived. They are flexible and reactive and their scope is not expressly limited by any standard understanding of the term 'maintenance'.

The remittance of arrears of periodical payments

8.25 Arrears can arise for a wide spectrum of reasons ranging from a genuine inability to pay to mistake or wilful default. The MCA 1973 provides opportunities to the payer for arrears to be remitted.[30] Swift action by the payee is important in all cases of non-payment, as any arrears that are more than 12 months old require the leave of the court as condition precedent to enforcement.[31] On an application by the payee for leave to enforce arrears that are more than 12 months old, the court can remit the payment of all or some of those arrears, depending on the particular circumstances of the case.[32]

THE FORMS

8.26 There are principally seven different types of periodical payments orders that the court can make (excluding orders for failure to maintain[33] and maintenance pending suit[34]). The appropriate order will depend on the circumstances of each individual case:

(a) *A substantive periodical payments order for the parties' joint lives*
An order, for example, for payment of £10,000 per annum, payable monthly at the rate of £833 per month to continue until either the payer or payee dies.[35]

(b) *A nominal periodical payments order for joint lives*
An order, for example, for payment of £1 per annum, payable annually to continue until either the payer or payee dies.[36]

(c) *A substantive or nominal periodical payments order for a limited term without a bar preventing the extension of the term*
An order for the payment of a nominal or substantive sum to continue until a specified date or event in the future, before which point in time the payee may apply to the court to extend the term for payment.

(d) *A substantive or nominal periodical payments order for a limited term with a bar preventing the extension of the term*

---

[30] MCA 1973, s 31(2A) and see also s 32(2) for applications to enforce arrears; CPA 2004, Sch 5, Part 11, para 52(1).
[31] MCA 1973, s 32(1).
[32] See **22.6-22.8**.
[33] See Chapter 4.
[34] See Chapter 5.
[35] Or the payee remarries.
[36] Or the payee remarries.

An order for the payment of a nominal or substantive sum to continue until a specified date or event in the future with an additional order preventing the payee from applying to the court to extend the term for payment.

(e) *An order for secured periodical payments*

An order that the payer secures, ie protects and retains, a sum out of which the periodical payments will be paid to the payee.

(f) *An order adjourning a claim for periodical payments*

An order adjourning a claim for periodical payments indefinitely or to a specified date in the future

(g) *An order dismissing any claims for periodical payments or secured periodical payments*[37]

---

[37] That is, any order pursuant to MCA 1973, s 23(1)(a) or (b); CPA 2004, Sch 5, Part 1, para 2(1)(a) or (b).

CHAPTER 9

THE QUANTIFICATION OF ORDERS FOR PERIODICAL PAYMENTS

'The parties need all the help they can get from previous authority to assist in negotiation. In a field as discretionary as this one, it is often hard to provide real guidance, which limits rather than promotes the debate. Pandora is constantly vigilant for opportunities to unlock the box'[1]

INTRODUCTION

9.1   The quantification of any periodical payments order, if consistency and predictability are *at all* valued, must be undertaken on a principled basis. Of course, the periodical payments order is only one of a number of financial orders available to the court in its ultimate pursuit of fairness and it cannot be seen in isolation from the lump sum, property or pension orders. Nevertheless, it is instructive to consider both how the quantum of a periodical payments order is calculated and the approaches and theories that inform that calculation. Periodical payments represent a prospective rather than a retrospective means of achieving a fair financial outcome for the parties to a divorce; as such, they invariably require judicial findings as to each party's income, earning capacity, health, expenditure and standard of living.[2]

9.2   The starting – and end – point for quantification must be the Matrimonial Causes Act 1973 (MCA 1973), s 25(1) and (2). However, this list of factors may direct the court to the relevant issues, but it does very little to guide the court as to how to convert its findings and judgments into raw pounds and pence. This chapter aims to steer the reader through the maze of numerous reported cases, which often involve assets and incomes that are stratospherically high compared with those of the population at large, to a position of some sense and clarity. It is broadly assumed, for the purpose of this chapter, that the court has divided capital and property so as to meet each

---

[1]   *Charman v Charman* [2006] EWHC 1879, per Coleridge J (of course, the case of *Charman v Charman* was the subject of an appeal to the Court of Appeal).

[2]   'The devious or the feckless husband will still be prevented from throwing his proper maintenance obligations on the state. The genuine struggler, on the other hand, will be spared the burden of having to pay to his former spouse indefinitely the last few pounds that separate him from total penury. Between those two extremes there will be ample opportunity for flexible orders which give proper weight to both heads of policy . . .': *Ashley v Blackman* [1988] Fam 85, [1988] FCR 699, at 92, per Waite J.

party's basic housing needs, and determined that a periodical payments order[3] is just and appropriate in the circumstances. How then should the quantum of that order be determined?

9.3   The enquiry must, of course, be in two stages,[4] computation and distribution: this applies to the quantification of periodical payments just as it does to the division of capital.

BACK TO BASICS

9.4   The approach to the quantification of a periodical payments order necessitates a return to the basic principles currently applicable to financial redistribution on divorce.

The two-stage approach

9.5   The court's enquiry in an application for a financial remedy, whether of a capital or income nature, is undertaken in two stages: the first is **computation** and the second is **distribution**. The computation stage in relation to an order for periodical payments requires the court, principally, to make findings as to the income[5], earning capacity and future needs of, and welfare or other benefits receivable by, each party. The distribution stage entails an analysis of the factors in s 25(1) and (2) of the MCA 1973 and the formulation of an order that achieves the overall objective of fairness (to both parties).

In pursuit of the elusive concept of fairness

9.6   Fairness is an elusive concept, grounded in [changeable] social and moral values, that is an instinctive response to a given set of facts.[6] However instinctive the response may be, the specific *requirements* of fairness are threefold: (1) **financial need**, (2) **compensation**, which is aimed at 'redressing any significant prospective economic disparity between the parties arising from the way they conducted their marriage'[7] and (3) **equal sharing**, unless there is good reason to the contrary.

9.7   All three requirements are connected to the parties' marriage, to the choices, decisions and sacrifices made and their enduring financial consequences. Baroness Hale expressed this principle as follows: 'The cardinal feature is that each [requirement] is looking at factors which are linked to the

---

3   Whether that will eventually be subject to a *Duxbury*-based capitalisation process or not.
4   *Charman v Charman (No 4)* [2007] 1 FLR 1246.
5   Note that, under the Universal Credit system – in transitional implementation at present – any maintenance paid to an ex-partner under a court order or agreement will count in full as income (not, however, maintenance for a child). '*The Welfare Benefits and Tax Credits Handbook*', Child poverty Action Group, 2013/2014, 15th Edition, London, page 274.
6   *Miller v Miller; McFarlane v McFarlane*, HL, at [4], per Lord Nicholls of Birkenhead.
7   Ibid, at [14], per Lord Nicholls of Birkenhead.

parties' relationship, either causally or temporally, and not to extrinsic, unrelated factors, such as a disability arising after the marriage has ended'.[8]

Periodical payments and the three requirements of fairness

9.8   There is a live and (as yet fully) unresolved debate as to whether the third requirement of fairness identified above – that of 'sharing' – applies to the assessment and quantification of an order for periodical payments. The vast majority of orders for periodical payments are resolved by reference to the payee's needs. A smaller number of orders may involve some uplift to, or enhancement of, the quantum (or term) of a periodical payments order to reflect a compensatory element for the payee: a recognition of the payee's financial disadvantage, for example, arising out of sacrificed career prospects. In *Miller v Miller; McFarlane v McFarlane*, Lord Nicholls had 'no difficulty' in extending the use of a periodical payments order as a means of affording compensation to the payee as well as meeting the payee's financial need.[9] The sharing 'principle', however, is almost impossible to apply to the quantification of a periodical payments order in the same way as it may be applied to the distribution of capital. The requirement is to share the fruits of the matrimonial partnership based on the principle that each party on divorce '*is entitled to an equal share of the assets of the partnership, unless there is good reason to the contrary*'.[10] The income of one party after separation is not an 'asset' in the sense of a home or an investment portfolio. However, in *Miller v Miller; McFarlane v McFarlane*, Baroness Hale referred to Mr McFarlane's earning power as the 'main family asset', which had been generated over a lengthy marriage in which the couple chose a life involving the wife's devotion to the home and family and the husband to his work and career. Therefore, Baroness Hale concluded that 'the wife is undoubtedly entitled to generous income provision for herself and for the sake of their children, including sums which will enable her to provide for her own old age and insure the husband's life. She is also entitled to a *share* in the very large surplus, on the principles both of *sharing the fruits of the matrimonial partnership* and of compensation for the comparable position which she might have been in had she not compromised her own career for the sake of them all' (emphasis added).[11]

> In the more recent case of *B v S (Financial Remedy: Marital Property Regime)*[12] Mostyn J undertook a survey of the case-law concerning the *apparent* application of the sharing principle to the assessment of periodical payments orders. Mostyn J outlined that the doubtful justification for such an application of the sharing principle is that the payer's income is, 'in some intangible way, a piece of matrimonial →

---

[8]   Ibid, at [137], per Baroness Hale.
[9]   Ibid, at [31], per Lord Nicholls of Birkenhead.
[10]   Ibid, at [16], per Lord Nicholls of Birkenhead.
[11]   At [154], per Baroness Hale of Richmond.
[12]   [2012] 2 FLR 502.

property there to be equitably or fairly shared'.[13] Mostyn J rejected this justification, as it fails to recognise the fact that the continued receipt of income in the future depends solely on the continued work of the party earning that income. The *ability* to earn at a high level may be the result of a career which, but for the sacrifices made by the other party to the marriage in caring for the family, children and home may not have developed to such a level, but the actual receipt of income relies on the payer's labour. In *B v S*, Mostyn J refused to allow consideration of the concept of sharing to intrude in the assessment of a periodical payments award, since such an approach is 'based on a doubtful principle, and is replete with problems of quantification by any sure standard. The sharing principle in relation to matrimonial property[14] is simple enough: it is usually 50/50, because in the division of the marital acquest, equity (or fairness) is (usually) equality. But if the concept of sharing is going to uplift above the assessment of need a periodical payments award which will be paid from post-separation earnings, how does a judge set about doing it? Is it a third? Or 40%? Or 20%? There are not even any signposts along the road to a fair award'.[15]

9.9   Mostyn J's conclusion that a periodical payments order should, save in exceptional circumstances, be adjudged or settled by reference to '[financial] need' alone, is driven by an aspiration to simplify the quantification of such an order. This is a welcome statement of general principle:[16] it also accords with the Court of Appeal's refusal in *Jones v Jones* to entertain any argument based upon the capitalisation of the husband's earning capacity (as an asset), whether at the date of the marriage or at the financial remedy hearing:

'There is, however, a separate, wider question whether it is ever necessary or appropriate for the court to attempt to capitalise the earning capacity which a party has at the date of the hearing. There is no denying the extreme importance of an inquiry into the earning capacity of each party at that date: indeed s 25(2)(a) of the Matrimonial Causes Act 1973 makes it mandatory. A spouse's earning capacity will usually be a central foundation of an order for periodical payments, and thus

---

[13]   *B v S*, at [76], per Mostyn J.

[14]   Not non-matrimonial property.

[15]   *B v S*, at [79], per Mostyn J.

[16]   As far as one can be made in such a discretion-based system. However, the House of Lords' opinion remains as to the applicability of the 'sharing' principle to an award of periodical payments, see also *P v P (Post-Separation Accruals and Earning Capacity)* [2007] EWHC 2877 (Fam), [2008] 2 FLR 1135 in which Moylan J stated: 'Baroness Hale of Richmond is not, in my view, qualifying her previous remarks when she refers to Mrs McFarlane as being entitled to a share of the husband's surplus income "on the principles both of sharing ... and of compensation". An issue had been raised in that case (see the Court of Appeal's decision: *Parlour v Parlour; McFarlane v McFarlane* [2004] EWCA Civ 872, [2005] Fam 171, [2004] 2 FLR 893) as to whether periodical payments could only be awarded to meet needs. The Court of Appeal decided that there was no such limitation. In that context, it is not surprising to read that, if an equal share of the capital is not sufficient to provide for need and compensate for disadvantage, the principles identified by the House of Lords (including sharing) continue to apply and can continue to apply to "surplus" income. For example, in *Parlour* the husband's future income was shared not on the basis of need, nor of compensation ...' (at [121]).

of any order by way of capitalisation thereof, pursuant to the principles of need and/or of compensation. Even if, however, an earning capacity may also sometimes be relevant to a fair distribution of the assets pursuant to the sharing principle, it does not follow that the earning capacity should itself be treated as one of those assets, still less that an attempt should be made to capitalise it.'[17]

Mostyn J's restriction of the quantification of a periodical payments order to need[18] has been expressly followed in the case of *G v B*,[19] which involved an asset base of some £6.1m. In *G v B* the husband was aged 62 and the wife, 46. The marriage had lasted some 8–10 years (depending on the date of cohabitation) and the parties had one child. The wealth in the case all emanated from the husband's father, who had died in 2005, and whose assets were now held in a Leichtenstein foundation to which the husband had recourse throughout the marriage. The husband had no real earning capacity and the wife's was also very modest. Blair J accepted that the parties' needs were the 'magnetic factor' in the case and that the derivation of the funds (from the husband's father) was to be given some weight.

9.10   Finally, it is also the case that a periodical payments order based on a (perhaps unlimited) period of 'sharing' the payer's income will offend against the principle of seeking to achieve a clean break and eventual financial independence between the parties.[20]

CAPITAL DIVISION AND INCOME PROVISION

9.11   As explained in the introduction to this chapter, a periodical payments order cannot be seen in isolation from the other lump sum, pension and property adjustment orders available to the court. If the capital assets are sufficiently large, an equal or even unequal division of those assets may be sufficient to meet a party's needs (for housing and income) and any latent claim for compensation. Nevertheless, where the capital assets are low and the income or earning capacity of one party is high, a periodical payments order may prove to be a crucial mechanism to redress 'a rapid decrease in the primary carer's standard of living and a rapid increase in the breadwinner's after an otherwise equal division of capital'.[21] In an exceptional case where the payer's earnings are very high, the periodical payments order may provide a significant surplus to the payee over and above his or her needs.

---

[17]   *Jones v Jones* [2011] 1 FLR 1723, at [27], per Wilson LJ.
[18]   Or, exceptionally, compensation.
[19]   [2013] EWHC 3414.
[20]   Although, this is not always the case and, exceptionally, as, for example, in *Miller/McFarlane*, the high income but low capital position may warrant and *require* some sharing of income surplus to needs.
[21]   *Miller v Miller; McFarlane v McFarlane*, at [142], per Baroness Hale of Richmond.

Marriage as a partnership: financial provision after separation

9.12 Case-law contains a number of general observations about the limitations of future financial provision after divorce. The partnership of marriage terminates on separation and, ultimately, decree absolute. The termination of the partnership is an important fact that should inform the distributive powers of the court. Baroness Hale puts it thus:

> 'In general, it can be assumed that the marital partnership does not stay alive for the purpose of sharing future resources unless this is justified by need or compensation. The ultimate objective is to give each party an equal start on the road to independent living'.[22]

FINANCIAL NEED AND COMPENSATION FOR RELATIONSHIP-GENERATED DISADVANTAGE

9.13 Given that financial need and, exceptionally, compensation, appear to be the principal bases for calculating the quantum of a periodical payments award, how are these two concepts to be understood?

What exactly is 'financial need'?

9.14

> '[138] The most common rationale is that the relationship has generated needs which it is right that the other party should meet. In the great majority of cases, the court is trying to ensure that each party and their children have enough to supply their needs, set at a level as close as possible to the standard of living which they enjoyed during the marriage (note that the House did not adopt a restrictive view of needs in *White*: see 608G–609A and 993 respectively). This is a perfectly sound rationale where the needs are the consequence of the parties' relationship, as they usually are. The most common source of need is the presence of children, whose welfare is always the first consideration, or of other dependent relatives, such as elderly parents. But another source of need is having had to look after children or other family members in the past. Many parents have seriously compromised their ability to attain self-sufficiency as a result of past family responsibilities. Even if they do their best to re-enter the employment market, it will often be at a lesser level than before, and they will hardly ever be able to make up what they have lost in pension entitlements. A further source of need may be the way in which the parties chose to run their life together. Even dual career families are difficult to manage with completely equal opportunity for both. Compromises often have to be made by one so that the other can get ahead. All couples throughout their lives together have to make choices about who will do what, sometimes forced upon them by circumstances such as redundancy or low pay, sometimes freely made in the ➥

---

[22] *Miller v Miller, McFarlane v McFarlane*, at [144].

> interests of them both. The needs generated by such choices are a perfectly
> sound rationale for adjusting the parties' respective resources in
> compensation.'[23]

The MCA 1973 directs the court to consider the financial needs, obligations
and responsibilities which each of the parties has or is likely to have in the
foreseeable future.[24] Over at least the last 50 years, the courts have striven in
various ways to interpret, expand upon and conceptualise this statutory
direction. Therefore, a variety of different expressions has arisen which are
designed to *assist*[25] the understanding of financial 'need': three that can be
identified are (1) 'reasonable requirements', (2) need 'generously interpreted'
and, perhaps, (3) 'real need'.

Reasonable requirements

9.15   The 'reasonable requirements' of the wife used to be a factor limiting any
financial award to her, and this concept applied to the assessment of both
capital and income provision. In *White v White*,[26] the House of Lords rejected
the notion that financial need – even interpreted more generously and called
'reasonable requirements' – should determine a party's financial award. The
House of Lords encouraged the lower courts to stop using the expression
'reasonable requirements' and to return to the language of the MCA 1973:
financial needs, obligations and responsibilities.

Need 'generously interpreted'

9.16   Despite the House of Lords in *White v White* equating the term
'reasonable requirements' with a generous interpretation of a party's financial
need – and then *rejecting* the utility of that term – this generous interpretation
of needs found renewed favour in the case of *Miller v Miller; McFarlane v
McFarlane*. A generous interpretation of needs implies an assessment that is not
parsimonious and which, if financial resources permit, is benevolently in excess
of a party's basic budget. The concept of a generous interpretation once again
became established as a means for deviating from a strict budgetary approach
to the assessment of financial need. However, the Court of Appeal intervened in
the case of *Robson v Robson*[27] to direct attention away from these judicial
interpretations on the words of the MCA 1973 and to return to the language
introduced by Parliament:

> 'Concentrate on s 25 of the Matrimonial Causes Act 1973 as amended because this
> imposes a duty on the court to have regard to all the circumstances of the case,
> first consideration being given to the welfare while a minor of any child of the
> family who has not attained the age of 18; and then requires that regard must be

---

[23]   *Miller v Miller; McFarlane v McFarlane*, at [138], per Baroness Hale.
[24]   MCA 1973, s 25(2)(b).
[25]   To what extent these expressions do assist this exercise is open to debate.
[26]   [2000] 2 FLR 981.
[27]   [2010] EWCA Civ 1171, [2011] 1 FLR 751.

had to the specific matters listed in s 25(2). Confusion will be avoided if resort is had to the precise language of the statute, not any judicial gloss placed upon the words, for example by the introduction of 'reasonable requirements' nor, dare I say it, upon need always having to be 'generously interpreted.'[28]

Judicial gloss on the term 'need' is conceptually both unnecessary and redundant, since the interpretation of 'need' must itself be informed by the other factors relevant to the court's discretionary assessment. Its assessment must be holistic. Therefore, 'the principle of need requires consideration of the financial needs, obligations and responsibilities of the parties (s 25(2)(b)); of the standard of living enjoyed by the family before the breakdown of the marriage (s 25(2)(c)); of the age of each party (half of s 25(2)(d)); and of any physical or mental disability of either of them (s 25(2)(e)).[29] In the calculation of the appropriate level of periodical payments, each party's income and earning capacity must be added to this list. Care must always be taken not to adopt judicial phrases, such as 'generously interpreted needs', and to treat them like statutory imperatives. Ryder J reminds the practitioner in *Lawrence v Gallagher*:[30]

> 'There is a prevalent practice of coining ever more sophisticated phrases which are intended by practitioners to highlight particular aspects of the notion of "fairness". That practice has created an expectation that the judge will consider the same in judgment. That expectation is inappropriate not least because the linguistic devices employed are not terms of art: they are no more than tools to assist in the interpretation of fact which should not be elevated to the status of factors that have to be considered alongside the s 25 criteria.'

Real need

9.17 'Real need' is a phrase that is arguably the opposite of need 'generously interpreted': it implies a more basic and less indulgent assessment of need, particularly given its articulation in the case-law as putting a person (who is in such real need) in a 'predicament'. This term appears, for example, in the case of *Radmacher (Formerly Granatino) v Granatino*, in which the Supreme Court doubted whether parties to an ante-nuptial agreement would have intended an agreement to leave one party in a 'predicament of real need' and the other enjoying a sufficiency of resources.[31] Unfortunately for Mr Granatino, the court's assessment was that he was not in such a position of real need after his marriage, albeit that his needs were severely diminished in a manner inconceivable had there been no ante-nuptial agreement.[32] It does appear, therefore, that the interpretation of 'financial need' can be qualified by, for

---

[28] At [43], per Ward LJ.
[29] *Charman v Charman (No 4)*, at [70], per Sir Mark Potter (President, as he then was).
[30] [2012] EWCA Civ 394, [2012] 2 FLR 643, at [57].
[31] At [81] and the example given of such a predicament was the husband having been incapacitated during the marriage such that he could not earn a living.
[32] As Mostyn J commented in *N v F (Financial Orders: Pre-Acquired Wealth)* [2011] EWHC 586 (Fam), [2011] 2 FLR 533.

example, the presence of an ante-nuptial agreement:[33] as Mostyn J commented in *N v F (Financial Orders: Pre-acquired Wealth)*, an ante-nuptial agreement to preserve one party's non-matrimonial property 'can have the effect of assessing [the other party's] need more conservatively'.[34]

Caution: need, the marital standard of living and the duration of the marriage

9.18 The *marital standard of living* is an aspect of each case to which the court's attention is directed.[35] This standard, if high and provided for by one party's financial resources, may justify a commensurate assessment of need, albeit that the shorter the marriage – and therefore the shorter the period during which such a standard of living was enjoyed – the more unfair it may be for the other party to expect to continue to live at that standard after separation.[36] In *McCartney v Mills McCartney*, Bennett J accepted counsel for the husband's submissions that 'in a short marriage case it is legitimate to look at the claimant's needs more conservatively than in a long marriage, because the standard of living which has a bearing on the assessment of need will have been enjoyed for a shorter period'.[37]

9.19 Equally, if the marital standard of living was extravagant and unjustified when compared to the financial resources of the parties, it will be unfair to assess a party's needs at the end of the marriage by reference to such a standard. For example, in *Robson v Robson*, the husband and wife had funded their profligate lifestyle by drawing on the husband's significant inheritances. At first instance, Charles J framed the wife's financial award to provide her with a continuation of the lifestyle enjoyed during the marriage. The Court of Appeal rejected such an approach. The facts that (1) the wealth of the husband came from inheritance, (2) the parties had both lived beyond their means from such wealth and (3) the wife had been fully aware of the husband's mismanagement of his inheritance did not justify a maintenance of the marital standard of living. The Court of Appeal reduced the assessment of the wife's immediate annual income need by 10% and her subsequent need at age 70 by some 28%. Ward LJ made the following observations:

---

[33] See also *V v V (Ancillary Relief: Prenuptial Agreement)* [2011] EWHC 3230 (Fam), [2012] 1 FLR 1315.

[34] At [19]: *N v F* was a case focusing on the division of assets brought into the marriage by the husband: in his judgment, Mostyn J considered the 'reasonable' need of the wife – both in terms of her housing and future expenditure – and awarded a *Duxbury* sum to provide income of £104,000 pa for life as opposed to the wife's requested budget of £187,000 pa. See also David Salter sitting as a Deputy Judge of the High Court in *B v B (Assessment of Assets: Pre-Marital Property)* [2012] EWHC 314 (Fam), [2012] 2 FLR 22: 'the assessment of need is not an insulated metric and the presence of pre-marital property may lead to a more conservative assessment of needs. In reaching my conclusion in relation to the wife's capital needs, I also have regard to the husband's pre-marital wealth.' (At [89].)

[35] MCA 1973, s 25(2)(c).

[36] *McCartney v Mills McCartney* at [240], per Bennett J.

[37] Ibid, from Mr Mostyn QC's submission at [214].

'[76] Since they had drawn upon capital to support their lifestyle, there can be no complaint about the fact that the judge required the inherited property to continue to be the source to fund the wife's future income needs. Given the husband's age, lack of earning capacity, and the loss of the farm income, he could hardly provide future support for the wife otherwise than by continuing to use his capital resources. The question is, however, whether the judge was correct to continue providing support at the level to maintain "the standard of living enjoyed by the family before the breakdown of the marriage". True it is that that is the statutory factor to which the court must have regard pursuant to s 25(2)(c). Ordinarily that would be the right approach. But this is not an ordinary case. First, the capital is inherited capital and as such deserves a special consideration. It is not to be inviolate having regard to the length of time during which and the extent to which the parties had relied upon it to subsidise the lifestyle they had individually, and jointly, established for themselves. Secondly, and more importantly, the circumstances of the case are relevant and the circumstances here are that they plundered the inheritance to indulge in a lifestyle which their income and efforts could not justify. They were living beyond their means. On the judge's findings it was the husband who was mainly at fault for failing to maximise the income of the estate and he, a trained accountant, was also at fault for permitting the state of affairs which tolerated enjoying the good life at a level which could not be afforded had prudence, and not profligacy, been the watchword. He is rightly criticised for his extravagance. But the wife does not escape criticism ... she was fully aware that they were living on a mismanaged inheritance, that the level of expenditure to support their lifestyle meant that the nature and consequence of that lifestyle, as the second generation in possession, was that the inheritance was being enjoyed to the full and put at risk rather than enjoyed and nurtured by them. In other words, she was complicit in their prodigality.

[77] It seems to me, therefore, to be inconsistent to criticise them, albeit one more than the other, for being recklessly wasteful of their bounty, a criticism which carries with it the implication that it ought reasonably to cease and that a more moderate lifestyle was called for in the future, yet at the same time, to allow the wife to live in the same extravagant way as she inappropriately had in days of yore. It also seems to me to be unfair to the husband to expect him to continue to plunder the inheritance in order to continue to maintain his former wife at a rate found to be beyond his means.'

A broad conclusion: one man's real need may be another man's luxury

9.20 Need is an *elastic* concept, whether applied to the question of housing or future income requirements: it must be so, in order to achieve the necessary degree of flexibility to respond justly to the circumstances of each case. A judicial finding as to a party's financial needs must also be the result of an *holistic* assessment and investigation. The scale of the income available to both parties, the presence of children and the marital standard of living are all factors relevant to determining what may be appropriate in an individual case. As Mostyn J so aptly remarked in *N v F*: 'just as there are inheritances and inheritances, there are needs and needs'.[38]

---

[38] *N v F*, at [17].

UNDERSTANDING AND QUANTIFYING COMPENSATION

9.21 Compensation for relationship-generated disadvantage is a rationale that has caused much consternation: in its original articulation in *Miller v Miller; McFarlane v McFarlane*, compensation was identified as a concept that may overlap with, but is distinct from, that of financial need.[39] Compensation is a difficult concept to apply to family law, as its traditional context is in the payment of money by one party to the other for damages caused by, usually, a negligent or criminal act. It is clear now from case-law that the financial remedy version of compensation is not to be treated (in a similar way) as a separate 'head of claim' that is pleaded by a party by reference to a financial schedule of loss.[40] In *RP v RP*,[41] Coleridge J rejected any approach to compensation on the basis of a damages claim or as an arithmetical calculation of a party's lost earning capacity as 'completely misconceived'. How then, if at all, is a compensatory element to a periodical payments order to be quantified?

9.22 A very comprehensible statement on compensation appears in the opinion of Lord Nicholls in *Miller v Miller; McFarlane v McFarlane*:

> '[it is] aimed at redressing any significant prospective economic disparity between the parties arising from the way they conducted their marriage. For instance, the parties may have arranged their affairs in a way which has greatly advantaged the husband in terms of his earning capacity but left the wife severely handicapped so far as her own earning capacity is concerned. Then the wife suffers a double loss: a diminution in her earning capacity and the loss of a share in her husband's enhanced income. This is often the case. Although less marked than in the past, women may still suffer a disproportionate financial loss on the breakdown of a marriage because of their traditional role as home-maker and child-carer.'[42]

In none of the reported cases has a periodical payments order ever been expressed as a sum of £y + z per annum with £y being the payee's needs and £z being an element of compensation. In *Lauder v Lauder*,[43] the wife, who was aged 50 at separation, had a modest earning capacity, which was attributable to the marriage and the parties' decision that she would be a wife and mother; a disadvantage that required proper compensation. At trial the wife's own needs budget was presented as £43,867 pa. The district judge uplifted/increased this figure by 14% to represent a 'generous interpretation' of the wife's needs. On appeal, Baron J ordered capitalised periodical payments to provide the wife with net spendable income of £65,000 pa, which represents some £21,000 more each year than presented in the wife's budget. The compensatory element of the wife's claim for periodical payments was expressly *not* separated from the 'generously interpreted' needs element.

---

[39] *Miller*, at [15], per Lord Nicholls.
[40] See *CR v CR* [2008] 1 FLR 323 in which Bodey J (at [83]) warned against elevating the components of fairness into separate 'heads of claim' or 'of loss' independent of the words of MCA 1973, s 25.
[41] [2007] 1 FLR 2105.
[42] Miller, at [13], per Lord Nicholls.
[43] [2007] 2 FLR 802.

9.23   In *VB v JP*[44] the wife sought an increase to her periodical payments order from £81,000 to £130,000 pa on the basis that she was entitled to a 'premium' over her stated budgetary needs by way of compensation for the loss of her earning capacity. The wife was 45 years of age and had spent 14 years caring for the family: it was accepted that she was unable to earn anything more than 'pin money' from employment. Sir Mark Potter found that the wife suffered 'undoubted relationship-generated disadvantage' but that it was inappropriate to quantify the element of compensation separately from that of the wife's needs generously assessed against the background of the standard of living during the marriage, the husband's considerably increased income and the reduced availability to the wife of a substantial proportion of the child maintenance originally provided'.[45] After a review of the case-law, Sir Mark Potter gave the following general guidance as to the approach to a case involving a dispute as to compensation:

> '[59] In my view, there emerge from the post-*Miller; McFarlane* authorities to which I have been referred the following propositions in elaboration of, but consistent with, the House of Lords decision. **First,** it is at the exit of the marriage and in relation to the division/redistribution of the family assets that the consideration of the element of compensation immediately arises, but as a feature of the concept of fairness rather than as a head of claim in its own right. **Second,** on the exit from the marriage, the partnership ends and in ordinary circumstances a wife has no right or expectation of continuing economic parity ("sharing") unless and to the extent that consideration of her needs, or compensation for relationship-generated disadvantage so require. A clean break is to be encouraged wherever possible. **Third,** in big money cases, where the matrimonial assets are sufficient for a clean break to be achieved, a wife with ordinary career prospects is likely to be have been compensated by an equal division of the assets and consideration of how the wife's career might have progressed is unnecessary and should be avoided. Where, however, that is not the case and the parties accept or the court decides that fairness can only be achieved by an award of continuing periodical payments in respect of a wife's maintenance, then the matter of compensation in respect of relationship-generated disadvantage requires consideration, again as a strand or element of fairness. **Fourth,** in cases other than big money cases, where a continuing award of periodic payments is necessary and the wife has plainly sacrificed her own earning capacity, compensation will rarely be amenable to consideration as a separate element in the sense of a premium susceptible of calculation with any precision. **Where it is necessary to provide ongoing periodical payments for the wife after the division of capital assets insufficient to cover her future maintenance needs, any element of compensation is best dealt with by a generous assessment of her continuing needs unrestricted by purely budgetary considerations, in the light of the contribution of the wife to the marriage and the broad effect of the sacrifice of her own earning capacity upon her ability to provide for her own needs** ➡

---

[44]   [2008] 1 FLR 742.
[45]   Ibid, at [66].

> following the end of the matrimonial partnership. These considerations are of course inherent in s 25(a)(b)(d) and (f) of the 1973 Act.' (emphasis added)

The very high income case and compensation/exceptional sharing

9.24 In 2009 Mrs McFarlane's ('the wife's') application for an upward variation of her periodical payments order came for hearing before Charles J.[46] The husband's income had increased from £750,000 to £1.1m net p a. The wife's original (spousal) periodical payments order was set at £250,000 pa on a joint lives basis. Charles J imposed a series of percentages on the husband's banded income to quantify the periodical payments order to the wife, as follows: 40% on net earnings up to £750,000 p a, 20% to a £1m p a limit and 10% on net income in excess of £1m p a. Charles J approached the resolution of the case not only on the basis of a compensatory element to the wife's award but also by reference to a 'sharing' of the husband's future income: the quid pro quo for such sharing was that the term of the periodical payments order would be limited to 7 years (to 2015). This term would enable the wife, who would significantly share in a surplus of income in excess of both parties' financial needs, to save and invest funds with the intention of amassing capital sufficient to provide for her future lifetime income needs:

> '[123] ... what is important is to remember when assessing the award to be made that the wife gave up her well-paid career. To my mind, this provides a solid foundation for an award that provides that by reference to what they both (but in particular she) gave up financially for their long-term financial security (whether they were together or apart) the wife is to continue to share in the product of the husband's success and thus the main (or only) source of income that they would rely on to fund their lifestyle (together or apart) before and after retirement.'

The facts of Mrs McFarlane's case are exceptional, as is Charles J's application of the 'sharing' requirement of fairness to the assessment of the wife's periodical payments. However, Charles J's approach to quantification can assist in other cases in which an argument in favour of compensation is well-founded. Charles J quantified the total income available to the parties and applied the needs principle to identify the surplus of income over needs; thereafter, the Judge applied all three principles of need, compensation and sharing to determine how that surplus was to be shared. Charles J also urged parties and their advisers to focus on the fairness of the net financial effect of a proposed order for periodical payments.[47]

---

[46] [2009] EWHC 891 (Fam), [2009] 2 FLR 1322.
[47] By looking, for example, at the percentage split of the combined income of the parties or the surplus income retained by each party after meeting their needs and fulfilling their obligations.

CONCLUSIONS AS TO QUANTIFICATION/POINTS OF PRACTICE AND THEORY

9.26 The case-law advocates against a formulaic approach to the quantification of a spousal periodical payments order. Thus, the vacuum left by the absence of a formula allows for the exercise of very broad discretionary powers. The starting point is the financial needs of both parties and the income available. Occasionally, the payee's continuing economic disadvantage, particularly after a long marriage, and in light of the choices made by the parties during the marriage, will justify a compensatory 'element' to an award of periodical payments: if so, that element will affect both the term and the quantum of the order. Exceptionally, it may still be *permissible* to apply the sharing principle to determine an order for periodical payments, particularly if any surplus receipt over and above financial need is to be used as part of a planned programme towards the payee's ultimate financial independence. It is, therefore, possible to draw from the case-law a broad approach to the quantification of an order for periodical payments:[48]

(1) Determine the net income of each party from all sources (salary, dividends, investment income, regular bonus payments, welfare benefits etc).

(2) Assess whether one party's reasonably achievable earning capacity is greater than their current income.

(3) Determine, by reference to a maintenance budget[49] and all the circumstances of the case, the appropriate and fair level of annual expenditure for both parties.

(4) Establish the level of any deficit between the payee's needs and his or her income.

(5) Examine the marital standard of living and the duration during which such standard was maintained: was this standard maintained with/without unaffordable extravagance? The marital standard of living may impact on the way in which the needs of the parties are approached, ie more or less generously.

(6) Establish the extent of any surplus available after both parties' needs are met from the total annual income available.

(7) Determine whether the facts of the case warrant arguments for a compensatory element to the payee's award by reference to his or her relationship-generated disadvantage.

---

[48] It being fully accepted that there is no formula(!) and that there is no particular incremental process to the calculation of an award, see further *Whaley v Whaley* [2012] 1 FLR 735.

[49] See Chapter 7 on Needs, Budgets and Expenditure.

(8) If compensation is a 'live' principle (1) can this be reflected without unfair detriment to the payer and, if so, (2) can it be expressed through a [more] generous assessment of the payee's continuing needs unconstrained by purely budgetary considerations?[50]

(9) Calculate the 'net effect' of the proposed order for periodical payments on both parties: what will be the level of each party's (a) net income from all sources, (b) ongoing financial needs and (c) available surplus over and above the budgeted needs.

---

[50] This may allow, by way of example, for savings, spending beyond the set budget, larger pension contributions or expenditure that was condoned during the marriage but challenged by the other party after separation.

CHAPTER 10

THE BONUS AND PERIODICAL PAYMENTS

INTRODUCTION

10.1 Bonus payments come in many different forms. They may be annual, quarterly or monthly; payable in cash, shares or options (or a mixture of all three) and at the recipient's election or imposed on him/her; guaranteed or deferred; large and small; performance-linked[1] or discretionary; consistent or unpredictable. The bonus may be anything from a negligible to a significant proportion of the recipient's overall annual remuneration package. Given the myriad types of bonus payments, there is no obvious one-size-fits-all solution or formula as to how they are to be approached by the court in the overall division of finances. A distinction, however, does need to be drawn between (a) cases in which the capital assets are sufficient to effect a clean break, and where an issue remains as to whether, and if so, how, the received or receivable bonuses of the payer are to be distributed between the parties and (b) cases in which the capital assets are insufficient or the circumstances inappropriate to effect a clean break and the payer's future bonus payments may be required to contribute – in part or in whole – to the payee's periodical payments award. This chapter will provide an overview of the different approaches (a) to those cases identified above but will focus latterly on (b) cases in which the payer's remuneration includes bonus payments and the payee is the beneficiary of an order for periodical payments.[2]

THE BONUS ANALYSIS: INFORMATION AND DISCLOSURE

10.2 In any case in which a bonus forms part of a party's overall remuneration package, it will fall for express consideration under the Matrimonial Causes Act 1973 (MCA 1973), s 25(2)(a) within the purview of the 'income, earning capacity, property and other financial resources which each of the parties has or is likely to have in the foreseeable future …'.[3] It is impossible, in the process of

---

[1] Linked to a company's results, a trading index (eg FTSE 100) or personal performance and targets, or a mixture of all three (or other applicable criteria).

[2] Whether on a joint lives basis or for a (non)-extendable term.

[3] Including, of course, in the case of earning capacity, any increase in that capacity which it would in the opinion of the court be reasonable to expect a party to the marriage to take steps to acquire.

disclosure and discovery, to predict every aspect or component of the information required in respect of bonus payments, but any initial analysis may include requests for the following:

(a)   What is the history of bonus payments over, say, the last 5 years? At what point was the bonus paid and at what level? (If elements of a bonus are deferred or paid in the form of share options, it may be difficult to assess this figure with any accuracy).[4]

(b)   What, if any, are the performance-linked criteria that apply to the receipt of the bonus? Are these criteria linked to the company's or recipient's performance (or a combination of both)?

(c)   What is the historical data available as to the company or recipient meeting the criteria for receipt [of all or part] of the bonus?

(d)   In what form is the bonus paid (cash, shares, options etc)? Has this method of payment been consistent over the 5-year analysis period?

(e)   If elements of the bonus are deferred (eg share options), over what period is the deferral made and what, if any, additional conditions apply to the deferred receipt?

(f)   What is the likelihood of the deferral conditions being met (ie if a conditional grant of shares will only vest if the price achieves a certain value for a defined period, is the target price or period unrealistic)?

(g)   What proportion of the recipient's total annual remuneration package is typically represented by the bonus payment?

(h)   How is the bonus payment taxed (ie at source from the monthly total wage or from encashment of shares; is Capital Gains Tax payable)?[5]

(i)   How have the bonus payments contributed towards the family's overall finances and expenditure (ie used as savings, put aside for educational expenses, funding property purchases or 'luxury' expenditure)?

10.3   The information acquired above can be collated to construct an analysis table which may subsequently be used by the practitioner or presented to the court as a summary of the matter in hand, the type of bonus involved, the method of receipt and the likelihood of future receipt.

---

[4]   If an order is eventually made that requires the division of future bonus payments, the order should address the method, timing and transmission of notice of such payment to the payee.

[5]   Does the scheme require the placing of bonus/shares/options in a trust for the deferral period as a tax saving measure for the company? This may act to increase the overall taxation when paid out.

Year	Basic salary gross	Date when bonus paid	Total amount of bonus paid gross	Performance-linked criteria (personal / company / other)	Performance-linked criteria met?	Form of payment	Date of deferred receipt / conditions of deferral	Bonus as % of total remuneration	Tax	Other notes
Year 5	£100,000	4 March	£90,000	50% linked to personal / 50% linked to company	H met personal / company element paid at 85% of total potential	£40,000 cash and £50,000 share options	Cash immediate / share options exercisable in 3 years	47%	Cash taxed at source / IT on shares deducted from award	Cash used to reduce FMH mortgage
Year 4	£90,000	5 March	£105,000	50% linked to personal / 50% linked to company	H met some personal, so paid at 80% of total potential / company performance met	£60,000 cash and £45,000 share options	Cash immediate / share options exercisable in 3 years	54%	As above and CGT may apply if shares later sold	Cash used to fund family holiday to Seychelles
Year 3	£85,000	1 April	£85,000	60% linked to personal / 20% linked to company / 20% linked to EPS[6]	All criteria met	£60,000 cash and £25,000 share options	£30,000 cash immediate / £30,000 cash deferred for 1 year / shares immediate	50%	As above and H sold shares 2 months after exercising option	Cash used to reduce FMH mortgage
Year 2										
Year 1										

---

[6] Earnings per share increase.

10.4 It is suggested that the following **documents** should be sought from the bonus recipient in order to substantiate the information provided at **10.2**:

(a) employment contracts and all amendments;

(b) company documents detailing in narrative form the bonus or incentive scheme, applicable taxation rules and performance criteria;

(c) tax returns for the analysis period;

(d) documentary evidence of the number of share options and share option price, if applicable;

(e) bank statements identifying the receipt of all bonus payments;

(f) company accounts for the analysis period/public information as to company stock performance (if floated).[7]

THE BONUS ANALYSIS: INCOME OR CAPITAL?

10.5 There are cases in which significant argument is devoted to whether the bonus payments received or receivable are to be treated by the court as the recipient's (existing or future) capital resources or income. It is submitted that care should be taken to not get 'drawn into' overly technical arguments regarding this issue but, broadly, regard can be had to the following factors:

(a) the original documents establishing the bonus structure;

(b) the manner in which the bonus is taxable (income tax or capital gains tax or a combination of both schemes);

(c) the contractual nature (or not) of the bonus;

(d) the regularity of the bonus payment/the deferred nature of payment.

10.6 Generally, if the bonus has been received after the parties' separation but before trial, its income status will have been transmuted into the capital resources available for division. If the bonus is receivable after trial, it will most likely represent the recipient's income (and be treated as such), although the level of the bonus may enable the recipient to significantly augment his/her capital resources. If the bonus payment is very large in comparison with the basic salary, or if it is paid by way of shares or options that may be exercised at a later date, there may be an argument that these 'payments' represent future capital receipt. If the payment has been 'earned' during the marriage by reference to the employment period over which the bonus accrued, the argument may be that such payment represents part of the 'fruits of the marriage' and can be subject to the sharing principle.

10.7 If the bonus is received before trial but after separation, it may justify an approach that subsumes the bonus into the capital available for division. However, as is seen further below, the fact that the bonus has been received

---

[7] If a public company, accounts and share information for similar trading companies may be useful to demonstrate market performance.

after the parties' separation may give good reason for the court to depart from an equal division of that element of the capital. The court will likely assess the capital at the date of trial as inclusive of the bonus payments already received, but it will also consider the 'nature and provenance' of that element of the capital in order to determine whether, and if so, how, it should be shared or divided between the parties.[8] The nature and provenance of the bonus payment refers to its source and, therefore, the contributions of the earning party.

BROAD PRINCIPLES: FUTURE FINANCIAL RESOURCES

10.8　Any approach to the division of future bonus payments received by one party must be seen in the context of general attitudes towards the appropriateness of sharing future financial resources after separation. Baroness Hale set the potential limit in *Miller; McFarlane*, thus:

> '[143] … there are many cases in which the approach of roughly equal sharing of the partnership assets with no continuing claims … is … feasible and fair.
>
> [144] In general, it can be assumed that the marital partnership does not stay alive for the purpose of sharing future resources unless this is justified by need or compensation. The ultimate objective is to give each party an equal start on the road to independent living.
>
> …
>
> [154] There is obviously a relationship between capital sharing and future income provision. If capital has been equally shared and is enough to provide for need and compensate for disadvantage, then there should be no need for continuing financial provision.'[9]

BIG[GER] MONEY, CLEAN BREAK CASES AND BONUS PAYMENTS RECEIVED AFTER SEPARATION

10.9　In a case in which the capital resources are enough to effect a clean break and, therefore, to provide the payee with sufficient assets to meet capital and housing needs and future income needs (on a capitalised basis),[10] the court may divide bonus payments principally in two ways.[11] First, if a bonus has already been received by the time of the trial but after the parties' physical separation, the fact of receipt after separation may justify an other-than-equal sharing (ie more or less than 50% of that element of the available resources) with the payee. Second, if a bonus or bonuses are receivable after trial, the court may provide the payee with a (reducing) percentage of such bonuses upon their

---

8　　*H v H* [2009] EWHC 3739 (Fam), [2010] 2 FLR 173, at [78].

9　　And accepted by Moylan J as a general submission that sharing ends at the end of the marital relationship *B v B (Ancillary Relief: Post-Separation Income)* [2010] 2 FLR 1214, at [48].

10　Whether by payment of a *Duxbury* Fund (see Chapter 15) or a non-amortised amount.

11　This assumes that it is not a case in which there is to be no division or sharing of the bonus.

receipt to enable the payee to *transition* from financial dependence to independence. In both cases, the court will seek to balance the particular contributions of the recipient of the bonus with the prior – and, even, perhaps – ongoing contributions of the payee to the overall employment position of the recipient which enabled him/her to receive the bonus payments. Care must be taken to ensure that any such factors that influence the court's final award are drawn from, and are directly referable to, the statutory list of considerations in MCA 1973, s 25(2).[12]

10.10 It is extremely important to note that, in determining how and, if so, to what extent, bonus payments received or receivable are to be divided in such cases, the court is undertaking an expressly discretionary, fact-specific exercise: this has been repeatedly noted in the case-law:

(a) 'In my view the quantification of any such additional award is fact sensitive and difficult to describe in general terms or by reference to a formula.'[13]

(b) 'There is no absolutely right or wrong answer or methodology to be applied in this situation.'[14]

(c) 'The weight to be given to the fact that some of the resources have accrued through the husband's earnings since the separation is a matter for my discretion.'[15]

Therefore, although this chapter may draw out a variety of approaches to bonus payments, the ultimate division will depend, almost entirely, on the particular circumstances of each individual case.

SOMETHING OTHER THAN EQUAL SHARING

10.11 In *B v B (Ancillary Relief: Post-Separation Income)*,[16] the principal issue for Moylan J was the extent to which, as part of a clean break award, the payee should receive part of the wealth which had accrued from income earned by the payer after the parties' separation. The parties in *B v B* were in their early 40s. They had been married for some 10 years and had three children aged 11, 6 and 5: the youngest child had special needs. Shortly after the marriage the wife (W) reduced her work to part-time hours and, thereafter, gave up paid employment altogether. The husband (H), by contrast, developed a successful career as a financial trader. H received significant bonuses in cash and deferred shares: his last bonus in 2008 was £9.2m gross. The exact amount of the deferred elements of H's bonus, payable in instalments over a 3-year period,

---

[12]   For example, the length of the marriage may be an important consideration if a wife and
      mother devoted herself to the family to enable the husband to develop a long-term career
      which, in the latter years of the marriage, has generated significant financial reward.

[13]   *H v H* [2007] EWHC 459 (Fam), [2007] 2 FLR 548, at [112], per Charles J.

[14]   *B v B* [2013] EWHC 1232 (Fam), [2013] Fam Law 1374, at [53], per Coleridge J.

[15]   *P v P* [2007] EWHC 2877 (Fam), [2008] 2 FLR 1135, at [123], per Moylan J.

[16]   [2010] EWHC 193 (Fam), [2010] 2 FLR 1214.

was unclear. Moylan J found the assets to be £15m[17] with a further estimated sum due to the husband of £3.5m arising out of deferred bonus payments. Moylan J assessed W's future income needs at £120,000 pa and adopted a capitalised figure for these needs of £6m, not on a *Duxbury* basis but by reference to a modest assumed rate of return. Additionally, her capital needs of £1m required a payment to her of £7m from the assessed assets of £15m or 46%. Furthermore, the award included payment to W of 15% of all net sums received by the husband from deferred instalments, which was estimated at trial at £3.5m but generally accepted that the figure was uncertain.

10.12   In *P v P (Post-Separation Accruals and Earning Capacity)*[18] the parties were in their early 50s and had enjoyed a long 24-year marriage. The three children of the marriage were all over 18 at the time of the trial before Moylan J. H's career in the financial services industry had generated significant wealth in the latter stages of the marriage: indeed, £6.8m of the total assets of £16.7m had been received by H in cash and deferred shares after the parties' separation. Moylan J rejected any need to draw a clear and specific boundary between matrimonial and non-matrimonial property by reference to the date of the parties' separation or any other particular date or event. Instead, Moylan J awarded W – on a needs basis[19] – a total of £8.4m of the assets (or 50.3%) including the post-separation income and bonuses earned by H. Moylan J could not ignore H's significant earning capacity, which is an express factor to which the court's consideration is directed in MCA 1973, s 25(2). Equally, W's claim to any future resources of H was rejected by the court, as her award comprised significant post-separation accruals by H.

THE TRANSITION OR 'RUN-OFF' AWARD

10.13   In *H v H*,[20] the parties were both in their 40s and had four children. They had chosen to conduct their marriage so that W cared for the home and family and H was thereby enabled to develop a hugely successful career. The assets at trial amounted to circa £29m.[21] The parties differed as to the extent to which W should (a) share equally in bonuses and income earned and 'cashed' after separation, and (b) whether W was entitled to an additional lump sum to represent her loss of a share in H's future income and earning capacity. Charles J rejected the notion that, after the parties' separation, 'contributions by a wife to the family after the end of the marital partnership can generally be said to warrant a conclusion that a proportion of the husband's future income continues to be attributable to the wife's domestic contribution and thus a fruit of the marital partnership'.[22] It was common ground in *H v H* that an equal

---

[17]   Including deferred instalments and bonus payments.
[18]   [2008] 2 FLR 1135.
[19]   For housing and income.
[20]   [2007] 2 FLR 548.
[21]   There was a dispute, of course, about what assets were to be treated as 'matrimonial' and 'non-matrimonial'.
[22]   *H v H* [2007], at [87], per Charles J.

division of the assets [even if] not including those bonuses earned by H after separation would amply meet W's claims for need, compensation and sharing. Therefore, the extent to which W's award should be further augmented to account for H's ability to earn significant future income and bonuses involved an obvious value judgment by the court: this, of course, was accepted by W, who herself did not advance a case for her entitlement to share in the future bonus income of H on a joint lives basis. Charles J recognised that such a value judgment did not yield easily to the application of any particular arithmetical formula. Therefore, in a case in which an order can be made:

(a)   on a clean break basis;

(b)   that provides the payee with sufficient capital to meet needs and all other aspects of compensation and sharing; and

(c)   enables the payee to live at a standard comparable to that enjoyed in the latter years of the marriage *and* to make substantial savings:

> 'the focus should be on the added effects of the provision to address the "run off" from the marital partnership, and thus the transition to independent living, considered in the context of the overall award.'[23]

10.14   The factors that will influence whether such a 'run-off' award should be made and, if so, at what level, will include:

> 'the length of time that the wife has enjoyed the fruits of the spadework and joint endeavours of the parties, the likely future product of that spadework and endeavour, an evaluation of the effects of the respective past and future contributions of the parties on the ability of the husband to earn his future income and thus on his earning capacity in the future (as opposed to an assessment of the effects of their contributions during the continuation of the marital partnership) and the overall effects of an award with and without a provision in respect of future income.'[24]

In reflecting these factors in *H v H*, Charles J awarded W a reducing 'run-off' award of one-third, one-sixth and one-twelfth of the income earned by H over a three-year period respectively.

10.15   In *B v B*[25] Coleridge J dealt with a case involving assets of £40m. W (54) was a 'full-time mother' and H (57) a private equity fund manager. The marriage had lasted for some 20 years and had produced two children, the youngest of whom was 13 years of age. The parties had enjoyed a very high standard of living. One key argument related to the way in which the wife should share in any future fortune generated by the husband's involvement in the private equity firm, MaisonBlau. MaisonBlau operated a complicated structure that generally provided for the investment executive (H), in addition to regular bonus payments, to invest in tandem with external investors (a

---

[23]   *H v H*, [2007] at [113], per Charles J.
[24]   *H v H*, [2007] at [114], per Charles J.
[25]   [2013] EWHC 1232 (Fam).

'co-investment'), from which a later individual profit could be drawn (if successful). H might also become entitled to 'carry' or carried interest if the investment generated profit above certain contractual levels. W proposed a tapered percentage approach to sharing the 'carry' from various funds. H offered an equal sharing of co-investments to the date of separation and proposed a tapered approach (on different percentages) to the carried interest. Coleridge J ultimately shared all co-investments equally and applied a tapered approach to the carried interest in two funds but excluded a third fund as 'the carry may not be established or ascertained ever or at least for many, many years and so [the wife's] entitlement to share in it is, I consider, miniscule'.[26] In so doing, Coleridge J set out some helpful guidance as to how to approach the tension between, on the one hand, terminating the sharing of future resources (and, in effect, bonus payments) and, on the other, ensuring that the payee's (perhaps) more indirect and unquantifiable contribution to those future resources is properly recognised:

'i) Fairness is what I am trying to achieve and both sides make sound points. Fairness (the somewhat diluted offspring of justice) is not just about arithmetic and precision of calculation but a broad recognition by the court, after considering all the factors, of the value of the claimant's (in this case the wife's) role in the whole marital partnership;

ii) The industry standard/general rule that the date of trial is the date when both the categorisation of the pot and its value is assessed, should not easily be circumvented. The proposition that merely because an asset comes into existence after the date of separation it should be excluded is far too simplistic and is not appropriate when, as here, a respondent's efforts are merely a seamless continuum of similar pre-separation activity and there is no obvious delay in the proceedings. It is as if the husband is banking his surplus income during the time between separation and trial;

iii) There is no absolutely right or wrong answer or methodology to be applied in this situation. To achieve fairness it is necessary to recognise fully the tension between the fact that the wealth was in part generated by the use of expertise built up during the marriage and in part by the expenditure of effort after the separation. Both elements are important. I do not think this part of the case can be analysed precisely either by reference to the time involved in each phase of the process and/or its relative importance. It is a product of both to some extent. But I make the general observation that the further into the future, post separation, the asset is created or achieves ascertainable value the less, it seems to me, it can be sensibly categorised as "matrimonial". Beyond that drilling down into the deepest subterranean springs of the arguments adds nothing to the achievement of fairness;'[27]

---

[26] At [53].
[27] *B v B*, at [53], per Coleridge J.

CASES IN WHICH A PERIODICAL PAYMENTS ORDER IS MADE AND THE TREATMENT OF (FUTURE) RECEIVABLE BONUS PAYMENTS

10.16 This section will assume that (a) the capital resources at trial are insufficient to achieve a clean break, (b) that the court imposes a periodical payments order and (c) that the payer is/will be in receipt of bonus payments as part of an overall remuneration package.

10.17 There are, broadly[28], six identified ways[29] in which future bonus payments may be accounted for and allocated to the payee within a periodical payments order:[30]

- The 'all-in' income method
- The exclusion method
- The capped method
- The transition method
- The deferred clean break method
- The 'other agreed' methods.

10.18 In order to analyse and elucidate these various methods, the following illustrative scenarios are offered:

- **SCENARIO 1:** *the payment of a regular annual bonus as an element of a party's remuneration package.* For example, a basic salary of £60,000 net pa and a bonus of up to 40% of the basic salary, which, historically, has been paid as follows:

2013	£20,000
2012	£21,000
2011	£19,000
2010	£19,200

- **SCENARIO 2:** *the payment of large performance-related 'bonus' made by way of deferred share options (basic guaranteed salary of £200,000 gross pa)*: bonus payments contingent upon company- and personal-performance targets being met over a 3-year period from the date of the award, as follows:

---

[28] This cannot, of course, be an exhaustive list, but it demonstrates some of the more common methods which must reflect the individual circumstances of each case and, indeed, some cases may justify a combination of such methods.

[29] According to the author and drawing on case-law and experience.

[30] Or, indeed, by way of an undertaking to pay money, which should be protected by a properly-drafted notice to, and undertaking of, the payer, pursuant to the Family Procedure Rules (FPR 2010), PD 33A: for further detail, see Chapter 22 on Enforcement.

2013	50,000 1p share options (share price 720pps[31]) due 2016
2012	60,000 1p share options (share price 720pps) due 2015
2011	80,000 1p share options (share price 720pps) due 2014
2010	70,000 1p share options (share price 720pps) due end 2013

- **SCENARIO 3**: *the payment of a regular but discretionary bonus approximately equivalent in value to the recipient's guaranteed basic salary* (eg annual salary of £100,000 gross and annual bonus of between £90,000 and £110,000 gross)
- **SCENARIO 4**: *the payment of an irregular and discretionary bonus, not forming part of the receiving party's contractual remuneration package,* which, historically, has been received as follows:

2013	£0
2012	£6,000
2011	£780
2010	£600
2009	£2,900
2008	£1,000

10.19 The following elements for the creation of formulae are adopted:

a	=	basic salary
b	=	bonus payment
c	=	% of bonus payment
d	=	capped % of bonus payment
x	=	total income of payer
y	=	assessed level of periodical payments
z	=	fixed sum of periodical payments

The 'all-in' income method (Scenarios 1 and 3)

10.20 The 'all-in' income method assimilates the bonus payments as an equal and predictable element of the recipient's future remuneration package. The indicators that may justify such an approach are:

(a) A history of bonus payments at a relatively consistent level.

(b) Security of tenure in employment (eg a permanent employment contract or a lengthy period of service).

(c) Contractual entitlement to a bonus, and to an identified level of bonus payment (ie up to 40% of gross salary).

---

[31] Price per share.

(d)   Consistently meeting or surpassing of performance targets (whether company or personal).

(e)   A bonus paid in cash or shares with no deferral of receipt.

(f)   A basic salary insufficient to meet the assessed level of any periodical payments order.

10.21   The 'all-in' income method proceeds on the basis that, for the purpose of calculating the payer's income, a bonus will continue to be paid in the future. Therefore, x = a + b and any periodical payments order is drafted on the basis that the payee receives a fixed sum of £y for whatever term is appropriate. An example of this approach is found in *H v H (Financial Provision)*.[32] In this case, the parties had enjoyed a marriage of approximately 7 years including cohabitation; they were in their early 30s and had one child. The capital assets of circa £2m were insufficient to achieve a clean break and a periodical payments order was made. H was a broker in exotic derivatives. His remuneration package included a basic salary (£250,000 gross pa) and guaranteed bonuses. Singer J treated H as having earned average bonuses over a 2-year period of £475,000 gross pa and added this figure to his basic gross salary. The resulting gross total figure of £725,000 netted down to £435,000 pa, which was adopted as the figure for H's net income from which the periodical payments order was to be made. The order for periodical payments was assessed at £125,000 for W in addition to agreed child maintenance of £15,000, which resulted in a total maintenance order to the payee wife of 32% of H's net annual remuneration. The disparity in spendable income (£100,000 for W and £295,000 for H) adequately reflected and rewarded the fact that H's income was hard-earned.[33]

The exclusion method (Scenario 4)

10.22   The exclusion method takes no account of any bonus payment received. If a bonus is negligible in comparison to the payer's basic salary, or if it is very inconsistent in terms of the amount and timing of receipt, this may justify its exclusion as a basis for calculating the payer's total income. If, in contrast, the bonus payment is included in such circumstances, it may require frequent attempts to negotiate a variation to the level of periodical payments and, ultimately, applications to the court to effect such a variation.

10.23   So x = a only, out of which £y is paid.

The capped method (Scenario 3)

10.24   The capped method acknowledges a difference in source between the basic salary (a) and the bonus payment (b). Rather than adopting an 'all-in' income method, any periodical payments order is expressed as emanating from these two sources of income but in different formats. For example, an assessed

---

[32]   [2009] 2 FLR 795.
[33]   *H v H*, [2009] at [101], per Singer J.

budget for the payee of £5,000 per month is payable as, first, a fixed amount of £3,000 per month based on the payer's basic salary (a) and, second, a percentage of the bonus (c), but capped at a level no higher than the remaining maintenance payable of £2,000 per month, (d).

10.25 So x = a + b, out of which y is paid as z + d.

10.26 The indicators that may favour the capped method are:

(a) Consistent history of bonus receipt.

(b) A standard of living during the marriage that relied to some extent on the receipt of bonus payments.

(c) A bonus payment forming a significant proportion of the payer's remuneration package.

(d) A fluctuating bonus payment or prospects of significant increases to the level of payment.

(e) An assessed level of periodical payments that is either (a) incapable of payment in full from a basic salary or (b) requires some sharing between the parties of the risk that a bonus may not be forthcoming.

10.27 The capped method presents obvious problems in cases in which a bonus is not paid on a monthly basis, as the parties must then have some formula to adjust any payments made or due. Furthermore, if the level of a payee's periodical payments order is predicated on his/her needs (without – or even with – a generous interpretation or room for additional and discretionary spending),[34] it may be unfairly risky to fund those needs from a bonus which may not materialise. Additionally, the balance must be carefully struck between the proportion of the overall remuneration package which derives from basic salary and that which is based on bonus payments. Finally, care must be taken in cases in which a bonus is comprised of a mixture of cash and deferred elements (shares, options or otherwise) to ensure, as far as possible, that the order shares the risks and rewards of guaranteed cash on the one hand, and shares or options on the other. That is no mean feat and will require some carefully drafted calculations, dependent on the circumstances of the individual case.

10.28 The need to 'cap' the percentage element of any bonus paid by way of an order for periodical payments arises from the uncontrollable nature of an *uncapped* percentage: if the order provides for the payee to receive a percentage of a bonus without a cap on the total financial receipt, this may result in

---

[34] See *AR v AR (Treatment of Inherited Wealth)* [2012] 2 FLR 1, at [71], per Moylan J: ' … in my judgment, the court's task when addressing this factor ["*needs*"] is not to arrive at a mathematically exact calculation of what constitutes an applicant's future income needs. It is to determine the notional annual income which, in the circumstances of the case, it would be fair for the [payee] to receive. Further, in a case such as this, the wife is entitled to have sufficient resources to enable her to spend money on additional, discretionary items which will vary from year to year and which are not reflected in her annual budget'.

significant over-payment to the payee, which removes the fairness of the overall financial division. Furthermore, if, as developing case-law suggests, a periodical payments order is invariably limited to meeting a party's needs,[35] allowing an uncapped percentage division of a bonus will stray improperly into the realms of 'sharing' the payer's future resources.[36]

10.29 The case of *Parr v Parr*[37] provides a recent example of the capped method. In this case the District Judge made an order providing for W to receive periodical payments of (a) £3,750 per month payable in advance and (b) a sum equal to 25% of H's annual bonuses (net of tax and National Insurance) on a joint lives basis. The history of H's remuneration from employment for the 3 years preceding the appeal before Eleanor King J evinced an annual salary of £250,000 and a non guaranteed bonus average of £200,000.[38] The District Judge attributed to W an earning capacity of £500 per month and a fair (basic) budget for her of £4,250 per month. The District Judge regarded H's bonus payments as an integral part of the periodical payments order but did not, as Eleanor King J saw it, frame the periodical payments order on anything but the basis of W's maintenance requirements. Given that the District Judge was unable to quantify the level of H's bonus in a way which would have allowed him to specify an exact figure with which to 'top-up' the basic maintenance figure of £3,750 per month, he was driven to using a percentage. However, Eleanor King J considered that the District Judge erred by failing to cap the amount receivable by the payee according to the 25% formula. Eleanor King J explained the reasoning, thus:

> '38. In my judgment where the Learned District Judge fell into error was in failing to identify a figure which would represent the [wife's] maximum reasonable maintenance entitlement taking into account all the circumstances of the case, namely a cap. In my judgment, where the family income is routinely made up of salary and bonus and the bonus represents such a significant proportion of the total that the Judge is driven to making a conventional monthly order for a sum less than that which he would otherwise feel to be appropriate, (taking into account all the s 25 factors and in particular the standard of living and the totality of the income available in the foreseeable future), he may well provide for a part of the [wife's] maintenance to be paid from the bonus. Such payment, given the intrinsic uncertainty of bonuses, can only be expressed in percentage terms.

> 39. The proper approach would be for the District Judge to calculate a total figure for maintenance which covers what he finds to be her ordinary expenditure together with such sum as would provide for what Moylan J described as '*additional, discretionary, items which will vary from year to year and which are not reflected in her annual budget*'. Having carried out this exercise the court will then make a monthly order to be paid for from salary at whatever rate the District

---

[35] See Chapter 9 on Quantification.
[36] If a particularly large future bonus is received, it may justify an application for variation and capitalisation to achieve a clean break, see further Chapters 17 and 18.
[37] [2013] EWHC 4105 (Fam).
[38] Paid part in cash and part in deferred cash and shares.

Judge feels to be fair, and the balance to be expressed as a percentage of the net bonus up to a stated maximum each year.

40. It should be made clear that such orders cannot be calculated with arithmetical precision. In determining the appropriate percentage the court will do the best it can looking at the historical pattern of bonuses to date and by factoring in such information as may be available in relation to the future prospects of H (or his company). The inherent uncertainty of bonus payments provides, in part, the reason why … the setting of a cap is essential in order to avoid the unintentional unfairness which may arise as a consequence of a wholly unanticipated substantial bonus paid to the H. Such a payment would result in W receiving a sum substantially in excess of that which the District Judge regarded as appropriate in order to maintain her maintenance at a fair level.

41. In common with most bonuses, H's bonus is made up of a number of elements in the form of stock or cash deferral. W''s percentage will apply pro rata across the various elements – it would not be fair for her to be entitled to receive the entirety of her maintenance percentage from the cash element leaving the H to take the risk on stock movements and the cash flow consequences of deferred cash payments.'[39]

The transition method (Scenarios 1 and 3)

10.30 In common with the 'run off' award considered above in cases involving a clean break, a similar award – and made for similar reasons – may be appropriate in cases in which a clean break is not possible, whether made by agreement or imposed by the court. If a payer's basic salary is sufficient to meet an assessed level of periodical payments, a fair overall result may nevertheless justify additional payment to the payee of a reducing share of the payer's bonus payments over a specified period. This transition may take into account a lengthy marriage, during which the payee made domestic contributions enabling the payer to develop the significant earning capacity. On occasion, the term for payment may be linked to a child's minority or to a period over which it is anticipated that the payee will progress to an independent earning capacity. The gradually reducing percentage of any bonus[40] received by the payee may represent the slow erosion of the link between the marriage and the parties' respective contributions to it, and the payer's personal input into the generation of each annual bonus payment. However, if capital resources are shared in a manner that meets both parties' capital needs, and if a periodical payments order provides for the payee's income needs and recognises any compensatory element to his/her award, it is reasonable to argue that no transition period of bonus-related payments should be permitted.

The deferred clean break method

10.31 The deferred clean break method refers to the payee receiving a share of future bonus payments with a view to such payments, if sufficient, resulting in

---

[39] There is some concern as to how this is to be achieved in practice.
[40] Most likely capped at a particular amount.

the termination of any periodical payments order[41] and, consequently, a clean break.[42] This method tends to treat future bonuses as akin to capital receipt in the hands of the payer. For example, evidence at trial may show that the payer may be due to receive significant future bonus payments, whether deferred or in shares or options, which, if large enough, would provide sufficient resources to the payee to capitalise his/her maintenance requirements. It may be possible, in such circumstances, to frame an order so that, if the payee receives a certain amount from such bonus payments, his/her financial dependency on the payer can be terminated. This potential is even stronger in cases in which the payer's high income is only possible over a limited period of time. There are obvious risks attached to such an order, as it is prospective in nature and may therefore conflict with a proposed dismissal of the payee's capital claims. The payee may prefer to seek to share in such bonus payments by way of a periodical payments order (if appropriate) and await any application to vary and capitalise that order in the future.[43]

The other agreed methods

10.32 The range of agreements that parties can make as to the division of future bonus payments is infinite: these may include diverting a proportion of each future bonus (for a specified term or otherwise) to (a) generate a savings fund for children of the family; (b) make savings for education expenses; (c) contribute towards trust funds; or (d) to offset the retention of other assets by the payee. If such agreements are to be enforced, they should be drafted by way of an undertaking, signed by the payer and with notice to him/her of the consequences of a breach.[44] Finally, if the capital resources are sufficient, the payee may agree to retain a larger share of those assets in lieu of any continuing claim against the payer's future bonus payments. If this agreement is adopted, the order should include a recital providing an explanation, so that the rationale for the calculation of any periodical payments order (and the exclusion of any bonus element therefrom) is clear at any later variation application.

CONCLUSION

10.33 There is no single method which fairly divides bonus payments received either after separation but before trial or such payments receivable after trial. The case law is unambiguous about the highly fact-specific nature of the

---

[41] Which may be made on a basis with or without a bar preventing the payee from applying to extend the term for payment.

[42] See, for example, *Q v Q* [2005] EWHC 402 (Fam), [2005] 2 FLR 640.

[43] See Chapter 18 on variation and capitalisation. Furthermore, care must be taken – if the payee's share is framed as a series of lump sums – to ensure that such an order makes clear whether each individual payment is capable of variation pursuant to MCA 1973, s 31(7): see *Hamilton v Hamilton* [2013] EWCA Civ 13.

[44] In compliance with FPR 2010, PD 33A.

discretion exercised by the judge. There is, however, a different approach discernible in cases in which a clean break is possible and those in which a dismissal of claims is not possible.

CHAPTER 11

TERMINATING FINANCIAL DEPENDENCY: THE IMMEDIATE AND DEFERRED CLEAN BREAK AND [NON]-EXTENDABLE TERM ORDERS

'An object of the modern law is to encourage [the parties] to put the past behind them and to begin a new life which is not overshadowed by the relationship which has broken down.'[1]

INTRODUCTION

11.1   The 'clean break' is the effective termination of divorcing parties' financial claims against, and obligations to, each other: it can be ordered immediately upon the parties determining all their financial claims or it can be deferred to a future date. On first blush, periodical payments orders – which perpetuate financial dependence – are the antithesis of the clean break. On the other hand, a periodical payments order for a limited term can be an important step on the road to an eventual (deferred) clean break.[2]

11.2   The search for the clean break, which is a duty imposed on the court in all cases, is founded on the preference for the severance of financial ties after divorce and on the encouragement towards financial independence and the pursuit of self-sufficiency. The clean break is a creation of modern matrimonial law[3] and its importance has elevated its status to that of a 'principle' within the court's discretionary assessment. Nevertheless, its prominence must not override the court's ultimate pursuit of fairness; it is at the point where 'principle' and fairness collide that the difficulties inherent in achieving a clean break are most visibly exposed.

11.3   This chapter analyses the court's duty to consider the viability of a clean break; it also identifies the key guidance as to when a clean break may be appropriate and how it is to be achieved and, latterly, illustrates circumstances deserving of a limited-term periodical payments order. The following questions are addressed:

---

[1]   *Minton v Minton* [1979] AC 593, at 608, per Lord Scarman.
[2]   At which point the order can 'bar' the payee from applying to extend the term of the periodical payments order pursuant to MCA 1973, s 28(1A).
[3]   Introduced in 1984.

(1) *To break cleanly or not?* Do the circumstances of the case warrant an immediate clean break (ie no periodical payments order and a termination of the right to apply for such an order)?

(2) *To term or not to term?* Do the circumstances of the case justify an order for periodical payments for any term other than the parties' joint lives?

(3) *To bar or not to bar?* Do the circumstances of the case make it appropriate to debar the payee from seeking to extend the term of any order for periodical payments[4] (ie a periodical payments order for a limited period and, upon the term expiring, a termination of the right to apply for – or to extend – such an order; a deferred clean break)?

THE GOAL OF AUTONOMY AND SELF-SUFFICIENCY VERSUS THE REALITIES OF LIFE POST- DIVORCE

11.4 The clean break principle[5] is the embodiment of the role of individual autonomy in family law, which itself is a relatively recent development away from dependence and reliance.[6] However, autonomy and self-sufficiency do not always dovetail easily with core themes in family law such as the responsibilities of parents to their children, the state interest in upholding marriage and the enforcement of financial obligations between spouses.[7] A marriage represents a catalogue of choices made by the persons involved that impact to a greater or lesser extent on their ability to achieve financial independence on divorce, the most obvious being the decision to have and raise a family. Despite the move away from the more traditional roles of spouses (one bread-winner and one child-carer) and a fresh focus on equality and non-discrimination, the reality that women still play the lead caring and home-based role within the family unit means that a system that advocates autonomy *can* also unfairly disadvantage women. Herring highlights that:

> 'In most, if not all, intimate relationships parties invest in varying ways and extents to the relationship. Putting central value on the autonomy of the parties to leave the relationship and purse their own life goal will disadvantage the party who has invested more in it and has suffered economic or social disadvantage as a result. In most relationships, especially where there are children, that will be women.'[8]

11.5 Many marriages, long or short, will generate dependence (by the husband on the wife and vice versa). Some ex-spouses will require financial support from one party for reasons other than dependence, for example, due to health

---

4   Pursuant to MCA 1973, s 28(1A).

5   As it is identified by Lord Nicholls in *Miller v Miller; McFarlane v McFarlane* [2006] UKHL 24, at [30].

6   Respect for autonomy is also a core principle behind the progression towards giving effect to nuptial agreements: by recognising the weight to be given to the choices and decisions made by the parties to a marriage (see, for example, *Radmacher (formerly Granatino) v Granatino* [2010] 2 FLR 1900 and *V v V* [2012] 1 FLR 1315).

7   Herring, Jonathan, 'Relational Autonomy and Family Law' in *Rights, Gender and Family Law*, Routledge, 2010, p 259.

8   Ibid, p 265.

problems. The court's duty is to unpack the choices and realities of the marriage and to search for, but not necessarily to achieve, a clean break, which may be immediate or deferred to some point in the future. The Matrimonial and Family Proceedings Act (MFPA) 1984 discarded the objective of returning the parties to a divorce to the position they would have been in had they not married, and rejected the idea that life-long support after divorce was appropriate. Inextricably bound to this principled rejection was the expectation that former spouses should become financially independent of each other wherever, and as soon as, possible after the divorce.[9] However, while the *ideal* may be a world in which divorce and separation is a neutral event that affects both parties in similar ways, the reality is that it is often devastatingly one-sided, both emotionally and financially. The periodical payments order, whether imposed for a lifetime or for a limited period, is an explicit recognition of this ongoing inequality.

THE OBJECTIVE OF THE CLEAN BREAK

11.6

> 'Periodical payments are a continuing source of stress for both parties. They are also insecure. With the best will in the world, the paying party may fall on hard times and be unable to keep them up. Nor is the best will in the world always evident between formerly married people. It is also the logical consequence of the retreat from the lifelong obligation. Independent finances and self-sufficiency are the aims.'[10]

The ultimate objective is fairness. The Matrimonial Causes Act 1973 (MCA 1973) explicitly recognises the *aim* of self-sufficiency. Whereas a lump sum payment, for example, draws a clear line under the past, periodical payments represent the opposite, as future earnings and future payments are presently indeterminate. There is undesirability in perpetuating financial ties after separation and the court, therefore, is encouraged and enabled to effect a clean break settlement[11] between parties to a divorce. The objective in doing so is to give each party an equal start on the road to independent living after their separation:

> '[133] Section 25A is a powerful encouragement towards securing the court's objective by way of lump sum and capital adjustment (which now includes pension sharing) rather than by continuing periodical payments. This is good practical sense ....'[12]

---

[9] *Bromley's Family Law*, 10th edn, p 1023.
[10] *Miller v Miller*, at [133], per Baroness Hale.
[11] Ibid, at [130].
[12] Ibid, per Baroness Hale.

THE LEGAL BASIS FOR THE CLEAN BREAK[13]

11.7 Section 25A provides the core tripartite basis for the clean break:

(1) Where on or after the grant of a decree of divorce or nullity of marriage the court decides to exercise its powers under section 23(1)(a), (b) or (c), 24 or 24A or 24B above in favour of a party to the marriage, it shall be the duty of the court to consider whether it would be appropriate so to exercise those powers that the financial obligations of each party towards the other will be terminated as soon after the grant of the decree as the court considers just and reasonable.

(2) Where the court decides in such a case to make a periodical payments or secured periodical payments order in favour of a party to the marriage, the court shall in particular consider whether it would be appropriate to require those payments to be made or secured only for such term as would in the opinion of the court be sufficient to enable the party in whose favour the order is made to adjust without undue hardship to the termination of his or her financial dependence on the other party.

(3) Where on or after the grant of a decree of divorce or nullity of marriage an application is made by a party to the marriage for a periodical payments or secured periodical payments order in his or her favour, then, if the court considers that no continuing obligations should be imposed on either party to make or secure periodical payments in favour of the other party, the court may dismiss the application with a direction that the applicant shall not be entitled to make any further application in relation to the marriage for an order under section 23(1)(a) or (b) above.

The clean break principle does not exist in a vacuum and its legal basis extends beyond the three statutory subsections above. For example, when deciding what financial provision to make on divorce, the court is directed to consider not only a party's earning capacity but also any *increase in that capacity which it is reasonable to expect a party to take steps to acquire.*[14] This direction to consider earning capacity is relevant to the ability of a party to achieve complete or partial self-sufficiency through their own efforts and earned income.

11.8 Section 25(2)(a) of the MCA 1973 mandates the court to consider:

'The income, earning capacity, property and other financial resources which each of the parties to the marriage has or is likely to have in the foreseeable future, including in the case of earning capacity any increase in that capacity which it would in the opinion of the court be reasonable to expect a party to the marriage to take steps to acquire.'

Furthermore, if the court rejects an immediate clean break and decides that a periodical payments order is fair and appropriate, it may limit the payment of the order to any term that it considers suitable. Before the term for payment

---

[13] In cases of civil partnership, see the Civil Partnership Act 2004, Sch 5, Part 5, para 23.
[14] MCA 1973, s 25(2)(a).

expires, the payee is entitled to apply to further extend that term. However, MCA 1973, s 28(1A) permits the court, in appropriate circumstances, to direct that the payee will not be able make such an application:

> 'Where a periodical payments or secured periodical payments order in favour of a party to a marriage is made on or after the grant of a decree of divorce or nullity of marriage, the court may direct that that party shall not be entitled to apply under section 31 below for the extension of the term specified in the order.'

The various legal bases for the clean break can be consolidated, so that in every case in which a periodical payments order[15] is required, the court must consider the following:

(1) whether the payee or payer can reasonably take steps to increase their respective earning capacities;

(2) whether it would be appropriate to formulate an order for periodical payments so that the financial obligations of each party towards the other can be terminated as soon after the divorce as is just and reasonable;

(3) if a periodical payments order is appropriate, whether those payments should be made[16] only for such term as is sufficient to enable the payee to adjust without undue hardship to the termination of the periodical payments; and

(4) whether the payee should be prevented from making any application to extend the term of the periodical payments.

TO BREAK CLEANLY OR NOT?

11.9 The immediate clean break is achieved by determining that a division of capital, property and pension arrangements provides for both parties' financial needs, meets any latent or co-existing claim for compensation for relationship-generated financial disadvantage, and fairly shares the matrimonial 'pot'.[17]

11.10 Given the innumerable different financial and personal circumstances of individual cases, it is impossible to list exhaustively those cases in which an immediate clean break may be appropriate. However, case authorities may furnish the practitioner with the following broad examples in which an immediate clean break may or may not be appropriate.

---

[15] Secured or unsecured, or a lump sum order, a property adjustment order, an order for sale of property, a pension sharing order or a pension compensation sharing order.

[16] Or secured (if a secured order for periodical payments is being made, see Chapter 16).

[17] See Chapter 9 on quantification.

Indicators in favour of a clean break

11.11

(a) *Cases with low or nil income*: If the parties are low earners or in receipt of state benefits, and if there is little prospect of a significant increase to a prospective payer's income, it may be appropriate to impose an immediate clean break: this is particularly so if there is sufficient capital to provide for housing and other financial requirements. However, if there are young children of the marriage, if the available capital is also limited and if there is evidence that a party's income-fortunes may improve, care should be taken to consider a nominal periodical payments order for a term at least linked to the child's minority.[18]

(b) *Cases with sufficient capital assets to achieve a clean break*: There are many cases in which the available capital assets, whether divided equally or in some other proportion, can provide for an immediate clean break by endowing the payee with a capital sum from which he or she can derive a future income.[19] These cases may arise where both parties wish to achieve a clean break[20] or, alternatively, where the court imposes a clean break. Furthermore, the immediate clean break may be achieved by (1) an [un]equal division of capital in 'big money' cases or (2) an unequal division of capital in 'smaller' or 'middle' money cases.

In *CR v CR*[21] the parties' marriage had lasted some 24 years; there were two adult children of the marriage and the husband ('H')was a high-earner with anticipated income of £1m net pa. The wife ('W') presented her case as requiring an equal division of the capital assets of circa £16m plus an uplift (capitalised) based on £350,000 pa for a period of 5 years to 'compensate' her for the loss of her own career prospects and in recognition of H's future income. Bodey J rejected W's arguments for an additional lump sum uplift by virtue of any 'compensation' claim:

> '[92] I say straight away that the wife does not, to my mind, succeed in demonstrating any significant lost career prospects, certainly not for which "compensation" should be factored into the outcome. Such prospects as there were are, in my view, far too speculative. In any event, a wife with (if I may so describe them) "ordinary" career prospects which are forfeited following her marriage to a husband who is or becomes a financial high-flyer, is highly likely to have been adequately "compensated" for that forfeiture by the very fact of an equal division of the family's resources.'

However, the wife in *CR v CR* did succeed in her case for an unequal capital division in her favour – taking her to some £9m or 56% of the total available assets – on the basis that she would derive her future

---

[18] See Chapter 12 on nominal periodical payments.
[19] Normally and broadly calculated on a *Duxbury* basis, see Chapter 15, but not necessarily so.
[20] See, for example, *RP v RP* [2007] 1 FLR 2105, in which the court ordered a 60/40 division of capital in the wife's favour to provide her with a housing fund and a capitalised *Duxbury* fund producing £50,000 net pa for her life.
[21] [2008] 1 FLR 323.

income for life from the investment of capital in excess of her 'housing fund' of £4m. Bodey J provided W with a capital fund of £5m in addition to her housing needs and calculated that this would provide W – without having to expend the fund itself[22] – with an income of approximately £160,000 net pa for her life.

(c) *Smaller- or middle-money cases but with sufficient capital funds to order a capital shift in the prospective payee's favour*: In *A v L (Departure From Equality: Needs)*[23] the wife ('W') was 49 and the husband ('H') 57 years of age at the time of the appeal before Moor J. The marriage had lasted 14 years; there were two children over the age of 18 and separation had occurred in 2000. The assets only amounted to £233,000, the vast majority of which represented the equity in the former matrimonial home, in which W continued to live. The district judge found W to have a low earning capacity and H to have an income of circa £28,000 pa. The district judge's order provided for (a) a delayed sale of the former matrimonial home (b) thereafter, a division of the net sale proceeds as to 70% to W and 30% to H and (c) periodical payments of £500 per month for the benefit of W for a period of 4 years[24]. On appeal, Moor J maintained the capital division but imposed a clean break. The district judge had, by reference to broad financial needs and the disparity in income between the parties, departed from capital equality in W's favour. However, in making an order for periodical payments for the benefit of W *in addition* to a favourable capital shift, the balance of fairness had been disturbed.

(d) *Cases with no children, shorter marriages and established earning capacities*: Three identifying characteristics of a case potentially suitable for an immediate clean break are:
   (i)   the absence of children;
   (ii) a shorter marriage;[25]
   (iii) established earning capacities of *both* parties.
   In *Murphy v Murphy*[26] the Court of Appeal replaced a nominal periodical payments order with an immediate clean break. The marriage was childless and had lasted for less than 8 years: both parties were aged approximately 40. The wife had retrained and she was developing a new career. The husband, who had worked as a successful banker until being made unemployed, had future employment prospects. The assets totalled £3m, which was sufficient to meet the parties' housing and immediate needs.[27] Thorpe LJ concluded that 'the case had all the hallmarks of clean break and equality' and that 'it should not be forgotten that in all these

---

[22]   Ie not on a strict *Duxbury* basis.
[23]   [2012] 1 FLR 985.
[24]   With a bar preventing her from extending this period.
[25]   See also *Hedges v Hedges* [1991] 1 FLR 196 for a very early analysis of the statutory provisions in MCA 1973 relating to a clean break.
[26]   [2011] 1 FLR 537.
[27]   Parker J at first instance had determined that there should be a 65/35 division of the assets in W's favour.

cases the judge has a statutory duty to achieve a clean break between the parties provided that that can be done without undue hardship'.[28]

(e)   *Cases in which the parties are at retirement age*: If both parties are in retirement and drawing on, or living off, income from pension arrangements, a pension sharing order on a clean break basis may provide adequately for both parties' future income needs. An additional periodical payments order may not be appropriate.

(f)   *Cases involving unreliable payers or significant obstacles to enforcement*: If a [prospective] payer demonstrates an intention to refuse to pay periodical payments or to frustrate the enforcement of any such order, the court may capitalise the payments and impose a lump sum order rather than an order for periodic maintenance.[29]

(g)   *The payee's remarriage or cohabitation*: the payee's remarriage automatically terminates any order for periodical payments; the payee's cohabitation with another person does not.[30] If a prospective payee is cohabiting or has an intention to marry at the time that a periodical payments order is contemplated, the partner's financial position and support may justify a clean break. Conversely, if a payee's claim to capitalised periodical payments can be met by the court's award of a *Duxbury* capital sum,[31] the court should 'not flinch' from ordering a clean break 'because there is a mere possibility that at some time in the future the wife might establish a new relationship and remarry'.[32]

Indicators against a clean break

11.12

(a)   *Cases with insufficient capital to achieve a clean break*: There exist a significant number of cases in which the capital assets are limited but the family's income is relatively high:[33] in such cases, the 'breadwinner's'

---

[28]   *Murphy v Murphy* at [34]–[35].

[29]   See, for example, *Fournier v Fournier* [1998] 2 FLR 990 in which an original order for periodical payments was replaced with a lump sum order capitalising the payments. The periodical payments had proved neither practical nor effective as the husband had refused to pay and the process of enforcement had been very expensive for the payee wife and a significant drain on family resources. Naturally, the court requires available capital to make such an order; furthermore, care must be taken to ensure that the payer's deliberate behaviour does not impact on the overall fairness of the award to the payee, whether made by lump sum or periodic payment.

[30]   See further, Chapter 14.

[31]   Capitalised maintenance.

[32]   As was the husband's argument in *Robson v Robson* [2011] 1 FLR 751, at [86], per Ward LJ.

[33]   For an earlier (and pre-*Miller; McFarlane*) example of this type of case, see also *B v B (No. 1) (Financial Provision Proceedings)* [1995] 2 FCR 813, at 825F, per Thorpe LJ: 'Of course, clean break orders are to be achieved wherever realistically appropriate. Of course, the intensity of feeling between these two [parties] is the strongest indicator for clean break if clean break is achievable. But it seems to me that the one class of case where clean break, however desirable, is not achievable is the case where the husband has the capacity to generate very substantial income and where the capital is not proportionately great. That is this case par excellence. What should be a substantial capital base has been dissipated. The only thing that remains is

earning capacity may be an important advantage[34] to him or her, developed over the course of the marriage, which it would be unfair not to share or divide. In the rather exceptional circumstances of Mrs McFarlane's divorce, for example, both parties had accepted before the district judge that a clean break was impossible, as an equal division of the £3m asset pot to meet the housing requirements of both parties was insufficient to thereafter provide for Mrs McFarlane's future income needs.[35]

> '[154] There is obviously a relationship between capital sharing and future income provision. If capital has been equally shared and is enough to provide for need and compensate for disadvantage, then there should be no continuing financial provision. In McFarlane, there has been an equal division of property, but this largely consisted of homes which can be characterised as family assets. This was not enough to provide for needs or compensate for disadvantage. The main family asset is the husband's very substantial earning power, generated over a lengthy marriage in which the couple deliberately chose that the wife should devote herself to home and family and the husband to work and career. The wife is undoubtedly entitled to generous income provision for herself and for the sake of their children, including sums which will enable her to provide for her own old age and insure the husband's life. She is also entitled to a share in the very large surplus, on the principles both of sharing the fruits of the matrimonial partnership and of compensation for the comparable position which she might have been in had she not compromised her own career for the sake of them all ...'[36]

Care must be taken, however, not to ascribe a capital value (ie to capitalise) to a party's income stream and, thereafter, to attempt to divide such value as a capital 'asset'.[37] Instead, the breadwinner's high income or earning capacity – seen in the context of the available capital assets, the marital standard of living, the length of the marriage and the employment sacrifices made by the other party – may demand a periodical payments order so as to meet needs[38] and achieve fairness in the overall division of finances.[39]

---

the husband's capacity to generate high income. I do not think, however desirable a clean break might be to meet the emotional and psychological needs of the parties, that it would be principled in this case.'

[34] Or, as Baroness Hale perhaps controversially saw it, as 'asset' to be divided (*Miller v Miller; McFarlane v McFarlane*).

[35] Mrs McFarlane sought a periodical payments order for £275,000 p a and Mr McFarlane proposed an order for £100,000 p a.

[36] *Miller v Miller; McFarlane v McFarlane*, per Baroness Hale, at [154].

[37] See, for example, Wilson LJ's comments in *Jones v Jones* [2011] 1 FLR 1723, CA, at [27]: 'Even if, however, an earning capacity may also sometimes be relevant to a fair distribution of the assets pursuant to the sharing principle, it does not follow that the earning capacity should itself be treated as one of those assets, still less that an attempt should be made to capitalise it'.

[38] Furthermore, if the payee is 'owed' compensation for relationship-generated disadvantage, the social desirability of a clean break should not, of itself, be sufficient to deprive the payee of that compensation (*Miller v Miller; McFarlane v McFarlane*, per Lord Nicholls, at [39]).

[39] There may also be cases in which the future receipt of significant capital provides an

(b)   *Cases involving longer marriages and/or the 'older' payee*: Generally, the longer the marriage endures, the more time that passes during which the consequences of the choices and decisions made by the parties will become entrenched. The decisions to have children, to leave employment or to take part-time or lower paid work, to move country, leave family or focus on a career, may all have enduring financial consequences. There is, of course, no general rule that older age or a longer marriage of itself necessitates an ongoing periodical payments order,[40] but it may make it very difficult for a non-working party to return to the employment market with any level of success. The focus should be on the financial and personal consequences for the parties of the way in which they chose to live their lives during the marriage, set in the narrative of older age and, perhaps, a longer period of dependence on the income of the 'breadwinner'. Charles J aptly described this approach as follows in *G v G (Financial Remedies: Short Marriage: Trust Assets)*:[41]

> '139. Naturally, I recognise that in many cases where a wife has stayed at home to look after the children she will be awarded a joint lives periodical payments order, but this is not because she can simply choose whether or not to work. Rather, it is because she cannot fairly be expected to do so having regard to her earning capacity and her past and continuing care of the children (and thus her relationship-generated needs and disadvantages) …'

(c)   *Cases involving a [family] business with no capital value*:[42] If it is inappropriate or impossible to ascribe a capital value to a business shareholding of one party and it is, instead, a source of income for a payer, it may be proper to make a time-unlimited periodical payments order so that the payer and payee can both derive future income benefits.[43]

(d)   *Cases involving a [family] business and an illiquid shareholding*: If one party has a share in a family business (or, indeed, a shareholding in a non-family business) but the shareholding or business is to be retained and not sold or transferred, a clean break may be inappropriate. The argument is that it is unfair for the shareholding party to reject or dispute a sale or

---

opportunity for the court to order a deferred clean break. See, for example, *R v R (Financial Remedies: Needs and Practicalities)* [2013] 1 FLR 120.

[40]   *Flavell v Flavell* [1997] 1 FLR 353, CA is often quoted as providing the basis for such a rule, in which Ward LJ stated that 'There is, in my judgment, often a tendency for [orders terminating dependency] to be made more in hope than in serious expectation. Especially in judging the case of ladies in their middle years, the judicial looking into the crystal ball very rarely finds enough of substance to justify a finding that adjustment can be made without undue hardship …'. However, in *Flavell v Flavell*, there was no evidence that the payee wife could indeed enter the employment market with any level of success. Given the fact of longer life expectancies, later dates for retirement and many 'older' people continuing to work later in life, *Flavell* must be seen in its contemporary context and with an eye to the specific facts of that case.

[41]   [2012] 2 FLR 48.

[42]   For an example of this approach, see *V v V (Financial Relief)* [2005] 2 FLR 697, per Coleridge J.

[43]   And such an order for periodical payments may be made for a fixed sum or on a percentage basis. See, for example, *V v V (Financial Relief)* [2005] 2 FLR 697 and *R v R (Financial Remedies)* [2012] EWHC 2390 (Fam), [2013] 1 FLR 106 at [52].

transfer of the shareholding on the one hand but seek to impose a clean break on the payee on the other. The real value of the shareholding may be difficult to ascertain and the risks and fortunes for the business may be impossible to predict. However, if the payee's needs for future income cannot be met by extracting sufficient capital from the shareholding/business, a clean break may be inappropriate: after all, the shareholder will continue to trade with 'locked-in' capital in the business that otherwise would have been paid to the payee by way of a lump sum payment to achieve a clean break. Furthermore, if the business develops in the future to a point at which liquidity is reached sufficient to capitalise the payee's periodical payments order, the clean break may then be achievable.[44]

TO TERM OR NOT TO TERM?

Adjusting without undue hardship to the termination of financial dependence

11.13

> If the court rejects an immediate clean break and instead makes a periodical payments order, it must consider on the evidence available *at the time of trial* whether it is appropriate that periodical payments should cease at some point *in the future*. In determining whether, and if so, when, such a position may be reached, the MCA 1973 guides the court only to assess the ability of the payee to adjust without undue hardship to the termination of the payer's financial support. In effect, the statute imposes a two-stage test, which was identified in *Fisher v Fisher*[45] thus:
>
> > 'The expression "adjust to the termination of the support" itself connotes a gradual but progressive effort on the part of the supported spouse. The court therefore has to enquire whether (a) the position has been reached in which such an order is appropriate; and (b) if, and only if, the court is so satisfied then to devise a programme of adjustment which will achieve partial or total financial viability without undue hardship.'
>
> This two-stage assessment is arguably one of the most difficult facing the court when it makes a periodical payments order. The date at which questions of adjustment and undue hardship must be assessed is the date of the termination of the order, which may be months or years in the future.[46] Therefore, the court must make a *prospective* assessment on ➙

---

[44] See, for example, *F v F (Clean Break: Balance of Fairness)* [2003] 1 FLR 847, per Singer J, at [90]–[91]: the court was unwilling to 'surrender fairness on the altar of finality' (at [89], per Singer J).

[45] [1989] 1 FLR 423, at 429.

[46] *D v D (Financial Provision: Periodical Payments)* [2004] 1 FLR 988.

> *current* evidence which, even though it will address the *future* financial circumstances of the payee, will inevitably embody a degree of expectation and risk.

11.14 The concept of 'undue hardship' is not further defined in the MCA 1973 or case-law. The Oxford English Dictionary defines hardship as 'the quality of being hard to bear; painful difficulty' or 'hardness of fate or circumstance; severe suffering or privation'. 'Undue' is defined as 'inappropriate, unsuitable, improper; unrightful' or 'going beyond what is warranted or natural; excessive, disproportionate'.[47]

Adjusting: evidence not expectation

11.15 The assessment of whether a payee can adjust without undue hardship is ultimately one of fact and degree taking into account all the circumstances of the case, including the welfare of minor children. The length of the marriage, the period during which the payee has been financially dependent (and the extent of this dependence), the standard of living enjoyed during the marriage and the needs and responsibilities of the payee will all impact on the assessment. The key to mounting or defending a case for a limited term of periodical payments is *evidence* and not expectation or vague assertions as to the payee's ability to adjust to the termination of financial support, or to the justice to the payer achieved by virtue of such an adjustment. In *Flavell v Flavell*,[48] Ward LJ warned against the tendency for orders terminating future financial support 'to be made more in hope than serious expectation'. Ultimately, the question that must be asked is: *is the evidence at trial sufficient and adequately cogent to demonstrate, on a balance of probabilities, that the payee will be in a position to adjust to termination of periodical payments without undue financial hardship?*

11.16 The gathering of such evidence should be addressed as a matter of priority, if the imposition of a term for periodical payments is an issue in a case. The evidence may include the following:

- the payee's curriculum vitae listing any qualifications, voluntary or paid work and promotions;
- information from previous employers about the roles and responsibilities of the payee in employed/voluntary positions;
- information as to the payee's final salary and bonus for each employed role;
- costs and timings for any proposed re-training schemes;
- expert evidence (employment consultant, for example) as to the employed roles for which the payee is capable and qualified;
- adverts for sample jobs for which the payee could apply;

---

[47] Shorter Oxford English Dictionary (5th edn, Oxford University Press, 2002).
[48] [1997] 1 FLR 353, CA.

- evidence as to the cost of any childcare required if the payee is to return to work or training.

11.17 The evidential test was the subject of more particular guidance in *C v C (Financial Relief: Short Marriage)*,[49] the facts of which make the case particularly unusual – not least the 9½ month marriage itself. However, the guidance summarised by Ward LJ as how to approach the question of adjustment to the termination of financial dependence is relevant to all cases:

> '(2) If there is to be no clean break, and a periodical payments order is to be made, then the court must decide pursuant to s 25 what amount is to be ordered. The duration of the marriage is a factor relevant to the determination of quantum.
>
> (3) If a periodical payments order is made, whether for 5p pa or whatever, the question is whether it would be appropriate to impose a term because in the absence of such a direction the order will endure for joint lives or until the remarriage of the payee: see s 28(1)(a).
>
> (4) The statutory test is this: is it appropriate to order periodical payments only for such a term as in the opinion of the court would be sufficient to enable the payee to adjust without undue hardship to the termination of financial dependence on the paying party?
>
> (5) What is appropriate must of necessity depend on all the circumstances of the case including the welfare of any minor child and the s 25 checklist factors, one of which is the duration of the marriage. It is, however, not appropriate simply to say, "This is a short marriage, therefore a term must be imposed".
>
> (6) Financial dependence being evident from the very making of an order for periodical payments, the question is whether, in the light of all the circumstances of the case, the payee can adjust – and adjust without undue hardship – to the termination of financial dependence and if so when. The question is, can she adjust, not should she adjust. In answering that question the court will pay attention not only to the duration of the marriage but to the effect the marriage and its breakdown and the need to care for any minor children has had and will continue to have on the earning capacity of the payee and the extent to which she is no longer in the position she would have been in but for the marriage, its consequences and its breakdown. It is highly material to consider any difficulties the payee may have in entering or re-entering the labour market, resuming a fractured career and making up any lost ground.
>
> (7) The court cannot form its opinion that a term is appropriate without evidence to support its conclusion. Facts supported by evidence must, therefore, justify a reasonable expectation that the payee can and will →

---

[49] [1997] 2 FLR 26, CA.

become self-sufficient. Gazing into the crystal ball does not give rise to such a reasonable expectation. Hope, with or without pious exhortations to end dependency, is not enough.

(8) It is necessary for the court to form an opinion not only that the payee will adjust, but also that the payee will have adjusted within the term that is fixed. The court may be in a position of such certainty that it can impose a deferred clean break by prohibiting an extension of the term pursuant to s 28(1A). If, however, there is doubt about when self-sufficiency will be attained, it is wrong to require the payee to apply to extend the term. If there is uncertainty about the appropriate length of the term, the proper course is to impose no term but leave the payer to seek the variation and if necessary go through the same exercise, this time pursuant to s 31(7)(a).'

11.18 In *C v C*, the Court of Appeal highlighted that the question for the judge is not '*should*' but '*can*' the payee adjust to the termination of financial dependence. This wording is clearly designed to shift the emphasis away from a principled or partisan assessment of the appropriateness of ongoing maintenance payments to one based on evidence. Nevertheless, the court is entitled to – and, if possible, should – make findings about any increase to a party's earning capacity that it is considered reasonable to expect that party to take steps to acquire.[50] Those increases may be immediate or they may be the result of a period of re-training, up-skilling or gaining qualifications. Therefore, the payee may be at risk of the court deciding that s/he should be training or seeking alternative employment to increase annual income figures. Additionally, the ages of the parties, the standard of living prior to their separation and the length of the marriage – and, therefore, the amount of time over which any financial dependency has developed – are factors that affect a court's assessment of whether a term shorter than that of joint lives should be imposed. Care must be taken, however, not to draw the focus away from the payee's *ability* to adjust, as these additional factors may narrowly and erroneously focus attention on whether the payee 'should' adjust to the termination of financial dependency.

11.19 The case of *L v L (Financial Remedies: Deferred Clean Break)*[51] is a more modern example of the appropriateness of a term order for periodical payments rather than one for joint lives. The wife ('W') was 44 years old and the husband ('H') 50. The marriage lasted some 10 years and produced two children, who were 12 and 9 years old. The capital assets at trial amounted to £3.4m. H argued for a clean break and W sought joint lives periodical payments at the rate of £60,000 p.a. W owned a farm and also worked as a fashion designer but made only a small profit. The farm had been run as a hobby during the marriage, but agent evidence at trial suggested it could generate a profit of circa £23,000 in the future. H worked as a General Practitioner; the District Judge at first instance did not make any specific finding as to his income but reference was made to £82,000 of annual profit

---

[50] MCA 1973, s 25(2)(a).
[51] [2011] EWHC 2207 (Fam), [2012] 1 FLR 1283.

after deductions for corporation tax. The District Judge assessed W's income needs at £47,500 pa and ordered H to pay global periodical payments to her at that rate on a joint lives basis.

11.20 On appeal, Eleanor King J rehearsed the approach of the Court of Appeal in *C v C* (above) and substituted a (remaining) 2 year and 5 months' term order for the joint lives order of the District Judge. W's farm was a significant capital asset and agricultural holding of some 350 acres, and it was capable of developing from a 'hobby' enterprise to one generating an income for her once H's horses had been removed. Alternatively, if the farm failed to produce an income sufficient to meet W's future needs, she could sell the farm (worth £2m net) in order to realise capital, re-house at a more moderate level and use the balance to generate an income in an alternative way. W was also relatively young and had worked throughout the marriage; the marriage itself had only been of a medium length and the children were subject to a shared care arrangement between the parents. Therefore, the facts of the case justified 'a reasonable expectation that the payee can and will become self-sufficient'[52]. Eleanor King J recorded her view that 'this wife is comparatively well placed – she has substantial capital of her own which covers her basic living costs even if she chooses to do little more to increase the income from the farm; she has never left the workplace and has her well-deserved reputation upon which to build a business in order to produce a more substantial income'.[53]

Term orders: whose uncertainty and whose burden?

11.21 The question of whether a term order for periodical payments is appropriate invariably depends on bold judicial findings as to, for example, earning capacity, employment prospects and the future burden of childcare responsibilities. Some judges are more cautious than others. If the balance of the evidence suggests that the payee may struggle to generate or develop personal income, and if there is a real risk of that struggle resulting in failure, the court is likely to err on the side of caution and reject a term order for periodical payments. The same applies if the fortunes of the payer are uncertain. *The court must essentially decide whether the burden should lie with the payer to apply to terminate a periodical payments order in the future (and thereby make a joint lives order) or whether that burden should rest with the payee to apply to extend the set period for the receipt of periodical payments (and thereby make a term order).* Judicial caution on this issue has been exercised for decades, as the older case *of Suter v Suter and Jones*[54] demonstrates. In *Suter v Suter* the marriage had endured for some 13 years and had produced two children aged 14 and 8. The parties were in their early thirties. The husband worked as a petty officer in the Royal Navy and the wife, who had a new partner, was employed as a cleaner. The trial judge ordered periodical payments at the rate of £100 per month for a 10-year term. The

---

[52] Ibid, at [70].
[53] Ibid.
[54] [1987] 2 All ER 336.

husband appealed and sought an immediate clean break or a termination of his obligation to pay earlier than the 10 years ordered.

11.22   Sir Roualeyn Cumming-Bruce (at 340j) said:

> '... I am clear that on the facts it is not possible at this date to predict with any more confidence than the registrar when the wife will have been able to make the adjustment which leads to the inference that it will then be just and reasonable to terminate her right to claim periodical payments from her husband. The children are growing up. It is likely that it will become progressively easier for the wife to organise and increase her earning capacity. But there are too many uncertainties to predict the development of events over the next 10 years.'

11.23   In the later case of *S v S*[55], Sir Mark Potter rejected the husband's request for a term order for periodical payments lasting 5 years and imposed a joint lives order. The marriage was childless and had lasted for 11 years. The husband was a successful investment banker who wanted to leave the pressures of working in the city, preferably within 12 to 18 months of the final order but, in any event, he claimed, within 5 years. The wife claimed that the husband was a hard and determined worker and that he was likely to develop his career and redouble his efforts to make up lost ground after the conclusion of the financial remedy proceedings. The wife herself claimed an earning capacity of £12,000 pa, which was accepted by the court. District Judge Segal considered that the expense and nuisance of returning to vary a joint lives order[56] was potentially less damaging than the risk of making an irreversible order that turned out to be based on incorrect figures. The District Judge had been unable to make a finding that the husband would leave (or be forced to leave) his lucrative employment in the city. Sir Mark Potter dismissed the husband's appeal against the imposition of a joint lives order:

> 'I consider that the district judge was entitled to take the course he did if, as he stated, he regarded it as the fairest course, compared with the alternative of a term periodical payments order which was likely to result in unfairness to one or both of the parties. While the terms of section 25A require the court to consider carefully the making of a term order, nothing in that section ... suggest[s] that the court is required to depart from the overall requirement of fairness between the parties ...'

11.24   In *Miller v Miller; McFarlane v McFarlane*, the House of Lords reversed the decision of the Court of Appeal that imposed a 5-year term of periodical payments for the benefit of Mrs McFarlane.[57] Lord Nicholls made reference to the test of 'exceptional justification' that may apply if a party is to succeed in extending an original term set for periodical payments.[58] Lord Nicholls was astutely careful to ensure that Mrs McFarlane, after a long marriage during

---

[55]   [2008] 2 FLR 113.
[56]   Whether the application was subsequently brought by the payer or payee.
[57]   The original order of the district judge having been for joint lives.
[58]   Arising out of the case of *Fleming v Fleming* [2004] 1 FLR 667.

which she had sacrificed a professional career in favour of her family, was not to be left facing the hurdle of applying to extend a short-term order for maintenance:

> '[96] This leads me to the point where I fundamentally disagree with the Court of Appeal: the replacement of a joint lives order with a 5-year order. I agree with the Court of Appeal that when the husband has repaid the mortgage on his new home, and the wife's earning capacity has revived, the time may be ripe for a reassessment of the parties' position to see if a deferred clean break is practicable. A clean break might then be achievable by the court exercising its power to order the husband to make a lump sum payment to the wife as consideration for discharging his liability to make further periodical payments. The court has this power under s 31(7A) and (7B) inserted into the 1973 Act by s 66 of the Family Law Act 1996.
>
> [97] That is something which will merit careful consideration at a suitably early date. But I do not see how this leads to the conclusion that the district judge's joint lives order should be set aside in favour of an extendable 5 years' order. The practice in the family courts seems to be that on an application for extension of a periodical payments order made for a finite period the applicant must surmount a high threshold: *Fleming v Fleming* [2003] EWCA Civ 1841; [2004] 1 FLR 667, at 670, paras [12]–[14]. In the present case it would be altogether inappropriate, indeed unjust, to make a 5-year order and place the wife in that position when 5 years has elapsed. In the present case a 5-year order is most unlikely to be sufficient to achieve a fair outcome. Further financial provision of some sort will be needed. So, far from compelling the wife to apply for an extension of a 5-year order, and requiring her to shoulder the heavy burden accompanying such an application, it is more appropriate for the husband to have to take the initiative in applying for a variation of a joint lives order when he considers circumstances make that appropriate. Certainly the district judge cannot be said to have erred in principle in making a joint lives order, especially when this was common ground between the parties. I would allow this appeal and restore the order of District Judge Redgrave.'

The short marriage and the clean break/term order

11.25   A shorter marriage[59] may of itself be an important fact in favour of an immediate clean break or a shorter term of periodical payments to enable the payee to make the transition from the marital lifestyle to that of independent living.[60] However, a short marriage may have involved very serious choices or decisions, the consequences of which may have a long-term financial impact for either the payer or the payee. The court may select a term order for periodical payments at a static level or it may reduce the quantum of the order over time in order to encourage the payee to achieve some level of self-sufficiency.

11.26   In *G v G (Financial Remedies: Short Marriage: Trust Assets)*[61] Charles J was faced with the following circumstances and arguments: the wife ('W') sought a joint lives periodical payments order whereas the husband ('H')

---

[59]   In this context, one of 6 years or less.
[60]   See, for example, *M-D v D* [2008] EWHC 1929 (Fam).
[61]   [2012] 2 FLR 48.

argued for a staged reduction in the level of periodical payments to their eventual termination when the child of the marriage reached 11 years of age. The marriage had endured for just 5 years and there was one child of the marriage who was 4 years old. W was 33, H 38 and he was a very high earner. W was also a beneficiary under family trusts and had been the recipient of financial support from her parents. W had worked and had an earning capacity but did not return to work after the birth of the parties' son. Charles J identified the issue as to how long, after a short marriage between two highly qualified persons, should a high earning spouse remain completely (or very substantially) responsible for supporting the other spouse, who has a good earning capacity but does not wish to pursue it to the full. Charles J undertook a broad analysis of the relevant case-law and provided the following assistance:

> '136. What I take from this guidance on the approach to the statutory task is that the objective of achieving a fair result (assessed by reference to the words of the statute and the rationales for their application identified by the House of Lords):
>
> i)   is not met by an approach that seeks to achieve a dependence for life (or until re-marriage) for the payee spouse to fund a lifestyle equivalent to that enjoyed during the marriage (or parity if that level is not affordable for two households), but
>
> ii)   is met by an approach that recognises that the aim is independence and self sufficiency based on all the financial resources that are available to the parties. From that it follows that:
>
> iii)   generally, the marital partnership does not survive as a basis for the sharing of future resources (whether earned or unearned). But, and they are important buts:
>
>> a)   the lifestyle enjoyed during the marriage sets a level or benchmark that is relevant to the assessment of the level of the independent lifestyles to be enjoyed by the parties,
>>
>> b)   the length of the marriage is relevant to determining the period for which that level of lifestyle is to be enjoyed by the payee (so long as this is affordable by the payor), and so also, if there is to be a return to a lesser standard of living for the payee, the period over which that transition should take place,
>>
>> c)   if the marriage is short, this supports the conclusion that the award should be directed to providing a transition over an appropriate period for the payee spouse to either a lower long term standard of living than that enjoyed during the marriage, or to one that is not contributed to by the other spouse,
>>
>> d)   the marriage, and the choices made by the parties during it, may have generated needs or disadvantages in attaining and funding self sufficient independence that (i) should be compensated, and (ii) make continuing dependence/provision fair,
>>
>> e)   the most common source of a continuing relationship generated need or disadvantage is the birth of children and their care,
>>
>> f)   a continuing relationship generated need is often reflected in a continuing contribution to the day to day care of the children of the relationship, that contribution being recognised by the continuing financial contribution of the paying spouse (which is a continuing contribution to the day to day care of the children),

g) the choices made by the parties as to the care of their children are an important factor in determining how that care should be provided and shared both by reference to day to day care and the funding of the independent households, and

h) the provisions of s 25A must be taken into account.

As to points (e), (f) and (g), s 25(1) provides that when the court is having regard to all the circumstances of the case first consideration is to be given to the welfare while a minor of a child of the family, and in my judgment this is a clear indicator that the impact of the manner in which that welfare has been, and is to be, promoted has particular weight.

140. As mentioned earlier, the wife placed great reliance on *C v C (Financial Relief: Short Marriage)* [1997] 2 FLR 26. She did so not only to resist a term being set for the periodical payments pursuant to s 25A(2), but also to support her contention that (apart from limited credit for trust income) the level of periodical payments she sought should only be reduced as a result of an application for variation.

141. Two preliminary points are relevant. Firstly, like all cases of its and earlier dates, *C v C* must be read and applied in the light of the significant changes that have resulted from *White*, and later cases (in particular *Miller and McFarlane*), and this is so notwithstanding that *C v C* is specifically directed to the application of s 25A(2). Secondly, s 25A(2), and so *C v C*, is expressly directed to the termination of financial dependence and not to the issue whether, applying other sections and the relevant rationales, the initial order for periodical payments should (a) take immediate account of the earnings and/or earning capacity of the payee, or (b) build in reductions to take account of them and so reduce rather than terminate financial dependence on the other spouse. There is of course an overlap, and so an analogy to be drawn, between reduction and termination ...

143. As argued, I accept that *C v C* confirms that s 25A(2) is directed to the payee's hardship, that the court must take an evidence based approach to whether the payee can and will adjust and that unless the court concludes, on that evidential basis, that a term should be imposed it should not impose one on the basis that the payee can seek an extension (or on any other basis). Further, I accept and acknowledge that, as with all its other conclusions the court has to base any reductions in periodical payments on an evidential foundation.

144. But, in my judgment this need for an evidential base does not mean that the wife can assert (which at times she seemed to be arguing) that she can avoid an evidence based finding on her likely earnings by not providing an estimate of her earnings from the work she is planning to do, and/or by not co-operating in obtaining a report from an expert on her earning potential. As to the latter point, I do not accept that the absence of such a report is an indication that she is unlikely to be able to earn significant sums from part time employment. Rather, in my view, by not quantifying her earnings, and/or co-operating in their quantification, the wife acted contrary to her duty to give full and frank disclosure of her business plans (and thus her s 25(2)(a) resources) and the overriding objective.'

Following the anticipated increases in the wife's future earnings over a 6-year period after the final order, Charles J reduced the periodical payments for her benefit from £95,500 to £35,000 p a.[62]

TO BAR OR NOT TO BAR? THE DEFERRED CLEAN BREAK

11.27   If the court determines that it is fair to impose a periodical payments order for a term of less than the parties' joint lives, it must also consider whether to prevent the payee from applying to the court to extend that term for payment. If the court imposes a 'bar' preventing such an application,[63] the order will result in a deferred clean break; that is, a termination of any further financial provision by way of periodical payments at the date when the term ends. The postponed finality inherent in such an order may give the court real cause for concern. The fact that a periodical payments order is required at all will normally arise out of the payee's needs and his or her inability to meet those needs through personal effort and income. If the periodical payments order involves an element of compensation[64] for the payee or, exceptionally, a 'sharing' of income in excess of needs (however generously interpreted), it may be difficult, or even impossible, to determine a specific future date when such payments should cease.

The broad approach

11.28

> The court will approach the question of whether to impose a bar by utilising the same evidential basis upon which it determined that a term order for periodical payments was justified. Whereas a term order with no bar enables the court to revisit the appropriateness of the term, if the justice of the case requires it, a term order with a bar imposes an irrevocable restriction which deprives the court of any future jurisdiction on the issue. Generally, therefore, if a bar is to be imposed, the court must find, on the balance of probabilities, not only that the payee *will* adjust to the termination of financial dependence, but also that the payee *will have* adjusted within the specific period.[65] Such a finding requires a position of *relative* confidence, which is more difficult to reach the more entrenched the financial dependence of the payee and the more fragile and risky the payee's expected route to self-sufficiency.

---

[62]   Thereafter to be increased according to the Retail Prices Index.
[63]   Pursuant to MCA 1973, s 28(1A).
[64]   For relationship-generated disadvantage: see further Chapter 9 on quantification.
[65]   *C v C* [1997] 2 FLR 26, CA.

Dates, life-events and the length of the term for periodical payments

11.29 It is common to seek to link the conclusion of a term for periodical payments to a specific future event or date. For example, the youngest child reaching 18 years of age, the payer's retirement or the payee's completion of a phase of re-training.

11.30 The length of the term for periodical payments may also affect the court's decision as to whether to impose a bar. A brief term order of, say, 3 years, after a short marriage and involving younger parties may justify the imposition of a bar. On the other hand, a longer term order after a lengthy marriage and predicated on the basis of the payee achieving certain goals to attain self-sufficiency, may involve a number of predictions as to the future which, if they are not realised, may leave the payee in a position of continuing hardship.

11.31 In *D v D (Financial Provision: Periodical Payments)*[66] the parties' long marriage had endured for 21 years. The husband was 51 years of age and the wife 55. The children of the family were over 18 and independent. Both parties worked; the husband as a solicitor earning £61,000 per annum and the wife as a legal secretary with income needs of £25,000 pa. The capital was divided equally, pension sharing orders were made and periodical payments were ordered for the wife's benefit of £10,000 a year on a joint lives basis. The husband appealed the joint lives periodical payments order and sought a limitation of the term to 10 years to coincide, broadly, with his anticipated retirement. Coleridge J allowed the appeal and imposed a 10-year term order but refused to also impose a bar preventing the wife from seeking to extend the term. Coleridge J recognised that the district judge had sought to provide broad equality for both parties upon retirement, which was endorsed as a proper objective. However, Coleridge J emphasised that, in also ordering joint lives maintenance, the balance of fairness could be upset, because 'if an order for periodical payments is left rampant, if I can use that word – without any restriction on it – then equality can later be destroyed because of intervening events and it potentially flies in the face of the attainment of the district judge's perfectly proper objective'.[67]

11.32 Coleridge J, however, also recognised that a 10-year term was a long period for continuing maintenance with a definite termination and no right for the wife to extend the period of support:

> '... I have come to the conclusion that with a term as long as this it is simply unsafe to dismiss her claim outright in 10 years' time, when plainly within that 10 year period there is a significant dependency. It is quite impossible for a court to look as far as 10 years hence with any degree of precision and, although, as I say, my clear view is (and I express it in this strong way) that there should be no further

---

[66]   [2004] 1 FLR 988.
[67]   Ibid, at [23], per Coleridge J.

payment by the husband beyond that term, I do not propose to put in place the bar under s 28(1A). If unforeseen events occur within the next 10 years which create for the wife financial embarrassment, it would be wrong after this length of marriage to prevent the court from having the ability to consider the matter again.'[68]

The presence of children

11.33 A payee who has ongoing care of the children of the family has an additional [financial] burden beyond seeking a route to financial self-sufficiency. The welfare of minor children must be the court's first consideration. In *N v N (Consent Order: Variation)*[69] Roch LJ was keen to emphasise that a payee with responsibility for minor children should not, generally, be the recipient of a term order for periodical payments with a bar preventing an extension application prior to the youngest child of the family reaching the age of 18:

> 'It can be anticipated that it will be an exceptional case that an order for periodical payments will be limited to a term under section 28(1) where there is a child of the family who remains in the care and control of the party in whose favour the order for periodical payments is being made and who has yet to attain the age of 18 years, and that it will only be in the most exceptional and unusual case that a direction under section 28(1A) will be made in such circumstances ...'

This broad statement of principle must, however, be seen in light of the current system of statutory child support and the more common sharing of care between parents after separation.[70] The payee with 'care and control' of a child – or the resident parent with a claim for child maintenance – will receive a fixed percentage of the payer's gross income[71] under the revised child support system. Nevertheless, if the court has determined that a fixed term for periodical payments is appropriate, the payee's responsibility for childcare may impact upon his or her ability to achieve the goals of qualifications, re-training or full-time work upon which the term order may have been based.

---

[68] Ibid, at [26], per Coleridge J.
[69] [1993] 2 FLR 868, at 883.
[70] See also *Mawson v Mawson* [1994] 2 FLR 985 and *Waterman v Waterman* [1989] 1 FLR 380.
[71] See Chapter 20 for more details.

POINTS OF PRACTICE AND THEORY

Clean break

11.34

(1) The marriage represents a catalogue of choices made by the persons involved that impact to a greater or lesser extent on their ability to achieve financial independence on divorce.

(2) Look for 'hallmarks' in favour of a clean break, as follows:
 (a) little income and no realistic prospect of significant increases;
 (b) sufficient capital assets to achieve clean break with equal or unequal division;
 (c) no children, shorter marriages and established earning capacities of both parties;
 (d) parties at retirement age;
 (e) unreliable payers and/or obstacles to enforcement;
 (f) the payee's remarriage or cohabitation.

(3) Indicators against a clean break:
 (a) insufficient capital assets;
 (b) older payee and longer marriages;
 (c) businesses with no capital value or illiquid shareholdings.

Term orders for periodical payments

11.35

(4) When assessing whether a term should be applied to a periodical payments order, the court must make a *prospective* assessment on *current* evidence which, even though it will address the *future* financial circumstances of the payee, will inevitably embody a degree of expectation and risk.

(5) The test is in two stages and requires a proper evidential foundation: the court has to enquire whether (a) the position has been reached in which such an order is appropriate; and (b) if, and only if, the court is so satisfied, then to devise a programme of adjustment which will achieve partial or total financial viability without undue hardship.

(6) Can (not should!) the payee adjust – and adjust without undue hardship – to the termination of financial dependence and if so when? The court will pay attention not only to the duration of the marriage but to the effect the marriage and its breakdown and the need to care for any minor children has had and will continue to have on the earning capacity of the payee and the extent to which s/he is no longer in the position s/he would have been in but for the marriage, its consequences and its breakdown. It is highly material to consider any difficulties the payee may have in entering or re-entering the labour market, resuming a fractured career and making up any lost ground.

CHAPTER 12

ORDERS FOR NOMINAL PERIODICAL PAYMENTS: JUSTIFICATION AND TRANSMUTABILITY[1]

INTRODUCTION

12.1 An order for nominal periodical payments ('nominal order') is a fully-fledged periodical payments order save for one element only; that the payment is expressed as a nominal sum. The Oxford dictionary defines nominal as 'very small; far below the real value or cost'. A nominal order is indeed expressed in a final order as a trifling sum of 5 pence or £1 per annum; however, its real value or cost is only known at a later date, years or perhaps decades in the future. Primarily, a nominal order is one which is often described as 'leaving the door ajar' at a later date for the payee, if the circumstances justify it, to seek an extension of the term for payments or an order transmuting the nominal order into a substantive periodical payments order. A transmuted order is then equally susceptible to capitalisation.[2]

12.2 Given that the nominal payment of, say, 5 pence per annum is of no real financial use, the only (and potentially significant) benefit of a nominal order is its capacity to be transmuted – at a later date – into a substantive periodical payments order. This may be a trite statement but it is indicative of the curious and sometimes awkward position such orders occupy in the court's armoury of financial remedies. The nominal amount of the payment places such orders – in strict monetary terms – in a precarious position on the cusp of a 'clean break',[3] for a court has no power to order periodical payments that provide for the payment of (literally) nothing.[4] However, as a nominal order is a type of periodical payments order, it fully engages the court's powers of variation, extension and capitalisation. It is no surprise, therefore, that a nominal order can prove difficult for the payer to accept, as it is an order tainted with significant future uncertainty. For the payee, the future benefits of a nominal order may be difficult to appreciate at the time of the final order or, in the battle for a speedy conclusion to litigation, apparently easier to relinquish than 'cash in hand'.

---

[1]   The ability to change from one form into another: in this context, transforming a nominal periodical payments order into a substantive one.
[2]   See Chapter 18.
[3]   If all other claims are settled or determined.
[4]   Ie, a periodical payments order requires the *payment* of something.

12.3 This chapter identifies the reasoning behind nominal orders, the circumstances in which such orders have been made, refused or successfully appealed and the principles governing the transmutability of a nominal order into a substantive order for periodical payments. As a nominal order shares all the attributes of a periodical payments order (save for the amount of the payment), the reader should also consult other chapters in The Guide dealing with the clean break principle and applications for variation and capitalisation.

JUSTIFICATION FOR A NOMINAL ORDER

Legal basis

12.4 The nominal order shares its legal basis with an order for substantive periodical payments under MCA 1973, s 23(1)(a). Therefore, the nominal order can be made for such term as the court deems fair, just and appropriate having regard to all the familiar factors outlined in MCA 1973, s 25(2). The court is under its common duty to consider whether a clean break is appropriate as soon after a decree absolute as it considers just and reasonable (MCA 1973, s 25A(1). Additionally, when the court makes a nominal order[5] it must 'in particular consider whether it would be appropriate to require those payments to be made ... only for such term as would in the opinion of the court be sufficient to enable the party in whose favour the order is made to adjust without undue hardship to the termination of his or her financial dependence on the other party' (MCA 1973, s 25A(2)).

The clean break versus the nominal order

12.5 In *Minton v Minton*,[6] Lord Scarman neatly encapsulated the importance of the clean break:

> 'The law now encourages spouses to avoid bitterness after family breakdown and to settle their money and property problems. An object of the modern law is to encourage each to put the past behind them and to begin a new life which is not overshadowed by the relationship which has broken down.'[7]

A nominal order is, in financial terms, separated from the imposition of a clean break by only 5 pence (or such nominal sum as is chosen) a year. The principal issue, therefore, in cases where a nominal order is sought is whether the circumstances of the case justify such an order and, if so, for how long. Whereas a substantive periodical payments order will invariably be made on the basis of either identifiable and future financial needs or sufficient income of the payer, the nominal order may claim no such justification: it can be designed instead to cater for a *potential* financial need or a potential increase in the payer's income position. Thus, the nominal order perpetuates the financial ties

---

[5]   Or a substantive order for periodical payments.
[6]   [1979] AC 593.
[7]   Ibid, at 608.

between separated parties contrary to the spirit of seeking to achieve financial independence, all in the name of a nominal sum.

12.6   On appeal in *Murphy v Murphy*[8] Parker J imposed a capital division of 65/35% in favour of the wife. The childless marriage had endured for 8 years and the parties were both approximately 40 years old. Parker J overturned the original order for nominal periodical payments, commenting that 'the case had all the hallmarks of clean break and equality'.[9] The nominal order was inappropriate as 'the judge had already rejected equality of division to reflect the disparity in future earning capacity and to add a nominal order suggests duplication. It should not be forgotten that in all these cases the judge has a statutory duty to achieve a clean break between the parties provided that that can be done without undue hardship. It seems to me that that responsibility may have been overlooked in the present case'.[10]

12.7   The justification for a nominal order (as opposed to a clean break) is principally made on two bases: first, as a device to make provision for uncertainties and risks and, secondly, as a practical means of keeping a periodical payments claim alive to address potential financial imbalances arising out of a final order.

Uncertainties and risks: the nominal order as a 'safety valve', 'last backstop' and 'long stop'

12.8   The nominal order can be – and is – made to cater principally for uncertainties in the financial position of either party. This rationale has endowed the relevant case-law with a number of catch-phrases to justify the rejection of a clean break in favour of the adoption of a nominal order. Common reasons for uncertainty are:

(a)   the presence of, and responsibility for, children;

(b)   a developing or tentative earning capacity of the payee (or payer);

(c)   employment risks or health concerns that may impact on future income and financial resources; and

(d)   temporary reductions to the payer's income.

In order for the court to make a nominal order it must ordinarily make findings as to the income and future earning capacity of the parties or it must be incapable of making such findings, which gives rise to the uncertainty upon which it must rely to justify imposing a nominal order. Three common terms to describe and validate the nominal order are as a 'safety valve', a 'last backstop' and a 'longstop'. All three catchphrases share a common purpose: to manage risk and uncertainty.

---

[8]   [2011] 1 FLR 537.
[9]   Ibid, at [34], per Thorpe LJ.
[10]   Ibid, at [35], per Thorpe LJ.

The safety valve

12.9   The parties in *Scallon v Scallon*[11] had ended a long marriage of some 44 years. The husband's earned income was approximately one-third more than that of the wife. The Recorder on appeal ordered a division of proceeds of sale of the matrimonial home to enable both parties to re-house and a nominal order in the wife's favour on a joint lives' basis. The Court of Appeal retained the nominal order. Purchas LJ commented that, in making a nominal order, the Recorder had 'guarded against unforeseen eventualities, which might strike at the wife's earning capacity and in that way also strike at her ability to service a mortgage, by providing the *safety valve* of the nominal order for periodical payments'[12] (emphasis added).

The last backstop

12.10   In *Whiting v Whiting*,[13] the Court of Appeal was divided over the justification for a nominal order. The parties had previously agreed upon a reduction of the original substantive periodical payments order in favour of the wife to a nominal sum. The wife had re-trained as a teacher and achieved financial independence. The parties' children were either working or attending university. The husband had remarried and, since redundancy, had undertaken some consultancy and lecturing work. However, at the hearing to determine whether the nominal order should be discharged, the wife was earning substantially more than the husband. The judge at trial considered the nominal order to be a last backstop which should be retained, despite there being no imminent likelihood of the wife needing financial support from the husband. However, in retaining the nominal order, Slade LJ stated that the court below, in exercising its discretion, could equally have dismissed the nominal order:

> 'However, I find myself unable to say that the judge was obviously wrong in taking the view that, on the particular facts of this case, the maintenance order should be kept alive as a *'last backstop'* (emphasis added). In my judgment, she was entitled in the exercise of her discretion on the particular facts to take the view that the maintenance order should be kept alive in case unforeseen contingencies, such as redundancy or illness, should in the future deprive the wife (who has done everything she could to put herself on her feet) of her ability to provide for herself and make it necessary for her again to look to the husband for her needs, so far as he might be able to meet them. In the meantime, the husband suffers no detriment except such anxiety as he may feel arising from the possibility of a future application. I do not say that I myself would necessarily have reached the same conclusion as the judge.'[14]

---

11   [1990] FCR 911, [1990] 1 FLR 194, CA.
12   [1990] 1 FLR 194, at 202D.
13   [1988] 2 All ER 275.
14   Ibid, at 287D.

The long stop

12.11   In *H v H (Financial Provision: Capital Allowance)*[15] the parties had been married for 12 years and had three children who were aged 10, 8 and 5. The district judge divided the capital 61/39% in the wife's favour and ordered periodical payments for the wife and children until further order. The wife had qualified as a teacher and a nurse as well as having a qualification in accountancy. On appeal, Thorpe J considered it likely that the doctor husband would increase his income by achieving consultancy status in 3 or 4 years' time. The wife was deemed to have a limited earning capacity despite her qualifications given her ongoing care of the children. In relation to the distribution of income Thorpe J considered it as a 'pretty straightforward case'[16] and increased the periodical payments for the children to a level which brought the wife's total income to a level that exceeded her stated expenditure. Regarding the wife's remaining financial claims for herself, Thorpe J stated:

> 'Obviously there can be no certainty as to how things will go for her, but I think it is reasonable to ascribe to her an earning capacity in that future time which will offset the loss of income flowing from the reduction in her investment portfolio. So I see no reason to anticipate that the wife will have a substantial right to periodical payments at that future stage either … In those circumstances, should the wife's right to periodical payments survive at all in light of the statutory requirements to look for conclusion? I have come to the decision that the circumstances of this case are not sufficiently secure to justify an outright dismissal at this stage. Although I do not myself today envisage circumstances in which the wife's claim for periodical payments might become substantive, I cannot ignore that possibility. I accordingly conclude that the wife's claim to periodical payments should result in a 5p order. I am sure that she will not interpret that as any invitation to renew [an] application in 3 or 4 years' time. Nor, am I sure, will she slacken her efforts towards a return to earning in any false reliance upon it. It is only there as a *long stop*.'[17] (emphasis added)

Practicalities: addressing financial imbalance

12.12   The nominal periodical payments order can also function as a means to address potential unfairness if there is evidence that any final award may be affected by future uncertain events. For example, in *Z v Z (No 2) (Financial Remedy: Marriage Contract)*[18] the French couple's assets after a marriage of 14 years amounted to just over £15m, of which approximately 10% was in the wife's name. The parties had married in France under the *separation de biens*[19] regime. The asset base of £15m did not include three potential tax liabilities of the husband, which, combined, amounted to a figure in excess of £4m. However, the case was presented at final hearing on the basis that it was 'pretty unlikely' that such tax charges would be due. Moor J assessed the wife's needs

---

[15]   [1993] 2 FLR 335.
[16]   Ibid, at 348.
[17]   Ibid, at 349C.
[18]   [2012] 1 FLR 1100.
[19]   Under which, all property is owned separately.

at £6m or 40% of the assets without taking account of the [unlikely] tax charges and despite the French marital contract. Given that the husband was the only person who had a real understanding of the likelihood of the tax liabilities crystallising, Moor J gave him a choice: either to accept sole liability for all tax charges and achieve a clean break OR to accept an indemnity from the wife for half of any tax charge over £3m, in which case the wife would have a nominal maintenance order in her favour. As the award to the wife had been assessed on the basis of her 'reasonable needs', the nominal maintenance order could be used to redress any shortfall to those needs arising out of her making a contribution pursuant to her indemnity towards the husband's tax liabilities in the future.

12.13 In all cases in which a nominal order is made, whether to cater for uncertainties or to provide a practical future solution to an issue incapable of resolution at a final hearing, it is best practice to recite within the order (or seek a recital in the judgment of it) the reasons why a nominal order has been made. Although the reasons will not bind a judge at any future variation hearing, they will undoubtedly impact on the court's discretionary exercise.

The dependence of children and nominal periodical payments orders

12.14 There is no principle that a nominal order *must* be made in favour of the parent with care of a minor child of the family. However, the court's first consideration in dealing with a family finance case must, of course, be the welfare of any minor child.[20] Therefore, there *are* strong arguments in favour of such an order, particularly if the child is the product of a longer marriage, the financial dependence of the payee is entrenched or the future risks for the payee more obviously necessitate the 'safety valve' of a nominal order.

12.15 For example, in *J (SR) v J (DW)*[21] the Court of Appeal made a nominal order on the wife's appeal against the dismissal of her financial claims. The parties had married in their twenties; they had four children, one of whom was still dependent at 10 years of age and living with the wife. The wife had not been in employment for many years, although she had undertaken some local voluntary work during the marriage. The husband was a chartered engineer and, at the time of the trial, his business had suffered significantly, although he continued to trade. After separation both the wife and the husband lived in rented accommodation. The wife was reliant on state benefits for her income. The district judge dismissed the wife's claims for periodical payments. The Court of Appeal recognised and highlighted several factors militating against a clean break including:

(1)   the responsibility of the wife for a dependent 10-year-old child;

---

[20]   MCA 1973, s 25(1).
[21]   [1999] 2 FLR 176, CA.

'The presence of such children does not rule out a clean break, but the courts recognise that it is difficult to achieve this when children and their carer are still dependent because there are so many uncertainties involved'.[22]

(2) that the wife was extremely unlikely to financially support herself without resorting to state benefits;

(3) the parties had had a long marriage of some 27 years;

(4) the ages of the parties (the wife being 49 and the husband 52 years old);

(5) the wife had given up work to care for the children, a decision which continued to impact on her earning capacity;

(6) the husband's future prospects to improve his financial position.

Hale J concluded that 'it is not only in [this wife's] interests but in the community's interests that parents ... should have a real choice between concentrating on breadwinning and concentrating on home-making and child-rearing, and do not feel forced, for fear of what might happen should their marriage break down much later in life, to abandon looking after the home and the family to other people for the sake of maintaining a career'.[23]

Short marriages, dependent children and nominal periodical payments orders

12.16 A short marriage may nevertheless warrant a nominal order if the circumstances of the case justify it. Even in a case in which the wife is younger, fully employable despite her childcare commitments and in receipt of a large capital sum[24] as a result of the divorce, the court has refused a husband's appeal against the imposition of a nominal order. In *S v B (Ancillary Relief: Costs)*[25] Wilson J dismissed the husband's appeal against a nominal order made for an extendable period of 10 years. The marriage was a short one of some 3 years producing one child, aged 3, who lived with wife in the former matrimonial home. At the time of the appeal, the wife was 29 years old and earning approximately £18,000 net per annum. The husband, 41, was unemployed but had previously worked in the lucrative merchant banking sector. The district judge found that the husband would generate earnings in the foreseeable future well in excess of the wife's. Wilson J said that, had he been the judge at final hearing, he would have dismissed the wife's application for periodical payments. However, he *did not* interfere with the trial judge's conclusions, stating that:

'I must accept that a fair number of my colleagues – be they High Court judges, circuit judges or district judges – would reasonably have exercised their discretion in favour of keeping alive, at least until the child was a teenager, the wife's right to

---

[22] Ibid, at 182, per Hale J.

[23] Ibid, at 182E, per Hale J.

[24] Enabling the wife to purchase a three-bed property in West London, which was in excess of her and the child's housing needs but would permit a live-in-nanny or a lodger.

[25] [2004] EWHC 2089 (Fam), [2005] 1 FLR 474.

seek to inflate a nominal order for periodical payments to a substantive level. They would regard it as a reasonable precaution against unforeseen developments, taken primarily for the sake of the child. I stress, however, that the circumstances in which it would be apt to vary the order are indeed unlikely to arise: if, for example, the wife fell seriously ill and if, by then, the husband was again a substantial earner, then, yes, there might be a needs-based variation of the order, providing always that the court bore in mind the amount of capital of which, after so short a marriage, the wife had by order relieved the husband'.[26]

12.17 However, in *Fallon v Fallon*[27] the parties had enjoyed a short marriage of only 4 years. There were two children of the marriage. The husband was 46 and the wife 41 years old at the time of the appeal to the Court of Appeal. Even though the wife had not maintained a claim for periodical payments at first instance after 8 years of separation and had secured financial independence, the district judge made an order for nominal periodical payments for a term of 9 years. Having regard to the brevity of the marriage, the husband's ongoing child support payments and a voluntary payment to the wife of £200 per month in addition, Thorpe J started with the conviction that a clean break should be achieved and concluded that 'I cannot see any possible justification for a nominal order which only invites the possibility for future litigation'.[28]

Balancing risk and opportunity

12.18 If the court is considering imposing a nominal order, it must attempt to ascertain the future financial risks and opportunities for both parties. The MCA 1973, of course, demands consideration of the income, earning capacity, property and financial needs a party is likely to have in the foreseeable future. Additionally, a nominal order requires the court to balance those financial risks and opportunities against the prospect of a party achieving financial independence. Where evidence and arguments militate against risk, the court will be more minded to impose a clean break.

12.19 In *A v A*[29] the parties had four children, the youngest being 10 years old, who remained living with the husband in the former matrimonial home. The marriage had lasted some 22 years. The wife had a 25% interest in a family company. Charles J set the wife's income at a minimum of £100,000 net per annum over the following few years, principally derived from her shareholding in the company. Both parties sought a clean break and Charles J acceded to this joint position but, obiter, made the following comment:

'I add that I considered whether, contrary to the stance of the parties, I should not order a clean break but include nominal orders, or a nominal order, for periodical payments to cater for the risks relating to the future income and more general financial positions of the parties. But I concluded that those risks, and thus the chances of my predictions being seriously wrong and an imbalance being created

---

26 Ibid, at [36], per Wilson J.
27 [2008] EWCA Civ 1653, [2010] 1 FLR 910.
28 Ibid, at [16], per Thorpe LJ.
29 [2004] EWHC 2818 (Fam), [2006] 2 FLR 115.

that would warrant a substantial award of periodical payments in the future, did not outweigh the clear advantages that would flow from a clean break as sought by both parties'.[30]

Avoiding further litigation

12.20   An ancillary objection to a nominal order is the future litigation such an order invites in the form of variation applications. If one or more of the parties has pursued unmerited applications, is prone to repeated applications to the court or is unperturbed by legal costs, or if the litigation has taken a significant toll on either party, the court may be persuaded that the benefits of a nominal order are outweighed by the desirability of closing down routes to further acrimony and litigation. Although not strictly dealing with the removal of a nominal periodical payments order, in *H v H (Financial Provision)*, Thorpe J took the parties' mutual experience of the financial litigation into account as one factor[31] in his decision to replace a joint lives periodical payments order with a clean break:

> 'So is it appropriate in this case to apply the clean break? These parties have had a very unhappy experience of litigation in this Division over the course of the last 7 years, and it is highly undesirable that they should be exposed to the risk or temptation for further litigation.'[32]

Cohabitation and nominal periodical payments

12.21   The cohabitation of the payee, whether at the time of an original order or upon a variation application, often results in the payer challenging the logic and fairness of his continuing payments. In *Grey v Grey*[33] the payee wife accepted only during cross-examination that she was in a fixed and permanent relationship with another man. The husband argued that her cohabitation should lead generally to no substantive order for maintenance being made or, if the court had a continuing concern about the payee's ability to be or become self-sufficient, and had no recourse to the cohabitant, a nominal order should be made.[34] The Court of Appeal restated the critical difference between marriage and cohabitation; the former generating statutory claims for financial support upon divorce and the latter providing no such equivalent jurisdiction upon separation. Thus, if cohabitation exists, this *may* lead to the imposition of a nominal periodical payments order or an immediate clean break; but only if (1) the court investigates the level of financial contribution that the cohabitant ought to be making to the payee's finances and (2) an assessment of all the financial circumstances – including the economic consequences of cohabitation – leads, in fairness, to such a conclusion.

---

[30]   Ibid, at [141], per Charles J.
[31]   The others being (1) the manifest disparity in the capital positions of the parties and (2) the fact that the original order for £5,000 p a was, in a sense, irrelevant to the wife's needs.
[32]   [1993] 2 FLR 35, at 46.
[33]   [2010] 1 FLR 1764.
[34]   Mr Pointer QC appeared on behalf of the Husband in the Court of Appeal.

THE TRANSMUTABILITY OF A NOMINAL ORDER

12.22 Transmutability is the capacity for a nominal order to be converted by the court into an order for the payment of a substantive sum by way of periodical payments. Transmutability is achievable only upon an application to vary the nominal order, which is made pursuant to MCA 1973, s 31(7). The procedure and principles applicable to a variation application are dealt with in detail in Chapter 17. A transmuted order is then fully capable of a further supplemental order for capitalisation (by way of lump sum, property adjustment order or pension sharing order) and may be subject to a term for payment with an eventual clean break.[35]

Special rules do not apply

12.23 The transmutability of a nominal order is not dependent upon the applicant satisfying any particular or exceptional conditions that do not apply to a standard application to vary a periodical payments order. In *N v N*,[36] in which the wife sought to vary a nominal order in her favour and to capitalise the varied order, it was argued on behalf of the husband that the wife must satisfy a condition precedent or 'trigger' to entitle the court to exercise its discretion, without which the (transmutable) safety net of a nominal order should not be available to her. Charles J swiftly rejected this argument, as the statutory language of MCA 1973, s 31(7) demands a consideration of all the circumstances of the case, which 'precludes the condition precedent or trigger approach advanced on behalf of the husband. This is because such an approach would isolate a relevant factor or factors and would demand that it (or they) are assessed in isolation and without any balancing with, or overview taken account of, all relevant factors, whereas ... the statutory provisions demand such a balancing exercise and overview'.[37] The Court of Appeal eventually allowed the husband's appeal against the varied and capitalised order made by Charles J in *North v North*[38] but endorsed the judge's rejection of the need for the applicant to satisfy a condition precedent or trigger.

Transmuted orders and the limits of the safety net

12.24

> *North v North* provides a salutary and cautionary tale to the payer who seeks to rely on the long-stop or safety net of a nominal periodical payments order. The parties' marriage endured for 13 years during which time three children were born. At that stage the wife was just 37 years old. A final ancillary relief order was made by consent in 1981 providing the wife with nominal periodical payments on a joint lives basis. The husband →

---

[35] See Chapter 18
[36] *N v N* [2006] EWHC 3269 (Fam), [2007] 1 FCR 749, at [36], per Charles J.
[37] Ibid.
[38] [2007] EWCA Civ 760, [2008] 1 FLR 158. See chapter 18 for further detail about this case.

had remarried; however, he had continued to show generosity to his first wife by, *inter alia*, transferring ground rents to her to increase her annual income and paying her shares of an inheritance that he received. The wife made no real effort to secure employment. In 2000, she sold her home and other assets and emigrated to Australia. She rented an expensive property and invested the balance of her monies with relatively disastrous financial consequences. At the date of the variation application, the husband's financial position had improved significantly since the divorce and his net assets amounted to circa £5m. Despite the district judge making assessments adverse to the wife's credibility and condemning many of her financial decisions, he varied the nominal order on the basis of needs of £16,500 pa and ordered a capitalised payment of £202,000 on a clean break basis. In the Court of Appeal, Thorpe LJ highlighted the distinction between financial needs arising, on the one hand, out of blameworthy mismanagement or irresponsibility and, on the other, those caused by misfortune:

> '[32] Once within the territory of discretion, the court's overarching objective is a fair result. There are, of course, two faces to fairness. The order must be fair both to the applicant in need and to the respondent who must pay. In any application under s 31 the applicant's needs are likely to be the dominant or magnetic factor. But it does not follow that the respondent is inevitably responsible financially for any established needs. He is not an insurer against all hazards nor, when fairness is the measure, is he necessarily liable for needs created by the applicant's financial mismanagement, extravagance or irresponsibility. The prodigal former wife cannot hope to turn to a former husband in pursuit of a legal remedy, whatever may be her hope that he might, out of charity, come to her rescue.
>
> [33] Thus in the present case the wife's failure to utilise her earning potential, her subsequent abandonment of the secure financial future provided for her by the husband, her choice of a more hazardous future in Australia, together with her lifestyle choices in Australia, were all productive of needs which she had generated and for which the husband should not as a matter of fairness be held responsible in law. Even the applicant's subjective sense of fairness should surely not encourage her to expect that someone from whom she was divorced so many years ago should be required in law to compensate her for the financial consequences of ill-advised choices.
>
> [34] However, I would not necessarily, as the district judge appeared to do, put the wife's investment losses into the same category. While it can, of course, be said that stock exchange investments are less secure than ground rents, they are a more conventional form of capital investment and carry the prospect of capital appreciation to offset the erosion of inflation. Thus even had the wife been content to remain in Sheffield, she might reasonably have decided to exchange the ground rents for a stock exchange portfolio. The consequential loss seems to me more the outcome of hazard and therefore to be characterised as misfortune rather than mismanagement.'

Therefore, the payee must be astute to the reality that, although a nominal order may be a 'safety valve' or a 'long-stop', the extent to which the payer will be held financially responsible for the payee's needs is not boundless and may be limited by the origin of those needs. If the payee seeks a variation of a nominal order to cater for self-evident needs, the fact that those needs are self-created[39] may justify a refusal to order substantive periodical payments at all or at the level sought by the application. The identification of those needs that should, in fairness, be insured by the payer, and those that should not, will depend on the particular circumstances of each case.[40]

Transmutability and the reasoning behind the original nominal order

12.25 Although special rules do not apply to an application to vary a nominal periodical payments order, it is arguable that the court considering a variation application will look more critically at any information revealing the circumstances in which it was originally anticipated that the nominal order may be transmuted. Judgments in cases imposing nominal orders invariably include the judge's express view as to the reasons for the nominal order and the risks for which it is designed to cater. Similarly, recitals in a consent order may indicate, for example, the payee's agreement not to apply for variation save in cases of loss of income through ill-health or redundancy. In *Cornick v Cornick (No 3)*[41] Charles J commented that the reasoning behind the original order (of which a variation was sought) was a relevant circumstance of the case and, therefore, 'on an application to vary it can be assessed whether the purpose of the earlier order has been fulfilled and, if it has, this would be a relevant (and perhaps a decisive) factor in favour of refusing an extension or variation …'.[42] In *J (SR) v J (DW)* (see **12.15**), Hale J, in making the nominal order in favour of the wife, stated that 'if there is to be a nominal periodical payments order, any variation application would have to be based on very solid grounds to suggest that it had merit, and any legal adviser would be most ill-advised to pursue it without such a solid basis'.[43] Gibson LJ added that the substantial grounds would require material evidence of a sound improvement in the husband's finances.[44]

12.26 These judicial views or consensual recitals attached to the original nominal order are not binding on the court considering a variation application. However, they may have significant influence on the future exercise of the court's discretion, depending on all the other circumstances of the case.

---

[39] *North v North*, at [58].
[40] In the Court of Appeal, the wife's periodical payments were capped at £3,000 pa, to be capitalised at a sum less than £50,000.
[41] [2001] 2 FLR 1240.
[42] *McFarlane v McFarlane* [2009] EWHC 891 (Fam), [2009] 2 FLR 1322, at [104].
[43] [1999] 2 FLR 176, at 182.
[44] Ibid, at 183G.

POINTS OF PRACTICE AND THEORY

12.27

(1) Nominal orders may be used to cater for future financial uncertainties; the case-law has referred to such orders as providing a safety valve, last backstop or longstop for the payee's benefit.

(2) However, the 'safety valve' argument does not extend to the payer being an insurer for all hazards or financial needs created by the payee's financial mismanagement, extravagance or irresponsibility.

(3) Indicators in favour of a nominal order may include:
   (a) responsibility for children;
   (b) a developing or tentative earning capacity;
   (c) employment risks or health concerns;
   (d) unknown or unquantifiable liabilities; and
   (e) temporary reductions to the payer's income.

(4) Care should be taken not to unreasonably impose a nominal order in cases in which contentious future litigation is to be avoided.

(5) The question whether to impose a nominal order involves the court striking a balance between financial risks and opportunities and the prospect of the payee achieving financial independence.

(6) Consideration should be given at the time when making the nominal order to recording in writing the reasons for such an order.

(7) The nominal order, if transmuted into a substantive one, is thereafter open to the court's powers to capitalise the value to the payee on a *Duxbury* basis.

(8) Transmuting a nominal order into a substantive one does not require the satisfaction of any specific conditions.

CHAPTER 13

BANKRUPTCY AND PERIODICAL PAYMENTS

'The Family Division is concerned with the division of the cake, but the size of the cake is liable to be diminished by any order made by the Insolvency Court.'[1]

INTRODUCTION

13.1 The law governing bankruptcy is a topic of such significant breadth and specialisation that it is beyond anything but a superficial treatment in this Guide. There are two books dedicated to the consequences of potential or actual bankruptcy proceedings for cases of family finance, which are worthy of further reading.[2] This chapter summarises some key concepts and consequences related to the bankruptcy process before considering, in some isolation, the impact of bankruptcy on claims and existing orders for periodical payments.

CORE PRINCIPLES

The bankruptcy petition and discharge

13.2 A creditor's petition can be presented to the court on the basis of the debtor's debt of just £750.[3] Alternatively, the debtor himself may present his own petition (with no minimum debt required) on the sole basis that he is unable to pay his debts.[4]

13.3 The bankruptcy of an individual commences with the day on which the bankruptcy order is made.[5] The bankrupt is discharged from bankruptcy

---

[1] *Albert v Albert (A Bankrupt)* [1996] BPIR 232, at para 235, per Millett LJ.
[2] Barker, Calhaem, Middleton and Schofield, *Bankruptcy and Divorce: A Practical Guide for the Family Lawyer*, Jordan Publishing, 2010 and Miller, Gareth, *The Family, Creditors & Insolvency*, Oxford, 2004.
[3] The present bankruptcy level.
[4] IA 1986, s 282(1): a bankruptcy order can be annulled if, on the grounds existing at the time, the bankruptcy order ought not to have been made, or the bankruptcy debts and expenses have all been paid or secured to the satisfaction of the court; see IA 1986, s 282 and *Paulin v Paulin* [2009] BPIR 572, CA for an example of a wife's application to annul her husband's bankruptcy on the basis that it was procured as a tactic to frustrate her financial claims on divorce.
[5] IA 1986, s 278(1)(a).

generally after the period of one year from the date of the bankruptcy order[6] unless a longer period or the fulfilment of conditions is specified by the bankruptcy court. The discharge releases the bankrupt from all the bankruptcy debts,[7] although the process of distributing the bankrupt's estate to the satisfaction of creditors may well extend beyond the one-year period.

Application to annul a bankruptcy order

13.4 A spouse or ex-spouse, whose financial claims may be prejudiced by a bankruptcy order may, in certain circumstances, apply for a bankruptcy order to be annulled or suspended. The prospect of annulment is a potential remedy to a person claiming that the presentation of a bankruptcy petition is a tactic to frustrate legitimate financial claims on divorce.[8] The basis for such an application is Insolvency Act 1986 (IA 1986), s 282(1), which provides as follows:

> 'The court may annul a bankruptcy order if at any time it appears to the court –
>
> (a)   that, on any grounds existing at the time the order was made, the order ought not to have been made, or
> (b)   that, to the extent required by the rules, the bankruptcy debts and the expenses of the bankruptcy have all, since the making of the order, been either paid or secured for, or to, the satisfaction of the court.'

In the case of a debtor's own petition for bankruptcy, the only ground on which a bankruptcy petition may be presented to the court is the debtor's inability to pay his or her debts.[9] Therefore, the bankruptcy court may[10] annul a bankruptcy order if it concludes that, on the day of that order, the bankrupt was able to pay his debts: the inquiry is not into whether the bankrupt's liabilities exceeded his assets ('balance sheet insolvency') but into whether he could meet his liabilities when they were due ('commercial insolvency').[11]

13.5 Unfortunately, there is no specific statutory machinery that provides automatic notice to a spouse or ex-spouse of the other party's [to a marriage] bankruptcy.[12] Within this context, if a spouse considers applying to annul a bankruptcy order, the following considerations are relevant:

---

[6]   IA 1986, s 279(1).
[7]   IA 1986, s 281(1) and see further **13.27**.
[8]   See further *Paulin v Paulin* [2009] BPIR 572, CA.
[9]   IA 1986, s 272(1).
[10] The court retains a discretion whether to annul the order, as to which see further *Artman v Artman* [1996] BPIR 511, at 514, per Robert Walker J.
[11] See also *Ella v Ella* [2008] EWHC 3258 (Ch), [2009] BPIR 441 in which Sir Edward Evans-Lombe annulled a bankruptcy order made in relation to a husband: the annulment was ordered on the basis, *inter alia*, that the bankruptcy proceedings had been used by the husband and wife as a weapon in their family dispute (upon divorce): the proceedings, therefore, amounted to an abuse of process, and were dismissed.
[12] Note that the 'Statement of Affairs' submitted by the Debtor within bankruptcy proceedings does provide for the disclosure by him/her of any current or previous involvement in divorce proceedings.

(1) action should be taken immediately to apply to annul the order before the bankruptcy costs reduce or eliminate the assets otherwise available;

(2) if it appears to the bankruptcy court that divorce proceedings are ongoing, the court should consider a short adjournment to give notice of the bankruptcy petition to the affected spouse or partner;

(3) if an adjournment is not ordered, any bankruptcy order should be served immediately on the spouse or partner;[13]

(4) it may be preferable for the annulment application to be transferred to the Family Division, if a petition for divorce has been presented.[14]

The warnings for immediate action were outlined clearly by Jackson J in *Mekarska v Ruiz & Boyden*:

Bankruptcy and notice to third parties

[5] This case emphatically shows that where a person affected by a bankruptcy order, such as a spouse or civil partner, considers that the order should not have been made, or that there are ways of getting it set aside, they must act immediately to have it annulled or suspended before the costs of the bankruptcy eat into or, as here, eat up, the family assets.

[6] In the case of a creditor's petition, the Insolvency Rules 1986 (as amended) make appropriate provision for the proceedings to be served on the debtor. There is no equivalent provision in the case of a debtor's petition, even though third parties may be affected as profoundly as the debtor himself. On the other hand, there is nothing to prevent the court taking bespoke measures to meet the needs of individual cases.

[7] The standard statement of affairs accompanying a debtor's petition requires the applicant to disclose whether they have been involved in divorce proceedings at any time in the past 5 years. A positive reply should alert the court to the likelihood that a spouse or partner may have a legitimate interest in the outcome of the petition. I propose that the bankruptcy court →

---

13 See *Mekarska v Ruiz & Boyden* [2011] EWHC 913 (Fam), [2011] 2 FCR 608, [2011] 2 FLR 1351.

14 See further *Arif v Zar* [2012] EWCA Civ 986, at [21], per Patten LJ: ... judges and registrars sitting in bankruptcy need to be alive to the real possibility that husbands (or wives) may attempt to use the protection of a bankruptcy order as a shield against the claims of their spouses for ancillary relief. Where there is credible evidence of this, they should not be afraid to use the powers they have to order full disclosure and to require the attendance and cross-examination of witnesses where this is necessary in order properly and fairly to determine the annulment application. In such cases the more convenient course may well be to transfer the annulment application itself to be heard along side the ancillary relief application in the Family Division, where the evidence and issues are likely to be similar and costs can be saved by having a single hearing of both applications.' See also the subsequent decision of Norris J in *Arif v Anwar* [2013] EWHC 624 (Fam) in which Norris J presided over a 'preliminary oral discovery' hearing to determine the consequences on the husband's financial resources of various transactions alleged in relation to the former matrimonial home (and following the procedure for, and reasoning behind, such a hearing that was initially outlined by Coleridge J in *OS v DS* [2004] EWHC 2376 (Fam)).

> should employ a simple expedient in cases where it is apparent that divorce proceedings are ongoing. When faced with such a petition, and particularly the petition of a debtor who is not being pressed for payment, the court should consider whether to adjourn for a short time to allow notice to be given to a spouse or partner who may be affected. They may be in a good position to say whether the debtor is in fact insolvent or, if he is, to make proposals for debts to be cleared without the need for bankruptcy and all it entails.
>
> [8] Even if adjournment is for some reason not appropriate, the bankruptcy order should at least be served on the spouse or partner at the time that it is made, so that they are immediately aware of what is going on. In the present case, it is of concern that the wife only became aware of the husband's bankruptcy by chance 3 months after the event, by which time the bankruptcy process was already gathering momentum.

The general effects of bankruptcy

13.6   On making a bankruptcy order the Official Receiver assumes control over, and protects, the bankrupt's estate. It is 'a cardinal principle of bankruptcy law ... that the bankrupt should transfer what he owns to his trustee for division amongst his creditors'.[15] The trustee in bankruptcy (or Official Receiver if no trustee is appointed) is under a duty to collect and realise the bankrupt's estate and to distribute the same to his creditors in satisfaction of his debts. The estate of the bankrupt – which vests in the trustee – includes all property belonging to, or vested in, him at the commencement of the bankruptcy. Therefore, once the bankrupt's property has vested in the trustee, no order under the Matrimonial Causes Act 1973 can affect it at that time.[16] Additionally, unless there is a clear surplus of assets over liabilities in the bankruptcy, it will not be possible to make an order in financial remedy proceedings.[17] However, the definition of 'property' that vests by operation of law in the trustee[18] does not include (a) *property acquired by the bankrupt after the commencement of proceedings* and (b) *the bankrupt's income*, which remains otherwise available, perhaps to a limited extent, to meet the family's claims for financial provision.

Void payments

13.7   From the date of the presentation of the petition for bankruptcy to the date on which the bankrupt's estate vests in the trustee,[19] any payment made by the bankrupt is void unless made with the consent of the (Bankruptcy) Court or

---

[15]   Miller, Stephen Schaw, *Personal Insolvency Law and Practice*, 2008, para 14.1.
[16]   The court, of course, can look to future foreseeable surplus assets of a bankrupt (*Hellyer v Hellyer (Lump Sum Payments)* [1996] 2 FLR 579).
[17]   See *Hellyer v Hellyer (Lump Sum Payments)* [1996] 2 FLR 579.
[18]   IA 1986, s 436.
[19]   Which is the date on which the trustee's appointment takes effect or, in the case of the Official Receiver, the date on which he becomes trustee (see IA 1986, s 306).

later ratified by that court.[20] However, a payment received in good faith by a person prior to the bankruptcy order being made, for value[21] and without notice that the bankruptcy petition had been presented, is not void.[22] A periodical payment made after the presentation of a bankruptcy petition, therefore, is prima facie void. However, although there is no obvious decided authority on the point, it is suggested in Rayden & Jackson[23] that, in practice, in most cases the trustee in bankruptcy will not challenge such a payment, as the bankruptcy court is likely to subsequently ratify it.[24]

After-acquired property, income increases and the bankrupt's duty to give notice

13.8 After the commencement of the bankruptcy and prior to discharge,[25] the bankrupt may acquire property and the trustee may seek to claim that property[26] for the bankrupt's estate and ultimate satisfaction of his creditors. As after-acquired property of the bankrupt does not automatically vest in the trustee, the power of the trustee to make a claim by way of notice against such property is provided for in IA 1986, s 307.

13.9 Under risk of an order for contempt of court, the bankrupt is under a duty to give notice to the trustee of (1) any property acquired after the commencement of the bankruptcy and (2) any increase in his income.[27] Notice must be given by the bankrupt to the trustee within 21 days of the accrual of the property or the increase in income.[28]

13.10 If a third party receives a bankrupt's after-acquired property (which can include money) in good faith, for value and without notice of the bankruptcy, s/he is protected from a claim against that property brought by the trustee.[29]

13.11 Any after-acquired property that constitutes 'income', however, is excluded from any claim by the trustee in bankruptcy under IA 1986, s 307(5). Instead, the trustee may make a claim for an *income payments order* in relation to the bankrupt's income pursuant to IA 1986, s 310 (see **13.12–13.21**). An income payments order may have serious implications for an ex-spouse's claim for an order for periodical payments.

---

[20] IA 1986, s 284(1).
[21] Which, presumably, must follow the *Hill v Haines* [2008] Ch 412 approach that the 'value' arises out of the rights to property and money claims upon divorce conferred and recognised by the law.
[22] IA 1986, s 284(4)(a).
[23] *Rayden & Jackson on Divorce and Family Matters* (2005), para 19.21.
[24] *Hill v Haines* [2008] Ch 412.
[25] IA 1986, s 307(2)(c).
[26] Which is widely defined in IA 1986, s 436 as 'money, goods, things in action, land and every description of property wherever situated and also obligations and every description of interest, whether present or future or vested or contingent, arising out of, or incidental to, property'.
[27] IA 1986, s 333(2).
[28] Rule 6.200. This is the Insolvency Rules 1986.
[29] IA 1986, s 307(4)(a).

Income payments orders

13.12 The bankrupt's income received after the commencement of bankruptcy proceedings does not automatically vest in the trustee. Income, for the purpose of an income payments order, is defined as *every payment in the nature of income made to the bankrupt from time to time*, and includes payments from businesses, employment and pension schemes,[30] which can be in the form of a single (not necessarily a regular) payment.[31] Prior to the bankrupt's discharge, the trustee is entitled to make an application to the court for an order claiming so much of the bankrupt's income as is specified in an order ('an income payments order').[32] An income payments order[33] can remain in force for up to 3 years from the date on which the order is made[34] and requires the bankrupt to pay the amounts specified in the order to the trustee or may require the person making the payment to pay that amount directly to the trustee. The sums received by the trustee pursuant to an income payments order form part of the bankrupt's estate.[35]

LEGAL BASIS FOR AN INCOME PAYMENTS ORDER

Income payments orders (IA 1986, s 310)

13.13 Section 310 of the IA 1986 provides:

'(1) The court may ... make an order ("an income payments order") claiming for the bankrupt's estate so much of the income of the bankrupt during the period for which the order is in force as may be specified in the order.

(1A) An income payments order may be made only on an application instituted –

(a)   by the trustee, and
(b)   before the discharge of the bankrupt.

(2) The court shall not make an income payments order the effect of which would be to reduce the income of the bankrupt when taken together with any payments to which subsection (8) applies below what appears to the court to be necessary for meeting the reasonable domestic needs of the bankrupt and his family.

(3) An income payments order shall, in respect of any payment of income to which it is to apply, either –

(a)   require the bankrupt to pay the trustee an amount equal to so much of that payment as is claimed by the order, or

---

[30]   IA 1986, s 310(7).
[31]   *Supperstone v Lloyd's Names Working Party* [1999] BPIR 832.
[32]   IA 1986, s 310(1), (1A).
[33]   IA 1986 also provides for the making of an income payments agreement pursuant to IA 1986, s 310A, which carries the same force and enforcement provisions as an income payments order.
[34]   And, therefore, can persist beyond the bankrupt's discharge.
[35]   IA 1986, s 310(5).

(b)   require the person making the payment to pay so much of it as is so claimed to the trustee, instead of to the bankrupt.

(4) Where the court makes an income payments order it may, if it thinks fit, discharge or vary any attachment of earnings order that is for the time being in force to secure payments by the bankrupt.

(5) Sums received by the trustee under an income payments order form part of the bankrupt's estate.

(6) An income payments order must specify the period during which it is to have effect; and that period –

(a)   may end after the discharge of the bankrupt, but
(b)   may not end after the period of three years beginning with the date on which the order is made.

(6A) An income payments order may (subject to subsection (6)(b)) be varied on the application of the trustee or the bankrupt (whether before or after discharge).

(7) For the purposes of this section the income of the bankrupt comprises every payment in the nature of income which is from time to time made to him or to which he from time to time becomes entitled, including any payment in respect of the carrying on of any business or in respect of any office or employment and (despite anything in section 11 or 12 of the Welfare Reform and Pensions Act 1999) any payment under a pension scheme but excluding any payment to which subsection (8) applies.

(8) This subsection applies to –

(a)   payments by way of guaranteed minimum pension; and
(b)   payments giving effect to the bankrupt's protected rights as a member of a pension scheme.

(9) In this section, "guaranteed minimum pension" and "protected rights" have the same meaning as in the Pension Schemes Act 1993.'

THE LIMITS OF AN INCOME PAYMENTS ORDER AND ITS INTERACTION WITH AN ORDER FOR PERIODICAL PAYMENTS

Limits: reasonable domestic needs

13.14 The ability of the trustee in bankruptcy to claim a share of the bankrupt's income for a period of 3 years can clearly have a drastic effect on any proposed or existing periodical payments order made in financial remedy proceedings. There is an obvious tension between the applicant's claims for financial provision on divorce and the trustee's duty within the bankruptcy proceedings (see also **19.21–19.23**).

13.15 The extent to which an income payments order can reduce the bankrupt's income is prescribed by statute. The IA 1986 provides basic financial protection to the bankrupt (and, in this scenario, the assumed payer of a periodical payments order) such that an income payments order cannot have the effect of reducing the bankrupt's income to a level below which it 'appears to the court to be necessary for meeting the reasonable domestic needs of the bankrupt and his family'.[36]

13.16 The extent of the bankrupt's 'reasonable domestic needs' depends on the circumstances of each individual case. For example, the definition can include private school fees paid for the benefit of children of the family, if the particular facts justify a continued payment. *Re Rayatt (A Bankrupt)*[37] established the principle that school fees are *capable* of falling within the definition of 'reasonable domestic needs'. Whether such payments do so or not will depend on the evidence before the court as to the particular need to continue such payments in each individual case. In *Re Rayatt*, the evidence from the school's headmistress was that the youngest child, who was due to take subjects in her GCSE courses, would be 'very seriously disadvantaged' should she be moved from her fee-paying school. The Registrar had been wrong to disregard this evidence and to proceed on a general assumption that payments for private education could never, as a matter of general principle, fall within the compass of 'reasonable domestic needs'.[38]

Limits: defining the 'family'

13.17 An important limitation to the bankrupt's reasonable domestic needs is the IA 1986 definition of the 'family' of the bankrupt as 'the persons (if any) who are living with [the bankrupt] and are dependent on him'.[39] Therefore, for the payee of an existing or potential periodical payments order who is living *physically apart* from the bankrupt, her financial needs will not form part of the Insolvency Court's consideration of what may be the maximum amount to be abstracted from the bankrupt's income. The same applies to children of the bankrupt who are not 'living with him'. Consequently, an income payments order can significantly reduce the available income, against which a periodical payments order can be made; the reduction to the bankrupt's income can be made with little, if any, reference to the payee's needs for ongoing financial support.

Interaction

13.18 The bankruptcy court and the Family Court approach the bankrupt's income in very different ways and with dissimilar motives. The Family Court has its focus on satisfying the payee's (and perhaps children's) need for financial support in a manner which is fair and consistent with an assessment of all the

---

[36]   IA 1986, s 310(2).
[37]   [1998] BPIR 495.
[38]   See also *Scott v Davis* [2003] BPIR 1009 (Ch).
[39]   IA 1986, s 385.

circumstances of the case and the first consideration being given to the welfare of the children of the family. The bankruptcy court seeks to appropriate the income of the bankrupt for the benefit of the bankrupt's estate and is limited only to ensuring that the bankrupt can meet his and his family's reasonable domestic needs.

13.19 In *Albert v Albert*,[40] the husband was an undischarged bankrupt. His wife brought ancillary relief proceedings against him, which were heard after the bankruptcy order had been made. Wall J made an order at that hearing joining the trustee as a respondent to the ancillary relief proceedings, despite the wife acknowledging that she was not seeking a lump sum or capital award, but rather just an order for periodical payments from the husband. The Court of Appeal allowed the appeal against the order joining the trustee. The trustee had not decided, or even considered, at that stage whether to apply for an income payments order and the trustee had not identified any issue in the ancillary relief proceedings in which he had a legitimate interest. The Court of Appeal identified how the issues to be considered by the Family Division and the trustee differed:

> 'The Family Division is concerned to ascertain the amount of the bankrupt's income and to decide how much of that income should be made available to maintain the wife and child. In making its determination it must ascertain the amount of the bankrupt's income, as best it may, on the evidence put before it. But the amount of that income will be affected by any order that the Insolvency Court has made, or may subsequently make, which has the effect of diverting the bankrupt's income in or towards payment of his creditors. The Family Division is concerned with the division of the cake, but the size of the cake is liable to be diminished by any order made by the Insolvency Court.'[41]

The reality for the payee of a periodical payments order is that an income payments order, if made, may significantly reduce the quantum of her claim for maintenance. The Family Court has no capacity to challenge an income payments order and is, in effect, bound by the reduction to the payer's income for the period the order remains in force. The IA 1986 permits only the bankrupt or the trustee in bankruptcy to apply for a variation of an income payments order.[42]

Will the bankruptcy court allow for an order for periodical payments when quantifying an income payments order?

13.20 The 'reasonable domestic needs' of the bankrupt include those of his 'family' who live with him and are dependent on him.[43] The statutory wording appears to exclude payments to an ex-spouse, or for the benefit of children who are not living with the bankrupt. Therefore, the payee of a periodical payments

---

[40] [1996] BPIR 232.
[41] Ibid, at 235D, per Millett LJ.
[42] IA 1986, s 310(6A).
[43] IA 1986, s 385.

order should be warned that his/her maintenance payments may be ignored by the Insolvency Court in deference to meeting the bankrupt's creditors' claims.

13.21 The case of *Re X (A Bankrupt)*[44] provides some potential relief for the payee of a periodical payments order or the recipient of a child support assessment[45], albeit that the comments of Singer J are obiter and appear to have been expressed more in hope than real anticipation. In *Re X*, the mother brought proceedings pursuant to the Children Act 1989, Sch 1, against the father, who was made subject of a bankruptcy order. The mother had already applied to the CSA for a maintenance assessment; therefore, the court was concerned only with a lump sum and settlement of property application. Singer J made an (interim) order for the father to make a lump sum payment to the mother of £4,260 representing, in part, the historical budget-deficit of the mother and, in the other, 4 months of rental payments on her property. Singer J gave an additional judgment in which he justified his jurisdiction to make such an order and stated the following regarding the restrictive definition of 'family' in the IA 1986 and the impact on maintenance payments for a separated ex-spouse:

> '... Mr Allen (Counsel for Mother) was able to tell me, and Mr Howard (the trustee) did not dissent from the proposition, that as a matter of practice, a Child Support Agency assessment, for instance, would be taken into account in the exercise of the [Insolvency] Court's discretion when considering an income payments order made which would deprive the child of the benefit of such an assessment. It seems to me, therefore, as a matter of analogy, that the bankruptcy court, if such an application were made in a situation such as this, might well favourably view the liability under a lump sum order as falling within the category of reasonable demands upon the bankrupt's income.'[46]

It can fairly be assumed that the Family Court will do what it can to protect the position of the payee of a periodical payments order in cases of potential or actual bankruptcy of the payee. There may be an expectation that the Insolvency Court will do likewise, particularly where children are involved, but there is no guarantee. Muir Hunter on Personal Insolvency suggests that 'it is not the normal practice of the bankruptcy court to ignore the needs of the dependants not living with the bankrupt.[47]

PERIODICAL PAYMENTS AND BANKRUPTCY: EFFECT AND IMPACT

13.22 The payment of a periodical payments order is a personal liability of the bankrupt and, as such, is enforceable only against the personal earnings of the

---

[44] [1996] BPIR 494.
[45] By the Child Support Agency or other applicable body.
[46] [1996] BPIR 494, at 499D.
[47] Muir Hunter on Personal Insolvency, para 3-1008.

bankrupt. For that reason, a periodical payments order can be made and continue to have effect, notwithstanding the bankruptcy of the payer.[48]

13.23 If a bankruptcy order has been made *before* a financial remedy order has been made, the payee's claim for a periodical payments order remains live, save that the presentation of a petition for bankruptcy or the making of a bankruptcy order may result in a stay of the financial remedy proceedings.[49]

13.24 If a bankruptcy order is made *after* a periodical payments order has been made, the bankrupt remains liable for the maintenance payments throughout the duration of the bankruptcy order and after discharge. However, as noted above, an income payments agreement or order can be made which may limit the amount of income available to the payee, against which a claim for periodical payments can be made.[50]

The [potential] bankrupt in receipt of periodical payments

13.25 Any payments made to a potential or actual bankrupt pursuant to a periodical payments order in family proceedings fall within the definition of the bankrupt's 'income' within the IA 1986; they are thus vulnerable to an income payments order. If a *payee's* bankruptcy appears likely, there is little point in the court making any periodical payments order for a sum in excess of the very basic domestic needs of the payee: any deemed 'surplus' is liable to invasion by an income payments order and the payer will effectively be paying funds to meet the bankrupt's creditors' claims. In the event of the payee's bankruptcy, immediate consideration should be given to making an application to vary, terminate or suspend any periodical payments order.[51] The bankruptcy is a significant change in circumstances relevant to an application to vary a periodical payments order and provides a sound basis for – at the very least – suspending any order throughout the duration of any income payments order.

Periodical payments and the proof of debts

13.26 The bankruptcy scheme provides various protections for the bankrupt. Firstly, once a bankruptcy order is made, no creditor of the bankrupt in respect of a debt *provable* in the bankruptcy has any remedy against the bankrupt in relation to that debt nor can the creditor, before the bankrupt's discharge,[52] commence legal proceedings or any action against the bankrupt without leave of the court. Furthermore, upon the bankrupt's discharge from a bankruptcy order, he is released from all his *bankruptcy debts*. This raises the questions of

---

[48]   See further in Miller, *The Family, Creditors and Insolvency*, para 8.3.

[49]   IA 1986, s 285(1).

[50]   An income payments order can only be varied on the application of the bankrupt or the trustee (IA 1986, s 310(6A)).

[51]   Matrimonial Causes Act 1973 (MCA 1973), s 31(7) and see Chapter 17 on Variation.

[52]   Which generally occurs one year after the commencement of bankruptcy (for a bankruptcy commenced after 1 April 2004).

whether a liability to pay periodical payments in family proceedings is (a) a 'provable' debt and (b) a debt from which the bankrupt is released upon his discharge.

Provable debts

13.27 Generally, all claims by creditors are provable debts, but an important exception is made in the context of periodical payments and maintenance orders; the following debts are not provable in bankruptcy:[53]

(a) Any obligations (other than an obligation to pay a lump sum or to pay costs) arising under an order made in family proceedings.[54]
(b) Any obligation made under a maintenance assessment made under the Child Support Act 1991.

It is clear, therefore, that (arrears, and future payments, of) periodical payments orders are not provable debts within the Insolvency Rules.[55] The payee is unable to stand as a creditor in the bankruptcy and seek a share of the bankrupt's estate from the trustee to satisfy the debt. This puts the payee of a periodical payments order at a significant disadvantage in relation to the bankrupt's other commercial creditors.

Bankruptcy debts

13.28 Discharge is the *quid pro quo* for the bankrupt surrendering his estate to the trustee for the benefit of his creditors. Discharge releases the bankrupt from all 'bankruptcy debts', which include any liability existing at the commencement of the bankruptcy as well as any liability which may apply after the commencement of the bankruptcy by reason of an obligation incurred beforehand. However, by specific exception, discharge does not release the bankrupt from any bankruptcy debt which arises under an order made in family proceedings or under a maintenance assessment made under the Child Support Act 1991.[56] Therefore, the payee has a claim, after discharge, to payment of any liability for an unpaid periodical payments order, subject, of course, to the bankrupt's ability to pay.[57]

Discretionary release

13.29 The bankruptcy court does retain a discretion to release a bankrupt from a debt from which he is not automatically released on discharge from

---

[53] On a bankruptcy order made on or after 1 April 2005.
[54] Which includes financial remedy proceedings.
[55] See rule 13.3(2)(a) of the Insolvency Rules 1986 and despite a sub-committee recommending that such arrears should have been provable debts.
[56] IA 1986, s 281(5) (except to such extent and on such conditions as the court may direct).
[57] Leave must also be granted to pursue arrears of periodical payments that are more than 12 months old, see further MCA 1973, s 32(1).

bankruptcy.[58] This discretionary release applies to debts arising under an order in family proceedings. The ultimate balance to be struck by the court in deciding whether a bankrupt should be released from such a debt is between (a) the prejudice to the payee in releasing the debt if there is or might be some prospect of any part of the debt being paid in the future and (b) the potential prejudice to the payer's chance of building a viable future for himself and his dependents if the debt remains payable.[59]

13.30 For example, in *McRoberts v McRoberts*,[60] Hildyard J was concerned with the potential release of a husband from a debt to pay the wife the sum of £244,966 that remained outstanding from an original lump sum order [payable by instalments] of £450,000. Hildyard J accepted that the circumstances relevant to the exercise of the court's discretion may include those identified in the case of *Hayes v Hayes*[61] and made further comment, as follows:

'[23] ... various circumstances that would be relevant [include]:

(1)   any lapse of time between the date when the discharge [from bankruptcy] occurred and the date of any application for release, and the reasons for any delay;
(2)   the future earning capacity of the applicant, the possibility of some future income or capital receipt or windfall, the prospect accordingly of the obligation being fulfilled in whole or in part if not released, and in the round whether there is any good reason for maintaining the obligation;
(3)   the risk of the respondent to the application using the fact of the obligation (if not released) to harass the applicant, for example by seeking to diminish the applicant in the eyes of the community, or his future prospects, by reference to the stigma still relating to bankruptcy, or by bringing new and abusive bankruptcy proceedings calculated to restrict the applicant in building a new life;
(4)   the duration of time that has elapsed since the relevant obligation arose.

[24] I agree that all these factors should be taken into account, although I doubt that the last will often weigh materially in the balance. As it seems to me, the ultimate balance to be struck is between (a) the prejudice to the respondent/obligee in releasing the obligation if otherwise there would or might be some prospect of any part of the obligation being met and (b) the potential prejudice to the applicant's realistic chance of building a viable financial future for himself and those dependent upon him if the obligation remains in place.

[25] In striking that balance I consider that the burden is on the applicant [seeking release from the debt]; unless satisfied that the balance of prejudice favours its release, the obligation should remain in place: that follows from the fact that continuance is the default option, and from the rationale of excluding such obligations from automatic discharge ...

---

58   IA 1986, s 281(5)(b).
59   See further, *Hayes v Hayes* [2012] EWHC 1240 (Ch), [2012] BPIR 739 and *McRoberts v McRoberts* [2012] EWHC 2966 (Ch), [2013] BPIR 77, [2013] 1 WLR 1601.
60   [2013] 1 WLR 1601.
61   [2012] BPIR 739.

[26] I would add this, since it is of relevance in this particular case: it seems to me that the purposes for which the discretion is conferred do not include review of the merits or overall fairness of the underlying obligation. In my view, the purpose of the discretion is to enable the Court, in order better to achieve the objectives of discharging a bankrupt, to release an obligation if persuaded that the likelihood of its being satisfied is not such that its continuance is likely to [have] be of any benefit to the obligee, and that, conversely, its release is necessary in order to assist the obligor in building a viable financial future.

[27] Further, as it seems to me, in the case of an obligation imposed in matrimonial proceedings, that is so, even if circumstances have changed such as might suggest that the obligation might fairly be reviewed or modified. In my view, any such review or modification of the underlying obligation should be reserved to the matrimonial courts in the exercise of its jurisdiction to do so (if any) conferred by the Matrimonial Causes Acts; and if review or modification is not within their jurisdiction under those Acts, I do not consider that section 281(5) of the IA was intended or should be deployed to supply some additional basis of review.'

Bankruptcy and an order for secured periodical payments

13.31   The order for secured periodical payments takes effect upon decree absolute.[62] If payments are secured on identified property and for security to be provided by execution of a deed, this creates an immediate equitable charge over the property and the trustee in bankruptcy will take (the estate) subject to that charge.[63]

Miscellaneous trustee powers: obtaining information from an ex-spouse

13.32   The trustee in bankruptcy or Official Receiver has quite remarkable investigatory powers,[64] which extend to applying to the court for an order to summon a bankrupt's spouse or former spouse or civil partner or former civil partner to appear before the court. The summons may extend to providing information containing 'an account of ... dealings with the bankrupt or to produce any documents in his possession or under his control relating to the bankrupt or the bankrupt's dealings, affairs or property'.[65] Therefore, in cases in which it is deemed just and reasonable to seek further financial information from an ex-spouse of a bankrupt, the court can order the provision of such information to enable the trustee to carry out his functions of, inter alia, realising assets, investigating the conduct of the bankrupt and enabling a distribution to his/her creditors.[66]

---

[62]   MCA 1973, s 23(5).
[63]   Miller, *The Family, Creditors and Insolvency*, para 8.4.
[64]   As described in *Muir Hunter on Personal Insolvency*, para 3-2511.
[65]   IA 1986, s 366(1).
[66]   Muir Hunter, para 3-2511.

CHAPTER 14

THE IMPACT OF REMARRIAGE AND COHABITATION ON ORDERS FOR PERIODICAL PAYMENTS

'So I suggest that the court must nowadays ... factor into its analysis and calculations not only numerically but in principle the existence of a lengthy and settled period of cohabitation and the likelihood of its continuing indefinitely. To confine its consideration to the arithmetic only is a judicial fudge, mixing principle with practicality and producing potential unfairness and enhanced forensic uncertainty.'[1]

INTRODUCTION

14.1   There *is* life after divorce: for some, it is one lived happily alone; for others, it is truly fulfilled only by living with, or marrying, another person. Whereas divorce[2] marks the severance of social and contractual marital ties and permits re-marriage, an order for periodical payments perpetuates one party's financial dependence on the other despite (or in spite of) the divorce.

14.2   Whilst the marriage rate in the United Kingdom between 1998 and 2010 evidenced a steady decline,[3] cohabitation[4] has been the fastest growing family type.[5] Despite the growing popularity of cohabitation as a family model in the UK, the financial claims of a cohabitant – as opposed to an ex-spouse – upon separation are limited[6] and concentrate on the provision for children, rather than the adults, of the relationship.[7]

14.3   The process of mutual disclosure in financial remedy proceedings demands information as to each party's actual or intended remarriage or

---

[1]   *K v K (Periodical Payment: Cohabitation)* [2005] EWHC 2886 (Fam), [2006] 2 FLR 468.
[2]   Decree absolute.
[3]   From 10.3 to 8.8 persons marrying per 1,000 of the population of all ages.
[4]   Ie living with a partner but not married or in a civil partnership.
[5]   Office for National Statistics, Cohabitation Report 2012, available at http://www.ons.gov.uk/ons/rel/family-demography/families-and-households/2012/cohabitation-rpt.html.
[6]   In 2007 the Law Commission examined the financial consequences of the breakdown of a cohabiting relationship and undertook a consultation, available at http://lawcommission.justice.gov.uk/docs/lc307_Cohabitation_summary.pdf.
[7]   See Sch 1 to the Children Act 1989.

cohabitation. The fact of the cohabitation of one party[8] in financial remedy proceedings on divorce often generates costly and contentious arguments as to the principled fairness and quantification of a periodical payments order. This chapter outlines the criteria for determining cohabitation and assesses the impact of the payer *and* payee's remarriage and cohabitation on an order for periodical payments, both at the originating application stage and upon a subsequent variation application.[9]

COHABITATION: THE STATISTICS

14.4   The incidence of cohabitation is increasing, both pre- and post-divorce and for same- and opposite-sex couples. By 2012 almost 5 million people were cohabiting, which was double the figure in 1996. Between 1996 and 2012 the number of same sex cohabiting couples rose by 345%. The biggest percentage increase since 1996 of those cohabiting (both opposite and same sex) is in the age range of 65 and over and, of those cohabiting in the age group 65–74, over three-fifths had previously divorced or dissolved a civil partnership. The incidence of children in cohabiting families is also high: in 2012 39% of opposite sex cohabiting couples had a dependent child compared with 38% of married couples.[10] See the diagram overleaf.

---

[8]   If it can be proved.
[9]   Which is further dealt with in Chapter 17 on Variation.
[10]   See the Office for National Statistics at www.ons.gov.uk.

People Cohabiting in the UK, 1996–2012

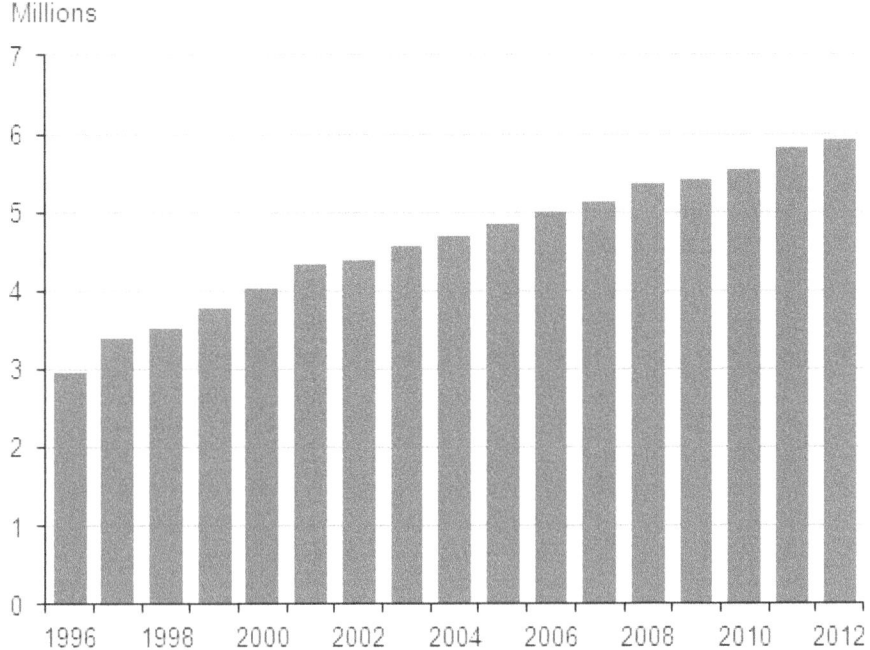

THE EFFECT OF REMARRIAGE ON AN ORDER FOR PERIODICAL PAYMENTS

Remarriage of the *payee* of a periodical payments order

14.5 The Matrimonial Causes Act 1973 (MCA 1973) applies a consistent and well-established policy of ending an ex-spouse's financial dependence upon his or her remarriage or formation of a civil partnership. First, the payee's remarriage automatically terminates any existing spousal periodical payment order.[11] Second, the remarriage of, or formation of a civil partnership by, a party to a marriage disentitles that party from applying for a financial provision order in relation to that prior marriage.[12] There is no discretion for the court to deviate from these statutory absolutes.

Remarriage of the *payer* of a periodical payments order

14.6

> The remarriage of the payer has no automatic effect on a periodical payments order. However, remarriage can impact upon the payer's ➡

---

[11]   MCA 1973, s 28(1).
[12]   MCA 1973, s 28(3).

available financial resources and ability to make payments, and it may form the basis of an application by the payer to vary the quantum or term of a periodical payments order.[13] The following broad provisions as to the impact of the payer's remarriage can be drawn from the case-law:

- the payer is *entitled* to order his or her life to balance responsibilities to an ex-spouse and a new married partner;
- the payer's financial needs, obligations and responsibilities[14] can legitimately include those relating to a new spouse, depending on the financial circumstances;
- no priority is given to the maintenance claims of an ex-spouse over the needs of a present spouse, or vice versa;
- the court will assess the financial position of the payer's new spouse (in terms of income and capital) and determine whether and, if so, to what extent, he or she is able to support the payer in meeting any financial obligations;
- upon remarriage, the complete financial position of the payer's household should be appraised by the court to determine the net effect on the payer of any periodical payments order.

The impact of the payer's subsequent marriage[15] on a periodical payments order (whether pursuant to an original order or upon an application for variation[16]) will depend on a full assessment of the circumstances of the case, including the new or increased financial responsibilities of the payer and the financial resources of the payer's new spouse.

A brief historical review: the payer's remarriage

14.7 Generally, the law has not been incognisant of the reality that new relationships often bring with them new financial responsibilities. When assessing the ability of a payer to meet any ongoing obligations to an ex-spouse, the court will have regard to the payer's *entitlement* to 'order his life in such a way as will hold in reasonable balance the responsibilities to his existing family, which he carries into his new life, as well as his proper aspirations for that new future'.[17] The court's choice of the word 'entitlement' in *Delaney v Delaney* is liberal and illuminating; however, achieving the appropriate balance is a much more difficult task than articulating it.

14.8 Despite there being no principle of prioritising an ex-spouse's claims over a present spouse's needs, the court will deprecate 'any notion that a former

---

[13] For more detail on applications to vary, see Chapter 17.

[14] MCA 1973, s 25(2)(b).

[15] Also classed as 'the second wife impact', as taken from my article, '*The Second Wife Impact and Ancillary Relief: Vaughan v Vaughan* [2010] EWCA Civ 349' published by Family Law Week, November 2010.

[16] MCA 1973, s 31(7), see further Chapter 17.

[17] *Delaney v Delaney* [1990] 2 FLR 457, CA, at 461, per Ward J.

husband and extant father may slough off the tight skin of familial responsibility and ... slither into and lose himself in the greener grass on the other side ...'.[18] The legitimate financial claims of the ex-spouse cannot, of course, be ignored. Equally, the payer's genuine and reasonable financial responsibilities towards a new spouse and family must also be taken into account. In the 1970 case of *Roberts v Roberts*,[19] the Divisional Court of Probate, Divorce and Admiralty held that no primacy could be given to the financial claims of a first wife[20] but rather that 'on general principle, a spouse must on marriage ... be presumed to take the other subject to all existing encumbrances, whether known or not – for example ... an obligation to support the wife or child of a dissolved marriage'.

14.9 In the later case *of Stockford v Stockford*[21] the Court of Appeal dismissed a first wife's claim for an increase in her periodical payments. The husband had subsequently remarried and the court at first instance was right to consider his financial needs as including obligations to support both his first wife *and* his second family. In *Slater v Slater*[22] the court considered the *reverse* impact of a second wife on a payer husband, ie to what extent the second wife's financial resources were relevant to the assessment of an existing periodical payments order. The Court of Appeal determined that the financial position of the second wife had relevance to the extent that, first, her resources could assist the husband to meet the financial obligations in respect of his 'new' family and, second, that the whole financial position of the new family should be brought into account when considering the net effect of any financial order arising out of the first marriage, on the husband. However, this assessment would not extend to 'treating the second wife's income as a joint fund together with the husband's income, out of which the first wife [would be] entitled to draw her entitlement ...'.[23]

The modern approach: the payer's remarriage

14.10 The Court of Appeal case of *Vaughan v Vaughan*[24] is the leading authority regarding the impact of remarriage on financial claims and orders arising out of a prior marriage.

14.11 In *Vaughan v Vaughan* the Court of Appeal was faced with a first wife's appeal against a decision discharging a periodical payments order for £15,175 pa in her favour (in addition to an annual payment of £12,000 pursuant to a deed of separation dating back to 1981). At the time of the appeal, the wife was 66 and the husband 71 years old. In 1985 the husband had remarried. His second wife was some 15 years his junior. He was previously a

---

[18] Ibid, at p 461E; see also *Furniss v Furniss* (1982) 3 FLR 46.
[19] [1970] P 1, [1968] 3 WLR 1181.
[20] As it was a wife in that case.
[21] (1982) 3 FLR 58.
[22] (1982) 3 FLR 364.
[23] Ibid, at 369F, per Sir John Arnold P.
[24] [2010] EWCA Civ 349, [2010] 2 FLR 242.

successful barrister but suffering from ill health. By the time of the appeal, the first wife had a home with a net value of just over £1m, a valuable antique desk worth £300,000 and a pension income of £5,000 gross pa. The first wife's pleaded income needs were £62,000 per annum, a sum which was reduced by the trial judge to circa £50,000. Conversely, the husband had a home in North Kensington with a net value of £3,628,000, a property in Wales and various other smaller investments. The husband also had a private pension fund with a value of £2,388,000 before commutation. Given the husband's ailing health and his second wife's relative youth, he was electing to exercise his right under the scheme to have an annuity paid to himself and his second wife during their joint lives and, upon death, at the same rate to the survivor (approximately £100,000 gross pa). The judge at first instance ascribed half of the husband's gross annual pension income (approx £50,000) to the second wife, thereby deducting 50% of this income from the husband's available income. The judge at trial was keen to highlight the second wife's positive and contributory influence on the husband's financial position, and assessed the value of her contribution as follows:

> 'I consider that the second wife has an entitlement to a substantial proportion of [the assets built up during the second marriage]. In view of the length of the [second] marriage and her contribution to the welfare of the family, particularly, being a mother of two children, I consider that she must be entitled to at least 50% of those assets.'

14.12

The Court of Appeal criticised the first instance judge's appraisal of the second wife's entirely theoretical financial claims against the husband (as neither party intended to divorce). The judge had elevated the second wife's potential 'claim' to the realms of an existing proprietary entitlement, to the extent that he treated it as eliminating the extant claims of the first wife. It was illogical and inconsistent to attribute one half of the husband's pension income to the second wife, despite her contributions to the marriage; that would be akin to attributing half of the husband's earnings during the marriage to her. The trial judge, therefore, had fallen into error in a number of respects. First, he assessed the first wife's claim as if it competed with that of the second wife, despite the second marriage continuing happily. Second, he trespassed beyond the real into the hypothetical, and, in so doing, gave priority to the second wife's supposed claims, contravening the standard that the second wife took the husband along with all his 'encumbrances', including the ongoing financial obligations to his first wife. Instead, 'all the judge should have done was to take into account the husband's obligation to maintain the second wife to the extent to which she could not maintain herself out of the income already judicially attributed to her'.[25] *Vaughan v Vaughan*, therefore, provides clear guidance that the court must strike a →

---

[25] *Vaughan v Vaughan*, at [39], per Wilson LJ.

balance between the 'shackles' of prior obligations and the freedom to invest in a new relationship. The remarriage of the payer of a periodical payment order is relevant in assessing:

(a) the extent to which the second spouse's financial position assists or enables the payer to meet all his or her financial obligations (past and present); and

(b) the ultimate net effect of any order for periodical payments on the payer's financial position, taking account of the reality of the payer's circumstances and obligations within a second family unit.

COHABITATION

14.13 Cohabitation of the payer or payee of a periodical payments order has no automatic effect on that order but it *can* influence both the *quantum and term* of an order in three principal ways. First, it may be relevant at the stage of making an original order as to how much and for how long maintenance should be paid. Second, it can provide an explicit reason within a financial order for terminating periodical payments. Third, cohabitation can instigate or affect an application to vary an order for periodical payments. Therefore, the impact of cohabitation on an existing or contemplated periodical payments order requires a staged assessment, as follows:

(1) What is cohabitation, how is it defined and how is it proved?

(2) What are the financial consequences of cohabitation on the payer/payee?

(3) To what extent should cohabitation and its financial consequences affect a periodical payments order?

Stage 1: defining and proving cohabitation: the difficulty with labels

14.14 Cohabitation is not statutorily defined for the purpose of the MCA 1973.[26] It is perhaps unfortunate that the word is used in financial orders, as any definition is imprecise and controversial. However, 'cohabitation' is the term used in the Form E financial statement and in many orders drafted by lawyers and approved by the court. Therefore, the court must generally approach the issue on a binary basis; either cohabitation is proved or not.

14.15 The oft-quoted and classic expression of the eight factors relevant to the determination of whether two people are cohabiting originates from the case of *Kimber v Kimber*.[27] In *Kimber v Kimber*, a periodical payments order was

---

[26] The Family Law Act 1996 provides a definition of 'cohabitants' in s 62(1)(a) as 'two persons who are neither married to each other nor civil partners of each other but are living together as husband and wife or as if they were civil partners'.

[27] [2000] 1 FLR 383.

drafted to terminate the wife's maintenance when she 'cohabit[ed] with another person for more than 3 months'. The applicable but non-exhaustive list of factors identified by the court and referable to the particular facts in *Kimber* included:

(1)   living under the same roof (save for times of illness, holidays, work and other periodic absences spent apart);

(2)   a sharing of tasks and duties;

(3)   stability and a degree of permanence in the relationship;

(4)   the way in which finances are handled and managed in the relationship;

(5)   the existence of a sexual relationship;

(6)   the presence of, or relationship with, children (of the relationship or of a prior marriage or relationship);[28]

(7)   the expressed intentions and motivations of the individuals involved;

(8)   the 'opinion of the reasonable person with normal perceptions' (of the relationship and its status).

However, these eight factors do not constitute a definitive checklist by any means. There is no box-ticking set of criteria for assessing whether a cohabiting relationship exists between two people.[29] Ultimately, the overall test must be both subjective and objective as the court will take into consideration the intentions and motivations of the individuals involved: 'the task of the judge is to stand back, to look at the totality of the evidence and to come to a common sense decision'.[30] To the eight factors listed above two more can be added:

(9)   evidence of mutual commitment (which is a very important factor in the context of financial responsibility for another's household);[31] and

(10) the length of the (cohabiting) relationship.

Indeed, a relationship may fall short of 'true' cohabitation if two parties maintain two separate households, yet it may be obvious from an appreciation of all other circumstances that the relationship is a 'committed partnership'[32] in which the two people are indeed a couple. Ultimately, the factual analysis may determine that such individuals are 'cohabiting' despite maintaining two separate residences.[33]

14.16   The task for the practitioner, therefore, is not to be wedded to the label of 'cohabitation' or to checklists of factors, but rather to survey the whole

---

[28]   Relevant in *Kimber v Kimber* was the wife's partner's involvement in the school, pastoral and extra-curricular activities of the child of the wife's previous marriage.

[29]   *Grey v Grey* [2009] EWCA Civ 1424, [2010] 1 FLR 1764.

[30]   *X v Y (Maintenance Arrears: Cohabitation)* [2012] EWHC 1 (Fam), at [84], per HHJ Bellamy (appeal brought unsuccessfully on procedural grounds in *Re H-J (Children)* [2012] EWCA Civ 1080).

[31]   *Re Grey (No 3)* [2010] EWHC 1055 (Fam), [2010] 2 FLR 1848, at [22], per Singer J.

[32]   Ibid, at [47].

[33]   For example, see *Re Grey (No 3)*.

course of the relationship, as alleged, and to query the duration of it and the level of commitment demonstrated by the evidence, financial and otherwise. Actual cohabitation in *one home* as a family will most likely be decisive. It is not, however, definitive. The vagaries and idiosyncrasies of relationships do not easily lend themselves to a simple pigeon-holing analysis, as Singer J commented in *Re Grey (No 3)*:[34]

> '[22] Certainly relationships, like Rome, are not built in a day. Maybe more than many human pursuits and endeavours they may embark tentatively or at full tilt. They may stop and they may start, they may founder and they may rekindle. Over days, months or years they may wax and wane. They take innumerable forms and no one size fits all. And the language we use to describe relationships and those in them is also unsatisfactory, lacking in precision, frequently ambiguous, signifying one thing or different things to one pair of partners or cohabitants and another, and often quite different things again to those who observe and attempt to categorise them. Many ingredients will fall for consideration into the mixing bowl of objective relationship appraisal, but I regard mutual commitment as a very important indicator in the context of financial responsibility for another's household.'

Proving cohabitation

14.17 It can be notoriously risky and costly to embark on a process of seeking to prove cohabitation in financial remedy proceedings. The following sources of evidence may assist but the list is non-exhaustive and evidence should be directed, if possible, to the ten factors identified above:

(a) the client's own observations;

(b) witness statements from neighbours, friends or work colleagues as to the relationship, attendance at events or school gatherings, parents' evenings etc;

(c) longer-term observations of a party's home or work by an enquiry agent;[35]

(d) joint financial transactions, eg purchasing a home or car or entering into joint financial commitments;

(e) bank statements exhibiting a sharing or exchange of funds or joint contributions to expenditure;[36]

(f) postal correspondence addressed to both parties jointly;

(g) claims for benefits or tax credits that incorporate joint incomes or resources;

(h) mobile phone records.

---

[34] [2010] 2 FLR 1848, at [22].
[35] Subject to the court's control over the admission of such evidence.
[36] An inspection appointment may be sought in relation to the financial information of a third party alleged to be cohabiting with a payer or payee of a periodical payments order.

Cohabitation: opportunities for disclosure, interrogation and adverse inferences

14.18   The fact – and financial effect – of cohabitation or of a divorcing party's intention to [re]marry requires disclosure at various stages in the process of mutual information exchange. Non-disclosure of cohabitation or the prospects of remarriage may lead to a subsequent application to set aside an order.[37]

14.19

- *Form E*: the financial statement requires a party to indicate whether that party has remarried, is living with a partner or has an intention to live with a new partner within 6 months (from the date of swearing the Form E). If a party has remarried (or formed a civil partnership) – or intends to do so – or is living with another person – or intends to do so – that party should disclose the other person's income, assets and liabilities, as far as they are known.

- *Questionnaire*:[38] the questionnaire is the opportunity to (a) seek confirmation that there has been no change to a party's relationship status and (b) request disclosure and evidence from a party as to a partner's financial circumstances.

- *Statement of Issues*: if the issue of a party's cohabitation is live within proceedings, both as to the fact of cohabitation and its impact on the court's discretionary exercise, this should be highlighted within the statement of issues.[39]

- *Schedule of Deficiencies*: if questions as to a party's alleged cohabitation are unanswered or answered with insufficient detail or precision, a Schedule of Deficiencies may be served. This document can also highlight a party's refusal to provide information or disclosure, which may support a request (a) for an inspection appointment (see below) or (b) that the court draw adverse inferences against that party in light of a refusal to provide the requested disclosure.

- *Witness statements*: a party may apply to file and serve narrative statements from neighbours or family members, for example, who are able to provide the court with evidence in support – or denial – of an allegation of cohabitation.

- *Admission of agent evidence*: inquiry agent evidence, which may have involved surveillance, tracking, observation, photographs and video material to establish the frequency of a partner's visits or overnight stays,

---

[37]   See *Livesey (Formerly Jenkins) v Jenkins* [1985] FLR 813 in which the wife's engagement to marry was the non-disclosed fact justifying the order being set aside and, for a modern approach to the test, *W v C (Financial Remedies: Appeal: Non-Disclosure)* [2012] EWHC 3788 (Fam), [2013] 2 FLR 115.

[38]   FPR 2010, r 9.14(5)(c).

[39]   FPR 2010, r 9.14(5)(a): the questionnaire must set out any further information or documents requested *by reference to* the statement of issues.

is likely to amount to expert evidence, for which permission is required from the court to adduce the same within the proceedings.

- *Third-party interrogation of the partner/cohabitant*: in certain circumstances, the court can order a third party (partner or cohabitant) to attend court for the purposes of an inspection appointment. The application for such an appointment is made pursuant to Part 18 of the Family Procedure Rules 2010 (FPR 2010) and provides for a third party to attend a hearing with specified documents for 'inspection'. However, a cautionary approach must be taken to applying for an inspection appointment: demanding financial disclosure from a third party is a personal infringement which must be balanced carefully against the need for, and relevance of, the disclosure sought. In *Frary v Frary*[40] the Court of Appeal highlighted that it 'will only be in the rarest cases where it will be possible to say that full information about the property and income of the third party, whether the third party is a new spouse, a new mistress, a new lover, a rich uncle ... will be relevant to the issue which the court has to consider under section 25 of the MCA [1973]'.

  However, *Frary v Frary* was decided in 1993 and, in light of the later decision in *Grey v Grey*, it is arguable that the need to establish a partner's financial position is heightened, as the court should enquire as to what contribution the partner ought to make to the household outgoings and budget.

  In the more recent case of *M v M (Third Party Subpoena: Financial Conduct)*[41] Peter Hughes QC provided some further guidance as to the considerations relevant to determining whether a third party should be ordered to provide evidence:[42]

  > '[116] ...
  >
  > (a) How important is the information to the issues in the proceedings?
  > (b) Has the applicant taken appropriate steps to obtain the information within the proceedings and to enforce orders for disclosure, without success, before applying for third party disclosure?
  > (c) Would it be sufficient for the court to draw inferences adverse to the respondent from the refusal to supply the information and comply with court orders?
  > (d) What is the relationship between the respondent and the third party?
  > (e) If disclosure is necessary and proportionate, do the documents contain private information that can be protected by editing?'

- *Drawing adverse inferences*: if a party is ordered to provide information as to a partner's financial circumstances or financial contribution and fails to

---

[40] [1993] 2 FLR 696: and for a successful application for an inspection appointment (but not in relation to a cohabitant's financial circumstances) see *D v D* [1995] 2 FLR 497.

[41] [2006] 2 FLR 1253.

[42] The order in this case was for a subpoena duces tecum (High Court) or witness summons (county court equivalent), although the considerations referred to are surely applicable to an inspection appointment application, which is also for the purpose of extracting disclosure from a third party.

do so, that party is at risk of adverse inferences being drawn by the court[43] as to the finances, and potential financial contributions, of a third party.

Stage 2: the financial consequences of cohabitation on the payer/payee

14.20 The cohabitation of the payer or payee may enhance or diminish that person's financial circumstances. A new partner may have capital or income that they are willing to share or they may strictly maintain individual finances; they may come to the relationship with children, debt, financial security or impecuniosity.

Stage 3: the extent to which cohabitation and its financial consequences may affect an order for periodical payments

14.21 There is no rule or principle that a payee's cohabitation justifies a clean break (ie no order for periodical payments), a dismissal of an existing periodical payments order or a reduction of a substantive periodical payments order to one of nominal payments.[44] Cohabitation is not to be equated with [re]marriage, despite the social trend towards engaging in such relationships and even in circumstances where the cohabitation is longer in duration than many marriages.[45] However, if cohabitation is admitted or found as a fact by the judge, the assessment thereafter is two-staged and is taken from the leading case of *Grey v Grey*:[46]

(1) What contribution is the payee's cohabitant making to the payee's budget or household expenditure?

(2) If the cohabitant is not making any such contribution (or an insufficient one), what contribution, in all the circumstances, does the court consider the partner *ought* to make (to the payee's budget or household expenditure)?[47]

The assessment requires information as to the payee's partner's income and financial resources which, if not provided voluntarily, places the payee at risk of the court drawing adverse inferences.[48] Even if the payee and the partner have carefully organised their financial affairs to remain ostensibly and financially independent of one another, the court must consider what contribution *ought* fairly to be made, particularly in light of the length of the relationship and the mutuality of other commitments between the partners. The longer and more settled the cohabitation, the stronger may be the argument that considerable

---

[43] See *Grey v Grey* [2009] EWCA Civ 1424, [2010] 1 FLR 1764.
[44] For more detail on nominal periodical payments orders, refer to Chapter 12.
[45] *Fleming v Fleming* [2004] 1 FLR 667.
[46] [2009] EWCA Civ 1424, [2010] 1 FLR 1764; which approved the law as stated in *Atkinson v Atkinson* [1988] Fam 93, [1988] 2 WLR 204, [1988] 2 FLR 353, CA and *Fleming v Fleming*.
[47] See *Grey v Grey* [2009] EWCA Civ 1424, [2010] 1 FLR 1764.
[48] See *Fleming v Fleming*.

weight should be attached to the fact of cohabitation in quantifying – and expressing a term for – periodical payments for an ex-spouse.[49]

14.22 The case of *Grey v Grey* witnessed the Court of Appeal returning the bitterly-fought battles of Lara and Richard Grey to Singer J's court. The husband's appeal had succeeded to the extent that (1) the judge's original conclusions as to the wife's relationship with Mr Thompson were inadequate and imprecise, and (2), as a result of their being a 'couple', the financial contribution that Mr Thompson ought to have made to the wife's finances should have been assessed within any final award as to spousal periodical payments.

14.23 The extent to which cohabitation may impact on an order was also considered by Coleridge J in *K v K (Periodical Payment: Cohabitation).*[50] In *K v K* the court dealt with an application to vary a periodical payments order in light of the payee wife's settled cohabitation for 3 years with a partner in circumstances in which the two people had fully involved themselves in each other's financial affairs. Coleridge J rejected the husband's argument that the wife's cohabitation should result in a nominal order. However, the judge was highly critical of the perceived unfairness of a payer providing financial support to a payee who was living in a settled relationship with A.N. Other:

> '[88] I do not shrink from saying that, in my judgment, nowadays the man on the Clapham omnibus (perhaps more likely now to be found on the crowded underground train) regards it as wholly anomalous and unfair for a cohabiting ex-wife in the circumstances of this wife to continue to receive income provision from a former husband indefinitely, perhaps for the rest of her life or until she chooses to remarry. If cohabitation is to be a social norm surely financial independence from a previous partner, whether married or not must go with it?'

Nevertheless, Coleridge J refused to reduce the wife's periodical payments order to a nominal sum. In light of the particular circumstances, the final order capitalised the wife's future periodical payments and reduced the lump sum payable by 20% to reflect the cohabitation factors. In so doing, Coleridge J did not apply any particular arithmetical formula to effect a reduction to the wife's future financial provision and instead factored into the analysis the reality of cohabitation and the likelihood of its continuing indefinitely 'not only numerically but in principle'.[51]

14.24 The law, therefore, remains wholly discretionary in relation to the impact of cohabitation on a periodical payments order. The longer the cohabitation of the payee, the more entwined the cohabitant's finances, the greater the mutual commitment, the stronger the ties and the more evident and normalised the sharing of resources, then the more powerful the argument for such cohabitation to reduce or even terminate a periodical payments order.

---

[49] See *Fleming v Fleming* at [9], per Thorpe LJ.
[50] [2005] EWHC 2886 (Fam), [2006] 2 FLR 468.
[51] *K v K*, at [91].

Orders that terminate a periodical payments order on the payee's cohabitation

14.25 It is permissible, fair, and indeed required, in certain cases to limit the term of a periodical payments order to the payee's cohabitation with another person. This can be done in a consent order or by judicial imposition by designating cohabitation as one of the specified events leading to the cessation of payments. The limit can be expressed in an order in a variety of ways, and by including or excluding criteria or time constraints, for example, 'to the [payee's] cohabitation with another person as husband and wife' or 'to the [payee's] cohabitation with another person for a continuous period of three/six months' or 'to the [payee's] cohabitation with another person' or 'to the payee's continuous cohabitation with another person ...'.

14.26 The legal basis for such an order is MCA 1973, s 23(1)(a), which provides that the court may make an order 'that either party to the marriage shall make to the other such periodical payments, for such term, as may be specified in the order'. In *K v K (Periodical Payment: Cohabitation)* Coleridge J offered his opinion in support of introducing 'cohabitation clauses' in orders for periodical payments:

> 'I see no reason why nowadays courts should not order a termination on 'cohabitation' after a certain period. Section 28(b) of the Matrimonial Causes Act 1973 by no means prohibits it and it would at least provide certainty for the parties. It would, I consider, better reflect modern mores and social behaviour.'[52]

The circumstances in which such a limit will be [in]appropriate are many and varied. Factors that may influence the court to accept or impose such a term will include the length of the marriage, the extent of the financial dependence, the presence of children and the existence of a fledgling relationship of the payee (that does not yet constitute cohabitation).

---

[52]   Ibid, at [104](a).

POINTS OF PRACTICE AND THEORY

14.27

(1) The payer is *entitled* to order his or her life to balance responsibilities to an ex-spouse and a new married partner; the payer's needs can legitimately include those relating to a new spouse, depending on the financial circumstances; no priority is given to the maintenance claims of an ex-spouse over the needs of a present spouse, or vice versa; the court will assess the financial position of the payer's new spouse (in terms of income and capital) and determine whether and, if so, to what extent, he or she is able to support the payer in meeting any financial obligations; upon remarriage, the complete financial position of the payer's household should be appraised by the court to determine the net effect on the payer of any periodical payments order.

(2) The remarriage of the payer of a periodical payment order is relevant in assessing:
   (a) the extent to which the second spouse's financial position assists or enables the payer to meet all his or her financial obligations (past and present); and
   (b) the ultimate net effect of any order for periodical payments on the payer's financial position, taking account of the reality of the payer's circumstances and obligations within a second family unit.

(3) If cohabitation is admitted or found as a fact by the judge, the assessment thereafter is two-staged and is taken from the leading case of *Grey v Grey*:
   (a) What contribution is the payee's cohabitant making to the payee's budget or household expenditure?
   (b) If the cohabitant is not making any such contribution (or an insufficient one), what contribution, in all the circumstances, does the court consider the partner *ought* to make (to the payee's budget or household expenditure)?

CHAPTER 15

PERIODICAL PAYMENTS AND *DUXBURY* CALCULATIONS: THE FABLE OF THE 'TOOL' AND THE 'PARADOX'

'... *the exercise upon which the court has to embark is one which is inherently unscientific and in which expert evidence can be of only the most limited assistance. Average life expectations can be actuarially ascertained, but to assess the probabilities of future political, economic and fiscal policies requires not the services of an actuary or an accountant but those of a prophet.*'[1]

WHAT IS A *DUXBURY* CALCULATION?

15.1   A *Duxbury* calculation is prophetic actuarial alchemy: it provides a lump sum figure ('the *Duxbury* fund') that, if suitably invested and amortised, represents the *present* value of a *future* income stream: the *Duxbury* fund, therefore, is broadly intended to provide a capital value of the payee's right to a periodical payments stream that it replaces.[2] The calculation's formula, however, relies on a number of assumptions, as will be seen below, which makes it impossible for a *Duxbury* fund to provide any *guarantee* of a payee's future income stream or spending power.

15.2   The *Duxbury* calculation relies on *Duxbury* tables (a selection of multipliers[3]), which provide the basis for the actuarial calculation. The *Duxbury* calculation therefore, is a paper-based exercise,[4] which avoids the significant costs and delay associated with the instruction of financial experts.[5] These tables are available in various formats; see for example, At A Glance, The Financial Tables within *Duckworth's Matrimonial Property* and Finance and the 'Capitalise' computer programme.

---

[1]   Lord Oliver of Aylmerton in *Hodgson v Trapp* [1988] 3 WLR 1281.
[2]   Lewis Marks QC, '*An Alternative View of Duxbury: A Reply*', June [2010] Fam Law 614.
[3]   Which are used in conjunction with a multiplicand representing the annual income figure.
[4]   Or computerised, particularly if using the Capitalise programme.
[5]   *F v F (Duxbury Calculation: Real Rate of Return)* [1996] 1 FLR 833.

WHEN IS A *DUXBURY* CALCULATION USEFUL?[6]

15.3 A *Duxbury* calculation can assist at any stage of proceedings when information as to the present capitalised value[7] of an income stream is required, for example:

(a) effecting a [partial or total] clean break by payment of a lump sum to a payee in lieu of a periodical payments order (whether on a joint lives or term basis);[8]

(b) effecting a clean break by payment of a lump sum to a payee upon an application to vary/capitalise a periodical payments order;[9]

(c) undertaking a reverse calculation[10] to gauge the income a payee may generate from a lump sum payment, or from other capital retained by the payee;

(d) undertaking a reverse calculation (as above at (c)) to verify that an equal (or other) sharing of capital resources will also meet a payee's future income needs;

(e) calculating the appropriate level of capital security required to impose an order for secured periodical payments.[11]

THE FUNDAMENTAL ASSUMPTIONS WITHIN A *DUXBURY* CALCULATION

15.4 A *Duxbury* calculation is an actuarial formula that relies on a number of fiscal and **physical** assumptions. These assumptions are important in (1) understanding the limitations of the calculated figure and (2) presenting arguments that a 'strict'[12] *Duxbury* calculation is [in]appropriate in any given case.

Fiscal assumptions

15.5

(a) *The lump sum is amortised*: the calculation assumes that the payee's income from the capital sum will be generated both through investment

---

[6] The Duxbury method, despite criticism, has been described and endorsed as the 'industry standard' in financial remedy proceedings (see, for example, *F v F (Duxbury Calculation: Real Rate of Return)* [1996] 1 FLR 833 and *Dharamshi v Dharamshi* [2001] 1 FLR 736).

[7] Amortised, and suitably invested.

[8] Particularly in big money cases: for example, Counsel in *AH v PH* [2013] EWHC 3873 (Fam), at [82] could not draw attention to any significant big money case in which the wife's maintenance had not been capitalised!

[9] Pursuant to MCA 1973, s 31(7B)(a); and see further, Chapter 18.

[10] Ie taken from the starting point of a lump sum, eg £300,000, to calculate the income that can be generated from the investment and amortisation of that sum over a given period of time.

[11] See further, Chapter 16.

[12] Ie the actual capital value provided by a *Duxbury* calculation without any amendment (based usually on the payee's age, personal income, pension age and income needs).

(of the capital) and from a gradual exhaustion of the fund, such that at the end of the term assumed for payments, the capital fund will be nil.

(b)   *Life expectancy*: the calculation relies upon tables that provide projected life expectancy figures for males and females: the life expectancy figures provide the basis for a calculation predicated on the payee receiving an income stream for the duration of his or her life;

(c)   *Inflation*: The At A Glance *Duxbury* tables assume consistent inflation at 3% pa.

(d)   *Rate of return/capital growth*: the payee receives a capital lump sum in lieu of future periodical payments, and it is assumed that s/he will invest the fund and generate an income higher than the prevailing rate of inflation. At A Glance predicts average capital growth of 3.75%[13] and income yield of 3%.

(e)   *Pension receipt/taxation*: The *Duxbury* tables usually account for the payee's receipt of a full state pension and for a consistent taxation regime.[14]

PHYSICAL ASSUMPTIONS

15.6   The fiscal assumptions inherent in the *Duxbury* calculation impact directly on the final capital figure. The physical assumptions, however, refer to those realities of life post-divorce that are not strictly accounted for within the calculation's formula, but are nevertheless important in determining whether the court should ultimately depart from the *Duxbury*-calculated figure. For example, the basic *Duxbury* calculation does not account for:

(1)   the potential for the payee to remarry or cohabit;[15]

There is no rule that a payee's *prospects* of remarriage must be taken into account in adjusting the result of a *Duxbury* calculation.[16] If there is a settled plan to remarry or good evidence in support of such a plan, this should affect both the principle of providing, and the calculation of, a capitalised *Duxbury* fund. However, remote prospects of remarriage will arguably have no impact. In *Dixon v Marchant*,[17] Ward LJ summarised the position in the standard case when dismissing a husband's appeal due to his wife's remarriage some 6 months after payment of a capitalised sum for maintenance:

'Payment of a lump sum carried risks for both parties – a risk for the husband that the wife would remarry so that he would have been better off

---

[13]   The At A Glance *Duxbury* tables assume a real rate of return of 4.25%.

[14]   As indicated in the At A Glance *Duxbury* Tables (Table 16, At A Glance, 2013–2014).

[15]   The tables in Duckworth's Matrimonial Property and Finance do provide alternative multipliers to notionally take account of the payee's prospect of remarriage. However, as remarriage terminates the payment of, and right to claim for, periodical payments, these alternative tables can arguably only provide a very broad alternative basis for calculation.

[16]   See *Duxbury v Duxbury* [1992] Fam 62, [1991] 2 WLR 639.

[17]   [2008] EWCA Civ 11, [2008] 1 FLR 655, Wall LJ dissenting.

paying her maintenance until that obligation ceased on her remarriage, and a risk for the wife that a lump sum crudely based, on the face of it, on a multiplicand of no more than 7 years or so at £15,000 pa might be exhausted during her lifetime so that she would have been better off preserving her rights to maintenance from him and his estate. There were no special features to the case: it was a run of the mill compromise.'[18]

In the recent case of *AH v PH*,[19] Moor J rejected an argument that the wife's prospects of remarriage should result in the adjustment of a *Duxbury* calculation. In *AH v PH*, the parties were in their early thirties, the marriage had been a short one of just 4 years and there were two children, the eldest of whom was 5 years old. All the capital assets in the case were classed as non-matrimonial (on the husband's side):

> 'I am quite satisfied that the law is that I must ignore the prospects of remarriage in calculating the appropriate figure for capitalisation. I accept that to do otherwise would involve a wholly inappropriate assessment of remarriage prospects that would be both invidious and unscientific.'

(2)   each party's present or future job security;

(3)   a significant change to the payer's or payee's financial circumstances;

(4)   the receipt by the payee of additional capital from an external source (eg an inheritance);[20] or

(5)   a reduction or increase to the payee's financial needs at certain life-stages (eg retirement or down-sizing from a larger property and releasing equity that may provide an additional investment resource[21]).

WHY IS A *DUXBURY* CALCULATION A 'TOOL AND NOT A RULE'?

15.7   The *Duxbury* calculation is nothing more than *one* method of representing a party's financial needs. As seen above, it is also predicated on a number of fiscal and physical assumptions. As such, it *may* assist in the pursuit

---

[18]   *Dixon v Marchant*, at [24], per Ward LJ.

[19]   [2013] EWHC 3873 (Fam) at [82]: in this case, Moor J also took account of the *Duxbury* paradox (see **15.8**) and capitalised the wife's maintenance award on a 14-year basis to take her to the youngest child of the family completing secondary education.

[20]   Care should be taken, as some courts are more open to an adjusted *Duxbury* award to account for the introduction of future capital. In *CO v CO (Ancillary Relief: Pre-Marriage Cohabitation)* [2004] EWHC 287 (Fam), [2004] 1 FLR 1095 at [85], for example, Coleridge J was 'not prepared to indulge in such a glorified speculation exercise in this case because it would be to impart a spurious accuracy to the calculations at this late stage in the balancing exercise when so many of the other underlying figures are shot through with uncertainty . . .' (taken from Coleridge J in *J v V (Disclosure: Offshore Corporations)* [2003] EWHC 3110 (Fam), [2004] 1 FLR 1042).

[21]   See, for example, *Y v Y (Financial Orders: Inherited Wealth)* [2013] 2 FLR 924 in which Baron J's calculated *Duxbury* fund allowed for a capital injection of £1.5m to the wife's finances in 15 years' time when it was expected that she would sell her home and down-size to a smaller property.

of achieving overall fairness, but it must also be seen in the context of, and must respond to, the multiple factors for the court's consideration in the Matrimonial Causes Act 1973 (MCA 1973), s 25. Therefore, in *White v White*[22] Thorpe LJ described *Duxbury* as 'a tool and not a rule'; it is a guide and not the answer to the determination of, and appropriate means of providing for, a payee's financial needs or maintenance entitlement. For the payer, whereas a periodical payments order is open to variation, suspension and termination, a lump sum payment in lieu of maintenance – and calculated on a *Duxbury* basis – is a final and irreversible order. For the payee, the *Duxbury* fund however, provides no guarantee of a future certain income level or spending power; the fund can only represent a broad guide as to the income potential. This is to be contrasted with an annuity,[23] which is a 'low risk solution with a high level of guarantee[24] but often at much higher capital cost.[25] If a *Duxbury* calculation is undertaken, it is then incumbent on the court to 'stand back and decide whether to uplift or depress the mathematical calculation to give proper reflection to the other statutory criteria and, finally, all the circumstances of the case'.[26] The *Duxbury* calculation must also be seen within the framework of the court's objective of achieving fairness, which may well engage the 'sharing' principle in relation to matrimonial and non-matrimonial assets.[27]

NEGOTIATING THE '*DUXBURY* PARADOX'

15.8 The *Duxbury* Paradox is the contradiction inherent in a *Duxbury* calculation (based on a payee's lifetime needs) that an older payee, and even after a long marriage, will require a smaller lump sum to provide for his or her future financial need than a younger payee. Therefore, if the *Duxbury* calculation is adopted as a *rule* in such circumstances, it can result in a significantly unfair award for the payee. The *Duxbury* Paradox means that, in certain cases involving younger parties, shorter marriages and significant 'non-matrimonial' resources,[28] care must be taken to ensure that a payee's overall financial award is not unduly high, and that in other cases involving longer marriages and an older payee, that the capitalised amount is not unfairly limited by reference to his or her needs only.[29]

---

22 [1998] 2 FLR 310, at 320.
23 A financial contract providing fixed payments over a specified period of time, usually the recipient's life, ie a life annuity.
24 Phillpotts, Deebie and Bruce, '*An Alternative View of Duxbury*', February [2010] Fam Law 161.
25 For example, according to At A Glance, a capital sum of £198,000 provides a 68-year-old woman – on a Duxbury basis – with £20,000 pa over her lifetime, whereas a sum of £200,000 will buy the same individual a gross annuity of just £8,294 pa (on an escalation rate of 3% pa).
26 *Dharamshi v Dharamshi* [2001] 1 FLR 736, at [9], per Thorpe LJ.
27 See *Miller v Miller; McFarlane v McFarlane* [2006] 1 FLR 1186.
28 Ie those resources that are not necessarily to be shared on an equal basis with the payee, depending on the court's approach to, and assessment of, the circumstances of the case.
29 This also applies to the issue of amortisation of the fund: for example, in *CR v CR* [2008] 1 FLR 323, Bodey J provided the wife with a fund of £5m in addition to her housing costs.

DEPARTING FROM THE *DUXBURY* CALCULATION: FINAL ORDERS VERSUS ORDERS FOR CAPITALISATION ON AN APPLICATION TO VARY A PERIODICAL PAYMENTS ORDER

15.9 The *Duxbury* calculation may be used, first, at the stage of a final order that determines each party's financial claims and, second, upon an application to vary and then capitalise[30] a periodical payments order. The case-law recognises a difference in the 'weight' to be attached to a *Duxbury* calculation in both instances and, therefore, a distinction in the extent to which the court has discretion to depart from the figure produced by the calculation. Broadly, the discretion to adjust up or down from a *Duxbury* calculation at the capitalisation stage is narrower than at the final order stage. The reason for the difference in weight is that, at a final order stage, the court is considering the appropriate overall division of capital, property, pension and income claims; whereas, upon a variation application, the focus is on the resolution of outstanding income claims only and the court is expressly directed *not* to revisit the parties' capital claims[31]. In *Pearce v Pearce*, Thorpe LJ explained the rationale, as follows:

> '... this discipline is necessary as a safeguard against the temptation to further adjust the capital division between the parties to reflect the factors which were not foreseen or which did not pertain at the date of the original division. This abstinence is required not only by authority, but also as a matter of policy. Families with not inconsiderable assets are obliged to achieve division by one means or another once the marriage has floundered. They are entitled to know that that obligation once completed does not revive. In cases where a complete clean break cannot be achieved at the date of redistribution of the family assets, it is important that the parties should not be encouraged to take advantage of any subsequent developments that permit the dismissal of the outstanding periodical payments order. The court has its duty under Section 31(7A). Therefore, a relatively simple, certain and predictable method for the calculation of the capital sum that can fairly be substituted for the periodical payments order is of great importance. It enables parties to see where they stand and to weigh the relative advantages and disadvantages of finality. It contributes to the compromise of the issue and thus to a reduction in contested cases.'[32]

Bodey J did not accept that such a sum should be amortised over the wife's remaining 38 years' life expectancy: 'it is quite difficult here to see the fairness of the wife having to spend through all her capital when, given the husband's very large ongoing net income and the possibility of his working many more years if he wishes, he will not have to do the same' (at [100]).

[30] For further detail, see Chapter 18.
[31] See also, Chapter 18 on Capitalisation.
[32] [2003] 2 FLR 1144, at [39]. See also *AR v AR (Treatment of Inherited Wealth)* [2012] 2 FLR 1, at [94], per Moylan J for endorsement of this approach.

CIRCUMSTANCES IN WHICH IT MAY BE APPROPRIATE TO DEPART FROM A *DUXBURY* CALCULATION[33]

15.10   The court has a discretion to depart from the *Duxbury* calculation and this is evident in a number of reported cases, as set out below. However, any digression from the calculation must be **evidenced and principled**, as Mostyn J reminds the practitioner in *DR v GR (Financial Remedies: Variation of Overseas Trust)*:[34]

'To depart from the Duxbury pathway when capitalising a lifetime income need risks an unprincipled, formless and impressionistic judgment replacing the tried and tested guideline. Of course the Duxbury figure is only ever a guideline but departure from it must surely be rationally and numerically justified by reference to clear evidence rather than just being, as here, a figure plucked out of the thin air ...'

Providing additional financial security and enabling discretionary expenditure

15.11   In *AR v AR (Treatment of Inherited Wealth)*, Moylan J uplifted the wife's *Duxbury* fund of £2.5m (to provide a lifetime income of £115,000 net pa[35]) to £3.2m to enable her to have sufficient resources to spend money on additional discretionary items, which may vary from year to year and were not reflected in the wife's annual budget. This additional measure of financial security was appropriate and fair given the husband's own additional expenditure; for example, providing a significant loan to the children of the marriage, purchasing an inheritance tax policy and funding a very expensive holiday for the parties' son.

Meeting concerns as to the assumed rate of return

15.12   In *W v W (Financial Provision: Form E)*[36] Mostyn J dealt with the variation and capitalisation of an original order for periodical payments at the rate of £27,000. The husband was aged 59 and the wife 61; their marriage had lasted for 21 years. The wife was in poor health and presented at trial as nervous, fragile and insecure. She was in receipt of state pension. The husband's financial and income position had improved significantly since the original order. Mostyn J determined the wife's future income needs by way of periodical payments at the level of £34,000. The judge also made reference to the amortisation of a *Duxbury* fund over the period of assumed life expectancy and commented that, if the wife outlived that expectancy, the consequences of her then having no capital or income would be 'disastrous' for her. Mostyn J also

---

[33]   These are innumerable and only a few of the more important examples are given here.

[34]   [2013] 2 FLR 1534, at [57]: in which Mostyn J rejected an argument to add £137,000 to the *Duxbury* calculation to provide a 'rainy day' fund for the wife.

[35]   Against a budget presented by the wife at trial of £136,000 pa, which was 'flawed' in a number of respects.

[36]   [2004] 1 FLR 494.

considered that the assumed rate of return/yield inherent in the *Duxbury* calculation should be reduced from 3.75% to 3.25%, which would provide the wife with a higher *Duxbury* fund. The resulting *Duxbury* fund of £560,000 was £25,000 higher than that produced on the basis of a yield of 3.75% and provided the wife with 'a sinking fund ... for the exigencies of life, death and [the] markets'.[37]

Foreign investment and tax

15.13 If the payee is living, or intending to live, abroad, and if any *Duxbury* fund is to be invested within a foreign jurisdiction, this may justify an amendment to the *Duxbury* calculation to account for specific investment costs or applicable taxes.[38] It is important to note, in addition, that a *Duxbury* calculation does not account for the costs associated with the payee's professional investment and management of any *Duxbury* fund (whether in the United Kingdom or elsewhere).

---

[37] *W v W*, at [97], per Mostyn J.
[38] See, for example, *F v F (Ancillary Relief: Substantial Assets)* [1995] 2 FLR 45.

CHAPTER 16

ORDERS TO PROVIDE SECURITY FOR PERIODICAL PAYMENTS

INTRODUCTION

16.1 Orders for periodical payments can be notoriously difficult and expensive to enforce.[1] In certain circumstances, the court may make an order for the payer of a periodical payments order to secure those payments[2] to the satisfaction of the court: this is termed a 'secured periodical payments order' in The Guide. However, the order to provide such security has been described by many commentators as a 'hybrid' financial order,[3] as it is not, in itself, an order of an income or capital nature. The secured periodical payments order is uncommon in modern matrimonial practice for a number of reasons, including the preference to effect a 'clean break' between divorcing parties[4] if fair and appropriate as well as the general antipathy towards restricting the payer's future access to a significant proportion of (secured) capital. Nevertheless, secured periodical payments orders can still prove useful in a small number of cases, and justify a short chapter in The Guide providing an overview of their legal basis, utility and application.

LEGAL BASIS, INTERPRETATION AND PROCEDURE

16.2 Pursuant to the Matrimonial Causes Act 1973 (MCA 1973), s 23(1)(b)[5] the court may make an order 'that either party to the marriage shall secure to the other such periodical payments, for such term, as may be so specified'.[6] The order can also be made in relation to an order for periodical payments for the benefit of, or directly payable to, a child.[7]

16.3 The order to *secure* periodical payments is *not* an order to *make* those periodical payments. The order to secure will be made in conjunction with a 'standard' order for periodical payments that provides for the payer to make

---

[1]   See, for further detail, Chapter 22 on enforcement.
[2]   Against property or capital, for example.
[3]   Bird, R and King, A 'Financial Remedies Handbook', 2013, para 3.1 and Duckworth, 'Matrimonial Property and Finance' section 4, para 60.
[4]   For more, see Chapter 11.
[5]   Civil Partnership Act 2004 (CPA 2004), Sch 5, Part 1, para 2(1)(b).
[6]   On granting a decree of divorce, a decree of nullity of marriage or a decree of judicial separation, or at any time thereafter.
[7]   MCA 1973, s 23(1)(e); CPA 2004, Sch 5, Part 1, para 2(1)(e).

payments to the payee of £x per month/annum for a specified term or for the parties' joint lives. The order for security may relate to all or only some of the quantum of and term for, the standard periodical payments order.

16.4 A secured periodical payments order is a 'financial remedy':[8] the standard Family Procedure Rules 2010 (FPR 2010) Part 9 procedure applies to an application for the order, and the general rule that the court will not make an order requiring one party to pay the costs of the other party, applies.[9]

16.5 The maximum term for a secured periodical payments order is the death or remarriage of the payee. In contrast to a non-secured order, the death of the *payer* does not terminate a secured periodical payments order.[10]

THE PROVISION OF SECURITY

16.6 The hallmark of the secured periodical payments order is the provision of security for the payments: the objective is to guarantee that the payee will receive his/her due payments for the life of the order. If the court determines that a secured periodical payments order is appropriate, the parties should be given an opportunity to try and agree the identity of the assets from which the security will derive.[11] There is no explicit restriction on what type of asset may be used to provide security (property, funds, bank accounts etc), although an income-generating asset will have the benefit of providing both security for payment *and* a source for the actual periodical payments themselves.

16.7 Whatever security is chosen by the parties or, in default, ordered by the court, it must be a specific and identifiable asset (or assets) rather than by way of a general charge on all assets of one party.[12]

16.8 The court's powers to order a sale of property are engaged when the court makes a secured periodical payments order.[13] If the payer defaults in paying the periodical payments, the payee may apply for property to be sold so as to receive (capitalised) payment.

FLEXIBILITY VERSUS FINALITY

16.9 Whenever the court is considering making a secured periodical payments order, it must examine its utility and fairness versus an outright capital order:[14]

---

[8]   FPR 2010, r 2.3.
[9]   As the order falls within the definition of 'financial remedy proceedings' in FPR 2010, r 28.3(4)(b).
[10] MCA 1973, s 28(1)(b).
[11] A *Duxbury* calculation may be required to assess the level of security required, see further Chapter 15 on *Duxbury* calculations.
[12] *Barker v Barker* [1952] P 184, CA.
[13] MCA 1973, s 24A.
[14] For example, an order for the payment of a lump sum or a property adjustment order.

that alternative capital order may, for example, provide the payee with a (capitalised) *Duxbury* fund in lieu of maintenance[15] or, in the case of an order for the benefit of a child, set a fund aside to pay future school fees. The secured periodical payments order benefits from flexibility: it is subject to the court's powers of variation,[16] discharge and suspension and, upon the payer's death, the payee or the personal representative of the deceased [payer] may apply to the court for an order of variation.[17] The lump sum or property adjustment order, by comparison, has the advantage of finality[18] and the effective termination of the parties' claims for financial provision arising out of their divorce. In *Tracey v Tracey*,[19] for example, the court was faced with a choice between a secured periodical payments order and a lump sum order to assure the future private education of the parties' children. Thorpe LJ weighed in the balance the competing advantages and disadvantages of both orders, as follows:

> '[22] The secured periodical payments have the advantage of flexibility, since they allow annual variation to reflect circumstances. Change of future circumstances can be divided between change in the payer's circumstances and change in the recipient's needs. By contrast, the lump sum has the great attraction of finality, eliminating the risk of future litigation between the parents.
>
> [23] Returning to the secured periodical payments route, as to the payer's circumstances there is a plain risk of a health collapse and an income collapse within the scale of [W – the child's] education at Cranleigh [school]. On the other hand, in many families, private education is frequently funded in whole or in part from capital. As to the recipients' needs, there cannot be much doubt as to [A – the other child's] need to complete his education at Cranmore [school] and of W's need to complete his education, so soon to begin, at Cranleigh, but A's need, in a future that would not commence until September 2009 and which would not terminate until July 2014, is much less easy to predict.
>
> [24] So, balancing all these considerations, in the end I favour the advantages of finality, but a finality that does not endeavour to reach beyond the reasonably predictable.'

DOCUMENTS, DEEDS AND DECREES

16.10 The secured periodical payments order in matrimonial proceedings should be supplemented by a deed to give effect to the terms of that order (to protect the asset used as security). The court may settle the terms of that deed

---

[15] From which the payee will derive an income for life or for some other defined period.

[16] MCA 1973, s 31(2)(c) and see further Chapter 17 on variation and Chapter 18 on capitalisation.

[17] See MCA 1973, s 31(6), (8) and (9): note than no such application can be made without the court's permission after the end of the period of 6 months from the date on which representation in regard to the estate is first taken out. Alternatively, a claim may be pursued under the Inheritance (Provision for Family and Dependants) Act 1975.

[18] If ensuring, in the case of a lump sum order, that it is not variable pursuant to MCA 1973, s 31(2)(d) and see also *Hamilton v Hamilton* [2013] EWCA Civ 13.

[19] [2007] 1 FLR 196.

or, if necessary, it has the power to direct that its terms are referred to a conveyancing counsel to finalise the proper instrument, which the parties to the case shall execute, as necessary.[20]

16.11   If there is concern about a party's willingness to execute an appropriate deed, the court may either (a) defer the grant of a decree absolute[21] until the deed has been executed or (b) make an order nominating an individual (eg a partner in a solicitor's firm) to execute the deed on behalf of the recalcitrant party.

Factors for the court's consideration

16.12

> The court's power to make a secured periodical payments order relies on the familiar discretionary exercise provided for in MCA 1973, s 25(1) and (2): the court must have regard to all the circumstances of the case, and first consideration is given to the welfare of any minor children of the family. In addition to the factors common to the making or refusing of financial orders, the following matters may be of importance to a case in which a secured order is being considered:
>
> (a)   *The extent of the available capital*: security can only be provided if sufficient assets are available to the court and, preferably, within its jurisdiction.[22] In most cases, the available capital will be required to meet each party's reasonable housing needs; in others, there may be sufficient additional capital to pay a lump sum to the payee to capitalise any future claim s/he may have for periodical payments.
>
> (b)   *The type of assets available*: the provision of security is only as good and 'safe' as the asset secured for the payee's benefit, together with the prospects of the payee being able to enforce that security, if necessary. For example, in *MT v OT (Financial Provision: Costs)*[23] Charles J rejected the payer's offer of security against a property owned by a trust, as it would place considerable difficulties in the way of the payee in enforcing the order. The court can order, instead, for example, that a certain amount of cash is held in a bank account or to a solicitor's order as security for payment.[24]
>
> (c)   *The impact of ordering the provision of security on the needs of the payer*: the court must make an order that is fair to both parties. It →

---

[20]   MCA 1973, s 30(a). Advice should also be taken as to the tax consequences of providing any security.

[21]   In proceedings for divorce, nullity of marriage or judicial separation.

[22]   The court will be unlikely to make an order for security in relation to assets held abroad unless there is good evidence of the court's ability to enforce the order, if necessary.

[23]   [2007] EWHC 838 (Fam), [2008] 2 FLR 1311 which, admittedly, is a case pursuant to Sch 1 to the Children Act 1989 for financial provision for the benefit of a child, but the same principles apply.

[24]   As Charles J intended to propose to the payer in *MT v OT*, ibid.

may be inappropriate and unfair for a secured periodical payments order to 'freeze' assets of the payer that s/he otherwise requires to meet immediate or foreseeable housing or capital needs.

(d) *The risk of the payer leaving the jurisdiction of the court/defaulting on making payment*: the secured periodical payments order is invariably made because of concerns that the payer will default in making the appropriate payments or take him/herself out of the jurisdiction of the court, thereby frustrating enforcement. The simple fact that a payer has defaulted is not likely, on its own, to be sufficient to convince the court that security is necessary. However, in *C v C (Financial Relief: Short Marriage)*,[25] Ward LJ refused the husband's appeal against a secured periodical payments order due to the combination of various identified 'risk factors', as follows:

> 'I turn to the question of the secured provision. It is agreed that the judge made this order for reasons partly, but I suspect minimally, in the light of early difficulties in maintaining payments. That by itself would not be enough. But given the husband's lies and deception, given the difficulties there were in obtaining information as to his means and given some move of residence and relocation from this country to Athens, it is not, in my judgment, wrong to secure the periodical payments as he did.'[26]

Naturally, an unreliable or irresponsible payer may, conversely – and even against his or her own case at trial – encourage the court to make an order for a clean break and a capitalised[27] payment to the payee rather than secured periodical payments: despite the security that may be provided, the variability of the secured order and the potential for further litigation may persuade the court that a termination of claims and proceedings is the preferred outcome. In *Robson v Robson*,[28] for example, the husband appealed an order made after a long 21-year marriage, at the end of which the parties had assets of circa £22.6m (of which £16m represented an estate inherited by the husband). The husband succeeded, on appeal, in lowering the lump sum to the wife from £8m to £7m on a clean break basis. However, the husband had argued late in the original trial – and without evidence as to any proposed security – that the court should make a secured periodical payments order in the wife's favour rather than a *Duxbury* capitalised payment to her[29] on the basis of her lifetime income needs. That argument failed. The Court of Appeal also rejected this aspect of the husband's appeal. Ward LJ stated:

> 'Secured periodical payments or a clean break?

---

[25] [1997] 2 FLR 26 and see also *Tavouleras v Tavouleras* [1998] 2 FLR 418, CA.
[26] *C v C*, at [47].
[27] *Duxbury*-based.
[28] [2010] EWCA Civ 1171, [2011] 1 FLR 751.
[29] See further, Chapter 15 on *Duxbury* calculations.

[78–79] This suggestion came 'late in the day' but it remains tenaciously pursued by Mr Amos. The judge very fairly gave the husband an opportunity to put in evidence of the security he was offering. In the event, as the judge found … no satisfactory evidence was offered of the detail of a viable plan to support the argument for secured provision. Small wonder the husband lost. I have already rejected his application after the hearing to plug the gaps that were so manifest at the hearing. Good administration of justice depends upon the finality of the judgments of the court. The judge's findings of fact that the evidence was insufficient to justify the relief being sought must be upheld …

… The judge found, and was entitled to find, that the husband was unreliable and irresponsible. His conduct of the litigation was criticised. The conclusion was that there was considerable doubt as to whether the husband would comply with a reasonable business plan so that an award of periodical payments and security would lead to further litigation in relation to them. All of those matters were clearly in the province of the judge to decide, and having had the advantage he had to assess the husband during a hearing which took 10 days, this court would be slow indeed to interfere. Far from the approach of the judge being shown to be plainly wrong, in my judgment, he was plainly right and on the facts as he found them he was in the exercise of his discretion fully entitled to reject the belated application to order secured periodical payments.'

POINTS OF PRACTICE AND THEORY

16.13

(1) The secured order prevents a clean break and restricts the payer's future access to significant capital resources.

(2) An order for security is not an order to *make* periodical payments.

(3) The death of the payer does not automatically terminate the order for security.

(4) The selected security must be identifiable; a general charge on the payer's assets is inappropriate.

(5) The secured order provides flexibility due to its variability, whereas the lump sum order provides finality.

(6) The secured order should be supplemented by a deed giving effect to the terms of the order: the court may direct that such a document is prepared by conveyancing counsel, if required.

CHAPTER 17

VARIATION, DISCHARGE, SUSPENSION AND REVIVAL: QUANTUM AND TERM

'... so far as is fairly possible, the court should take an approach that seeks to avoid a repeat of the emotional and financial cost of these proceedings in an application for variation, by setting parameters that the court can take into account as and when there is such an application.'[1]

INTRODUCTION

17.1 The contradictory virtue of an order for periodical payments is that, despite its immediate and future utility, it remains variable during its existence. Periodical payments orders benefit from an innate facility to respond to the changing financial circumstances and fortunes of both parties, whilst also suffering from the uncertainty demanded by such responsiveness. The variability of periodical payments orders may be expressed as an increase or decrease to the quantum of the original order, by extension of the period for payment, by dismissal, suspension or revival of the order or by consequential 'capitalisation' of the order's future value. This chapter considers the procedure and principles pertaining to an application to vary the quantum and/or term of a periodical payments order. The principles are divided into those arising from statute and those that have evolved through case-law interpretation. The principles upon which the court acts in an application for capitalisation are dealt with in detail in Chapter 18.[2]

17.2 An application to vary a periodical payments order is approached in a similar way to a substantive and original application for a financial remedy. As a result, variation applications can be costly and lengthy and are often hotly disputed. An application for an increase in the quantum of periodical payments may be met with a cross-application from the payer for a decrease to, or discharge of, the order. In determining a variation application the court exercises a full and broad discretion. This chapter seeks to draw on common themes in the case-law to guide the practitioner towards the relevant considerations at an early stage, so as to assist in advising upon, and presenting, a case involving any application to vary the quantum or term of a periodical payments order.

---

[1]   *G v G* [2012] 2 FLR 48, at [195], per Charles J.
[2]   And should be read in conjunction with this chapter.

QUANTUM VARIATION

Legal basis

17.3 The Matrimonial Causes Act 1973 (MCA 1973), s 31 provides that:[3]

> '(1) Where the court has made an order to which this section applies, then, subject to the provisions of this section and of section 28(1A) above, the court shall have the power to vary or discharge the order or to suspend any provision thereof temporarily and to revive the operation of any provision so suspended.'

The orders relevant to The Guide to which MCA 1973, s 31 applies are an order for maintenance pending suit and any order for interim maintenance, any periodical payments order (including for a child) and any secured periodical payments order.[4]

17.4 On an application to vary, the court has the power under MCA 1973, s 31(7B)(c) – if it varies or discharges the original order – to direct that the party in whose favour the original order was made is not entitled to make any further application for:

(i)   a periodical payments or secured periodical payments order, or

(ii) an extension of the period to which the original order is limited by any variation of the court.

Pursuant to MCA 1973, s 31(10), if the court decides to vary or discharge a periodical payments or secured periodical payments order:

> '... then, subject to section 28(1) and (2) above, the court shall have the power to direct that the variation or discharge shall not take effect until the expiration of such period as may be specified in the order.'

Procedure

17.5 A variation application requires the court to consider the circumstances of the case de novo[5] or afresh, which demands a full investigation into all the relevant financial circumstances of both parties. It is therefore of no surprise that an application pursuant to MCA 1973, s 31(1) is an application for a 'financial order', which is, in itself, a 'financial remedy'[6] and subject to the full Family Procedure Rules 2010 (FPR 2010), Part 9 procedure.[7]

---

[3]   Civil Partnership Act 2004 (CPA 2004), Sch 5, Part 11.

[4]   MCA 1973, s 31(2)(a)–(c); the court may also vary an order for payment of a lump sum by instalments (see *Hamilton v Hamilton* [2013] EWCA Civ 13 for recent guidance) and a deferred order for payment of a lump sum relevant to pension rights or pension compensation rights.

[5]   *Flavell v Flavell* [1997] 1 FLR 353, CA.

[6]   FPR 2010, r 2.3(1).

[7]   FPR 2010, rr 9.1 and 9.3(1) define a 'variation order' as proceedings for an order under s 31 of the MCA 1973 (or the equivalent Part 11 of Sch 5 to the Civil Partnership Act 2004).

17.6   A party cannot rely on the usual 'liberty to apply' provision included in most orders to seek a variation, which is outside the jurisdiction provided by MCA 1973, s 31.[8]

17.7   The parties will be required to file financial statements (Forms E) and make full financial disclosure. Disclosure is not necessarily limited to income and expenditure matters, as capital investments may (or should) generate income, and pension and capital[9] provision may be important if capitalisation is an option for resolution of the claim.[10]

Case analysis on a variation application

17.8   The diagram overleaf highlights the different factors that will influence the court's discretionary exercise in determining a variation application. They are divided according to their source: from statute or case-law. A factual analysis, using the headings provided to assess the particular facts of the case, will focus attention on the salient elements.

Principles on which the court acts (statutory)

17.9   The court's task is to undertake a full re-assessment of all the circumstances of the case[11] and to achieve a fair result for both parties. A change in any matters to which the court had regard at the time of making the original order will normally provide the trigger for the variation application, although such a change is not a *prerequisite* for an application to vary. The principles for the court are derived from the statute in the first instance. MCA 1973, s 31(7) mandates the court, when considering whether to vary, discharge, suspend or revive an applicable order, to consider the following four factors:

The welfare of a minor child (as the court's first consideration)

17.10   In keeping with MCA 1973, s 25(2), the court's first consideration is the welfare of any minor child of the family, an aspect of a case which often impacts on the other discretionary factors, particularly those of income and earning capacity of the payee. In *N v N (Consent Order: Variation)*[12] Roch LJ stated that the words 'first consideration' mean that 'where there is a child of the family who has not attained the age of 18, the court must consider the welfare of such a child first before any other relevant matter and the welfare of such a child will be the most important consideration, more important than any other single factor, but it will not be paramount in the sense that it can be overridden by a combination of other relevant and applicable factors'.

---

[8]   *Thompson v Thompson* [1985] 2 All ER 243, CA.
[9]   Including property.
[10]   See Chapter 18: depending on the full assessment of the parties' financial circumstances (and in particular their ages), it may be appropriate to terminate periodical payments and to substitute a pension sharing order.
[11]   MCA 1973, s 25(1) and (2).
[12]   [1993] 2 FLR 868, at 882.

Variation Application: Case Analysis Example

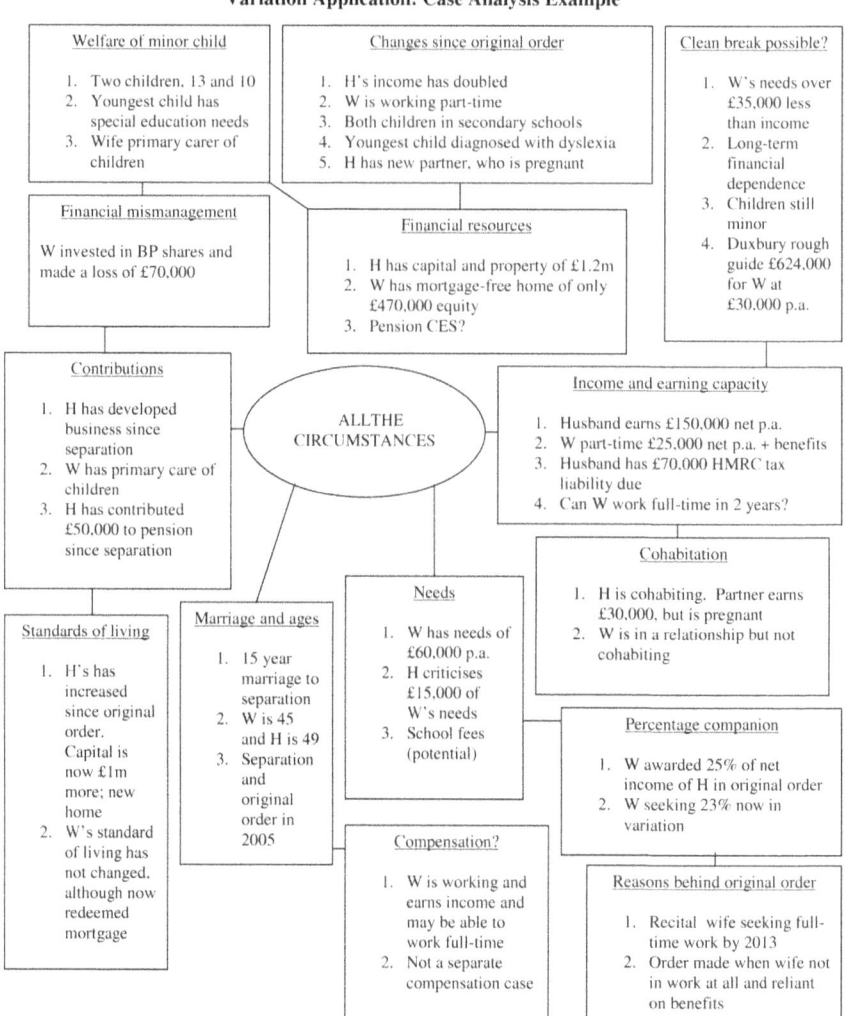

All the circumstances of the case

17.11 The court's investigation and assessment of a variation application is no more limited than that applicable to an original application for a financial order. In the majority of cases, the investigation has its focus on the financial needs and obligations of the parties, particularly the payee. However, 'needs' 'are now no more a determinative or limiting factor on an application for a periodical payments order than they are on an application for a lump sum'.[13] The court will seek to weigh in the balance all the relevant circumstances of the case, which will be assessed, in practice, against the familiar discretionary factors in MCA 1973, s 25(2).

---

[13] *Miller v Miller* [2006] 2 AC 618, at [34], per Lord Nicholls of Birkenhead.

Any change in any of the matters to which the court was required to have regard when making the original order

17.12 The changes most commonly, but not exclusively, associated with a variation application are an increase or decrease in either party's income or expenditure, the children of the family reaching majority, the cohabitation of one party, the remarriage of the payer or the retirement and ill-health of either party; all of which can result in an application to vary a periodical payments order. The statutory mandate to account for any changes since the original order is a contextual one, which pitches the historical against the contemporary circumstances in order to assist the court in determining whether a variation is now due and, if so, what the fair quantum of payment (and its duration) should be.

17.13 In practice, therefore, it is important to obtain – at the minimum – the following historical information:

- the parties' original Forms E;[14]
- the original order (with all recitals and undertakings);
- any original judgment or note of judgment;
- any open correspondence leading to a consent order;[15]
- in a case involving a business or a shareholding, the company accounts available at the date of the original order;
- any information indicating the income of the payer and payee on which the original order was based.

The pervasive search for the clean break

17.14 Every application to vary a periodical payments order re-engages the court's duty to consider whether a termination of the payments can be achieved (MCA 1973, s 25A). The somewhat modified obligation is provided in MCA 1973, s 31(7),[16] as follows:

> '(a) in the case of a periodical payments or secured periodical payments order made on or after the grant of a decree of divorce or nullity of marriage, the court shall consider whether in all the circumstances and after having regard to any such change it would be appropriate to vary the order so that payments under the order are required to be made or secured only for such further period as will in the opinion of the court be sufficient (in light of any proposed exercise by the court, where the marriage has been dissolved, of its powers under subsection (7B) below) to enable the party in whose favour the order was made to adjust without undue hardship to the termination of those payments;

---

[14] Necessary to get a broad understanding of the financial information at the time and to make a more specific calculation of the percentage of the payer's net income ordered to be paid to the payee by way of periodical payments.

[15] And any 'without prejudice' correspondence from previous files to which the client is entitled.

[16] CPA 2004, Sch 5, Part 11, para 59(4).

(b)   in a case where the party against whom the order was made has died, the circumstances of the case shall also include the changed circumstances resulting from his or her death.'

The court must enquire whether an immediate or deferred clean break can be achieved without causing the payee undue (financial) hardship. This enquiry is considered in more detail in **10.14–10.20**, to which reference should be made. The enquiry is also relevant to the variation or extension of the term for payment of a periodical payments order.[17]

Principles on which the court acts (case-law)

17.15   In addition to – and by extrapolation from – the statutory principles on which the court acts, case-law indicates that the following factors may be of relevance to the determination of a variation application, depending on the facts of the case:

The reasons for, and the purpose of, the original order

17.16   Any reasoning behind the original order subject of the variation application, whether derived from the original judgment, written materials available from files (if disclosable and disclosed) or from recitals to, or undertakings contained in, the order itself, should be investigated. As a variation application is designed to effect a change to an existing payment regime established by the court, the rationale for the original regime is a relevant consideration, particularly as the court is directed to consider any changes in matters originally taken into account by the court. For example, recitals in the original order may express the limited circumstances in which it was envisaged that the payee would seek to increase the level of payments; or the court's judgment may indicate why a staged reduction in payments was ordered, for example, in recognition of the payee's developing earning capacity. The reasoning for, and purpose of, the original order will not bind the court on a variation application, but these factors may provide a useful opportunity for the payer or payee to challenge the reasons relied upon for an upward or downward variation of the quantum of the order.[18] For the same reason, it may prove important when agreeing an order at the original stage, to include a recital as to the income of the payer and payee on which the periodical payments order is based.

> In *Cornick v Cornick (No 3)*[19] the wife's second variation (and, then, capitalisation) application was motivated by a significant increase in the husband's capital and income. Charles J carefully considered the reasoning given by the district judge at the time of the original order and →

---

[17]   For which see **17.35–17.40**.
[18]   Equally, therefore, it is important to consider including any recitals in an original order for periodical payments by way of explanation of the basis of, and reasoning behind, its quantum and term.
[19]   [2001] 2 FLR 1240.

of Hale J[20] on the first variation application. District Judge White had originally found that forcing a sale of Mr Cornick's shares in Perpetual – the business in which he worked – would have been devastating for him. The district judge regarded the husband's shareholding, instead, as part of his overall employment package, which was to be the source of his income and, therefore, the ongoing periodical payments order for the benefit of the wife. Charles J concluded that a factor generally likely to be relevant on an application to vary is 'the reason for the original orders (ie the lump sum and periodical payments order)'[21]. In *Cornick*, the parties agreed that a lump sum payment would be made to capitalise the wife's outstanding financial claims and to achieve a clean break. Nevertheless, the need to consider the reasons for the original order is of general relevance to any variation application; Charles J commented as follows:

> '... the fact that Mr Cornick joined Perpetual during the marriage and acquired and consolidated his position in that company during the marriage, with the result that the "employment package" District Judge White decided he should retain was so acquired and consolidated, is an important factor to be taken into account both in respect of the decision to order a lump sum and in quantifying it. District Judge White decided that Mr Cornick should retain that "employment package" on the basis that it would be the source of the payments made by him to his wife and children which would set their standard of living. This reasoning, or underlying purpose, supports the view that the massive rise in Mr Cornick's resources from that source is an important factor to be taken into account both in respect of the decision to order a lump sum and in quantifying it.'[22]

In the variation application in *McFarlane v McFarlane*,[23] the husband's income had increased since the original order to over £1m per annum. The wife sought an upwards variation of her joint lives periodical payments order, which stood at the rate of £250,000 per annum, and an uplift to the order for periodical payments for the children payable then at £20,000 pa. The wife had found employment as a trainee trade mark attorney. The husband had remarried; he had been promoted to high-level equity partner and his net income had increased commensurately. Charles J revisited his conclusions in *Cornick v Cornick (No 3)* and reassured himself that the reasoning behind the original order was a relevant circumstance of the case and, therefore, 'on an application to vary it can be assessed whether the purpose of the earlier order has been fulfilled and, if it has, this would be a relevant (and perhaps a decisive) factor in favour of refusing an extension or variation ...'.[24]

The purposes of the original order may be many and varied but may include, for example, providing a transition for the payee to some level of →

---

[20] As she then was.
[21] At [121(a)].
[22] *Cornick*, at [166].
[23] *McFarlane v McFarlane* [2009] 2 FLR 1322.
[24] *McFarlane v McFarlane* [2009] EWHC 891 (Fam), [2009] 2 FLR 1322 at [104].

income and independence, assisting the payee during the children's minority, providing compensation to the payee for a 'lost' earning capacity after a long marriage, or assisting during a period of the payee's ill-health.

The fact that the original order [for periodical payments] has governed the rights of the parties and has set a pattern to their lives after their divorce[25]

17.17 A circumstance of the case linked to the assessment of a party's standard of living is invariably the fact that the original order for periodical payments has established a financial regime to which the parties have become accustomed. The payee will have organised financial affairs and determined a standard of living according to personal means and the maintenance paid; the payer will have budgeted for maintenance payments alongside other financial commitments. The pattern set by the original order extends beyond the *reasons* for that order to a consideration of the way in which the ordered payments have governed the parties' financial lives and choices since their divorce.

Compensation for relationship-generated disadvantage

17.18 A periodical payments order is a vehicle for meeting financial need as well as affording compensation to a party to the marriage for relationship-generated financial disadvantage; not as a separate 'head of claim'[26] but as an element of fairness.[27] Lord Nicholls explained the rationale in *Miller v Miller*:

> 'If one party's earning capacity has been advantaged at the expense of the other party during the marriage it would be extraordinary if, where necessary, the court could not order the advantaged party to pay compensation to the other out of his enhanced earnings when he receives them. It would be most unfair if absence of capital assets were regarded as cancelling his obligation to pay compensation in respect of a continuing economic advantage he has obtained from the marriage.'[28]

At the original-order stage, an element of compensation may justify an increase to the amount of a periodical payments order; in a variation application, the concept of compensation remains relevant and *can* impact on the amount of any variation.

17.19 In *VB v JP*[29] the wife sought an upward variation of a periodical payments order from £33,000 to £130,000 per annum. The marriage had lasted for 11 years. The original periodical payments order was made on a joint lives basis. The husband's income had increased from £340,000 net to £470,000 net per annum by the date of the variation application. The wife's case was that the lifestyle choices made by the parties during their marriage

---

[25] *Cornick v Cornick (No 3)* [2001] 2 FLR 1240, at [121], per Charles J.
[26] As in a personal injury schedule of loss.
[27] See further, Chapter 9 on quantification.
[28] *Miller* at [32].
[29] [2008] EWHC 112 (Fam), [2008] 1 FLR 742.

prevented her pursuing her career and that her variation application should, therefore, include an element of compensation. The court rejected the husband's argument that the consideration of compensation is limited only to the original order determining the parties' financial claims on exiting the marriage. Equally, the court did not approve an approach that sought to quantify separately the wife's claim for compensation. Sir Mark Potter stated:

> 'Where it is necessary to provide ongoing periodical payments for the wife after the division of capital assets insufficient to cover her future maintenance needs, any element of compensation is best dealt with by a generous assessment of her continuing needs unrestricted by purely budgetary considerations, in the light of the contribution of the wife to the marriage and the broad effect of the sacrifice of her own earning capacity upon her ability to provide for her own needs following the end of the matrimonial partnership.'[30]

17.20   In *Lauder v Lauder*[31] the court was concerned with an appeal relating to the variation of an order made originally in 1988, the terms of which had been suspended by agreement between the parties. At the time of the appeal the wife was 70 and suffered from ongoing health complaints. The original order had awarded her circa 35% of the husband's net income but only 26% of the capital asset base. At the date of the trial the husband's assets had increased through various property investments to not less than £4.5m and he was generating a long term net income of £200,000 per annum. Baron J was clear that the suspension of the original order was to the much greater economic disadvantage of the wife, who was entitled to an element of compensation:

> 'On analysis, therefore, this case merits an award which includes an element of compensation for relationship-related disadvantage. This wife cannot claim to be a Mrs McFarlane, but there can be little doubt that the length of the marriage and her age at separation ... (50 years old) ... put her at a severe disadvantage in the labour market. She did not have the ability, given the manner in which these parties conducted their life and their suspension of a 1998 order, to make herself fully independent given that she is 70 years old.'[32]

17.21   The compensation element of the wife's award was not calculated separately from, and added to, her needs (generously interpreted); but rather it acted to justify a higher annual sum of periodical payments over a figure limited *purely* by needs.[33]

Compensation for relationship-generated disadvantage has its limits as a concept. It should not be pleaded or calculated as a separate 'head of claim' of the applicant payee. On a variation application, which may occur many years after the original order, it may be inappropriate to attempt to calculate the financial 'premium' or increase to a periodical →

---

[30]   *VB v JP*, at [59].
[31]   [2007] 2 FLR 802.
[32]   *Lauder*, at [69], per Baron J.
[33]   A periodic sum that was eventually capitalised.

payments order at all on the basis of a compensatory claim: the longer the period since the original order, the more artificial and unwelcome this calculation becomes. The President in *VB v JP* put it thus:

> 'Attempts under the rubric of compensation to isolate and quantify the level of income or earning capacity sacrificed by a wife years after the event for the purpose of calculating a premium element on the award, constitutes a search for precision which is to be discouraged both on the grounds of policy and practicality, and which goes beyond what is required or generally appropriate in the exercise required of the court under s 25.'

In *W v W (Periodical Payments: Variation)*,[34] when increasing the wife's periodical payments, Moylan J also sought to limit the scope for relying on a 'compensatory' element to a periodical payments claim as a means of restricting (rather than augmenting) a financial award:

> 'I do not consider that the concept of relationship-generated disadvantage was intended to place a ceiling on the spouse's (or former spouse's) claims by reference to what she (in this case) would have been able to earn if marriage and motherhood had not intervened. It seems clear to me that the proposition is intended principally to ensure that the court does not overlook the effect on a spouse of a loss of career, because the principles of need and sharing can more easily accommodate the more broader claims (and consequences) based on contributions and other aspects of section 25. However, this debate again highlights one of the potential disadvantages of a formulaic application of the principles identified by the House of Lords ... It is trite to say that these principles are intended to be guides on the route to fairness and not obstacles to the achievement of fairness.'[35]

In *Hvorostovsky v Hvorostovsky*[36] the Russian baritone husband's income had increased significantly since an agreement was reached upon divorce regarding the wife's periodical payments (from £550,000 to £1.86m gross pa). At the time of the divorce, the parties had agreed a regime of payments increasing to £117,000 per annum to the wife and subject to indexation. The wife appealed against the quantum imposed by the court on her variation application, stating that the judge had wrongly failed to include an element of compensation in the calculation. The Court of Appeal allowed the wife's appeal and increased the quantum but did *not* do so on the basis of a compensation 'claim' for relationship-generated disadvantage. The wife's career had ended shortly before its natural conclusion. There was no evidence of any specific sacrifice made by the wife – and for which she should be 'compensated' – as she had given up her career at a time very near its natural close in any event: →

---

[34]   [2010] 2 FLR 985.
[35]   *W v W*, at [97], per Moylan J.
[36]   [2009] EWCA Civ 791, [2009] 3 FCR 650.

'[38] ... Whatever she gave to him and to the children is aptly assessed under the heading of 'contribution'. That, rather than relationship-related disadvantage is the language of the statute.

[39] Of course compensation for relationship-related disadvantage may be a very important ingredient in many cases, particularly in the assessment of the original division of capital and foreseeable income. If reflected at that stage it will find its continuing reflection on a variation hearing without fresh assessment.'[37]

The standard of living of the parties

17.22   MCA 1973, s 25(2) directs the court to consider the standard of living enjoyed by the family *before the breakdown* of the marriage. However, an increase in the payer's income *after* the original order will normally mean that the payer's standard of living has increased commensurately *since* the marriage. On a variation application, the court will take account not only of the standard of living prior to separation but also the standard of living enjoyed by the parties at the time of the variation application, as this may be an important 'matter' that has changed since the original order. A comparison, therefore, between the parties' abilities to spend, save, invest, purchase or rent property, for example, may contribute to an argument that fairness requires an increase or decrease to the quantum of periodical payments. In *Cornick v Cornick (No 3)* Charles J put it as follows

'... If the payor's available resources decreased dramatically the payee would not be able to argue successfully against a downward variation because the payee's standard of living would then fall below the standard enjoyed by the family before the breakdown of the marriage. In my judgment in those circumstances the payee would be likely to have to suffer the consequences of the inability of the payor to pay as much. It is therefore logical that a payee is not precluded from deriving benefit from an increase in the payor's fortunes even if this results in the payee enjoying a higher standard of living that she did during the marriage.'[38]

The standard of living prior to the separation and during the marriage does not constitute a ceiling in the assessment of a payee's application to vary the quantum.[39]

Financial mismanagement, extravagance or irresponsibility

17.23   The stimulus behind a variation application remains the pursuit of fairness. Elusive as this concept may be, the case of *North v North*[40] makes it abundantly clear that there are 'two faces to fairness',[41] which demand fairness

---

[37]   *Hvorostovsky*, at [38] and [39], per Thorpe LJ.
[38]   At [105].
[39]   *W v W*, at [985], per Moylan J: this is just as true for the payee's financial needs, which are not necessarily a determinative or limiting factor when assessing quantum on a variation application.
[40]   [2007] EWCA Civ 760, [2008] 1 FLR 158.
[41]   *North*, at [32], per Thorpe LJ.

to the applicant in need and to the respondent who must pay. In *North v North* the original order was made at a time when the court's power to dismiss a periodical payments claim was limited to dismissal by consent. Therefore, a nominal order for periodical payments was made for the benefit of the wife on a joint lives basis. In subsequent years, the husband transferred ground rents to the wife[42] to augment her income and allowed her to purchase properties at a discount through his company. In 1998 the wife decided to sell her assets and moved to Australia; she invested her money in the stock market with disastrous consequences and made significant losses. The wife sought an upward variation of her nominal periodical payments order to meet her needs. Despite findings that the wife's financial situation was entirely of her own making, the district judge acceded to her claim and ordered periodical payments of £16,500 pa capitalised as a lump sum payment from the husband of £202,000 to terminate her periodical payments claim. The Court of Appeal acknowledged the importance of having regard to the financial needs of the payee in a variation application. However, the court rejected the notion that the (voluntarily generous) husband should have to meet the wife's needs that arose as a result of her failure to utilise her earning potential, her abandonment of financial security in the UK and her choice of a more hazardous future in Australia:

> 'In any application under s 31 the applicant's needs are likely to be the dominant or magnetic factor. But it does not follow that the respondent is inevitably responsible financially for any established needs. He is not an insurer against all hazards nor, when fairness is the measure, is he necessarily liable for needs created by the applicant's financial mismanagement, extravagance or irresponsibility.'[43]

However, this general statement as to the 'responsibility' of the payer is a qualified one. He is not *necessarily* responsible, but he may well be. For example, in *North v North*, Thorpe LJ made a distinction between financial losses of the wife which were the result of 'ill-advised choices' or mismanagement and those losses that were better characterised as the result of misfortune. Ultimately, the Court of Appeal substituted for the benefit of the wife an order for periodical payments at £3,000 pa to be capitalised at a sum not exceeding £50,000.

The choices made by the parties since the original order

17.24 The parties' financial choices and decisions made after the original order for periodical payments may, whether or not characterised as extravagant or irresponsible, affect the court's assessment of the overall fairness of ordering the payer to meet financial needs arising as a result of such choices. The same rationale applies to the payer who, having chosen to waste resources, invest unwisely and spend extravagantly, or has failed to maximise an earning capacity, approaches the court on a variation application pleading poverty and an inability to continue to pay maintenance.

---

[42] In addition to those transferred to her by the original order to provide her with some income.
[43] *North v North*, at [32], Thorpe LJ.

17.25   In the more recent case of *Yates v Yates*[44] the wife received a lump sum of £978,000 by virtue of the original order, almost half of which was designed to enable her to discharge a mortgage. The periodical payments order in her favour was set for a 3-year term. However, the wife chose not to redeem the mortgage on her property and instead re-mortgaged the property for £100,000 and invested that sum in a non-income-producing bond. On the wife's variation application the district judge, in setting the revised level of needs for the wife's periodical payments, accounted for the wife's mortgage interest payments of £500 per month. The Court of Appeal allowed the husband's challenge against the inclusion of mortgage interest payments that were the result not only of the wife's personal choice but also ran contrary to the intention behind payment to her of the original lump sum. Thorpe LJ summarised the position as follows:

> 'it seems to me little more than common sense that if a recipient of a lump sum twice the size of the mortgage on the final matrimonial home **elects** to hold back capital made available for the mortgage discharge in order to invest in a bond that bears no income, she cannot look to the payer thereafter for indemnity or contribution to the continuing mortgage interest payments. That seems to me to be an absolutely self-evident point.' (emphasis added)[45]

Cohabitation

17.26   One party's cohabitation in a settled relationship with another may affect the quantum of a periodical payments order in a variation application just as it may in an original application for periodical payments. Indeed, the cohabitation of one party may be one of the important changes in circumstances since the original order relied upon by the applicant. The financial impact of the cohabitation, whether this manifests as an additional drain on the payer's resources or as a sharing of otherwise individual outgoings, may justify an argument for an increase or decrease to the quantum of payments. The impact of cohabitation on a periodical payments order is dealt with in detail in Chapter 14 and the principles outlined therein are fully applicable in variation cases.

Comparing the percentage of income payable or receivable under the original order with that payable under the variation order

17.27   Fairness has a broad horizon: to that extent, courts are reminded of the importance of 'standing back' from the minutiae of arguments and figures to assess objectively the overall fairness of a financial remedy order. Upon an application to vary, one method for assessing the overall proportionality and fairness of a proposed order is to calculate the percentage of the payer's income proposed to be paid [after the variation] and compare that figure with the percentage of the payer's income subject of the original periodical payments order. The comparison may also be relevant to the extent that the proportion of

---

[44]   [2012] EWCA Civ 532, [2013] 2 FLR 1070.
[45]   At [12], per Thorpe LJ.

the payer's income paid to the payee under the original order may be a 'circumstance of the case' in its own right.

17.28   In *Lauder v Lauder*, the high proportion of the husband's income paid to the wife under the original consent order (35%) was accepted as a relevant circumstance of the case and, albeit not solely determinative of the applicable percentage of his income to be paid at the variation stage, was regarded as one of the background and relevant factors in the case.[46] The order in *Lauder v Lauder* was varied to provide the wife with 30% of the husband's increased income, which was 'in line' with the proportion agreed in the original order.

17.29   In *Hvorostovsky v Hvorostovsky* the Court of Appeal criticised the first instance decision as the judge had not undertaken the percentage-comparison task and, therefore, 'did not stand back from the figures to judge the overall proportionality of his conclusion'.[47]

Backdating upon an application to vary a periodical payments order

17.30   The court has the power to backdate an order made as a result of an application to vary a periodical payments order: this power exists whether the variation provides for an increase or a decrease to the quantum of payment.[48] In principle, the court has a discretion to backdate any variation before the date of making the application to vary. Indeed, the court can, in certain circumstances, backdate the variation to the date of the original order, which is the subject of the variation. In *Grey v Grey*[49] Wall LJ positively endorsed the proposition made in *Rayden & Jackson on Divorce and Family Matters* that 'The court, in so far as its own orders are concerned, has an almost unrestricted power to vary them retrospectively and, moreover, to backdate any variation which it makes in a pre-existing order beyond the date of the application for variation.'

17.31   In *Cornick v Cornick (No 2)*[50] the original order for periodical payments was made in December 1992 and the wife's application for variation (on the basis of a significant increase in the husband's wealth) was determined in September 1994. Hale J backdated the increase in periodical payments upon the wife's variation application to December 1992, on the basis that the husband's income had risen substantially and quickly; indeed, in the first year after the order was made it had nearly doubled. The Court of Appeal did not interfere with Hale J's determination:

> 'No question arises as to the backdating of the order to the date when the application to vary was made, but she went further and adopted what, in *S v S*

---

[46]   *Lauder*, at [66], per Baron J.
[47]   Per Thorpe LJ, at [33].
[48]   MCA 1973, s 31(14).
[49]   [2009] EWCA Civ 1424, [2010] 1 FLR 1764.
[50]   [1995] 2 FLR 490.

[1987] 2 FLR 342, was described as an exceptional step. She back-dated part of the order to the date when the district judge made his award, because of the fact that the husband's income had risen substantially during that period and the wife had not in fact received what had been expected. In the first year after the order as made by the district judge the husband's income had nearly doubled. She took the view that that was an exceptional circumstance which justified her in making an order backdating a partial increase to the date of the district judge's order. Mr Mostyn submits that she thereby exceeded her jurisdiction and wrongly exercised her discretion. I am quite unable to say that she was plainly wrong in exercising her discretion in that way. I believe that it was within the reasonable limits of her discretion and she set out clearly the basis upon which she proceeded to make that order.'[51]

17.32   The only restriction on the court's discretion to backdate a payment is reasonableness. In the case of *S v S*,[52] the order under appeal backdated a variation of periodical payments some 7 years.

'Whilst it is clear on authority and the wording of section 31, as amended, that the power to give an order retrospective effect is unlimited, subject to constraints not relevant to this appeal, this power must be exercised reasonably. There may well be cases, albeit exceptional ones, where in order to right a wrong order made in the past the backdating of the order over a period of years can be justified ... Normally the countervailing effects of a shortfall in proper financial support in the past and the effect of the increase in the size of the order eventually made as a result in the fall in the value of the pound will be compensated in a rough and ready way over a relatively short period of retroactive effect by the exercise of his general discretion by the judge in determining both the size of the order and the length of the backdating.'

Arrears

17.33   The counterweight to the court's ability to backdate any order upon a variation application is its power to remit the payment of any arrears due. Pursuant to MCA 1973, s 31(2A), in the event that the court varies an order for maintenance pending suit, an interim order for maintenance or a periodical payments order (whether secured or not), the court has power to remit the payment of any arrears.[53]

Costs

17.34   An application for variation of a periodical payments order is an application for a 'variation order'[54], which is a 'financial order' within the meaning of the FPR 2010. Therefore, the general rule as to costs applies in that the court will not make an order requiring one party to pay the costs of the other unless one party's conduct of the litigation justifies such an order.[55]

---

[51]   At 495, per Sir Stephen Brown P.
[52]   [1987] 2 All ER 312, at 319h, per Purchas LJ.
[53]   MCA 1973, s 31(2A); CPA 2004, Sch 5, Part 11, para 52.
[54]   See FPR 2010, r 9.3.
[55]   FPR 2010, r 28.3(4), (5) and (7).

VARIATION OF THE TERM OF A PERIODICAL PAYMENTS ORDER

17.35   In the absence of an order preventing the payee from applying to extend the term for a periodical payments order (a 'bar'),[56] the payee can apply to vary the order and extend the term for payment. Commonly, an order for periodical payments will be drafted to terminate on specific events, for example, the youngest child of the family reaching 18 years of age, a certain future calendar date or the payee's cohabitation. Occasionally, an order may also provide for the periodical payments to continue 'until further order'. These words are arguably superfluous, as the court is always entitled to revisit a periodical payments order and to vary its terms or suspend or terminate its application. If a periodical payments order is subject to a term, and that term has expired, the words 'until further order' do not provide a basis for applying to extend the term for payment. The term is absolute unless an application is made to extend: the phrase 'until further order' does not mean 'that only the obligation to pay comes to an end leaving the order comatose but capable of being kissed back to life by an application to vary'.[57]

When to apply to extend the term

17.36   The application to extend a term for payment must be made before the expiration of the term. The final order after an application to extend a term may be made after the expiry of the term, but the application itself must be made beforehand. In *Jones v Jones*[58] the wife was the beneficiary of a 5-year term order for periodical payments with no bar preventing an application to extend the term. Four days before the expiration of the term the wife applied to extend the order to one of joint lives and to increase the amount of the payment. Thorpe LJ, giving the lead judgment, made it clear that only the application must be made before the end of the term and the hearing to determine the application can be held at a later date.

The reasons for the original term order

17.37   Whether by recital in the original [consent] order or by inclusion in the judgment of the court, it can be good practice – depending on the circumstances and the individual represented – to make reference to the reasons for imposing a term order for periodical payments. The reasoning can be a useful tool at a subsequent variation stage to justify or defend an application to extend the term. For example, in *D v D (Financial Provision: Periodical Payments)*[59] Coleridge J provided for a 10-year term with no bar but explicitly stated the following:

---

[56]   MCA 1973, s 28(1A).
[57]   *G v G (Periodical Payments)* [1997] 2 All ER 272, at 284b, per Ward LJ.
[58]   [2000] 2 FLR 307.
[59]   [2004] EWHC 445 (Fam), [2004] 1 FLR 988.

'[26] So it is my clear intention that, all things being equal, there should be no further periodical commitment by the husband to the wife after 10 years. However, I have come to the conclusion that with a term as long as this it is simply unsafe to dismiss her claim outright in 10 years' time, when plainly within that 10-year period there is a significant dependency. It is quite impossible for a court to look as far as 10 years hence with any degree of precision and, although, as I say, my clear view is (and I express it in this strong way) that there should be no further payment by the husband beyond that term, I do not propose to put in place the bar under s 28(1A). If unforeseen events occur within the next 10 years which create for the wife financial embarrassment, it would be wrong after this length of marriage and after this length of dependency after marriage to prevent the court from having the ability to consider the matter again. So there will be no s 28(1A) bar but the order will terminate automatically unless the wife succeeds in extending it within the term.'

In the case of *N v N (Financial Orders: Appellate Role)*[60] the parties compromised their financial claims in 2005 with, amongst others, an order for the husband to pay to the wife periodical payments of £1,000 per month for a period of 5 years with no bar on the wife's ability to apply to extend the term. The consent order included a number of recitals, as follows:

'(1) It is both parties' intention that the wife will become financially independent from the husband within five years of this order.
(2) The wife shall keep the husband informed that any increase to her current income of £1,000 per month or more which takes place at any point during the term of any maintenance order in her favour.'

The District Judge made findings that, despite these recitals, the wife had made no serious attempts to update her skills during the period of the original term order and that the husband had been slow in providing financial disclosure, which had increased the legal costs. Notwithstanding the criticisms of the wife, the district judge extended the periodical payments order for a further 2 years but imposed a bar preventing any further extension thereafter. The wife successfully appealed and the Circuit Judge extended the term for payment for a further 3 years and imposed a nominal periodical payments order afterwards on a joint lives basis. Understandably, the husband appealed. The Court of Appeal reverted to the District Judge's original order. Although the appeal judgment in *N v N* has its focus on the limited role of an appellate court, it is a clear example of the usefulness of including reasoning, rationale and expectations within the body of an original term order for periodical payments. If an order is made by consent, those recitals are too numerous and varied to list but may include, for example, the following matters:

•   A broad expectation of the payee achieving financial independence by a certain date.   →

---

60   [2011] EWCA Civ 940, [2012] 1 FLR 622.

- Reference to any training or further qualifications that the payee intends to take and the timescales involved.

- A note of an expected level of income that the payee can achieve from sources other than periodical payments.

- An agreement that the payee will inform the payer if his/her income from sources other than periodical payments reaches a certain level (information which can be used by the payer to then seek a variation or dismissal of periodical payments).

- A reference to the reasons for a shorter term or a staged reduction in periodical payments over time: for example, linked to the children moving to secondary school or to provide a period of adjustment, re-training or job-seeking.

Applying to extend the term for periodical payments and the requirement of 'exceptional justification'?

17.38 Section 31 of the MCA 1973 makes no reference to any test of 'exceptional justification' that an applicant must satisfy to successfully apply for an order extending a term for periodical payments. However, in the case of *Fleming v Fleming*[61] the Court of Appeal allowed the husband's appeal against an order extending the term of a periodical payments order from 4 years to joint lives but on a reduced quantum. Thorpe LJ stated that the obligations on the court to seek to achieve a clean break, if achievable without undue hardship to the payee, 'are much enhanced in any case where there has been a previous term ordered ... in such circumstances the exercise of the power to extend obligations requires some exceptional justification'.[62] *Fleming v Fleming*, therefore, appears to set a high evidential hurdle for the application to succeed, as the original term order provides a legitimate expectation for the payer that, at the end of the term, the payments will come to an end and the period for payment will not be extended.

17.39 However, the test of 'exceptional justification' has been the subject of an ambivalent approach by the higher courts and the law is arguably unclear as to whether the test has survived. The House of Lords in *Miller; McFarlane* expressly accounted for the *Fleming v Fleming* test in its decision to overturn the Court of Appeal's 5-year term periodical payments order and to reinstate Mrs McFarlane's joint lives order:

> '[97] That is something which will merit careful consideration at a suitably early date. But I do not see how this leads to the conclusion that the district judge's joint lives order should be set aside in favour of an extendable 5 years' order. The practice in the family courts seems to be that on an application for extension of a periodical payments order made for a finite period the applicant must surmount a high threshold: *Fleming v Fleming* [2003] EWCA Civ 1841; [2004] 1 FLR 667, at 670, paras [12]—[14]. In the present case it would be altogether inappropriate,

---

[61] [2003] EWCA Civ 1841, [2004] 1 FLR 667.
[62] *Fleming*, at [13].

indeed unjust, to make a 5-year order and place the wife in that position when 5 years has elapsed. In the present case a 5-year order is most unlikely to be sufficient to achieve a fair outcome. Further financial provision of some sort will be needed. So, far from compelling the wife to apply for an extension of a 5-year order, and requiring her to shoulder the heavy burden accompanying such an application, it is more appropriate for the husband to have to take the initiative in applying for a variation of a joint lives order when he considers circumstances make that appropriate.'[63]

17.40   In Mrs McFarlane's subsequent variation application,[64] Charles J stated obiter that the test for 'exceptional justification' was neither appropriate nor applicable: instead, the focus should be on the *reasoning* behind an original order for a term for periodical payments; therefore, 'on an application to vary it can be assessed whether the purpose of the earlier order has been fulfilled and, if it has, this would be a relevant (and perhaps a decisive) factor in favour of refusing an extension or variation'.[65] Charles J reaffirmed his view as to the inapplicability of the 'exceptional justification' test in the case of *G v G (Financial Remedies: Short Marriage: Trust Assets).*[66] In *G v G*, Charles J was not concerned with a term order for periodical payments but rather one that provided for a reducing amount to the payments over a 6-year period to reflect the wife's predicted earnings. Charles J commented that, if the *Fleming v Fleming* test did survive, the mere fact that an order for periodical payments provided for a staged reduction to the quantum of periodical payments over time did not, of itself, provide a reason for the applicant to prove 'exceptional justification':

> '[145] I remain of the view I expressed about *Fleming v Fleming* [2003] EWCA Civ 1841, [2004] 1 FLR 667 in para [104] of my judgment in *McFarlane v McFarlane* [2009] EWHC 891 (Fam), [2009] 2 FLR 1322. But, if that is wrong and in any event, *Fleming v Fleming* does not have direct application to an order that provides for reductions in periodical payments to take account of the predicted earnings of a spouse rather than its termination pursuant to s 25A(2). Notwithstanding the overlap between a termination and a reduction by reference to an assessment of future earnings, in my view the intention of the court in so ordering reductions would not normally found the legitimate expectation referred to in *Fleming v Fleming*, and thus the need for the payee to provide an exceptional justification for a variation. Rather, when reductions are ordered it seems to me that the expectation is, and the approach on a variation would be, that the court will look at the reasons why, in the events that have happened, the predictions upon which the reductions are founded have been shown to have been wrong, the reasons for this and their impact in all the circumstances (including the reasons for the original award).'

It is not absolutely clear whether an applicant seeking to extend the term for an order for periodical payments must plead and evidence an 'exceptional

---

[63]   Per Lord Nicholls of Birkenhead and see also at [155], per Baroness Hale of Richmond, in which she did not question whether the *Fleming v Fleming* test was wrong in principle.
[64]   *McFarlane v McFarlane* [2009] 2 FLR 1322.
[65]   *McFarlane* [2009], at [104].
[66]   [2012] 2 FLR 48.

justification'. However, without a judgment from the Court of Appeal or higher overturning *Fleming v Fleming*,[67] the test must be considered by any potential applicant. Until then, the need for 'exceptional justification' will continue to support arguments that (a) a joint lives order is more appropriate in cases in which the potential harm of a term order is greater to the payee than the payer and (b) the payer should bear the burden of applying to vary or terminate a joint lives order, an application which does not require 'exceptional justification'.

---

[67]   Unfortunately, Eleanor King J did not deal expressly with the question of whether the *Fleming v Fleming* test remained applicable in the case of *L v L (Financial Remedies: Deferred Clean Break)* [2012] 1 FLR 1283.

POINTS OF PRACTICE AND THEORY

17.41

(1) In an application to vary a periodical payments order, the following considerations are/may be relevant (depending on the circumstances of the case)

   (a) the welfare of a minor child of the family;

   (b) any change in any of the matters to which the court was required to have regard when making the original order;

   (c) the pervasive search for a clean break;

   (d) the reasons for, and purpose of, the original order (why is a change to the existing payments regime necessary and appropriate?);

   (e) the fact that the original order has set a pattern to the parties' lives since divorce (assess the parties' standards of living at the time of the variation application);

   (f) any ongoing compensatory element (for relationship-generated disadvantage);

   (g) the impact of a party's financial mismanagement, extravagance or irresponsibility since the original order;

   (h) the financial choices and decisions made by the parties since the original order;

   (i) a party's cohabitation with another person;

   (j) the difference between the percentage of income payable under the original order and the percentage of income payable under the varied order.

(2) The court has a discretion to backdate any variation to a point before the date of making the application to vary.

(3) The application to extend a term for periodical payments must be made before the expiration of the term, albeit that the hearing of, and judgment on, the application may take place after the end of the term.

(4) The law remains unclear as to whether a condition of 'exceptional justification' is required to apply successfully for an order extending a term for periodical payments. An assessment may be undertaken at the variation stage to ascertain whether the purpose of the original order has been fulfilled and, if it has, this may be a relevant (and perhaps a decisive) factor in favour of refusing an extension to the term. Pending clarification from the Court of Appeal, the need for 'exceptional justification' will continue to support arguments that:

   (a) a joint lives order is more appropriate in cases in which the potential harm of a term order is greater to the payee than the payer; and

   (b) the payer should bear the burden of applying to vary or terminate a joint lives order, an application which does not require 'exceptional justification'.

CHAPTER 18

CAPITALISATION UPON AN APPLICATION TO VARY A PERIODICAL PAYMENTS ORDER

'What the judge is endeavouring to do is to express as a capital sum what is a fair capital sum in the circumstances in substitution for the periodical payments which would otherwise have been appropriate.'[1]

INTRODUCTION

18.1   Capitalisation is the term given to the process of substituting an order of a capital nature for an order for periodical payments, whether those payments are secured or not. In this chapter, the term also includes the substitution of a pension sharing[2] or property adjustment order, even though such an order is not strictly 'capital' in nature, in the sense of an order for the payment of a lump sum. Capitalisation can also be a method of achieving a clean break.[3] Therefore, just as a Cash Equivalent (Value) is a method for valuing the benefits which have accrued to a pension scheme member, the process of capitalisation seeks – in its simplest terms – to attribute a fair cash value to a future income stream from an existing or varied periodical payments order.

18.2   The court is provided with options as to how such an attributed value is to be paid to the payee, whether by payment of a lump sum or by the making of a property adjustment order; or, alternatively, by imposition of a pension sharing order[4] to replace the income generated by the periodical payments order.

18.3   Capitalisation, if it is ordered, is the result of a staged assessment, which begins with the court's evaluation of the underlying application to vary a periodical payments order and ends with the capitalised order. Therefore, this chapter should be read after, and in conjunction with, Chapter 17, which deals with the court's approach to the assessment of variation applications.

---

[1]   *Harris v Harris* [2001] 1 FCR 68, at [44], per Pill LJ.
[2]   Or pension compensation order.
[3]   See Chapter 15 on *Duxbury* calculations.
[4]   In cases involving a petition filed on or after 1 December 2000.

18.4   For the payer, capitalisation represents, on the one hand, income-freedom through the termination of ongoing duties to pay maintenance but, on the other, the risk of over-payment. For the payee, capitalisation provides capital security and independence with the danger of under-payment. Any capital sum that appears appropriate at the time of the application may be shown, as a result of future events, to have worked in favour of, or against, one or other of the parties.[5] Therein lies the difficulty with all capitalisation claims: the court must strive to value a *future* income stream, which is the result of an *historical* order in light of the *current* and *anticipated* circumstances of the parties. In so doing, the court must also strive to impose an order that is fair in all the circumstances.

LEGAL BASIS

18.5   The legal basis is statutory and is found in the Matrimonial Causes Act 1973 (MCA 1973), s 31(7),[6] which provides as follows:

'(7A) Subsection (7B) below applies where, after the dissolution of a marriage, the court –

(a)   discharges a periodical payments order or secured periodical payments order made in favour of a party to the marriage; or
(b)   varies such an order so that payments under the order are required to be made or secured only for such further period as is determined by the court.

(7B) The court has power, in addition to any power it has apart from this subsection, to make supplemental provision consisting of any of –

(a)   an order for the payment of a lump sum in favour of a party to the marriage;
(b)   one or more property adjustment orders in favour of a party to the marriage;
(ba) one or more pension sharing orders;
(c)   a direction that the party in whose favour the original order discharged or varied was made is not entitled to make any further application for –
       (i)   a periodical payments or secured periodical payments order, or
       (ii)   an extension of the period to which the original order is limited by any variation made by the court.

(7C) An order for the payment of a lump sum made under subsection (7B) above may –

(a)   provide for the payment of that sum by instalments of such amount as may be specified in the order; and
(b)   require the payment of the instalments to be secured to the satisfaction of the court.'

---

[5]   *Harris v Harris*, at [77], per Pill LJ.
[6]   Civil Partnership Act 2004 (CPA 2004), Sch 5, Part 11, para 53.

APPLICABILITY AND PROCEDURE

18.6   The court has the power to capitalise only if it *discharges* a periodical payments order or *varies* a periodical payments order so that payments are only to be made (or secured) for a fixed period i e if the court imposes a term for payment. Additionally, even though an order for capitalisation is a 'supplemental' order within the wording of MCA 1973, a party seeking capitalisation should apply specifically for such an order (in addition to the variation application) so that the respondent is fully aware of the case that will be presented at trial. In *NG v SG (Appeal: Non-Disclosure)*[7] the husband appealed an order capitalising a periodical payments order in favour of the wife. The wife had not applied for capitalisation and the possibility of such an order was only mentioned by counsel in final written submissions. Mostyn J stated the following:

> 'My first conclusion is that the decision to invoke the capitalisation provisions in s 31(7A) and (7B) MCA 1973 and to make an award of £675,000 thereunder in the circumstances which I have described was demonstrably wrong in principle and flawed. It is noteworthy that in the principal authority concerning capitalisation, *Pearce v Pearce* [2003] 2 FLR 1144, CA (which was not cited to the court) both parties had formally applied for capitalisation. It must be elementary that the proposed payer of a capitalisation award should actually receive, with ample notice, an application for that relief. Moreover, the directions of the court and the evidence would need specifically to address the relief sought. All manner of bespoke Duxbury calculations would likely need to be done. The fact that H's representatives did not raise a complaint about this change of tack by W after 21 April 2011 does not cure this fundamental defect.'[8]

ORDERS AVAILABLE ON AN APPLICATION FOR 'CAPITALISATION'

18.7   The court may order the following relief in favour of one of the parties to the marriage:

(1)   *Payment of a lump sum*:[9] the lump sum may be ordered to be paid on a 'one-off' basis or in instalments,[10] and the court may require security for payment.[11] Interest can be charged on late payments and the order can specify the rate of applicable interest.[12]

---

[7]   [2011] EWHC 3270 (Fam), [2012] 1 FLR 1211.

[8]   At [46].

[9]   MCA 1973, s 31(7B)(a); CPA 2004, Sch 5, Part 11, para 53(2)(a).

[10]   See, for example, *Grocholewska-Mullins v Mullins* [2013] EWCA Civ 1121: at the time of writing, this is only a judgment giving permission to appeal against an order providing for staged lump sum payments by way of capitalisation. If the court is replacing an income stream with a capital sum, it must have regard to the transition period from one to the other and ensure that its order provides for short-term income protection for the payee before receipt of the capital sum.

[11]   MCA 1973, s 31(7C) ; CPA 2004, Sch 5, Part 11, para 54.

[12]   See MCA 1973, s 23(6).

(2)   *One or more property adjustment orders:*[13] albeit that if the court makes more than one property adjustment order in favour of the same party to the marriage, each order must be of a different category of property adjustment order (ie order for transfer of property OR settlement of property OR variation of settlement).[14]

(3)   *One or more pension sharing orders:*[15] such relief is available where the petition was filed after 1 December 2000 AND the pension to be shared has not been the subject of a previous pension sharing order in relation to the marriage of the parties involved in the variation application.[16]

(4)   *A pension compensation order.*[17]

(5)   *A direction of the court* prohibiting the payee of the original order from making a further application for periodical payments OR a bar on extending the period of the original order for the payment of periodical payments[18] (a clean break).

This battery of orders provides the court with the power and means to effect a clean break between the parties at a date shortly or significantly after the original order for periodical payments. Irrespective of any prior order for a clean break as to the capital, property and pension claims of the parties, the existence of an ongoing periodical payments order may entitle the payee to further capital, property and pension sharing orders upon an application to vary and/or capitalise. It is *crucial* for the payer to be aware of his or her exposure to this future risk at the time of the initial periodical payments order, particularly in relation to cases in which no pension sharing order is made at that stage. If a pension sharing order has been made, the payer of a periodical payments order may have good reason to continue investing in the pension scheme that has already been shared, as a pension scheme cannot be subject to more than one pension sharing order.

THE BENEFITS AND DISADVANTAGES OF CAPITALISATION UPON A VARIATION APPLICATION

18.8

> Whether capitalisation is appropriate or not will depend, of course, on the circumstances of each individual case, the prevailing economic conditions and the financial position of each party. The following general benefits and disadvantages usually apply:[19]   ➡

---

[13]   MCA 1973, s 31(7B)(b); CPA 2004, Sch 5, Part 11, para 53(2)(b).
[14]   MCA 1973, s 31(7E).
[15]   MCA 1973, s 31(7B)(ba); CPA 2004, Sch 5, Part 11, para 53(2)(c).
[16]   MCA 1973, s 24B(3); CPA 2004, Sch 5, Part 4, para 18.
[17]   MCA 1973, s 31(7B)(bb).
[18]   MCA 1973, s 31(7B)(c); CPA 2004, Sch 5, Part 11, para 53(2)(d).
[19]   In this sense, capitalisation is taken as effecting a full clean break between the parties.

(a) *Security*: periodical payments orders are always variable (upwards or downwards) and are, therefore, inherently insecure, particularly in cases where the payer's income relies, for example, on bonus payments, dividend drawings or payments from a discretionary trust.[20] Capitalisation offers the security of a fixed capital receipt and payment for both the payee and payer respectively.

(b) *Cohabitation and re-marriage*: the payee's cohabitation can affect the quantum of a periodical payments order, depending on the cohabitee's financial position. The payee's remarriage automatically terminates a periodical payments order. Therefore, capitalisation can afford some future income/capital security, 'freeing' the payee to enter into a new relationship without the risk of a subsequent reduction or cessation of financial support.

(c) *Court applications*: periodical payments are vulnerable to court applications for the enforcement of payments, the enforcement (or remittance) of arrears, variation, suspension and termination. The payment of a capital sum to terminate periodical payments affords protection from the costs and uncertainty of negotiation and litigation.

(d) *Achieving a clean break*: capitalisation and the termination of periodic financial dependence meets the law's expectation of considering and effecting a clean break, if it is possible to do so without the payee suffering undue hardship.

(e) *Recession or growth-proofing*: in times of recession and financial uncertainty, a periodical payments order (assessed as a percentage of the payer's income) may provide more flexibility to meet a payer's unpredictable financial future. Capitalisation may result in a significant overpayment by the payer should his income reduce significantly thereafter. Conversely, in times of prosperity, the payee may receive a capital sum and submit to a clean break, which precludes the possibility of benefiting from a significant improvement in the payer's earnings.

(f) *Payer's prosperity*: for the payer, the release from the obligation to make periodical payments permits room to focus on career-development and the rebuilding of wealth and financial security without the looming shadow (as it may be seen) of financial disclosure, investigation and criticism of economic decisions.

(g) *Payee's freedom*: equally, the payee's receipt of a capital sum allows freedom to control, invest, spend and otherwise employ the proceeds without similar risks of disclosure, investigation and criticism.

---

[20] See, for example, *Whaley v Whaley* [2011] EWCA Civ 617, [2012] 1 FLR 735.

CAPITALISATION AND THE PROHIBITION AGAINST CAPITAL READJUSTMENT

18.9 A claim for capitalisation is essentially a claim for capital or other financial provision representing the value of a *future* income stream, assessed as a fair outcome having regard to all the circumstances of the case. The claim will always be made[21] after the court has already provided for a fair distribution of any capital assets, property and pension provision between the parties; therefore, the claim is not an opportunity for the parties (or the court) to revisit or revise the original capital claims between the parties or to make a further distribution of capital 'by the back door' (*Lauder v Lauder*):[22]

> '[70] I do not consider that this case merits any provision for 'sharing' the husband's wealth. Even though this is an unusual case, the capital claims have already been dealt with and I am clear that this application cannot be used as a basis to distribute capital by the back door. Accordingly, where the husband has been successful since the separation and some 20 years have elapsed, no element of sharing is to be provided.'

The Court of Appeal affirmed this prohibition in the leading case of *Pearce v Pearce*.[23] In *Pearce*, the marriage had lasted some 14 years. The original order provided the wife with periodical payments of £36,000 per annum on a joint lives basis. In the following years the wife made a loss of £50,000 on a property that she had purchased in Ireland. At the time of the variation hearing, the husband's capital had increased but his income had decreased from £270,000 per annum at the time of the original hearing to £130,000 per annum. At the capitalisation hearing the wife's needs were found to be £47,000 per annum, which, according to the *Duxbury* tables,[24] produced a capitalised figure of £635,000. The judge ordered a lump sum payment from the husband of £740,000. The Court of Appeal substituted the Judge's order with the lesser figure of £655,000 and definitively concluded that 'there is simply no power or discretion to embark on further adjustment of capital to reflect the outcome of unwise or unfortunate investment on one side or prudent or lucky investment on the other ...'.[25] Thorpe LJ provided the skeleton process for courts to follow in claims for capitalisation (see further below and **18.10**) in order to respect the finality of the original order on the one hand, whilst, on the other, doing justice to the changed financial circumstances that exist at the time of a variation and capitalisation order:

> '[39] I believe that this discipline is necessary as a safeguard against the temptation to further adjust the capital division between the parties to reflect the factors which were not foreseen or which did not pertain at the date of the original division. This abstinence is required not only by authority but ➡

---

21   Unless, in rare cases, claims for lump sums, for example, have been adjourned.
22   *Lauder v Lauder* [2007] EWHC 1227, [2007] 2 FLR 802, at [70], per Baron J.
23   [2003] 3 FCR 178.
24   For more detail on *Duxbury* calculations, see Chapter 15.
25   *Pearce* at [36], per Thorpe LJ.

also as a matter of policy. Families with not inconsiderable assets are obliged to achieve division, by one means or another, once the marriage has foundered. They are entitled to know that that obligation once completed does not revive. In cases where a complete clean break cannot be achieved at the date of redistribution of the family assets it is important that the parties should be encouraged to take advantage of any subsequent developments that permit the dismissal of the outstanding periodical payments order. The court has its duty under s 31(7)(a). Therefore a relatively simple, certain and predictable method for the calculation of the capital sum that can fairly be substituted for the periodical payments order is of great importance. It enables parties to see where they stand and to weigh the relative advantages and disadvantages of finality. It contributes to the compromise of the issue and thus to a reduction in contested cases.'

THE STAGED-ASSESSMENT APPROACH (LUMP SUM PAYMENT)

18.10   The court's approach to capitalisation (in terms of quantifying the lump sum payable to achieve a clean break) is now relatively well settled by case-law, particularly in cases involving a joint lives periodical payments order.[26] However, even though the procedure and formulae for the parties and the court to follow are clear, the result will, in no unusual sense, very much depend on the particular facts of each case.

The staged-assessment should guide the preparation and presentation of any capitalisation case; it involves asking a series of questions,[27] as follows:

(1)   Should periodical payments continue at all – ie can the payee adjust to their termination without undue hardship (within the meaning of MCA 1973, s 31(7)(a))?[28]

(2)   If ongoing periodical payments are necessary and fair, should the level of payment provided for in the original order vary upwards or downwards?

(3)   If a variation is required, what is the fair revised figure for ongoing periodical payments?

(4)   From what date should the variation commence? Should this be backdated?   →

---

[26]   That is, an order for periodical payments that is not limited by a specific term for payment, eg 5 years.

[27]   Originally consisting of three questions (*Pearce v Pearce*) but extended in this text to demonstrate the ancillary and additional questions introduced in subsequent case-law.

[28]   *Vaughan v Vaughan*, [2010] 2 FLR 242, at [28], per Wilson LJ.

(5)   What capital payment, calculated in accordance with the *Duxbury* tables, should be substituted for the income stream that is being terminated?[29]

(6)   Does the payer own property (which may be transferred) or have rights in a pension scheme (which may be shared) that can provide an alternative means of achieving capitalisation?

(7)   Is it fair[30] to both parties to capitalise the periodical payments and, in particular, is it reasonably practicable for the payer to pay the capital sum (or transfer property or share a pension, as appropriate) rather than make ongoing periodical payments?[31]

Stages 1–4 are dealt with comprehensively in Chapter 17 on Variation and the principles on which the court acts in following these stages will not be repeated here. The following analysis will focus on the enquiry relevant to stages 5 to 7 above.

Stage 5: Quantification of the lump sum

18.11   The substitution of a lump sum payment and the achievement of a clean break is entirely consistent with the ethos of financial remedy litigation. In *Minton v Minton*[32] Lord Scarman highlighted the importance of the 'clean break' principle in the Matrimonial Causes Act 1973 because 'an object of the modern law is to encourage each [party] to put the past behind them and to begin a new life which is not overshadowed by the relationship that has broken down'.[33] The question of *whether* to capitalise a periodical payments order rarely proves as contentious as the question of '*how* to quantify the recipient's compensation for the dismissal of a statutory right'[34] (emphasis added). It is generally obvious upon financial disclosure whether the payer has capital, property or pension provision sufficient to capitalise a periodical payments order. How the level of the appropriate lump sum (or other order) is calculated often proves more problematic.

The use of a *Duxbury* calculation

18.12   The *Duxbury* calculation can and should be used to assist in calculating the appropriate figure to capitalise a claimant's future income need both at the stage of a final order (when a full clean break will be imposed[35]) and upon any

---

[29]   *Pearce*, at [37]. If capitalisation is to be achieved by means of a property adjustment order, stages 1–5 should be followed but any capital sum should be 'paid' by transfer, settlement or variation of settlement of property to the value of the capitalised sum.

[30]   Fairness will also require the court to consider whether, despite the uncertainties in future events which often plague these applications, a solution can be reached that is fair to both parties (*W v W (Periodical Payments: Variation)* [2010] 2 FLR 985).

[31]   Wilson LJ, at [28].

[32]   [1979] AC 593.

[33]   Ibid, at 608.

[34]   *Harris v Harris* [2001] 1 FCR 68, CA, at 74A, per Thorpe LJ.

[35]   Terminating any right to apply for or receive periodical payments.

later application for capitalisation.[36] Stage 5 in the capitalisation process above suggests that a *Duxbury* calculation is the *only* solution in capitalisation cases in which a joint lives periodical payments order remains appropriate but is being discharged and capitalised.[37] However, despite the Court of Appeal in *Pearce v Pearce* promoting the use of the *Duxbury* tables in capitalisation cases in order to encourage consistency and certainty, it has proved impossible in other cases to avoid deviating from the strictures of *Duxbury* figures in order to accommodate fairly the unique circumstances of each case.

18.13 Stage 5, therefore, *requires* initial recourse to the *Duxbury* tables, which represent the approved and accepted method for translating the (varied) future income stream into a lump sum. For a large number of cases, if the payer has sufficient resources, the calculation of the appropriate figure in line with the *Duxbury* tables will stand. In other cases, however, the case-law is not consistent as to (1) how much latitude the judge in a capitalisation case has to deviate from the lump sum figure produced by the *Duxbury* calculation, and (2) for what reasons.

18.14 The extent to which the court may deviate from the *Duxbury* calculation necessarily reflects the substantive differences between final orders and subsequent capitalisation orders. The former seek to determine all live financial claims upon divorce. The latter, in contrast, do not provide any opportunity to revisit the original capital distribution AND have a much more limited focus on the determination of an ongoing periodical payments claim. In final clean break orders upon divorce, *Duxbury* 'is a tool and not a rule'[38] (*White v White*); *Duxbury* tables 'have an obvious utility but they can never amount to more than the offer of a starting point' (*Harris v Harris*).[39] In capitalisation cases, the Duxbury calculation is not a straightjacket that binds the court's hands, but the discretion retained by the judge is more severely curtailed: the discretion is 'a *narrower* one, in departing from the mathematics of the Duxbury tables to reflect *special factors* which individual cases will regularly generate'[40] (emphasis added).

18.15 Following *Pearce v Pearce*, Wilson LJ in the case of *Vaughan v Vaughan*[41] stated that 'the court has, thank goodness, only a narrow discretion to arrive at a capital sum otherwise than by application of the Duxbury formula and it should exercise it in order only to reflect special factors'.[42] These special factors are potentially limitless in nature but the following can be drawn from the case-law.

---

[36] For a more detailed assessment of the *Duxbury* calculation, its parameters and limitations, see Chapter 15.
[37] The same basic formula can also be used if the capitalisation is referable to a fixed term of payments rather than to a predicted lifetime of payments; for example, the Capitalise programme enables such a calculation to be undertaken.
[38] [1998] 3 FCR 45, at 56.
[39] At 74G (and on a joint life basis not a whole life basis).
[40] *Pearce*, at [38].
[41] [2010] 2 FLR 242.
[42] *Vaughan*, at [28] (in which case the court did not deviate from the *Duxbury* figure).

The Duxbury calculation and the capitalisation of a term order for periodical payments

18.16   The *Duxbury* calculation is based on a party's future lifetime income needs. If, on a variation application, the court capitalises a *term* order for periodical payments or varies an original order but only for a *limited term* (as opposed to a joint lives order), the use of a 'straight'[43] *Duxbury* calculation to quantify the appropriate lump sum payment will be inappropriate. For example, if a wife, who is 40 years old, has the benefit of a 3-year order for periodical payments at the rate of £20,000 per annum which, on her variation application, is increased to £25,000 per annum and extended by 10 years, the '*Duxbury*' calculation for a woman of 43 years of age to provide a similar *lifetime* income is £505,000.[44] By contrast, a simple formula multiplying 10 years by £25,000 results in a lump sum of £250,000. However, such a 'straight-line' calculation ignores, for example, the inherent variables included in the *Duxbury* formula such as the wife's ability to invest the lump sum to generate an income or the discount for the early receipt of capital.[45]

18.17   There are a number of ways to calculate the appropriate lump sum to capitalise a limited term of periodical payments. It is arguably good practice to have reference to a number of different sources for the calculation to cross-check its accuracy.[46]

Special factors justifying a departure from the Duxbury calculation

18.18   Special factors must be drawn from those listed in MCA 1973, s 25(2), which include the 'catch-all' reference to 'all the circumstances of the case'. The following three examples illustrate cases in which special factors existed and their influence on the eventual award.

The 'Duxbury paradox', old age and ill-health

18.19   In *Lauder v Lauder*,[47] the original consent order was made in 1988 after a 24-year marriage. At that time, the youngest of the three children was 14 years old. The wife, who suffered from ill-health during the marriage, received approximately 26% of the capital assets and a periodical payments order at the rate of 35% of the husband's income on a joint lives basis. In the event, the original order – which was made on the understanding that the wife would receive financial support for life from the husband – was put into suspension by the parties and not implemented. That was a very unusual circumstance of the case. The wife suffered from ongoing mobility and health problems during the

---

[43]   Ie without any amendments to cater for a term much shorter that the payee's life expectancy.
[44]   At A Glance 2013–2014, Table 16, *Duxbury* Calculations.
[45]   See also *Yates v Yates* [2012] EWCA Civ 532, [2013] 2 FLR 1070.
[46]   For example, the Capitalise computer programme and the Financial Tables in Duckworth's 'Matrimonial Property and Finance'.
[47]   [2007] 2 FLR 802.

marriage and subsequently, but had nevertheless secured work as a secretary after separation. By the date of the variation hearing, the husband had generated an asset base of no less than £4.5m and a net income of £200,000 per annum. Conversely, the wife had assets of £487,900 and £9,000 gross income per annum from pension payments and benefits. The wife's periodical payments order (as suspended) was varied at first instance to £40,000 per annum and capitalised at a figure of £500,000 using a *Duxbury* calculation.

18.20   On appeal before Baron J, the wife was 70 and the husband 68 years old. Baron J accepted the *Duxbury* calculation as the starting point and used it as a basis for reaching a fair outcome. However, the judge was concerned that the use of a *Duxbury* calculation alone could lead to unfairness to an older wife after a long marriage and a significant period of post-separation financial dependence, particularly in circumstances where the figure adopted for the wife's annual income needs was too low. Therefore, Baron J's view was that *Duxbury* 'is not the entire answer, given this lady's age, unless the multiplicand is sufficiently high. It is, however, a check against such order as I consider is appropriate'.[48] In the circumstances, Baron J adopted a reverse approach to the *Duxbury* calculation[49] and imposed a lump sum payment of £725,000, which provided the wife with £60,000 per annum net income.

18.21   The wife's age and ill-health, her long-term financial dependence on the husband and the length of the marriage justified a higher capitalisation figure, albeit that the calculation was based on a level of periodical payments £20,000 per annum higher than determined at first instance. Baron J concluded that:

> 'she also needs sufficient capital to enable her to live the rest of her life without having to worry about finances. At her age, she should not feel that she is confined to a budget without there being some margin for error. Twenty-four years of marriage give her that entitlement.'[50]

Arrears and miscellaneous compensation

18.22   Additional special factors justifying a departure from the Duxbury calculation may be the existence of arrears of periodical payments or the subsequent loss of rights that were acquired under the original order for financial relief. In *Pearce v Pearce* the Court of Appeal allowed the wife to recover £25,000 additional capital for the husband's release from an undertaking he gave within the original order to share with the wife the use of a holiday home in Italy. Furthermore, the lump sum payment ordered included £10,000 towards the payment of arrears of periodical payments.

---

[48]   *Lauder*, at [71], per Baron J.
[49]   Ie deciding an appropriate lump sum award and then considering the level of income that such a lump sum would produce.
[50]   At [73].

The payee's cohabitation/shorter marriages

18.23 In *K v K (Periodical Payment: Cohabitation)*[51] Coleridge J was concerned with a case in which the wife was in a settled relationship of cohabitation at the time of the variation application. The *Duxbury* calculation to capitalise periodical payments of £12,000 per annum (which the judge had determined was appropriate) for a lady of 54 years of age required a lump sum of £175,000. Coleridge J reduced this sum to account for a reversionary annuity purchased by the husband for the benefit of the wife (which had an actuarial value of £47,000).[52] Additionally, the judge made a further reduction to reflect the fact of the wife's settled cohabitation and the consequent shorter period of financial support expected by the husband. The final figure of £100,000 was reached as follows:

> 'The Duxbury model has been approved by the Court of Appeal in the context of these applications to capitalise. But it seems to me at this stage of the calculation the fact that the wife and Mr B have been in a settled relationship for 3 years and show every sign of continuing to remain in that state (having become fully involved in each others' financial affairs) must impact on any capitalisation process by way of reduction of the period of dependency ...'[53]

> 'In rough and ready terms that is about a 20% reduction for the fact and financial impact of [the wife's] cohabitation and the financial implications which flow from it'.[54]

In *W v W (Periodical Payments: Variation)*[55] Moylan J departed considerably from the *Duxbury* figure produced when capitalising an annual periodical payments claim of £40,000. In *W v W* the marriage had been short (2 years), there was one child of the family and both parties were cohabiting with new partners. The wife (W) had not worked after the divorce whereas the husband had sold his business for circa £11.4m net. At trial W sought a capitalised sum of £985,000 as the Duxbury figure but accepted a reduction to £800,000 to reflect, in particular, the short length of the marriage and the fact of her cohabitation. Moylan J reduced the 'straight' *Duxbury* figure for capitalisation of £940,000 to a lump sum payment by the husband of £625,000 to enable W to adjust to the termination of periodical payments without undue hardship. The judge placed some weight on the ongoing contributions of W to the care of the parties' child, which necessarily extended well beyond the short period of the marriage itself. The reasons for the reduction were explained as follows by Moylan J: →

---

[51] [2005] EWHC 2886 (Fam), [2006] 2 FLR 468.
[52] Alternatively, by notionally increasing the wife's age by the number of years during which the annuity would be paid, which resulted in a similar reduction of £53,000.
[53] *K v K*, at [101].
[54] *K v K*, at [103].
[55] [2010] 2 FLR 985.

'[99] I do not consider it appropriate to capitalise the wife's income claims by the application of what has been called a straight Duxbury. That would produce a sum very broadly of £940,000. Nor do I consider that the sum proposed by Mr Cohen, namely £800,000 is appropriate. This would not give proper weight to the matters referred to by Miss Boyd, including the length of the marriage, the manner in which the husband's wealth has accrued and the wife's cohabitation with Mr N ...'

'[100] ... in my judgment ... the husband's case does not give sufficient weight in particular to the contributions that the wife has made and will make to the welfare of the family and instead gives too much weight to the length of the marriage and to the wife's relationship with Mr N. The wife's contribution to the welfare of the family will have extended over a period of approximately 24 years, if measured from the date when the parties started living together to when T [the child] will reach the age of 21. This is a very substantial period of time. The consequences of these years of contribution will continue for the rest of the wife's life. Accordingly, it is her contributions as a mother to which I give significant weight in contrast to her contributions as a wife which existed for a relatively short period, even if the years of pre-marital cohabitation are included, and to which I ascribe considerably less weight. In my view also, her contributions as a mother entitle the wife to a measure of financial independence.'

'[101] ... £625,000 ... is a significant discount from a straight Duxbury but is an award which properly reflects the *dominant factors* in this case to which I have already referred' (emphasis added).

Stage 6: pension sharing orders and capitalisation

18.24   It is common for the payer to make an application to vary and capitalise a periodical payments order in expectation of imminent retirement. The court may, upon such an application, substitute a periodical payments order with one or more pension sharing orders, if appropriate, in lieu of, or in addition to, the payment of a capital sum. This resolution is not a 'capitalisation' of maintenance in the literal sense, as it replaces one income stream (periodical payments) with another (payments from a pension fund or annuity). However, it can be the court's preferred resolution to a claim for 'capitalisation' if the circumstances of the case justify recourse to a pension sharing order.[56]

18.25   In *Pearce v Pearce*, Thorpe LJ commented that, given the simplicity in replacing one income stream with another whilst terminating the dependency of periodical payments, 'in my judgment, in any case in which the court can exercise jurisdiction under s 31(7B)(ba), it should endeavour to conclude the issue by so doing, only considering capital orders, whether alternatively or

---

[56]   Note that a pension sharing order may also provide the transferee recipient with a (tax-free) lump sum in addition to an ongoing income stream.

additionally, where the circumstances would not permit the court to achieve a fair outcome by substituting a pension sharing order for the periodical payments order'.[57]

18.26   The circumstances relevant to the question of whether imposition of a pension sharing order is fair will include:

(a)   the ages of the parties;
(b)   the size, value and types of the pension funds available for division;
(c)   whether the payee is at (or close to) an age allowing access to the income benefits from any pension sharing order;
(d)   whether the payer's pension pot will, on its own or in conjunction with other income streams, also provide sufficiently and fairly for the payer's retirement (either on its own or in conjunction with other capital and investments).

If a pension sharing order is appropriate, actuarial evidence will be required to assess the pension fund's value, any lump sum payment available under the pension scheme and the future income derivable.

Pension peculiarities

18.27   Pension sharing orders made on a variation and capitalisation application must observe the limitations and peculiarities applicable in any substantive claim for a financial remedy, as follows:

(a)   Expert actuarial evidence will be necessary to calculate the appropriate percentage of the pension sharing order needed to generate the income required by the payee.
(b)   The court cannot make a pension sharing order in relation to a pension arrangement or shareable state scheme rights, which is/are already the subject of a pension sharing order in relation to the marriage in question.[58]
(c)   Beware, in addition, the possibility of 'income gap syndrome', which can be created if the pension to be shared is in payment but the recipient of the pension sharing order cannot access the pension benefits for a period of time.[59]

---

[57]   *Pearce*, at [15], per Thorpe LJ.
[58]   MCA 1973, s 24B(3), (4).
[59]   Salter, Rae and Ellison, *Pensions on Divorce, Law, Practice and Precedents* (2009), p 136: income gap syndrome occurs 'where a pension sharing order is made against a pension in payment, as a result of which the pension debit brings about an immediate reduction in the pension in payment. The person with the benefit of the pension credit, however, may not receive any instantaneous corresponding benefit as, under the terms applicable to her internal pension credit membership or, on an external transfer, the destination arrangement ... she may not be able to take benefits for a number of years'.

Stage 7: Is it right and fair to capitalise?: resources and uncertainty

18.28 The final stage for the court is to assess whether, in all the circumstances of the case, it is fair to impose a capitalised order. This stage will involve consideration of the available financial resources (particularly of the payer), any risks associated with the parties' future income, their contingent debts and assets and the age and health of either party etc. In cases in which the financial resources of the payer are sufficient to withstand a capitalised order, the court will generally only decline to make such an order if the financial or personal uncertainties[60] are such as to preclude the achievement of fairness through the process of capitalisation. The standard, therefore, is relatively high for the court to decline to make a capitalised order. For example, in *W v W*, Moylan J rejected the husband's argument that the wife's cohabitation made capitalisation inappropriate because of the uncertainty as to whether she would marry her partner (and thereby terminate her right to periodical payments):

> '[94] The first issue I propose to address is whether I should capitalise the wife's income claims. The case in which there is no element of uncertainty will be rare. Uncertainty is not in itself a reason for postponing adjudication and not, in my view, in itself a reason for refusing to capitalise an income claim unless the uncertainty is such that a fair outcome cannot be achieved until the uncertainty is resolved. In my judgment, I can capitalise the wife's claims on the evidence available to me in a way which is fair to both parties and in a way which gives proper weight to the wife's relationship with Mr N.'

---

[60] Principally of the payer but the principle applies to both parties.

POINTS OF PRACTICE AND THEORY

18.29

(1) For the payer, capitalisation represents, on the one hand, income-freedom through the termination of ongoing duties to pay maintenance but, on the other, the risk of over-payment. For the payee, capitalisation provides capital security and independence with the danger of under-payment and/or unfavourable future changes to his/her financial position.

(2) A specific application should be made for capitalisation.

(3) Capitalisation is not an opportunity for the parties (or the court) to revisit or revise the original [and concluded] capital claims of the parties or to make a further distribution of capital 'by the back door'.

(4) The staged-assessment applies to the capitalisation process:
   (a) Should periodical payments continue at all?
   (b) If ongoing periodical payments are required, should the level of payment provided for in the original order vary upwards or downwards?
   (c) If a variation is required, what is the fair revised figure for ongoing periodical payments?
   (d) From what date should the variation commence? Should this be backdated?
   (e) What capital payment, calculated in accordance with the *Duxbury* tables, should be substituted for the income stream that is being terminated?
   (f) Does the payer own property or have rights in a pension scheme that can provide an alternative means of achieving capitalisation?
   (g) Is it fair to both parties to capitalise the periodical payments and, in particular, is it reasonably practicable for the payer to pay the capital sum rather than make ongoing periodical payments?

(5) Departure from the *Duxbury* calculation may be justified to account for, inter alia:
   (a) the *Duxbury* paradox;
   (b) lost payments of arrears or other (quantifiable) rights;
   (c) the payee's cohabitation; and
   (d) shorter marriages.

(6) Subject to the statutory limitations regarding pension sharing, consideration should be given, if appropriate, to 'capitalising' the [varied] periodical payments order by way of a pension sharing order.

CHAPTER 19

PENSION ORDERS & PERIODICAL PAYMENTS: ATTACHMENT, SHARING & INTERACTION

'… the problem is that, notwithstanding divorce, the wife who has the benefit only of an attachment order remains hitched to the husband's wagon.'[1]

INTRODUCTION

19.1   A pension sharing order, so common to family practitioners, is a financial order in its own right.[2] A pension attachment order[3], less often encountered but just as legitimate a tool for distributing pension rights upon divorce, is, by contrast, a derivative form of a periodical payments order: it attaches the payee's entitlement to periodical payments[4] to the pension scheme of the payer. Consequently, a pension attachment order is predisposed to the possibilities of variation and dismissal[5] inherent in a 'standard' periodical payments order, and it prohibits a clean break between the parties. The pension sharing order's principal advantages are its finality and general irreversibility. Nevertheless, in certain cases, a pension attachment order can provide a useful alternative to the distribution of pension rights.

19.2   This chapter addresses some general issues applicable to pension benefits and the relevant procedure and guidance relating to their division, and proceeds to highlight the advantages and disadvantages of a pension attachment order.[6] Commentary is also provided on the interaction of a periodical payments order with a pension sharing order.

---

[1]   *R (Smith) v Secretary of State for Defence and Secretary of State for Work and Pensions* [2005] 1 FLR 97, at [15], per Wilson J.
[2]   FPR 2010, r 2.3.
[3]   Civil Partnership Act 2004 (CPA 2004), Sch 5, Part 6, paras 25, 26.
[4]   And other, secondary, benefits.
[5]   On the death of either party or remarriage of the payee.
[6]   Whereas in cases of a pension sharing order, the terminology often refers to the transferor and transferee, in cases of pension attachment, reference is made instead to the 'member' and 'non-member' spouse (that is, the member of the pension scheme subject of the pension attachment order).

TERMINOLOGY

19.3

[Pension scheme] member	=	the member of a pension arrangement against which a pension attachment order is made[7]
Non-member	=	the payee/recipient of a pension attachment order
Transferor	=	the member of a pension arrangement in the case of a pension sharing order: it is the transferor's pension scheme from which a pension debit is made
Transferee	=	the recipient of the pension credit created by virtue of a pension sharing order

PENSION BENEFITS

19.4   Pension benefits are paid to a pension scheme member in a variety of different ways; principally as monthly income when a scheme is in payment, by way of lump sum upon retirement – often tax free[8] – or as payment to specified dependants upon death.

19.5   In determining a fair division of finances on divorce, the court is directed to have regard to (a) the benefits under a pension arrangement which a party to the marriage has or is likely to have, and (b) any benefits under a pension arrangement which, by reason of the divorce, a party to the marriage will lose the chance of acquiring.[9]

THE NATURE OF A PENSION ATTACHMENT ORDER: PRIMARY AND SECONDARY POWERS

19.6

> Pension attachment is a form of immediate or deferred financial provision, which provides for the making of a periodical payments order or lump sum order payable upon the member's retirement or taking of pension benefits.
>
> Pension attachment orders are available in respect of petitions for divorce, nullity or judicial separation issued on or after 1 July 1996. The order itself can be made at any time but payment pursuant to the order is only made upon the member's retirement and taking of pension benefits, which ➙

---

[7]   The payer.
[8]   Sometimes automatic and sometimes enhanced by an ability to commute some of the pension entitlement.
[9]   MCA 1973, s 25B(1)(a) and (b).

may be many years after the date of the order. The pension attachment order must be expressed as a percentage[10] of the payment due to the member: the order for payment should be calculated and expressed as a percentage of the *net* figure[11] received by the member from the pension scheme, as any pension income will be taxable income for the member but not the payee recipient of the attachment order[12].

Pension attachment orders include *primary* and *secondary* powers enabling the court to distribute and allocate the member's pension benefits from income payments, lump sums and death benefits, to the advantage of the non-member.

Primary power

19.7 The primary power is to order that a specified percentage[13] of any pension income paid to the member is instead paid by the pension scheme to the non-member.

19.8 The Matrimonial Causes Act 1973 (MCA 1973), s 25B[14] reads as follows:

'(4) To the extent to which the order is made having regard to any benefits under a pension arrangement, the order may require the [person responsible for] the pension arrangement in question, if at any time any payment in respect of any benefits under the arrangement becomes due to the party with pension rights, to make a payment for the benefit of the other party.

(5) The order must express the amount of any payment required to be made by virtue of subsection (4) above as a percentage of the payment which becomes due to the party with pension rights.

(6) Any such payment by the person responsible for the arrangement –

(a)   shall discharge so much of his liability to the party with pension rights as corresponds to the amount of the payment, and

(b)   shall be treated for all purposes as a payment made by the party with pension rights in or towards the discharge of his liability under the order.'

---

[10]   As must an order for pension sharing as against the CE value calculated at the time the order takes effect, see *H V H (Financial Relief: Pensions)* [2009] EWHC 3739 (Fam), [2010] 2 FLR 173, per Baron J.

[11]   Ie net of all income tax, costs and charges.

[12]   Care should be taken to enquire directly with the pension scheme as to how the pension attachment order will work in practice. Tax advice should also be sought: for example, a £9,000 annual income of a 60-year-old will incur no tax if it is the only income received, but may well be taxed from age 65 or 66 when the state pension is receivable.

[13]   This is the only method for describing a pension attachment order (MCA 1973, s 25B(5)).

[14]   In cases of civil partnership dissolution, the rules relating to pension benefits are found in CPA 2004, Sch 5, Part 6.

Secondary powers

19.9 The secondary powers provide the court with the ability to exercise control over the various ways in which the member spouse or the person responsible[15] for the pension arrangement may elect to *take, define or direct* the application of other available pension benefits within a scheme. The court can order:

- the member to exercise a right of commutation[16] available under the pension arrangement to any extent (ie up to 100% of the limit authorised by the pension scheme, or not at all);[17] or
- the member spouse to nominate the non-member spouse as the recipient of all or some of any lump sum payable in respect of the member's death;[18] or
- the person responsible for the member's pension scheme to pay to the non-member any lump sum payable in respect of the member's death.[19]

19.10 Secondary powers may direct the member to maximise the commuted lump-sum available to him, which can provide additional capital in a case with otherwise limited resources. The court can also direct that no right to commutation is exercised by the member, thereby maximising the future pension income for both parties if an attachment order is made. However, the court has no power to order the date upon which the member must take his pension benefits: therefore, an undertaking is advisable from the member specifying the date upon which the pension benefits will be taken.

---

[15] Defined in MCA 1973, s 5D(4) and dependent on the type of pension arrangement.
[16] Payment of a lump sum in lieu of a portion of future income benefits payable under the pension scheme.
[17] MCA 1973, s 25B(7).
[18] MCA 1973, s 25C(2)(b).
[19] MCA 1973, s 25C(2)(a).

Pension Attachment Flow Chart

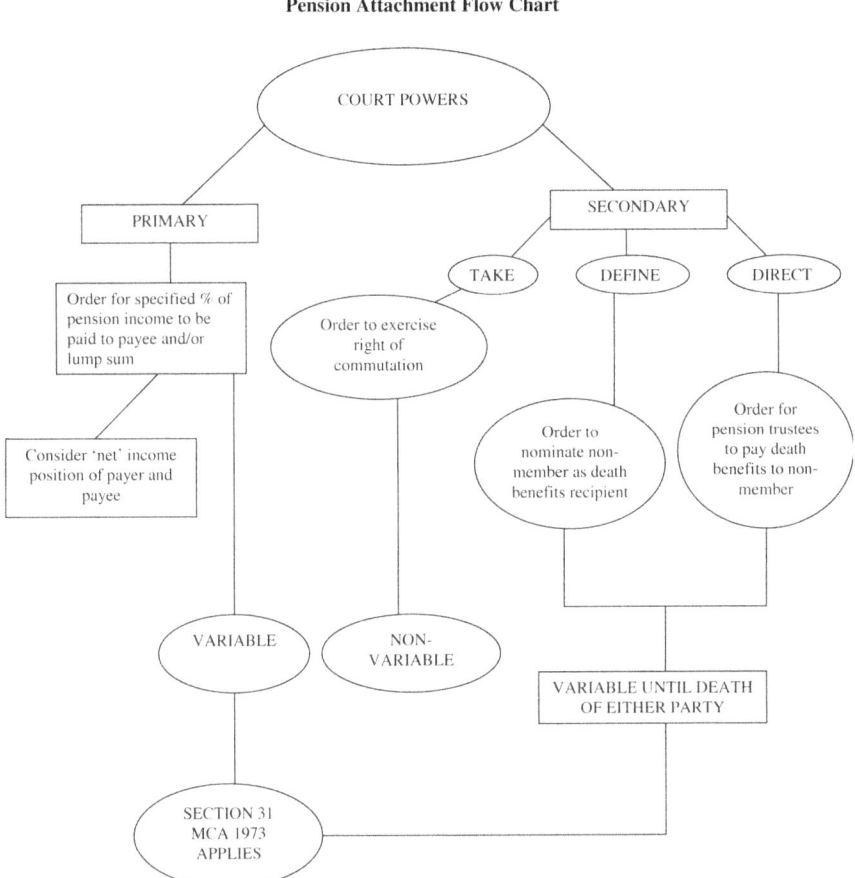

Pension attachment orders versus pension sharing orders

19.11

> Pension attachment orders differ from pension sharing orders in a number of key ways.
>
> (a) First, a pension attachment order leaves the member's pension scheme intact, whereas a pension sharing order irreversibly debits and reduces the transferor's pension scheme for the purpose of providing a corresponding pension credit to the transferee. ➡

(b) Second, a pension attachment order is a mechanism for enforcing (periodical and other) payments, or securing benefits from, a pension scheme,[20] whereas the pension sharing order is a substantive financial order in its own right.[21]

(c) Third, a pension attachment order, as a form of periodical payments order, remains variable (upwards or downwards) during its lifetime and will terminate on the death of either party or on the remarriage of the non-member. The pension sharing order, by contrast, is final[22] and survives the death of either party and the remarriage of the transferee.

(d) Fourth, the pension attachment order allows the non-member to benefit from any subsequent contributions to, or growth of, the attached pension scheme;[23] a pension sharing order creates independent pension credits[24] for the transferee and disentitles the transferee from any further contributions made to the transferor's pension after the order has taken effect.

VALUATIONS AND EXPERT EVIDENCE IN PENSION MATTERS

19.12 The prescribed methodology for valuing pension benefits upon divorce, whether for the purpose of a pension sharing or pension attachment order (and if the pension is in payment or not),[25] is the cash equivalent ('CE') value.[26] However, the restriction to the CE does not make other valuations and expert opinion superfluous, such as, valuations of the future income or lump sum benefits payable by the pension scheme. In cases in which the parties are close(r) to retirement age, are determined to achieve a 'target income' from any pension order[27] or are seeking to replace a periodical payments order with a pension order of some kind, actuarial evidence as to likely future benefits[28] from the scheme is important. Such expert evidence may also be relevant in cases involving more unusual pension schemes[29] or certain public sector schemes[30] and those in which there is a significant age difference between the

---

[20] What is otherwise described as a derivative order, see Hay, Hess and Lockett, *Pensions on Divorce: A Practitioner's Handbook* (2008), para 5.6.

[21] See also FPR 2010, r 2.3: a 'financial order' is defined as including a pension sharing order.

[22] Upon it taking effect and being implemented.

[23] If the member chooses to continue to make such contributions after a pension attachment order has been made.

[24] Which may be subject of an internal (within the member's scheme) or external (to another scheme or annuity) transfer.

[25] The Cash Equivalent of Benefits (CEB) valuation is no longer applicable.

[26] Divorce etc (Pensions) Regulations 2000, SI 2000/1123 and Pensions on Divorce etc (Provision of Information) Regulations 2000, SI 2000/1048.

[27] *Butterworths Family Law Service*, 4(1), para 1598.

[28] With and without a commutation of pension benefits, if applicable.

[29] Eg a defined benefit or contribution scheme, SIPPs (Self Invested Personal Pension) schemes or SSASs (Small Self-Administered Schemes).

[30] Eg Civil Service, Teachers, Police and Armed Forces schemes.

parties.[31] The actuarial calculations are complex and often rely heavily on financial projections of inflation or investment return. For example, if pension income is payable immediately, the older the recipient of a pension sharing order, generally the lower the pension sharing order percentage required to provide for that person's future income. However, if the transferee is not going to draw pension income for some time, the younger the recipient of a pension sharing order, the lower the percentage required may be, as the transferee's pension credits have longer to earn an investment return.

19.13   In pension attachment order cases, actuarial evidence is an *imperative*, as the primary order must be expressed as a percentage deduction against the member's future pension income. The CE figure alone – which provides a capitalised figure for the value of the benefits within a pension scheme – is of little, if any, use to the court or the parties to the proceedings. Therefore, expert evidence is required to provide an opinion as to the current and projected future income and benefits derived and derivable from the relevant pension scheme.[32]

Examples of questions to ask, and issues to address to, an expert actuary in cases of pension attachment:[33]

- From what date can the member take pension benefits?
- What death-in-service benefits are payable under the pension arrangement?
- What lump sum, if any, is payable upon the scheme member taking his/her pension benefits?
- What are the pension scheme's rules regarding the nomination of beneficiaries of death-in-service benefits?
- What right of commutation does the member have under the pension arrangement?
- What is the impact of any commutation on future pension income?
- What is the member's projected net income/lump sum from the pension arrangement calculated on the basis of the benefits accrued to date?
- What is the maximum amount of annual contribution the member can make to the pension arrangement between now and retirement? What is the scheme member's current contribution and what options does s/he have to change the contribution?
- What level of inflation and what other financial additions to the pension arrangement are assumed in the calculations?   ➡

---

[31]   See, for example, *B v B (Assessment of Assets)* [2012] 2 FLR 22, at [50], per David Salter (sitting as a Deputy Judge of the High Court).

[32]   This will necessarily depend on a variety of factors including the member's future contributions (if any), inflation, fund performance etc.

[33]   Non-exhaustive and dependent on the particular circumstances of each case.

> • What is the member's projected net income/lump sum from the pension arrangement calculated on the basis of full contributions being made until retirement?[34]

PENSION ATTACHMENT ORDERS AND VARIATION

19.14 As noted above, a significant disadvantage (or advantage) to a pension attachment order is the fact that, with only limited exception, it remains variable during its lifetime. Chapter 17, which considers that law applicable to the variation of a periodical payments order, provides a framework for the way in which the court will approach such an application. The following table sets out the variable and non-variable pension attachment orders available under the MCA 1973, s 31:

Order	Variable/non-variable	Statutory reference
Percentage of pension income paid to the non-member	Variable	MCA 1973, s 31(2)(b) and (dd)(i)
Lump sum paid to non-member	Variable	MCA 1973, s 31(2)(dd)(ii)
Attachment of pension compensation	Variable	MCA 1973, s 31(2)(dd)(iii)
For payment of death-in-service benefits	Non-variable *after* the death of either party to the marriage	MCA 1973, s 31(2B)

CONTRIBUTIONS AND PENSION BENEFITS ACCRUED BEFORE, DURING AND AFTER THE MARRIAGE: GENERAL APPROACH

19.15 An actuary instructed to provide a report as to pension provision may be asked to calculate the percentage pension sharing order required to provide equality of income for the parties to the marriage from their respective pension schemes at age 60 or 65, but only taking account of the pension provision 'accrued' during the marriage. This instruction is often given to the expert to offer the opportunity for the court to account in some way for the fact that some or all of the pension provision of a party may have been acquired prior to the marriage or during a lengthy period of separation prior to the issue of financial proceedings. The only direct statutory basis for such an account to be taken is the direction to the court to consider the contributions of the parties to the welfare of the family.[35] However, those contributions can be familial as well

---

[34] The actuarial calculation would have to assume that salary remains the same in the future in real terms and that there are no relevant changes to the pension scheme.
[35] MCA 1973, s 25(2)(f).

as financial, retrospective and prospective, and the court must not discriminate against the party who has adopted the domestic and caring role[36] in weighing the value of different contributions. The fact of non-marital accrual of pension provision can be a circumstance of a particular case, but the case-law does not specifically support a division of pension benefits that excludes those benefits which have been accrued by one party before the marriage or after separation.

19.16 For example, reference can be made to the case of *H v H*,[37] which is often misquoted as authority for an approach that only takes into account the pension accrued during the years of the marriage. In reality, Thorpe LJ was instead expressing his rejection of the wife's arguments – prior to the reliance on the CE valuation – that the court should look to the *future* 26 years of contributions likely to be made by the doctor husband (as against those of the wife) in determining the appropriate division of pension benefits:

> 'I think that in deciding what weight to attach to pension rights it is more important in this case to look to the value of what has been earned during cohabitation than to look to the prospective value of what may be earned during the course of the 25 or 30 years between separation and retirement age. Of course, I bear in mind that in the future accumulation of pension rights the husband has very great advantages ... but I do not think that this disparity in [the parties'] ability to accumulate pension rights over decades post separation should be given undue weight in the performance of the balancing exercise.'[38]

19.17 In certain cases the fact that pension benefits (or perhaps even a significant proportion of it) were accrued by one party before the marriage *and* that other assets and income are sufficient and available to otherwise meet a party's needs, *may* justify excluding that pension provision or part of it from the overall financial division. This argument carries more weight in cases in which the marriage has not been particularly lengthy and the parties are younger and facing a longer period to retirement age. For example, in *GS v L (Financial Remedies: Pre-Acquired Assets, Needs)*[39] the court dealt with financial matters ancillary to a 10-year marriage, which produced two children and involved parties who were in their early 40s. The husband had brought significant assets into the marriage including pension provision with a value of £384,000. Eleanor King J recognised the special facts regarding the husband's pension benefits, as follows:

> 'So far as the pension is concerned, it can and should in my judgment properly be excluded from the division of assets, a position effectively, but not absolutely, conceded by the wife. The pension cannot be drawn down for many years and was accrued in its entirety before the marriage; the fund cannot be used to provide for the wife's needs in either the short or medium term. Given the benefit of the capital

---

[36] *White v White* [2001] 1 AC 596, [2000] 3 WLR 1571, [2000] 2 FLR 981, HL.
[37] [1993] 2 FCR 308.
[38] At 318B, per Thorpe LJ.
[39] [2011] EWHC 1759, [2013] 1 FLR 300.

with which she will leave the marriage and a working life of 25 years ahead of her, fairness in my judgment requires that the husband should retain his pension fund absolutely.'[40]

CONTRIBUTIONS AND PENSION BENEFITS ACCRUED BEFORE, DURING AND AFTER THE MARRIAGE: PENSION ATTACHMENT

19.18 It is in the nature of a pension attachment order that it is only effective[41] against the member's pension when he or she chooses to take those pension benefits. Furthermore, at the time of the attachment order, the parties may be many years from retirement. The member may choose not to make any further contributions to the 'attached' pension scheme, if an order is made, thereby depriving the non-member of any benefit from those future contributions. Conversely, the member may seek to argue that the percentage of an attachment order should be reduced to reflect any future contributions made to the pension arrangement. Finally, as noted above, the pension attachment order remains variable, which exposes the percentage figure to an application for variation at a future date, depending on the circumstances at the time of the variation application.

PENSIONS AND BANKRUPTCY

19.19 The general rule in bankruptcy is that the bankrupt's estate vests in the trustee in bankruptcy for subsequent distribution amongst the creditors. The effect that bankruptcy may have on applications and orders for, and payment of, periodical payments is considered in more detail in Chapter 13.

Bankruptcy and pensions in payment

19.20 If a bankruptcy petition is filed on or after 29 May 2000, pension rights in approved schemes (and linked annuities) are *excluded* from the bankrupt's estate. However, any lump sum or income payment arising out of a pension scheme and paid to the bankrupt is liable to an income payments order,[42] which can significantly reduce the amount of the pension payment received by the bankrupt: this equally reduces the income available against which a periodical payments order can be made for the duration of the income payments order.[43]

---

[40] At [86].
[41] In the sense that the order results in payment.
[42] Please see **12.12–12.21**.
[43] Income payments orders, their effect, operation and duration are considered in detail in Chapter 13.

Bankruptcy and pensions not in payment but capable of payment

19.21 If a bankrupt is *able* to elect to take pension benefits (lump sum or income) but has chosen *not to do so* – and, therefore, is frustrating the trustee's claim to financial resources that would otherwise be available to satisfy the creditors – the court can force the bankrupt's election to take pension benefits and, thereafter, capture any benefit paid to the bankrupt through an income payments order.[44]

19.22 In *Raithatha v Williamson*,[45] the trustee applied to the court for an income payments order in relation to the bankrupt's pension entitlements under a pension scheme estimated to be worth £900,000 (including a lump sum of £248,000 and annual income of up to £43,000). However, the bankrupt, although entitled by age and circumstance to draw his pension benefits, had not elected to do so at the date of the application. First, the court held that any lump sum payment made to the bankrupt could be classed as 'income' and therefore subject to an income payments order. Second, although the bankrupt had the right to elect whether to take his pension entitlements or not, that did not prevent the court from making an income payments order in relation to unelected entitlements.

> '[W]hy should a person who elected [to take pension benefits] on the day preceding his bankruptcy be in a position where his entitlement to enjoy the fruits of his pension is subject to the right of the trustee to apply for them to go to his creditors ... whereas the person who had not yet elected is immune ... and can enjoy the full fruits of his pension to the detriment of his creditors?'[46]

19.23 An applicant in financial remedy proceedings cannot procure an order under MCA 1973 forcing a pension member to elect to draw pension benefits. The Bankruptcy Court may do so by virtue of the power to make an income payments order. Therefore, the potential or actual payee of a periodical payments order, faced with the payer's bankruptcy, must be aware of the possibility that pension income and lump sum payments may be 'siphoned off' to meet the bankrupt's creditors' claims. The duration of an income payments order is limited to 3 years.

---

[44] Most pension schemes allow the beneficiary to choose when to start to draw the pension, with a minimum age of 55 and a maximum age of 75. It is also usually possible to draw down a tax free lump sum of up to 25% of the value of the member's interest, as an advance payment of pension.

[45] [2012] EWHC 909 (Ch), [2012] BPIR 621.

[46] At [36], per Bernard Livesey QC.

PENSION ATTACHMENT ORDERS AND ALTERNATIVES

19.24

> There are various methods for distributing or accounting for the parties'
> pension provision on divorce in addition, or as an alternative, to making a
> pension attachment order[47]. The principal methods are:
>
> (1)　*offsetting*: providing for one party to receive cash or property in lieu
> 　　　of an order sharing or attaching the member's pension;
>
> (2)　*a pension sharing order*: an order providing the transferee with
> 　　　pension credits drawn from the transferor's pension arrangement;
>
> (3)　*a joint lives periodical payments order*: a standard periodical
> 　　　payments order to provide for the payee's future maintenance, not
> 　　　linked in any formal way to the payer's pension arrangements;
>
> (4)　*a nominal periodical payments order*:[48] combined, perhaps, with an
> 　　　undertaking from the payee not to apply to vary the payment to a
> 　　　substantive level (eg £500 per month) until a certain date or occasion
> 　　　linked to the payer's retirement;
>
> (5)　*an order for periodical payments for a specified term*: (with or
> 　　　without an order preventing an application to extend that term)[49]
> 　　　combined with a pension sharing order: the term for the periodical
> 　　　payments order will run to the date on which the payee may take the
> 　　　benefits of the pension sharing order;[50]
>
> (6)　*an undertaking given by the pension scheme member to take the
> 　　　pension benefits*: (lump sum and/or income) at a specified date in
> 　　　order to fund a periodical payments order;
>
> (7)　*an order for secured periodical payments*.[51]

COMPARING THE PENSION SHARING ORDER AND THE PENSION ATTACHMENT ORDER

19.25　For the reasons noted above, the pension sharing order is often
preferable to the making of a pension attachment order. The limitations of the

---

[47]　Included but not specified in this list are orders relating to pension compensation: see, for
　　　example, MCA 1973, s 24F (pension compensation sharing orders) and MCA 1973, s 25F
　　　(attachment of pension compensation).

[48]　For a term or not and with a bar on applying to extend the term or not (MCA 1973, s 28(1A)).

[49]　MCA 1973, s 28(1A).

[50]　See *D v D (Financial Provision: Periodical Payments)* [2004] EWHC 445 (Fam), [2004] 1 FLR
　　　988.

[51]　See further, Chapter 16.

latter type of order were succinctly addressed by Wilson J in *R (Smith) v Secretary of State for Defence and Secretary of State for Work and Pensions*:[52]

> '[The pension attachment order] does not carve out of his rights, pension rights for her, bespoke to her needs and in particular to the length of her life. It merely impresses upon whatever may be payable to the husband under a pension scheme a compulsory redirection to the wife in satisfaction of his obligations under court orders. Thus no part of his pension is payable to the wife, whatever her age and however great her need, until, within the limits open to him under the scheme, the husband chooses to retire. Even more significantly, no further payment falls to be made to her in the event that, following his retirement, he predeceases her ...'

Pension sharing order versus pension attachment order

	Pension sharing order	Pension attachment order
Clean break	Compliant with a clean break[53]	Contrary to the clean break
Finality	Final and only capable of variation before decree absolute[54]	Variable throughout its life
Death	No effect	The payer or payee's death terminates the order[55]
Remarriage	No effect	The payee's remarriage terminates the order: an order cannot be made after the remarriage of the intended payee
Future contributions	The pension member's contributions to a shared fund after the pension sharing order are protected	The percentage deduction by way of attachment order includes all pension benefits, including those accrued after the date of the pension attachment order
Date for taking pension benefits	Both parties free to retire and draw benefits in accordance with scheme rules	Pension member may be subject of undertaking to take benefits on specific date

---

[52] [2005] 1 FLR 97 at [15]: see also Singer J in *T v T (Financial Relief: Pensions)* [1998] 1 FLR 1072.

[53] Whether immediate or deferred (ie a pension sharing order is combined with a term periodical payments order to run to the date on which the payee's periodical payments cease and pension benefits are payable).

[54] MCA 1973, s 31(2)(g) and (4A): an application may be brought only before the pension sharing order has, or would have, taken effect.

[55] Consider attachment of death benefits.

	Pension sharing order	Pension attachment order
Taxation	Provider and recipient of pension debits and credits respectively are individually taxable on any future benefits	Pension member remains taxable on the pension income received prior to division under the pension attachment order[56]

Advantages of Pension Attachment

19.26 Pension attachment orders do, however, have some (often overlooked) advantages in comparison with a pension sharing order.

(a) *A pension attachment order preserves the gross value of the pension benefits.* If a pension sharing order is made and the transferee takes an external transfer,[57] this will invariably result in a loss of value of the transferee's pension credits. Conversely, the pension attachment order leaves the value of the whole pension benefits unchanged. The loss of value in the case of the pension sharing order is attributable to two reasons. First, the transferee will incur costs associated with the management of the externally transferred pension and, second, if the CE value of the transferor's pension benefits is an undervalue, the transferee's pension credit does not necessarily account for that undervalue.

(b) *A pension attachment order avoids 'income gap syndrome'.* For certain pension schemes,[58] the transferee of a pension sharing order made against a pension in payment may not be entitled to receive income from the transferred pension credits for some years, whereas the transferor's pension income suffers an immediate reduction. The attachment order, by contrast, can provide immediate payment to the non-member, thereby avoiding a period of 'income gap' and loss.

CLEAN BREAK

19.27 A full clean break[59] is not possible if a pension attachment order is made, as the attachment of the pension is simply a specialised form of a periodical payments order.

---

[56] Note that this fact may prove particularly inefficient if the scheme member is a higher rate tax payer and the payee is not.

[57] Ie not an internal transfer where the transferee's pension credit remains within the transferor's pension scheme.

[58] For example, the Armed Forces Pension Scheme 1975.

[59] Dismissing the payee's claims against the payer.

PENSION ATTACHMENT ORDERS AND STATUTORY PROHIBITIONS

19.28   If a pension arrangement is, or has been, the subject of a pension sharing order in relation to the parties' marriage, the court cannot make a pension attachment order[60] in relation to the same pension arrangement.[61] The same prohibition applies to lump sum orders and payments or nominations relating to death-in-service benefits.[62] These prohibitions do not apply if the pension sharing order was made in relation to a different marriage.

19.29   Equally, if a pension attachment order (periodical payments or lump sum) is in force[63] in relation to a pension arrangement, that same pension arrangement cannot be made the subject of a pension sharing order. This prohibition applies in relation to a pension attachment order made in relation to any marriage.[64]

PROCEDURE

19.30   The Family Procedure Rules 2010 (FPR 2010), r 9.33–9.36 provide for a particular procedure to be followed if an application is made for a pension attachment order, which is not replicated here but appears in the appendix to The Guide. The applicant for a pension attachment order must send to the person responsible for the pension arrangement (a) address details for the applicant and for payment (from the pension scheme) to the applicant and (b) address details for the applicant's bank, if payment is to be made to the bank direct.[65]

19.31   The person responsible for the pension arrangement subject of the attachment order may request a copy of the pension member's Form E detailing the pension rights disclosed and, thereafter, may file a statement and attend the FDA or other court hearing,[66] if appropriate.

19.32   FPR 2010 details the manner in which the pension attachment order is to be drafted by reference to the pension attachment annex. Each individual pension attachment order requires a separate annex (Form P2).[67]

19.33   The pension attachment annex sets out clearly the different orders the court may make and divides the annex into sections to provide for periodical

---

[60]   Including an order that a member party exercises his or her right of commutation and makes payment to the non-member.
[61]   MCA 1973, s 25B(7B) and s 25C(4).
[62]   MCA 1973, s 25C(4).
[63]   Which suggests that, if discharged, a pension sharing order could be made.
[64]   MCA 1973, s 24B(5).
[65]   FPR 2010, r 9.33(1)(a)–(c).
[66]   FPR 2010, r 9.33.
[67]   See Appendix.

payments, directions as to the commutation of benefits and/or the allocation of death-in-service benefits under the pension arrangement.

PENSION SHARING AND ORDERS FOR PERIODICAL PAYMENTS

19.34 Pension sharing orders are usually only one component of a broader set of orders designed to distribute assets and income fairly on divorce. In certain cases, pension sharing orders may be combined with a periodical payments order to cater, for example, for the years between a final financial order and the taking of pension benefits. In cases in which the pension provision is very small compared to the income presently available,[68] circumstances may justify a periodical payments order extending beyond the anticipated dates of the parties taking their pension benefits. However, in cases in which equality is the objective and in which pension sharing orders are made to provide broadly equally for the parties' needs on retirement, it may be appropriate to limit the term of a periodical payments to the date upon which pension benefits are likely to be drawn.

19.35 In *D v D (Financial Provision: Periodical Payments)*[69] the parties were in their 50s and the marriage had been a long one of some 21 years producing two (now adult) children. The District Judge had undertaken a careful assessment of the parties' respective financial positions at trial and, as best as could be achieved, prospectively upon retirement. The order was predicated on achieving equality in terms of capital and broad equality of pension provision at a date 10 years hence. The court imposed a pension sharing order against the husband's pension arrangements and additionally made a periodical payments order for the benefit of the wife for £10,000 per annum on a *joint lives basis*. The husband appealed, principally against the joint lives nature of the periodical payments order in light of the orders for lump sum and pension sharing, and he argued that a 10-year term order for periodical payments was the only fair conclusion: the term for payment should have a bar,[70] he argued, preventing the wife from applying to extend the term.

On appeal, Coleridge J allowed the appeal and made an order for a 10-year term for periodical payments but did not impose a bar on the right of the wife to apply for an extension of the term for payment. First, the District Judge had failed to recognise that the lump sum paid to the wife in addition to the pension sharing order in her favour would provide an income adequate to meet her needs on retirement. Second, in exercising the discretion afresh on appeal, Coleridge J was careful to recognise that 'if an order for periodical payments is left rampant ... without any ➡

---

[68] And, particularly, if the marriage is lengthy and the payee's future needs cannot be met by the pension sharing orders made.

[69] [2004] EWHC 445 (Fam), [2004] 1 FLR 988.

[70] MCA 1973, s 29(1A).

restriction on it – then equality can later be destroyed because of intervening events and it potentially flies in the face of the attainment of the district judge's perfectly proper objective [of achieving equality]'.[71] Therefore, the combination of a joint lives periodical payments order with other orders designed to provide for broad equality at a specific point in time in the future, tipped the scales of fairness too heavily in favour of the wife:

> '[25] I propose to limit the wife's order to 10 years. I have no doubt at all that that is the fair way in which this matter should have been dealt with, given the other correct findings that the district judge adopted and given his approach in relation to the capital. All things being equal, in my judgment, the wife's periodical payments should not extend beyond the husband's retirement in 10 years' time, even if he in the intervening period prospers relative to her. It is not, in my judgment, fair to the parties for the courts to carry out a careful, equal division of the assets in the way that this district judge did and then leave open, in an unrestricted way, the possibility for "the basis of" that fairness to be revisited in years to come.'

19.36 Finally, it should also be noted, as is dealt with in detail in Chapter 18 on 'Capitalisation', that where the court discharges a periodical payments order or varies such an order so that the payments are to be made only for a specified period, the court may at that stage make a pension sharing order.[72]

---

[71] At [23].
[72] Whether or not a pension sharing order was made at the time of the original order (as long as the pension scheme to be shared is not, or has not been, the subject of a pension sharing order), see MCA 1973, s 24B(3). See also the statutory prohibitions in **19.30–19.31**.

POINTS OF PRACTICE AND THEORY

19.37

(1) Pension attachment is a form of immediate or deferred financial provision, which provides for the making of a periodical payments order or lump sum order payable upon the member's retirement or taking of pension benefits.

(2) The pension attachment order is contrary to the 'clean break' principle, variable throughout its lifetime, terminates on either party's death and on the payee's remarriage and applies a percentage deduction to income that includes all present and future contributions to the pension scheme.

(3) A pension attachment order is predisposed to the possibilities of variation and dismissal inherent in a 'standard' periodical payments order, and it prohibits a clean break between the parties.

(4) Actuarial input is advised in cases in which the parties are close(r) to retirement age, are determined to achieve a 'target income' from any pension order or are seeking to replace a periodical payments order with a pension order of some kind: actuarial opinion is required, inter alia, as to the projected future income and benefits derived and derivable from the relevant pension scheme.

(5) A bankrupt, who has the right to elect whether to take pension entitlements or not, may be ordered (by the Bankruptcy Court) to take such benefits and the subsequent income may be made subject of an income payments order. By contrast, an applicant in financial remedy proceedings cannot procure an order under MCA 1973 forcing a pension member to elect to draw pension benefits.

(6) If the court makes a pension sharing order, care should be taken to assess whether the circumstances of the case justify a term order for periodical payments that runs only to the date on which the transferee may take the pension benefits (whether on an extendable or non-extendable term basis).

CHAPTER 20

PERIODICAL PAYMENTS FOR THE BENEFIT OF A CHILD: SCHOOL FEES, DISABILITY EXPENSES, TOP-UP ASSESSMENTS AND WRITTEN AGREEMENTS

'The duty of parents to provide for the maintenance of their children is a principle of natural law; an obligation laid on them not only by nature herself, but by their own proper act, in bringing them into the world: for they would be in the highest manner injurious to their issue, if they only gave their children life, that they might afterwards see them perish. By begetting them, therefore, they have entered into a voluntary obligation, to endeavour, so far as in them lies, that the life which they have bestowed shall be supported and preserved. And thus the children will have a perfect right of receiving maintenance from their parents.'[1]

INTRODUCTION AND CONTEXT

20.1 The statutory child support system is a mix of public and private law designed as a nationalised system to assess and enforce the financial obligations owed by parents to their children.[2]

20.2 Statutory recognition of the duty to provide financial support to children can be traced back to the Poor Relief Act of 1601,[3] which provided for fathers, mothers and the wider family, at their own cost, to relieve and maintain poor persons. The law, therefore, has for centuries recognised the right of the child who is too young to fend for him/herself to be provided for by his/her parents.[4] In the case of *R (on the application of Kehoe) v Secretary of State for Work and Pensions*, Baroness Hale was clear in her assessment that 'children have a civil right to be maintained by their parents, which is such to engage Article 6 of the European Convention on Human Rights.'[5]

---

[1]   Blackstone, *Commentaries on the Laws of England*, Book 1, Chapter XVI (and quoted by Baroness Hale of Richmond in *R (on the application of Kehoe) v Secretary of State for Work and Pensions* [2005] 2 FLR 1249, HL, at [50]).
[2]   *Huxley v Child Support Officer* [2000] 1 FLR 898, at 908, per Hale J.
[3]   43 Elizabeth, c 2, s 7.
[4]   [2005] 2 FLR 1249, HL, at [51], per Baroness Hale.
[5]   Ibid, at [71].

20.3 The Child Support Act of 1991 (CSA 1991) removed jurisdiction from the courts for the assessment and enforcement of these parental financial obligations, save in exceptional and limited circumstances. The Child Support Agency (CSA)[6] was provided with both authority and a formula for assessment of the appropriate level of child maintenance payable by the non-resident parent ('NRP') together with enforcement mechanisms to collect payment. Furthermore, the CSA 1991 prescribed the limited occasions when the court retained a residual power to make orders for the payment of maintenance to, or for the benefit of, a child.

20.4 This chapter does not provide a detailed commentary on the myriad rules and regulations governing the present statutory child support system.[7] Rather, it has its focus on the four key powers retained by the court in cases of divorce and the dissolution of civil partnerships, namely the capacity to order:

(1) the payment of school fees;

(2) the payment of expenses attributable to a child's disability;

(3) a 'top-up' assessment in those cases in which the payer's weekly income exceeds the assessable maximum within the applicable child support system; and

(4) the payment of maintenance for a limited period (12 months) reflecting, in all material respects, an agreement by the parents to make a specified payment.

20.5 The powers of the court pursuant to the Children Act 1989 to make orders for the benefit of children of unmarried parents are considered in detail in Bazley et al, *Applications under Schedule 1 to the Children Act 1989* (2010).

A BASIC OVERVIEW OF THE STATUTORY CHILD SUPPORT SYSTEM

20.6 The statutory system for the assessment of child maintenance is divided into three broad schemes: the applicable scheme depends generally on the date of the application for an assessment by the CSA: the 'pre-2003 scheme', the 'net income' scheme and the 'gross income' scheme.

20.7 The *pre-2003 scheme* applies only to applications made before 3 March 2003 and is not covered further in this Guide as it has now only very limited application.

20.8 The *net income scheme* applies to all applications made after 4 March 2003, save for those applications that fall under the gross income scheme, as set out below.

---

[6] And its later incarnations.

[7] Reference can be made instead, for example, to the comprehensive *Child Support Handbook 2013/2014* (15th edn, Child Poverty Action Group, updated by Mark Brough).

20.9 The *gross income scheme* was introduced for assessment applications made after 10 December 2013; initially for families with at least four qualifying children but it is being extended in phases to eventually cover all new applications.[8]

20.10 Responsibility for operating the child support system lies with the Department for Work and Pensions. The two organisations with duties to implement the system are the Child Support Agency (CSA) and the Child Maintenance Service (CMS).[9]

20.11 The recently-introduced gross income scheme has been coupled with a distinct policy drive to encourage parents to negotiate their own child maintenance agreements by, for example, providing advice and support services to them[10] and imposing fees for making an application for assessment.

20.12 The schemes apply a formula to the NRP's income in order to determine the appropriate level of child maintenance. The following tables show the basic percentages used to calculate child maintenance in both net and gross income scheme applications.[11] Generally, both schemes require consideration of:

(1)   the weekly [net or gross] income of the NRP;

(2)   the number of other relevant children for whom the NRP is responsible; and

(3)   the number of nights that the qualifying child spends with the NRP.

---

[8]   At the time of writing, the scheme has been extended to new applications involving two or more relevant children. See also the article by Jody Atkinson for a summary of this new scheme and further explanation of its detailed rules, '*Child Support: Here Comes the New Gross Income Scheme*' in Family Law Week, August 2013 available online http://www.familylawweek.co.uk/site.aspx?i=ed113401.

[9]   Broadly, the CMS deals with all new gross income scheme applications and the CSA is responsible for net income scheme applications. The plan is to graduate the scheme so that the CMS will eventually deal with all cases.

[10] See the Child Maintenance Options (CMO) service, which provides telephone, web-based and face-to-face support and guidance: tel 0800 988 0988 or visit www.cmoptions.org.

[11] On the basic or basic rate plus basis only, ie not for those very low income applications (less than £200 per week net or gross) in which the nil or flat rate band applies.

Table 20.1 NET INCOME SCHEME: basic rate for NRP with weekly net income in excess of £200

Number of relevant children subject of the application	Percentage rate of net weekly income payable	Number of other children for whom NRP is responsible	Reduction to net weekly income for other relevant children[12]
1	15%	1	15%
2	20%	2	20%
3+	25%	3	25%

Table 20.2 GROSS INCOME SCHEME: basic rate and basic rate 'plus' for NRP with weekly gross income in excess of £200

Number of relevant children subject of the application	BASIC RATE Percentage rate of gross weekly income payable (up to amounts of £800 per week)	BASIC RATE PLUS Percentage rate of gross weekly income payable (on amounts in excess of £800 per week)	Number of other children for whom NRP is responsible	Reduction to gross weekly income for other relevant children[13]
1	12%	9%	1	11%
2	16%	12%	2	14%
3+	19%	15%	3	16%

---

[12] Reduction is applied to the net weekly income figure before calculating the appropriate child maintenance figure.

[13] Reduction is applied to the weekly income figure before calculating the appropriate child maintenance figure.

Table 20.3 Percentage reductions applicable to the weekly maintenance assessment in cases in which the NRP shares the care of the children (for net and gross income schemes)

Number of nights spent with NRP	Reduction to maintenance figure
52–103	1/7th or
104–155	2/7th or
156–174	3/7th or
175+	½ or

Periodical Payments for the Benefit Of Children

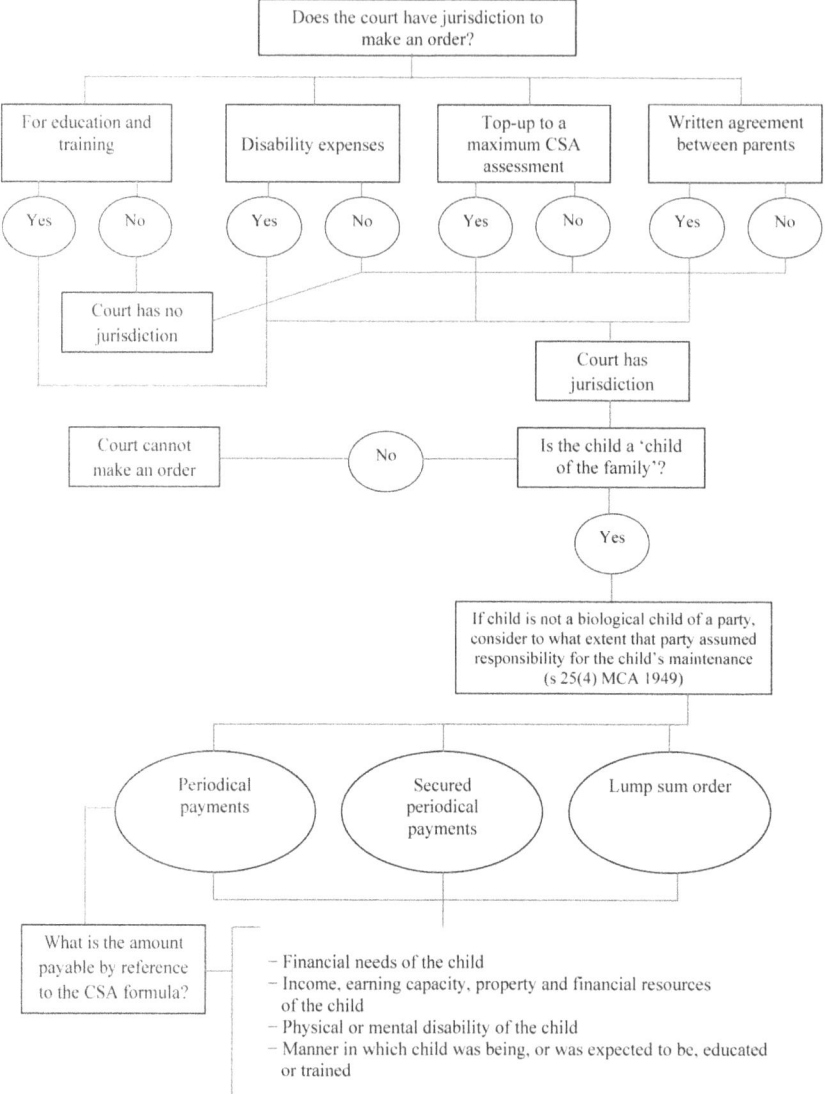

THE COURT'S RESIDUAL JURISDICTION

20.13   The legal basis for the court's four principal residual powers to make orders against a party to pay school fees, disability expenses and periodical payments, either in excess of the maximum statutory assessment (a 'top-up order') or in reflection of an agreement to make payment, is found in s 8 of the CSA 1991.[14]

Legal basis: school fees

20.14   CSA 1991, s 8:

> '(7) This section shall not prevent a court from exercising any power which it has to make a maintenance order[15] in relation to a child if –
>
> (a)   the child is, will be or (if the order were to be made) would be receiving instruction at an educational establishment or undergoing training for a trade, profession or vocation (whether or not while in gainful employment); and
> (b)   the order is made solely for the purposes of requiring the person making or securing the making of periodical payments fixed by the order to meet some or all of the expenses incurred in connection with the provision of the instruction or training.'

20.15   Private school fees are expensive. It is not uncommon for parties to make significant financial sacrifice in an attempt to provide their children with what they view as first-class education, facilities and opportunities.[16] Upon divorce, and the splitting of capital and incomes, the affordability of, and ability to pay,[17] such fees may be put under even more significant strain and scrutiny. If resources permit the continued payment of school fees, and if a party refuses to make future payments, the court may make a 'school fees order', which may cover tuition costs and boarding fees or both. The recipient

---

[14]   The court also retains the power to vary a maintenance order made on or after 3 March 2003 (if no calculation has been made) or an order made after that date in certain circumstances (CSA 1991, s 8(3A)); and to make an order against the parent with care of the child (CSA 1991, s 8(10)).

[15]   Defined in CSA 1991, s 8(11) as an order requiring the making or securing of periodical payments to or for the benefit of [the] child and which is made under, inter alia, Part II of the MCA 1973, Sch 1 to the Children Act 1989 and Sch 5, 6 or 7 to the Civil Partnership Act 2004 (CPA 2004).

[16]   Parties should be aware that an agreement to make voluntary payment of school fees may not necessarily be taken into account by the CSA in its discretion when calculating a maintenance assessment: see *R (Green) v Secretary of State for the Department for Work and Pensions* [2010] EWHC 1278. See also *DB v CMEC* [2010] UKUT 356 (AAC); CCS/2705/2009 in which the Upper Tribunal determined that 'school fees cannot simply be deducted from the variation [of a child maintenance assessment] that would otherwise be agreed. That would be a rigid rule and inconsistent with the nature of a discretion. The issue is whether those fees can be taken into account as part of the assessment whether it would be just and equitable to agree to a particular variation ... The child support legislation leaves to the courts the power to make orders that a parent pay tuition fees for a child's education: section 8(7) [MCA 1973]. The Commission has power to agree to a variation in respect of boarding fees under regulation 13 (of the Child Support (Variations) Regulations 2000.' (para 31 and 32 per Edward Jacobs).

[17]   See also *Parra v Parra* [2003] 1 FLR 942, CA at para 28 in which Thorpe LJ matched the equality of capital receipt with equality of financial obligation: 'Secondly, the parents should contribute equally to future education costs. Equal division of assets should ordinarily be matched by equal division of obligation.'

of a periodical payments order for the benefit of a child is not limited to the other party to the divorce proceedings but extends to 'such person as may be specified in the order':[18] therefore, a school fees order can be expressed for the payer to make payment direct to the bursar/school authority/appropriate individual in satisfaction of the liability. Although parents can agree that school fees payments should be in discharge of a (non-resident) parent's maintenance liability, the CSA only has power to agree to a variation of a maintenance assessment in respect of boarding fees (and not tuition fees).[19] If the (non-resident) parent's overall liability for child maintenance and school fees is excessive, that parent should approach the family court to reconsider the payment of fees under the Matrimonial Causes Act 1973 (MCA 1973), s 8(7). The CSA is designed to determine the amount of maintenance payable to cover living, clothing, housing and (non fee-paying) school expenses. Private education is an additional cost chosen by the parents. In *DB v CMEC*[20] the Upper Tribunal (Administrative Appeals Chamber) reasoned thus:

> '[34] I have not found it easy to decide whether the deputy Commissioner was correct that the amount of school fees paid by a non-resident parent cannot be taken into account in applying the just and equitable test [on a variation]. On the one hand, that test provides a largely unrestricted discretion to take account of the whole of the financial circumstances relevant to both the non-resident parent and the person with care. On the other hand, it must be applied within the context of the child support scheme, which expressly leaves to the court the issue of tuition fees. I have decided that the express legislative division of responsibility between the courts and the Commission indicates that school fees are a matter for the courts and not to be taken into account under the just and equitable test.

> [35] This does not leave the non-resident parent without recourse. It may be that his combined liability for child support maintenance and his share of the school fees is excessive. There should be a legal mechanism by which his overall liabilities can be taken into account. Section 8(7) [MCA 1973] preserves that mechanism for the court. The non-resident parent can apply to the court for a more appropriate order in respect of the school fees.'

20.16 Naturally, the court is alive to the needs of children after divorce as its first consideration, particularly if there is a risk of their removal from schooling to which they have become accustomed or which is to their obvious benefit. In *T v T (Financial Provision: Private Education)*,[21] Bennett J had great concern for the welfare of the 12-year-old boy who, faced with a loss of school fees payments by his father, would undoubtedly exit from a route to public school: 'I am confident he will [pass his common entrance exam] comfortably. To pull the plug on him now would not just be unfair, but I believe damaging to him'.[22]

---

[18] MCA 1973, s 23(1)(d).

[19] See reg 13 of the Child Support (Variation) Regulations 2000.

[20] [2010] UKUT 356 (AAC), per Edwards Jacobs at paras 34–35.

[21] [2006] 1 FLR 903; the decision having been successfully appealed in *Tracey v Tracey* [2007] 1 FLR 196.

[22] *T v T*, at [54]. *T v T* was successfully appealed in part but the welfare consideration still stands as of 'first', if not paramount, importance. In *Tracey v Tracey* [2007] 1 FLR 196, Thorpe LJ

20.17 It is also common ground that a school fees order – if appropriate – can be made by way of periodical payments (secured or otherwise) or by order for payment of a lump sum to meet the estimated cost of future fees. The choice between the two orders will depend on the balancing exercise between the need for flexibility for payment (periodical payments) versus the attraction of finality (lump sum), the level of available capital and the security of any income stream from which the school fees are to be paid.[23]

Legal basis: disability expenses

20.18

'(8) This section shall not prevent a court from exercising any power which it has to make a maintenance order in relation to a child if –

(a)   an allowance under Part 4 of the Welfare Reform Act 2012 (personal independence payment) or a disability living allowance is paid to or in respect of him; or

(b)   no such allowance is paid but he is disabled,

and the order is made solely for the purpose of requiring the person making or securing the making of periodical payments fixed by the order to meet some or all of any expenses attributable to the child's disability.'

20.19 MCA 1973 does not provide a definition of the term 'disabled' if the child is not in receipt of a disability living allowance.[24] The CSA 1991 does provide such a definition in s 8(9) as follows: 'For the purposes of subsection (8), a child is disabled if he is blind, deaf or dumb or is substantially and permanently handicapped by illness, injury, mental disorder[25] or congenital deformity or such other disability as may be prescribed.' There are various other statutory definitions of 'disabled': for example, the Equality Act 2010[26] and the Children Act 1989.[27]

> Despite MCA 1973 expressly limiting payments made 'solely' for the purpose of meeting expenses attributable to the child's disability, the Court of Appeal has urged as broad an interpretation of such expenses as →

---

was also convinced that 'my first conclusion is that there must be security for the future private education of these boys: enough to say that the history of the case demands it ...' (at [21]).

[23]   See *Tracey v Tracey* [2007].

[24]   https://www.gov.uk/disability-living-allowance-children.

[25]   See Mental Health Act 1983, s 1(2): a mental disorder is a 'mental illness, arrested or incomplete development of mind, psychopathic disorder and any other disorder or disability of [the] mind and 'mentally disordered' shall be construed accordingly'.

[26]   Section 6: a person has a disability if he/she has a physical or mental impairment and the impairment has a substantial and long-term adverse effect on his/her ability to carry out normal day-to-day activities.

[27]   Section 17(11): a child is disabled if 'he is blind, deaf or dumb or suffers from mental disorder of any kind or is substantially and permanently handicapped by illness, injury or congenital deformity or such other disability as may be prescribed ...' (for the purpose of CA 1989, s 17 by reference to provision of services for children in need).

possible. In *C v F (Disabled Child)*[28] – a case involving a child of unmarried parents – the child, T, was born severely disabled and suffered from autism, hyperactivity, double incontinence and brain damage. Butler-Sloss LJ accepted that the court's discretion to make an order was circumscribed by CSA 1991, s 8(8) but that 'it is implicit in any periodical payments application that the court will have to exercise its discretion after considering all the relevant circumstances of each individual case ... in general a court considering this difficult assessment should take into account in *the broadest sense* the expenses attributable to the child's disability. The additional help needed, the cost of fees and subsistence allowance for additional help, a larger or better-appointed house, heating, clothing, car expenses, respite care are only some of the expenses which immediately spring to mind. The expenses attributable to the disability, broadly assessed, the income and allowances coming into the family housing the child with a disability have to be weighed in the balance against the income, assets, liabilities and outgoings of the person asked to meet some or all of those expenses ...'[29] (emphasis added).

20.20 The approach of the court should be two-pronged. First, there must be an assessment of the financial resources available to all parties (including the child and any benefits payable by reason of the disability). Second, the court should assess broadly the expenses related to the disability.

Legal basis: 'top-up' order

20.21

'(6) This section shall not prevent a court from exercising any power which it has to make a maintenance order in relation to a child if –

(a)   a maintenance assessment is in force with respect to the child;

(b)   the amount of the child support maintenance payable in accordance with the assessment was determined by reference to the alternative formula mentioned in paragraph 4(3) of Schedule 1; and

(c)   the court is satisfied that the circumstances of the case make it appropriate for the absent parent to make or secure the making of periodical payments under a maintenance order in addition to the child support maintenance payable by him in accordance with the maintenance assessment.'

20.22 It remains unclear whether a maximum assessment *must* have been made by the CSA[30] before the court's power to make a 'top up' order is invoked, or whether the court can make its own independent assessment of

---

[28]   *C v F (Disabled Child: Maintenance Orders)* [1998] 2 FLR 1, CA, at 6.

[29]   *C v F* at 6–7.

[30]   Under the gross income scheme, this is an assessment on income up to £3,000 per week. The author, however, cautions against not having such an assessment given the statutory wording, particularly in cases in which the payer's income is not significantly in excess of the maximum level.

whether the payer's income is in excess of the amount prescribed for a maximum CSA assessment. In *CF v KM (Financial Provision for a Child: Costs of Legal Proceedings)*,[31] Charles J did not determine the question on appeal but queried the logic of having to await a maximum CSA assessment if the court had a full appraisal of the payer's income and the facts made it clear that the payer's weekly income exceeded the amount prescribed by the CSA:

> '[4] The premise for that stance was and is that, unless and until the Commission make a maximum assessment, the court's power to order "top-up" periodical payments pursuant to s 8(6) of the Child Support Act 1991 is not engaged. I queried this, because it is not what s 8(6) expressly provides, and I was referred to *Re P (Child: Financial Provision)* [2003] EWCA Civ 837, [2003] 2 WLR 865, [2003] 2 FLR 865 and *H v C* [2009] EWHC 1527 (Fam), [2009] 2 FLR 1540. It seemed to me arguable that the court could determine the issue of fact that is part of the trigger to its jurisdiction set by s 8(6)(b), namely whether the father has a net weekly income in excess of the figure set in regulations (at present £2,000 per week). It was common ground that the jurisdictional issue of fact set by s 8(6)(a) is satisfied.'

Legal basis: written agreements

20.23

> '(5) ... this section shall not prevent a court from exercising any power which it has to make a maintenance order in relation to a child if –
>
> (a) a written agreement (whether or not enforceable) provides for the making, or securing, by an absent parent of the child of periodical payments to or for the benefit of the child; and
> (b) the maintenance order which the court makes is, in all material respects, in the same terms as that agreement.'

20.24 If the parties record in writing an agreement for the payer to make periodical payments for the benefit of a child, that agreement provides the court with power to make an order for child maintenance in the terms of the agreement. The order remains in force for a period of 12 months, after which date either party (payer or payee) can apply to the CSA for an assessment to be made.

Legal basis for quantification and payment: child maintenance in cases of a petition for divorce

20.25 The power to order periodical payments for the benefit of a child of the family is provided for in MCA 1973, s 23(1)(d).[32]

---

[31] [2010] EWHC 1754 (Fam), [2011] 1 FLR 208. This was a case pursuant to Schedule 1 of the Children Act 1989.

[32] See s 23 for additional provisions relating to lump sum payments and secured periodical payments for the benefit of a child; in cases of civil partnership dissolution, see CPA 2004, Sch 5, Part 1, para 2(1)(d).

'(d) an order that a party to the marriage shall make to such person as may be specified in the order for the benefit of a child of the family, or to such a child, such periodical payments, for such term, as may be so specified;

(2) The court may also, subject to those restrictions, make any one or more of the orders mentioned in subsection (1)(d), (e) and (f) above –

(a) in any proceedings for divorce, nullity of marriage or judicial separation, before granting a decree; and
(b) where any such proceedings are dismissed after the beginning of the trial, either forthwith or within a reasonable period after the dismissal.'

20.26 An order for periodical payments for an adult can only be made after decree nisi.[33] An order for the benefit of a child can be made notwithstanding the lack of a decree nisi and, even if divorce proceedings are dismissed, the court is empowered to make such an order within a reasonable period of time after the dismissal.[34]

20.27 Unlike orders for periodical payments between parties to a marriage,[35] an order for periodical payments for the benefit of a child can specify payment to 'such person as may be specified in the order' or to the child himself directly.[36] It is acceptable for an order to be framed to provide part-payment to a parent and part-payment to the child directly, particularly in cases involving older children, as 'it is not uncommon for older children, and especially undergraduate children, to operate their own bank account and to manage an allowance paid to them. It may be wholly appropriate that children learn from having personal control over a modest allowance ...'.[37]

DEFINING A 'CHILD OF THE FAMILY'

20.28

> The court's ability to make a child maintenance order is restricted to a 'child of the family'. A child of the family is defined as a [biological] child of both parties to the marriage or 'any other child, not being a child who is placed with those parties as foster parents by a local authority or voluntary organisation, who has been treated by both of those parties as a child of their family'.[38] Whether or not a child is to be treated as a 'child of the family' for the purpose of MCA 1973, s 23 is a fact-specific question in each case. →

---

[33] MCA 1973, s 23(1).
[34] MCA 1973, s 23(2).
[35] Which can only be ordered from one party to the other.
[36] MCA 1973, s 23(1)(d).
[37] *G v G (Periodical Payments: Jurisdiction)* [1997] 1 FLR 368, at 381, per Ward LJ.
[38] MCA 1973, s 52(1).

In *Re A (Child Of The Family)*[39] the Court of Appeal rejected a husband's appeal against an order concluding that his grandchild was a 'child of the family' within the meaning of MCA 1973, s 52(1). The court emphasised that the test to determine whether a child is a child of the family is an objective one, which requires an examination of all the circumstances of the individual case. In *Re A* the circumstances went beyond those of the 'normal' provision of support by grandparents to their family; instead, the grandparents had effectively assumed primary responsibility for the child for the foreseeable future. They alone had made decisions regarding the child's schooling; they were called 'Mum' and 'Dad' by the child (in contrast to their other grandchildren), and they had refused the return of the child to her mother and assumed primary responsibility for the costs of the child's maintenance and upbringing.

There is also no minimum amount of time required for a child to be accepted by a party to the marriage and treated by the court as a child of the family. In *Teeling v Teeling*[40] the Court of Appeal upheld a wife's appeal against an order that a child born to her during a separation and an affair was not a child of the family in circumstances in which the husband allowed the wife and child to return to live with him for a period of 6 months. Ormrod LJ concluded that 'de facto, the child has been treated as a child of the family. The husband did various things for the child and was obviously willing, if the wife had been prepared, to accept the child as his own child and to live together as a family, and they did so for 6 months'.[41]

The counterweight to the open, objective and time-unlimited test applied to determine whether a child is a child of the family is found in MCA 1973, s 25(4). This provision applies to cases in which the potential payer is not the biological parent of the child concerned: it requires the court to have regard to whether the potential payer *'assumed any responsibility for the child's maintenance*, and, if so, the *extent to which, and the basis upon which*, that party assumed such responsibility and to the *length of time* for which that party discharged such responsibility' (emphasis added).[42]

FACTORS FOR THE COURT'S CONSIDERATION

20.29   When determining whether a child periodical payments order should be made and, if so, its quantification and duration, the court must have regard to all the circumstances of the case; first consideration is given to the welfare of

---

[39]   [1998] 1 FLR 347.
[40]   [1984] FLR 808.
[41]   Ibid, at 809.
[42]   The court must also consider whether the payer knew that the child was not biologically his when he assumed and discharged any responsibility and the liability of any other person to maintain the child (MCA 1973, s 23(4)).

the minor child of the family. In addition to the financial resources,[43] income, earning capacity, needs, obligations and disabilities of the parties to the marriage and the standard of living of the family,[44] the court is specifically directed to consider:

(a) the financial needs of the child (as distinct from those of his/her parent);

(b) the income, earning capacity (if any), property and other financial resources of the child (for example, income or capital entitlements under a trust);

(c) any physical or mental disability of the child;

(d) the manner in which the child was being, and the manner in which the parties expected the child to be, educated or trained.

THE NUMBER AND DURATION OF ORDERS

20.30 The court may make a periodical payments order for the benefit of a child from 'time to time'.[45] The court is empowered, therefore, to make more than one order for periodical payments for the benefit of the child and, if the term of a previous order has expired, to make another order for periodical payments thereafter.[46] The 'clean break' provision does not apply as it does in the case of periodical payments orders for ex-spouses.[47]

20.31 MCA 1973 broadly limits the making of periodical payments orders in favour of a child to his/her 18th birthday[48]. The general rule is that no order for financial provision for the benefit of a child shall be made by the court if the child is 18 years old, and any order made shall not extend beyond the child's 18th birthday.[49] However, this rule is subject to an important exception, which permits an order to be made after a child's 18th birthday and for an order made before such date to extend beyond the child's 18th birthday if it appears to the court that:

(a) the child is, or will be, or if an order were made without complying with either or both of those provisions, would be, receiving instruction at an educational establishment or undergoing training for a trade, profession or vocation, whether or not he is also, or will also be, in gainful employment; or

(b) there are special circumstances which justify the making of an order without complying with either or both of those provisions.[50]

---

[43] Including any resources from trust structures, see *Whaley v Whaley* [2012] 1 FLR 735.
[44] See MCA 1973, s 25(3)(e).
[45] MCA 1973, s 23(4).
[46] As long as the requirements in MCA 1973, s 29(3) are met.
[47] See also *Jackson's Matrimonial Finance* (2012), para 10.7.
[48] MCA 1973, s 29(1).
[49] MCA 1973, s 29(1) and (2)(b).
[50] MCA 1973, s 29(3).

QUANTIFICATION OF AN ORDER FOR CHILD PERIODICAL PAYMENTS

20.32 If the court's power is engaged to make a periodical payments order for the benefit of a child, the amount of the payment will depend on its purpose (ie general 'top-up' maintenance or more specific school fees or disability expenses) in conjunction with a full assessment of the applicable factors.[51]

20.33 In *GW v RW (Financial Provision: Departure From Equality)*[52] – a case in which both parents were habitually resident in Australia – Mostyn J[53] concluded that 'the appropriate starting point for a child maintenance award should almost invariably be the figure thrown up by the new child support rules'.[54] The figure for child maintenance calculated by reference to the CSA formula applicable at the time can provide, therefore, a rule of thumb[55] to guide the court, but it does not fetter the court's ultimate discretion. In *N v F (Financial Orders: Pre-acquired Wealth)*[56] the husband was to receive a *Duxbury* fund of £3.487 million, which would provide him with an annual income of £184,000 in addition to his schoolmaster's salary of £36,000 net per annum. Mostyn J applied the CSA formula to the husband's total annual income of £220,000 and reduced it according to the relevant percentage deduction for the number of nights the children were in the husband's care.

PROCEDURE

20.34 An order for child periodical payments is a financial order[57] and, thereby, a financial remedy: the application for such an order follows the standard Family Procedure Rules 2010 (FPR 2010), Part 9 procedure.[58]

20.35 FPR 2010, r 9.10 specifies those classes of people who may apply for a financial remedy in respect of children. The child of the family is a potential applicant, if the court has given permission for the child to apply for a financial remedy.

SEGAL ORDERS

20.36 As an interim measure, and pending an assessment by the relevant statutory agency responsible for child maintenance, the court may make a

---

[51] As set out above at 20.29.
[52] [2003] 2 FLR 108.
[53] Sitting as a Deputy Judge of the High Court.
[54] *GW v RW*, at 129.
[55] *SW v RC* [2008] 1 FLR 1703, at [18], per Singer J.
[56] [2011] 2 FLR 533.
[57] FPR 2010, r 2.3.
[58] FPR 2010, r 29.8 also provides a route for the court, without a hearing, to indicate the rejection of an application for an order which, in its opinion, it would be prevented from making under CSA 1991, s 8 or 9.

'Segal' order.[59] This order is predicated on two conditions: first, that the amount of maintenance that is ordered reduces 'pro tanto'[60] upon an assessment being made by the statutory agency and, second, that the amount ordered includes a substantial element of spousal periodical payments. In *Dorney-Kingdom v Dorney-Kingdom*,[61] Thopre LJ explained the jurisdiction as follows:

> [14] It is necessary now to refer to the mechanism which the judges thought might confer upon them jurisdiction. A practice has grown up, finding its origins before District Judge Segal in the Principal Registry, to make an order for spousal maintenance under s 23(1)(a) of the Matrimonial Causes Act 1973 that incorporates some of the costs of supporting the children as part of a global order. When a 'Segal order' is made an important ingredient is that the overall sum will reduce pro tanto from the date upon which the Child Support Agency brings in an assessment. The utility of the "Segal order" is obvious, since in many cases the determination of the ancillary relief claims will come at a time when the Child Support Agency has yet to complete its assessment of liability. It is therefore very convenient for a district judge to have a form of order which will carry the parent with primary care over that interim pending the Agency's determination.
>
> [15] The proscription on the court making orders for child periodical payments other than by agreement, expressed in s 8(3) of the statute, could be said to be challenged, if not breached, by the mechanism of the Segal order. However, it seems to me to be just within the bounds of legitimacy, since it is no sort of ouster of or challenge to the jurisdiction of the Agency, but merely a holding until such time as the Agency can carry out its proper function. But it seems to me absolutely crucial that if legitimacy is to be preserved, there must be a substantial ingredient of spousal support in the Segal order. If in any case there is a determination that the primary carer has no entitlement to periodical payments on her own account, any form of order that is not an agreed order plainly circumvents the statutory prohibition ...

A Segal order should, however, only be interim in nature as the court's jurisdiction to make an order determining the level of child maintenance payable is severely limited by CSA 1991, s 8, as set out at **20.18**. Therefore, the Segal order differs from the 'global [maintenance] order', which may be made in cases in which the court's jurisdiction to make a child maintenance order is engaged, for example, by virtue of the circumstances meriting a 'top-up' order. In such a case, the court may make an order providing for a sum £x to be paid to the payee, which comprises £a as spousal periodical payments and £b as child maintenance. The global sum of £x will then reduce automatically as each respective child reaches a specified age or event[62] that is recorded in the order as a basis for such payment to cease: the spousal element will continue until the conclusion of the relevant term.

---

[59] Which takes its name from a decision of DJ Segal.
[60] For so much.
[61] [2000] 2 FLR 855.
[62] For example, completion of secondary education.

CHAPTER 21

MAINTENANCE AGREEMENTS AND MCA 1973, SS 34–35

'Throughout history there has been a tension between those who see marriage as essentially a matter of contract negotiated between husband and wife or, more frequently, their families, and those who see it as a matter of status imposed first by the church and then by the state. We do not need to regard marriage as a religious sacrament to believe that it is more than a mere individual contract. All the text books say that it is a status. The parties freely contract into it but they are not free to write all the terms for themselves. Their relationship affects third parties, most notably their children, as well as themselves …'[1]

INTRODUCTION

21.1 The modern law of financial remedies has a rapidly-developing preference for respecting the individual autonomy of, and choices made by, the parties to a marriage.[2] Albeit that there is (as yet)[3] no automatic statutory enforcement of ante- or post-nuptial agreements,[4] MCA 1973, ss 34 and 35 do contain alternative provisions regulating the validity and alteration of 'maintenance agreements'.[5] These provisions originate from 1957[6] and, indeed, find historical origins in the private separation deeds that became more popular in the 18th and 19th centuries:[7] they remain within the Matrimonial Causes Act 1973 (MCA 1973), despite the landscape of matrimonial practice having changed drastically over the last 40 years. In 1957, the continuation of proceedings through to a final divorce was still uncommon[8] but some statutory construct was important to allow separating parties to conclude agreements as to future financial provision. This chapter summarises the court's remaining powers to vary and revoke these financial arrangements that parties have agreed upon to govern their rights and liabilities when living separately.

---

[1] Baroness Hale of Richmond, 'What's the Deal? Marital Property Agreements Past, Present and Future' [2011] IFL 282.

[2] See, for the ultimate expression of this, *Radmacher (Formerly Granatino) v Granatino* [2010] UKSC 42, [2010] 2 FLR 1900.

[3] The Law Commission recommendations are awaited.

[4] The Law Commission has consulted on this issue.

[5] Referred to as dead letters for more than 30 years by Wilson LJ in the Court of Appeal hearing in the case of *Radmacher v Granatino* [2009] 2 FLR 1181, at [134].

[6] Maintenance Agreements Act 1957.

[7] For more detail, see Chapter 1 on the historical development of maintenance and alimony.

[8] Circa 25,000 per year in the 1950s rising to 120,000 in 2010.

LEGAL BASIS: ELEMENTS AND EFFECT OF A MAINTENANCE AGREEMENT

21.2 A maintenance agreement (within the terms of MCA 1973, s 34) is:

(a)   any written agreement

(b)   made between the parties to a marriage[9]

(c)   during the continuance or after the dissolution or annulment of the marriage

(d)   containing financial arrangements[10] (ie 'provisions governing the rights and liabilities of the parties towards one another when living separately … in respect of the making or securing of payments or the disposition or use of any property, including rights and liabilities with regard to the maintenance or education of any child)'.[11]

21.3 A maintenance agreement professing to restrict either party's ability to apply to the court for an order for financial provision does not invalidate the whole agreement: whereas the purported restriction itself is void, the remaining terms of the agreement will be binding on the parties. The court retains a power (a) to vary or revoke any financial arrangements within the agreement and (b) to insert new financial arrangements into the agreement for the benefit of a party or a child of the family.[12]

21.4 The provisions in MCA 1973, ss 34–35, however, do not affect either party's right to apply for, nor the court's ability to make, an order for financial provision.[13] Therefore, whatever the terms of a maintenance agreement concluded by the parties to a marriage, either party may still apply for the full panoply of financial remedies[14] in the traditional manner pursuant to MCA 1973, s 23(1).[15]

---

9   Or a separation agreement containing no financial arrangements (MCA 1973, s 34(2)(b)).

10   The definition of financial arrangements has also been construed in *F v F (Financial Remedies: Premarital Wealth)* [2012] EWHC 438 (Fam), [2012] 2 FLR 1212 as covering 'only those agreements made with the expressed or clearly implied purpose of governing the parties' financial affairs, including in the event of separation and not those that could do so only if certain terms of the agreement were reconstituted'. In *F v F*, at [24], per Macur J.

11   See MCA 1973, s 34(2).

12   Defined in MCA 1973, s 52(1).

13   Eg any order pursuant to MCA 1973, s 23(1) or indeed an order brought under any other enactment. See MCA 1973, s 34(6).

14   'If parties who have made such an agreement, whether ante-nuptial or post-nuptial, then decide to live apart, we can see no reason why they should not be entitled to enforce their agreement. This right will, however, prove nugatory if one or other objects to the terms of the agreement, for this is likely to result in the party who objects initiating proceedings for divorce or judicial separation and arguing in ancillary relief proceedings that he or she should not be held to the terms of the agreement' (*Radmacher v Granatino*, at [52], per Lord Phillips).

15   In which circumstances, the court should 'give effect to a nuptial agreement that is freely entered into by each party with a full appreciation of its implications unless, in the circumstances prevailing, it would not be fair to hold the parties to their agreement' (*Radmacher v Granatino*): subject, also, to whether there is evidence of any material lack of disclosure, information or advice at the time of entering into the agreement.

THE ALTERATION OF MAINTENANCE AGREEMENTS: VARYING, REVOKING AND INSERTING FINANCIAL ARRANGEMENTS

21.5 The court has power to vary or revoke *any* financial arrangements contained in a maintenance agreement or to insert new financial arrangements into the agreement for the benefit of either party or a child of the family.[16] These powers can be exercised having regard to all the circumstances of the case.

Process, procedure and costs

21.6 An order pursuant to MCA 1973, s 35 is a 'financial remedy' and a 'financial order'[17]. Therefore, first, the Family Procedure Rules 2010 (FPR 2010), Part 9 application procedure applies,[18] as it does to applications for the more common financial orders;[19] and second, the general rule, that the court will not make an order requiring one party to pay the costs of another party, applies.[20] An application can be made to the High Court, a county court or, in certain circumstances, the magistrates' court.[21]

Conditions for altering a maintenance agreement

21.7 The court must be satisfied that:

(a) a maintenance agreement is for the time being subsisting;[22] and

(b) each of the parties to the agreement is domiciled or resident in England and Wales;[23] and

(c) the court is satisfied either that:
   (i)   by reason of a change in the circumstances in the light of which any financial arrangements contained in the agreement were made or, as the case may be, financial arrangements were omitted from it (including a change foreseen by the parties when making the agreement), the agreement should be altered so as to make different, or, as the case may be, so as to contain financial arrangements; or
   (ii) the agreement does not contain proper financial arrangements with respect to any child of the family.

---

[16] MCA 1973, s 35(2)(b)(i) and (ii).
[17] FPR 2010, r 2.3.
[18] Not in the case of an application to alter a maintenance agreement after the death of one party (pursuant to MCA 1973, s 36 but not otherwise dealt with in The Guide).
[19] Eg lump sum, property adjustment and periodical payments orders etc.
[20] FPR 2010, r 28.3(4)(b)(i), which defines 'financial remedy proceedings' as proceedings for, inter alia, a 'financial order'.
[21] For the applicable limitations on applications to the Magistrates' Court see MCA 1973, s 35(3).
[22] MCA 1973, s 35(1): and that the circumstances in which it came to being are not vitiated, for example, by undue influence or pressure to enter into the agreement being placed on one party (see *NA v MA* [2007] 1 FLR 1760).
[23] Ibid.

21.8 The court will make such changes to the maintenance agreement as it considers just and by having regard to 'all the circumstances'. The agreement itself can be based on the state of affairs at the time the agreement is made or by reference to prospective changes to those conditions in the future. The agreement is 'designed to take effect immediately and to address the circumstances prevailing at the time that it is made, as well, of course, as those contemplated in the future. It will have regard to any children of the family, to the assets of husband and wife, to their incomes and to their pension rights. Thus it makes sense to look for a significant change of circumstances as the criterion justifying a departure from the agreement'.[24]

21.9 If the court inserts a new arrangement for the making of periodical payments, or increases the agreed rate of periodical payments, the term for such periodical payments shall not extend beyond the death of either party or the remarriage of the payee.[25]

---

[24] *Radmacher v Granatino*, at [65].
[25] In the same manner as a 'standard' order for periodical payments pursuant to MCA 1973, s 28.

CHAPTER 22

ENFORCEMENT OF MAINTENANCE ORDERS AND ARREARS[1] WITHIN ENGLAND & WALES

'... I have counted that I was constrained to quote from eight sections or subsections of six statutes, spanning over 100 years from 1869 to 1980, and also two different rules of court. To the respondent wife in this case, who acts in person, this judgment must have seemed, and to the lay reader, and perhaps even a lawyer, this judgment must now seem like gobbledegook, and the eyes glaze over. The issue was the very serious one of whether a man was lawfully sent to prison. It ought to be possible to resolve and be clear about it by a much more simple process, particularly as the jurisdiction is one which may frequently be exercised by lay magistrates in circumstances where (as in this case) one or both parties may increasingly act in person. This area of the law is in dire need of modernisation, simplification and reform.'[2]

INTRODUCTION

22.1 The enforcement within England & Wales[3] of orders made in financial remedy proceedings is a confusing and often disconnected network of statutes, rules, forms and procedures that, collectively, has been described as 'hopelessly complex and procedurally tortuous'.[4] The Law Commission is undertaking a project to make wide-ranging proposals for reform, but the specific recommendations arising from this welcome development will not be available for a number of years.[5] The Family Procedure Rules 2010 (FPR 2010) were intended to simplify and codify the applicable enforcement procedure and, in relation to applications for a judgment summons, to make the process compliant with the European Convention on Human Rights (ECHR).

22.2 The broad and unwieldy topic of 'enforcement' could easily justify a full practitioner's text running to hundreds of pages. Therefore, this chapter provides a broad overview of the principal methods for, and essential procedure

---

[1]   Collectively, in this context, orders for maintenance pending suit and periodical payments.
[2]   *Constantinides v Constantinides* [2013] EWHC 3688 (Fam), at [37], per Holman J.
[3]   The international enforcement of financial orders is beyond the scope of this work and is dealt with comprehensively elsewhere, see for example, *Rayden & Jackson on Divorce and Family Matters*.
[4]   http://lawcommission.justice.gov.uk/areas/family-financial-orders.htm.
[5]   The current estimate is 2016, if the proposals develop into a formal Bill.

relevant to, the enforcement of a periodical payments order or a related undertaking to pay a sum of money (which may indeed be on a periodic basis). This chapter also details some of the methods available to secure location and financial information in relation to a non-complying payer, and addresses the circumstances in which leave to enforce arrears of maintenance is required.[6]

22.3 Within this chapter, the expressions 'judgment creditor' and 'judgment debtor' are used – where appropriate – to describe, respectively, the person entitled to enforce an order or judgment[7] and the person against whom an order has been made.[8] Otherwise, the terms of 'payer' and 'payee' are used.

22.4 The various specific forms required for making or responding to applications in enforcement proceedings can be found at http://www.justice.gov. uk/courts/procedure-rules/family/formspage. A number of the more commonly used forms are also reproduced in the Appendix to The Guide.

SECURING LOCATION AND FINANCIAL INFORMATION IN RELATION TO A JUDGMENT DEBTOR

22.5 Effective enforcement proceedings require the judgment creditor to identify and serve proceedings on the judgment debtor,[9] and are often assisted by providing the court with some knowledge of the judgment debtor's financial affairs, even if such information is not provided by the judgment debtor him/herself. Three useful methods for securing such information are as follows:

(a) *An application to the Department for Work and Pensions*[10] *(or the appropriate branch of Her Majesty's Forces) to trace the address of a judgment debtor.*

 The Practice Direction providing for the disclosure of addresses by government departments[11] has survived the new FPR 2010 and is to be found in FPR 2010, PD 6C. The court may request address information on behalf of an individual seeking to enforce an order for financial provision either for him/herself or for the benefit of children of a former marriage. The Practice Direction sets out the information required by the government department(s) in order to assist the tracing process.[12] The Practice Direction also provides information as to the correct Departments to contact in the case of a tracing exercise relating to serving or recently serving members of HM Forces.

---

[6]   It does not deal with matters of the reciprocal enforcement of maintenance orders (within UK or externally)
[7]   Otherwise known in The Guide as the payee.
[8]   Otherwise known in The Guide as the payer.
[9]   Often by means of personal service.
[10] Previously the Department for Social Security.
[11] 'Disclosure of Addresses by Government Departments' [1988] 2 FLR 183.
[12] The Practice Direction is provided in the Appendix to The Guide.

(b) *An application for an order that a judgment debtor attends court to provide information for the purpose of enabling the judgment creditor to enforce a judgment.*[13]

The Civil Procedure Rules (CPR) Part 71 provides an avenue for a judgment creditor to apply to the court for the judgment debtor to attend court to provide information about his/her means or 'any other matter about which information is needed to enforce a judgment or order'.[14] An order to attend court must be served personally on the judgment debtor[15] and, on attendance at court, s/he will be questioned on oath. If the judgment debtor fails to attend court, the matter will be referred to a High Court judge or circuit judge and a committal order may be made against the judgment debtor.[16]

(c) *An application for a[n interim] third party debt order*[17], *which requires a bank or building society to make disclosure of a judgment debtor's accounts.*[18]

A third party debt order directs a third party to pay a judgment creditor a specific sum of money, if the judgment debtor holds an account that is in credit with that third party bank or building society.[19] An application for a third party debt order is dealt with initially by the court without a hearing and the court may make an interim order at that stage:[20] if it does so, and if the third party is a bank or building society, it is under an obligation to (a) search for all accounts held with the bank or building society by the judgment creditor and (b) disclose to the court and the judgment creditor within 7 days of service of the order the account number(s) and any credit standing in those account(s). Therefore, armed with the name of a non-disclosing judgment debtor (and any other helpful identifying information), the judgment creditor has a means to obtain basic financial information from the relevant bank or building society directly.[21]

---

[13] Pursuant to CPR Part 71 as applied by FPR 2010, r 33.23; see also CPR, PD 71 for details as to the process and the requirements on the applicant.

[14] CPR, r 71.2(1) and application should be made using Form N316.

[15] CPR, r 71.3.

[16] CPR, r 71.8.

[17] Using form N349 and see the Practice Direction to CPR Part 72 for the detailed procedure (these orders used to be called 'garnishee' orders).

[18] CPR, r 72.6 as imported into the FPR 2010 by r 33.24 (with some minor modifications).

[19] A bank account in credit is a debt due by the bank to its customer.

[20] If a third party debt order is not an appropriate remedy, the judgment creditor may consider an application for a freezing order to protect any assets against which enforcement may be pursued. The freezing order may contain directions to the judgment debtor to provide financial information. See also *O'Farrell v O'Farrell* [2013] 1 FLR 77.

[21] The third party must be within this jurisdiction: the phrase 'bank or building society' refers to any person carrying on a business in the course of which he lawfully accepts deposits in the United Kingdom (see CPR, r 72.1(1) and (2)).

ENFORCING THE PAYMENT OF ARREARS UNDER A PERIODICAL PAYMENTS ORDER[22]

22.6 If a payer fails to make periodical payments pursuant to an order, the payee must act relatively swiftly to protect his/her ability to recover any unpaid sums. Leave of the court is required to enforce arrears due under an order for maintenance pending suit and an interim or final order for periodical payments *if the arrears became due more than 12 months before the date on which proceedings for enforcement were commenced.*[23] The court hearing an application for leave to enforce arrears may:

(a)   refuse leave; or

(b)   grant leave subject to restrictions or conditions that the court deems proper; or

(c)   remit all or some of the arrears due.[24]

Granting leave to enforce arrears or remitting them

22.7 The court has discretion as to whether to enforce 'stale' arrears;[25] older case-law makes reference to a rule of practice[26] that it is *usual* to remit or decline to enforce arrears that have accrued more than 12 months before the application to enforce. Therefore, in exercising its discretion, the court will consider the reasons behind any delay in bringing enforcement proceedings:

> 'The philosophy underlying the rule must therefore have been that if the complainant waited a year to seek enforcement of the order, she did not need the money, or at least had managed well enough without it, and the husband might reasonably regard the liability as something which he could forget about. This is not to say that the rule has changed in modern times when a wife might reasonably live on her savings for a period and expect to be reimbursed by a single large payment. However it does point to the fact that the courts should take account of the extent to which the complainant has sought to assert her rights.'[27]

This practice has also been described as a 'starting point': that stale arrears are not to be enforced unless there are special circumstances[28] justifying such

---

[22]   This includes periodical payments for a spouse and/or a child.
[23]   MCA 1973, s 32(1).
[24]   MCA 1973, s 32(2).
[25]   Those over 12 months old from the date of application to enforce.
[26]   In the High Court, but expressly not a rule of law (as the MCA 1973 makes no reference to any such rule). However, this rule of practice has been referred to without criticism by the Court of Appeal in *Shaw v Shaw* [2002] EWCA Civ 1298, [2002] 2 FLR 1204.
[27]   *Russell v Russell* [1986] 1 FLR 465, at 473, per Sir John Donaldson MR.
[28]   *B v C (Maintenance: Enforcement of Arrears)* [1995] 1 FLR 467, at 469, per Johnson J; however, see *Lumsden v Lumsden* (unreported but available on Lexis Nexis) 11 November 1998, Court of Appeal, in which Butler-Sloss LJ questioned the origin and correctness of a rule of practice requiring 'special circumstances'.

enforcement. The question for the court must be whether to exercise its discretion to *enforce* the stale maintenance arrears, *not* whether to exercise its discretion to *remit* the arrears.

22.8 The payer's circumstances and behaviour will impact on the court's discretionary exercise. A flagrant defiance or disregard of the order to make payments may support an order to enforce stale arrears.[29] The payer's culpability is a relevant and sometimes decisive factor.[30] Conversely, the payer's debt, poor financial circumstances or unemployment may support an argument not to enforce.[31] If delay has been occasioned by the court process itself, or by unmeritorious cross-applications by the payer to remit certain arrears, these may amount to special circumstances justifying the enforcement of stale arrears.[32] It is good practice – whether pursuing or defending an application to enforce stale arrears – to divide the periods of non-payment into sections of time referable to the payee's (and payer's) arguments in support of enforcement or remission: this approach will assist the court in analysing the reasons for non-payment and deducing whether 'special circumstances' exist to substantiate the enforcement of stale arrears.

Case analysis example: enforcement of stale arrears

Period of time	Arrears accrued (non-cumulative)	Payee's position	Payer's position
Jan–July 2011	£14,000	Emailed payer requesting payment	Able to pay/in same employment
July 2011–July 2012	£24,000	Emailed payer's family/first solicitor letter/drawing on savings	Able to pay/in same employment save for August 2012 when off sick
July–Dec 2012	£10,000	Solicitor correspondence/ payee represents herself	Payer on reduced pay due to illness August 2012–Dec 2012 (£3,200 per month)

---

[29] See *Purba v Purba* [2000] 1 FLR 444 in which the husband made no payment at all consequent upon an order for interim periodical payments of £1,000 per month (even when unsuccessfully appealed).
[30] See *Lumsden v Lumsden* (above).
[31] *King v Bunyon* [2007] EWHC 3281 (Admin), [2008] 1 FLR 1564.
[32] *C v S (Maintenance Order: Enforcement)* [1997] 1 FLR 298.

Dec 2012–Nov 2013	£22,000	Payee applies (without solicitor) to court to enforce but struck out for lack of subsequent action	Payer made redundant January 2013. On JSA until August 2013. New job £6,000 per month net basic
Nov 2013–Date of application to enforce	£4,000	Payee applies after instructing new solicitor	Payer in new job at same salary
TOTAL TIME: 3 years	TOTAL ARREARS: £74,000	–	–

ENFORCING AN ORDER FOR PERIODICAL PAYMENTS

'Pre-emptive' enforcement

Enforcement pursuant to the Maintenance Enforcement Act 1991 (MEA 1991)

22.9 An attachment of earnings order[33] is normally sought by the applicant *after* the original order for payment has been made and *after* the respondent's failure to comply with that order. The MEA 1991, however, enables the High Court or a county court – on application or of its own motion – to make orders to assist the enforcement of periodical payments at the time that the original order for payment is made.[34] If the respondent is ordinarily resident in England and Wales and has been ordered to pay periodical payments, the court may:

(a) order the respondent to make payments to the applicant by standing order;

(b) order the respondent to make payment to the applicant by any other specified method (eg direct debit) and without the need for further authority from the respondent to require the continued and periodic payment;

(c) order the respondent to open a bank account from which payments to the applicant can be made;[35]

(d) make an attachment of earnings order.[36]

---

[33] See further **22.15–22.18**.
[34] Or at a later time.
[35] If the respondent has been given an opportunity to open such an account and has, without reasonable excuse, failed to do so.
[36] MEA 1991, s 1(4)(b).

If there has been a history of non-compliance with previous orders, for example, for maintenance pending suit, an applicant may be well advised to seek an order at an early stage to maximise the possibility of future payment.

'1 Maintenance orders in the High Court and county courts: means of payment, attachment of earnings and revocation, variation, etc

(1) Where the High Court or a county court makes a qualifying periodical maintenance order, it may at the same time exercise either of its powers under subsection (4) below in relation to the order, whether of its own motion or on an application made under this subsection by an interested party.

(2) For the purposes of this section, a periodical maintenance order is an order –

(a)   which requires money to be paid periodically by one person ("the debtor") to another ("the creditor"); and
(b)   which is a maintenance order;

and such an order is a "qualifying periodical maintenance order" if, at the time it is made, the debtor is ordinarily resident in England and Wales.

(3) Where the High Court or a county court has made a qualifying periodical maintenance order, it may at any later time –

(a)   on an application made under this subsection by an interested party, or
(b)   of its own motion, in the course of any proceedings concerning the order,

exercise either of its powers under subsection (4) below in relation to the order.

(4) The powers mentioned in subsections (1) and (3) above are –

(a)   the power to order that payments required to be made by the debtor to the creditor under the qualifying periodical maintenance order in question shall be so made by such a method of payment falling within subsection (5) below as the court may specify in the particular case; or
(b)   the power, by virtue of this section, to make an attachment of earnings order under the Attachment of Earnings Act 1971 to secure payments under the qualifying periodical maintenance order in question.

(5) The methods of payment mentioned in subsection (4)(a) above are –

(a)   payment by standing order; or
(b)   payment by any other method which requires the debtor to give his authority for payments of a specific amount to be made from an account of his to an account of the creditor's on specific dates during the period for which the authority is in force and without the need for any further authority from the debtor.

(6) In any case where –

(a)   the court proposes to exercise its power under paragraph (a) of subsection (4) above, and
(b)   having given the debtor an opportunity of opening an account from which payments under the order may be made in accordance with the method of payment proposed to be ordered under that paragraph, the court is satisfied that the debtor has failed, without reasonable excuse, to open such an account,

the court in exercising its power under that paragraph may order that the debtor open such an account.

(7) Where in the exercise of its powers under subsection (1) or (3) above the High Court or a county court has made in relation to a qualifying periodical maintenance order such an order as is mentioned in subsection (4)(a) above (a "means of payment order"), it may at any later time –

(a)   on an application made under this subsection by an interested party, or
(b)   of its own motion, in the course of any proceedings concerning the qualifying periodical maintenance order,

revoke, suspend, revive or vary the means of payment order.

(8) In deciding whether to exercise any of its powers under this section the court in question having (if practicable) given every interested party an opportunity to make representations shall have regard to any representations made by any such party.

(9) Nothing in this section shall be taken to prejudice –

(a)   any power under the Attachment of Earnings Act 1971 which would, apart from this section, be exercisable by the High Court or a county court; or
(b)   any right of any person to make any application under that Act;

and subsection (7) above is without prejudice to any other power of the High Court or a county court to revoke, suspend, revive or vary an order.

(10) For the purposes of this section –

"debtor" and "creditor" shall be construed in accordance with subsection (2) above;

"interested party" means any of the following, that is to say –

(a)   the debtor;
(b)   the creditor; and
(c)   in a case where the person who applied for the qualifying periodical maintenance order in question is a person other than the creditor, that other person;

"maintenance order" means any order specified in Schedule 8 to the Administration of Justice Act 1970 and includes any such order which has been discharged, if any arrears are recoverable under it;

"qualifying periodical maintenance order" shall be construed in accordance with subsection (2) above, and the references to such an order in subsections (3) and (7) above are references to any such order, whether made before or after the coming into force of this section;

and the reference in subsection (2) above to an order requiring money to be paid periodically by one person to another includes a reference to an order requiring a lump sum to be paid by instalments by one person to another.'

Post-default enforcement

The Family Procedure Rules 2010

22.10   The FPR 2010 devotes three of its Parts to the procedure applicable to the enforcement of orders made in family proceedings. Part 32 deals with the registration and enforcement of orders, Part 33 provides general rules on enforcement in the High Court and county court and Part 34 covers the cross-border enforcement of maintenance orders. The FPR 2010 also imports Part 70 of the CPR,[37] which governs the general procedure relevant to the enforcement of judgments or orders.

GENERAL: commencing the enforcement process in relation to an order for periodical payments

22.11   The FPR 2010 permits the applicant to apply to the court for either (a) an order for enforcement by a particular method (of the applicant's choosing) or (b) an order for such method of enforcement as the court may consider appropriate.[38]

22.12   The applicant is likely to select a particular method of enforcement if s/he has proper information as to the respondent's financial means and position. Alternatively, if the applicant elects for the court to determine the appropriate enforcement method, the respondent will automatically be ordered to attend court,[39] to produce (financial) documents in his control as described in the court's order and, thereafter, to answer on oath such questions as the court may require.[40] The applicant should indicate in the application notice any specific financial documents of which disclosure is sought. The CPR indicates that the examination as to the respondent's means can be undertaken by an officer of the court[41] or by a judge.[42] An examination before a judge – at which the

---

[37]   Rule 33.2 (as well as other Parts of the CPR).
[38]   Rule 33.3(2).
[39]   Under sanction of contempt of court if the respondent fails to attend.
[40]   CPR, r 71.2(6) and (7) and see the Practice Direction for Part 71 for further detail.
[41]   Using the Form EX140, 'Record of [individual] examination'.
[42]   CPR, r 71.6.

applicant must attend and conduct the questioning[43] – will prove more effective in eliciting financial details and documents from the judgment debtor.[44] The court may make an order for enforcement from a menu of options (as listed on the appropriate application form), including an attachment of earnings order, a third party debt order, a charging order, a writ of execution or by way of the appointment of a receiver.[45]

GENERAL: commencing the enforcement process in relation to an undertaking for the payment of money

22.13 An undertaking to pay a sum of money (whether periodic or not) as a component of an order must be accompanied by both *notice* and *confirmation*: a *notice* to the person giving that undertaking that s/he may be sent to prison if it is proved that s/he has or has had the means to pay the sum of money promised and has refused or neglected, or is refusing or neglecting, to pay that sum.[46] Additionally, the person giving the undertaking must make a signed statement of *confirmation* that s/he understands the consequence of breaking a promise to pay a sum of money. This statement does not need to be given before the court in person.[47]

22.14 An undertaking to pay a sum of money that complies with the notice and confirmation requirements above[48] may be enforced as if it was an order, and the procedure in FPR 2010, Part 33 applies.[49]

THE METHODS OF ENFORCEMENT[50]

An attachment of earnings order[51]

22.15 A common method for enforcing a periodical payments order is an order directly instructing a person who has the respondent in his employment to make periodical deductions from the respondent's earnings[52] (an attachment of earnings order). The order is only effective against the earnings (wages, fees,

---

[43] CPR, r 71.6(3)(b).

[44] CPR, PD 71, para 2.2 states that the order will provide for questioning to take place before a judge only if the judge considering the request decides that there are compelling reasons to make such an order.

[45] NB: none of which involve the judgment debtor's potential imprisonment.

[46] FPR 2010, PD 33A, paras 2.1–2.4.

[47] FPR 2010, PD 33A, para 2.4: 'The statement need not be given before the court in person. It may be endorsed on the court copy of the undertaking or may be filed in a separate document such as a letter.'

[48] And has effect as if it was an order made under Part 2 of the MCA 1973.

[49] FPR 2010, PD 33A, paras 2.1–2.4.

[50] For guidance on additional orders regarding, for example, the retention of a passport, see *Young v Young* [2012] EWHC 138 (Fam), [2012] 2 FLR 470 and *B v B (Injunction: Restraint on Leaving Jurisdiction)* [1997] 2 FLR 148.

[51] Form N337 'Request for attachment of earnings order' and Form N56 'Form for replying to an attachment of earnings application'.

[52] AEA 1971, s 6.

bonus, commission and pension payments[53]) of an employee.[54] The Attachment of Earnings Act 1971 (AEA 1971) is a comprehensive piece of legislation and its contents are not repeated here in full.[55]

22.16 The attachment of earnings order provides some protection to the respondent by prescribing (a) a normal deduction rate and (b) a protected earnings rate. The former sets the amount of the appropriate deduction from the respondent's earnings and the latter imposes a limit to the permissible deductions from the respondent's earnings.[56]

22.17 The duty to comply with an attachment of earnings order rests with the respondent's employer.[57] If the respondent leaves the employment of the person to whom an attachment of earnings order has been made, the order will lapse unless and until the order is re-directed to any subsequent employer.[58]

22.18 The money deducted and collected by means of the attachment of earnings order is used to discharge firstly, payable and unpaid sums of maintenance and, secondly, any costs incurred in proceedings related to the maintenance order which were payable by the respondent at the time the attachment of earnings order was made.[59]

Enforcement against the earnings of members of the Armed Forces

22.19 The AEA 1971 expressly prohibits the making of an attachment of earnings order against the pay or allowances of a respondent who is a member of Her Majesty's forces.[60] However, the Armed Forces (Forfeitures and Deductions) Regulations 2009[61] empowers the Defence Council to make an order in similar terms authorising a deduction to be made from the pay of a respondent (member of the Armed Forces) to meet the terms of a maintenance order.[62]

---

[53] The court has the power to determine whether particular payments received by the respondent are to be treated as 'earnings' for the purposes of an attachment of earnings order (AEA 1971, s 16).

[54] Defined in AEA 1971, ss 6(2) and 24. Section 24 provides an interpretation of earnings and makes it clear that an attachment order can be made in relation to pension payments.

[55] The AEA 1971 is reproduced in the Appendix to The Guide.

[56] AEA 1971, s 6(5).

[57] AEA 1971, s 7.

[58] AEA 1971, s 9(4).

[59] AEA 1971, s 13(2).

[60] AEA 1971, s 24(2)(b) and despite apparently contradictory legislation in the Armed Forces Act 1996, s 356(4)(a).

[61] SI 2009/1109.

[62] See reg 7.

Charging order[63]

22.20   In any case in which a judgment or order requires a person to pay a sum of money to another[64] (which includes an order to make periodical payments), the court may charge the property of the respondent as security for the payment of any money due or to become due. The Charging Orders Act 1979 (COA 1979) provides the legal basis for such an order and CPR Part 73 deals comprehensively with the applicable procedure.[65] The charging order is not a direct means of enforcement that compels immediate payment: instead, it provides a means for securing assets, which may be the subject of enforcement proceedings.

22.21   The initial application for a charging order is dealt with by the court without a hearing. The court may at that stage make an interim charging order[66] or list the matter for a hearing. A charging order may be made with or without conditions[67]. If the applicant secures a charging order over the respondent's interest in property,[68] the ultimate sanction is an order for sale of that property.[69] Both the imposition of the initial charging order and any subsequent order for sale are subject to the court's discretion.

JUDGMENT SUMMONS[70]

22.22

> 'There are scant means of enforcement open to a person (usually a wife) who has achieved ancillary relief orders, unless there are assets within the jurisdiction against which the order can be readily enforced and it is important that the power to apply for committal under the Debtors Act should be seen by debtors as a real and lively threat.'[71]

On an application for a judgment summons, a judgment debtor who has failed to comply with an order to pay a debt, and who has or has had the means to comply, may be committed to prison for a period of up to 6 weeks or until his or her compliance with the order.[72] The legal basis for a judgment summons is s 5 of the Debtors Act 1869:

---

63   Form N379 'Application for a charging order on land or property'.
64   Which can include an order for the payment of maintenance pending suit (see *M v M (Maintenance Pending Suit: Enforcement: on Dismissal of Suit)* [2009] 1 FLR 790.
65   FPR 2010, r 33.25 lists the applicable modifications in financial remedy proceedings.
66   CPR, r 73.4.
67   COA 1979, s 3.
68   Which is defined widely in COA 1979, s 2 to include land, stock, unit trusts and funds in court.
69   See CPR, r 73.10 for the applicable procedure.
70   Form D62 'Request for issue of judgment summons'.
71   *Zuk v Zuk* [2012] EWCA 1871, [2013] 2 FLR 1466, at [16], per Thorpe LJ.
72   This can include an order for the payment of school fees, even where the amount of future payments is not specified in the order, see *L v L (School Fees: Maintenance: Enforcement)* [1997] 2 FLR 252. There is a right of appeal (without permission) against a committal order pursuant to CPR r 52.3(1)(a)(i).

'(1) Subject to the provisions herein-after mentioned, and to the prescribed rules, any court may commit to prison for a term not exceeding 6 weeks, or until payment of the sum due, any person who makes default in payment of any debt or instalment of any debt due from him in pursuance of any order or judgment of that or any other competent court.

(2) That such jurisdiction shall only be exercised where it is proved to the satisfaction of the court that the person making default either has or has had since the date of the order or judgment the means to pay the sum in respect of which he has made default, and has refused or neglected, or refuses or neglects, to pay the same.'

22.23 The application for a judgment summons may be made in relation to a periodical payments order or an order for maintenance pending suit. Generally speaking, the application for a judgment summons is a method of enforcement that should only be deployed as a means of last resort:[73] the procedural obligations placed upon the judgment creditor are significant and the potential consequences for the judgment debtor are, of course, very serious.[74] Furthermore, the judgment creditor will usually have more interest in securing the payment of arrears of periodical payments, and the judgment debtor's committal to prison may severely affect his or her employment and income prospects.

22.24 The fact that an application for a judgment summons has penal consequences for the judgment debtor means that the constituent elements of the 'offence'[75] within the Debtors Act 1869 must be proved to the criminal standard of proof, ie beyond a reasonable doubt.[76] The respondent cannot be compelled to give evidence.[77]

22.25

> The procedure governing an application for judgment summons is provided for in FPR 2010, Part 33.[78] It is imperative that the applicant complies with the relevant rules, which are detailed and specific and include, for example, providing to, or offering, the respondent a sum of money reasonably sufficient to cover the expenses of travelling to and from the court at which s/he is summoned to appear.[79] In *Bhura v Bhura*,[80] Mostyn J carefully collated the guidance relevant to any application for a judgment summons under the Debtors Act 1869, as follows: →

---

[73] *Bhura v Bhura* [2013] 2 FLR 44, at [15], per Mostyn J.
[74] For the interaction of orders for the production of documents in proceedings in which the respondent is compellable and non-compellable, see *Mohan v Mohan* [2013] EWCA Civ 586.
[75] Stated with caution, as the proceedings are civil proceedings.
[76] *Mubarak v Mubarak* [2001] 1 FLR 698, CA.
[77] FPR 2010, r 33.14(2).
[78] Rule 33.10–33.18.
[79] FPR 2010, r 33.11(3).
[80] [2013] 2 FLR 44.

'[13] Stated shortly it seems to me that the applicable principles are these:

(i)   Section 5 requires the court to be satisfied to the criminal standard that:
        (a)   the respondent has had at any point since the date of the order the means to pay the sums due under the order; and
        (b)   has refused or neglected to pay them.

(ii)   The use of the present and past tenses in the phrases "either has or has had" and "and has refused or neglected, or refuses or neglects" means that the section will be satisfied if proof of both ability to pay and refusal or neglect to pay is made at any single point from the date of the order right up to the date of the hearing.

(iii)   The use of the alternative verbs "refuse" and "neglect" means that the court is not confined to proof of a positive wilful refusal to pay; the section will be equally satisfied if proof is made of a culpable indifference to the obligation to pay.

(iv)   It is essential that the applicant adduces sufficient evidence to establish at least a case to answer. Generally speaking, this need not be an elaborate exercise. Proof of the order and of non-payment will likely give rise to an inference which establishes the case to answer.

(v)   The respondent is not required to give evidence or to incriminate himself. In the absence of a case to answer being demonstrated the respondent is entitled to have the application dismissed without more.

(vi)   If the applicant establishes a case to answer an evidential burden shifts to the respondent to answer it. If he fails to discharge that evidential burden then the terms of s 5 will be found proved against him or her to the requisite standard.

(vii)   The applicant does not have to serve evidence prior to the hearing but if he or she fails to do so the court will be astute to ensure that the respondent is not taken by surprise and that the hearing can proceed without unfairness to him or her.

(viii) It is perfectly permissible for both the inquiry into the respondent's means at all points since the making of the order and the inquiry into whether he or she has been guilty of a refusal or neglect to pay to take place in one conflated hearing.

(ix)   Provided that principles (i)–(viii) are carefully observed then the procedure will be European Convention-compliant.'

22.26 *Zuk v Zuk*[81] is a further warning for judgment creditors and debtors to take the greatest care to ensure that all the procedural and substantive safeguards are observed in any application for a judgment summons. In *Zuk v Zuk*, the judge wrongly committed a husband to 9 months' imprisonment for non-payment of a lump sum, when the judge's powers of committal should have been limited to the 6-week maximum provided for by the Debtor's

---

[81]   [2012] EWCA 1871, [2013] 2 FLR 1466.

Act 1869.[82] *Zuk v Zuk* also highlights the need for the court to observe CCR Order 29 in committal proceedings – which is imported into the FPR 2010[83] – which states that:

'The court should also have regard to the need for the respondent to be –

(1) allowed a reasonable time for responding to the committal application including, if necessary, preparing a defence;
(2) made aware of the availability of assistance from the Community Legal Service and how to contact the Service;
(3) given the opportunity, if unrepresented, to obtain legal advice; and
(4) if unable to understand English, allowed to make arrangements, seeking the assistance of the court if necessary, for an interpreter to attend the hearing.'

Judgment summons and 'the means to pay'

22.27   In the case of *Constantinides v Constantinides*,[84] Holman J identified a material difference in the statutory tests for imprisonment depending on whether the proceedings for judgment summons take place in a magistrates' court, county court or in the High Court.[85] Holman J concluded that the same test must apply in all courts in which an application for a judgment summons is heard: the court must be satisfied, therefore, in every case, that the debtor has or has had the 'means to pay' the sums due under the order. Having the 'means to pay' relates to the income or assets of the debtor and does not extend to his or her earning capacity:[86]

'It would, frankly, be intolerable if a person was liable to be imprisoned on an argument that although he was, say, earning £20,000 a year he ought to be earning £30,000 a year. It is scarcely more tolerable to imprison somebody on an argument that although he is in fact not earning, and has no income, he could and should be earning. It seems to me that those sorts of considerations are far too speculative a foundation for the ultimate and grave sanction of imprisonment.'[87]

22.28   If the court makes an order of committal against the debtor, it may suspend the order (ie not commit the debtor to prison immediately) on terms that the debtor pays to the creditor at a specified time or by instalments (a) the amount due, (b) the costs of the judgment summons and (c) any sums accruing

---

[82]   The court must also be astute to ensure (1) that the judgment debtor is given the opportunity to present mitigation and/or to purge his or her contempt and (2) that the court considers the options available to it other than immediate committal, eg variation of the order to extend the date for payment or establishing a regime of instalment payments (see further the procedural direction to the court in FPR 2010, r 33.16(1)).

[83]   FPR 2010, r 33.1(2).

[84]   [2013] EWHC 3688 (Fam).

[85]   The Debtors Act 1869 makes reference to the debtor having the 'means to pay' whereas the Magistrates' Courts Act 1980, s 93(6) makes no such explicit reference and refers instead to the debtor's 'wilful refusal' or 'culpable neglect' to pay any sum due.

[86]   As explicitly brought into the court's discretionary exercise by MCA 1973, s 25(2)(a).

[87]   *Constantinides*, at [33].

due under the original order.[88] If the debtor subsequently fails to pay according to the terms of the suspended order, the judgment creditor must file a further statement setting out the default.[89]

22.29   If application is made for a judgment summons relating to an order for maintenance pending suit, maintenance pending outcome of proceedings or an order for other periodical payments, the judgment debtor may be able to avoid committal if the court considers that 'the [original] order for payment would have been varied or suspended if the debtor had made an application for that purpose'.[90] It is preferable for the debtor to make an application for a variation of the order (pursuant to MCA 1973, s 31(2))[91] in order for that application to be heard prior to or at the hearing of the application for a judgment summons.[92] Albeit that such an application by the debtor is not strictly necessary, the court will require sufficient financial information and disclosure to enable it to consider whether the original order would have been varied or suspended. If the court finds that a variation would have been made, it may 'make a new order for payment of the amount due under the original order together with the costs of the judgment summons, either at a specified time or by instalments.'[93]

---

[88]   FPR 2010, r 33.16(2).
[89]   FPR 2010, r 33.16(4)(b).
[90]   FPR 2010, r 33.16(1)(b).
[91]   For more information as to the circumstances relevant to such an application, see Chapter 17.
[92]   Under the old rules and regime, see *Corbett v Corbett* [2003] 2 FLR 385.
[93]   FPR 2010, r 33.16(1).

POINTS OF PRACTICE AND THEORY

22.30

(1) Location and financial information can be sought, as follows:
   (a) by application to the Department for Work and Pensions (or the appropriate branch of Her Majesty's Forces) to trace the address of a judgment debtor;
   (b) by application for an order that a judgment debtor attends court to provide information for the purpose of enabling the judgment creditor to enforce a judgment;
   (c) by application for a[n interim] third party debt order, which requires a bank or building society to make disclosure of a judgment debtor's accounts.

(2) Permission is required to enforce 'stale arrears' (over 12 months old): the question for the court must be whether to exercise its discretion to *enforce* the stale maintenance arrears, *not* whether to exercise its discretion to *remit* the arrears.

(3) FPR 2010-compliant enforcement permits either (a) a general application for an order from a pre-determined list [of orders] or (b) a specific application for an order of the judgment creditor's choosing. The general application does not include orders that result in the judgment debtor's committal.

(4) Application for a judgment summons requires (a) that the judgment debtor has failed to comply with an order to pay a debt and (b) that s/he has or has had the means to comply with that order. Strict rules of procedure and evidence apply.

(5) Consider an urgent application for variation or suspension of the original order for periodical payments or maintenance pending suit if the circumstances would warrant such an order for variation or suspension.

APPENDIX 1

STATUTES

ATTACHMENT OF EARNINGS ACT 1971

Cases in which attachment is available

1 Courts with power to attach earnings

(1) The High Court may make an attachment of earnings order to secure payments under a High Court maintenance order.

(2) A county court may make an attachment of earnings order to secure –

    (a)   payments under a High Court or a county court maintenance order,

    (b)   the payment of a judgment debt, other than a debt of less than £5 or such other sum as may be prescribed by county court rules; or

    (c)   payments under an administration order.

(3)   A magistrates' court may make an attachment of earnings order to secure–

    (a)   payments under a magistrates' court maintenance order or;

    (b)   *(repealed)*

    (c)   the payment of any sum required to be paid under regulations under section 23 or 24 of the Legal Aid, Sentencing and Punishment of Offenders Act 2012

(4) *(repealed)*

(5) Any power conferred by this Act to make an attachment of earnings order includes a power to make such an order to secure the discharge of liabilities arising before the coming into force of this Act.

Amendments—Access to Justice Act 1999; SI 2006/1737; Criminal Defence Service Act 2006; Legal Aid, Sentencing and Punishment of Offenders Act 2012.

1A Orders to which this Act applies

The following provisions of this Act apply, except where otherwise stated, to attachment of earnings orders made, or to be made, by any court under this Act or under Schedule 5 to the Courts Act 2003, or by a fines officer under that Schedule.

Amendments—SI 2006/1737.

2 Principal definitions

In this Act–

(a) 'maintenance order' means any order, decision, settlement or instrument specified in Schedule 1 to this Act and includes one which has been discharged or has otherwise ceased to operate if any arrears are recoverable thereunder;

(b) 'High Court maintenance order', 'county court maintenance order' and 'magistrates' court maintenance order' mean respectively a maintenance order enforceable by the High Court, a county court and a magistrates' court;

(c) 'judgment debt' means a sum payable under –
   (i) a judgment or order enforceable by a court in England and Wales (not being a magistrates' court);
   (ii) an order of a magistrates' court for the payment of money recoverable summarily as a civil debt; or
   (iii) an order of any court which is enforceable as if it were for the payment of money so recoverable;
   but does not include any sum payable under a maintenance order or an administration order;

(d) 'the relevant adjudication', in relation to any payment secured or to be secured by an attachment of earnings order, means the conviction, judgment, order or other adjudication from which there arises the liability to make the payment; and

(e) 'the debtor', in relation to an attachment of earnings order, or to proceedings in which a court has power to make an attachment of earnings order, or to proceedings arising out of such an order, means the person by whom payment is required by the relevant adjudication to be made.

Amendments—SI 2011/1484.

3 Application for order and conditions of court's power to make it

(A1) This section shall not apply to an attachment of earnings order to be made under Schedule 5 to the Courts Act 2003.

(1) The following persons may apply for an attachment of earnings order –

(a) the person to whom payment under the relevant adjudication is required to be made (whether directly or through [any court or] an officer of any court);

(b) where the relevant adjudication is an administration order, any one of the creditors scheduled to the order;

(c) *without prejudice to paragraph (a) above, where the application is to a magistrates' court for an order to secure maintenance payments, and there is in force an order under section 59 of the Magistrates' Courts Act 1980, or section 19(2) of the Maintenance Orders Act 1950, that those payments be made to the designated officer for a magistrates' court, that officer;*

[(c)   without prejudice to paragraph (a) above, an officer of the family court if the application is to the family court for an order to secure maintenance payments and there is in force an order that those payments be made to the court or an officer of the court;]

[(ca) without prejudice to paragraph (a) above, where the application is to a magistrates' court to secure maintenance payments under a maintenance order described in paragraph 13, 14, 14A or 14B of Schedule 1 and those payments are to be made to the designated officer for a magistrates' court, that officer;]

(d)   in the following cases the debtor –
    (i)   where the application is to a magistrates' court; or
    (ii)   where the application is to the High Court or a *county court* [the county court] [the family court] for an order to secure maintenance payments.

(2) (*repealed*)

(3) Subject to subsection (3A) below for an attachment of earnings order to be made on the application of any person other than the debtor it must appear to the court that the debtor has failed to make one or more payments required by the relevant adjudication.

(3A) Subsection (3) above shall not apply when the relevant adjudication is a maintenance order.

(3B) (*repealed*)

(3C) (*repealed*)

(4) Where proceedings are brought –

(a)   in the High Court or a *county court* [the county court] [the family court] for the enforcement of a maintenance order by committal under section 5 of the Debtors Act 1869; or

(b)   in a magistrates' court for the enforcement of a maintenance order under section 76 of the Magistrates' Courts Act 1980 (*distress* [taking control of goods] *or committal*),

Then the court may make an attachment of earnings order to secure payments under the maintenance order, instead of dealing with the case under section 5 of the said Act of 1869 or, as the case may be, section 76 of the said Act of 1980.

(5) (*repealed*)

(6) Where proceedings are brought in a *county court* [the county court] for an order of committal under section 5 of the Debtors Act 1869 in respect of a judgment debt for any of the taxes, contributions [premiums] or liabilities specified in Schedule 2 to this Act, the court may, in any circumstances in which it has power to make such an order, make instead an attachment of earnings order to secure the payment of the judgment debt.

(7) A *county court* [The county court] shall not make an attachment of earnings order to secure the payment of a judgment debt if there is in force an order or warrant for the debtor's committal, under section 5 of the Debtors

Act 1869, in respect of that debt; but in any such case the court may discharge the order or warrant with a view to making an attachment of earnings order instead.

Amendments—Magistrates' Courts Act 1980; Maintenance Enforcement Act 1991; Criminal Procedure and Investigations Act 1996; Powers of Criminal Courts (Sentencing) Act 2000; Courts Act 2003; SI 2006/1737;SI 2012/2814.

Prospective Amendments—Words in italics prospectively repealed and subsequent words in square brackets prospectively substituted and inserted Crime and Courts Act 2013, s 17(6), Sch 10, Pt 2, paras 20, 23(1), (2) with effect from a date to be appointed ; word "distress" in italics repealed and subsequent words in square brackets substituted by the Tribunals, Courts and Enforcement Act 2007 with effect from a date to be appointed.

Administration orders in the county court

4 Extension of power to make administration order

(1) Where, on an application to a *county court* [the county court] for an attachment of earnings order to secure the payment of a judgment debt, it appears to the court that the debtor also has other debts, the court –

   (a)   shall consider whether the case may be one in which all the debtor's liabilities should be dealt with together and that for that purpose an administration order should be made; and

   (b)   if of opinion that it may be such a case, shall have power (whether or not it makes the attachment of earnings order applied for), with a view to making an administration order, to order the debtor to furnish to the court a list of all his creditors and the amounts which he owes to them respectively.

(2) If, on receipt of the list referred to in subsection (1)(b) above, it appears to the court that the debtor's whole indebtedness amounts to not more than the amount which for the time being is the county court limit for the purposes of section 112 of the County Courts Act 1984 (limit of total indebtedness governing county court's power to make administration order on application of debtor), the court may make such an order in respect of the debtor's estate.

(2A) Subsection (2) above is subject to section 112(3) and (4) of the County Courts Act 1984 (which require that, before an administration order is made, notice is to be given to all the creditors and thereafter restrict the right of any creditor to institute bankruptcy proceedings).

[(2) The court may make an administration order in respect of the debtor's estate if, after receipt of the list referred to in subsection (1)(b) above, the court is satisfied that the conditions in sections 112B(2) to (7) of the County Courts Act 1984 (conditions to power to make administration orders) are met in relation to the debtor.]

(3)   *(repealed)*

(4) Nothing in this section is to be taken as prejudicing any right of a debtor to apply, under *section 112* [section 112J] of the County Courts Act 1984 for an administration order.

Amendments—Insolvency Act 1976; County Courts Act 1984.

Prospective Amendments—Words in italics prospectively repealed and subsequent words in square brackets prospectively substituted and inserted Crime and Courts Act 2013, s 17(6), Sch 10, Pt 2, paras 20, 23(1), (2) with effect from a date to be appointed; Sub-ss (2), (2A): substituted, by subsequent sub-s (2), by the Tribunals, Courts and Enforcement Act 2007, s 106(2), Sch 16, para 1(1), (2); for transitional provisions see s 106(3) thereof. Word "section 112" in italics repealed and subsequent words in square brackets substituted by the Tribunals, Courts and Enforcement Act 2007 with effect from a date to be appointed.

5 Attachment of earnings to secure payments under administration order

(1) Where a *county court* [the county court] makes an administration order in respect of a debtor's estate, it may also make an attachment of earnings order to secure the payments required by the administration order.

(2) At any time when an administration order is in force a *county court* [the county court] may (with or without an application) make an attachment of earnings order to secure the payments required by the administration order, if it appears to the court that the debtor has failed to make any such payment.

(3) The power of a county court under this section to make an attachment of earnings order to secure the payments required by an administration order shall, where the debtor is already subject to an attachment of earnings order to secure the payment of a judgment debt, include power to direct that the last-mentioned order shall take effect *(with or without variation under section 9 of this Act)* [(with the variation required by paragraph 11 of Schedule 3A and such other variations, if any, as the court thinks appropriate)] as an order to secure the payments required by the administration order.

Prospective Amendments—Words in italics prospectively repealed and subsequent words in square brackets prospectively substituted and inserted Crime and Courts Act 2013, s 17(6), Sch 10, Pt 2, paras 20, 23(1), (2) with effect from a date to be appointed; Word "(with or without variation under section 9 of this Act)" in italics repealed and subsequent words in square brackets substituted by the Tribunals, Courts and Enforcement Act 2007 with effect from a date to be appointed

Consequences of attachment order

6 Effect and contents of order

(1) An attachment of earnings order shall be an order directed to a person who appears to the court, or as the case may be the fines officer, making the order to have the debtor in his employment and shall operate as an instruction to that person –

(a) *to make periodical deductions from the debtor's earnings in accordance with Part I of Schedule 3 to this Act; and*

[(a) to make periodical deductions from the debtor's earnings, as specified in the order; and]

(b) at such times as the order may require, or as the court, or where the order is made under Schedule 5 to the Courts Act 2003, as the court or the fines officer as the case may be, may allow, to pay the amounts deducted to the collecting officer of the court, as specified in the order.

[(1A) If a county court [the county court] makes an attachment of earnings order to secure payment of a judgment debt, the order must specify that periodical deductions are to be made in accordance with the fixed deductions scheme.

(1B) If a court (whether a county court [the county court] or another court) makes any other attachment of earnings order, the order must specify that periodical deductions are to be made in accordance with Part 1 of Schedule 3.]

(2) For the purposes of this Act, the relationship of employer and employee shall be treated as subsisting between two persons if one of them, as a principal and not as a servant or agent, pays to the other any sums defined as earnings by section 24 of this Act.

(3) An attachment of earnings order shall contain prescribed particulars enabling the debtor to be identified by the employer.

(4) Except where it is made to secure maintenance payments, the order shall specify the whole amount payable under the relevant adjudication (or so much of that amount as remains unpaid), including any relevant costs.

(5) Subject to subsection (5A) below, *the order* [a Schedule 3 deductions order] shall specify–

    (a)   the normal deduction rate, that is to say, the rate (expressed as a sum of money per week, month or other period) at which the court thinks it reasonable for the debtor's earnings to be applied to meeting his liability under the relevant adjudication; and

    (b)   the protected earnings rate, that is to say the rate (so expressed) below which, having regard to the debtor's resources and needs, the court thinks it reasonable that the earnings actually paid to him should not be reduced.

(5A) If the order is made under Schedule 5 to the Courts Act 2003 then it shall specify the percentage deduction rate in accordance with fines collection regulations made under that Schedule.

(6) In the case of an order made to secure payments under a maintenance order (not being an order for the payment of a lump sum), the normal deduction rate–

    (a)   shall be determined after taking account of any right or liability of the debtor to deduct income tax when making the payments; and

    (b)   shall not exceed the rate which appears to the court necessary for the purpose of–

        (i)   securing payment of the sums falling due from time to time under the maintenance order, and

        (ii)   securing payment within a reasonable period of any sums already due and unpaid under the maintenance order.

(7) For the purposes of an attachment of earnings order, the collecting officer of the court shall be (subject to later variation of the order under section 9 of this Act) –

(a) in the case of an order made by the High Court, either –
  (i) the proper officer of the High Court, or
  (ii) the appropriate officer of the family court or *such county court as the order may specify* [the county court if the order so specifies];
[(aa) in the case of an order made by the family court, the appropriate officer of that court;]
(b) in the case of an order made by a *county court* [the county court], the appropriate officer of that court; and
(c) in the case of an order made by a magistrates' court, the designated officer for that court or for another magistrates' court specified in the order.

(8) In subsection (7) above 'appropriate officer' means an officer designated by the Lord Chancellor.

[(9) The Lord Chancellor may by order make such provision as he considers expedient (including transitional provision) with a view to providing for the payment of amounts deducted under attachment of earnings orders to be made to such officers as may be designated by the order rather than to collecting officers of the court.

(10) Any such order may make such amendments in this Act, in relation to functions exercised by or in relation to collecting officers of the court as he considers expedient in consequence of the provision made by virtue of subsection (9) above.

(11) The power to make such an order shall be exercisable by statutory instrument.

(12) Any such statutory instrument shall be subject to annulment in pursuance of a resolution of either House of Parliament.]

Amendments—Administration of Justice Act 1977; Courts Act 2003; SI 2006/1737.

Prospective amendments—Sub-ss (9)–(12): inserted by the Courts and Legal Services Act 1990,with effect from a date to be appointed.: para (a),(1A), (1B) substituted by the Tribunals, Courts and Enforcement Act 2007, words "the order" in italics repealed and subsequent words in square brackets substituted by the Tribunals, Courts and Enforcement Act 2007with effect from a date to be appointed; Sub-ss (1A), (1B): words "a county court" in italics repealed and subsequent words in square brackets substituted by the Crime and Courts Act 2013 with effect from a date to be appointed: in para (a)(ii) words "the family court or" in square brackets inserted by the Crime and Courts Act 2013, Sub-s (7): in para (a)(ii) words "such county court as the order may specify" in italics repealed and subsequent words in square brackets substituted by the Crime and Courts Act 2013 with effect from a date to be appointed.

[6A The fixed deductions scheme]

[(1) In this Act "fixed deductions scheme" means any scheme that the Lord Chancellor makes which specifies the rates and frequencies at which deductions are to be made under attachment of earnings orders so as to secure the repayment of judgment debts.

(2) The Lord Chancellor is to make the fixed deductions scheme by regulations.

(3) The power to make regulations under subsection (2) is exercisable by statutory instrument.

(4) The Lord Chancellor may not make a statutory instrument containing the first regulations under subsection (2) unless a draft of the instrument has been laid before, and approved by resolution of, each House of Parliament.

(5) A statutory instrument containing any subsequent regulations under subsection (2) is subject to annulment in pursuance of a resolution of either House of Parliament.]

Prospective Amendments—Prospectively inserted by the Tribunals, Courts and Enforcement Act 2007, with effect from a date to be appointed.

7 Compliance with order by employer

(1) Where an attachment of earnings order has been made, the employer shall, if he has been served with the order, comply with it; but he shall be under no liability for non-compliance before seven days have elapsed since the service.

(2) Where a person is served with an attachment of earnings order directed to him and he has not the debtor in his employment, or the debtor subsequently ceases to be in his employment, he shall (in either case), within ten days from the date of service or, as the case may be, the cesser, give notice of that fact to the court.

(3) Part II of Schedule 3 to this Act shall have effect with respect to the priority to be accorded as between two or more attachment of earnings orders directed to a person in respect of the same debtor.

(4) On any occasion when the employer makes, in compliance with the order, a deduction from the debtor's earnings –

   (a)   he shall be entitled to deduct, in addition, £1.00, or such other sum as may be prescribed by order made by the Lord Chancellor, towards his clerical and administrative costs; and
   (b)   he shall give to the debtor a statement in writing of the total amount of the deduction.

(5) An order of the Lord Chancellor under subsection (4)(a) above –

   (a)   may prescribe different sums in relation to different classes of cases;
   (b)   may be varied or revoked by a subsequent order made under that paragraph; and
   (c)   shall be made by statutory instrument subject to annulment by resolution of either House of Parliament.

Amendments—SI 1991/356.

8 Interrelation with alternative remedies open to creditor

(1) Where an attachment of earnings order has been made to secure maintenance payments, no order or warrant of commitment shall be issued in

consequence of any proceedings for the enforcement of the related maintenance order begun before the making of the attachment of earnings order.

(2) Where a *county court* [the county court] has made an attachment of earnings order to secure the payment of a judgment debt–

(a) no order or warrant of commitment shall be issued in consequence of any proceedings for the enforcement of the debt begun before the making of the attachment of earnings order; and

(b) so long as the order is in force, no execution for the recovery of the debt shall issue against any property of the debtor without the leave of the county court.

(3) An attachment of earnings order made to secure maintenance payments shall cease to have effect upon the making of an order of commitment or the issue of a warrant of commitment for the enforcement of the related maintenance order, *or upon the exercise for that purpose of the power conferred on a magistrates' court by section 77(2) of the Magistrates' Courts Act 1980 to postpone the issue of such a warrant.*

(4) An attachment of earnings order made to secure the payment of a judgment debt shall cease to have effect on the making of an order of commitment or the issue of a warrant of commitment for the enforcement of the debt.

(5) An attachment of earnings order made to secure –

(a) any payment mentioned in section 1(3)(c) of this Act; or

(b) the payment of any sum mentioned in paragraph 1 of Schedule 5 to the Courts Act 2003,

shall cease to have effect on the issue of a warrant committing the debtor to prison for default in making that payment.

Amendments—Magistrates' Courts Act 1980; SI 2006/1737.

Prospective Amendments—Words in italics repealed and subsequent words substituted Crime and Courts Act 2013,with effect from a date to be appointed.

Subsequent proceedings

9 Variation, lapse and discharge of orders

(1) The court, or where an attachment of earnings order is made under Schedule 5 to the Courts Act 2003, the court or the fines officer as the case may be, may make an order discharging or varying an attachment of earnings order.

[(1A) Subsection (1) is subject to Schedule 3A (which deals with the variation of certain attachment of earnings orders by changing the basis of deductions).]

(2) Where an order is varied, the employer shall, if he has been served with notice of the variation, comply with the order as varied; but he shall be under no liability for non-compliance before seven days have elapsed since the service.

(3) Rules of court may make provision –

(a) as to the circumstances in which an attachment of earnings order made under this Act may be varied or discharged by the court of its own motion:

(aa) as to the circumstances in which an attachment of earnings order made under Schedule 5 to the Courts Act 2003 may be varied or discharged by the court or the fines officer of its or his own motion;

(b) in the case of an attachment of earnings order made by a magistrates' court, for enabling a single justice, on an application made by the debtor on the ground of a material change in his resources and needs since the order was made or last varied, to vary the order for a period of not more than four weeks by an increase of the protected earnings rate.

(4) Where an attachment of earnings order has been made and the person to whom it is directed ceases to have the debtor in his employment, the order shall lapse (except as respects deduction from earnings paid after the cesser and payment to the collecting officer of amounts deducted at any time) and be of no effect unless and until the court, or where the order was made under Schedule 5 to the Courts Act 2003, unless and until the court or the fines officer as the case may be, again directs it to a person (whether the same as before or another) who appears to the court or the fines officer (as the case may be) to have the debtor in his employment.

(5) The lapse of an order under subsection (4) above shall not prevent its being treated as remaining in force for other purposes.

Amendments—SI 2006/1737.

Prospective Amendments—Sub-s (1A): inserted by the Tribunals, Courts and Enforcement Act 2007 with effect from a date to be appointed.

[9A Suspension of fixed deductions orders]

[(1) A county court [The county court] must make an order suspending a fixed deductions order if the court is satisfied of either or both of the following –

(a) that the fixed deductions order requires periodical deductions to be made at a rate which is not appropriate;

(b) that the fixed deductions order requires periodical deductions to be made at times which are not appropriate.

(2) The county court is to make the suspension order on the following terms –

(a) if the condition in subsection (1)(a) is met: on terms specifying the rate at which the debtor must make repayments (whether higher or lower than the rate at which the order requires the deductions to be made);

(b) if the condition in subsection (1)(b) is met: on terms specifying the times at which the debtor must make repayments;

(c) if either or both conditions are met: on any additional terms that the court thinks appropriate.

(3) If the employer is given notice of the suspension order, the employer must cease to make the deductions required by the fixed deductions order; but the employer is under no liability for non-compliance before seven days have elapsed since service of the notice.

(4) A county court [The county court] –

- (a) must revoke the suspension order if any of the terms of the suspension order are broken;
- (b) may revoke the suspension order in any other circumstances if the court thinks that it is appropriate to do so.

(5) Rules of court may make provision as to the circumstances in which a county court [the county court] may of its own motion –

- (a) make a suspension order; or
- (b) revoke a suspension order.

(6) The suspension of a fixed deductions order under this section does not prevent the order from being treated as remaining in force subject to the provisions of this section.

(7) This section is without prejudice to any other powers of a court to suspend attachment of earnings orders or to revoke the suspension of such orders.

(8) In this section, in relation to a fixed deductions order, "repayments" means repayments of the judgment debt to which the order relates.]

Amendments—SI 2006/1737.

Prospective Amendments—Prospectively inserted by the Tribunals, Courts and Enforcement Act 2007 with effect from a date to be appointed. Words in italics repealed and subsequent words in square brackets substituted by Crime and Courts Act 2013 with effect from a date to be appointed.

10 Normal deduction rate to be reduced in certain cases

(1) The following provisions shall have effect, in the case of an attachment of earnings order made to secure maintenance payments, where it appears to the collecting officer of the court that –

- (a) the aggregate of the payments made for the purposes of the related maintenance order by the debtor (whether under the attachment of earnings order or otherwise) exceeds the aggregate of the payments required up to that time by the maintenance order; and
- (b) the normal deduction rate specified by the attachment of earnings order (or, where two or more such orders are in force in relation to the maintenance order, the aggregate of the normal deduction rates specified by those orders) exceeds the rate of payments required by the maintenance order; and
- (c) no proceedings for the variation or discharge of the attachment of earnings order are pending.

(2) In the case of an order made by the High Court or *a county* [family]court, the collecting officer shall give the prescribed notice to the person to whom he

is required to pay sums received under the attachment of earnings order, and to the debtor; and the court shall make the appropriate variation order, unless the debtor requests it to discharge the attachment of earnings order, or to vary it in some other way, and the court thinks fit to comply with the request.

(3) In the case of an order made by a magistrates' court, the collecting officer shall apply to the court for the appropriate variation order; and the court shall grant the application unless the debtor appears at the hearing and requests the court to discharge the attachment of earnings order, or to vary it in some other way, and the court thinks fit to comply with the request.

(4) In this section, 'the appropriate variation order' means an order varying the attachment of earnings order in question by reducing the normal deduction rate specified thereby so as to secure that that rate (or, in the case mentioned in subsection (1)(b) above, the aggregate of the rates therein mentioned) –

    (a)   is the same as the rate of payments required by the maintenance order; or

    (b)   is such lower rate as the court thinks fit having regard to the amount of the excess mentioned in subsection (1)(a).

Prospective Amendments—Sub-s (3) prospectively repealed and words in italics repealed and subsequent words substituted Crime and Courts Act 2013, with effect from a date to be appointed.

11 Attachment order in respect of maintenance payments to cease to have effect on the occurrence of certain events

(1) An attachment of earnings order made to secure maintenance payments shall cease to have effect–

    (a)   upon the grant of an application for registration of the related maintenance order under section 2 of the Maintenance Orders Act 1958 *(which provides for the registration in a magistrates' court of a High Court or county court maintenance order, and for registration in the High Court of a magistrates' court maintenance order)*; [for the registration in the family court of a High Court maintenance order)];

    (b)   where the related maintenance order is registered under Part I of the said Act of 1958, upon the giving of notice with respect thereto under section 5 of that Act (notice with view to cancellation of registration);

    (c)   subject to subsection (3) below, upon the discharge of the related maintenance order while it is not registered under Part I of the said Act of 1958;

    (d)   upon the related maintenance order ceasing to be registered in a court in England or Wales, or becoming registered in a court in Scotland or Northern Ireland, under Part II of the Maintenance Orders Act 1950.

(2) Subsection (1)(a) above shall have effect, in the case of an application for registration under section 2(1) of the said Act of 1958, notwithstanding that the grant of the application may subsequently become void under subsection (2) of that section.

(3) Where the related maintenance order is discharged as mentioned in subsection (1)(c) above and it appears to the court discharging the order that arrears thereunder will remain to be recovered after the discharge, that court may, if it thinks fit, direct that subsection (1) shall not apply.

Prospective Amendments—Words in italics repealed and subsequent words substituted Crime and Courts Act 2013, with effect from a date to be appointed.

12 Termination of employer's liability to make deductions

(1) Where an attachment of earnings order ceases to have effect under section 8 or 11 of this Act, the proper officer of the prescribed court shall give notice of the cesser to the person to whom the order was directed.

(2) Where, in the case of an attachment of earnings order made otherwise than to secure maintenance payments, the whole amount payable under the relevant adjudication has been paid, and also any relevant costs, the court shall give notice to the employer that no further compliance with the order is required.

(3) Where an attachment of earnings order –

(a) ceases to have effect under section 8 or 11 of this Act; or
(b) is discharged under section 9,

the person to whom the order has been directed shall be under no liability in consequence of his treating the order as still in force at any time before the expiration of seven days from the date on which the notice required by subsection (1) above or, as the case may be, a copy of the discharging order is served on him.

Administrative provisions

13 Application of sums received by collecting officer

(1) Subject to subsection (3) below, the collecting officer to whom a person makes payments in compliance with an attachment of earnings order shall, after deducting such court fees, if any, in respect of proceedings for or arising out of the order, as are deductible from those payments, deal with the sums paid in the same way as he would if they had been paid by the debtor to satisfy the relevant adjudication.

(2) Any sums paid to the collecting officer under an attachment of earnings order made to secure maintenance payments shall, when paid to the person entitled to receive those payments, be deemed to be payments made by the debtor (with such deductions, if any, in respect of income tax as the debtor is entitled or required to make) so as to discharge–

(a) first, any sums for the time being due and unpaid under the related maintenance order (a sum due at an earlier date being discharged before a sum due at a later date); and
(b) secondly, any costs incurred in proceedings relating to the related maintenance order which were payable by the debtor when the attachment of earnings order was made or last varied.

(3) Where a *county court* [the county court] makes an attachment of earnings order to secure the payment of a judgment debt and also, under section 4(1) of this Act, orders the debtor to furnish to the court a list of his creditors, sums paid to the collecting officer in compliance with the attachment of earnings order shall not be dealt with by him as mentioned in subsection (1) above, but shall be retained by him pending the decision of the court whether or not to make an administration order and shall then be dealt with by him as the court may direct.

14 Power of court to obtain statement of earnings etc

(1) Where in any proceedings a court has power under this Act or under Schedule 5 to the Courts Act 2003, or a fines officer has power under that Schedule, to make *an attachment of earnings order* [a Schedule 3 deductions order], the court or the fines officer, as the case may be, may –

   (a)   order the debtor to give to the court or the fines officer, as the case may be, within a specified period, a statement signed by him of –
         (i)   the name and address of any person by whom earnings are paid to him;
         (ii)   specified particulars as to his earnings and anticipated earnings, and as to his resources and needs; and
         (iii) specified particulars for the purpose of enabling the debtor to be identified by any employer of his;
   (b)   order any person appearing to the court or the fines officer, as the case may be, to have the debtor in his employment to give to the court or the fines officer, as the case may be, within a specified period, a statement signed by him or on his behalf of specified particulars of the debtor's earnings and anticipated earnings.

[(1A) Where in any proceedings a county court [the county court] has power to make a fixed deductions order, the court may order the debtor to give to the court, within a specified period, a statement signed by him of—

   (a)   the name and address of any person by whom earnings are paid to him; and
   (b)   specified particulars for enabling the debtor to be identified by any employer of his.]

(2) *Where an attachment of earnings order has been made, the court or the fines officer, as the case may be, may at any time thereafter while the order is in force* [At any time when a Schedule 3 deductions order is in force, the court or the fines officer, as the case may be, may –]

   (a)   make such an order as is described in subsection (1)(a) or (b) above; and
   (b)   order the debtor to attend before the court on a day and at a time specified in the order to give the information described in subsection (1)(a) above.

[(2A) At any time when a fixed deductions order is in force, the court may –

(a)   make such an order as is described in subsection (1A) above; and
(b)   order the debtor to attend before it on a day and at a time specified in the order to give the information described in subsection (1A) above.]

(3) In the case of an application to a magistrates' court for an attachment of earnings order, or for the variation or discharge of such an order, the power to make an order under subsection (1) or (2) above shall be exercisable also, before the hearing of the application, by a single justice.

(4) Without prejudice to subsections (1) to (3) above, rules of court may provide that where notice of application for an attachment of earnings order is served on the debtor, it shall include a requirement that he shall *give to the court, within such period and in such manner as may be prescribed, a statement in writing of the matters specified in subsection (1)(a) above and of any other prescribed matters which are, or may be, relevant under section 6 of this Act to the determination of the normal deduction rate and the protected earnings rate to be specified in any order made on the application.* [, within such period and in such manner as may be prescribed, give the court a statement in accordance with subsection (4A) or (4B)].

This subsection does not apply to an attachment of earnings order to be made under Schedule 5 to the Courts Act 2003.

[(4A) In a case where the attachment of earnings order would, if made, be a Schedule 3 deductions order, the debtor must give a statement in writing of –

(a)   the matters specified in subsection (1)(a) above, and
(b)   any other prescribed matters which are, or may be, relevant under section 6 of this Act to the determination of the normal deduction rate and the protected earnings rate to be specified in any attachment of earnings order made on the application.

(4B) In a case where the attachment of earnings order would, if made, be a fixed deductions order, the debtor must give a statement in writing of the matters specified in subsection (1A) above.]

(5) In any proceedings in which a court has the power under this Act or under Schedule 5 to the Courts Act 2003, or a fines officer has power under that Schedule, to make an attachment of earnings order, and in any proceedings for the making, variation or discharge of such an order, a document purporting to be a statement given to the court or the fines officer, as the case may be, in compliance with an order under subsection (1)(a) or (b) [(or 1A)] above, or with any such requirement of a notice of application for an attachment of earnings order as is mentioned in subsection (4) above, shall, in the absence of proof to the contrary, be deemed to be a statement so given and shall be evidence of the facts stated therein.

Amendments—Administration of Justice Act 1982; SI 2006/1737.

Prospective Amendments—Sub-s (1A), (2A),(4A),(4B), prospectively inserted and words in italics repealed and subsequent words in square brackets substituted by Tribunals, Courts and

Enforcement Act 2007 with effect from a date to be appointed. Words "a county court" in italics repealed and subsequent words in square brackets substituted by the Crime and Courts Act 2013 with effect from a day to be appointed.

15 Obligation of debtor and his employers to notify changes of employment and earnings

(1)   While an attachment of earnings order is in force –

(a)   the debtor shall from time to time notify the court in writing of every occasion on which he leaves any employment, or becomes employed or re-employed, not later (in each case) than seven days from the date on which he did so;

(b)   [if the order is a Schedule 3 deductions order,] the debtor shall, on any occasion when he becomes employed or re-employed, include in his notification under paragraph (a) above particulars of his earnings and anticipated earnings from the relevant employment; and

(c)   any person who becomes the debtor's employer and knows that the order is in force and by, or (if the order was made by a fines officer) for, which court it was made shall, within seven days of his becoming the debtor's employer or of acquiring that knowledge (whichever is the later) notify that court in writing that he is the debtor's employer, *and include* [and, if the order is a Schedule 3 deductions order, include] in his notification a statement of the debtor's earnings and anticipated earnings.

(2) In the case of an attachment of earnings order made by a fines officer, the reference to 'the court' in subsection (1)(a) above shall mean the court for which that order was made.

Amendments—SI 2006/1737.

Prospective Amendments—Words in italics repealed and subsequent words substituted Tribunals, Courts and Enforcement Act 2007 with effect from a date to be appointed.

16   Power of court to determine whether particular payments are earnings

(1) Where an attachment of earnings order is in force, the court shall, on application of a person specified in subsection (2) below, determine whether payments to the debtor of a particular class or description specified by the application are earnings for the purposes of the order; and the employer shall be entitled to give effect to any determination for the time being in force under this section.

(2) The persons referred to in subsection (1) above are –

(a)   the employer;

(b)   the debtor;

(c)   the person to whom payment under the relevant adjudication is required to be made (whether directly or through the officer of any court); and

(d) without prejudice to paragraph (c) above, where the application is in respect of an attachment of earnings order made to secure payments under *a magistrates' court* [family court] maintenance order, the collecting officer.

(3) Where an application under this section is made by the employer, he shall not incur any liability for non-compliance with the order as respects any payments of the class or description specified by the application which are made by him to the debtor while the application, or any appeal in consequence thereof, is pending; but this subsection shall not, unless the court otherwise orders, apply as respects such payments if the employer subsequently withdraws the application or, as the case may be, abandons the appeal.

Prospective Amendments—Words in italics repealed and subsequent words substituted Crime and Courts Act 2013 with effect from a date to be appointed.

CHILD SUPPORT ACT 1991

* * * *

8 Role of the courts with respect to maintenance for children

(1) This subsection applies in any case where the Secretary of State would have jurisdiction to make a maintenance assessment with respect to a qualifying child and an absent parent of his on an application duly made by a person entitled to apply for such an assessment with respect to that child.

(2) Subsection (1) applies even though the circumstances of the case are such that the Secretary of State would not make an assessment if it were applied for.

(3) In any case where subsection (1) applies, no court shall exercise any power which it would otherwise have to make, vary or revive any maintenance order in relation to the child and absent parent concerned.

(3A) In any case in which section 4(10) or 7(10) prevents the making of an application for a maintenance assessment, and—

(a) no application has been made for a maintenance assessment under section 6, or
(b) such an application has been made but no maintenance assessment has been made in response to it,

subsection (3) shall have effect with the omission of the word 'vary'.

(4) Subsection (3) does not prevent a court from revoking a maintenance order.

(5) The Lord Chancellor or in relation to Scotland the Lord Advocate may by order provide that, in such circumstances as may be specified by the order, this section shall not prevent a court from exercising any power which it has to make a maintenance order in relation to a child if—

(a) a written agreement (whether or not enforceable) provides for the making, or securing, by an absent parent of the child of periodical payments to or for the benefit of the child; and

(b)   the maintenance order which the court makes is, in all material respects, in the same terms as that agreement.

(5A) The Lord Chancellor may make an order under subsection (5) only with the concurrence of the Lord Chief Justice.

(6) This section shall not prevent a court from exercising any power which it has to make a maintenance order in relation to a child if—

(a)   a maintenance assessment is in force with respect to the child;

(b)   the amount of the child support maintenance payable in accordance with the assessment was determined by reference to the alternative formula mentioned in paragraph 4(3) of Schedule 1; and

(c)   the court is satisfied that the circumstances of the case make it appropriate for the absent parent to make or secure the making of periodical payments under a maintenance order in addition to the child support maintenance payable by him in accordance with the maintenance assessment.

(7) This section shall not prevent a court from exercising any power which it has to make a maintenance order in relation to a child if—

(a)   the child is, will be or (if the order were to be made) would be receiving instruction at an educational establishment or undergoing training for a trade, profession or vocation (whether or not while in gainful employment); and

(b)   the order is made solely for the purposes of requiring the person making or securing the making of periodical payments fixed by the order to meet some or all of the expenses incurred in connection with the provision of the instruction or training.

(8) This section shall not prevent a court from exercising any power which it has to make a maintenance order in relation to a child if—

(a)   an allowance under Part 4 of the Welfare Reform Act 2012 (personal independence payment) or a disability living allowance is paid to or in respect of him; or

(b)   no such allowance is paid but he is disabled,

and the order is made solely for the purpose of requiring the person making or securing the making of periodical payments fixed by the order to meet some or all of any expenses attributable to the child's disability.

(9) For the purposes of subsection (8), a child is disabled if he is blind, deaf or dumb or is substantially and permanently handicapped by illness, injury, mental disorder or congenital deformity or such other disability as may be prescribed.

(10) This section shall not prevent a court from exercising any power which it has to make a maintenance order in relation to a child if the order is made against a person with care of the child.

(11) In this Act 'maintenance order', in relation to any child, means an order which requires the making or securing of periodical payments to or for the benefit of the child and which is made under—

(a)   Part II of the Matrimonial Causes Act 1973;

(b)   the Domestic Proceedings and Magistrates' Courts Act 1978;

(c)   Part III of the Matrimonial and Family Proceedings Act 1984;

(d)   the Family Law (Scotland) Act 1985;

(e)   Schedule 1 to the Children Act 1989;

(ea) Schedule 5, 6 or 7 to the Civil Partnership Act 2004, or

(f)   any other prescribed enactment,

and includes any order varying or reviving such an order.

(12) The Lord Chief Justice may nominate a judicial office holder (as defined in section 109(4) of the Constitutional Reform Act 2005) to exercise his functions under this section.

Amendments—Child Support Act 1995; Social Security Act 1998; Civil Partnership Act 2004; Constitutional Reform Act 2005; Child Maintenance and Other Payments Act 2008; Public Bodies (Child Maintenance and Enforcement Commission: Abolition and Transfer of Functions) Order 2012, SI 2012/2007, Welfare Reform Act 2012.

9 Agreements about maintenance

(1) In this section 'maintenance agreement' means any agreement for the making, or for securing the making, of periodical payments by way of maintenance, or in Scotland aliment, to or for the benefit of any child.

(2) Nothing in this Act shall be taken to prevent any person from entering into a maintenance agreement.

(2A) The Secretary of State may, with a view to reducing the need for applications under sections 4 and 7—

(a)   take such steps as the Secretary of State considers appropriate to encourage the making and keeping of maintenance agreements, and

(b)   in particular, before accepting an application under those sections, invite the applicant to consider with the Secretary of State whether it is possible to make such an agreement.

(3) Subject to section 4(10)(a) and (ab) and section 7(10), the existence of a maintenance agreement shall not prevent any party to the agreement, or any other person, from applying for a maintenance assessment with respect to any child to or for whose benefit periodical payments are to be made or secured under the agreement.

(4) Where any agreement contains a provision which purports to restrict the right of any person to apply for a maintenance assessment, that provision shall be void.

(5) Where section 8 would prevent any court from making a maintenance order in relation to a child and an absent parent of his, no court shall exercise any power that it has to vary any agreement so as—

(a)   to insert a provision requiring that absent parent to make or secure the making of periodical payments by way of maintenance, or in Scotland aliment, to or for the benefit of that child; or

(b)   to increase the amount payable under such a provision.

(6) In any case in which section 4(10) or 7(10) prevents the making of an application for a maintenance assessment, subsection (5) shall have effect with the omission of paragraph (b).

Amendments—Child Support Act 1995; Child Maintenance and Other Payments Act 2008; Welfare Reform Act 2012; SI 2012/2007; SI 2013/2947.

[9A Maintenance agreements: indicative calculations

(1) A person with care or non-resident parent in relation to any qualifying child or qualifying children may apply to the Secretary of State for an indicative calculation with respect to that child or any of those children.

(2) A qualifying child who has attained the age of 12 years and is habitually resident in Scotland may apply to the Secretary of State for an indicative calculation with respect to himself or herself.

(3) An indicative calculation is a calculation of the amount of child support maintenance which the Secretary of State considers would in accordance with section 11 be fixed by a maintenance calculation if such a calculation were made with respect to the child or children in question.

(4) An indicative calculation does not create any liability on any person to pay child support maintenance.

(5) The Secretary of State may limit the number of applications the Secretary of State will accept under this section in any particular case in such manner as the Secretary of State thinks fit.

(6) Where a person who is alleged to be the parent of a child with respect to whom an application for an indicative calculation has been made denies being one of the child's parents, the Secretary of State shall not make the indicative calculation on the assumption that the person is one of the child's parents unless the case falls within paragraph (b) of Case A3 in section 26(2).]

Amendments—SI 2012/2007.

Prospective Amendments—Section inserted by Welfare Reform Act 2012, ss 138, 150(3).

10 Relationship between maintenance assessments and certain court orders and related matters

(1) Where an order of a kind prescribed for the purposes of this subsection is in force with respect to any qualifying child with respect to whom a maintenance assessment is made, the order—

(a)   shall, so far as it relates to the making or securing of periodical payments, cease to have effect to such extent as may be determined in accordance with regulations made by the Secretary of State; or
(b)   where the regulations so provide, shall, so far as it so relates, have effect subject to such modifications as may be so determined.

(2) Where an agreement of a kind prescribed for the purposes of this subsection is in force with respect to any qualifying child with respect to whom a maintenance assessment is made, the agreement—

(a) shall, so far as it relates to the making or securing of periodical payments, be unenforceable to such extent as may be determined in accordance with regulations made by the Secretary of State; or

(b) where the regulations so provide, shall, so far as it so relates, have effect subject to such modifications as may be so determined.

(3) Any regulations under this section may, in particular, make such provision with respect to—

(a) any case where any person with respect to whom an order or agreement of a kind prescribed for the purposes of subsection (1) or (2) has effect applies to the prescribed court, before the end of the prescribed period, for the order or agreement to be varied in the light of the maintenance assessment and of the provisions of this Act;

(b) the recovery of any arrears under the order or agreement which fell due before the coming into force of the maintenance assessment,

as the Secretary of State considers appropriate and may provide that, in prescribed circumstances, an application to any court which is made with respect to an order of a prescribed kind relating to the making or securing of periodical payments to or for the benefit of a child shall be treated by the court as an application for the order to be revoked.

(4) The Secretary of State may by regulations make provision for—

(a) notification to be given by the Secretary of State to the prescribed person in any case where the Secretary of State considers that the making of a maintenance assessment has affected, or is likely to affect, any order of a kind prescribed for the purposes of this subsection;

(b) notification to be given by the prescribed person to the Secretary of State in any case where a court makes an order which it considers has affected, or is likely to affect, a maintenance assessment.

(5) Rules may be made under section 144 of the Magistrates' Courts Act 1980 (rules of procedure) requiring any person who, in prescribed circumstances, makes an application to a magistrates' court for a maintenance order to furnish the court with a statement in a prescribed form, and signed by an officer of the Secretary of State, as to whether or not, at the time when the statement is made, there is a maintenance assessment in force with respect to that person or the child concerned.

In this subsection—

'maintenance order' means an order of a prescribed kind for the making or securing of periodical payments to or for the benefit of a child; and

'prescribed' means prescribed by the rules.

Amendments—Social Security Act 1998; Child Maintenance and Other Payments Act 2008; Public Bodies (Child Maintenance and Enforcement Commission: Abolition and Transfer of Functions) Order 2012, SI 2012/2007.

* * * *

DEBTORS ACT 1869

* * * *

5 Saving of power of committal for small debts

Subject to the provisions herein-after mentioned, and to the prescribed rules, any court may commit to prison for a term not exceeding six weeks, or until payment of the sum due, any person who makes default in payment of any debt or instalment of any debt due from him in pursuance of any order or judgment of that or any other competent court.

Provided—(1) That the jurisdiction by this section given of committing a person to prison shall, in the case of *any court other than the superior courts of law and equity, be exercised only subject to the following restrictions; that is to say,* [the county court] –

(a) Be exercised only by a judge or his *deputy* [of the court], and by an order made in open court and showing on its face the ground on which it is issued:

(b) (*repealed*)

(c) *Be exercised only as respects a judgment of a county court by a county court judge or his deputy.*

(2) That such jurisdiction shall only be exercised where it is proved to the satisfaction of the court that the person making default either has or has had since the date of the order or judgment the means to pay the sum in respect of which he has made default, and has refused or neglected, or refuses or neglects, to pay the same.

Proof of the means of the person making default may be given in such manner as the court thinks just.

For the purpose of considering whether to commit a debtor to prison under this section, the debtor may be summoned in accordance with the prescribed rules.

Any jurisdiction by this section given to the *superior courts* [High Court or family court] may be exercised by a judge sitting in chambers, or otherwise, in the prescribed manner.

Persons committed under this section *by a superior court* [by the High Court or family court] may be committed to the prison in which they would have been confined if arrested on a writ of capias ad satisfaciendum, and every order of committal *by any superior court* [by the High Court or family court] shall, subject to the prescribed rules, be issued, obeyed, and executed in the like manner as such writ.

This section, so far as it relates to *any county court* [the county court], shall be deemed to be substituted for sections ninety-eight and ninety-nine of the County Courts Act 1846 and that Act and the Acts amending the same shall be construed accordingly, and shall extend to orders made by the county court with respect to sums due in pursuance of any order or judgment of any court *other than a* [other than the] county court.

No imprisonment under this section shall operate as a satisfaction or extinguishment of any debt or demand or cause of action, or deprive any person of any right to take out execution against the lands, goods, or chattels of the person imprisoned, in the same manner as if such imprisonment had not taken place.

Any person imprisoned under this section shall be discharged out of custody upon a certificate signed in the prescribed manner to the effect that he has satisfied a debt or instalment of a debt in respect of which he was imprisoned, together with the prescribed costs (if any).

[Section 31E(1)(b) of the Matrimonial and Family Proceedings Act 1984 (family court has county court's powers) does not apply in relation to the powers given by this section to the county court.]

Amendments—Bankruptcy Act 1883; Statute Law (Repeals) Act 2004; SI 2002/439.

Prospective Amendments—Words in italics repealed and subsequent words in square brackets substituted by Crime and Courts Act 2013, with effect from a date to be appointed

INSOLVENCY ACT 1986

* * *

281 Effect of discharge

(1) Subject as follows, where a bankrupt is discharged, the discharge releases him from all the bankruptcy debts, but has no effect –

  (a) on the functions (so far as they remain to be carried out) of the trustee of his estate, or
  (b) on the operation, for the purposes of the carrying out of those functions, of the provisions of this Part;

and, in particular, discharge does not affect the right of any creditor of the bankrupt to prove in the bankruptcy for any debt from which the bankrupt is released.

(2) Discharge does not affect the right of any secured creditor of the bankrupt to enforce his security for the payment of a debt from which the bankrupt is released.

(3) Discharge does not release the bankrupt from any bankruptcy debt which he incurred in respect of, or forbearance in respect of which was secured by means of, any fraud or fraudulent breach of trust to which he was a party.

(4) Discharge does not release the bankrupt from any liability in respect of a fine imposed for an offence or from any liability under a recognisance except, in the case of a penalty imposed for an offence under an enactment relating to the public revenue or of a recognisance, with the consent of the Treasury.

(4A) In subsection (4) the reference to a fine includes a reference to a confiscation order under Part 2, 3 or 4 of the Proceeds of Crime Act 2002.

(5) Discharge does not, except to such extent and on such conditions as the court may direct, release the bankrupt from any bankruptcy debt which—

(a) consists in a liability to pay damages for negligence, nuisance or breach of a statutory, contractual or other duty, or to pay damages by virtue of Part I of the Consumer Protection Act 1987, being in either case damages in respect of personal injuries to any person, or

(b) arises under any order made in family proceedings or under a *maintenance assessment* [maintenance calculation] made under the Child Support Act 1991.

(6) Discharge does not release the bankrupt from such other bankruptcy debts, not being debts provable in his bankruptcy, as are prescribed.

(7) Discharge does not release any person other than the bankrupt from any liability (whether as partner or co-trustee of the bankrupt or otherwise) from which the bankrupt is released by the discharge, or from any liability as surety for the bankrupt or as a person in the nature of such a surety.

(8) In this section –

'family proceedings' means –
  (a) *family proceedings within the meaning of the Magistrates' Courts Act 1980 and any proceedings which would be such proceedings but for section 65(1)(ii) of that Act (proceedings for variation of order for periodical payments); and*
  [(a) proceedings in the family court;] and
  (b) family proceedings within the meaning of Part V of the Matrimonial and Family Proceedings Act 1984.

'fine' means the same as in the Magistrates' Courts Act 1980; and
'personal injuries' includes death and any disease or other impairment of a person's physical or mental condition.

Amendments—Consumer Protection Act 1987; Children Act 1989; Child Support Act 1991; Proceeds of Crime Act 2002.

Prospective Amendments—Words in italics prospectively substituted by Child Support, Pensions and Social Security Act 2000, s 26, Sch 3, para 6. Sub-s (8): in definition "family proceedings" para (a) substituted by the Crime and Courts Act 2013 with effect from a date to be appointed.

281A Post-discharge restrictions

Schedule 4A to this Act (bankruptcy restrictions order and bankruptcy restrictions undertaking) shall have effect.

Amendment—Enterprise Act 2002.

282 Court's power to annul bankruptcy order

(1) The court may annul a bankruptcy order if it at any time appears to the court—

    (a)   that, on any grounds existing at the time the order was made, the order ought not to have been made, or

    (b)   that, to the extent required by the rules, the bankruptcy debts and the expenses of the bankruptcy have all, since the making of the order, been either paid or secured for to the satisfaction of the court.

(2) The court may annul a bankruptcy order made against an individual on a petition under paragraph (a), (b) or (c) of section 64(1) if it at any time appears to the court, on an application by the Official Petitioner –

    (a)   that the petition was pending at a time when a criminal bankruptcy order was made against the individual or was presented after such an order was so made, and

    (b)   no appeal is pending (within the meaning of section 277) against the individual's conviction of any offence by virtue of which the criminal bankruptcy order was made;

and the court shall annul a bankruptcy order made on a petition under section 264(1)(d) if it at any time appears to the court that the criminal bankruptcy order on which the petition was based has been rescinded in consequence of an appeal.

(3) The court may annul a bankruptcy order whether or not the bankrupt has been discharged from the bankruptcy.

(4) Where the court annuls a bankruptcy order (whether under this section or under section 261 or 263D in Part VIII) –

    (a)   any sale or other disposition of property, payment made or other thing duly done, under any provision in this Group of Parts, by or under the authority of the official receiver or a trustee of the bankrupt's estate or by the court is valid, but

    (b)   if any of the bankrupt's estate is then vested, under any such provision, in such a trustee, it shall vest in such person as the court may appoint or, in default of any such appointment, revert to the bankrupt on such terms (if any) as the court may direct;

and the court may include in its order such supplemental provisions as may be authorised by the rules.

(5) *(repealed)*

Amendment—Enterprise Act 2002.

Prospective Amendments—Prospective repeal of sub-section (2) by the Criminal Justice Act 1988 with effect from a date to be appointed.

Chapter II
Protection of bankrupt's estate and investigation of his affairs

283 Definition of bankrupt's estate

(1) Subject as follows, a bankrupt's estate for the purposes of any of this Group of Parts comprises –

- (a) all property belonging to or vested in the bankrupt at the commencement of the bankruptcy, and
- (b) any property which by virtue of any of the following provisions of this Part is comprised in that estate or is treated as falling within the preceding paragraph.

(2) Subsection (1) does not apply to—

- (a) such tools, books, vehicles and other items of equipment as are necessary to the bankrupt for use personally by him in his employment, business or vocation;
- (b) such clothing, bedding, furniture, household equipment and provisions as are necessary for satisfying the basic domestic needs of the bankrupt and his family.

This subsection is subject to section 308 in Chapter IV (certain excluded property reclaimable by trustee).

(3) Subsection (1) does not apply to—

- (a) property held by the bankrupt on trust for any other person, or
- (b) the right of nomination to a vacant ecclesiastical benefice.

(3A) Subject to section 308A in Chapter IV, subsection (1) does not apply to –

- (a) a tenancy which is an assured tenancy or an assured agricultural occupancy, within the meaning of Part I of the Housing Act 1988, and the terms of which inhibit an assignment as mentioned in section 127(5) of the Rent Act 1977, or
- (b) a protected tenancy, within the meaning of the Rent Act 1977, in respect of which, by virtue of any provision of Part IX of that Act, no premium can lawfully be required as a condition of assignment, or
- (c) a tenancy of a dwelling-house by virtue of which the bankrupt is, within the meaning of the Rent (Agriculture) Act 1976, a protected occupier of the dwelling-house, and the terms of which inhibit an assignment as mentioned in section 127(5) of the Rent Act 1977, or
- (d) a secure tenancy, within the meaning of Part IV of the Housing Act 1985, which is not capable of being assigned, except in the cases mentioned in section 91(3) of that Act.

(4) References in any of this Group of Parts to property, in relation to a bankrupt, include references to any power exercisable by him over or in respect of property except in so far as the power is exercisable over or in respect of property not for the time being comprised in the bankrupt's estate and—

(a) is so exercisable at a time after either the official receiver has had his release in respect of that estate under section 299(2) in Chapter III or a meeting summoned by the trustee of that estate under section 331 in Chapter IV has been held, or

(b) cannot be so exercised for the benefit of the bankrupt;

and a power exercisable over or in respect of property is deemed for the purposes of any of this Group of Parts to vest in the person entitled to exercise it at the time of the transaction or event by virtue of which it is exercisable by that person (whether or not it becomes so exercisable at that time).

(5) For the purposes of any such provision in this Group of Parts, property comprised in a bankrupt's estate is so comprised subject to the rights of any person other than the bankrupt (whether as a secured creditor of the bankrupt or otherwise) in relation thereto, but disregarding –

(a) any rights in relation to which a statement such as is required by section 269(1)(a) was made in the petition on which the bankrupt was adjudged bankrupt, and

(b) any rights which have been otherwise given up in accordance with the rules.

(6) This section has effect subject to the provisions of any enactment not contained in this Act under which any property is to be excluded from a bankrupt's estate.

Amendments-Housing Act 1988.

283A Bankrupt's home ceasing to form part of estate

(1) This section applies where property comprised in the bankrupt's estate consists of an interest in a dwelling-house which at the date of the bankruptcy was the sole or principal residence of –

(a) the bankrupt;
(b) the bankrupt's spouse or civil partner, or
(c) a former spouse or former civil partner of the bankrupt.

(2) At the end of the period of three years beginning with the date of the bankruptcy the interest mentioned in subsection (1) shall –

(a) cease to be comprised in the bankrupt's estate, and
(b) vest in the bankrupt (without conveyance, assignment or transfer).

(3) Subsection (2) shall not apply if during the period mentioned in that subsection –

(a) the trustee realises the interest mentioned in subsection (1);
(b) the trustee applies for an order for sale in respect of the dwelling-house;
(c) the trustee applies for an order for possession of the dwelling-house;
(d) the trustee applies for an order under section 313 in Chapter IV in respect of that interest, or
(e) the trustee and the bankrupt agree that the bankrupt shall incur a specified liability to his estate (with or without the addition of interest

from the date of the agreement) in consideration of which the interest mentioned in subsection (1) shall cease to form part of the estate.

(4) Where an application of a kind described in subsection (3)(b) to (d) is made during the period mentioned in subsection (2) and is dismissed, unless the court orders otherwise the interest to which the application relates shall on the dismissal of the application—

(a) cease to be comprised in the bankrupt's estate, and
(b) vest in the bankrupt (without conveyance, assignment or transfer).

(5) If the bankrupt does not inform the trustee or the official receiver of his interest in a property before the end of the period of three months beginning with the date of the bankruptcy, the period of three years mentioned in subsection (2) –

(a) shall not begin with the date of the bankruptcy, but
(b) shall begin with the date on which the trustee or official receiver becomes aware of the bankrupt's interest.

(6) The court may substitute for the period of three years mentioned in subsection (2) a longer period –

(a) in prescribed circumstances, and
(b) in such other circumstances as the court thinks appropriate.

(7) The rules may make provision for this section to have effect with the substitution of a shorter period for the period of three years mentioned in subsection (2) in specified circumstances (which may be described by reference to action to be taken by a trustee in bankruptcy).

(8) The rules may also, in particular, make provision –

(a) requiring or enabling the trustee of a bankrupt's estate to give notice that this section applies or does not apply;
(b) about the effect of a notice under paragraph (a);
(c) requiring the trustee of a bankrupt's estate to make an application to the Chief Land Registrar.

(9) Rules under subsection (8)(b) may, in particular –

(a) disapply this section;
(b) enable a court to disapply this section;
(c) make provision in consequence of a disapplication of this section;
(d) enable a court to make provision in consequence of a disapplication of this section;
(e) make provision (which may include provision conferring jurisdiction on a court or tribunal) about compensation.

Amendments—Enterprise Act 2002; Civil Partnership Act 2004.

284 Restrictions on dispositions of property

(1) Where a person is adjudged bankrupt, any disposition of property made by that person in the period to which this section applies is void except to the extent that it is or was made with the consent of the court, or is or was subsequently ratified by the court.

(2) Subsection (1) applies to a payment (whether in cash or otherwise) as it applies to a disposition of property and, accordingly, where any payment is void by virtue of that subsection, the person paid shall hold the sum paid for the bankrupt as part of his estate.

(3) This section applies to the period beginning with the day of the presentation of the petition for the bankruptcy order and ending with the vesting, under Chapter IV of this Part, of the bankrupt's estate in a trustee.

(4) The preceding provisions of this section do not give a remedy against any person –

  (a)   in respect of any property or payment which he received before the commencement of the bankruptcy in good faith, for value and without notice that the petition had been presented, or
  (b)   in respect of any interest in property which derives from an interest in respect of which there is, by virtue of this subsection, no remedy.

(5) Where after the commencement of his bankruptcy the bankrupt has incurred a debt to a banker or other person by reason of the making of a payment which is void under this section, that debt is deemed for the purposes of any of this Group of Parts to have been incurred before the commencement of the bankruptcy unless –

  (a)   that banker or person had notice of the bankruptcy before the debt was incurred, or
  (b)   it is not reasonably practicable for the amount of the payment to be recovered from the person to whom it was made.

(6) A disposition of property is void under this section notwithstanding that the property is not or, as the case may be, would not be comprised in the bankrupt's estate; but nothing in this section affects any disposition made by a person of property held by him on trust for any other person.

* * * *

Chapter IV
Administration by trustee

Acquisition, control and realisation of bankrupt's estate

306 Vesting of bankrupt's estate in trustee

(1) The bankrupt's estate shall vest in the trustee immediately on his appointment taking effect or, in the case of the official receiver, on his becoming trustee.

(2) Where any property which is, or is to be, comprised in the bankrupt's estate vests in the trustee (whether under this section or under any other provision of this Part), it shall so vest without any conveyance, assignment or transfer

307 After-acquired property

(1) Subject to this section and section 309, the trustee may by notice in writing claim for the bankrupt's estate any property which has been acquired by, or has devolved upon, the bankrupt since the commencement of the bankruptcy.

(2) A notice under this section shall not be served in respect of –

(a) any property falling within subsection (2) or (3) of section 283 in Chapter II;

(aa) any property vesting in the bankrupt by virtue of section 283A in Chapter II;

(b) any property which by virtue of any other enactment is excluded from the bankrupt's estate, or

(c) without prejudice to section 280(2)(c) (order of court on application for discharge), any property which is acquired by, or devolves upon, the bankrupt after his discharge.

(3) Subject to the next subsection, upon the service on the bankrupt of a notice under this section the property to which the notice relates shall vest in the trustee as part of the bankrupt's estate; and the trustee's title to that property has relation back to the time at which the property was acquired by, or devolved upon, the bankrupt.

(4) Where, whether before or after service of a notice under this section –

(a) a person acquires property in good faith, for value and without notice of the bankruptcy, or

(b) a banker enters into a transaction in good faith and without such notice,

the trustee is not in respect of that property or transaction entitled by virtue of this section to any remedy against that person or banker, or any person whose title to any property derives from that person or banker.

(5) References in this section to property do not include any property which, as part of the bankrupt's income, may be the subject of an income payments order under section 310.

Amendments—Enterprise Act 2002.

* * * *

310 Income payments orders

(1) The court may make an order ('an income payments order') claiming for the bankrupt's estate so much of the income of the bankrupt during the period for which the order is in force as may be specified in the order.

(1A) An income payments order may be made only on an application instituted –

  (a) by the trustee, and
  (b) before the discharge of the bankrupt.

(2) The court shall not make an income payments order the effect of which would be to reduce the income of the bankrupt when taken together with any payments to which subsection (8) applies below what appears to the court to be necessary for meeting the reasonable domestic needs of the bankrupt and his family.

(3) An income payments order shall, in respect of any payment of income to which it is to apply, either –

  (a) require the bankrupt to pay the trustee an amount equal to so much of that payment as is claimed by the order, or
  (b) require the person making the payment to pay so much of it as is so claimed to the trustee, instead of to the bankrupt.

(4) Where the court makes an income payments order it may, if it thinks fit, discharge or vary any attachment of earnings order that is for the time being in force to secure payments by the bankrupt.

(5) Sums received by the trustee under an income payments order form part of the bankrupt's estate.

(6) An income payments order must specify the period during which it is to have effect; and that period –

  (a) may end after the discharge of the bankrupt, but
  (b) may not end after the period of three years beginning with the date on which the order is made.

(6A) An income payments order may (subject to subsection (6)(b)) be varied on the application of the trustee or the bankrupt (whether before or after discharge).

(7) For the purposes of this section the income of the bankrupt comprises every payment in the nature of income which is from time to time made to him or to which he from time to time becomes entitled, including any payment in respect of the carrying on of any business or in respect of any office or employment and despite anything in section 11 or 12 of the Welfare Reform and Pensions Act 1999 any payment under a pension scheme but excluding any payment to which subsection (8) applies.

(8) This section applies to –

  (a) payments by way of guaranteed minimum pension; and
  (b) (*repealed*)

(9) In this section, 'guaranteed minimum pension' has the same meaning as in the Pension Schemes Act 1993.

Amendments—Pensions Act 1995; Welfare Reform and Pensions Act 1999; Enterprise Act 2002; Pensions Act 2008; SI 2011/1730; SI 2012/709.

310A Income payments agreement

(1) In this section 'income payments agreement' means a written agreement between a bankrupt and his trustee or between a bankrupt and the official receiver which provides-

- (a) that the bankrupt is to pay to the trustee or the official receiver an amount equal to a specified part or proportion of the bankrupt's income for a specified period, or
- (b) that a third person is to pay to the trustee or the official receiver a specified proportion of money due to the bankrupt by way of income for a specified period.

(2) A provision of an income payments agreement of a kind specified in subsection (1)(a) or (b) may be enforced as if it were a provision of an income payments order.

(3) While an income payments agreement is in force the court may, on the application of the bankrupt, his trustee or the official receiver, discharge or vary an attachment of earnings order that is for the time being in force to secure payments by the bankrupt.

(4) The following provisions of section 310 shall apply to an income payments agreement as they apply to an income payments order—

- (a) subsection (5) (receipts to form part of estate), and
- (b) subsections (7) to (9) (meaning of income).

(5) An income payments agreement must specify the period during which it is to have effect; and that period—

- (a) may end after the discharge of the bankrupt, but
- (b) may not end after the period of three years beginning with the date on which the agreement is made.

(6) An income payments agreement may (subject to subsection (5)(b)) be varied—

- (a) by written agreement between the parties, or
- (b) by the court on an application made by the bankrupt, the trustee or the official receiver.

(7) The court –

- (a) may not vary an income payments agreement so as to include provision of a kind which could not be included in an income payments order, and
- (b) shall grant an application to vary an income payments agreement if and to the extent that the court thinks variation necessary to avoid the effect mentioned in section 310(2).

Amendments—Enterprise Act 2002.

* * * *

436 Expressions used generally

(1)   In this Act, except in so far as the context otherwise requires (and subject to Parts VII and XI)—

'the appointed day' means the day on which this Act comes into force under section 443;

'associate' has the meaning given by section 435;

'body corporate' includes a body incorporated outside Great Britain, but does not include—

(a)   a corporation sole, or

(b)   a partnership that, whether or not a legal person, is not regarded as a body corporate under the law by which it is governed;

'business' includes a trade or profession;

'the Companies Acts' means the Companies Acts (as defined in section 2 of the Companies Act 2006) as they have effect in Great Britain;

'conditional sale agreement' and 'hire-purchase agreement' have the same meanings as in the Consumer Credit Act 1974;

'the EC Regulation' means Council Regulation (EC) No 1346/2000;

'EEA State' means a state that is a Contracting Party to the Agreement on the European Economic Area signed at Oporto on 2nd May 1992 as adjusted by the Protocol signed at Brussels on 17th March 1993;

'employees' share scheme' means a scheme for encouraging or facilitating the holding of shares in or debentures of a company by or for the benefit of—

(a)   the bona fide employees or former employees of—

(i)   the company,

(ii)   any subsidiary of the company, or

(iii) the company's holding company or any subsidiary of the company's holding company, or

(b)   the spouses, civil partners, surviving spouses, surviving civil partners, or minor children or step-children of such employees or former employees.

'modifications' includes additions, alterations and omissions and cognate expressions shall be construed accordingly;

'property' includes money, goods, things in action, land and every description of property wherever situated and also obligations and every description of interest, whether present or future or vested or contingent, arising out or, or incidental to, property;

'records' includes computer records and other non-documentary records;

'subordinate legislation' has the same meaning as in the Interpretation Act 1978; and

'transaction' includes a gift, agreement or arrangement, and references to entering into a transaction shall be construed accordingly.

(2)   The following expressions have the same meaning in this Act as in the Companies Acts—

'articles', in relation to a company (see section 18 of the Companies
Act 2006);

'debenture' (see section 738 of that Act);

'holding company' (see sections 1159 and 1160 of, and Schedule 6 to, that
Act);

'the Joint Stock Companies Acts' (see section 1171 of that Act);

'overseas company' (see section 1044 of that Act);

'paid up' (see section 583 of that Act);

'private company' and 'public company' (see section 4 of that Act);

'registrar of companies' (see section 1060 of that Act);

'share' (see section 540 of that Act);

'subsidiary' (see sections 1159 and 1160 of, and Schedule 6 to, that Act).

Amendments—Insolvency Act 1986 (Amendment) Regulations 2002; Insolvency Act 1986
(Amendment) Regulations 2005; SI 2007/2194; SI 2009/1941.

436A Proceedings under EC Regulation: modified definition of property

In the application of this Act to proceedings by virtue of Article 3 of the EC
Regulation, a reference to property is a reference to property which may be
dealt with in the proceedings.

Amendments—Insolvency Act 1986 (Amendment) (No 2) Regulations 2002.

436B References to things in writing

(1) A reference in this Act to a thing in writing includes that thing in electronic
form.

(2) Subsection (1) does not apply to the following provisions –

(a)   section 53 (mode of appointment by holder of charge),

(b)   section 67(2) (report by receiver),

(c)   section 70(4) (reference to instrument creating a charge),

(d)   section 111(2) (dissent from arrangement under s 110),

(e)   in the case of a winding up of a company registered in Scotland,
      section 111(4),

(f)   section 123(1) (definition of inability to pay debts),

(g)   section 198(3) (duties of sheriff principal as regards examination),

(h)   section 222(1) (inability to pay debts: unpaid creditor for £750 or
      more), and

(i)   section 223 (inability to pay debts: debt remaining unsatisfied after
      action brought).

Amendments—SI 2010/18.

* * * *

MAINTENANCE ENFORCEMENT ACT 1991

The High Court and county courts

1 Maintenance orders in the High Court and county courts: means of payment, attachment of earnings and revocation, variation, etc

(1) Where the High Court or a county court makes a qualifying periodical maintenance order, it may at the same time exercise either of its powers under subsection (4) below in relation to the order, whether of its own motion or on an application made under this subsection by an interested party.

(2) For the purposes of this section, a periodical maintenance order is an order –

- (a) which requires money to be paid periodically by one person ("the debtor") to another ("the creditor"); and
- (b) which is a maintenance order;

and such an order is a "qualifying periodical maintenance order" if, at the time it is made, the debtor is ordinarily resident in England and Wales.

(3) Where the High Court or a county court has made a qualifying periodical maintenance order, it may at any later time—

- (a) on an application made under this subsection by an interested party, or
- (b) of its own motion, in the course of any proceedings concerning the order,

exercise either of its powers under subsection (4) below in relation to the order.

(4) The powers mentioned in subsections (1) and (3) above are –

- (a) the power to order that payments required to be made by the debtor to the creditor under the qualifying periodical maintenance order in question shall be so made by such a method of payment falling within subsection (5) below as the court may specify in the particular case; or
- (b) the power, by virtue of this section, to make an attachment of earnings order under the Attachment of Earnings Act 1971 to secure payments under the qualifying periodical maintenance order in question.

(5) The methods of payment mentioned in subsection (4)(a) above are –

- (a) payment by standing order; or
- (b) payment by any other method which requires the debtor to give his authority for payments of a specific amount to be made from an account of his to an account of the creditor's on specific dates during the period for which the authority is in force and without the need for any further authority from the debtor.

(6) In any case where –

(a)　the court proposes to exercise its power under paragraph (a) of subsection (4) above, and

(b)　having given the debtor an opportunity of opening an account from which payments under the order may be made in accordance with the method of payment proposed to be ordered under that paragraph, the court is satisfied that the debtor has failed, without reasonable excuse, to open such an account,

the court in exercising its power under that paragraph may order that the debtor open such an account.

(7) Where in the exercise of its powers under subsection (1) or (3) above, the High Court or a county court has made in relation to a qualifying periodical maintenance order such an order as is mentioned in subsection (4)(a) above (a "means of payment order"), it may at any later time –

(a)　on an application made under this subsection by an interested party, or

(b)　of its own motion, in the course of any proceedings concerning the qualifying periodical maintenance order,

revoke, suspend, revive or vary the means of payment order.

(8) In deciding whether to exercise any of its powers under this section the court in question having (if practicable) given every interested party an opportunity to make representations shall have regard to any representations made by any such party.

(9) Nothing in this section shall be taken to prejudice –

(a)　any power under the Attachment of Earnings Act 1971 which would, apart from this section, be exercisable by the High Court or a county court; or

(b)　any right of any person to make any application under that Act;

and subsection (7) above is without prejudice to any other power of the High Court or a county court to revoke, suspend, revive or vary an order.

(10) For the purposes of this section –

"debtor" and "creditor" shall be construed in accordance with subsection (2) above;

"interested party" means any of the following, that is to say –

(a)　the debtor;

(b)　the creditor; and

(c)　in a case where the person who applied for the qualifying periodical maintenance order in question is a person other than the creditor, that other person;

"maintenance order" means any order specified in Schedule 8 to the Administration of Justice Act 1970 and includes any such order which has been discharged, if any arrears are recoverable under it;

"qualifying periodical maintenance order" shall be construed in accordance with subsection (2) above, and the references to such an order in subsections (3) and (7) above are references to any such order, whether made before or after the coming into force of this section;

and the reference in subsection (2) above to an order requiring money to be paid periodically by one person to another includes a reference to an order requiring a lump sum to be paid by instalments by one person to another.

Amendment—To be appointed.

* * * *

MATRIMONIAL CAUSES ACT 1973

* * * *

PART II
FINANCIAL RELIEF FOR PARTIES TO MARRIAGE AND CHILDREN OF FAMILY

Financial provision and property adjustment orders

21 Financial provision and property adjustment orders

(1) The financial provision orders for the purposes of this Act are the orders for periodical or lump sum provision available (subject to the provisions of this Act) under section 23 below for the purpose of adjusting the financial position of the parties to a marriage and any children of the family in connection with proceedings for divorce, nullity of marriage or judicial separation and under section 27(6) below on proof of neglect by one party to a marriage to provide, or to make a proper contribution towards, reasonable maintenance for the other or a child of the family, that is to say–

(a) any order for periodical payments in favour of a party to a marriage under section 23(1)(a) or 27(6)(a) or in favour of a child of the family under section 23(1)(d), (2) or (4) or 27(6)(d);

(b) any order for secured periodical payments in favour of a party to a marriage under section 23(1)(b) or 27(6)(b) or in favour of a child of the family under section 23(1)(e), (2) or (4) or 27(6)(e); and

(c) any order for lump sum provision in favour of a party to a marriage under section 23(1)(c) or 27(6)(c) or in favour of a child of the family under section 23(1)(f), (2) or (4) or 27(6)(f);

and references in this Act (except in paragraphs 17(1) and 23 of Schedule 1 below) to periodical payments orders, secured periodical payments orders, and orders for the payment of a lump sum are references to all or some of the financial provision orders requiring the sort of financial provision in question according as the context of each reference may require.

(2) The property adjustment orders for the purposes of this Act are the orders dealing with property rights available (subject to the provisions of this Act) under section 24 below for the purpose of adjusting the financial position of the

parties to a marriage and any children of the family on or after the grant of a decree of divorce, nullity of marriage or judicial separation, that is to say–

    (a)   any order under subsection (1)(a) of that section for a transfer of property;

    (b)   any order under subsection (1)(b) of that section for a settlement of property; and

    (c)   any order under subsection (1)(c) or (d) of that section for a variation of settlement.

21A Pension sharing orders

(1) For the purposes of this Act, a pension sharing order is an order which–

    (a)   provides that one party's–
        (i)   shareable rights under a specified pension arrangement, or
        (ii)   shareable state scheme rights,
        be subject to pension sharing for the benefit of the other party, and

    (b)   specifies the percentage value to be transferred.

(2) In subsection (1) above–

    (a)   the reference to shareable rights under a pension arrangement is to rights in relation to which pension sharing is available under Chapter I of Part IV of the Welfare Reform and Pensions Act 1999, or under corresponding Northern Ireland legislation,

    (b)   the reference to shareable state scheme rights is to rights in relation to which pension sharing is available under Chapter II of Part IV of the Welfare Reform and Pensions Act 1999, or under corresponding Northern Ireland legislation, and

    (c)   'party' means a party to a marriage.

Amendments—Welfare Reform and Pensions Act 1999.

21B Pension compensation sharing orders

(1) For the purposes of this Act, a pension compensation sharing order is an order which –

    (a)   provides that one party's shareable rights to PPF compensation that derive from rights under a specified pension scheme are to be subject to pension compensation sharing for the benefit of the other party, and

    (b)   specifies the percentage value to be transferred.

(2) In subsection (1) –

    (a)   the reference to shareable rights to PPF compensation is to rights in relation to which pension compensation sharing is available under Chapter 1 of Part 3 of the Pensions Act 2008 or under corresponding Northern Ireland legislation;

    (b)   "party" means a party to a marriage;

    (c)   "specified" means specified in the order.

Amendments—Pensions Act 2008.

21C Pension compensation: interpretation

In this Part –

"PPF compensation" means compensation payable under the pension compensation provisions;

"the pension compensation provisions" means –

(a)   Chapter 3 of Part 2 of the Pensions Act 2004 (pension protection) and any regulations or order made under it,

(b)   Chapter 1 of Part 3 of the Pensions Act 2008 (pension compensation on divorce etc) and any regulations or order made under it, and

(c)   any provision corresponding to the provisions mentioned in paragraph (a) or (b) in force in Northern Ireland.

Amendments—Pensions Act 2008.

Ancillary relief in connection with divorce proceedings etc

22 Maintenance pending suit

(1) On a petition for divorce, nullity of marriage or judicial separation, the court may make an order for maintenance pending suit, that is to say, an order requiring either party to the marriage to make to the other such periodical payments for his or her maintenance and for such term, being a term beginning not earlier than the date of the presentation of the petition and ending with the date of the determination of the suit, as the court thinks reasonable.

(2) An order under this section may not require a party to a marriage to pay to the other party any amount in respect of legal services for the purposes of the proceedings.

(3) In subsection (2) "legal services" has the same meaning as in section 22ZA.

Amendments—Legal Aid, Sentencing and Punishment of Offenders Act 2012.

22ZA Orders for payment in respect of legal services

(1) In proceedings for divorce, nullity of marriage or judicial separation, the court may make an order or orders requiring one party to the marriage to pay to the other ("the applicant") an amount for the purpose of enabling the applicant to obtain legal services for the purposes of the proceedings.

(2) The court may also make such an order or orders in proceedings under this Part for financial relief in connection with proceedings for divorce, nullity of marriage or judicial separation.

(3) The court must not make an order under this section unless it is satisfied that, without the amount, the applicant would not reasonably be able to obtain appropriate legal services for the purposes of the proceedings or any part of the proceedings.

(4) For the purposes of subsection (3), the court must be satisfied, in particular, that –

(a) the applicant is not reasonably able to secure a loan to pay for the services, and

(b) the applicant is unlikely to be able to obtain the services by granting a charge over any assets recovered in the proceedings.

(5) An order under this section may be made for the purpose of enabling the applicant to obtain legal services of a specified description, including legal services provided in a specified period or for the purposes of a specified part of the proceedings.

(6) An order under this section may –

(a) provide for the payment of all or part of the amount by instalments of specified amounts, and

(b) require the instalments to be secured to the satisfaction of the court.

(7) An order under this section may direct that payment of all or part of the amount is to be deferred.

(8) The court may at any time in the proceedings vary an order made under this section if it considers that there has been a material change of circumstances since the order was made.

(9) For the purposes of the assessment of costs in the proceedings, the applicant's costs are to be treated as reduced by any amount paid to the applicant pursuant to an order under this section for the purposes of those proceedings.

(10) In this section "legal services", in relation to proceedings, means the following types of services –

(a) providing advice as to how the law applies in the particular circumstances,

(b) providing advice and assistance in relation to the proceedings,

(c) providing other advice and assistance in relation to the settlement or other resolution of the dispute that is the subject of the proceedings, and

(d) providing advice and assistance in relation to the enforcement of decisions in the proceedings or as part of the settlement or resolution of the dispute,

and they include, in particular, advice and assistance in the form of representation and any form of dispute resolution, including mediation.

(11) In subsections (5) and (6) "specified" means specified in the order concerned.

Amendments—Legal Aid, Sentencing and Punishment of Offenders Act 2012.

22ZB Matters to which court is to have regard in deciding how to exercise power under section 22ZA

(1) When considering whether to make or vary an order under section 22ZA, the court must have regard to –

(a) the income, earning capacity, property and other financial resources which each of the applicant and the paying party has or is likely to have in the foreseeable future,

(b) the financial needs, obligations and responsibilities which each of the applicant and the paying party has or is likely to have in the foreseeable future,

(c) the subject matter of the proceedings, including the matters in issue in them,

(d) whether the paying party is legally represented in the proceedings,

(e) any steps taken by the applicant to avoid all or part of the proceedings, whether by proposing or considering mediation or otherwise,

(f) the applicant's conduct in relation to the proceedings,

(g) any amount owed by the applicant to the paying party in respect of costs in the proceedings or other proceedings to which both the applicant and the paying party are or were party, and

(h) the effect of the order or variation on the paying party.

(2) In subsection (1)(a) "earning capacity", in relation to the applicant or the paying party, includes any increase in earning capacity which, in the opinion of the court, it would be reasonable to expect the applicant or the paying party to take steps to acquire.

(3) For the purposes of subsection (1)(h), the court must have regard, in particular, to whether the making or variation of the order is likely to –

(a) cause undue hardship to the paying party, or

(b) prevent the paying party from obtaining legal services for the purposes of the proceedings.

(4) The Lord Chancellor may by order amend this section by adding to, omitting or varying the matters mentioned in subsections (1) to (3).

(5) An order under subsection (4) must be made by statutory instrument.

(6) A statutory instrument containing an order under subsection (4) may not be made unless a draft of the instrument has been laid before, and approved by a resolution of, each House of Parliament.

(7) In this section "legal services" has the same meaning as in section 22ZA.

Amendments—Legal Aid, Sentencing and Punishment of Offenders Act 2012.

23 Financial provision orders in connection with divorce proceedings etc

(1) On granting a decree of divorce, a decree of nullity of marriage or a decree of judicial separation or at any time thereafter (whether, in the case of a decree of divorce or of nullity of marriage, before or after the decree is made absolute), the court may make any one or more of the following orders, that is to say–

(a) an order that either party to the marriage shall make to the other such periodical payments, for such term, as may be specified in the order;

(b) an order that either party to the marriage shall secure to the other to the satisfaction of the court such periodical payments, for such term, as may be so specified;

(c) an order that either party to the marriage shall pay to the other such lump sum or sums as may be so specified;

(d) an order that a party to the marriage shall make to such person as may be specified in the order for the benefit of a child of the family, or to such a child, such periodical payments, for such term, as may be so specified;

(e) an order that a party to the marriage shall secure to such person as may be so specified for the benefit of such a child, or to such a child, to the satisfaction of the court, such periodical payments, for such term, as may be so specified;

(f) an order that a party to the marriage shall pay to such person as may be so specified for the benefit of such a child, or to such a child, such lump sum as may be so specified;

subject, however, in the case of an order under paragraph (d), (e) or (f) above, to the restrictions imposed by section 29(1) and (3) below on the making of financial provision orders in favour of children who have attained the age of eighteen.

(2) The court may also, subject to those restrictions, make any one or more of the orders mentioned in subsection (1)(d), (e) and (f) above–

(a) in any proceedings for divorce, nullity of marriage or judicial separation, before granting a decree; and

(b) where any such proceedings are dismissed after the beginning of the trial, either forthwith or within a reasonable period after the dismissal.

(3) Without prejudice to the generality of subsection (1)(c) or (f) above–

(a) an order under this section that a party to a marriage shall pay a lump sum to the other party may be made for the purpose of enabling that other party to meet any liabilities or expenses reasonably incurred by him or her in maintaining himself or herself or any child of the family before making an application for an order under this section in his or her favour;

(b) an order under this section for the payment of a lump sum to or for the benefit of a child of the family may be made for the purpose of enabling any liabilities or expenses reasonably incurred by or for the benefit of that child before the making of an application for an order under this section in his favour to be met; and

(c) an order under this section for the payment of a lump sum may provide for the payment of that sum by instalments of such amount as may be specified in the order and may require the payment of the instalments to be secured to the satisfaction of the court.

(4) The power of the court under subsection (1) or (2)(a) above to make an order in favour of a child of the family shall be exercisable from time to time; and where the court makes an order in favour of a child under subsection (2)(b)

above, it may from time to time, subject to the restrictions mentioned in subsection (1) above, make a further order in his favour of any of the kinds mentioned in subsection (1)(d), (e) or (f) above.

(5) Without prejudice to the power to give a direction under section 30 below for the settlement of an instrument by conveyancing counsel, where an order is made under subsection (1)(a), (b) or (c) above on or after granting a decree of divorce or nullity of marriage, neither the order nor any settlement made in pursuance of the order shall take effect unless the decree has been made absolute.

(6) Where the court–

(a)   makes an order under this section for the payment of a lump sum; and
(b)   directs–
    (i)   that payment of that sum or any part of it shall be deferred; or
    (ii)   that the sum or any part of it shall be paid by instalments,

the court may order that the amount deferred or the instalments shall carry interest at such rate as may be specified by the order from such date, not earlier than the date of the order, as may be so specified, until the date when payment of it is due.

Amendments—Administration of Justice Act 1982.

24 Property adjustment orders in connection with divorce proceedings etc

(1) On granting a decree of divorce, a decree of nullity of marriage or a decree of judicial separation or at any time thereafter (whether, in the case of a decree of divorce or of nullity of marriage, before or after the decree is made absolute), the court may make any one or more of the following orders, that is to say–

(a)   an order that a party to the marriage shall transfer to the other party, to any child of the family or to such person as may be specified in the order for the benefit of such a child such property as may be so specified, being property to which the first-mentioned party is entitled, either in possession or reversion;
(b)   an order that a 'settlement' of such property as may be so specified, being property to which a party to the marriage is so entitled, be made to the satisfaction of the court for the benefit of the other party to the marriage and of the children of the family or either or any of them;
(c)   an order varying for the benefit of the parties to the marriage and of the children of the family or either or any of them any ante-nuptial or post-nuptial settlement (including such a settlement made by will or codicil) made on the parties to the marriage , other than one in the form of a pension arrangement (within the meaning of section 25D below);
(d)   an order extinguishing or reducing the interest of either of the parties to the marriage under any such settlement , other than one in the form of a pension arrangement (within the meaning of section 25D below);

subject, however, in the case of an order under paragraph (a) above, to the restrictions imposed by section 29(1) and (3) below on the making of orders for a transfer of property in favour of children who have attained the age of eighteen.

(2) The court may make an order under subsection (1)(c) above notwithstanding that there are no children of the family.

(3) Without prejudice to the power to give a direction under section 30 below for the settlement of an instrument by conveyancing counsel, where an order is made under this section on or after granting a decree of divorce or nullity of marriage, neither the order nor any settlement made in pursuance of the order shall take effect unless the decree has been made absolute.

Amendments—Welfare Reform and Pensions Act 1999.

24A Orders for sale of property

(1) Where the court makes an order under section 22ZA or makes under section 23 or 24 of this Act a secured periodical payments order, an order for the payment of a lump sum or a property adjustment order, then, on making that order or at any time thereafter, the court may make a further order for the sale of such property as may be specified in the order, being property in which or in the proceeds of sale of which either or both of the parties to the marriage has or have a beneficial interest, either in possession or reversion.

(2) Any order made under subsection (1) above may contain such consequential or supplementary provisions as the court thinks fit and, without prejudice to the generality of the foregoing provision, may include–

    (a)   provision requiring the making of a payment out of the proceeds of sale of the property to which the order relates, and

    (b)   provision requiring any such property to be offered for sale to a person, or class of persons, specified in the order.

(3) Where an order is made under subsection (1) above on or after the grant of a decree of divorce or nullity of marriage, the order shall not take effect unless the decree has been made absolute.

(4) Where an order is made under subsection (1) above, the court may direct that the order, or such provision thereof as the court may specify, shall not take effect until the occurrence of an event specified by the court or the expiration of a period so specified.

(5) Where an order under subsection (1) above contains a provision requiring the proceeds of sale of the property to which the order relates to be used to secure periodical payments to a party to the marriage, the order shall cease to have effect on the death or re-marriage of, or formation of a civil partnership by, that person.

(6) Where a party to a marriage has a beneficial interest in any property, or in the proceeds of sale thereof, and some other person who is not a party to the marriage also has a beneficial interest in that property or in the proceeds of sale

thereof, then, before deciding whether to make an order under this section in relation to that property, it shall be the duty of the court to give that other person an opportunity to make representations with respect to the order; and any representations made by that other person shall be included among the circumstances to which the court is required to have regard under section 25(1) below.

Amendments—Matrimonial Homes and Property Act 1981; Matrimonial and Family Proceedings Act 1984; Civil Partnership Act 2004; Legal Aid, Sentencing and Punishment of Offenders Act 2012.

24B Pension sharing orders in connection with divorce proceedings etc

(1) On granting a decree of divorce or a decree of nullity of marriage or at any time thereafter (whether before or after the decree is made absolute), the court may, on an application made under this section, make one or more pension sharing orders in relation to the marriage.

(2) A pension sharing order under this section is not to take effect unless the decree on or after which it is made has been made absolute.

(3) A pension sharing order under this section may not be made in relation to a pension arrangement which–

(a) is the subject of a pension sharing order in relation to the marriage, or
(b) has been the subject of pension sharing between the parties to the marriage.

(4) A pension sharing order under this section may not be made in relation to shareable state scheme rights if–

(a) such rights are the subject of a pension sharing order in relation to the marriage, or
(b) such rights have been the subject of pension sharing between the parties to the marriage.

(5) A pension sharing order under this section may not be made in relation to the rights of a person under a pension arrangement if there is in force a requirement imposed by virtue of section 25B or 25C below which relates to benefits or future benefits to which he is entitled under the pension arrangement.

24C Pension sharing orders: duty to stay

(1) No pension sharing order may be made so as to take effect before the end of such period after the making of the order as may be prescribed by regulations made by the Lord Chancellor.

(2) The power to make regulations under this section shall be exercisable by statutory instrument which shall be subject to annulment in pursuance of a resolution of either House of Parliament.

Amendments—Divorce etc (Pensions) Regulations 2000.

24D Pension sharing orders: apportionment of charges

If a pension sharing order relates to rights under a pension arrangement, the court may include in the order provision about the apportionment between the parties of any charge under section 41 of the Welfare Reform and Pensions Act 1999 (charges in respect of pension sharing costs), or under corresponding Northern Ireland legislation.

Amendments—Welfare Reform and Pensions Act 1999.

24E Pension compensation sharing orders in connection with divorce proceedings

(1) On granting a decree of divorce or a decree of nullity of marriage or at any time thereafter (whether before or after the decree is made absolute), the court may, on an application made under this section, make a pension compensation sharing order in relation to the marriage.

(2) A pension compensation sharing order under this section is not to take effect unless the decree on or after which it is made has been made absolute.

(3) A pension compensation sharing order under this section may not be made in relation to rights to PPF compensation that –

    (a)   are the subject of pension attachment,

    (b)   derive from rights under a pension scheme that were the subject of pension sharing between the parties to the marriage,

    (c)   are the subject of pension compensation attachment, or

    (d)   are or have been the subject of pension compensation sharing between the parties to the marriage.

(4) For the purposes of subsection (3)(a), rights to PPF compensation "are the subject of pension attachment" if any of the following three conditions is met.

(5) The first condition is that –

    (a)   the rights derive from rights under a pension scheme in relation to which an order was made under section 23 imposing a requirement by virtue of section 25B(4), and

    (b)   that order, as modified under section 25E(3), remains in force.

(6) The second condition is that –

    (a)   the rights derive from rights under a pension scheme in relation to which an order was made under section 23 imposing a requirement by virtue of section 25B(7), and

    (b)   that order –

        (i)   has been complied with, or

        (ii)   has not been complied with and, as modified under section 25E(5), remains in force.

(7) The third condition is that –

(a)   the rights derive from rights under a pension scheme in relation to which an order was made under section 23 imposing a requirement by virtue of section 25C, and

(b)   that order remains in force.

(8) For the purposes of subsection (3)(b), rights under a pension scheme "were the subject of pension sharing between the parties to the marriage" if the rights were at any time the subject of a pension sharing order in relation to the marriage or a previous marriage between the same parties.

(9) For the purposes of subsection (3)(c), rights to PPF compensation "are the subject of pension compensation attachment" if there is in force a requirement imposed by virtue of section 25F relating to them.

(10) For the purposes of subsection (3)(d), rights to PPF compensation "are or have been the subject of pension compensation sharing between the parties to the marriage" if they are or have ever been the subject of a pension compensation sharing order in relation to the marriage or a previous marriage between the same parties.

Amendments—Pensions Act 2008.

24F Pension compensation sharing orders: duty to stay

(1) No pension compensation sharing order may be made so as to take effect before the end of such period after the making of the order as may be prescribed by regulations made by the Lord Chancellor.

(2) The power to make regulations under this section shall be exercisable by statutory instrument which shall be subject to annulment in pursuance of a resolution of either House of Parliament.

Amendments—Pensions Act 2008.

24G Pension compensation sharing orders: apportionment of charges

The court may include in a pension compensation sharing order provision about the apportionment between the parties of any charge under section 117 of the Pensions Act 2008 (charges in respect of pension compensation sharing costs), or under corresponding Northern Ireland legislation.

Amendments—Pensions Act 2008.

25 Matters to which court is to have regard in deciding how to exercise its powers under ss 23, 24, 24A, 24B and 24E

(1) It shall be the duty of the court in deciding whether to exercise its powers under section 23, 24 , 24A, 24B or 24E above and, if so, in what manner, to have regard to all the circumstances of the case, first consideration being given to the welfare while a minor of any child of the family who has not attained the age of eighteen.

(2) As regards the exercise of the powers of the court under section 23(1)(a), (b) or (c), 24 , 24A, 24B or 24E above in relation to a party to the marriage, the court shall in particular have regard to the following matters–

(a) the income, earning capacity, property and other financial resources which each of the parties to the marriage has or is likely to have in the foreseeable future, including in the case of earning capacity any increase in that capacity which it would in the opinion of the court be reasonable to expect a party to the marriage to take steps to acquire;

(b) the financial needs, obligations and responsibilities which each of the parties to the marriage has or is likely to have in the foreseeable future;

(c) the standard of living enjoyed by the family before the breakdown of the marriage;

(d) the age of each party to the marriage and the duration of the marriage;

(e) any physical or mental disability of either of the parties to the marriage;

(f) the contributions which each of the parties has made or is likely in the foreseeable future to make to the welfare of the family, including any contribution by looking after the home or caring for the family;

(g) the conduct of each of the parties, if that conduct is such that it would in the opinion of the court be inequitable to disregard it;

(h) in the case of proceedings for divorce or nullity of marriage, the value to each of the parties to the marriage of any benefit which, by reason of the dissolution or annulment of the marriage, that party will lose the chance of acquiring.

(3) As regards the exercise of the powers of the court under section 23(1)(d), (e) or (f), (2) or (4), 24 or 24A above in relation to a child of the family, the court shall in particular have regard to the following matters–

(a) the financial needs of the child;

(b) the income, earning capacity (if any), property and other financial resources of the child;

(c) any physical or mental disability of the child;

(d) the manner in which he was being and in which the parties to the marriage expected him to be educated or trained;

(e) the considerations mentioned in relation to the parties to the marriage in paragraphs (a), (b), (c) and (e) of subsection (2) above.

(4) As regards the exercise of the powers of the court under section 23(1)(d), (e) or (f), (2) or (4), 24 or 24A above against a party to a marriage in favour of a child of the family who is not the child of that party, the court shall also have regard–

(a) to whether that party assumed any responsibility for the child's maintenance, and, if so, to the extent to which, and the basis upon which, that party assumed such responsibility and to the length of time for which that party discharged such responsibility;

(b) to whether in assuming and discharging such responsibility that party did so knowing that the child was not his or her own;

(c) to the liability of any other person to maintain the child.

Amendments—Pensions Act 1995; Welfare Reform and Pensions Act 1999; Matrimonial and Family Proceedings Act 1984; Pensions Act 2008.

25A Exercise of court's powers in favour of party to marriage on decree of divorce or nullity of marriage

(1) Where on or after the grant of a decree of divorce or nullity of marriage the court decides to exercise its powers under section 23(1)(a), (b) or (c), 24 , 24A, 24B or 24E above in favour of a party to the marriage, it shall be the duty of the court to consider whether it would be appropriate so to exercise those powers that the financial obligations of each party towards the other will be terminated as soon after the grant of the decree as the court considers just and reasonable.

(2) Where the court decides in such a case to make a periodical payments or secured periodical payments order in favour of a party to the marriage, the court shall in particular consider whether it would be appropriate to require those payments to be made or secured only for such term as would in the opinion of the court be sufficient to enable the party in whose favour the order is made to adjust without undue hardship to the termination of his or her financial dependence on the other party.

(3) Where on or after the grant of a decree of divorce or nullity of marriage an application is made by a party to the marriage for a periodical payments or secured periodical payments order in his or her favour, then, if the court considers that no continuing obligation should be imposed on either party to make or secure periodical payments in favour of the other, the court may dismiss the application with a direction that the applicant shall not be entitled to make any future application in relation to that marriage for an order under section 23(1)(a) or (b) above.

Amendments—Pensions Act 1995; Welfare Reform and Pensions Act 1999; Matrimonial and Family Proceedings Act 1984; Pensions Act 2008.

25B Pensions

(1) The matters to which the court is to have regard under section 25(2) above include–

   (a)   in the case of paragraph (a), any benefits under a pension arrangement which a party to the marriage has or is likely to have, and
   (b)   in the case of paragraph (h), any benefits under a pension arrangement which, by reason of the dissolution or annulment of the marriage, a party to the marriage will lose the chance of acquiring,

and, accordingly, in relation to benefits under a pension arrangement, section 25(2)(a) above shall have effect as if 'in the foreseeable future' were omitted.

(2) (*repealed*)

(3) The following provisions apply where, having regard to any benefits under a pension arrangement, the court determines to make an order under section 23 above.

(4) To the extent to which the order is made having regard to any benefits under a pension arrangement, the order may require the person responsible for the pension arrangement in question, if at any time any payment in respect of any benefits under the arrangement becomes due to the party with pension rights, to make a payment for the benefit of the other party.

(5) The order must express the amount of any payment required to be made by virtue of subsection (4) above as a percentage of the payment which becomes due to the party with pension rights.

(6) Any such payment by the person responsible for the arrangement–

  (a) shall discharge so much of his liability to the party with pension rights as corresponds to the amount of the payment, and
  (b) shall be treated for all purposes as a payment made by the party with pension rights in or towards the discharge of his liability under the order.

(7) Where the party with pension rights has a right of commutation under the arrangement, the order may require him to exercise it to any extent; and this section applies to any payment due in consequence of commutation in pursuance of the order as it applies to other payments in respect of benefits under the arrangement.

(7A) The power conferred by subsection (7) above may not be exercised for the purpose of commuting a benefit payable to the party with pension rights to a benefit payable to the other party.

(7B) The power conferred by subsection (4) or (7) above may not be exercised in relation to a pension arrangement which–

  (a) is the subject of a pension sharing order in relation to the marriage, or
  (b) has been the subject of pension sharing between the parties to the marriage.

(7C) In subsection (1) above, references to benefits under a pension arrangement include any benefits by way of pension, whether under a pension arrangement or not.

Amendments—Welfare Reform and Pensions Act 1999.

25C Pensions: lump sums

(1) The power of the court under section 23 above to order a party to a marriage to pay a lump sum to the other party includes, where the benefits which the party with pension rights has or is likely to have under a pension arrangement include any lump sum payable in respect of his death, power to make any of the following provision by the order.

(2) The court may–

(a) if the person responsible for the pension arrangement in question has power to determine the person to whom the sum, or any part of it, is to be paid, require him to pay the whole or part of that sum, when it becomes due, to the other party,

(b) if the party with pension rights has power to nominate the person to whom the sum, or any part of it, is to be paid, require the party with pension rights to nominate the other party in respect of the whole or part of that sum,

(c) in any other case, require the person responsible for the pension arrangement in question to pay the whole or part of that sum, when it becomes due, for the benefit of the other party instead of to the person to whom, apart from the order, it would be paid.

(3) Any payment by the person responsible for the arrangement under an order made under section 23 above by virtue of this section shall discharge so much of his liability in respect of the party with pension rights as corresponds to the amount of the payment.

(4) The powers conferred by this section may not be exercised in relation to a pension arrangement which–

(a) is the subject of a pension sharing order in relation to the marriage, or

(b) has been the subject of pension sharing between the parties to the marriage.

Amendments—Welfare Reform and Pensions Act 1999.

25D Pensions: supplementary

(1) Where–

(a) an order made under section 23 above by virtue of section 25B or 25C above imposes any requirement on the person responsible for a pension arrangement ('the first arrangement') and the party with pension rights acquires rights under another pension arrangement ('the new arrangement') which are derived (directly or indirectly) from the whole of his rights under the first arrangement, and

(b) the person responsible for the new arrangement has been given notice in accordance with regulations made by the Lord Chancellor,

the order shall have effect as if it had been made instead in respect of the person responsible for the new arrangement.

(2) The Lord Chancellor may by regulations–

(a) in relation to any provision of sections 25B or 25C above which authorises the court making an order under section 23 above to require the person responsible for a pension arrangement to make a payment for the benefit of the other party, make provision as to the person to whom, and the terms on which, the payment is to be made,

(ab) make, in relation to payment under a mistaken belief as to the continuation in force of a provision included by virtue of section 25B or 25C above in an order under section 23 above, provision about the rights or liabilities of the payer, the payee or the person to whom the payment was due,

(b) require notices to be given in respect of changes of circumstances relevant to such orders which include provision made by virtue of sections 25B and 25C above,

(ba) make provision for the person responsible for a pension arrangement to be discharged in prescribed circumstances from a requirement imposed by virtue of section 25B or 25C above,

(c) *(repealed)*

(d) *(repealed)*

(e) make provision about calculation and verification in relation to the valuation of–

    (i)   benefits under a pension arrangement, or

    (ii) shareable state scheme rights,

for the purposes of the court's functions in connection with the exercise of any of its powers under this Part of this Act.

(2A) Regulations under subsection (2)(e) above may include–

(a) provision for calculation or verification in accordance with guidance from time to time prepared by a prescribed person, and

(b) provision by reference to regulations under section 30 or 49(4) of the Welfare Reform and Pensions Act 1999.

(2B) Regulations under subsection (2) above may make different provision for different cases.

(2C) Power to make regulations under this section shall be exercisable by statutory instrument which shall be subject to annulment in pursuance of a resolution of either House of Parliament.

(3) In this section and sections 25B and 25C above–

'occupational pension scheme' has the same meaning as in the Pension Schemes Act 1993;

'the party with pension rights' means the party to the marriage who has or is likely to have benefits under a pension arrangement and 'the other party' means the other party to the marriage;

'pension arrangement' means–

    (a)   an occupational pension scheme,

    (b)   a personal pension scheme,

    (c)   a retirement annuity contract,

    (d)   an annuity or insurance policy purchased, or transferred, for the purpose of giving effect to rights under an occupational pension scheme or a personal pension scheme, and

    (e)   an annuity purchased, or entered into, for the purpose of discharging liability in respect of a pension credit under section 29(1)(b) of the Welfare Reform and Pensions Act 1999 or under corresponding Northern Ireland legislation;

'personal pension scheme' has the same meaning as in the Pension Schemes Act 1993;

'prescribed' means prescribed by regulations;

'retirement annuity contract' means a contract or scheme approved under Chapter III of Part XIV of the Income and Corporation Taxes Act 1988;

'shareable state scheme rights' has the same meaning as in section 21A(1) above; and

'trustees or managers', in relation to an occupational pension scheme or a personal pension scheme, means–

    (a)   in the case of a scheme established under a trust, the trustees of the scheme, and

    (b)   in any other case, the managers of the scheme.

(4) In this section and sections 25B and 25C above, references to the person responsible for a pension arrangement are–

(a)   in the case of an occupational pension scheme or a personal pension scheme, to the trustees or managers of the scheme,

(b)   in the case of a retirement annuity contract or an annuity falling within paragraph (d) or (e) of the definition of 'pension arrangement' above, the provider of the annuity, and

(c)   in the case of an insurance policy falling within paragraph (d) of the definition of that expression, the insurer.

Amendments—Welfare Reform and Pensions Act 1999; Divorce etc (Pensions) Regulations 2000.

25E The Pension Protection Fund

(1) The matters to which the court is to have regard under section 25(2) include –

(a)   in the case of paragraph (a), any PPF compensation to which a party to the marriage is or is likely to be entitled, and

(b)   in the case of paragraph (h), any PPF compensation which, by reason of the dissolution or annulment of the marriage, a party to the marriage will lose the chance of acquiring entitlement to,

and, accordingly, in relation to PPF compensation, section 25(2)(a) shall have effect as if 'in the foreseeable future' were omitted.

(2) Subsection (3) applies in relation to an order under section 23 so far as it includes provision made by virtue of section 25B(4) which –

(a)   imposed requirements on the trustees or managers of an occupational pension scheme for which the Board has assumed responsibility in accordance with Chapter 3 of Part 2 of the Pensions Act 2004 (pension protection) or any provision in force in Northern Ireland corresponding to that Chapter, and

(b)   was made before the trustees or managers of the scheme received the transfer notice in relation to the scheme.

(3) The order is to have effect from the time when the trustees or managers of the scheme receive the transfer notice –

(a) as if, except in prescribed descriptions of case –
    (i) references in the order to the trustees or managers of the scheme were references to the Board, and
    (ii) references in the order to any pension or lump sum to which the party with pension rights is or may become entitled under the scheme were references to any PPF compensation to which that person is or may become entitled in respect of the pension or lump sum, and
(b) subject to such other modifications as may be prescribed.

(4) Subsection (5) applies to an order under section 23 if –

(a) it includes provision made by virtue of section 25B(7) which requires the party with pension rights to exercise his right of commutation under an occupational pension scheme to any extent, and
(b) before the requirement is complied with the Board has assumed responsibility for the scheme as mentioned in subsection (2)(a).

(5) From the time the trustees or managers of the scheme receive the transfer notice, the order is to have effect with such modifications as may be prescribed.

(6) Regulations may modify section 25C as it applies in relation to an occupational pension scheme at any time when there is an assessment period in relation to the scheme.

(7) Where the court makes a pension sharing order in respect of a person's shareable rights under an occupational pension scheme, or an order which includes provision made by virtue of section 25B(4) or (7) in relation to such a scheme, the Board subsequently assuming responsibility for the scheme as mentioned in subsection (2)(a) does not affect –

(a) the powers of the court under section 31 to vary or discharge the order or to suspend or revive any provision of it, or
(b) on an appeal, the powers of the appeal court to affirm, reinstate, set aside or vary the order.

(8) Regulations may make such consequential modifications of any provision of, or made by virtue of, this Part as appear to the Lord Chancellor necessary or expedient to give effect to the provisions of this section.

(9) In this section –

'assessment period' means an assessment period within the meaning of Part 2 of the Pensions Act 2004 (pension protection) (see sections 132 and 159 of that Act) or an equivalent period under any provision in force in Northern Ireland corresponding to that Part;
'the Board' means the Board of the Pension Protection Fund;
'occupational pension scheme' has the same meaning as in the Pension Schemes Act 1993;
'prescribed' means prescribed by regulations;
(*repealed*)
'regulations' means regulations made by the Lord Chancellor;

'shareable rights' are rights in relation to which pension sharing is available under Chapter 1 of Part 4 of the Welfare Reform and Pensions Act 1999 or any provision in force in Northern Ireland corresponding to that Chapter;

'transfer notice' has the same meaning as in section 160 of the Pensions Act 2004 or any corresponding provision in force in Northern Ireland.

(10) Any power to make regulations under this section is exercisable by statutory instrument, which shall be subject to annulment in pursuance of a resolution of either House of Parliament.

Amendments—Pensions Act 2004.

25F Attachment of pension compensation

(1) This section applies where, having regard to any PPF compensation to which a party to the marriage is or is likely to be entitled, the court determines to make an order under section 23.

(2) To the extent to which the order is made having regard to such compensation, the order may require the Board of the Pension Protection Fund, if at any time any payment in respect of PPF compensation becomes due to the party with compensation rights, to make a payment for the benefit of the other party.

(3) The order must express the amount of any payment required to be made by virtue of subsection (2) as a percentage of the payment which becomes due to the party with compensation rights.

(4) Any such payment by the Board of the Pension Protection Fund –

(a) shall discharge so much of its liability to the party with compensation rights as corresponds to the amount of the payment, and

(b) shall be treated for all purposes as a payment made by the party with compensation rights in or towards the discharge of that party's liability under the order.

(5) Where the party with compensation rights has a right to commute any PPF compensation, the order may require that party to exercise it to any extent; and this section applies to any payment due in consequence of commutation in pursuance of the order as it applies to other payments in respect of PPF compensation.

(6) The power conferred by subsection (5) may not be exercised for the purpose of commuting compensation payable to the party with compensation rights to compensation payable to the other party.

(7) The power conferred by subsection (2) or (5) may not be exercised in relation to rights to PPF compensation that –

(a) derive from rights under a pension scheme that were at any time the subject of a pension sharing order in relation to the marriage, or a previous marriage between the same parties, or

(b) are or have ever been the subject of a pension compensation sharing order in relation to the marriage or a previous marriage between the same parties.

Amendments—Pensions Act 2008.

25G Pension compensation: supplementary

(1) The Lord Chancellor may by regulations –

(a) make provision, in relation to any provision of section 25F which authorises the court making an order under section 23 to require the Board of the Pension Protection Fund to make a payment for the benefit of the other party, as to the person to whom, and the terms on which, the payment is to be made;

(b) make provision, in relation to payment under a mistaken belief as to the continuation in force of a provision included by virtue of section 25F in an order under section 23, about the rights or liabilities of the payer, the payee or the person to whom the payment was due;

(c) require notices to be given in respect of changes of circumstances relevant to orders under section 23 which include provision made by virtue of section 25F;

(d) make provision for the Board of the Pension Protection Fund to be discharged in prescribed circumstances from a requirement imposed by virtue of section 25F;

(e) make provision about calculation and verification in relation to the valuation of PPF compensation for the purposes of the court's functions in connection with the exercise of any of its powers under this Part.

(2) Regulations under subsection (1)(e) may include –

(a) provision for calculation or verification in accordance with guidance from time to time prepared by a prescribed person;

(b) provision by reference to regulations under section 112 of the Pensions Act 2008.

(3) Regulations under subsection (1) may make different provision for different cases.

(4) The power to make regulations under subsection (1) is exercisable by statutory instrument which shall be subject to annulment in pursuance of a resolution of either House of Parliament.

(5) In this section and section 25F –

"the party with compensation rights" means the party to the marriage who is or is likely to be entitled to PPF compensation, and "the other party" means the other party to the marriage;

"prescribed" means prescribed by regulations.

Amendments—Pensions Act 2008.

26 Commencement of proceedings for ancillary relief etc

(1) Where a petition for divorce, nullity of marriage or judicial separation has been presented, then, subject to subsection (2) below, proceedings for maintenance pending suit under section 22 above, for a financial provision order under section 23 above, or for a property adjustment order may be begun, subject to and in accordance with rules of court, at any time after the presentation of the petition.

(2) Rules of court may provide, in such cases as may be prescribed by the rules–

(a)   that applications for any such relief as is mentioned in subsection (1) above shall be made in the petition or answer; and

(b)   that applications for any such relief which are not so made, or are not made until after the expiration of such period following the presentation of the petition or filing of the answer as may be so prescribed, shall be made only with the leave of the court.

Financial provision in case of neglect to maintain

27 Financial provision orders etc in case of neglect by party to marriage to maintain other party or child of the family

(1) Either party to a marriage may apply to the court for an order under this section on the ground that the other party to the marriage (in this section referred to as the respondent)–

(a)   has failed to provide reasonable maintenance for the applicant, or

(b)   has failed to provide, or to make a proper contribution towards, reasonable maintenance for any child of the family.

(2) The court may not entertain an application under this section unless it has jurisdiction to do so by virtue of the Maintenance Regulation and Schedule 6 to the Civil Jurisdiction and Judgments (Maintenance) Regulations 2011.

(3) Where an application under this section is made on the ground mentioned in subsection (1)(a) above then, in deciding–

(a)   whether the respondent has failed to provide reasonable maintenance for the applicant, and

(b)   what order, if any, to make under this section in favour of the applicant,

the court shall have regard to all the circumstances of the case including the matters mentioned in section 25(2) above, and where an application is also made under this section in respect of a child of the family who has not attained the age of eighteen, first consideration shall be given to the welfare of the child while a minor.

(3A) Where an application under this section is made on the ground mentioned in subsection (1)(b) above then, in deciding–

(a)　whether the respondent has failed to provide, or to make a proper contribution towards, reasonable maintenance for the child of the family to whom the application relates, and

(b)　what order, if any, to make under this section in favour of the child,

the court shall have regard to all the circumstances of the case including the matters mentioned in section 25(3)(a) to (e) above, and where the child of the family to whom the application relates is not the child of the respondent, including also the matters mentioned in section 25(4) above.

(3B) In relation to an application under this section on the ground mentioned in subsection (1)(a) above, section 25(2)(c) above shall have effect as if for the reference therein to the breakdown of the marriage there were substituted a reference to the failure to provide reasonable maintenance for the applicant, and in relation to an application under this section on the ground mentioned in subsection (1)(b) above, section 25(2)(c) above (as it applies by virtue of section 25(3)(e) above) shall have effect as if for the reference therein to the breakdown of the marriage there were substituted a reference to the failure to provide, or to make a proper contribution towards, reasonable maintenance for the child of the family to whom the application relates.

(4) (*repealed*)

(5) Where on an application under this section it appears to the court that the applicant or any child of the family to whom the application relates is in immediate need of financial assistance, but it is not yet possible to determine what order, if any, should be made on the application, the court may make an interim order for maintenance, that is to say, an order requiring the respondent to make to the applicant until the determination of the application such periodical payments as the court thinks reasonable.

(6) Where on an application under this section the applicant satisfies the court of any ground mentioned in subsection (1) above, the court may make any one or more of the following orders, that is to say–

(a)　an order that the respondent shall make to the applicant such periodical payments, for such term, as may be specified in the order;

(b)　an order that the respondent shall secure to the applicant, to the satisfaction of the court, such periodical payments, for such term, as may be so specified;

(c)　an order that the respondent shall pay to the applicant such lump sum as may be so specified;

(d)　an order that the respondent shall make to such person as may be specified in the order for the benefit of the child to whom the application relates, or to that child, such periodical payments, for such term, as may be so specified;

(e)　an order that the respondent shall secure to such person as may be so specified for the benefit of that child, or to that child, to the satisfaction of the court, such periodical payments, for such term, as may be so specified;

(f) an order that the respondent shall pay to such person as may be so specified for the benefit of that child, or to that child, such lump sum as may be so specified;

subject, however, in the case of an order under paragraph (d), (e) or (f) above, to the restrictions imposed by section 29(1) and (3) below on the making of financial provision orders in favour of children who have attained the age of eighteen.

(6A) An application for the variation under section 31 of this Act of a periodical payments order or secured periodical payments order made under this section in favour of a child may, if the child has attained the age of sixteen, be made by the child himself.

(6B) Where a periodical payments order made in favour of a child under this section ceases to have effect on the date on which the child attains the age of sixteen or at any time after that date but before or on the date on which he attains the age of eighteen, then, if at any time before he attains the age of twenty-one an application is made by the child for an order under this subsection, the court shall have power by order to revive the first-mentioned order from such date as the court may specify, not being earlier than the date of the making of the application, and to exercise its powers under section 31 of this Act in relation to any order so revived.

(7) Without prejudice to the generality of subsection (6)(c) or (f) above, an order under this section for the payment of a lump sum–

(a) may be made for the purpose of enabling any liabilities or expenses reasonably incurred in maintaining the applicant or any child of the family to whom the application relates before the making of the application to be met;

(b) may provide for the payment of that sum by instalments of such amount as may be specified in the order and may require the payment of the instalments to be secured to the satisfaction of the court.

(8) (*repealed*)

Amendments—Domestic Proceedings and Magistrates Courts Act 1978; Family Law Reform Act 1987; Matrimonial and Family Proceedings Act 1984; Civil Jurisdiction and Judgments (Maintenance) Regulations 2011.

Additional provisions with respect to financial provision and property adjustment orders

28 Duration of continuing financial provision orders in favour of party to marriage, and effect of remarriage or formation of civil partnership

(1) Subject in the case of an order made on or after the grant of a decree of a divorce or nullity of marriage to the provisions of sections 25A(2) above and 31(7) below, the term to be specified in a periodical payments or secured periodical payments order in favour of a party to a marriage shall be such term as the court thinks fit, except that the term shall not begin before or extend beyond the following limits, that is to say–

(a) in the case of a periodical payments order, the term shall begin not earlier than the date of the making of an application for the order, and shall be so defined as not to extend beyond the death of either of the parties to the marriage or, where the order is made on or after the grant of a decree of divorce or nullity of marriage, the remarriage of, or formation of a civil partnership by, the party in whose favour the order is made; and

(b) in the case of a secured periodical payments order, the term shall begin not earlier than the date of the making of an application for the order, and shall be so defined as not to extend beyond the death or, where the order is made on or after the grant of such a decree, the remarriage of, or formation of a civil partnership by, the party in whose favour the order is made.

(1A) Where a periodical payments or secured periodical payments order in favour of a party to a marriage is made on or after the grant of a decree of divorce or nullity of marriage, the court may direct that that party shall not be entitled to apply under section 31 below for the extension of the term specified in the order.

(2) Where a periodical payments or secured periodical payments order in favour of a party to a marriage is made otherwise than on or after the grant of a decree of divorce or nullity of marriage, and the marriage in question is subsequently dissolved or annulled but the order continues in force, the order shall, notwithstanding anything in it, cease to have effect on the remarriage of, or formation of a civil partnership by, that party, except in relation to any arrears due under it on the date of the remarriage or formation of the civil partnership.

(3) If after the grant of a decree dissolving or annulling a marriage either party to that marriage remarries whether at any time before or after the commencement of this Act or forms a civil partnership, that party shall not be entitled to apply, by reference to the grant of that decree, for a financial provision order in his or her favour, or for a property adjustment order, against the other party to that marriage.

Amendments—Civil Partnership Act 2004; Maintenance Orders (Backdating) Order 1993; Matrimonial and Family Proceedings Act 1984.

29 Duration of continuing financial provision orders in favour of children, and age limit on making certain orders in their favour

(1) Subject to subsection (3) below, no financial provision order and no order for a transfer of property under section 24(1)(a) above shall be made in favour of a child who has attained the age of eighteen.

(2) The term to be specified in a periodical payments or secured periodical payments order in favour of a child may begin with the date of the making of an application for the order in question or any later date or a date ascertained in accordance with subsection (5) or (6) below but—

(a) shall not in the first instance extend beyond the date of the birthday of the child next following his attaining the upper limit of the compulsory school age (that is to say, the age that is for the time being that limit by virtue of section 35 of the Education Act 1944 together with any Order in Council made under that section) unless the court considers that in the circumstances of the case the welfare of the child requires that it should extend to a later date; and

(b) shall not in any event, subject to subsection (3) below, extend beyond the date of the child's eighteenth birthday.

(3) Subsection (1) above, and paragraph (b) of subsection (2), shall not apply in the case of a child, if it appears to the court that—

(a) the child is, or will be, or if an order were made without complying with either or both of those provisions would be, receiving instruction at an educational establishment or undergoing training for a trade, profession or vocation, whether or not he is also, or will also be, in gainful employment; or

(b) there are special circumstances which justify the making of an order without complying with either or both of those provisions.

(4) Any periodical payments order in favour of a child shall, notwithstanding anything in the order, cease to have effect on the death of the person liable to make payments under the order, except in relation to any arrears due under the order on the date of the death.

(5) Where—

(a) a *maintenance assessment* [maintenance calculation] ('the *current assessment* [current calculation]') is in force with respect to a child; and

(b) an application is made under Part II of this Act for a periodical payments or secured periodical payments order in favour of that child –
  (i) in accordance with section 8 of the Child Support Act 1991, and
  (ii) before the end of the period of 6 months beginning with the making of the *current assessment* [current calculation],

the term to be specified in any such order made on that application may be expressed to begin on, or at any time after, the earliest permitted date.

(6) For the purposes of subsection (5) above, 'the earliest permitted date' is whichever is the later of –

(a) the date 6 months before the application is made; or

(b) the date on which the *current assessment* [current calculation] took effect or, where successive *maintenance assessments* [maintenance calculations] have been continuously in force with respect to a child, on which the first of *those assessments* [those calculations] took effect.

(7) Where—

(a)　a *maintenance assessment* [maintenance calculation] ceases to have effect *or is cancelled* by or under any provision of the Child Support Act 1991; and

(b)　an application is made, before the end of the period of 6 months beginning with the relevant date, for a periodical payments or secured periodical payments order in favour of a child with respect to whom that *maintenance assessment* [maintenance calculation] was in force immediately before it ceased to have effect *or was cancelled*,

the term to be specified in any such order made on that application may begin with the date on which that *maintenance assessment* [maintenance calculation] ceased to have effect *or, as the case may be, the date with effect from which it was cancelled*, or any later date.

(8) In subsection (7)(b) above—

(a)　where the *maintenance assessment* [maintenance calculation] ceased to have effect, the relevant date is the date on which it so ceased; and

(b)　where the maintenance assessment was cancelled, the relevant date is the later of—

(i)　the date on which the person who cancelled it did so, *and*

(ii)　the date from which the cancellation first had effect.

Amendments—Matrimonial and Family Proceedings Act 1984; Maintenance Orders (Backdating) Order 1993; Education Act 1993; SI 1993/623.

Prospective Amendments—Words in square brackets substituted for preceding words in italics and words in italics repealed for certain purposes by Child Support, Pensions and Social Security Act 2000, ss 26, 85, Sch 3, para 3(1), (2), Sch 9, Pt I (not in force otherwise).

30 Direction for settlement of instrument for securing payments or effecting property adjustment

Where the court decides to make a financial provision order requiring any payments to be secured or a property adjustment order—

(a)　it may direct that the matter be referred to one of the conveyancing counsel of the court for him to settle a proper instrument to be executed by all necessary parties; and

(b)　where the order is to be made in proceedings for divorce, nullity of marriage or judicial separation it may, if it thinks fit, defer the grant of the decree in question until the instrument has been duly executed.

Variation, discharge and enforcement of certain orders, etc

31 Variation, discharge etc of certain orders for financial relief

(1) Where the court has made an order to which this section applies, then, subject to the provisions of this section and of section 28(1A) above, the court shall have power to vary or discharge the order or to suspend any provision thereof temporarily and to revive the operation of any provision so suspended.

(2) This section applies to the following orders, that is to say—

(a) any order for maintenance pending suit and any interim order for maintenance;

(b) any periodical payments order;

(c) any secured periodical payments order;

(d) any order made by virtue of section 23(3)(c) or 27(7)(b) above (provision for payment of a lump sum by installments);

(dd) any deferred order made by virtue of section 21(1)(c) (lump sums) which includes provision made by virtue of—

    (i) section 25B(4),

    (ii) section 25C, or

    (iii) section 25F(2),

    (provision in respect of pension rights or pension compensation rights);

(e) any order for a settlement of property under section 24(1)(b) or for a variation of settlement under section 24(1)(c) or (d) above, being an order made on or after the grant of a decree of judicial separation;

(f) any order made under section 24A(1) above for the sale of property.

(g) a pension sharing order under section 24B above, or a pension compensation sharing order under section 24E above, which is made at a time before the decree has been made absolute.

(2A) Where the court has made an order referred to in subsection (2)(a), (b) or (c) above, then, subject to the provisions of this section, the court shall have power to remit the payment of any arrears due under the order or of any part thereof.

(2B) Where the court has made an order referred to in subsection (2)(dd)(ii) above, this section shall cease to apply to the order on the death of either of the parties to the marriage.

(3) The powers exercisable by the court under this section in relation to an order shall be exercisable also in relation to any instrument executed in pursuance of the order.

(4) The court shall not exercise the powers conferred by this section in relation to an order for a settlement under section 24(1)(b) or for a variation of settlement under section 24(1)(c) or (d) above except on an application made in proceedings—

(a) for the rescission of the decree of judicial separation by reference to which the order was made, or

(b) for the dissolution of the marriage in question.

(4A) In relation to an order which falls within paragraph (g) of subsection (2) above ('the subsection (2) order')—

(a) the powers conferred by this section may be exercised—

    (i) only on an application made before the subsection (2) order has or, but for paragraph (b) below, would have taken effect; and

    (ii) only if, at the time when the application is made, the decree has not been made absolute; and

(b)   an application made in accordance with paragraph (a) above prevents the subsection (2) order from taking effect before the application has been dealt with.

(4B) No variation of a pension sharing order, or a pension compensation sharing order, shall be made so as to take effect before the decree is made absolute.

(4C) The variation of a pension sharing order, or a pension compensation sharing order, prevents the order taking effect before the end of such period after the making of the variation as may be prescribed by regulations made by the Lord Chancellor.

(5) Subject to subsections (7A) to (7G) below and without prejudice to any power exercisable by virtue of subsection (2)(d), (dd), (e) or (g) above or otherwise than by virtue of this section, no property adjustment order or pension sharing order, or a pension compensation sharing order, shall be made on an application for the variation of a periodical payments or secured periodical payments order made (whether in favour of a party to a marriage or in favour of a child of the family) under section 23 above, and no order for the payment of a lump sum shall be made on an application for the variation of a periodical payments or secured periodical payments order in favour of a party to a marriage (whether made under section 23 or under section 27 above).

(6) Where the person liable to make payments under a secured periodical payments order has died, an application under this section relating to that order (and to any order made under section 24A(1) above which requires the proceeds of sale of property to be used for securing those payments) may be made by the person entitled to payments under the periodical payments order or by the personal representatives of the deceased person, but no such application shall, except with the permission of the court, be made after the end of the period of six months from the date on which representation in regard to the estate of that person is first taken out.

(7) In exercising the powers conferred by this section the court shall have regard to all the circumstances of the case, first consideration being given to the welfare while a minor of any child of the family who has not attained the age of eighteen, and the circumstances of the case shall include any change in any of the matters to which the court was required to have regard when making the order to which the application relates, and—

(a)   in the case of a periodical payments or secured periodical payments order made on or after the grant of a decree of divorce or nullity of marriage, the court shall consider whether in all the circumstances and after having regard to any such change it would be appropriate to vary the order so that payments under the order are required to be made or secured only for such further period as will in the opinion of the court be sufficient (in the light of any proposed exercise by the court, where the marriage has been dissolved, of its powers under subsection (7B) below) to enable the party in whose favour the order was made to adjust without undue hardship to the termination of those payments;

(b) in a case where the party against whom the order was made has died, the circumstances of the case shall also include the changed circumstances resulting from his or her death.

(7A) Subsection (7B) below applies where, after the dissolution of a marriage, the court—

(a) discharges a periodical payments order or secured periodical payments order made in favour of a party to the marriage; or

(b) varies such an order so that payments under the order are required to be made or secured only for such further period as is determined by the court.

(7B) The court has power, in addition to any power it has apart from this subsection, to make supplemental provision consisting of any of—

(a) an order for the payment of a lump sum in favour of a party to the marriage;

(b) one or more property adjustment orders in favour of a party to the marriage;

(ba) one or more pension sharing orders;

(bb) a pension compensation sharing order;

(c) a direction that the party in whose favour the original order discharged or varied was made is not entitled to make any further application for—

(i) a periodical payments or secured periodical payments order, or

(ii) an extension of the period to which the original order is limited by any variation made by the court.

(7C) An order for the payment of a lump sum made under subsection (7B) above may—

(a) provide for the payment of that sum by instalments of such amount as may be specified in the order; and

(b) require the payment of the instalments to be secured to the satisfaction of the court.

(7D) Section 23(6) above applies where the court makes an order for the payment of a lump sum under subsection (7B) above as it applies where the court makes such an order under section 23 above.

(7E) If under subsection (7B) above the court makes more than one property adjustment order in favour of the same party to the marriage, each of those orders must fall within a different paragraph of section 21(2) above.

(7F) Sections 24A and 30 above apply where the court makes a property adjustment order under subsection (7B) above as they apply where it makes such an order under section 24 above.

(7G) Subsections (3) to (5) of section 24B above apply in relation to a pension sharing order under subsection (7B) above as they apply in relation to a pension sharing order under that section.

(7H) Subsections (3) to (10) of section 24E above apply in relation to a pension compensation sharing order under subsection (7B) above as they apply in relation to a pension compensation sharing order under that section.

(8) The personal representatives of a deceased person against whom a secured periodical payments order was made shall not be liable for having distributed any part of the estate of the deceased after the expiration of the period of six months referred to in subsection (6) above on the ground that they ought to have taken into account the possibility that the court might permit an application under this section to be made after that period by the person entitled to payments under the order; but this subsection shall not prejudice any power to recover any part of the estate so distributed arising by virtue of the making of an order in pursuance of this section.

(9) In considering for the purposes of subsection (6) above the question when representation was first taken out, a grant limited to settled land or to trust property shall be left out of account and a grant limited to real estate or to personal estate shall be left out of account unless a grant limited to the remainder of the estate has previously been made or is made at the same time.

(10) Where the court, in exercise of its powers under this section, decides to vary or discharge a periodical payments or secured periodical payments order, then, subject to section 28(1) and (2) above, the court shall have power to direct that the variation or discharge shall not take effect until the expiration of such period as may be specified in the order.

(11) Where—

(a)   a periodical payments or secured periodical payments order in favour of more than one child ('the order') is in force;

(b)   the order requires payments specified in it to be made to or for the benefit of more than one child without apportioning those payments between them;

(c)   a *maintenance assessment* [maintenance calculation] ('*the assessment* [the calculation]') is made with respect to one or more, but not all, of the children with respect to whom those payments are to be made; and

(d)   an application is made, before the end of the period of 6 months beginning with the date on which *the assessment* [the calculation] was made, for the variation or discharge of the order,

the court may, in exercise of its powers under this section to vary or discharge the order, direct that the variation or discharge shall take effect from the date on which *the assessment* [the calculation] took effect or any later date.

(12) Where—

(a)   an order ('the child order') of a kind prescribed for the purposes of section 10(1) of the Child Support Act 1991 is affected by a *maintenance assessment* [maintenance calculation];

(b)   on the date on which the child order became so affected there was in force a periodical payments or secured periodical payments order ('the spousal order') in favour of a party to a marriage having the care of the child in whose favour the child order was made; and

(c) an application is made, before the end of the period of 6 months beginning with the date on which the *maintenance assessment* [maintenance calculation] was made, for the spousal order to be varied or discharged,

the court may, in exercise of its powers under this section to vary or discharge the spousal order, direct that the variation or discharge shall take effect from the date on which the child order became so affected or any later date.

(13) For the purposes of subsection (12) above, an order is affected if it ceases to have effect or is modified by or under section 10 of the Child Support Act 1991.

(14) Subsections (11) and (12) above are without prejudice to any other power of the court to direct that the variation of discharge of an order under this section shall take effect from a date earlier than that on which the order for variation or discharge was made.

(15) The power to make regulations under subsection (4C) above shall be exercisable by statutory instrument which shall be subject to annulment in pursuance of a resolution of either House of Parliament.

Amendments—Matrimonial and Family Proceedings Act 1984; Matrimonial Homes and Property Act 1981; Administration of Justice Act 1982; Maintenance Orders (Backdating) Order 1993; Pensions Act 1995, s 166(3), Family Law Act 1996; Welfare Reform and Pensions Act 1999.

Prospective Amendments—Words in square brackets substituted for preceding words in italics for certain purposes by Child Support, Pensions and Social Security Act 2000, ss 26, 85, Sch 3, para 3(1), (3) (not in force otherwise). ; Sub-s (7FA): inserted with savings by the Family Law Act 1996 with effect from a date to be appointed. Subsections (2), (4B), (4C), (5), (7B) amended and (7H) inserted by Pensions Act 2008, s 120, Sch 6, Pt 1, paras 1, 8.

32 Payment of certain arrears unenforceable without the leave of the court

(1) A person shall not be entitled to enforce through the High Court or any county court the payment of any arrears due under an order for maintenance pending suit, an interim order for maintenance or any financial provision order without the leave of that court if those arrears became due more than twelve months before proceedings to enforce the payment of them are begun.

(2) The court hearing an application for the grant of leave under this section may refuse leave, or may grant leave subject to such restrictions and conditions (including conditions as to the allowing of time for payment or the making of payment by instalments) as that court thinks proper, or may remit the payment of the arrears or of any part thereof.

(3) An application for the grant of leave under this section shall be made in such manner as may be prescribed by rules of court.

33 Orders for repayment in certain cases of sums paid under certain orders

(1) Where on an application made under this section in relation to an order to which this section applies it appears to the court that by reason of–

(a) a change in the circumstances of the person entitled to, or liable to make, payments under the order since the order was made, or

(b) the changed circumstances resulting from the death of the person so liable,

the amount received by the person entitled to payments under the order in respect of a period after those circumstances changed or after the death of the person liable to make payments under the order, as the case may be, exceeds the amount which the person so liable or his or her personal representatives should have been required to pay, the court may order the respondent to the application to pay to the applicant such sum, not exceeding the amount of the excess, as the court thinks just.

(2) This section applies to the following orders, that is to say–

(a) any order for maintenance pending suit and any interim order for maintenance;

(b) any periodical payments order; and

(c) any secured periodical payments order.

(3) An application under this section may be made by the person liable to make payments under an order to which this section applies or his or her personal representatives and may be made against the person entitled to payments under the order or her or his personal representatives.

(4) An application under this section may be made in proceedings in the High Court or a county court for–

(a) the variation or discharge of the order to which this section applies, or

(b) leave to enforce, or the enforcement of, the payment of arrears under that order;

but when not made in such proceedings shall be made to a county court, and accordingly references in this section to the court are references to the High Court or a county court, as the circumstances require.

(5) The jurisdiction conferred on a county court by this section shall be exercisable notwithstanding that by reason of the amount claimed in the application the jurisdiction would not but for this subsection be exercisable by a county court.

(6) An order under this section for the payment of any sum may provide for the payment of that sum by instalments of such amount as may be specified in the order.

Consent orders

33A Consent orders for financial provision on property adjustment

(1) Notwithstanding anything in the preceding provisions of this Part of this Act, on an application for a consent order for financial relief the court may, unless it has reason to think that there are other circumstances into which it ought to inquire, make an order in the terms agreed on the basis only of the prescribed information furnished with the application.

(2) Subsection (1) above applies to an application for a consent order varying or discharging an order for financial relief as it applies to an application for an order for financial relief.

(3) In this section–

'consent order', in relation to an application for an order, means an order in the terms applied for to which the respondent agrees;
'order for financial relief' means an order under any of sections 23, 24, 24A, 24B or 27 above; and
'prescribed' means prescribed by rules of court.

Amendments—Matrimonial and Family Proceedings Act 1984; Welfare Reform and Pensions Act 1999.

Maintenance agreements

34 Validity of maintenance agreements

(1) If a maintenance agreement includes a provision purporting to restrict any right to apply to a court for an order containing financial arrangements, then–

(a) that provision shall be void; but
(b) any other financial arrangements contained in the agreement shall not thereby be rendered void or unenforceable and shall, unless they are void or unenforceable for any other reason (and subject to sections 35 and 36 below), be binding on the parties to the agreement.

(2) In this section and in section 35 below–

'maintenance agreement' means any agreement in writing made, whether before or after the commencement of this Act, between the parties to a marriage, being–
(a) an agreement containing financial arrangements, whether made during the continuance or after the dissolution or annulment of the marriage; or
(b) a separation agreement which contains no financial arrangements in a case where no other agreement in writing between the same parties contains such arrangements;

'financial arrangements' means provisions governing the rights and liabilities towards one another when living separately of the parties to a marriage (including a marriage which has been dissolved or annulled) in respect of the making or securing of payments or the disposition or use of any property, including such rights and liabilities with respect to the maintenance or education of any child, whether or not a child of the family.

35 Alteration of agreements by court during lives of parties

(1) Where a maintenance agreement is for the time being subsisting and each of the parties to the agreement is for the time being either domiciled or resident in England and Wales, then, subject to subsections (1A) and (3) below, either party may apply to the court or to a magistrates' court for an order under this section.

(1A) If an application or part of an application relates to a matter where jurisdiction falls to be determined by reference to the jurisdictional requirements of the Maintenance Regulation and Schedule 6 to the Civil Jurisdiction and Judgments (Maintenance) Regulations 2011 –

    (a)   the requirement as to domicile or residence in subsection (1) does not apply to the application or that part of it, but

    (b)   the court may not entertain the application or that part of it unless it has jurisdiction to do so by virtue of that Regulation and that Schedule.

(2) If the court to which the application is made is satisfied either–

    (a)   that by reason of a change in the circumstances in the light of which any financial arrangements contained in the agreement were made or, as the case may be, financial arrangements were omitted from it (including a change foreseen by the parties when making the agreement), the agreement should be altered so as to make different, or, as the case may be, so as to contain, financial arrangements, or

    (b)   that the agreement does not contain proper financial arrangements with respect to any child of the family,

then subject to subsections (3), (4) and (5) below, that court may by order make such alterations in the agreement–

    (i)   by varying or revoking any financial arrangements contained in it, or

    (ii)   by inserting in it financial arrangements for the benefit of one of the parties to the agreement or of a child of the family,

as may appear to that court to be just having regard to all the circumstances, including, if relevant, the matters mentioned in section 25(4) above; and the agreement shall have effect thereafter as if any alteration made by the order had been made by agreement between the parties and for valuable consideration.

(3) A magistrates' court shall not entertain an application under subsection (1) above unless both the parties to the agreement are resident in England and Wales the court acts in, or is authorised by the Lord Chancellor to act for, a local justice area in which at least one of the parties is resident, and shall not have power to make any order on such an application except–

    (a)   in a case where the agreement includes no provision for periodical payments by either of the parties, an order inserting provision for the making by one of the parties of periodical payments for the maintenance of the other party or for the maintenance of any child of the family;

(b) in a case where the agreement includes provision for the making by one of the parties of periodical payments, an order increasing or reducing the rate of, or terminating, any of those payments.

(4) Where a court decides to alter, by order under this section, an agreement by inserting provision for the making or securing by one of the parties to the agreement of periodical payments for the maintenance of the other party or by increasing the rate of the periodical payments which the agreement provides shall be made by one of the parties for the maintenance of the other, the term for which the payments or, as the case may be, the additional payments attributable to the increase are to be made under the agreement as altered by the order shall be such term as the court may specify, subject to the following limits, that is to say–

(a) where the payments will not be secured, the term shall be so defined as not to extend beyond the death of either of the parties to the agreement or the remarriage of, or formation of a civil partnership by, the party to whom the payments are to be made;

(b) where the payments will be secured, the term shall be so defined as not to extend beyond the death or remarriage of, or formation of a civil partnership by, that party.

(5) Where a court decides to alter, by order under this section, an agreement by inserting provision for the making or securing by one of the parties to the agreement of periodical payments for the maintenance of a child of the family or by increasing the rate of the periodical payments which the agreement provides shall be made or secured by one of the parties for the maintenance of such a child, then, in deciding the term for which under the agreement as altered by the order the payments, or as the case may be, the additional payments attributable to the increase are to be made or secured for the benefit of the child, the court shall apply the provisions of section 29(2) and (3) above as to age limits as if the order in question were a periodical payments or secured periodical payments order in favour of the child.

(6) For the avoidance of doubt it is hereby declared that nothing in this section or in section 34 above affects any power of a court before which any proceedings between the parties to a maintenance agreement are brought under any other enactment (including a provision of this Act) to make an order containing financial arrangements or any right of either party to apply for such an order in such proceedings.

Amendments—Civil Partnership Act 2004; Courts Act 2003; Matrimonial and Family Proceedings Act 1984; Civil Jurisdiction and Judgments (Maintenance) Regulations 2011.

36 Alteration of agreements by court after death of one party

(1) Where a maintenance agreement within the meaning of section 34 above provides for the continuation of payments under the agreement after the death

of one of the parties and that party dies domiciled in England and Wales, the surviving party or the personal representatives of the deceased party may, subject to subsections (2) and (3) below, apply to the High Court or a county court for an order under section 35 above.

(2) An application under this section shall not, except with the permission of the High Court or a county court, be made after the end of the period of six months from the date on which representation in regard to the estate of the deceased is first taken out.

(3) A county court shall not entertain an application under this section, or an application for permission to make an application under this section, unless it would have jurisdiction by virtue of section 22 of the Inheritance (Provision for Family and Dependants) Act 1975 (which confers jurisdiction on county courts in proceedings under that Act if the value of the property mentioned in that section does not exceed £5,000 or such larger sum as may be fixed by order of the Lord Chancellor) to hear and determine proceedings for an order under section 2 of that Act in relation to the deceased's estate.

(4) If a maintenance agreement is altered by a court on an application made in pursuance of subsection (1) above, the like consequences shall ensue as if the alteration had been made immediately before the death by agreement between the parties and for valuable consideration.

(5) The provisions of this section shall not render the personal representatives of the deceased liable for having distributed any part of the estate of the deceased after the expiration of the period of six months referred to in subsection (2) above on the ground that they ought to have taken into account the possibility that a court might permit an application by virtue of this section to be made by the surviving party after that period; but this subsection shall not prejudice any power to recover any part of the estate so distributed arising by virtue of the making of an order in pursuance of this section.

(6) Section 31(9) above shall apply for the purposes of subsection (2) above as it applies for the purposes of subsection (6) of section 31.

(7) Subsection (3) of section 22 of the Inheritance (Provision for Family and Dependants) Act 1975 (which enables rules of court to provide for the transfer from a county court to the High Court or from the High Court to a county court of proceedings for an order under section 2 of that Act) and paragraphs (a) and (b) of subsection (4) of that section (provisions relating to proceedings commenced in county court before coming into force of order of the Lord Chancellor under that section) shall apply in relation to proceedings consisting of any such application as is referred to in subsection (3) above as they apply in relation to proceedings for an order under section 2 of that Act.

Amendments—Inheritance (Provision for Family and Dependants) Act 1975.

* * * *

52 Interpretation

(1) In this Act—

'child', in relation to one or both of the parties to a marriage, includes an illegitimate child of that party or, as the case may be, of both parties;

'child of the family', in relation to the parties to a marriage, means—

(a)   a child of both of those parties; and

(b)   any other child, not being a child who is placed with those parties as foster parents by a local authority or voluntary organisation, who has been treated by both of those parties as a child of their family;

'the court' (except where the context otherwise requires) means the High Court or, where a county court has jurisdiction by virtue of Part V of the Matrimonial and Family Proceedings Act 1984, a county court;

'education' includes training;

'*maintenance assessment* [maintenance calculation]' has the same meaning as it has in the Child Support Act 1991 by virtue of section 54 of that Act as read with any regulations in force under that section.

'the Maintenance Regulation' means Council Regulation (EC) No 4/2009 including as applied in relation to Denmark by virtue of the Agreement made on 19th October 2005 between the European Community and the Kingdom of Denmark;

(2) In this Act—

(a)   references to financial provision orders, periodical payments and secured periodical payments orders and orders for the payment of a lump sum, and references to property adjustment orders, shall be construed in accordance with section 21 above;

(aa)   references to pension sharing orders shall be construed in accordance with section 21A above; and

(b)   references to orders for maintenance pending suit and to interim orders for maintenance shall be construed respectively in accordance with section 22 and section 27(5) above.

(3) For the avoidance of doubt it is hereby declared that references in this Act to remarriage include references to a marriage which is by law void or voidable.

(3A) References in this Act to the formation of a civil partnership by a person include references to a civil partnership which is by law void or voidable.

(4) Except where the contrary intention is indicated, references in this Act to any enactment include references to that enactment as amended, extended or applied by or under any subsequent enactment, including this Act.

Amendments—Children Act 1975; Children Act 1989; Matrimonial and Family Proceedings Act 1984; Maintenance Orders (Backdating) Order 1993, SI 1993/623; Welfare Reform and Pensions Act 1999; Civil Partnership Act 2004; definition 'the Maintenance Regulation' inserted by Civil Jurisdiction and Judgments (Maintenance) Regulations 2011, SI 2011/1484.

Prospective Amendments—Words in square brackets substituted for preceding words in italics for certain purposes by Child Support, Pensions and Social Security Act 2000, ss 26, 85, Sch 3, para 3(1), (4) (not in force otherwise).

* * * *

APPENDIX 2

STATUTORY INSTRUMENTS

ARMED FORCES (FORFEITURES AND DEDUCTIONS) REGULATIONS 2009

SI 2009/1109

PART 1

Forfeitures and Deductions

1 Citation and commencement

These Regulations may be cited as the Armed Forces (Forfeitures and Deductions) Regulations 2009 and shall come into force on 31st October 2009.

2 Interpretation

In these Regulations—

"the Act" means the Armed Forces Act 2006 and, unless expressly provided otherwise, a reference in these Regulations to a numbered section is a reference to that section of the Act;

"AA 1955" means the Army Act 1955;

"AFA 1955" means the Air Force Act 1955;

"NDA 1957" means the Naval Discipline Act 1957;

"the 2000 Council Regulation" means Council Regulation (EC) No 44/2001 of 22nd December 2000 on jurisdiction and the recognition and enforcement of judgments in civil and commercial matters, as amended from time to time and as applied by the Agreement made on 19th October 2005 between the European Community and the Kingdom of Denmark on jurisdiction and the recognition and enforcement of judgments in civil and commercial matters;

"the 2007 Hague Convention" means the Convention on the International Recovery of Child Support and other forms of Family Maintenance done at The Hague on 23rd November 2007;

"the Maintenance Regulation" means Council Regulation (EC) No 4/2009 including as applied in relation to Denmark by virtue of the Agreement made on 19th October 2005 between the European Community and the Kingdom of Denmark;

"Sovereign Base Areas" means the Sovereign Base Areas of Akrotiri and Dhekelia.

Amendments—SI 2012/2814; SI 2012/1484.

* * * *

4 Deduction from pay—amount paid to meet sum ordered to be paid by civilian court

(1) Subject to paragraph (2), the Defence Council, or an officer authorised by them, may make an order authorising a deduction to be made from the pay of a relevant person and to be appropriated in or towards satisfaction of any amount paid by or on behalf of a service authority to meet the whole or part of a relevant sum.

(2) An order made under paragraph (1) may only authorise a deduction to be made on or after the date on which the relevant sum is required to be paid.

(3) Subject to paragraph (2), the Defence Council, or an officer authorised by them, may by order vary an order made under paragraph (1).

(4) The Defence Council, or an officer authorised by them, may by order revoke an order made under paragraph (1).

(5) In this regulation "relevant sum" means a sum that a relevant person has been ordered to pay by a civilian court (anywhere).

* * * *

7 Deduction from pay—United Kingdom or Sovereign Base Areas maintenance order

(1) Subject to paragraph (2), the Defence Council, or an officer authorised by them, may make an order authorising a deduction to be made from the pay of a relevant person and to be appropriated in or towards satisfaction of a payment which he is required to make under a maintenance order of a court in the United Kingdom or the Sovereign Base Areas.

(2) An order made under paragraph (1) may only authorise a deduction to be made on or after the date on which the payment is required to be made.

(3) Subject to paragraph (2), the Defence Council, or an officer authorised by them, may by order vary an order made under paragraph (1).

(4) The Defence Council, or an officer authorised by them, may by order revoke an order made under paragraph (1).

(5) The Defence Council, or an officer authorised by them, may treat an order made under paragraph (1) as being in suspense during any period in which the relevant person's pay is suspended.

8 Deduction from pay—external maintenance order

(1) This regulation applies with respect to a maintenance order of a court, tribunal or person outside the United Kingdom and the Sovereign Base Areas (an "external maintenance order").

(2) Subject to paragraph (4), if an external maintenance order has been registered in or confirmed by a court in the United Kingdom, the Defence Council, or an officer authorised by them, may make an order authorising a deduction to be made from the pay of a relevant person and to be appropriated in or towards satisfaction of a payment which he is required to make under the maintenance order as so registered or confirmed, subject to any variation for the time being made to the maintenance order by such a court.

(2A) Subject to paragraph (5), if an external maintenance order is enforceable in the United Kingdom without prior registration by virtue of Section 1 of Chapter IV of the Maintenance Regulation, the Defence Council, or an officer authorised by them, may make an order authorising a deduction to be made from the pay of a relevant person and to be appropriated in or towards satisfaction of a payment which he is required to make under the maintenance order.

(3) Subject to paragraph (5), if an external maintenance order has not been registered in or confirmed by a court in the United Kingdom, but the Defence Council are, or the authorised officer is, satisfied either—

    (a)   that the maintenance order is capable of being registered in a court in the United Kingdom, or

    (b)   that the maintenance order would be capable of being so registered but for the fact that the relevant person is serving in the Armed Forces outside the United Kingdom,

the Defence Council or the authorised officer may make an order authorising a deduction to be made from the pay of a relevant person and to be appropriated in or towards satisfaction of a payment which he is required to make under the maintenance order.

(4) order made under paragraph (2) may only authorise a deduction to be made on or after the date on which the payment is required to be made under the maintenance order as registered in, or confirmed by, the court in the United Kingdom, including any variation for the time being made to that order by such a court.

(5) An order made under paragraph (2A) or (3) may only authorise a deduction to be made on or after the date on which the payment is required to be made under the maintenance order.

(6) An order made under paragraph (3) may provide –

  (a)   that it shall continue in force for a specified period, or
  (b)   that it shall continue in force until the occurrence of a specified event,

and for the earlier termination of the order if a specified event has not occurred within a specified period.

(7) Subject to paragraphs (4) and (5), the Defence Council, or an officer authorised by them, may by order vary an order made under this regulation.

(8) The Defence Council, or an officer authorised by them, may by order revoke an order made under this regulation.

(9) The Defence Council, or an officer authorised by them, may treat an order made under this regulation as being in suspense during any period in which the relevant person's pay is suspended.

(10) In this regulation—

- (a) a reference to a maintenance order being registered in a court in the United Kingdom means registered in such a court under –
    - (i) the Maintenance Orders (Facilities for Enforcement) Act 1920;
    - (ii) Part 1 of the Maintenance Orders (Reciprocal Enforcement) Act 1972;
    - (iii) Part 1 of the Civil Jurisdiction and Judgments Act 1982;
    - (iv) the 2000 Council Regulation;
    - (v) Section 2 of Chapter IV of the Maintenance Regulation; or
    - (vi) the 2007 Hague Convention,
- (b) a reference to a maintenance order confirmed by a court in the United Kingdom means confirmed in such a court under the Maintenance Orders (Facilities for Enforcement) Act 1920.

Amendments—SI 2011/1484; SI 2012/2814.

9 "Maintenance order", "spouse" and "civil partner"

(1) Subject to paragraph (2), in regulations 7 and 8 "maintenance order" means an order requiring a relevant person to make a payment for or in respect of –

- (a) the maintenance of his spouse or civil partner;
- (b) the maintenance of any child of his, his spouse or his civil partner;
- (c) the maintenance of any other child who has been treated by him and his spouse, or by him and his civil partner, as a child of their family;
- (d) any costs incurred in obtaining an order within sub-paragraph (a), (b) or (c); or
- (e) any costs incurred in proceedings on appeal against, or for the variation, revocation or revival of an order within sub-paragraph (a), (b) or (c).

(2) For the purposes of regulation 8, "order" in paragraph (1) includes an authentic instrument or court settlement as referred to in –

- (a) section 13 of the Civil Jurisdiction and Judgments Act 1982
- (b) the 2000 Council Regulation, or]
- (c) the Maintenance Regulation,

and the expression "maintenance order" is to be read accordingly.

(2A) For the purposes of regulation 8, a reference to a maintenance order is to include a reference to a maintenance arrangement which is to be recognised and enforceable in the same way as a maintenance decision by virtue of Article 30 of the 2007 Hague Convention.

(3) References in paragraph (1) to the spouse of a relevant person include, in relation to an order made in proceedings in connection with the dissolution or annulment of a marriage, references to the person who would have been his spouse if the marriage had subsisted.

(4) References in paragraph (1) to the civil partner of a relevant person include, in relation to an order made in proceedings in connection with the dissolution or annulment of a civil partnership, references to the person who would have been his civil partner if the civil partnership had subsisted.

Amendments—SI 2011/1484; SI 2012/2814.

10 Deduction from pay—child maintenance

(1) Subject to paragraph (2), the Defence Council, or an officer authorised by them, may make an order authorising a deduction to be made from the pay of a relevant person and to be appropriated in or towards satisfaction of any obligation of his to make a periodical payment in respect of a child in accordance with a maintenance calculation or maintenance assessment made under the 1991 Act or the 1991 Order.

(2) An order made under paragraph (1) may only authorise a deduction to be made on or after the date on which the relevant person is obliged to make the periodical payment.

(3) Subject to paragraph (2), the Defence Council, or an officer authorised by them, may by order vary an order made under paragraph (1).

(4) The Defence Council, or an officer authorised by them, may by order revoke an order made under paragraph (1).

(5) The Defence Council, or an officer authorised by them, may treat an order made under paragraph (1) as being in suspense during any period in which the relevant person's pay is suspended.

(6) In this regulation –

(a) "the 1991 Act" means the Child Support Act 1991;
(b) "the 1991 Order" means the Child Support (Northern Ireland) Order 1991.

11 Deduction from pay—judgment or order enforceable by a United Kingdom court

(1) Subject to paragraphs (2) and (3), the Defence Council, or an officer authorised by them, may make an order authorising a deduction to be made from the pay of a relevant person and to be appropriated in or towards satisfaction of any amount required to be paid by him by virtue of any judgment or order enforceable by a court in the United Kingdom.

(2) Paragraph (1) shall not apply to –

(a) a relevant sum within regulation 4(1);

(b) any payment in respect of which a deduction may be authorised under regulation 7(1), 8(2) or 8(2A); or

(c) any sum in respect of which a deduction may be made by virtue of section 32(2)(b) of the Court Martial Appeals Act 1968.

(3) An order made under paragraph (1) may only authorise a deduction to be made on or after the date on which the amount is required to be paid.

(4) Subject to paragraph (3), the Defence Council, or an officer authorised by them, may by order vary an order made under paragraph (1).

(5) The Defence Council, or an officer authorised by them, may by order revoke an order made under paragraph (1).

(6) The Defence Council, or an officer authorised by them, may treat an order made under paragraph (1) as being in suspense during any period in which the relevant person's pay is suspended.

Amendments—SI 2011/1484.

CHILD SUPPORT (MEANING OF CHILD AND NEW CALCULATION RULES) (CONSEQUENTIAL AND MISCELLANEOUS AMENDMENT) REGULATIONS 2012

SI 2012/2785

PART 1
GENERAL

1 Citation, commencement and interpretation

(1) These Regulations may be cited as the Child Support (Meaning of Child and New Calculation Rules) (Consequential and Miscellaneous Amendment) Regulations 2012.

(2) This regulation and regulation 11 come into force on 10th December 2012.

(3) Regulations 2 and 3 come into force on the day on which section 42 of the 2008 Act (meaning of "child") comes into force.

(4) Subject to paragraph (5), regulations 4 to 10 and 12 come into force in relation to a particular case on the day on which paragraph 2 of Schedule 4 to the 2008 Act (calculation by reference to gross weekly income) comes into force in relation to that type of case.

(5) Regulations 4(3) to (6) and 12 come into force in relation to an arrears-only case on 10th December 2012, subject to the saving in regulation 11(1).

(6) In these Regulations –

"2008 Act" means the Child Maintenance and Other Payments Act 2008.

"arrears of child support maintenance" means any payment of child support maintenance

    (a)   which has become due in relation to a maintenance assessment, or a maintenance calculation made under 2003 scheme rules, and not paid; and

    (b)   in respect of which the Secretary of State is arranging collection under section 29 of the 1991 Act;

"arrears-only case" means a case in which –

    (a)   there are arrears of child support maintenance; and

    (b)   there is –

        (i)   no maintenance assessment, or maintenance calculation made under 2003 scheme rules, still in force; and

        (ii)   no application for a maintenance assessment, or a maintenance calculation falling to be made under 2003 scheme rules, still to be determined;

"the Collection and Enforcement Regulations" means the Child Support (Collection and Enforcement) Regulations 1992.

(7) For the purposes of this regulation, a maintenance calculation is made (or will fall to be made) under 2003 scheme rules if the amount of the periodical payments required to be paid in accordance with it is (or will be) determined otherwise than in accordance with Part 1 of Schedule 1 to the Child Support Act 1991 as amended by Schedule 4 to the Child Maintenance and Other Payments Act 2008

Amendments—SI 2013/1517.

PART 2
MEANING OF "CHILD"

2 Amendment of the Child Support (Maintenance Assessment Procedure) Regulations 1992

(1) Schedule 1 (meaning of "child" for the purposes of the Act) to the Child Support (Maintenance Assessment Procedure) Regulations 1992 is amended as follows.

(2) For paragraph 1, substitute –

    "**1**

    (1) A person satisfies such conditions as may be prescribed for the purposes of section 55(1)(of the Act if that person satisfies any of the conditions in sub-paragraphs (2) and (3).

    (2) The person is receiving full-time education (which is not advanced education) –

        (a)   by attendance at a recognised educational establishment; or

        (b)   elsewhere, if the education is recognised by the Secretary of State.

    (3) The person is a person in respect of whom child benefit is payable.".

(3) Omit paragraph 1A.

(4) In paragraph 2 –

  (a) for "section 55 of the Act" substitute "this Schedule"; and
  (b) in sub-paragraph (a), after "education" insert ", a higher national certificate".

(5) In paragraph 3, for "section 55 of the Act" substitute "this Schedule".

(6) In paragraph 4, for "section 55(1)(b) of the Act" substitute "paragraph 1(2)".

(7) For paragraph 6, substitute –

"6

In this Schedule, "recognised educational establishment" means an establishment recognised by the Secretary of State for the purposes of this Schedule as being, or as comparable to, a university, college or school."

(8) After paragraph 6 insert –

"7 Education otherwise than at a recognised educational establishment

For the purposes of paragraph 1(2), the Secretary of State may recognise education provided for a person otherwise than at a recognised educational establishment only if satisfied that education was being so provided for that person immediately before that person attained the age of 16.".

3 Amendment of the Child Support (Maintenance Calculation Procedure) Regulations 2000

(1) Schedule 1 (meaning of "child" for the purposes of the Act) to the Child Support (Maintenance Calculation Procedure) Regulations 2000 is amended as follows.

(2) For paragraph 1, substitute –

"1

(1) A person satisfies such conditions as may be prescribed for the purposes of section 55(1)(of the Act if that person satisfies any of the conditions in sub-paragraphs (2) and (3).

(2) The person is receiving full-time education (which is not advanced education) –

  (a) by attendance at a recognised educational establishment; or
  (b) elsewhere, if the education is recognised by the Secretary of State.

(3) The person is a person in respect of whom child benefit is payable.".

(3) Omit paragraph 1A.

(4) In paragraph 2—

  (a) for "section 55 of the Act" substitute "this Schedule"; and

(b)   in sub-paragraph (a), after "education" insert ", a higher national certificate".

(5) In paragraph 3, for "section 55 of the Act" substitute "this Schedule".

(6) In paragraph 4, for "section 55(1)(b) of the Act" substitute "paragraph 1(2)".

(7) For paragraph 6, substitute –

"6

In this Schedule, "recognised educational establishment" means an establishment recognised by the Secretary of State for the purposes of this Schedule as being, or as comparable to, a university, college or school."

(8) After paragraph 6 insert –

"7

Education otherwise than at a recognised educational establishment

For the purposes of paragraph 1(2), the Secretary of State may recognise education provided for a person otherwise than at a recognised educational establishment only if satisfied that education was being so provided for that person immediately before that person attained the age of 16.".

PART 3
NEW CALCULATION RULES—CONSEQUENTIAL AND MISCELLANEOUS AMENDMENTS

4 Amendment of the Child Support (Collection and Enforcement) Regulations 1992

(1) The Collection and Enforcement Regulations are amended as follows.

(2) For regulation 4 (intervals of payment) and its heading, substitute –

"**4 Payments to be scheduled over reference period**

(1) The Secretary of State may, for the purposes of determining the frequency and amount of the payments of child support maintenance required to be made by a liable person –

(a)   determine the total amount payable for the reference period on the assumption that the weekly rate of child support maintenance will not change over that period; and

(b)   require that amount to be paid by equal instalments over that period at intervals determined by the Secretary of State.

(2) The reference period in relation to the maintenance calculation is, subject to paragraph (3), the period of 52 weeks mentioned in section 29(3A) of the Act beginning with –

(a)   the initial effective date (where it is the first such period in relation to the maintenance calculation); or

(b)   the review date.

(3) In this regulation "initial effective date" and "review date" have the meanings given by regulations 12 and 19 of the Child Support Maintenance Calculation Regulations 2012 respectively.".

(3) In regulation 8(1) (interpretation of Part 3), in the definition of "normal deduction rate" for "week, month or other period" substitute "month and the equivalent of that sum for a 1, 2 and 4 week period".

(4) For regulation 10 (normal deduction rate), substitute –

"10

(1) The period by reference to which the normal deduction rate is set must be the period by reference to which the liable person is normally paid where that period is a 1, 2 or 4 weekly or monthly period.

(2) The employer must select the normal deduction rate which applies depending on the period by reference to which the liable person's earnings are normally paid.

(3) Where the liable person is paid by reference to a period other than at a 1, 2 or 4 weekly or monthly period, the Secretary of State must discharge the deduction from earnings order in accordance with regulation 20.".

(5) For regulation 11 (protected earnings proportion and protected earnings rate) and its heading, substitute –

"11 Protected earnings proportion

(1) The period by reference to which the protected earnings proportion is set must be the same as the period by reference to which the normal deduction rate is set in accordance with regulation 10(1).

(2) The protected earnings proportion in respect of any period shall be 60% of the liable person's net earnings in respect of that period as calculated at the pay-day of the liable person by the employer.".

(6) In regulation 20 (discharge of deduction from earnings orders) –

(a)   omit "or" at the end of paragraph (1)(e);
(b)   at the end of paragraph (1)(f) insert –

"; or
(g)   the circumstances in regulation 10(3) apply.".

(7) In regulations 25C(1)(a) (maximum deduction rate for regular deduction order) and 25G(2)(d) (review of a regular deduction order) for "net" substitute "gross".

5 Amendment of the Child Support (Maintenance Arrangements and Jurisdiction) Regulations 1992

(1) The Child Support (Maintenance Arrangements and Jurisdiction) Regulations 1992 are amended as follows.

(2) In regulation 1(2) (interpretation) omit the definitions of "Maintenance Calculation Procedure Regulations" and "Maintenance Calculations and Special Cases Regulations".

(3) In regulation 5(3)(c) (notifications by the Secretary of State) for "regulation 8 of the Maintenance Calculations and Special Cases Regulations" substitute "regulation 50 of the Child Support Maintenance Calculation Regulations 2012".

(4) In regulation 8A(d) (maintenance calculations and maintenance orders—payments) omit the words from "in accordance with" to the end of that paragraph.

6 Amendment of the Social Security and Child Support (Decisions and Appeals) Regulations 1999

(1) The Social Security and Child Support (Decisions and Appeals) Regulations 1999 are amended as follows.

(2) In regulation 1(3) (interpretation), omit the definitions of "the Arrears, Interest and Adjustment of Maintenance Assessments Regulations", "the Maintenance Calculation Procedure Regulations", "the Maintenance Calculations and Special Cases Regulations", "relevant other child", "relevant person" and "Variations Regulations".

(3) Omit regulations 3A, 5A, 6A, 6B, 7B, 7C, 15A, 15B, 15C, 23 and 24.

(4) In regulation 4 (late application for a revision) –

    (a)   in paragraph (1), omit "or 3A(1)(a)";
    (b)   in paragraph (2), omit "the relevant person";
    (c)   in sub-paragraph (c) of paragraph (4), omit "or 3A"; and
    (d)   in paragraph (5), omit "and regulation 3A(1)(a)".

(5) In the heading to regulation 30 (appeal against a decision which has been replaced or revised) omit "replaced or".

(6) In regulation 30 (appeal against a decision which has been revised)—

    (a)   for paragraph (1) substitute –

> "(1) An appeal against a decision of the Secretary of State or the Board or an officer of the Board shall not lapse where—
>
>   (a)   the decision is revised under section 9 before the appeal is determined; and
>   (b)   the decision as revised is not more advantageous to the appellant than the decision before it was revised.";

    (b)   for paragraph (3) substitute –

> "(3) Where a decision as revised under section 9 is not more advantageous to the appellant than the decision before it was revised, the appeal shall be treated as though it had been brought against the decision as revised."; and

      (c)   in paragraphs (4) and (5), omit "replaced or".

(7) In regulation 33 (notice of appeal), omit paragraph (2)(d).

(8) Omit Schedule 3D (effective dates for supersession of child support decisions).

7 Amendment of the Child Support (Voluntary Payments) Regulations 2000

(1) The Child Support (Voluntary Payments) Regulations 2000 are amended as follows.

(2) In regulation 1(2) (interpretation) –

   (a) omit the definition of "the Maintenance Calculations and Special Cases Regulations";
   (b) in the definition of "the qualifying child's home" omit the words from "and "home" has" to the end; and
   (c) in the definition of "relevant person", in paragraph (c), for the words from "regulation 8" to the end substitute "regulation 50 of the Child Support Maintenance Calculation Regulations 2012".

(3) In regulation 2(1)(c) (voluntary payment) omit the words from "and for this purpose" to "2000".

8 Amendment of the Child Support Information Regulations 2008

(1) The Child Support Information Regulations 2008 are amended as follows.

(2) In regulation 2 (interpretation) –

   (a) in paragraph (1), for the definition of "Maintenance Calculation Procedure Regulations" substitute –

   ""the Maintenance Calculation Regulations" means the Child Support Maintenance Calculation Regulations 2012;"; and

   (b) omit paragraphs (2) and (3).

(3) In regulation 7 (duty of persons from whom information requested) omit paragraph (3).

(4) After regulation 9 (duty to notify change of address) insert –

   "**9A Duty to notify increase in current income**

   (1) In a case falling within paragraphs (2) or (3), the Secretary of State may notify the non-resident parent that that parent is required to notify the Secretary of State of any relevant change of circumstances in relation to that income.

   (2) A case falls within this paragraph if, in relation to a maintenance calculation in force –

      (a) gross weekly income is determined by reference to the non-resident parent's current income as an employee or officeholder (in accordance with regulation 38 of the Maintenance Calculation Regulations); and
      (b) paragraph 5(b) of Schedule 1 to the 1991 Act (nil rate) does not apply.

   (3) A case falls within this paragraph if, in relation to a maintenance calculation in force –

      (a) gross weekly income is determined by reference to the non-resident parent's current income (in accordance with regulation 37 of the Maintenance Calculation Regulations); and
      (b) paragraph 5(b) of Schedule 1 to the 1991 Act applies (nil rate).

(4) A notification by the Secretary of State under paragraph (1) must be in writing.

(5) Where a relevant change of circumstances occurs after the non-resident parent has been notified of a requirement under paragraph (1), the non-resident parent must notify the Secretary of State of that change—

(a)   within fourteen days beginning with the day on which the change occurs; or

(b)   within such other period as the Secretary of State has specified in the notification.

(6) For the purposes of a case falling within paragraph (2), a relevant change of circumstances occurs where—

(a)   the non-resident parent –
    (i)   commences a new employment or office; or
    (ii)   in relation to an existing employment or office, commences a new rate of remuneration or a new working pattern,

and could reasonably be expected to know that would result in an increased liability under the maintenance calculation in force if reported to the Secretary of State; or

(b)   the non-resident parent receives from their employment or office the following number of consecutive payments, each of which (if it were taken as a weekly average) exceeds the gross weekly income taken into account in the maintenance calculation in force by 25% or more –
    (i)   five payments, in the case of a non-resident parent paid weekly;
    (ii)   three payments, in the case of a non-resident parent paid fortnightly;
    (iii)   two payments, in the case of a non-resident parent paid four weekly or monthly.

(7) The payments referred to in paragraph (6)(b) are the gross remuneration from the employment or office in question less any pension contributions deducted under net pay arrangements.

(8) In paragraph (7)—

"net pay arrangements" means arrangements for relief in respect of pension contributions under section 193 of the Finance Act 2004.

(9) For the purposes of a case falling within paragraph (3), a relevant change of circumstances occurs where the non-resident parent's income increases to a gross weekly income of £5 or more.

(10) For the purposes of paragraph (9), gross weekly income is to be calculated in accordance with regulation 45(2) of the Maintenance Calculation Regulations.".

(5) In regulation 13 (disclosure of information to other persons) –

(a)   in paragraph (1)(d), for "regulation 23" to "Procedure Regulations" substitute "regulation 25 of the Maintenance Calculation Regulations (notification of a maintenance calculation)"; and

(b)   in paragraph (2)(c), for "regulation 34" to "Regulations 1999" substitute "paragraph 4 of the Schedule to the Maintenance Calculation Regulations".

9 (*repealed*)

Amendments—SI 2013/1517.

10 Revocations

The following Regulations are revoked –
(a)   the Child Support (Maintenance Assessment Procedure) Regula-
      tions 1992;
(b)   the Child Support (Maintenance Assessments and Special Cases)
      Regulations 1992;
(c)   the Child Support (Maintenance Assessments and Special Cases)
      Amendment Regulations 1993;
(d)   the Child Support Departure Direction and Consequential Amend-
      ments Regulations 1996;
(e)   the Child Support (Maintenance Calculations and Special Cases)
      Regulations 2000;
(f)   the Child Support (Variations) Regulations 2000; and
(g)   the Child Support (Maintenance Calculation Procedure) Regula-
      tions 2000.

PART 4
SAVINGS AND TRANSITIONAL PROVISION

11 Saving where arrears-only case

(1) Regulations 8, 10, 11 and 20 of the Collection and Enforcement
Regulations continue to apply in relation to an arrears-only case, as they were
in force immediately before the amendments made by regulation 4(3) to (6)
come into force, until notice is given to the non-resident parent by the Secretary
of State that the provisions of the Regulations as amended by regulation 4(3) to
(6) apply to that case.

(2) Any notice given under paragraph (1) must be in writing and sent by post
to the non-resident parent's last known or notified address and will be treated
as having been given on the second day following the day on which it is posted.

(3) For the purposes of this regulation any reference to a non-resident parent
includes reference to an absent parent.

12 Transitional provision

(1) Where, in any case, a deduction from earnings order was made before the
date on which the Collection and Enforcement Regulations as amended by
regulation 4(3) to (6) apply in relation to that case, this regulation shall apply in
respect of that order.

(2) Where the deduction from earnings order still has effect immediately before
regulation 4(3) to (6) comes into force in relation to that case –

(a) the order continues to take effect for the purposes of any deductions which are required to be made under the order until it is discharged or lapses;

(b) the Collection and Enforcement Regulations, as they were in force before the amendments made by regulation 4(3) to (6) came into force, continue to apply in relation to the order until it is discharged or lapses; and

(c) the order is to be treated as discharged, if it has not otherwise lapsed or been discharged, on the date that the first deduction from earnings order made under the Collection and Enforcement Regulations as amended by regulation 4(3) to (6) takes effect.

CIVIL PROCEDURE RULES 1998

SI 1998/3132

* * * *

PART 70
GENERAL RULES ABOUT ENFORCEMENT OF JUDGMENTS AND ORDERS

Practice Direction—This Part is supplemented by a practice direction – PD70 – which is set out below.

70.1 Scope of this Part and interpretation

(1) This Part contains general rules about enforcement of judgments and orders.

(Rules about specific methods of enforcement are contained in Parts 71 to 73, Schedule 1 RSC Orders 45 to 47 and 52 and Schedule 2 CCR Orders 25 to 29)

(2) In this Part and in Parts 71 to 73 –

(a) 'judgment creditor' means a person who has obtained or is entitled to enforce a judgment or order;

(b) 'judgment debtor' means a person against whom a judgment or order was given or made;

(c) 'judgment or order' includes an award which the court has –
   (i) registered for enforcement;
   (ii) ordered to be enforced; or
   (iii) given permission to enforce
   as if it were a judgment or order of the court, and in relation to such an award, 'the court which made the judgment or order' means the court which registered the award or made such an order; and

(d) 'judgment or order for the payment of money' includes a judgment or order for the payment of costs, but does not include a judgment or order for the payment of money into court.

Amendments—SI 2001/2792;SI 2002/2058.

70.2 Methods of enforcing judgments or orders

(1) Practice Direction 70 sets out methods of enforcing judgments or orders for the payment of money.

(2) A judgment creditor may, except where an enactment, rule or practice direction provides otherwise –

  (a) use any method of enforcement which is available; and
  (b) use more than one method of enforcement, either at the same time or one after another.

Amendments—SI 2001/2792; SI 2009/3390.

70.3 Transfer of proceedings for enforcement

(1) A judgment creditor wishing to enforce a High Court judgment or order in a county court must apply to the High Court for an order transferring the proceedings to that county court.

(2) A practice direction may make provisions about the transfer of proceedings for enforcement.

  (CCR Order 25 rule 13 contains provisions about the transfer of county court proceedings to the High Court for enforcement)

Amendments—Inserted by SI 2001/2792.

70.4 Enforcement of judgment or order by or against non-party

If a judgment or order is given or made in favour of or against a person who is not a party to proceedings, it may be enforced by or against that person by the same methods as if he were a party.

Amendments—SI 2001/2792.

70.5 Enforcement of decisions of bodies other than the High Court and county courts and compromises enforceable by enactment

(1) This rule applies, subject to paragraph (2), where an enactment provides that –

  (a) a decision of a court, tribunal, body or person other than the High Court or a county court; or
  (b) a compromise,

may be enforced as if it were a court order or that any sum of money payable under that decision or compromise may be recoverable as if payable under a court order.

(2) This rule does not apply to –

  (a) any judgment to which Part 74 applies;
  (b) arbitration awards;
  (c) any order to which RSC Order 115 applies; or
  (d) proceedings to which Part 75 (traffic enforcement) applies.

(2A) Unless paragraph (3) applies, a party may enforce the decision or compromise by applying for a specific method of enforcement under Parts 71 to 73, Schedule 1 RSC Orders 45 to 47 and 52 and Schedule 2 CCR Orders 25 to 29 and must –

(a) file with the court a copy of the decision or compromise being enforced; and

(b) provide the court with the information required by Practice Direction 70.

(3) If an enactment provides that a decision or compromise is enforceable or a sum of money is recoverable if a court so orders, an application for such an order must be made in accordance with paragraphs (4) to (7A) of this rule.

(4) The application –

(a) may, unless paragraph (4A) applies, be made without notice; and

(b) must be made to the court for the district where the person against whom the order is sought, resides or carries on business, unless the court otherwise orders.

(4A) Where a compromise requires a person to whom a sum of money is payable under the compromise to do anything in addition to discontinuing or not starting proceedings ("a conditional compromise"), an application under paragraph (4) must be made on notice.

(5) The application notice must –

(a) be in the form; and

(b) contain the information

required by Practice Direction 70.

(6) A copy of the decision or compromise must be filed with the application notice.

(7) An application other than in relation to a conditional compromise may be dealt with by a court officer without a hearing.

(7A) Where an application relates to a conditional compromise, the respondent may oppose it by filing a response within 14 days of service of the application notice and if the respondent –

(a) does not file a response within the time allowed, the court will make the order; or

(b) files a response within the time allowed, the court will make such order as appears appropriate.

(8) If an enactment provides that a decision or compromise may be enforced in the same manner as an order of the High Court if it is registered, any application to the High Court for registration must be made in accordance with Practice Direction 70.

Amendments—SI 2001/2792; SI 2001/4015; SI 2002/2058; SI 2003/2113; SI 2008/3327; SI 2009/3390.

70.6 Effect of setting aside judgment or order

If a judgment or order is set aside, any enforcement of the judgment or order shall cease to have effect unless the court otherwise orders.

Amendments—SI 2001/2792.

**PRACTICE DIRECTION –
PD70: ENFORCEMENT OF JUDGMENTS AND ORDERS**

This Practice Direction supplements CPR Part 70 (PD70)

Enforcement of Judgments and Orders for the Payment of Money

Section 1 – General

Methods of Enforcing Money Judgments – Rule 70.2

1.1 A judgment creditor may enforce a judgment or order for the payment of money by any of the following methods:

(1) a writ of fieri facias or warrant of execution (see RSC Orders 46 and 47 and CCR Order 26);

(2) a third party debt order (see Part 72);

(3) a charging order, stop order or stop notice (see Part 73);

(4) in a county court, an attachment of earnings order (see CCR Order 27);

(5) the appointment of a receiver (see Part 69);

1.2 In addition the court may make the following orders against a judgment debtor –

(1) an order of committal, but only if permitted by –
  (a) a rule; and
  (b) the Debtors Acts 1869 and 1878
  (See Part 81 – Applications and proceedings in relation to contempt of court, in particular Sections 2 and 8 and the Practice Direction supplementing Part 81, and CCR Order 28; and

(2) in the High Court, a writ of sequestration, but only if permitted by rule 81.20.

1.3 The enforcement of a judgment or order may be affected by –

(1) the enactments relating to insolvency; and

(2) county court administration orders.

Transfer of County Court Proceedings to another Court for Enforcement – Rule 70.3

2.1 Subject to section 2 of this practice direction, if a judgment creditor is required by a rule or practice direction to enforce a judgment or order of one county court in a different county court, he must first make a request in writing to the court in which the case is proceeding to transfer the proceedings to that other court.

2.2 Subject to section 2 of this practice direction, on receipt of such a request, a court officer will transfer the proceedings to the other court unless a judge orders otherwise.

2.3 The court will give notice of the transfer to all the parties.

2.4 When the proceedings have been transferred, the parties must take any further steps in the proceedings in the court to which they have been transferred, unless a rule or practice direction provides otherwise.

> (Part 52 and Practice Directions 52A and 52B provide to which court or judge an appeal against the judgment or order, or an application for permission to appeal, must be made)

Enforcement of High Court Judgment or Order in a County Court – Rule 70.3

3.1 If a judgment creditor wishes to enforce a High Court judgment or order in a county court, he must file the following documents in the county court with his application notice or request for enforcement –

(1) a copy of the judgment or order;
(2) a certificate verifying the amount due under the judgment or order;
(3) if a writ of execution has previously been issued in the High Court to enforce the judgment or order, a copy of the relevant enforcement officer's return to the writ; and
(4) a copy of the order transferring the proceedings to the county court.

3.2 In this paragraph and paragraph 7 –

(1) 'enforcement officer' means an individual who is authorised to act as an enforcement officer under the Courts Act 2003; and
(2) 'relevant enforcement officer' means –
    (a) in relation to a writ of execution which is directed to a single enforcement officer, that officer;
    (b) in relation to a writ of execution which is directed to two or more enforcement officers, the officer to whom the writ is allocated.

Enforcement of decisions of bodies other than the High Court and county courts and compromises enforceable by enactment

4.1 The information referred to in rule 70.5(2A) must –

(a) be included in practice form N322B or where paragraph 4.1A applies, in the practice form required by paragraph 4.1A(2);
(b) specify the statutory provision under which enforcement or the recovery of a sum of money is sought;
(c) state the name and address of the person against whom enforcement or recovery is sought;
(d) where the decision or compromise requires that person to pay a sum of money, state the amount which remains unpaid; and
(e) confirm that, where a sum of money is being recovered pursuant to a compromise, the compromise is not a conditional compromise.

4.1A

(1) This paragraph applies where –
    (a) either –
        (i) the decision to be enforced is a decision of an employment tribunal in England and Wales; or
        (ii) the application is for the recovery of a compromise sum under section 19A(3) of the Employment Tribunals Act 1996; and
    (b) the party seeking to enforce the decision wishes to enforce by way of a writ of fieri facias.
(2) The practice form which is to be used is –
    (a) where paragraph (1)(a)(i) applies, practice form N471;
    (b) where paragraph (1)(a)(ii) applies, practice form N471A.

4.2 An application under rule 70.5(3) for an order to enforce a decision or compromise must be made by filing an application notice in practice form N322A.

4.3 The application notice must state –

(a) the name and address of the person against whom the order is sought;
(b) how much remains unpaid or what obligation remains to be performed; and
(c) where the application relates to a conditional compromise, details of what under the compromise the applicant is required to do and has done under the compromise in addition to discontinuing or not starting proceedings.

4.4 Where –

(a) the application relates to a conditional compromise; and
(b) the application notice is served by the applicant on the respondent, the applicant must file a certificate of service with the court within 7 days of service of the application notice.

Registration of decisions in the High Court for enforcement – rule 70.5(8)

5.1 An application to the High Court under an enactment to register a decision for enforcement must be made in writing to the head clerk of the Action Department at the Royal Courts of Justice, Strand, London WC2A 2LL.

5.2 The application must –

(1) specify the statutory provision under which the application is made;
(2) state the name and address of the person against whom it is sought to enforce the decision;
(3) if the decision requires that person to pay a sum of money, state the amount which remains unpaid.

Interest on Judgment Debts

6 If a judgment creditor is claiming interest on a judgment debt, he must include in his application or request to issue enforcement proceedings in relation to that judgment details of –

(1) the amount of interest claimed and the sum on which it is claimed;
(2) the dates from and to which interest has accrued; and
(3) the rate of interest which has been applied and, where more than one rate of interest has been applied, the relevant dates and rates.

(Interest may be claimed on High Court judgment debts under section 17 of the Judgments Act 1838. The County Courts (Interest on Judgment Debts) Order 1991 specifies when interest may be claimed on county court judgment debts)

Enforcing a judgment or order against a partnership

6A.1 A judgment or order made against a partnership may be enforced against any property of the partnership within the jurisdiction.

6A.2 Subject to paragraph 6A.3, a judgment or order made against a partnership may be enforced against any person who is not a limited partner and who –

(1) acknowledged service of the claim form as a partner;
(2) having been served as a partner with the claim form, failed to acknowledge service of it;
(3) admitted in his statement of case that he is or was a partner at a material time; or
(4) was found by the court to have been a partner at a material time.

6A.3 A judgment or order made against a partnership may not be enforced against a limited partner or a member of the partnership who was ordinarily resident outside the jurisdiction when the claim form was issued unless that partner or member –

(1) acknowledged service of the claim form as a partner;
(2) was served within the jurisdiction with the claim form as a partner; or
(3) was served out of the jurisdiction with the claim form, as a partner, with the permission of the court given under Section IV of Part 6.

6A.4 A judgment creditor wishing to enforce a judgment or order against a person in circumstances not set out in paragraphs 6A.2 or 6A.3 must apply to the court for permission to enforce the judgment or order.

Payment of Debt after Issue of Enforcement Proceedings

7.1 If a judgment debt or part of it is paid –

(1) after the judgment creditor has issued any application or request to enforce it; but
(2) before –
    (a) any writ or warrant has been executed; or

(b) in any other case, the date fixed for the hearing of the application;

the judgment creditor must, unless paragraph 7.2 applies, immediately notify the court in writing.

7.2 If a judgment debt or part of it is paid after the judgment creditor has applied to the High Court for a writ of execution, paragraph 7.1 does not apply, and the judgment creditor must instead immediately notify the relevant enforcement officer in writing.

Section 2 – Automatic transfer of proceedings in designated money claims

Scope

8.1 This section applies to applications for orders to obtain information from judgment debtors and applications for enforcement of judgments made in Northampton County Court in respect of designated money claims where the proceedings have not been transferred to another county court.

Applications under Parts 71, 72 and 73

9.1 Where an application is made to which rule 71.2(2)(b)(ii), 72.3(1)(b)(ii) or 73.3(2)(e) applies, it must be filed in the court for the district in which the judgment debtor resides or carries on business.

Applications under Order 27

10.1 Where an application is made under rule 3(2), the application must be filed in the court for the district in which the judgment creditor resides or carries on business.

10.2 Where an application is made under rule 3(3), the application must be filed in the court for the district in which one or more of the debtors resides or carries on business.

Automatic transfer

11.1 Unless the court is satisfied that the application does not comply with the Rules, it will transfer the proceedings to the court in which the application was filed and a court officer will inform the County Court Money Claims Centre of the transfer.

PART 71
ORDERS TO OBTAIN INFORMATION FROM JUDGMENT DEBTORS

Practice Direction—This Part is supplemented by a practice direction – PD71 – which is set out below.

71.1 Scope of this Part

This Part contains rules which provide for a judgment debtor to be required to attend court to provide information, for the purpose of enabling a judgment creditor to enforce a judgment or order against him.

Amendments—SI 2001/2792.

71.2 Order to attend court

(1) A judgment creditor may apply for an order requiring –

(a) a judgment debtor; or
(b) if a judgment debtor is a company or other corporation, an officer of that body;

to attend court to provide information about –

(i) the judgment debtor's means; or
(ii) any other matter about which information is needed to enforce a judgment or order.

(2) An application under paragraph (1) –

(a) may be made without notice; and
(b) must be issued in the court which made the judgment or order which it is sought to enforce, except that –
(i) if the proceedings have since been transferred to a different court, it must be issued in that court; or
(ii) subject to subparagraph (b)(i), if it is to enforce a judgment made in Northampton County Court in respect of a designated money claim, it must be issued in accordance with section 2 of Practice Direction 70.

(3) The application notice must –

(a) be in the form; and
(b) contain the information

required by Practice Direction 71.

(4) An application under paragraph (1) may be dealt with by a court officer without a hearing.

(5) If the application notice complies with paragraph (3), an order to attend court will be issued in the terms of paragraph (6).

(6) A person served with an order issued under this rule must –

(a) attend court at the time and place specified in the order;
(b) when he does so, produce at court documents in his control which are described in the order; and
(c) answer on oath such questions as the court may require.

(7) An order under this rule will contain a notice in the following terms , or in terms to substantially the same effect –

If you the within-named   do not comply with this order you may be held to be in contempt of court and imprisoned or fined, or your assets may be seized.

Amendments—SI 2001/2792; SI 2009/3390; SI 2012/505; SI 2012/2208.

71.3 Service of order

(1) An order to attend court must, unless the court otherwise orders, be served personally on the person ordered to attend court not less than 14 days before the hearing.

(2) If the order is to be served by the judgment creditor, he must inform the court not less than 7 days before the date of the hearing if he has been unable to serve it.

Amendments—SI 2001/2792.

71.4 Travelling expenses

(1) A person ordered to attend court may, within 7 days of being served with the order, ask the judgment creditor to pay him a sum reasonably sufficient to cover his travelling expenses to and from court.

(2) The judgment creditor must pay such a sum if requested.

Amendments—SI 2001/2792.

71.5 Judgment creditor's affidavit

(1) The judgment creditor must file an affidavit$^{(GL)}$ or affidavits –

    (a)   by the person who served the order (unless it was served by the court) giving details of how and when it was served;

    (b)   stating either that –

        (i)   the person ordered to attend court has not requested payment of his travelling expenses; or

        (ii)   the judgment creditor has paid a sum in accordance with such a request; and

    (c)   stating how much of the judgment debt remains unpaid.

(2) The judgment creditor must either –

    (a)   file the affidavit$^{(GL)}$ or affidavits not less than 2 days before the hearing; or

    (b)   produce it or them at the hearing.

Amendments—SI 2001/2792.

71.6 Conduct of the hearing

(1) The person ordered to attend court will be questioned on oath.

(2) The questioning will be carried out by a court officer unless the court has ordered that the hearing shall be before a judge.

(3) The judgment creditor or his representative –

    (a)   may attend and ask questions where the questioning takes place before a court officer; and

    (b)   must attend and conduct the questioning if the hearing is before a judge.

Amendments—SI 2001/2792.

71.7 Adjournment of the hearing

If the hearing is adjourned, the court will give directions as to the manner in which notice of the new hearing is to be served on the judgment debtor.

Amendments—SI 2001/2792.

71.8 Failure to comply with order

(1) If a person against whom an order has been made under rule 71.2 –

(a)   fails to attend court;
(b)   refuses at the hearing to take the oath or to answer any question; or
(c)   otherwise fails to comply with the order;

the court will refer the matter to a High Court judge or circuit judge.

(2) That judge may, subject to paragraphs (3) and (4), make a committal order against the person.

(3) A committal order for failing to attend court may not be made unless the judgment creditor has complied with rules 71.4 and 71.5.

(4) If a committal order is made, the judge will direct that –

(a)   the order shall be suspended provided that the person –
      (i)   attends court at a time and place specified in the order; and
      (ii)   complies with all the terms of that order and the original order; and
(b)   if the person fails to comply with any term on which the committal order is suspended, he shall be brought before a judge to consider whether the committal order should be discharged.

(Part 81 contains provisions in relation to committal.)

Amendments—SI 2001/2792; SI 2001/4015; SI 2012/2208.

PRACTICE DIRECTION –
PD71: ORDERS TO OBTAIN INFORMATION FROM JUDGMENT DEBTORS

This Practice Direction supplements CPR Part 71 (PD71)

Orders to Obtain Information from Judgment Debtors

Application Notice – Rule 71.2

1.1 An application by a judgment creditor under rule 71.2(1) must be made by filing an application notice in Practice Form N316 if the application is to question an individual judgment debtor, or N316A if the application is to question an officer of a company or other corporation.

1.2 The application notice must –

(1)   state the name and address of the judgment debtor;
(2)   identify the judgment or order which the judgment creditor is seeking to enforce;
(3)   if the application is to enforce a judgment or order for the payment of money, state the amount presently owed by the judgment debtor under the judgment or order;
(4)   if the judgment debtor is a company or other corporation, state –
    (a)   the name and address of the officer of that body whom the judgment creditor wishes to be ordered to attend court; and
    (b)   his position in the company;
(5)   if the judgment creditor wishes the questioning to be conducted before a judge, state this and give his reasons;
(6)   if the judgment creditor wishes the judgment debtor (or other person to be questioned) to be ordered to produce specific documents at court, identify those documents; and
(7)   if the application is to enforce a judgment or order which is not for the payment of money, identify the matters about which the judgment creditor wishes the judgment debtor (or officer of the judgment debtor) to be questioned.

1.3 The court officer considering the application notice –

(1)   may, in any appropriate case, refer it to a judge (rule 3.2); and
(2)   will refer it to a judge for consideration, if the judgment creditor requests the judgment debtor (or officer of the judgment debtor) to be questioned before a judge.

Order to Attend Court – Rule 71.2

2.1 The order will provide for the judgment debtor (or other person to be questioned) to attend the county court for the district in which he resides or carries on business, unless a judge decides otherwise.

2.2 The order will provide for questioning to take place before a judge only if the judge considering the request decides that there are compelling reasons to make such an order.

Service of Order to Attend Court – Rule 71.3

3 Service of an order to attend court for questioning may be carried out by –

(a)   the judgment creditor (or someone acting on the judgment creditor's behalf);
(b)   a High Court enforcement officer; or
(c)   a county court bailiff.

Attendance at Court: Normal Procedure – Rule 71.6

4.1 The court officer will ask a standard series of questions, as set out in the forms in Appendixes A and B to this practice direction. The form in

Appendix A will be used if the person being questioned is the judgment debtor, and the form in Appendix B will be used if the person is an officer of a company or other corporation.

4.2 The judgment creditor or his representative may either –

(1) attend court and ask questions himself; or
(2) request the court officer to ask additional questions, by attaching a list of proposed additional questions to his application notice.

4.3 The court officer will –

(1) make a written record of the evidence given, unless the proceedings are tape recorded;
(2) at the end of the questioning, read the record of evidence to the person being questioned and ask him to sign it; and
(3) if the person refuses to sign it, note that refusal on the record of evidence.

Attendance at Court: Procedure Where the Order is to Attend Before a Judge – Rule 71.6

5.1 Where the hearing takes places before a judge, the questioning will be conducted by the judgment creditor or his representative, and the standard questions in the forms in Appendixes A and B will not be used.

5.2 The proceedings will be tape recorded and the court will not make a written record of the evidence.

Failure to Comply with Order: Reference to Judge – Rule 71.8(1)

6 If a judge or court officer refers to a High Court judge or circuit judge the failure of a judgment debtor to comply with an order under rule 71.2, he shall certify in writing the respect in which the judgment debtor failed to comply with the order.

Suspended Committal Order – Rule 71.8(2) And (4)(a)

7.1 A committal order will be suspended provided that the person attends court at a time and place specified in the order (rule 71.8(4)(a)(i)). The appointment specified will be –

(1) before a judge, if –
     (a)   the original order under rule 71.2 was to attend before a judge; or
     (b)   the judge making the suspended committal order so directs; and
(2) otherwise, before a court officer.

7.2 Rule 71.3 and paragraph 3 of this practice direction (service of order), and rule 71.5(1)(a) and (2) (affidavit of service), apply with the necessary changes to a suspended committal order as they do to an order to attend court.

Breach of Terms on which Committal Order is Suspended – Rule 71.8(4)(b)

8.1 If –

(1)   the judgment debtor fails to attend court at the time and place specified in the suspended committal order; and

(2)   it appears to the judge or court officer that the judgment debtor has been duly served with the order,

the judge or court officer will certify in writing the debtor's failure to attend.

8.2 If the judgment debtor fails to comply with any other term on which the committal order was suspended, the judge or court officer will certify in writing the non-compliance and set out details of it.

8.3 A warrant to bring the judgment debtor before a judge may be issued on the basis of a certificate under paragraph 8.1 or 8.2.

8.4 The hearing under rule 71.8(4)(b) may take place before a master or district judge.

8.5 At the hearing the judge will discharge the committal order unless he is satisfied beyond reasonable doubt that –

(1)   the judgment debtor has failed to comply with –
      (a)   the original order to attend court; and
      (b)   the terms on which the committal order was suspended; and
(2)   both orders have been duly served on the judgment debtor.

8.6 If the judge decides that the committal order should not be discharged, a warrant of committal shall be issued immediately.

PART 72
THIRD PARTY DEBT ORDERS

Practice Direction—This Part is supplemented by a practice direction – PD72 – which is set out below.

72.1 Scope of this Part and interpretation

(1) This Part contains rules which provide for a judgment creditor to obtain an order for the payment to him of money which a third party who is within the jurisdiction owes to the judgment debtor.

(2) In this Part, 'bank or building society' includes any person carrying on a business in the course of which he lawfully accepts deposits in the United Kingdom.

Amendments—SI 2001/2792; SI 2001/4015.

72.2 Third party debt order

(1) Upon the application of a judgment creditor, the court may make an order (a 'final third party debt order') requiring a third party to pay to the judgment creditor –

(a)   the amount of any debt due or accruing due to the judgment debtor from the third party; or

(b)   so much of that debt as is sufficient to satisfy the judgment debt and the judgment creditor's costs of the application.

(2) The court will not make an order under paragraph 1 without first making an order (an 'interim third party debt order') as provided by rule 72.4(2).

(3) In deciding whether money standing to the credit of the judgment debtor in an account to which section 40 of the Senior Courts Act 1981 or section 108 of the County Courts Act 1984 relates may be made the subject of a third party debt order, any condition applying to the account that a receipt for money deposited in the account must be produced before any money is withdrawn will be disregarded.

> (Section 40(3) of the Senior Courts Act 1981 and section 108(3) of the County Courts Act 1984 contain a list of other conditions applying to accounts that will also be disregarded)

Amendments—SI 2001/2792; Constitutional Reform Act 2005.

72.3 Application for third party debt order

(1) An application for a third party debt order –

(a)   may be made without notice; and
(b)   must be issued in the court which made the judgment or order which it is sought to enforce, except that –
    (i)   if the proceedings have since been transferred to a different court, it must be issued in that court; or
    (ii)   subject to subparagraph (b)(i), if it is to enforce a judgment made in Northampton County Court in respect of a designated money claim, it must be issued in accordance with section 2 of Practice Direction 70.

(2) The application notice must –

(a)   (i)   be in the form; and
    (ii)   contain the information
    required by Practice Direction 72; and
(b)   be verified by a statement of truth.

Amendments—SI 2001/2792; SI 2009/3390; SI 2012/505.

72.4 Interim third party debt order

(1) An application for a third party debt order will initially be dealt with by a judge without a hearing.

(2) The judge may make an interim third party debt order –

(a)   fixing a hearing to consider whether to make a final third party debt order; and
(b)   directing that until that hearing the third party must not make any payment which reduces the amount he owes the judgment debtor to less than the amount specified in the order.

(3) An interim third party debt order will specify the amount of money which the third party must retain, which will be the total of –

    (a)   the amount of money remaining due to the judgment creditor under the judgment or order; and

    (b)   an amount for the judgment creditor's fixed costs of the application, as specified in Practice Direction 72.

(4) An interim third party debt order becomes binding on a third party when it is served on him.

(5) The date of the hearing to consider the application shall be not less than 28 days after the interim third party debt order is made.

Amendments—SI 2001/2792; SI 2009/3390.

72.5 Service of interim order

(1) Copies of an interim third party debt order, the application notice and any documents filed in support of it must be served –

    (a)   on the third party, not less than 21 days before the date fixed for the hearing; and

    (b)   on the judgment debtor not less than –

        (i)   7 days after a copy has been served on the third party; and

        (ii)   7 days before the date fixed for the hearing.

(2) If the judgment creditor serves the order, he must either –

    (a)   file a certificate of service not less than 2 days before the hearing; or

    (b)   produce a certificate of service at the hearing.

Amendments—SI 2001/2792.

72.6 Obligations of third parties served with interim order

(1) A bank or building society served with an interim third party debt order must carry out a search to identify all accounts held with it by the judgment debtor.

(2) The bank or building society must disclose to the court and the creditor within 7 days of being served with the order, in respect of each account held by the judgment debtor –

    (a)   the number of the account;

    (b)   whether the account is in credit; and

    (c)   if the account is in credit –

        (i)   whether the balance of the account is sufficient to cover the amount specified in the order;

        (ii)   the amount of the balance at the date it was served with the order, if it is less than the amount specified in the order; and

    (iii)   whether the bank or building society asserts any right to the money in the account, whether pursuant to a right of set-off or otherwise, and if so giving details of the grounds for that assertion.

(3) If –

    (a)   the judgment debtor does not hold an account with the bank or building society; or

    (b)   the bank or building society is unable to comply with the order for any other reason (for example, because it has more than one account holder whose details match the information contained in the order, and cannot identify which account the order applies to),

the bank or building society must inform the court and the judgment creditor of that fact within 7 days of being served with the order.

(4) Any third party other than a bank or building society served with an interim third party debt order must notify the court and the judgment creditor in writing within 7 days of being served with the order, if he claims –

    (a)   not to owe any money to the judgment debtor; or

    (b)   to owe less than the amount specified in the order.

Amendments—SI 2001/2792; SI 2001/4015.

72.7 Arrangements for debtors in hardship

(1) If –

    (a)   a judgment debtor is an individual;

    (b)   he is prevented from withdrawing money from his account with a bank or building society as a result of an interim third party debt order; and

    (c)   he or his family is suffering hardship in meeting ordinary living expenses as a result,

the court may, on an application by the judgment debtor, make an order permitting the bank or building society to make a payment or payments out of the account ('a hardship payment order').

(2) An application for a hardship payment order may be made –

    (a)   in High Court proceedings, at the Royal Courts of Justice or to any district registry; and

    (b)   in county court proceedings, to any county court.

(3) A judgment debtor may only apply to one court for a hardship payment order.

(4) An application notice seeking a hardship payment order must –

    (a)   include detailed evidence explaining why the judgment debtor needs a payment of the amount requested; and

    (b)   be verified by a statement of truth.

(5) Unless the court orders otherwise, the application notice –

(a) must be served on the judgment creditor at least 2 days before the hearing; but

(b) does not need to be served on the third party.

(6) A hardship payment order may –

(a) permit the third party to make one or more payments out of the account; and

(b) specify to whom the payments may be made.

Amendments—SI 2001/2792.

72.8 Further consideration of the application

(1) If the judgment debtor or the third party objects to the court making a final third party debt order, he must file and serve written evidence stating the grounds for his objections.

(2) If the judgment debtor or the third party knows or believes that a person other than the judgment debtor has any claim to the money specified in the interim order, he must file and serve written evidence stating his knowledge of that matter.

(3) If –

(a) the third party has given notice under rule 72.6 that he does not owe any money to the judgment debtor, or that the amount which he owes is less than the amount specified in the interim order; and

(b) the judgment creditor wishes to dispute this,

the judgment creditor must file and serve written evidence setting out the grounds on which he disputes the third party's case.

(4) Written evidence under paragraphs (1), (2) or (3) must be filed and served on each other party as soon as possible, and in any event not less than 3 days before the hearing.

(5) If the court is notified that some person other than the judgment debtor may have a claim to the money specified in the interim order, it will serve on that person notice of the application and the hearing.

(6) At the hearing the court may –

(a) make a final third party debt order;

(b) discharge the interim third party debt order and dismiss the application;

(c) decide any issues in dispute between the parties, or between any of the parties and any other person who has a claim to the money specified in the interim order; or

(d) direct a trial of any such issues, and if necessary give directions.

Amendments—SI 2001/2792.

72.9 Effect of final third party order

(1) A final third party debt order shall be enforceable as an order to pay money.

(2) If –

    (a)   the third party pays money to the judgment creditor in compliance with a third party debt order; or

    (b)   the order is enforced against him,

the third party shall, to the extent of the amount paid by him or realised by enforcement against him, be discharged from his debt to the judgment debtor.

(3) Paragraph (2) applies even if the third party debt order, or the original judgment or order against the judgment debtor, is later set aside.

Amendments—SI 2001/2792.

72.10 Money in court

(1) If money is standing to the credit of the judgment debtor in court –

    (a)   the judgment creditor may not apply for a third party debt order in respect of that money; but

    (b)   he may apply for an order that the money in court, or so much of it as is sufficient to satisfy the judgment or order and the costs of the application, be paid to him.

(2) An application notice seeking an order under this rule must be served on –

    (a)   the judgment debtor; and

    (b)   the Accountant General at the Court Funds Office.

(3) If an application notice has been issued under this rule, the money in court must not be paid out until the application has been disposed of.

Amendments—Inserted by SI 2001/2792.

72.11 Costs

If the judgment creditor is awarded costs on an application for an order under rule 72.2 or 72.10 –

    (a)   he shall, unless the court otherwise directs, retain those costs out of the money recovered by him under the order; and

    (b)   the costs shall be deemed to be paid first out of the money he recovers, in priority to the judgment debt.

Amendments—SI 2001/2792.

PRACTICE DIRECTION –
PD72: THIRD PARTY DEBT ORDERS

This Practice Direction supplements CPR Part 72 (PD72)

Third Party Debt Orders

Application Notice – Rule 72.3

1.1 An application for a third party debt order must be made by filing an application notice in Practice Form N349.

1.2 The application notice must contain the following information –

    (1)   the name and address of the judgment debtor;

    (2)   details of the judgment or order sought to be enforced;

    (3)   the amount of money remaining due under the judgment or order;

    (4)   if the judgment debt is payable by instalments, the amount of any instalments which have fallen due and remain unpaid;

    (5)   the name and address of the third party;

    (6)   if the third party is a bank or building society –

        (a)   its name and the address of the branch at which the judgment debtor's account is believed to be held; and

        (b)   the account number;

        or, if the judgment creditor does not know all or part of this information, that fact;

    (7)   confirmation that to the best of the judgment creditor's knowledge or belief the third party –

        (a)   is within the jurisdiction; and

        (b)   owes money to or holds money to the credit of the judgment debtor;

    (8)   if the judgment creditor knows or believes that any person other than the judgment debtor has any claim to the money owed by the third party –

        (a)   his name and (if known) his address; and

        (b)   such information as is known to the judgment creditor about his claim;

    (9)   details of any other applications for third party debt orders issued by the judgment creditor in respect of the same judgment debt; and

   (10)   the sources or grounds of the judgment creditor's knowledge or belief of the matters referred to in (7), (8) and (9).

1.3 The court will not grant speculative applications for third party debt orders, and will only make an interim third party debt order against a bank or building society if the judgment creditor's application notice contains evidence to substantiate his belief that the judgment debtor has an account with the bank or building society in question.

Interim Third Party Debt Order – Rule 72.4

2 An interim third party debt order will specify the amount of money which the third party must retain (rule 72.4(3)). This will include, in respect of the judgment creditor's fixed costs of the application, the amount which would be allowed to the judgment creditor under rule 45.8 if the whole balance of the judgment debt were recovered.

Interim Orders Relating to Bank or Building Society Accounts –
Rule 72.6(1)–(3)

3.1 A bank or building society Obligations of the third party served with an interim third party debt order is only required by rule 72.6, unless the order states otherwise –

    (1)   to retain money in accounts held solely by the judgment debtor (or, if there are joint judgment debtors, accounts held jointly by them or solely by either or any of them); and

    (2)   to search for and disclose information about such accounts.

3.2 The bank or building society is not required, for example, to retain money in, or disclose information about –

    (1)   accounts in the joint names of the judgment debtor and another person; or

    (2)   if the interim order has been made against a firm, accounts in the names of individual members of that firm.

Attachment of debts owed by a partnership

3A.1 This paragraph relates to debts due or accruing due to a judgment creditor from a partnership.

3A.2 An interim third party debt order under rule 72.4(2) relating to such debts must be served on –

    (1)   a member of the partnership within the jurisdiction;

    (2)   a person authorised by a partner; or

    (3)   some other person having the control or management of the partnership business.

3A.3 Where an order made under rule 72.4(2) requires a partnership to appear before the court, it will be sufficient for a partner to appear before the court.

Transfer

4 The court may, on an application by a judgment debtor who wishes to oppose an application for a third party debt order, transfer it to the court for the district where the judgment debtor resides or carries on business, or to another court.

Applications for Hardship Payment Orders – Rule 72.7

5.1 The court will treat an application for a hardship payment order as being made –

    (1)   in the proceedings in which the interim third party debt order was made; and

    (2)   under the same claim number,

regardless of where the judgment debtor makes the application.

5.2 An application for a hardship payment order will be dealt with by the court to which it is made.

(Rule 72.7(2) provides that an application may be made –

- in High Court proceedings, in the Royal Courts of Justice or to any district registry; and
- in county court proceedings, to any county court.)

5.3 If the application is made to a different court from that dealing with the application for a third party debt order –

(1) the application for a third party debt order will not be transferred; but
(2) the court dealing with that application will send copies of –
    (a) the application notice; and
    (b) the interim third party debt order
    to the court hearing the application for a hardship payment order.

5.4 Rule 72.7(3) requires an application for a hardship payment order to be served on the judgment creditor at least 2 days before the court is to deal with the application, unless the court orders otherwise. In cases of exceptional urgency the judgment debtor may apply for a hardship payment order without notice to the judgment creditor and a judge will decide whether to –

(1) deal with the application without it being served on the judgment creditor; or
(2) direct it to be served.

5.5 If the judge decides to deal with the application without it being served on the judgment creditor, where possible he will normally –

(1) direct that the judgment creditor be informed of the application; and
(2) give him the opportunity to make representations,

by telephone, fax or other appropriate method of communication.

5.6 The evidence filed by a judgment debtor in support of an application for a hardship payment order should include documentary evidence, for example (if appropriate) bank statements, wage slips and mortgage statements, to prove his financial position and need for the payment.

Final Orders Relating to Building Society Accounts

6 A final third party debt order will not require a payment which would reduce to less than £1 the amount in a judgment debtor's account with a building society or credit union.

PART 73
CHARGING ORDERS, STOP ORDERS AND STOP NOTICES

Practice Direction—This Part is supplemented by a practice direction – PD73 – which is set out below.

73.1 Scope of this Part and interpretation

(1) This Part contains rules which provide for a judgment creditor to enforce a judgment by obtaining –

    (a)   a charging order (Section I);
    (b)   a stop order (Section II); or
    (c)   a stop notice (Section III),

over or against the judgment debtor's interest in an asset.

(2) In this Part –

    (a)   'the 1979 Act' means the Charging Orders Act 1979;
    (b)   'the 1992 Regulations' means the Council Tax (Administration and Enforcement) Regulations 1992;
    (c)   'funds in court' includes securities held in court;
    (d)   'securities' means securities of any of the kinds specified in section 2(2)(b) of the 1979 Act.

Amendments—SI 2001/2792.

Section I – Charging Orders

73.2 Scope of this Section

This Section applies to an application by a judgment creditor for a charging order under –

    (a)   section 1 of the 1979 Act; or
    (b)   regulation 50 of the 1992 Regulations.

Amendments—SI 2001/2792.

73.3 Application for charging order

(1) An application for a charging order may be made without notice.

(2) An application for a charging order must be issued in the court which made the judgment or order which it is sought to enforce, unless –

    (a)   the proceedings have since been transferred to a different court, in which case the application must be issued in that court;
    (b)   the application is made under the 1992 Regulations, in which event it must be issued in the county court for the district in which the relevant dwelling (as defined in regulation 50(3)(b) of those Regulations) is situated;
    (c)   the application is for a charging order over an interest in a fund in court, in which event it must be issued in the court in which the claim relating to that fund is or was proceeding;...
    (d)   the application is to enforce a judgment or order of the High Court and it is required by section 1(2) of the 1979 Act to be made to a county court; or

(e) the application is to enforce a judgment made in Northampton County Court in respect of a designated money claim, in which event the application must be issued in accordance with section 2 of Practice Direction 70.

(3) Subject to paragraph (2), a judgment creditor may apply for a single charging order in respect of more than one judgment or order against the same debtor.

(4) The application notice must –

(a) (i) be in the form; and
     (ii) contain the information,
     required by Practice Direction 73; and
(b) be verified by a statement of truth.

Amendments—SI 2001/2792; SI 2009/3390; SI 2012/505.

73.4 Interim charging order

(1) An application for a charging order will initially be dealt with by a judge without a hearing.

(2) The judge may make an order (an 'interim charging order') –

(a) imposing a charge over the judgment debtor's interest in the asset to which the application relates; and
(b) fixing a hearing to consider whether to make a final charging order as provided by rule 73.8(2)(a).

Amendments—SI 2001/2792.

73.5 Service of interim order

(1) Copies of the interim charging order, the application notice and any documents filed in support of it must, not less than 21 days before the hearing, be served on the following persons –

(a) the judgment debtor;
(b) such other creditors as the court directs;
(c) if the order relates to an interest under a trust, on such of the trustees as the court directs;
(d) if the interest charged is in securities other than securities held in court, then –
     (i) in the case of stock for which the Bank of England keeps the register, the Bank of England;
     (ii) in the case of government stock to which (i) does not apply, the keeper of the register;
     (iii) in the case of stock of any body incorporated within England and Wales, that body;
     (iv) in the case of stock of any body incorporated outside England and Wales or of any state or territory outside the United

Kingdom, which is registered in a register kept in England and Wales, the keeper of that register;

(v) in the case of units of any unit trust in respect of which a register of the unit holders is kept in England and Wales, the keeper of that register; and

(e) if the interest charged is in funds in court, the Accountant General at the Court Funds Office.

(2) If the judgment creditor serves the order, he must either –

(a) file a certificate of service not less than 2 days before the hearing; or

(b) produce a certificate of service at the hearing.

Amendments—SI 2001/2792.

73.6 Effect of interim order in relation to securities

(1) If a judgment debtor disposes of his interest in any securities, while they are subject to an interim charging order which has been served on him, that disposition shall not, so long as that order remains in force, be valid as against the judgment creditor.

(2) A person served under rule 73.5(1)(d) with an interim charging order relating to securities must not, unless the court gives permission –

(a) permit any transfer of any of the securities; or

(b) pay any dividend, interest or redemption payment relating to them.

(3) If a person acts in breach of paragraph (2), he will be liable to pay to the judgment creditor –

(a) the value of the securities transferred or the amount of the payment made (as the case may be); or

(b) if less, the amount necessary to satisfy the debt in relation to which the interim charging order was made.

Amendments—SI 2001/2792.

73.7 Effect of interim order in relation to funds in court

If a judgment debtor disposes of his interest in funds in court while they are subject to an interim charging order which has been served on him and on the Accountant General in accordance with rule 73.5(1), that disposition shall not, so long as that order remains in force, be valid as against the judgment creditor.

Amendments—SI 2001/2792.

73.8 Further consideration of the application

(1) If any person objects to the court making a final charging order, he must –

(a) file; and

(b) serve on the applicant,

written evidence stating the grounds of his objections, not less than 7 days before the hearing.

(2) At the hearing the court may –

(a) make a final charging order confirming that the charge imposed by the interim charging order shall continue, with or without modification;
(b) discharge the interim charging order and dismiss the application;
(c) decide any issues in dispute between the parties, or between any of the parties and any other person who objects to the court making a final charging order; or
(d) direct a trial of any such issues, and if necessary give directions.

(3) If the court makes a final charging order which charges securities other than securities held in court, the order will include a stop notice unless the court otherwise orders.

(Section III of this Part contains provisions about stop notices)

(4) Any order made at the hearing must be served on all the persons on whom the interim charging order was required to be served.

Amendments—Inserted by SI 2001/2792.

73.9 Discharge or variation of order

(1) Any application to discharge or vary a charging order must be made to the court which made the charging order.

(Section 3(5) of the 1979 Act and regulation 51(4) of the 1992 Regulations provide that the court may at any time, on the application of the debtor, or of any person interested in any property to which the order relates, or (where the 1992 Regulations apply) of the authority, make an order discharging or varying the charging order)

(2) The court may direct that –

(a) any interested person should be joined as a party to such an application; or
(b) the application should be served on any such person.

(3) An order discharging or varying a charging order must be served on all the persons on whom the charging order was required to be served.

Amendments—SI 2001/2792.

73.10 Enforcement of charging order by sale

(1) Subject to the provisions of any enactment, the court may, upon a claim by a person who has obtained a charging order over an interest in property, order the sale of the property to enforce the charging order.

(2) A claim for an order for sale under this rule should be made to the court which made the charging order, unless that court does not have jurisdiction to make an order for sale.

(A claim under this rule is a proceeding for the enforcement of a charge, and section 23(c) of the County Courts Act 1984 provides the extent of the county court's jurisdiction to hear and determine such proceedings)

(3) The claimant must use the Part 8 procedure.

(4) A copy of the charging order must be filed with the claim form.

(5) The claimant's written evidence must include the information required by Practice Direction 73.

Amendments—SI 2001/2792; SI 2009/3390.

Section II – Stop Orders

73.11 Interpretation

In this Section, 'stop order' means an order of the High Court not to take, in relation to funds in court or securities specified in the order, any of the steps listed in section 5(5) of the 1979 Act.

Amendments—SI 2001/2792.

73.12 Application for stop order

(1) The High Court may make –

    (a) a stop order relating to funds in court, on the application of any person –
        (i) who has a mortgage or charge on the interest of any person in the funds; or
        (ii) to whom that interest has been assigned; or
        (iii) who is a judgment creditor of the person entitled to that interest; or
    (b) a stop order relating to securities other than securities held in court, on the application of any person claiming to be beneficially entitled to an interest in the securities.

(2) An application for a stop order must be made –

    (a) by application notice in existing proceedings; or
    (b) by Part 8 claim form if there are no existing proceedings in the High Court.

(3) The application notice or claim form must be served on –

    (a) every person whose interest may be affected by the order applied for; and
    (b) either –
        (i) the Accountant General at the Court Funds Office, if the application relates to funds in court; or
        (ii) the person specified in rule 73.5(1)(d), if the application relates to securities other than securities held in court.

Amendments—SI 2001/2792.

73.13 Stop order relating to funds in court

A stop order relating to funds in court shall prohibit the transfer, sale, delivery out, payment or other dealing with –

(a)   the funds or any part of them; or
(b)   any income on the funds.

Amendments—SI 2001/2792.

73.14 Stop order relating to securities

(1) A stop order relating to securities other than securities held in court may prohibit all or any of the following steps –

(a)   the registration of any transfer of the securities;
(b)   the making of any payment by way of dividend, interest or otherwise in respect of the securities; and
(c)   in the case of units of a unit trust, any acquisition of or other dealing with the units by any person or body exercising functions under the trust.

(2) The order shall specify –

(a)   the securities to which it relates;
(b)   the name in which the securities stand;
(c)   the steps which may not be taken; and
(d)   whether the prohibition applies to the securities only or to the dividends or interest as well.

Amendments—SI 2001/2792.

73.15 Variation or discharge of order

(1) The court may, on the application of any person claiming to have a beneficial interest in the funds or securities to which a stop order relates, make an order discharging or varying the order.

(2) An application notice seeking the variation or discharge of a stop order must be served on the person who obtained the order.

Amendments—SI 2001/2792.

Section III – Stop Notices

73.16 General

In this Section –

(a)   'stop notice' means a notice issued by the court which requires a person or body not to take, in relation to securities specified in the notice, any of the steps listed in section 5(5) of the 1979 Act, without first giving notice to the person who obtained the notice; and
(b)   'securities' does not include securities held in court.

Amendments—Inserted by SI 2001/2792.

73.17 Request for stop notice

(1) The High Court may, on the request of any person claiming to be beneficially entitled to an interest in securities, issue a stop notice.

> (A stop notice may also be included in a final charging order, by either the High Court or a county court, under rule 73.8(3))

(2) A request for a stop notice must be made by filing –

    (a)   a draft stop notice; and
    (b)   written evidence which –
        (i)   identifies the securities in question;
        (ii)   describes the applicant's interest in the securities; and
        (iii) gives an address for service for the applicant.

> (A sample form of stop notice is annexed to Practice Direction 73)

(3) If a court officer considers that the request complies with paragraph (2), he will issue a stop notice.

(4) The applicant must serve copies of the stop notice and his written evidence on the person to whom the stop notice is addressed.

Amendments—SI 2001/2792; SI 2009/3390.

73.18 Effect of stop notice

(1) A stop notice –

    (a)   takes effect when it is served in accordance with rule 73.17(4); and
    (b)   remains in force unless it is withdrawn or discharged in accordance with rule 73.20 or 73.21.

(2) While a stop notice is in force, the person on whom it is served –

    (a)   must not –
        (i)   register a transfer of the securities described in the notice; or
        (ii)   take any other step restrained by the notice,

without first giving 14 days' notice to the person who obtained the stop notice; but

    (b)   must not, by reason only of the notice, refuse to register a transfer or to take any other step, after he has given 14 days' notice under paragraph (2)(a) and that period has expired.

Amendments—SI 2001/2792.

73.19 Amendment of stop notice

(1) If any securities are incorrectly described in a stop notice which has been obtained and served in accordance with rule 73.17, the applicant may request an amended stop notice in accordance with that rule.

(2) The amended stop notice takes effect when it is served.

Amendments—SI 2001/2792.

73.20 Withdrawal of stop notice

(1) A person who has obtained a stop notice may withdraw it by serving a request for its withdrawal on –

(a) the person or body on whom the stop notice was served; and
(b) the court which issued the stop notice.

(2) The request must be signed by the person who obtained the stop notice, and his signature must be witnessed by a practising solicitor.

Amendments—SI 2001/2792.

73.21 Discharge or variation of stop notice

(1) The court may, on the application of any person claiming to be beneficially entitled to an interest in the securities to which a stop notice relates, make an order discharging or varying the notice.

(2) An application to discharge or vary a stop notice must be made to the court which issued the notice.

(3) The application notice must be served on the person who obtained the stop notice.

Amendments—SI 2001/2792.

73.22 Practice Direction 73 makes provision for the procedure to be followed when applying for an order under section 23 of the Partnership Act 1890.

Amendments—Inserted by SI 2006/1689; SI 2009/3390.

PRACTICE DIRECTION –
PD73: CHARGING ORDERS, STOP ORDERS AND STOP NOTICES

This Practice Direction supplements CPR Part 73 (PD73)

Charging Orders, Stop Orders and Stop Notices

Section I – Charging Orders

Application Notice – Rule 73.3

1.1 An application for a charging order must be made by filing an application notice in Practice Form N379 if the application relates to land, or N380 if the application relates to securities.

1.2 The application notice must contain the following information –

(1) the name and address of the judgment debtor;
(2) details of the judgment or order sought to be enforced;
(3) the amount of money remaining due under the judgment or order;

(4)   if the judgment debt is payable by instalments, the amount of any instalments which have fallen due and remain unpaid;

(5)   if the judgment creditor knows of the existence of any other creditors of the judgment debtor, their names and (if known) their addresses;

(6)   identification of the asset or assets which it is intended to charge;

(7)   details of the judgment debtor's interest in the asset; and

(8)   the names and addresses of the persons on whom an interim charging order must be served under rule 73.5(1).

1.3 A judgment creditor may apply in a single application notice for charging orders over more than one asset, but if the court makes interim charging orders over more than one asset, it will draw up a separate order relating to each asset.

High Court and County Court Jurisdiction

2 The jurisdiction of the High Court and the county court to make charging orders is set out in section 1(2) of the 1979 Act.

Transfer

3 The court may, on an application by a judgment debtor who wishes to oppose an application for a charging order, transfer it to the court for the district where the judgment debtor resides or carries on business, or to another court.

Enforcement of Charging Orders by Sale – Rule 73.10

4.1 A county court has jurisdiction to determine a claim under rule 73.10 for the enforcement of a charging order if the amount owing under the charge does not exceed the county court limit.

4.2 A claim in the High Court for an order for sale of land to enforce a charging order must be started in Chancery Chambers at the Royal Courts of Justice, or a Chancery district registry.

(There are Chancery district registries at Birmingham, Bristol, Caernarfon, Cardiff, Leeds, Liverpool, Manchester, Mold, Newcastle upon Tyne and Preston)

4.3 The written evidence in support of a claim under rule 73.10 must –

(1)   identify the charging order and the property sought to be sold;

(2)   state the amount in respect of which the charge was imposed and the amount due at the date of issue of the claim;

(3)   verify, so far as known, the debtor's title to the property charged;

(4)   state, so far as the claimant is able to identify –

    (a)   the names and addresses of any other creditors who have a prior charge or other security over the property; and

    (b)   the amount owed to each such creditor; and

(5)   give an estimate of the price which would be obtained on sale of the property.

(6)   if the claim relates to land, give details of every person who to the best of the claimant's knowledge is in possession of the property; and

(7)   if the claim relates to residential property –

    (a)   state whether –

       (i)   a land charge of Class F; or

       (ii)   a notice under section 31(10) of the Family Law Act 1996, or under any provision of an Act which preceded that section,

   has been registered; and

    (b)   if so, state –

       (i)   on whose behalf the land charge or notice has been registered; and

       (ii)   that the claimant will serve notice of the claim on that person.

4.4 The claimant must take all reasonable steps to obtain the information required by paragraph 4.3(4) before issuing the claim.

4.5 Sample forms of orders for sale are set out in Appendix A to this practice direction for guidance. These are not prescribed forms of order and they may be adapted or varied by the court to meet the requirements of individual cases.

4A.1 A charging order or interim charging order may be made against any property, within the jurisdiction, belonging to a judgment debtor that is a partnership.

4A.2 For the purposes of rule 73.5(1)(a) (service of the interim order), the specified documents must be served on –

(1)   a member of the partnership within the jurisdiction;

(2)   a person authorised by a partner; or

(3)   some other person having the control or management of the partnership business.

4A.3 Where an order requires a partnership to appear before the court, it will be sufficient for a partner to appear before the court.

Section II – Stop Notices

5 A sample form of stop notice is set out in Appendix B to this practice direction.

Section III – Applications for orders made under section 23 of the Partnership Act 1890

6.1 This paragraph relates to orders made under section 23 of the Partnership Act 1890 ('Section 23').

6.2 The following applications must be made in accordance with Part 23 –

(1)   an application for an order under Section 23 of the 1890 Act made by a judgment creditor of a partner;

(2)   an application for any order by a partner of the judgment debtor in consequence of any application made by the judgment creditor under Section 23.

6.3 The powers conferred on a judge by Section 23 may be exercised by –

(1)   a Master;
(2)   the Admiralty Registrar; or
(3)   a district judge.

6.4 Every application notice filed under this paragraph by a judgment creditor, and every order made following such an application, must be served on the judgment debtor and on any of the other partners that are within the jurisdiction.

6.5 Every application notice filed under this paragraph by a partner of a judgment debtor, and every order made following such an application, must be served –

(1)   on the judgment creditor and the judgment debtor; and
(2)   on the other partners of the judgment debtor who are not joined in the application and who are within the jurisdiction.

6.6 An application notice or order served under this paragraph on one or more, but not all, of the partners of a partnership shall be deemed to have been served on all the partners of that partnership.

Appendix A

| **ORDER FOR SALE** | In the | Claim No |
| following a charging order | | Appn No |

(property solely owned by judgment debtor)

Claimant

Defendant

On the   20 ,   sitting at

Heard

The claimant is entitled to an equitable charge upon the defendant's interest in the property

registered at HM Land Registry under Title No

('the property')

under a charging order made on the

in the   in Claim No

and the court orders that

1 The remainder of this order will not take effect if the defendant by 4.00 pm on the　　　　　　20 pays to the claimant the judgment debt of £　　　　secured by the charge and his costs to date of this application assessed at £　　　, making together £　　　　together with interest at the rate of £　　　per day from the date of this order until payment is received by the claimant.

2 The property shall be sold without further reference to the court at a price not less than £　　　, unless that figure is changed by a further order of the court.

3 The claimant claimant's solicitor will have conduct of the sale.

4 To enable the claimant to carry out the sale, there be created and vested in the claimant pursuant to section 90 of the Law of Property Act 1925 a legal term in the property of 3000 years one day less than the remaining period of the term created by the lease under which the defendant holds the property.

5 The defendant must deliver possession of the property to the claimant on or before the　　　　　　20 within　　　　　days of this order being served on him.

6 The claimant shall first apply the proceeds of sale of the property –

(i) to pay the costs and expenses of effecting the sale; and

(ii) to discharge any charges or other securities over the property which have priority over the charging order.

7 Out of the remaining proceeds of sale the claimant shall –

(i) retain the amount due to him as stated in paragraph 1; and

(ii) pay the balance (if any) to the Defendant to　　　　　　into court.

8 Either party may apply to the court to vary any of the terms of this order, or for further directions about the sale or the application of the proceeds of sale, or otherwise.

ORDER FOR SALE	In the
following a charging order	Claim No
(property owned by judgment debtor and another person)	

Claimant

Defendants

On the　　　　　20 ,　　　　　　　　　sitting at

Heard

The claimant is entitled to an equitable charge upon the first defendant's interest in the property

registered at HM Land Registry under Title No

('the property')

under a charging order made on the

in the   in Claim No

and the court orders that

1 The remainder of this order will not take effect if the defendant by 4.00 pm on the   20 pays to the claimant the judgment debt of £   secured by the charge and his costs to date of this application assessed at £   , making together £   together with interest at the rate of £   per day from the date of this order until payment is received by the claimant.

2 The property shall be sold without further reference to the court at a price not less than £   , unless that figure is changed by a further order of the court.

3 The claimant claimant's solicitor will have conduct of the sale.

4 The court pursuant to section 50 of the Trustee Act 1925 appoints the claimant claimant's solicitor to convey the property.

5 The defendant must deliver possession of the property to the claimant on or before the   20 within   days of this order being served on him.

6 The claimant shall first apply the proceeds of sale of the property –

(i) to pay the costs and expenses of effecting the sale; and

(ii) to discharge any charges or other securities over the property which have priority over the charging order.

7 The claimant shall then divide the remaining proceeds of sale into two equal shares and –

(i) pay one equal share to the second defendant; and

(ii) out of the other equal share, retain the amount due to him stated in paragraph 1, and pay the balance (if any) to the first defendant to   into court.

8 Any party may apply to the court to vary any of the terms of this order, or for further directions about the sale or the application of the proceeds of sale, or otherwise.

FAMILY PROCEDURE RULES 2010

SI 2010/2955

PRACTICE DIRECTION 6C –
DISCLOSURE OF ADDRESSES BY GOVERNMENT DEPARTMENTS
(AMENDING PD OF 13 FEBRUARY 1989 [AS AMENDED BY PRACTICE DIRECTION 20 JULY 1995])

This Practice Direction supplements FPR Part 6

The arrangements set out in the Registrar's Direction of 26 April 1988 whereby the court may request the disclosure of addresses by government departments have been further extended. These arrangements will now cover:

(a)   tracing the address of a person in proceedings against whom another person is seeking to obtain or enforce an order for financial provision either for himself or herself or for the children of the former marriage; and,

(b)   tracing the whereabouts of a child, or the person with whom the child is said to be, in proceedings under the Child Abduction and Custody Act 1985 or in which a [Part I order] is being sought or enforced.

Requests for such information will be made officially by the [district judge]. The request, in addition to giving the information mentioned below, should certify:

1 *In financial provision applications either*

(a)   that a financial provision order is in existence, but cannot be enforced because the person against whom the order has been made cannot be traced; or

(b)   that the applicant has filed or issued a notice, petition or originating summons containing an application for financial provision which cannot be served because the respondent cannot be traced.

[A 'financial provision order' means any of the orders mentioned in s 21 of the Matrimonial Causes Act 1973, except an order under s 27(6) of that Act].

2 *In wardship proceedings* that the child is the subject of wardship proceedings and cannot be traced, and is believed to be with the person whose address is sought.

3 *(deleted)*

The following notes set out the information required by those departments which are likely to be of the greatest assistance to an applicant.

(1) Department of Social Security

The department most likely to be able to assist is the Department of Social Security, whose records are the most comprehensive and complete. The possibility of identifying one person amongst so many will depend on the particulars given. An address will not be supplied by the department unless it is satisfied from the particulars given that the record of the person has been reliably identified.

The applicant or his solicitor should therefore be asked to supply as much as possible of the following information about the person sought:

(i)   National Insurance number;
(ii)   surname;
(iii)   forenames in full;
(iv)   date of birth (or, if not known, approximate age);
(v)   last known address, with date when living there;

(vi) any other known address(es) with dates;

(vii) if the person sought is a war pensioner, his war pension and service particulars (if known);

and in applications for financial provision:

(viii) the exact date of the marriage and the wife's forenames.

Enquiries should be sent by the [district judge] to:

Contribution Agency
Special Section A, Room 101B
Longbenton
Newcastle upon Tyne
NE98 1YX

The department will be prepared to search if given full particulars of the person's name and date of birth, but the chances of accurate identification are increased by the provision of more identifying information.

Second requests for records to be searched, provided that a reasonable interval has elapsed, will be met by the Department of Social Security.

Income Support [/Supplementary Benefit]

Where, in the case of applications for financial provision, the wife is or has been in receipt of [income support/supplementary benefit], it would be advisable in the first instance to make enquiries of the manager of the local Social Security office for the area in which she resides in order to avoid possible duplication of enquiries.

(2) [Office for National Statistics]

National Health Service Central Register

[The Office for National Statistics] administers the National Health Service Central Register for the Department of Health. The records held in the Central Register include individuals' names, with dates of birth and National Health Service number, against a record of the Family Practitioner Committee area where the patient is currently registered with a National Health Service doctor. The Central Register does not hold individual patients' addresses, but can advise courts of the last Family Practitioner Committee area registration. Courts can then apply for information about addresses to the appropriate Family Practitioner Committee for independent action.

When application is made for the disclosure of Family Practitioner Committee area registrations from these records the applicant or his solicitor should supply as much as possible of the following information about the person sought:

(i)   National Health Service number;
(ii)   surname;
(iii) forenames in full;
(iv)   date of birth (or, if not known, approximate age);
(v)   last known address;

(vi)   mother's maiden name.

Enquiries should be sent by the [district judge] to:

[The Office for National Statistics]
National Health Service Central Register
Smedley Hydro, Trafalgar Road
Southport
Merseyside PR8 2HH

(3) Passport Office

If all reasonable enquiries, including the aforesaid methods, have failed to reveal an address, or if there are strong grounds for believing that the person sought may have made a recent application for a passport, enquiries may be made to the Passport Office. The applicant or his solicitor should provide as much of the following information about the person as possible:

(i)   surname;
(ii)   forenames in full;
(iii)   date of birth (or, if not known, approximate age);
(iv)   place of birth;
(v)   occupation;
(vi)   whether known to have travelled abroad, and, if so, the destination and dates;
(vii)   last known address, with date living there;
(viii) any other known address(es), with dates.

The applicant or his solicitor must also undertake in writing that information given in response to the enquiry will be used solely for the purpose for which it was requested, ie to assist in tracing the husband in connection with the making or enforcement of a financial provision order or in tracing a child in connection with a [Part 1 order] or wardship proceedings, as the case may be.

Enquiries should be sent to:

The Chief Passport Officer
[UK Passport Agency]
Home Office
Clive House, Petty France
London SW1H 9HD

(4) Ministry of Defence

In cases where the person sought is known to be serving or to have recently served in any branch of HM Forces, the solicitor representing the applicant may obtain the address for service of financial provision or [Part I] and wardship proceedings direct from the appropriate service department. In the case of army servicemen, the solicitor can obtain a list of regiments and of the various manning and record offices from the Officer in Charge, Central Manning Support Office, Higher Barracks, Exeter EC4 4ND.

The solicitor's request should be accompanied by a written undertaking that the address will be used for the purpose of service of process in those proceedings and that so far as is possible the solicitor will disclose the address only to the court and not to the applicant or any other person, except in the normal course of the proceedings.

Alternatively, if the solicitor wishes to serve process on the person's commanding officer under the provisions contained in s 101 of the Naval Act 1957, s 153 of the Army Act 1955 and s 153 of the Air Force Act 1955 (all of which as amended by s 62 of the Armed Forces Act 1971) he may obtain that officer's address in the same way.

Where the applicant is acting in person the appropriate service department is prepared to disclose the address of the person sought, or that of his commanding officer, to a [district judge] on receipt of an assurance that the applicant has given an undertaking that the information will be used solely for the purpose of serving process in the proceedings.

In all cases, the request should include details of the person's full name, service number, rank or rating, and his ship, arm or trade, corps, regiment or unit or as much of this information as is available. The request should also include details of his date of birth, or, if not known, his age, his date of entry into the service and, if no longer serving, the date of discharge, and any other information, such as his last known address. Failure to quote the service number and the rank or rating may result in failure to identify the serviceman or at least in considerable delay.

Enquiries should be addressed as follows:

[(a)   Officers of Royal Navy and Women's Royal Naval Service

The Naval Secretary
Room 161
Victory Building
HM Naval Base
Portsmouth
Hants PO1 3LS

Ratings in the Royal Navy
WRNS Ratings
QARNNS Ratings

Captain
Naval Drafting
Centurion Building
Grange Road
Gosport
Hants PO13 9XA

RN Medical and Dental Officers

The Medical Director General (Naval)
Room 114
Victory Building
HM Naval Base
Portsmouth
Hants PO1 3LS

	Naval Chaplains	Director General Naval Chaplaincy Service Room 201 Victory Building HM Naval Base Portsmouth Hants PO1 3LS
(b)	Royal Marine Officers	The Naval Secretary Room 161 Victory Building HM Naval Base Portsmouth Hants PO1 3LS
	Royal Marine Ranks	HQRM (DRORM) West Battery Whale Island Portsmouth Hants PO2 8DX
(c)	Army Officers (including WRAC and QARANC)	Army Officer Documentation Office Index Department Room F7 Government Buildings Stanmore Middlesex
	Other Ranks, Army	The Manning and Record Office which is appropriate to the Regiment or Corps
(d)	Royal Air Force Officers and Other Ranks Women's Royal Air Force Officers and Other Ranks (including PMRA FNS)	Ministry of Defence RAF Personnel Management 2b1(a) (RAF) Building 248 RAF Innsworth Gloucester GL3 1EZ]

General notes

Records held by other departments are less likely to be of use, either because of their limited scope or because individual records cannot readily be identified. If, however, the circumstances suggest that the address may be known to another department, application may be made to it by the [district judge], all relevant particulars available being given.

When the department is able to supply the address of the person sought to the [district judge], it will be passed on by him to the applicant's solicitor (or, in proper cases, direct to the applicant if acting in person) on an understanding to use it only for the purpose of the proceedings.

Nothing in this practice direction affects the service in matrimonial causes of petitions which do not contain any application for financial provision, etc. The existing arrangements whereby the Department of Social Security will at the request of the solicitor forward a letter by ordinary post to a party's last known address remain in force in such cases.

The Registrar's Direction of 26 April 1988 is hereby revoked.

Issued [in its original form] with the concurrence of the Lord Chancellor.

****

28.3 Costs in financial remedy proceedings

(1) This rule applies in relation to financial remedy proceedings.

(2) Rule 44.2 (1), (4) and (5) of the CPR do not apply to financial remedy proceedings.

(3) Rules 44.2(6) to (8) and 44.12 of the CPR apply to an order made under this rule as they apply to an order made under rule 44.3 of the CPR.

(4) In this rule –

    (a) 'costs' has the same meaning as in rule 44.1(1)(c) of the CPR; and

    (b) 'financial remedy proceedings' means proceedings for –

        (i) a financial order except an order for maintenance pending suit, an order for maintenance pending outcome of proceedings, an interim periodical payments order[, an order for payment in respect of legal services or any other form of interim order for the purposes of rule 9.7(1)(a), (b), (c) and (e);

        (ii) an order under Part 3 of the 1984 Act;

        (iii) an order under Schedule 7 to the 2004 Act;

        (iv) an order under section 10(2) of the 1973 Act;

        (v) an order under section 48(2) of the 2004 Act.

(5) Subject to paragraph (6), the general rule in financial remedy proceedings is that the court will not make an order requiring one party to pay the costs of another party.

(6) The court may make an order requiring one party to pay the costs of another party at any stage of the proceedings where it considers it appropriate to do so because of the conduct of a party in relation to the proceedings (whether before or during them).

(7) In deciding what order (if any) to make under paragraph (6), the court must have regard to –

    (a) any failure by a party to comply with these rules, any order of the court or any practice direction which the court considers relevant;

    (b) any open offer to settle made by a party;

    (c) whether it was reasonable for a party to raise, pursue or contest a particular allegation or issue;

(d)   the manner in which a party has pursued or responded to the application or a particular allegation or issue;

(e)   any other aspect of a party's conduct in relation to proceedings which the court considers relevant; and

(f)   the financial effect on the parties of any costs order.

(8) No offer to settle which is not an open offer to settle is admissible at any stage of the proceedings, except as provided by rule 9.17.

Costs and financial remedy proceedings			
Type of financial application	(1) Financial remedy[1]	(2) Financial order[2]	(3) Financial remedy proceedings[3]
Avoidance of disposition order	*	*	*
Maintenance pending suit	*	*	+
Maintenance pending outcome of proceedings	*	*	+
Order for periodical payments or lump sum under MCA 1973 (save for under s 27(6))	*	*	*
The same: under CPA 2004, Sch 5, Pt 1	*	*	*
Property adjustment order (r 2.3(1))	*	*	*
A variation order (r 9.3(1))	*	*	*
A pension sharing order (r 9.3(1))	*	*	*
Order under MCA 1973, s 27 (and under CPA 2004, Sch 5, Pt 9)	*		
MFPA 1984, Pt 3 (and under CPA 2004, Sch 7)	*		*
MCA 1973, s 35 (and CPA 2004)	*		
DPMCA 1978 (and CPA 2004, Sch 6)	*		
MCA 1973, s 10(2) (and CPA 2004, s 48(2))			*
CA 1989, Sch 1	*		
Order preventing disposition (including MCA 1973, s 37(2)(a), CPA 2004 and MFPA 1984)	*		
Interim financial order (r 9.17)			+
Other Pt 18 applications Trial of prelim issue (eg *Baker v Rowe Baker v Rowe* [2009] EWCA Civ 1162) Set aside application *Barder* appeal			+
Appeal; Pt 30			

Costs and financial remedy proceedings			
Type of financial application	(1) Financial remedy[1]	(2) Financial order[2]	(3) Financial remedy proceedings[3]
Appeal to Court of Appeal: CPR 1998, Pt 52			

1   FPR 2010, Pt 9

2   FPR 2010, rr 2.3(1) and 9.4

3   FPR 2010, r 28.3(4)

Amendments—SI 2013/530; SI 2013/1472.

****

PRACTICE DIRECTION 28A –
COSTS

This Practice Direction supplements FPR Part 28

Application and modification of the CPR

1.1 Rule 28.2 provides that subject to rule 28.3 of the FPR and to paragraph (2) of rule 28.2, Parts 43, 44 (except rules 44.3(2) and (3), 44.9 to 44.12C, 44.13(1A) and (1B) and 44.18 to 20), 47 and 48 and rule 45.6 of the CPR apply to costs in family proceedings with the modifications listed in rule 28.2(1)(a) to (d). Rule 28.2(1)(c) refers to modifications in accordance with this Practice Direction.

1.2 In addition to the modifications to the CPR listed in rule 28.2(1), in rule 48.1(1)(b) after paragraph (ii) insert "(iii) section 68A of the Magistrates' Courts Act 1980.".

1.3 Rule 28.2(2) provides that Part 47 and rules 44.3C and 45.6 of the CPR do not apply to proceedings in a magistrates' court.

Application and modification of the Practice Direction supplementing CPR Parts 43 to 48

2.1 For the purpose of proceedings to which these Rules apply, the Practice Direction about costs which supplements Parts 43 to 48 of the CPR ("the costs practice direction") will apply, but with the exclusions and modifications explained below to reflect the exclusions and modifications to those Parts of the CPR as they are applied by Part 28 of these Rules.

2.2 Rule 28.2(1) applies, with modifications and certain exceptions, Parts 43 to 48 of the CPR to costs in family proceedings. Paragraph 1.2 of this Practice Direction modifies rule 48.1(1)(b) when it applies to family proceedings. Rule 28.2(2), by way of exception, disapplies Part 47, rules 44.3C and 45.6 of the CPR in the case of family proceedings in a magistrates' court. Rule 28.3, again by way of exception, additionally disapplies CPR rule 44.3(1), (4) and (5) in the case of financial remedy proceedings, regardless of court.

2.3 The costs practice direction does not, therefore, apply in its entirety but with the exclusion of certain sections reflecting the non-application of certain rules of the CPR which those sections supplement.

2.4 The costs practice direction applies as follows –

- to family proceedings generally, other than in magistrates' courts, with the exception of sections 6, 15, 16, 17 and 23A;
- to family proceedings generally, in magistrates' courts only, with the exception of sections 6, 15, 16, 17, 23A and sections 28–49A;
- to financial remedy proceedings, other than in magistrates' courts, with the exception of section 6, paragraphs 8.1 to 8.4 of section 8 and sections 15, 16, 17 and 23A;
- to a financial remedy proceedings, in magistrates' courts only, with the exception of section 6, paragraphs 8.1 to 8.4 of section 8, sections 15, 16, 17, 23A and sections 28–49A.

2.5 All subsequent editions of the costs practice direction as and when they are published and come into effect shall in the same way extend to all family proceedings.

2.6 The costs practice direction includes provisions applicable to proceedings following changes in the manner in which legal services are funded pursuant to the Access to Justice Act 1999. It should be noted that although the cost of the premium in respect of legal costs insurance (section 29) or the cost of funding by a prescribed membership organisation (section 30) may be recoverable, family proceedings (within section 58A(2) of the Courts and Legal Services Act 1990) cannot be the subject of an enforceable conditional fee agreement.

2.7 Paragraph 1.4 of section 1 of the costs practice direction shall be modified as follows –

in the definition of "counsel" for "High court or in the county courts" substitute "High Court, county courts or in a magistrates' court".

General interpretation of references in CPR

3.1 References in the costs practice direction to "claimant" and "defendant" are to be read as references to equivalent terms used in proceedings to which these Rules apply and other terms and expressions used in the costs practice direction shall be similarly treated.

3.2 References in CPR Parts 43 to 48 to other rules or Parts of the CPR shall be read, where there is an equivalent rule or Part in these Rules, to that equivalent rule or Part.

Costs in financial remedy proceedings

4.1 Rule 28.3 relates to the court's power to make costs orders in financial remedy proceedings. For the purposes of rule 28.3, "financial remedy proceedings" are defined in accordance with rule 28.3(4)(b). That definition, which is more limited than the principal definition in rule 2.3(1), includes:

(a)   an application for a financial order, except:
  (i)   an order for maintenance pending suit or an order for maintenance pending outcome of proceedings;
  (ii)   an interim periodical payments order or any other form of interim order for the purposes of rule 9.7(1)(a), (b), (c) and (e);
(b)   an application for an order under Part 3 of the Matrimonial and Family Proceedings Act 1984 or Schedule 7 to the Civil Partnership Act 2004; and
(c)   an application under section 10(2) of the Matrimonial Causes Act 1973 or section 48(2) of the Civil Partnership Act 2004.

4.2 Accordingly, it should be noted that:

(a)   while most interim financial applications are excluded from rule 28.3, the rule does apply to an application for an interim variation order within rule 9.7(1)(d),
(b)   rule 28.3 does not apply to an application for any of the following financial remedies:
  (i)   an order under Schedule 1 to the Children Act 1989;
  (ii)   an order under section 27 of the Matrimonial Causes Act 1973 or Part 9 of Schedule 5 to the Civil Partnership Act 2004;
  (iii)   an order under section 35 of the Matrimonial Causes Act 1973 or paragraph 69 of Schedule 5 to the Civil Partnership Act 2004; or
  (iv)   an order under Part 1 of the Domestic Proceedings and Magistrates' Courts Act 1978 or Schedule 6 to the Civil Partnership Act 2004.

4.3 Under rule 28.3 the court only has the power to make a costs order in financial remedy proceedings when this is justified by the litigation conduct of one of the parties. When determining whether and how to exercise this power the court will be required to take into account the list of factors set out in that rule. The court will not be able to take into account any offers to settle expressed to be "without prejudice" or "without prejudice save as to costs" in deciding what, if any, costs orders to make.

4.4 In considering the conduct of the parties for the purposes of rule 28.3(6) and (7) (including any open offers to settle), the court will have regard to the obligation of the parties to help the court to further the overriding objective (see rules 1.1 and 1.3) and will take into account the nature, importance and complexity of the issues in the case. This may be of particular significance in applications for variation orders and interim variation orders or other cases where there is a risk of the costs becoming disproportionate to the amounts in dispute.

4.5 Parties who intend to seek a costs order against another party in proceedings to which rule 28.3 applies should ordinarily make this plain in open correspondence or in skeleton arguments before the date of the hearing. In any case where summary assessment of costs awarded under rule 28.3 would be appropriate parties are under an obligation to file a statement of costs in CPR Form N260.

4.6 An interim financial order which includes an element to allow a party to deal with legal fees (see *A v A (maintenance pending suit: provision for legal fees)* [2001] 1 WLR 605; *G v G (maintenance pending suit; costs)* [2002] EWHC 306 (Fam); *McFarlane v McFarlane, Parlour v Parlour* [2004] EWCA Civ 872; *Moses-Taiga v Taiga* [2005] EWCA Civ 1013; *C v C (Maintenance Pending Suit: Legal Costs)* [2006] Fam Law 739; *Currey v Currey (No 2)* [2006] EWCA Civ 1338) is an order made pursuant to section 22 of the Matrimonial Causes Act 1973 or an order under paragraph 38 of Schedule 5 of the 2004 Act, and is not a "costs order" within the meaning of rule 28.3.

4.7 By virtue of rule 28.2(1), where rule 28.3 does not apply, the exercise of the court's discretion as to costs is governed by the relevant provisions of the CPR and in particular rule 44.3 (excluding r 44.3(2) and (3)).

* * * *

PART 33
ENFORCEMENT

Chapter 1
General Rules

33.1 Application

(1) The rules in this Part apply to an application made in the High Court and a county court to enforce an order made in family proceedings.

(2) Part 50 of, and Schedules 1 and 2 to, the CPR apply, as far as they are relevant and with necessary modification (including the modifications referred to in rule 33.7), to an application made in the High Court and a county court to enforce an order made in family proceedings.

Section 1
Enforcement of orders for the payment of money

33.2 Application of the Civil Procedure Rules

Part 70 of the CPR applies to proceedings under this Section as if –

    (a)   in rule 70.1, in paragraph (2)(d), 'but does not include a judgment or order for the payment of money into court' is omitted; and

    (b)   rule 70.5 is omitted.

33.3 How to apply

(1) Except where a rule or practice direction otherwise requires, an application for an order to enforce an order for the payment of money must be made in a notice of application accompanied by a statement which must –

(a) state the amount due under the order, showing how that amount is arrived at; and

(b) be verified by a statement of truth.

(2) The notice of application may either –

(a) apply for an order specifying the method of enforcement; or

(b) apply for an order for such method of enforcement as the court may consider appropriate.

(3) If an application is made under paragraph (2)(b), an order to attend court will be issued and rule 71.2 (6) and (7) of the CPR will apply as if the application had been made under that rule.

33.4 Transfer of orders

(1) This rule applies to an application for the transfer –

(a) to the High Court of an order made in a designated county court; and

(b) to a designated county court of an order made in the High Court.

(2) The application must be –

(a) made without notice; and

(b) accompanied by a statement which complies with rule 33.3(1).

(3) The transfer will have effect upon the filing of the application.

(4) Where an order is transferred from a designated county court to the High Court –

(a) it will have the same force and effect; and

(b) the same proceedings may be taken on it,

as if it were an order of the High Court.

(5) This rule does not apply to the transfer of orders for periodical payments or for the recovery of arrears of periodical payments.

Section 2
Committal and injunction

33.5 General rule – committal hearings to be in public

(1) The general rule is that proceedings in the High Court for an order of committal will be heard in public.

(2) An order of committal may be heard in private where this is permitted by rule 6 of Order 52 of the RSC (cases in which a court may sit in private).

33.6 Proceedings in the principal registry treated as pending in a designated county court

(1) This rule applies where an order for the warrant of committal of any person to prison has been made or issued in proceedings which are –

(a) in the principal registry; and

(b)   treated as pending in a designated county court or a county court.

(2) The person subject to the order will, wherever located, be treated for the purposes of section 122 of the County Courts Act 1984 as being out of the jurisdiction of the principal registry.

(3) Where –

(a)   a committal is for failure to comply with the terms of an injunction^(GL); or

(b)   an order or warrant for the arrest or committal of any person is made or issued in proceedings under Part 4 of the 1996 Act in the principal registry which are treated as pending in a county court,

the order or warrant may, if the court so directs, be executed by the tipstaff within any county court.

33.7 Specific modifications of the CCR

(1) CCR Order 29, rule 1 (committal for breach of an order or undertaking) applies to –

(a)   section 8 orders, except those referred to in paragraph (2)(a); and
(b)   orders under the following sections of the 1989 Act –
   (i)   section 14A (special guardianship orders);
   (ii)   14B(2)(b) (granting of permission on making a special guardianship order to remove a child from the United Kingdom);
   (iii) section 14C(3)(b) (granting of permission to remove from the United Kingdom a child who is subject to a special guardianship order); and
   (iv)   section 14D (variation or discharge of a special guardianship order),

as if paragraph (3) of that rule were substituted by the following paragraph –

'(3) In the case of a section 8 order (within the meaning of section 8(2) of the Children Act 1989) or an order under section 14A, 14B(2)(b), 14C(3)(b) or 14D of the Children Act 1989 enforceable by committal order under paragraph (1), the judge or the district judge may, on the application of the person entitled to enforce the order, direct that the proper officer issue a copy of the order, endorsed with or incorporating a notice as to the consequences of disobedience, for service in accordance with paragraph (2), and no copy of the order shall be issued with any such notice endorsed or incorporated save in accordance with such a direction.'.

(2) CCR Order 29, rule 1 applies to –

(a)   contact orders to which a notice has been attached under section 11I of the 1989 Act or under section 8(2) of the Children and Adoption Act 2006;
(b)   orders under section 11J of the 1989 Act (enforcement orders); and
(c)   orders under paragraph 9 of Schedule A1 to the 1989 Act (orders following breach of enforcement orders),

as if paragraph (3) were omitted.

33.8 Section 118 County Courts Act 1984 and the tipstaff

For the purposes of section 118 of the County Courts Act 1984 in its application to the hearing of family proceedings at the Royal Courts of Justice or the principal registry, the tipstaff is deemed to be an officer of the court.

Chapter 2
Committal by way of Judgment Summons

33.9 Interpretation

In this Chapter, unless the context requires otherwise –

'order' means an order made in family proceedings for the payment of money;
'judgment creditor' means a person entitled to enforce an order under section 5 of the Debtors Act 1869;
'debtor' means a person liable under an order; and
'judgment summons' means a summons under section 5 of the Debtor's Act 1869 requiring a debtor to attend court.

33.10 Application

(1) An application for the issue of a judgment summons may be made –

  (a) in the case of an order of the High Court –
    (i) where the order was made in matrimonial proceedings, to the principal registry, a district registry or a divorce county court, whichever in the opinion of the judgment creditor is most convenient;
    (ii) where the order was made in civil partnership proceedings, to the principal registry, a district registry or a civil partnership proceedings county court, whichever in the opinion of the judgment creditor is the most convenient; and
    (iii) in any other case, to the principal registry, a district registry or a designated county court, whichever in the opinion of the judgment creditor is most convenient;
  (b) in the case of an order of a divorce county court, to whichever divorce county court is in the opinion of the judgment creditor most convenient; and
  (c) in the case of an order of a civil partnership proceedings county court, to whichever civil partnership proceedings county court is in the opinion of the judgment creditor most convenient,

having regard (in any case) to the place where the debtor resides or carries on business and irrespective of the court or registry in which the order was made.

(2) An application must be accompanied by a statement which –

  (a) complies with rule 33.3(1);
  (b) contains all the evidence on which the judgment creditor intends to rely; and
  (c) has exhibited to it a copy of the order.

33.11 Judgment summons

(1) If the debtor is in default under an order of committal made on a previous judgment summons in respect of the same order, a judgment summons must not be issued without the court's permission.

(2) A judgment summons must –

    (a)   be accompanied by the statement referred to in rule 33.10(2) and

    (b)   be served on the debtor personally not less than 14 days before the hearing.

(3) A debtor served with the judgment summons under paragraph (2)(b) must be paid or offered a sum reasonably sufficient to cover the expenses of travelling to and from the court at which the debtor is summoned to appear.

33.12 Successive judgment summonses

Subject to rule 33.11(1), successive judgment summonses may be issued even if the debtor has ceased to reside or carry on business at the address stated in the application for the issue of a judgment summons since the issue of the original judgment summons.

33.13 Requirement for personal service

In proceedings for committal by way of judgment summons, the following documents must be served personally on the debtor –

    (a)   where the court has summonsed the debtor to attend and the debtor has failed to do so, the notice of the date and time fixed for the adjourned hearing; and

    (b)   copies of the judgment summons and the documents mentioned in rule 33.10(2).

33.14 Committal on application for judgment summons

(1) No person may be committed on an application for a judgment summons unless –

    (a)   where the proceedings are in the High Court, the debtor has failed to attend both the hearing that the debtor was summonsed to attend and the adjourned hearing;

    (b)   where the proceedings are in a county court, an order is made under section 110(2) of the County Courts Act 1984; or

    (c)   the judgment creditor proves that the debtor –

        (i)   has, or has had, since the date of the order the means to pay the sum in respect of which the debtor has made default; and

        (ii)   has refused or neglected, or refuses or neglects, to pay that sum.

(2) The debtor may not be compelled to give evidence.

33.15 Orders for the benefit of different persons

Where an applicant has obtained one or more orders in the same application but for the benefit of different persons –

(a) where the judgment creditor is a child, the applicant may apply for the issue of a judgment summons in respect of those orders on behalf of the judgment creditor without seeking permission to act as the child's litigation friend; and

(b) only one judgment summons need be issued in respect of those orders.

33.16 Hearing of judgment summons

(1) On the hearing of the judgment summons the court may –

(a) where the order is for lump sum provision or costs; or

(b) where the order is an order for maintenance pending suit, an order for maintenance pending outcome of proceedings or an order for other periodical payments and it appears to the court that the order would have been varied or suspended if the debtor had made an application for that purpose,

make a new order for payment of the amount due under the original order, together with the costs of the judgment summons, either at a specified time or by instalments.

(2) If the court makes an order of committal, it may direct its execution to be suspended on terms that the debtor pays to the judgment creditor –

(a) the amount due;

(b) the costs of the judgment summons; and

(c) any sums accruing due under the original order,

either at a specified time or by instalments.

(3) All payments under a new order or an order of committal must be made to the judgment creditor unless the court directs otherwise.

(4) Where an order of committal is suspended on such terms as are mentioned in paragraph (2) –

(a) all payments made under the suspended order will be deemed to be made –

(i) first, in or towards the discharge of any sums from time to time accruing due under the original order; and

(ii) secondly, in or towards the discharge of a debt in respect of which the judgment summons was issued and the costs of the summons; and

(b) the suspended order must not be executed until the judgment creditor has filed a statement of default on the part of the debtor.

33.17 Special provisions as to judgment summonses in the High Court

(1) The court may summons witnesses to give evidence to prove the means of the debtor and may issue a witness summons for that purpose.

(2) Where the debtor appears at the hearing, the court may direct that the travelling expenses paid to the debtor be allowed as expenses of a witness.

(3) Where the debtor appears at the hearing and no order of committal is made, the court may allow the debtor's proper costs including compensation for any loss of earnings.

(4) When the court makes –

    (a)   a new order; or
    (b)   an order of committal,

a court officer must send notice of the order to the debtor and, if the original order was made in another court, to that court.

(5) An order of committal must be directed –

    (a)   where the order is to be executed by the tipstaff, to the tipstaff; or
    (b)   where the order is to be executed by a deputy tipstaff, to the county court within the district of which the debtor is to be found.

33.18 Special provisions as to judgment summonses in designated county courts

(1) Rules 1, 2, 3(2), 5, 7(3) and 9(2) of Order 28 of the CCR (which deal with the issue of a judgment summons in a county court and the subsequent procedure) do not apply to judgment summons issued in a designated county court.

(2) Rule 9(1) of Order 28 of the CCR (notification of order on judgment of High Court) applies to such a summons as if for the words 'the High Court' there were substituted the words –

    (a)   'any other court' where they first appear; and
    (b)   'that other court' where they next appear.

(3) Rule 7(1) and (2) of Order 28 of the CCR (suspension of a committal order) apply to such a summons subject to rule 33.16(2) and (3).

Chapter 3
Attachment of Earnings

33.19 Proceedings in the Principal Registry

The Attachment of Earnings Act 1971 and Order 27 of the CCR (attachment of earnings) apply to the enforcement of an order made in family proceedings in the principal registry which are treated as pending in a designated county court as if they were an order made by such a court.

Chapter 4
Warrant of Execution

33.20 Applications to vary existing orders

Where an application is pending for a variation of –

(a) a financial order;
(b) an order under section 27 of the 1973 Act; or
(c) an order under Part 9 of Schedule 5 to the 2004 Act,

no warrant of execution may be issued to enforce payment of any sum due under those orders, except with the permission of the district judge.

33.21 Section 103 County Courts Act 1984

Where a warrant of execution has been issued to enforce an order made in family proceedings pending in the principal registry which are treated as pending in a designated county court, the goods and chattels against which the warrant has been issued must, wherever they are located, be treated for the purposes of section 103 of the County Courts Act 1984 as being out of the jurisdiction of the principal registry.

Chapter 5
Court's Power to Appoint a Receiver

33.22 Application of the CPR

Part 69 of the CPR applies to proceedings under this Part.

Chapter 6
Orders to Obtain Information from Judgment Debtors

33.23 Application of the CPR

Part 71 of the CPR applies to proceedings under this Part.

Chapter 7
Third Party Debt Orders

33.24 Application of the CPR

(1) Part 72 of the CPR applies to proceedings under this Part with the following modifications.

(2) In rule 72.4 –

(a) in paragraph (1), for 'a judge' there is substituted 'the court'; and
(b) in paragraph (2), for 'judge' there is substituted 'court'.

(3) In rule 72.7, in paragraph (2)(a), after 'the Royal Courts of Justice' insert ', or the principal registry'.

(4) Rule 72.10 is omitted.

Chapter 8
Charging Order, Stop Order, Stop Notice

33.25 Application of the CPR

(1) Part 73 of the CPR applies to proceedings under this Part with the following modifications.

(2) In rule 73.1, paragraph (2), sub-paragraphs (b) and (c) are omitted.

(3) For rule 73.2, there is substituted 'This Section applies to an application by a judgment creditor for a charging order under section 1 of the 1979 Act.'.

(4) In rule 73.3, paragraph (2), sub-paragraphs (b) and (c) are omitted.

(5) In rule 73.4 –

    (a)   in paragraph (1), for 'a judge' there is substituted 'the court,'; and
    (b)   in paragraph (2), for 'judge' there is substituted 'court'.

(6) In rule 73.9, in the parenthesis after paragraph (1) –

    (a)   'and regulation 51.4 of the 1992 Regulations' is omitted;
    (b)   for 'provides' there is substituted 'provide', and
    (c)   ', or (where the 1992 Regulations apply) of the authority,' is omitted.

(7) In rule 73.10 –

    (a)   in paragraph (1), for 'a claim' there is substituted 'an application';
    (b)   in paragraph (2) and the parenthesis following it, for 'A claim' each time it appears there is substituted 'An application';
    (c)   in paragraph (3), for 'claimant' there is substituted 'applicant';
    (d)   in paragraph (4), for 'claim form' there is substituted 'application'; and
    (e)   in paragraph (5), for 'claimant's' there is substituted 'applicant's'.

(8) In rule 73.11, 'funds in court or' is omitted.

(9) In rule 73.12 –

    (a)   paragraph (1)(a) is omitted;
    (b)   in paragraph (1)(b) 'other than securities held in court' is omitted;
    (c)   in paragraph (2), in sub-paragraph (b), for 'claim form' there is substituted 'application notice'; and
    (d)   in paragraph (3) –
        (i)   'or claim form' is omitted; and
        (ii)   for sub-paragraph (b) there is substituted 'the person specified in rule 73.5(1)(d)'.

(10) Rule 73.13 is omitted.

(11) In rule 73.14, in paragraph (1), 'other than securities held in court' is omitted.

(12) In rule 73.16 –

    (a)   in paragraph (a) for '; and' there is substituted '.'; and
    (b)   paragraph (b) is omitted.

PRACTICE DIRECTION 33A –
ENFORCEMENT OF UNDERTAKINGS

This Practice Direction supplements FPR Part 33

Enforcement of undertaking to do or abstain from doing any act other than the payment of money

1.1 Rule 33.1(2) provides that Part 50 of, and Schedules 1 and 2 to, the CPR (which contain the Rules of the Supreme Court (RSC) and County Court Rules (CCR) respectively) apply, as far as they are relevant and with necessary modification, to an application made in the High Court and a county court to enforce an order made in family proceedings.

1.2 Subject to the Debtors Act 1869 (which makes provision in relation to orders for the payment of money), RSC Order 45.5 and CCR Order 29.1 enable a judgment or order to be enforced by committal for contempt of court where –

(a)   a person who is required by a judgment or order to do an act has refused or neglected to do that act within the specified time; or

(b)   a person disobeys a judgment or order requiring him to abstain from doing an act.

1.3 These Rules apply to undertakings as they apply to orders, with necessary modifications.

1.4 The form of an undertaking to do or abstain from doing any act must be endorsed with a notice setting out the consequences of disobedience, as follows:

> 'You may be sent to prison for contempt of court if you break the promises that you have given to the court'.

1.5 The person giving the undertaking must make a signed statement to the effect that he or she understands the terms of the undertaking being given and the consequences of failure to comply with it, as follows:

> 'I understand the undertaking that I have given, and that if I break any of my promises to the court I may be sent to prison for contempt of court'.

1.6 The statement need not be given before the court in person. It may be endorsed on the court copy of the undertaking or may be filed in a separate document such as a letter.

Enforcement of undertaking for the payment of money

2.1 Any undertaking for the payment of money that has effect as if it was an order made under Part 2 of the Matrimonial Causes Act 1973 may be enforced as if it was an order and Part 33 applies accordingly.

2.2 The form of an undertaking for the payment of money that has effect as if it were an order under Part 2 of the Matrimonial Causes Act 1973 must be endorsed with a notice setting out the consequences of disobedience, as follows:

'If you fail to pay any sum of money which you have promised the court that you will pay, a person entitled to enforce the undertaking may apply to the court for an order. You may be sent to prison if it is proved that you –

(a) have, or have had since the date of your undertaking, the means to pay the sum; and

(b) have refused or neglected, or are refusing or neglecting, to pay that sum.'

2.3 The person giving the undertaking must make a signed statement to the effect that he or she understands the terms of the undertaking being given and the consequences of failure to comply with it, as follows:

'I understand the undertaking that I have given, and that if I break my promise to the court to pay any sum of money, I may be sent to prison'.

2.4 The statement need not be given before the court in person. It may be endorsed on the court copy of the undertaking or may be filed in a separate document such as a letter.

INSOLVENCY RULES 1986

SI 1986/1925

* * * *

12.3 Provable debts

* * * *

(2) The following are not provable –

(a) in bankruptcy, any fine imposed for an offence, and any obligation (other than an obligation to pay a lump sum or to pay costs) arising under an order made in family proceedings or any obligation arising under a maintenance assessment made under the Child Support Act 1991;

Amendments—SI 1993/602; SI 2005/527.

* * * *

APPENDIX 3

FORMS

FORM N349 APPLICATION FOR THIRD-PARTY DEBT ORDER

Application for third party debt order

In the

Claim No.

Click here to reset form

Appn. No.

Claimant

Defendant

Third Party

The [claimant] [defendant] ('the judgment creditor') applies for an order that the third party pay to the judgment creditor the debt which the third party owes to the [defendant] [claimant] ('the judgment debtor') (or so much of it as is necessary to discharge the amount owing under the judgment or order given on   20   [by the   in claim no.   ] and the costs of this application).

1. **Judgment debtor**
    The judgment debtor is
    whose address is

    Postcode

2. **Judgment debt**
    The judgment or order required the judgment debtor to pay £   (including any costs and interest). The amount now due is £   [which includes further interest].
    ☐ £   of the instalments due under the judgment or order has fallen due and remains unpaid.

    ☐ The judgment or order did not provide for payment by instalments.

3. **Third party**
    The third party is within England and Wales and owes money to (or holds money to the credit of) the judgment debtor.

    The third party is a bank or building society.
    Its name is
    Its head office address in England and Wales is:

    The branch at which the account is held is
    ☐ not known

    ☐ the
        whose address is

    The account number is   The sort code is
    ☐ not known   ☐ not known
    ☐   ☐

N349 Application for third party debt order (03.02)   HMCS

[The third party is not a bank or building society.

☐ the third party is

whose address in England and Wales is

4.   **Other persons' interests**
The persons (in addition to the judgment debtor) who have a claim to the money owed by the third party are

☐ None

☐ The following: *(names and address(es))*

Information known about each person's claim:

5.   **Sources and grounds of information**
The judgment creditor knowns or believes that the information in section 3 and 4 is correct because:

6.   **Other applications**
In respect of the judgment debt,

☐ the judgment creditor has made no other applications for third party debt orders.

☐ the judgment creditor has already made the following application(s) for third party debt order:
Details of application(s)

Third party's name
Address

Postcode

Statement of Truth

*I believe (the judgment creditor believes) that the facts stated in this application form are true.

*I am duly authorised by the judgment creditor to sign this statement

signed _____ date _____

*(Judgment creditor)(Litigation friend *(where judgment creditor is a child or a patient)*)(Judgment creditor's solicitor)

*delete as appropriate

Full name _____

Name of judgment creditor's solicitor's firm _____

position or office held _____ *(if signing on behalf of a firm or company)*

Judgment creditor's or
judgment creditor's
solicitor's address to
which documents
should be sent.

if applicable

Ref. no.	
fax no.	
DX no.	
e-mail	
Tel. no.	

Postcode

FORM N337 REQUEST FOR ATTACHMENT OF EARNINGS ORDER

Click here to reset form	Click here to print form

Request for Attachment of Earnings Order
to be completed and signed by the claimant or their solicitor and sent to the court with the appropriate fee

Name of county court

1 Claimant's details
name, address, and phone number

Postcode

Phone no.

Claim number

For court use only

A/E application no.

Issue date:

Hearing date:

2 Name and address for service and payment
(if different from above)
Ref/Phone no.

Postcode

Phone no.

on

at   o'clock

at (address)

6 Employment details *(continued)*

Debtor's place of work
(if different from employer's address)

3 Debtor's details
name, address and phone number

Postcode

Phone no.

The debtor is employed as

Works No. / Pay Ref.

4 Judgment details

Court where judgment/order made if not court of issue

7 Other details
Give any other details about the debtor's circumstances which may be relevant to the application.

5 Outstanding debt

Balance due at date of request*
(excluding issue fee but including unsatisfied warrant costs)

* you may also be entitled to interest to the date of request where judgment is for £5,000 or more, or is in respect of a debt which attracts contractual or statutory interest for late payment

Issue fee

AMOUNT NOW DUE

6 Employment details *(please give as much information as you can – it will help the court to make an order more quickly)*

Employer's name and address

Postcode

Phone no.

I apply for an attachment of earnings order

I certify that the whole or part of any instalments due under the judgment or order have not been paid and the balance now due is as shown.

Signed

Claimant (Claimants solicitor)

Date

IMPORTANT
You must tell the court immediately of any payments you receive after you have sent this request to the court

N337 Request for attachment of earnings order (06.09)   © Crown copyright 2009

FORM N379 APPLICATION FOR CHARGING ORDER ON LAND OR PROPERTY

**Application
for charging order
on land or property**

Click here to reset form

In the

Claim No.

Appn. No.

Claimant

Defendant

The [claimant] [defendant] ('the judgment creditor') applies for an order imposing a charge on
the interest of the [defendant] [claimant] ('the judgment debtor') in the land or
property mentioned below to secure payment of the amount owing under the judgment or order
given on   20   [by the   in
claim no.   ].

1. **Judgment debtor**
The judgment debtor is
whose address is

Postcode

2. **Judgment debt**
The judgment or order required the judgment debtor to pay £   (including any costs and
interest). The amount now owing is £   [which includes further
interest payable on the judgment debt].

☐ £   of the instalments due under the judgment or order has fallen due and remains
unpaid.

☐ The judgment or order did not provide for payment by instalments.

3. **The land or property**
The address of the land or property upon which it is sought to impose a to charge is

[the title to which is registered at H. M. Land Registry under Title No.
An Office Copy of the Land Register entries for this title is attached.]

4. **Judgment debtor's interest in the land or property**
The judgment debtor is:

☐ the sole owner   ☐ a joint owner   ☐ a beneficiary under a trust

☐ This is shown by the Office Copy Land Register entries attached.

☐ The judgment creditor believes this to be so because

5. **Other creditors**

    ☐ The judgment creditor does not know of any other creditors of the judgment debtor.

    ☐ The judgment creditor knows of the following other creditors of the judgment debtor:
    (names and addresses and, if known, nature of debt and amount)

6. **Other persons to be served**

    ☐ No other person has an interest in the property (including any co-owners, trustees and persons with rights of occupation).

    ☐ The following persons have or may have an interest in the property:
    (name and address and, if known, nature of interest)

7. **Further information**

    The judgment creditor asks the court to take account of the following:

8. **Sources of information** *(Complete only where the judgment creditor is a firm or a company or other corporation)*

    [The information in this application is given [by me] [by   of
                                                    who is the   of the
    judgment creditor] after making proper enquiry of all persons within the judgment creditor's
    organisation who might have knowledge of the facts.]

Statement of Truth
*I believe (the judgment creditor believes) that the facts stated in this application form are true.
*I am duly authorised by the judgment creditor to sign this statement
signed _____ date _____
*(Judgment creditor)(Litigation friend *(where judgment creditor is a child or a patient)*)(Judgment creditor's solicitor)
*delete as appropriate
Full name _____
Name of judgment creditor's solicitor's firm _____
position or office held _____ *(if signing on behalf of a firm or company)*

Judgment creditor's or judgment creditor's solicitor's address to which documents should be sent.		*if applicable*	
		Ref. no.	
		fax no.	
		DX no.	
		e-mail	
		Tel. no.	
	Postcode		

FORM EX140 RECORD OF EXAMINATION

Record of examination
(Individual)

Click here to reset form.

In the	
Claim No.	
Appn No.	

Judgment Creditor:

Judgment Debtor:

---

1 Personal Information

Full Name

Your age?

Present address

National insurance no.

Are you
- [ ] married?
- [ ] single?
- [ ] separated?
- [ ] divorced?
- [ ] living with partner?

Phone numbers:

home

work

mobile

other

Do you intend moving to another address?
- [ ] Yes
- [ ] No

If Yes, what will your new address be and when are you moving?

Date

Do you have any dependant children?
- [ ] Yes
- [ ] No

If Yes, what are their names and ages?

Name	Age

Do you have other dependants living with you, *eg. elderly relatives*?
- [ ] Yes
- [ ] No

If Yes, what are their names and ages and to what extent are they dependant?

(2) Employment Status

Are you ☐ employed?
Go to section 3
below

☐ self employed?
Go to section 4
page 3

☐ unemployed?
Go to section 5
page 5

☐ retired?
Go to section 6
page 5

(3) Employment Details

What is your
occupation?

Where is your
place of work
if different?

What is the
name and
address of your
employer and
your employee
number?

employee number

What is your gross pay
*ie. before tax, national
insurance deductions?*

£   per

What is your average take
home pay including
overtime and commission?

£   per

Do you receive Working
Tax Credit?

☐ Yes
☐ No

If Yes, how much? £   per

How often are you paid?

☐ weekly   ☐ monthly   ☐ other _____

On which day are you
paid?

Is your pay paid

☐ in cash   ☐ by cheque   ☐ direct to bank or building society account?

If direct to bank or building
society account what is
the name and address of
the branch and account
number?

account
number

Do you have any jobs other
than your main job?

☐ Yes
☐ No

If Yes, ask for all the above details in relation to
all other jobs and set out information below.

2

—[Go to Section 7 page 5]—

④ Self Employed

How long have you been self employed?		What work do you do?

What is the name of your business?

Do you have business premises? eg. shop, yard, lockup
☐ Yes   If Yes, what is their address?
☐ No

What is your annual turnover? £ _____

What amount of profit did the business make over the last year? £ _____

How much do you draw from the business? £ _____ per _____

What were your total drawings in last 12 months? £ _____

Are you a ☐ sole trader?   ☐ partner?   If a partner,
(a) How many partners are there? _____

How many employees do you have? _____

(b) What is your share of the partnership ? _____ %

Do you complete Inland Revenue self assessment? ☐ Yes   ☐ No

Do you have accounts? ☐ Yes   ☐ No

Do you employ an accountant? ☐ Yes ☐ No   If Yes, what is the accountant's name and address?

If you don't have an accountant are accounts audited by a third party? ☐ Yes ☐ No   If Yes, give name and address and say when audit takes place?

Will you allow the creditor to approach your accountant or auditor or Inland Revenue to verify the information you have given in this section? ☐ Yes ☐ No

Date of audit

Are you working on any contracts at the moment? ☐ Yes ☐ No   If Yes, give details below

Name and address of customer	Nature of work	Contract price £	Amount outstanding £	Date payment expected

3

Is any money still due to you for work already done? ☐ Yes   ☐ No   If Yes, give details below

Name and address of customer	Nature of work	Contract price £	Amount outstanding £	Date payment expected

If money (see above) is overdue what steps are you taking to recover it?

Do you have contracts for work in the future? ☐ Yes   ☐ No   If Yes, give details below

Name and address of customer	Nature of work	Expected price £

—[Go to Section 7 page 5]—

4

5 Unemployed

How long have you been unemployed?

What is your trade / training /profession?

What steps are you taking to obtain employment?

Do you have any outstanding job interviews?

☐ Yes   If Yes, when?
☐ No

What state benefits do you receive?
(Housing benefit, if any should be included section 8b on page 7)

Type of benefit	Amount	Frequency of payment	DSS/BA ref.

—{ Go to Section 7 below }—

6 Retired

When did you retire?

By whom are your pension(s) paid, how much is paid and when?
(include both state and private pensions)

Pension from	Amount	Frequency of payment

—{ Go to Section 7 below }—

7 Other Income

Is there anyone else in your household who is employed? *(Do not include tenants/lodgers. See section 8 on page 6)*

☐ Yes   If Yes, how much do they contribute to the running of the home?   £   per
☐ No

What other state benefits do you receive?
(Housing benefit, if any should be included section 8b on page 7)

Type of benefit	Amount	Frequency of payment	DSS/BA ref.

—{ Go to Section 8 page 6 }—

5

8 Residence

Is your home

- [ ] your own property? Go to 8a below
- [ ] lodgings? Go to 8b page 7
- [ ] rented from a council or housing association? Go to 8b page 7
- [ ] rented unfurnished from a private landlord? Go to 8b page 7
- [ ] rented furnished from a private landlord? Go to 8b page 7
- [ ] other _____ (e.g. mobile home) Go to 8b page 7

8a Your own property

Are you the sole owner?
- [ ] Yes
- [ ] No   If No, name joint owner(s) _____

Do you own the
- [ ] freehold?
- [ ] leasehold?

When did you buy the property? _____

Is your home a
- [ ] house?
- [ ] bungalow?
- [ ] flat?

Is it
- [ ] detached?
- [ ] semi-detached?
- [ ] terraced?

How many of the following rooms does it have?
- [ ] living rooms?
- [ ] kitchens?
- [ ] bedrooms?
- [ ] bath/shower rooms?

How much Council Tax do you pay per year? £ _____

What was the purchase price of property? £ _____

What is its value now? £ _____

Is your home mortgaged?
- [ ] Yes
- [ ] No

If Yes, what is the name and address of your mortgage lender? _____

How much are your mortgage payments per month? £ _____

What type of mortgage do you have? eg. repayment, endowment etc. _____

How long is the mortgage for? _____ years

When did you take out the mortgage? _____

How much is currently owed under the mortgage? £ _____

Is some or all of the interest paid by the Benefits Agency?
- [ ] Yes
- [ ] No

If Yes, how much is paid each month? £ _____

6

Do you let any part of your home?

☐ Yes
☐ No

If Yes, give names of the tenants/lodgers and details of rent received

Do you have any loans secured on your home? (e.g. further mortgage)

☐ Yes
☐ No

If Yes, give the same details as for the first mortgage

—{ Go to Section 9 page 8 }—

8b Rented property

Do you rent

☐ on your own? ☐ jointly?

What is the name and address of your landlord?

How long have you lived at the property?

_____ months _____ years

Do you share parts of your home with someone unconnected with you?

☐ Yes
☐ No

Do you pay any additional service charges in connection with the premises?

☐ Yes
☐ No

If Yes, give details

£ _____ per

How much rent do you pay?

£ _____ per

none ☐

How much Council Tax do you pay a year?

£ _____

none ☐

Do you sub-let any part of your home?

☐ Yes
☐ No

If Yes, give names of tenants/lodgers and details of rent received.

Do you receive housing benefit?

☐ Yes
☐ No

If Yes, give details

£ _____ per

paid to

—{ Go to Section 9 page 8 }—

7

9 Savings, Investments and other Assets

Do you own any property
other than your home?   ☐ Yes   If Yes, give the address and
                         ☐ No   value and details of any
                                    mortgages and lettings

Do you have any bank, building society or other accounts?   ☐ Yes   ☐ No

If Yes, give details below

Name & Address of Bank Building Society	Account No.	Type of Account	Balance	Sole or joint A/c	Name(s) of joint account holder(s)

Do you have any shares, investments (eg. ISAs, Tessas etc.),   ☐ Yes   ☐ No
insurance/assurance policies or premium bonds?   If Yes, give details below

Are you making
contributions to a pension   ☐ Yes   If Yes, give
scheme?   ☐ No   details

Do you have any of the following items and how long have you had them?

	Age (years)	Is it owned by you, on hire purchase credit sale or rented?	If not owned by you, give; Name of Creditor	Amount still owed	Payments
☐ Microwave					
☐ Hi-fi / surround sound					
☐ Television (No.___)					
☐ Video					
☐ Camcorder					
☐ Computer					
☐ Dishwasher					
☐ Camera					
☐ Dining Room suite					
☐ Caravan					
☐ Mobile telephone					
☐ Musical instruments..					
☐ Other items....					

8

Do you own a motor vehicle?	☐ Yes ☐ No	If Yes, give age, make, model value and registration number. State whether it is owned by you, or subject to a hire purchase/ rental agreement.

Do you have any assets not previously mentioned?	☐ Yes ☐ No	If Yes, give details

Assets	Value

Does anyone owe you money, which is not a business debt or for work you have done?	☐ Yes ☐ No	If Yes, who owes you money and how much do they owe?

	Value

🔟 Other Debts or regular payments and court orders

Expenses
Do not include payments made by other members of your household out of their own income or priority debts listed opposite

Priority Debts
This section is for arrears only. DO NOT include regular expenses listed left

Expenses			Priority Debts			Total arrears outstanding
Mortgage	£	per	Rent arrears	£	per	£
Rent	£	per	Mortgage arrears	£	per	£
Council tax	£	per	Council tax/Community charge arrears	£	per	£
Gas	£	per				
Electricity	£	per	Water charge arrears	£	per	£
Water charges	£	per				
Housekeeping, food, school meals	£	per	Fuel arrears: Gas	£	per	£
Travelling expenses	£	per	Electricity	£	per	£
Children's clothing	£	per	Other	£	per	£
Maintenance/child support payments	£	per	Maintenance arrears	£	per	£
Student loan repayments	£	per	Income tax	£	per	£
Mail order payments	£	per	VAT	£	per	£
HP repayments	£	per	National Insurance	£	per	£
Digital/satellite TV subscriptions	£	per				
Telephone	£	per	Others *(give details below)*	£	per	£
Mobile phone	£	per		£	per	£
Other expenses	£	per		£	per	£
(not court orders, priority debts or credit debts listed left)	£	per		£	per	£
	£	per				
Total Expenses	£	per	Total Priority Debts	£	per	£

9

Have any court orders been made against you? ☐ Yes ☐ No   If Yes, give details below

Name of court and case number	Date of Judgment or order	Amount of Judgment or order	Instalments payable per month	Name of creditor	Total still owed	Are payments up to date? (yes/no)	If no, how much in arrears?
TOTALS							

Do you owe money on credit cards or any other loans (not mortage or business)? ☐ Yes ☐ No   If Yes, give details below

Name of Creditor	Total amount owing	Instalments payable per month	Are payments up to date? (yes/no)	If no, how much in arrears?
TOTALS				

Have any bankruptcy proceedings been issued against you? ☐ Yes ☐ No

If Yes, what is the court name and case no.

Is the petition

☐ still pending?　☐ order made but discharged?

☐ order has been made but not discharged?　☐ other outcome? *(give details below)*

Has an Individual Voluntary Arrangement been made? ☐ Yes ☐ No

If Yes, give the date

If No, is there a current proposal for one?　☐ Yes　☐ No

Give details of Trustee/ Insolvency Practitioner/ Administrator, supervisor

10

11 Offer of Payment

Can you make an offer of payment? ☐ Yes   ☐ No

If No, please explain why

What is your offer of payment?

Pay in full by [   ] day of [   ]

Instalments of [£   per   ] to start on [   ]

Method of payment   ☐ postal order   ☐ cheque   ☐ direct debit
                    ☐ standing order   ☐ payment book   ☐ cash

I certify that this is a correct record of the answers I gave to the questions in this document.

Signed .... Judgment Debtor
Print name ....
Date ....

The judgment debtor refused to sign this record of evidence.

Signed .... Court Officer
Print name ....
Date ....

The following costs of the examination have been allowed and added to the judgment debt £ [   ]

11

12 Documents produced

The judgment debtor produced the following documents:

FORM D62 REQUEST FOR ISSUE OF JUDGMENT SUMMONS

Request for issue of judgment summons

Judgment creditor's full name and address

Judgment debtor's full name and address

Click here to reset form

To be completed by the relevant party	
Name of court	Case No.
Name of Petitioner	
Name of Respondent	
Name of Co-Respondent (if applicable)	

If completing this form by hand, please use **black ink** and **BLOCK CAPITAL LETTERS** and tick the boxes that apply.

I apply for the issue of a judgment summons against the above named debtor in respect of an order made in this court on the [ ]/[ ]/[ ]
for (please give details of the order)

☐ I intend to apply to the Court at the hearing for the proposed judgment summons for leave to enforce arrears which became due more than twelve months before the date of the judgment summons.

☐ I am aware that if I do not prove to the satisfaction of the Court at the hearing that the debtor has, or has had since the date of the order, the means to pay the sum in respect of which he has made default and that he has refused or neglected, or refuses or neglects, to pay it, I may have to pay the costs of the judgment summons.

☐ I certify that the order has not been modified or discharged and that there is no order of commitment in this matter which remains unsatisfied.

☐ I further certify that no [writ or] warrant of execution has been issued to enforce the order.

Dated [ ]/[ ]/[ ]

Signed [   ]

[Solicitor for the] judgment creditor

Amount claimed as due and unpaid in respect of the order and any costs	£
Court fee paid to issue this judgment summons	£
Amount (if any) paid to you for your travelling expenses to the Court	£
Total Amount	£ 0.00

FORM P2 PENSION ATTACHMENT ANNEX UNDER [SECTION 25B OR 25C OF THE MATRIMONIAL CAUSES ACT 1973] [PARAGRAPH 25 OR 26 OF SCHEDULE 5 TO THE CIVIL PARTNERSHIP ACT 2004]

Click here to reset form

Pension Attachment Annex under [section 25B or 25C of the Matrimonial Causes Act 1973] [paragraph 25 or 26 of Schedule 5 to the Civil Partnership Act 2004]	In the	*[County Court] *[Principal Registry of the Family Division]
	Case No. (Always quote this)	
	Applicant's Solicitor's reference	
	Respondent's Solicitor's reference	

Between _____ (Petitioner)

and _____ (Respondent)

Take Notice that:

On _____ the court   *(delete as appropriate)

* made an order including provision under [section [25B][25C]* of the Matrimonial Causes Act 1973]* [paragraph [25][26]* or Schedule 5 to the Civil Partnership Act 2004]*.

* [varied] [discharged] an order which included provision under [section [25B][25C]* of the Matrimonial Causes Act 1973] [paragraph [25][26] of Schedule 5 to the Civil Partnership Act 2004]* and dated [ ] / [ ] / [   ]

This annex to the order provides the person responsible for the pension arrangement with the information required by virtue of rules of court:

1.   Name of the party with the pension rights:

2.   Name of the other party:

3.   The National Insurance Number of the party with pension rights:

4.   Details of the Pension Arrangement:

     (i) Name and address of the person responsible for the pension arrangement:

     (ii) Policy Reference Number:

     (iii) if appropriate, such other details to enable the pension arrangement to be identified:

5A. **(i) To be completed where a Periodical Payments Order is made under s.25B of the Matrimonial Causes Act 1973.**

The specified percentage of any payment due to the party with the pension rights that is to be paid for the benefit of the other party: ___ · ___ %

(ii) To be completed where the court orders that the party with pension rights commutes a percentage of his pension to a tax free lump sum on retirement under s.25B of the Matrimonial Causes Act 1973.

(a) the specified percentage of the maximum lump sum available that is to be commuted: ___ · ___ %

(b) the specified percentage of the commuted sum which is to be paid to the spouse or the former spouse of the party with pension rights: ___ · ___ %

(iii) To be completed where the court orders, under s.25C of the Matrimonial Causes Act 1973, that all or part of a lump sum payable to the party with pension rights in respect of his death be paid to the other party.

(a) the percentage of the lump sum to be paid by the person responsible for the pension arrangement to the other party: ___ · ___ %

(b) the percentage of the lump sum payable (in accordance with a nomination by the party with pension rights) to the other party: ___ · ___ %

(c) the percentage of the lump sum to be paid by the person responsible for the pension arrangement for the benefit of the other party: ___ · ___ %

5B. **(i) To be completed where a Periodical Payments Order is made under paragraph 25 of Schedule 5 to the Civil Partnership Act 2004.**

The specified percentage of any payment due to the civil partner with the pension rights that is to be paid for the benefit of the other civil partner: ___ · ___ %

(ii) To be completed where the court orders that the civil partner with pension rights commutes a percentage of his pension to a tax free lump sum on retirement under paragraph 25 of Schedule 5 to the Civil Partnership Act 2004.

(a) the specified percentage of the maximum lump sum available that is to be commuted: ___ · ___ %

(b) the specified percentage of the commuted sum which is to be paid to the civil partner or the former civil partner of the civil partner with pension rights: ___ · ___ %

(iii) To be completed where the court orders, under paragraph 26 of Schedule 5 to the Civil Partnership Act 2004, that all or part of a lump sum payable to the civil partner with pension rights in respect of his death be paid to the other civil partner.

(a) the percentage of the lump sum to be paid by the person responsible for the pension arrangement to the other civil partner: __ . __ %

(b) the percentage of the lump sum payable (in accordance with a nomination by the civil partner with pension rights) to the other civil partner: __ . __ %

(c) the percentage of the lump sum to be paid by the person responsible for the pension arrangement for the benefit of the other civil partner: __ . __ %

To the person responsible for the pension arrangement:
*(delete if this information has already been provided to the person responsible for the pension arrangement)

1. *You are required to serve any notice under the Divorce etc. (Pensions) Regulations 2000 or the Dissolution etc. (Pensions) Regulations 2005 on the other party at the following address:

2. *You are required to make any payments due under the pension arrangement to the other party at the following address:

3. *If the address at 2. above is that of a bank, building society or the Department of National Savings the following details will enable you to make payment into the account of the other party (e.g. Account Name, Number, Bank/Building Society/etc. Sort code):

Note: Where the order to which this annex applies was made by consent the following section should also be completed.

The court also confirms: *(delete as appropriate)

- *That notice has been served on the person responsible for the pension arrangement and that no objection has been received.

- *That notice has been served on the person responsible for the pension arrangement and that the court has considered any objection received.

3

FORM PPF2 PENSION PROTECTION FUND (PPF) ATTACHMENT ANNEX TO A PENSION COMPENSATION ATTACHMENT ORDER [SECTION 25F OF THE MATRIMONIAL CAUSES ACT 1973] [PARAGRAPH 34A OF SCHEDULE 5 TO THE CIVIL PARTNERSHIP ACT 2004]

Click here to reset form

Pension Protection Fund (PPF) Attachment Annex to a Pension Compensation Attachment Order [section 25F of the Matrimonial Causes Act 1973] [paragraph 34A of Schedule 5 to the Civil Partnership Act 2004]	In the	
		*[County Court] *[Principal Registry of the Family Division]
	Case No. (Always quote this)	
	Applicant's Solicitor's reference	
	Respondent's Solicitor's reference	

Between _____ (Petitioner)

and _____ (Respondent)

Take Notice that:

On _____ the court

*(delete as appropriate)

- made an order including provision under section 25F of the Matrimonial Causes Act 1973 or paragraph 34A of Schedule 5 to the Civil Partnership Act 2004*

- [varied] [discharged]* an order dated ☐ ☐ / ☐ ☐ / ☐ ☐ ☐ ☐ which included provision under section 25F of the Matrimonial Causes Act 1973 or paragraph 34A of Schedule 5 to the Civil Partnership Act 2004*

This annex to the order provides the PPF Board with the information required by virtue of rules of court:

1.	Name of the party who has the PPF compensation entitlement:	
2.	Name of the other party:	
3.	The National Insurance Number of the party with PPF compensation entitlement:	
4.	The name of the pension scheme for which the PPF Board assumed responsibility and to which the pension compensation relates:	
	(i) if appropriate, such other details to enable the PPF compensation to be identified:	

continued over the page ⇨

5A. (i) **To be completed where a periodical payments order is made under s.23 of the Matrimonial Causes Act 1973 making provision under s25F of the 1973 Act.**

The specified percentage of any payment due to the party with the PPF compensation entitlement that is to be paid for the benefit of the other party:　　　　　__ . __ %

(ii) **To be completed where the court orders that the party with PPF compensation entitlement commutes a percentage of his PPF compensation to a tax free lump sum on retirement under s.25F(5) of the Matrimonial Causes Act 1973.**

(a) the specified percentage of the maximum lump sum available that is to be commuted:　　　　__ . __ %

(b) the specified percentage of the commuted sum which is to be paid to the spouse or the former spouse of the party with PPF compensation entitlement:　　　　__ . __ %

5B. (i) **To be completed where a periodical payments order is made under Part 1 of Schedule 5 of the Civil Partnership Act 2004 making provision under paragraph 34A of Schedule 5 of the 2004 Act.**

The specified percentage of any payment due to the civil partner with the PPF compensation entitlement that is to be paid for the benefit of the other civil partner:　　　　__ . __ %

(ii) **To be completed where the court orders that the civil partner with PPF compensation entitlement commutes a percentage of the PPF compensation to a tax free lump sum on retirement under paragraph 34A(5) of Schedule 5 to the Civil Partnership Act 2004.**

(a) the specified percentage of the maximum lump sum available that is to be commuted:　　　　__ . __ %

(b) the specified percentage of the commuted sum which is to be paid to the civil partner or the former civil partner of the civil partner with PPF compensation entitlement:　　　　__ . __ %

continued over the page ➪

2

To the PPF Board:

(*delete if this information has already been provided
to the PPF Board)

1.* You are required to make any payments due
under the PPF compensation to the other party
at the following address:

2.* If the address at 1. above is that of a bank,
building society or the Department of National
Savings the following details will enable you to
make payment into the account of the other party
(e.g. Account Name, Number, Bank/Building
Society/etc. Sort code):

Note: Where the order to which this annex applies was made by consent the following section should also
be completed.

The court also confirms:
(*delete as appropriate)

- That notice has been served on the PPF Board and the Board is not aware of the member's PPF
compensation, or the pension rights from which it was derived, being subject to any order or provision
referred to in regulation 5(2)(b) of the Pension Protection Fund (Pension Compensation Sharing and
Attachment on Divorce etc) Regulations 2011, SI 2011/731.*

- That notice has been served on the PPF Board and that any order or provision referred to in regulation
5(2)(b) of the Pension Protection Fund (Pension Compensation Sharing and Attachment on Divorce etc)
Regulations 2011, SI 2011/731 has been considered and that there is the power to make this order.*

INDEX

References are to paragraph numbers.

Accounting for bonus payments
formula elements   10.19
methods
   all-in income method   10.20, 10.21
   capped method   10.24–10.29
   deferred clean break method   10.31
   exclusion method   10.22, 10.23
   generally   10.17
   other agreed methods   10.32
   transition method   10.30
scenarios   10.18

After-acquired property
bankruptcy   13.8–13.11

All-in income method
accounting for bonus payments   10.20, 10.21

Annulment
bankruptcy   13.4, 13.5

Armed forces personnel
enforcement against   22.19

Arrears
capitalisation of periodical
   payments   18.22
enforcement   22.6–22.8
maintenance pending suit   5.27, 5.28
periodical payments orders   8.14, 8.25
variation of quantum   17.33

Attachment of earnings order
enforcement   22.15–22.18
periodical payments orders   8.20

Backdating
periodical payments orders   8.4

Bank accounts
periodical payments orders   8.20

Bankruptcy
after-acquired property   13.8–13.11
annulment   13.4, 13.5
discharge   13.3
effects of   13.6
income payments orders
   allowance for periodical
     payments when
     quantifying   13.20, 13.21
   family, meaning of   13.17
   generally   13.12
   interaction with periodical
     payments   13.18, 13.19

Bankruptcy—*continued*
income payments orders—*continued*
   legal basis   13.13
   limits of   13.14–13.17
   reasonable domestic needs   13.16
introduction   3.20, 13.1
pensions
   general rule   19.19
   pensions capable of
     payment   19.21–19.23
   pensions in payment   19.20
periodical payments, and
   bankrupt in receipt of   13.25
   generally   3.20, 13.22–13.24
   income payments orders,
     interaction with   13.18, 13.19
   proof of debts   13.26–13.29
   secured payments   13.31
petition   13.2
proof of debts
   bankruptcy debts   13.28
   discretionary release   13.29, 13.30
   generally   13.26
   provable debts   13.27
spouses, obtaining information
   from   13.32
trustees' powers   13.32
void payments   13.7

Bonus payments
accounting for
   all-in income method   10.20, 10.21
   capped method   10.24–10.29
   deferred clean break method   10.31
   exclusion method   10.22, 10.23
   formula elements   10.19
   methods   10.17
   other agreed methods   10.32
   scenarios   10.18
   transition method   10.30
analysis
   disclosure   10.2–10.4
   income or capital   10.5–10.7
clean break   10.9
conclusions   10.33
division of,   10.10
future financial resources   10.8
future receivable   10.16, 10.17
introduction   10.1
run-off awards   10.13–10.15
unequal sharing   10.11, 10.12

Budget
  broad-brush versus fine toothcomb 7.8
  documents 7.5
  drafting 7.6, 7.7
  exaggeration 7.9, 7.10
  full and frank disclosure 7.11
  generally 3.14
  particular expenditure for particular
    people 7.12
  purpose of 7.3, 7.4
  traps and pitfalls 7.13
Burden of proof *see also* Proof
  costs allowances 6.10
  legal services orders 6.25

Capital division
  quantification of orders, and 9.11
Capital readjustment, prohibition
  against
  capitalisation of periodical
    payments 18.9
Capitalisation of periodical payments
  applicability, 18.6
  benefits 18.8
  clean break 18.8
  cohabitation 18.8, 18.23
  disadvantages of 18.8
  Duxbury calculations 3.17, 18.12–18.21
  introduction 18.1–18.4
  legal basis 18.5
  orders available 18.7
  original final orders 3.17
  periodical payments orders 8.7
  procedure, 18.6
  prohibition against capital
    readjustment 18.9
  recession-proofing 18.8
  remarriage 18.8
  staged-assessment approach
    arrears 18.22
    cohabitation 18.23
    Duxbury calculation 18.12–18.21
    fairness 18.28
    generally 18.10
    pension sharing orders 18.24–18.27
    quantification of lump sum 18.11
    shorter marriages 18.23
  supplemental orders 3.16
  variation, on 3.16
Capped method
  accounting for bonus
    payments 10.24–10.29
Charging orders
  enforcement 22.20, 22.21
Children, maintenance of
  'child of the family' 20.28
  clean break 11.33
  duration 20.31
  factors for court's consideration 20.29
  failure to maintain orders 4.15
  interim orders 20.36
  introduction 20.1–20.5

Children, maintenance of—*continued*
  nominal periodical
    payments 12.14–12.17
  number of orders 20.30
  procedure 20.34, 20.35
  quantification 20.25, 20.32, 20.33
  residual powers of court
    disability expenses 20.18–20.20
    divorce, and 20.26
    generally 20.13
    payment 20.27
    quantification 20.25
    school fees 20.14–20.17
    top-up orders 20.21, 20.22
    written agreements 20.23, 20.24
  Segal orders 20.36
  statutory child support
    system 20.6–20.12
  types of orders
    spouses and civil partners 3.9
    unmarried couples 3.10
Civil partners *see also* Spouses
  children, maintenance of 3.9
Clean break
  bonus payments 10.9
  capitalisation 18.8
  children 11.33
  deferred
    bar to extension of term 11.27
    broad approach 11.28
    children 11.33
    length of term 11.29–11.32
  generally 3.18
  immediate 11.9, 11.10
  indicators against 11.12
  indicators in favour of 11.11
  introduction of concept 2.32
  legal basis 11.7, 11.8
  nominal periodical payments
    versus 12.5–12.7
  objectives 11.6
  pensions 19.27
  practice points 11.34
  self-sufficiency versus realities of
    life post-divorce 11.4, 11.5
  short marriages 11.25, 11.26
  variation of quantum 17.14
Cohabitation
  capitalisation of periodical
    payments 18.8, 18.23
  defining 14.14–14.16
  disclosure 14.18, 14.19
  financial consequences for payer/
    payee 14.20
  generally 3.21, 14.13
  impact on periodical payments
    extent of 14.21–14.24
    introduction 14.1–14.3
    statistics 14.4
  nominal periodical payments 12.21
  orders that terminate periodical
    payments on 14.25, 14.26
  practice points 14.27

Cohabitation—*continued*
proving 14.17
variation of quantum 17.26
Compensation
periodical payments orders 8.24
quantification of orders
generally 9.21–9.23
very high income cases 9.24
Contributions to pensions
general approach 19.15–19.17
pension attachment 19.18
Costs
failure to maintain orders 4.17
legal services orders 6.29
maintenance agreements 21.6
maintenance pending suit 5.31
variation of quantum 17.34
Costs allowances *see also* Legal
services orders
amount 6.11
applicability 6.6
burden of proof 6.10
case law 6.7
discretionary standards 6.9
duration 6.12
maintenance pending suit
introduction 6.1, 6.2
legal services orders 6.13–6.29
old law 6.3–6.12
practice points 6.30
minimum standards 6.8
rationale 6.3, 6.4
statutory basis 6.5
types of orders 3.4
Criminal conversion
historical maintenance 2.19, 2.20

Default term *see* Duration
Deferred clean break *see* Clean break
Deferred clean break method
accounting for bonus payments 10.31
Disability expenses
children, maintenance of 20.18–20.20
Discharge
bankruptcy 13.3
periodical payments orders 3.15
Disclosure
bonus payments 10.2–10.4
budgets 7.11
cohabitation 14.18, 14.19
enforcement 22.5
need 7.11
Divorce *a mensa et thoro*
historical maintenance 2.10–2.15
Divorce Act 1857
historical maintenance 2.24
Divorce by Parliamentary Act
historical maintenance 2.21, 2.22
Duration
children, maintenance of 20.31
costs allowances 6.12
extendable term orders 3.19

Duration—*continued*
failure to maintain orders 4.12, 4.13
legal services orders 6.27
non-extendable term orders 3.19
periodical payments orders
default term 8.9, 8.10
extension of term 8.12, 8.13
generally 3.19
Duxbury calculations
assumptions
fiscal assumptions 15.5
generally 15.4
physical assumptions 15.6
capitalisation 3.17, 18.12–18.21
departing from
additional security 15.11
application to vary order 15.9
appropriate circumstances 15.10
enabling discretionary
expenditure 15.11
foreign investments 15.13
meeting concerns on assumed
rate of return 15.12
tax 15.13
meaning 15.1, 15.2
negotiating Duxbury paradox 15.8
tool not rule 15.7
use of 15.3

Ecclesiastical courts
historical maintenance 2.10–2.15
Enforcement
armed forces personnel 22.19
arrears 22.6–22.8
attachment of earnings
order 22.15–22.18
charging orders 22.20, 22.21
disclosure of financial information 22.5
introduction 22.1–22.4
judgment summons
generally 22.22–22.26
means to pay 22.27–22.29
legal services orders 6.22
location of judgment debtor 22.5
periodical payments orders
armed forces personnel 22.19
arrears 22.6–22.8
attachment of earnings
order 22.15–22.18
charging orders 22.20, 22.21
generally 3.22
methods 22.15–22.21
post-default enforcement 22.10–22.14
pre-emptive enforcement 22.9
practice points 22.30
Exclusion method
accounting for bonus payments 10.22, 10.23
Expenses
failure to provide reasonable
maintenance 4.14
generally 3.14

Extendable term orders *see* Duration
Extension of term *see* Duration
Extravagance
  variation of quantum   17.23

Failure to maintain orders
  applicability   4.3, 4.4
  children   4.15
  costs   4.17
  duration   4.12, 4.13
  expenses   4.14
  'failure to maintain'   4.8, 4.9
  final orders   4.6, 4.7
  interim orders   4.5
  introduction   4.1
  practice points   4.18
  prior liabilities   4.14
  procedure   4.16
  reasonableness   4.10, 4.11
  statutory basis   4.2
  types of orders   3.2
Fairness
  capitalisation of periodical
    payments   18.28
  quantification of orders   9.6–9.10
Foreign divorce
  periodical payments orders   3.12
Foreign investments
  Duxbury calculations   15.13
Forms
  periodical payments orders   8.26

High income cases
  quantification of orders   9.24
Historical perspective
  clean break, introduction of   2.32
  conclusion   2.44
  Divorce Act 1857   2.24
  financial support on separation
    criminal conversion   2.19, 2.20
    divorce *a mensa et thoro*   2.10–2.15
    divorce by Parliamentary Act   2.21,
           2.22
    ecclesiastical courts   2.10–2.15
    generally   2.5
    private separation deeds   2.16–2.18
    wife-sale   2.6–2.9
  introduction   2.1, 2.2
  Matrimonial Causes Act 1857   2.25–2.31
  medieval England   2.3, 2.4
  position by 1857   2.23
  quantum case law
    generally   2.33, 2.34
    post-1970   2.37–2.43
    pre-1970   2.35, 2.36

Immediate clean break *see* Clean break
Income payments orders
  allowance for periodical payments
    when quantifying   13.20, 13.21
  family, meaning of   13.17

Income payments orders—*continued*
  generally   13.12
  interaction with periodical
    payments   13.18, 13.19
  legal basis   13.13
  limits of   13.14–13.17
  reasonable domestic needs   13.16
Indexation
  periodical payments orders   8.21–8.23
Interim orders
  children, maintenance of   20.36
  failure to maintain orders   4.5
  maintenance pending suit   5.10
  types of orders   3.7
Irresponsibility
  variation of quantum   17.23

Judgment summons
  enforcement
    generally   22.22–22.26
    means to pay   22.27–22.29

Legal services orders *see also* Costs
  allowances
    applicability   6.15, 6.16
    burden of proof   6.25
    costs   6.29
    discretion   6.26
    dismissing   6.14
    duration   6.27
    enforcement   6.22
    introduction   6.13
    LAPSO changes   6.14
    legal services, meaning of   6.17, 6.18
    minimum standards   6.23, 6.24
    orders for sale of property   6.22
    payment   6.20, 6.21
    security   6.21
    timing   6.19
    types of orders   3.4
    variation   6.28

Maintenance agreements
  introduction   21.1
  meaning   21.2
  types of orders   3.13
  variation
    conditions for   21.7–21.9
    costs   21.6
    generally   21.5
    procedure   21.6
    void restrictions   21.3, 21.4
Maintenance pending suit
  applicability   5.3
  applicant's procedure   5.4–5.6
  arrears   5.27, 5.28
  cases   5.22
  costs   5.31
  costs allowances
    introduction   6.1, 6.2
    new law   6.13–6.29
    old law   6.3–6.12

Maintenance pending suit—*continued*

costs allowances—*continued*

practice points	6.30
discretion	5.15–5.17
hearing	5.8, 5.9
interim order	5.10
introduction	5.1

key concepts

arrears	5.27, 5.28
assumptions	5.23
balancing interests	5.26
discretion	5.15–5.17
generally	5.11
impact of agreement	5.29
inferences	5.23
maintenance, meaning of	5.12–5.15
reasonableness	5.16–5.18
standard of living	5.19, 5.20
third party support for applicant	5.21, 5.22
third party support for respondent	5.24, 5.25
legal basis	5.2

legal services orders

applicability	6.15, 6.16
burden of proof	6.25
costs	6.29
discretion	6.26
dismissing	6.14
duration	6.27
enforcement	6.22
introduction	6.13
LAPSO changes	6.14
legal services, meaning of	6.17, 6.18
minimum standards	6.23, 6.24
orders for sale of property	6.22
payment	6.20, 6.21
security	6.21
timing	6.19
variation	6.28

periodical payments orders

translating maintenance pending suit into	5.32
reasonableness	5.16–5.18
respondent's procedure	5.7
standard of living	5.19, 5.20

third party support

for applicant	5.21, 5.22
for respondent	5.24, 5.25
types of orders	3.3
variation	5.30

Maintenance, failure to provide reasonable

applicability	4.3, 4.4
children	4.15
costs	4.17
duration	4.12, 4.13
expenses	4.14
failure to maintain	4.8, 4.9
final orders	4.6, 4.7
interim orders	4.5
introduction	4.1
practice points	4.18

Maintenance, failure to provide reasonable—*continued*

prior liabilities	4.14
procedure	4.16
reasonableness	4.10, 4.11
statutory basis	4.2

Married couples *see* Spouses

Matrimonial Causes Act 1857

historical maintenance	2.25–2.31

Need

budget

broad-brush versus fine

toothcomb	7.8
documents	7.5
drafting	7.6, 7.7
exaggeration	7.9, 7.10
full and frank disclosure	7.11

particular expenditure for

particular people	7.12
purpose of	7.3, 7.4
traps and pitfalls	7.13
generally	3.14
historical maintenance	2.42, 2.43
income payments orders	13.16
introduction	7.1, 7.2
macro-economic approach	7.14, 7.15
practice points	7.16

relationship-generated disadvantage

financial need	9.14–9.17
generally	9.13
interpretation of need	9.16
marital standard of living	9.18, 9.19
need versus luxury	9.20
real need	9.17
reasonable requirements	9.15

Net income calculators

periodical payments orders	8.16

Nominal periodical payments

addressing financial imbalance	12.12, 12.13
avoiding further litigation	12.20
children	12.14–12.17
clean break versus	12.5–12.7
cohabitation	12.21
introduction	12.1–12.3
legal basis	12.4
practicalities	12.12, 12.13
practice points	12.27
risk versus opportunity	12.18, 12.19
short marriages	12.16, 12.17

transmutability

generally	12.22
limits of safety net	12.24
reasoning behind original order	12.25, 12.26
special rules do not apply	12.23
types of orders	3.6

uncertainties of

generally	12.8
last backstop	12.10
long stop	12.11
safety valve	12.9

Non-extendable term orders *see*
  Duration

One-third rule
  historical maintenance   2.38
Orders for sale of property
  legal services orders   6.22
Overseas divorce
  periodical payments orders   3.12

Payments *see also* Bonus payments
  children, maintenance of   20.27
  interim payments   3.7, 8.5
  legal services orders   6.20, 6.21
  periodical payments orders   8.18, 8.19
  void payments in bankruptcy   13.7
Pension attachment orders
  alternatives   19.24
  contributions   19.18
  nature of   19.6
  pension sharing orders versus   19.11,
                                           19.26
  primary powers   19.7, 19.8
  secondary powers   19.9, 19.10
  statutory prohibitions   19.28, 19.29
  variation   19.14
Pension sharing orders
  capitalisation of periodical
          payments   18.24–18.27
  pension attachment orders versus   19.11,
                                           19.25, 19.26
  periodical payments, and   19.34–19.36
Pensions
  bankruptcy
    general rule   19.19
    pensions capable of
            payment   19.21–19.23
    pensions in payment   19.20
  clean break   19.27
  contributions
    general approach   19.15–19.17
    pension attachment   19.18
  expert evidence   19.13
  introduction   19.1, 19.2
  pension attachment orders
    alternatives   19.24
    contributions   19.18
    nature of   19.6
    pension sharing orders versus   19.11,
                                           19.26
    primary powers   19.7, 19.8
    secondary powers   19.9, 19.10
    statutory prohibitions   19.28, 19.29
    variation   19.14
  pension benefits   19.4, 19.5
  pension sharing orders
    capitalisation of periodical
            payments   18.24–18.27
    pension attachment orders
            versus   19.11, 19.25, 19.26
    periodical payments, and   19.34–19.36
  practice points   19.37

Pensions—*continued*
  procedure   19.30–19.33
  terminology   19.3
  types of orders   3.11
  valuations   19.12
Periodical payments orders
  absolutes   8.2
  arrears   8.14, 8.25
  attachment of earnings   8.20
  backdating   8.4
  bank accounts   8.20
  bankruptcy,
    bankrupt in receipt of   13.25
    generally   13.22–13.24
    income payments orders,
            interaction with   13.18, 13.19
    proof of debts   13.26–13.29
    secured payments   13.31
  capitalisation   3.16, 3.17, 8.7
  children, maintenance of
    spouses and civil partners   3.9
    unmarried couples   3.10
  cohabitation   3.21
  compensation   8.24
  decree absolute for effectiveness   8.11
  discharge   3.15
  duration
    default term   8.9, 8.10
    extension of term   8.12, 8.13
    generally   3.19
  elements   8.3
  enforcement
    armed forces personnel   22.19
    arrears   8.14, 22.6–22.8
    attachment of earnings
            order   22.15–22.18
    charging orders   22.20, 22.21
    generally   3.22
    methods   22.15–22.21
    post-default enforcement   22.10–22.14
    pre-emptive enforcement   22.9
  flexibility   8.24
  forms   8.26
  game rules   8.17
  indexation   8.21–8.23
  interim payments   3.7, 8.5
  introduction   8.1
  maintenance pending suit,
            translating   5.32
  net income calculators   8.16
  nominal   3.6
  non-taxable position   8.15
  overseas divorce   3.12
  payment   8.18, 8.19
  remarriage   3.21, 8.8
  secured   3.8
  standing orders   8.20
  start date   8.4
  substantive   3.5
  suspension   3.15
  types of orders
    interim orders   3.7
    nominal orders   3.6

Periodical payments orders—*continued*
    types of orders—*continued*
        secured orders   3.8
        substantive orders   3.5
    unmarried couples   3.10
    variation   3.15, 8.6
Private separation deeds
    historical maintenance   2.16–2.18
Prohibition against capital
    readjustment
    capitalisation of periodical
        payments   18.9
Proof
    burden of proof
        costs allowances   6.10
        legal services orders   6.25
    cohabitation   14.17
    debts
        bankruptcy debts   13.28
        discretionary release   13.29, 13.30
        generally   13.26
        provable debts   13.27

Quantification of lump sum
    capitalisation of periodical
        payments   18.11
Quantification of orders
    approach
        fairness   9.6–9.10
        generally   9.4
        two-stage approach   9.5
    capital division, impact of   9.11
    children, maintenance of   20.25, 20.32,
         20.33
    compensation
        generally   9.21–9.23
        very high income cases   9.24
    introduction   9.1–9.3
    practice points   9.26
    relationship-generated disadvantage
        financial need   9.14–9.17
        generally   9.13
        interpretation of need   9.16
        marital standard of living   9.18, 9.19
        need versus luxury   9.20
        real need   9.17
        reasonable requirements   9.15
    separation   9.12
Quantum, variation of
    arrears   17.33
    case analysis on   17.8
    case law principles
        choices made by parties since
            original order   17.24, 17.25
        extravagance   17.23
        facts of original order   17.17
        financial management   17.23
        generally   17.15
        irresponsibility   17.23
        purpose of original order   17.16
        reasons for original order   17.16

Quantum, variation of—*continued*
    case law principles—*continued*
        relationship-generated
            disadvantage   17.17–17.21
        standard of living   17.22
    clean break   17.14
    cohabitation   17.26
    costs   17.34
    extravagance   17.23
    introduction   17.1, 17.2
    irresponsibility   17.23
    legal basis   17.3, 17.4
    percentage of income
        payable   17.27–17.32
    procedure   17.5–17.7
    standard of living   17.22
    statutory principles
        all circumstances of case   17.11
        changes in matters regarded for
            original order   17.12, 17.13
        generally   17.9
        search for clean break   17.14
        welfare of child   17.10
    welfare of child   17.10

Reasonableness
    failure to maintain orders   4.10, 4.11
    historical maintenance   2.39–2.41
    maintenance pending suit   5.16–5.18
Recession-proofing
    capitalisation of periodical
        payments   18.8
Relationship-generated disadvantage
    quantification of orders
        financial need   9.14–9.17
        generally   9.13
        interpretation of need   9.16
        marital standard of living   9.18, 9.19
        need versus luxury   9.20
        real need   9.17
        reasonable requirement   9.15
    variation of quantum   17.17–17.21
Remarriage
    capitalisation of periodical
        payments   18.8
    impact on periodical payments
        generally   3.21, 8.8
        payee's remarriage   14.5
        payer's remarriage   14.6–14.10, 14.12
Run-off awards
    bonus payments   10.13–10.15

Sale of property
    orders for
        legal services orders   6.22
School fees
    children, maintenance of   20.14–20.17
Security for periodical payments
    bankruptcy, and   13.31
    documents   16.10, 16.11
    factors for court's consideration   16.12
    flexibility versus finality   16.9

Security for periodical payments—*continued*
 interpretation 16.3, 16.4
 introduction 16.1
 legal basis 16.2
 legal services orders 6.21
 maximum term 16.5
 practice points 16.13
 provision of 16.6–16.8
Segal orders
 children, maintenance of 20.36
Self-sufficiency
 realities of life post-divorce 11.4, 11.5
Separation
 quantification of orders 9.12
Short marriages
 capitalisation of periodical
  payments 18.23
 clean break 11.25, 11.26
 nominal periodical payments 12.16, 12.17
Spouses
 bankruptcy
  obtaining information from 13.32
 children, maintenance of 3.9
Standard of living
 maintenance pending suit 5.19, 5.20
 quantification of orders 9.18, 9.19
 variation of quantum 17.22
Standing orders
 periodical payments orders 8.20
Supplemental orders
 capitalisation of periodical
  payments 3.16
Suspension
 generally 3.15

Tax
 Duxbury calculations 15.13
Term *see* Duration
Term orders
 appropriateness 11.21–11.24
 deferred clean break
  bar to extension of term 11.27
  broad approach 11.28
  children 11.33
  length of term 11.29–11.32
  practice points 11.35
  short marriages 11.25, 11.26
Terminating financial dependency
 adjusting without undue hardship
  evidence not expectation 11.15–11.20
  generally 11.13, 11.14
 clean break *see also* Clean break
  deferred 11.27–11.33
  generally 3.18
  immediate 11.9, 11.10
  indicators against 11.12
  indicators in favour of 11.11
  legal basis 11.7, 11.8
  objectives 11.6
  practice points 11.34

Terminating financial dependency—*continued*
 clean break —*continued*
  self-sufficiency versus realities of
   life post-divorce 11.4, 11.5
   short marriages 11.25, 11.26
  deferred clean break
   bar to extension of term 11.27
   broad approach 11.28
   children 11.33
   length of term 11.29–11.32
  introduction 11.1–11.3
  term orders
   appropriateness 11.21–11.24
   practice points 11.35
   short marriages 11.25, 11.26
Third party support
 maintenance pending suit
  for applicant 5.21, 5.22
  for respondent 5.24, 5.25
Top-up orders
 children, maintenance of 20.21, 20.22
Transition method
 accounting for bonus payments 10.30
Trustees in bankruptcy *see* Bankruptcy

Unequal sharing
 bonus payments 10.11, 10.12
Unmarried couples
 children, maintenance of 3.10

Valuation
 pensions 19.12
Variation
 capitalisation on application for
  applicability, 18.6
  arrears 18.22
  benefits 18.8
  clean break 18.8
  cohabitation 18.8
  cohabitation of payee 18.23
  disadvantages of 18.8
  Duxbury calculation 18.12–18.21
  fairness 18.28
  generally 3.16
  introduction 18.1–18.4
  legal basis 18.5
  orders available 18.7
  pension sharing orders 18.24–18.27
  procedure, 18.6
  prohibition against capital
   readjustment 18.9
  quantification of lump sum 18.11
  recession-proofing 18.8
  remarriage 18.8
  shorter marriages 18.23
  staged-assessment approach 18.10
 generally 3.15
 legal services orders 6.28
 maintenance agreements
  conditions for 21.7–21.9
  costs 21.6
  generally 21.5

Variation—*continued*
  maintenance agreements—*continued*
    procedure — 21.6
  practice points — 17.41
  quantum
    arrears — 17.33
    case analysis on — 17.8
    case law principles — 17.15–17.25
    cohabitation — 17.26
    costs — 17.34
    introduction — 17.1, 17.2
    legal basis — 17.3, 17.4
    percentage of income
      payable — 17.27–17.32
    procedure — 17.5–17.7
    statutory principles — 17.9–17.14
  supplemental orders on — 3.16

Variation—*continued*
  term
    exceptional justification — 17.38–17.40
    generally — 17.35
    reasons for original order — 17.37
    when to apply to extend — 17.36
Very high income cases
  quantification of orders — 9.24
Void payments
  bankruptcy — 13.7

Welfare of child
  variation of quantum — 17.10
Wife-sale
  historical maintenance — 2.6–2.9
Written agreements
  children, maintenance of — 20.23, 20.24